Consciousness and the World

Consciousness and the World

Brian O'Shaughnessy

King's College London

CLARENDON PRESS · OXFORD

OXFORD

UNIVERSITY PRESS

Great Clarendon Street, Oxford OX2 6DP

Oxford University Press is a department of the University of Oxford.
It furthers the University's objective of excellence in research, scholarship,
and education by publishing worldwide in

Oxford New York

Athens Auckland Bangkok Bogotá Buenos Aires Calcutta
Cape Town Chennai Dar es Salaam Delhi Florence Hong Kong Istanbul
Karachi Kuala Lumpur Madrid Melbourne Mexico City Mumbai
Nairobi Paris São Paulo Singapore Taipei Tokyo Toronto Warsaw

and associated companies in Berlin Ibadan

Oxford is a registered trade mark of Oxford University Press
in the UK and certain other countries

Published in the United States
by Oxford University Press Inc., New York

British Library Cataloguing in Publication Data

Library of Congress Cataloging in Publication Data
O'Shaughnessy, Brian.
Consciousness and the world / Brian O'Shaughnessy.
Includes index.
1. Consciousness. I. Title.

B808.9 .O74 1999 126—dc21 99–045064
ISBN 0–19–823893–2

1 3 5 7 9 10 8 6 4 2

Typeset by Best-set Typesetter Ltd., Hong Kong
Printed in Great Britain
on acid-free paper by
Biddles Ltd
Guildford and King's Lynn

For Edna

Contents

Introduction

The purpose of this work is to provide a theory of Consciousness, a phenomenon of pivotal importance in the mind, intimately linked to the other phenomena to be studied, and of the relation of consciousness through perception with the World towards which essentially it is directed. To be in the state consciousness is to be in the experiential condition of being aware of the World. As we say of the conscious, they are 'in touch' with Reality as those lost in a trance or dream are not. My interest lies in this fundamental mental phenomenon and the way it engages with Reality.

The work begins with an analytical inquiry into consciousness, the main enterprise at the outset being the dismantling of this state into its constituents. Thereafter the discussion moves to an investigation of the closely related phenomenon of the Attention, a phenomenon sometimes referred to as 'The Stream of Consciousness'. Now one of the prime functions of the attention is to enable the mind to open out attentively or perceptually onto outer reality. Here we have an occurrence of great moment, indeed a watershed in the development of mind. In perception we encounter the phenomenon in which consciousness must originally have travelled beyond its own confines and engaged with the rest of the World. This event, in which two diverse realms come together, in which the mind establishes concrete contact with the World, and in its ultimate ontological physical form, must be of great importance to consciousness. And it must in addition be a matter of major significance so far as consciousness is concerned that in the final analysis perception is the only conceivable avenue that could lead consciousness out onto the contents of physical reality. It is in any case via such an avenue that consciousness acquires the substance for its representations and the setting for its deeds.

The discussion which follows sets out to give an analysis of the main participants in this interaction, to show in close-up how such a concrete connection between consciousness and the World is effected, and reveal just what in the end it accomplishes. Starting out from the phenomenon of consciousness, together with an analytic account of what it brings to the epistemological transaction, I attempt to set out in intelligible stages the manner in which a bridge of awareness, arising in the experiential core of consciousness, spans the divide between two diverse realms and leads the mind out onto that spatio-temporal scene of physical objects from which ultimately, through the phenomenon of internalization, the mind itself in the first place developed. And I try to bring out how this cannot be just one encounter amongst others for the mind, but is rather to be understood as a foundational phenomenon. Then the starting point in this basic epistemological interaction is consciousness. Thus it begins in a mental phenomenon which is at once vastly familiar to us all, yet liable on reflection to generate puzzlement.

1. Mystery

(1) Why such an interest in consciousness at the present time? Could it be because of a feeling that we might in this phenomenon be in the presence of something absolutely inexplicable? After all, not everything is explicable. The greatness of a particular work of art, while not pure mystery, is a matter of 'noumenal' depth, a bottomless well, beyond demonstration. Is consciousness such a thing? Are we in this phenomenon running our heads up against the limits of explanation?

This seems unlikely. It is worth remembering that at some point during the history of the life-system of which we are part, consciousness evolved into being, and that the laws of physics cannot have relaxed their hold upon physical phenomena as it did. And it seems equally certain that supervenience must have characterized the emergence of consciousness upon such a physical basis, and that it is inconsistent with a radical contingency. If one physical condition corresponds to consciousness in one animal in one life-system in one sector of physical space, it is not going to correspond to unconsciousness or something quite other either in another animal or in a different life-system in another part of the universe. These considerations suggest that there cannot be much to the idea that consciousness is an essentially inexplicable phenomenon. What that explanation is, and whether we can ever hope to find it, are naturally enough other matters.

Perhaps the central question is, whether the falsity of the theory of radical contingency is a logical necessity. Is it simply inconceivable that one physical state corresponds to consciousness in one place, and the identical physical state corresponds to nothing psychological elsewhere? Locke was of the opinion that God could as easily 'annex' the sensation of (say) blue to one lot of 'motions' as to any other. This is tantamount to the supposition that the relation between mental phenomena of this kind and the body is one of pure contingency, comparable to the contingency of the Laws of Physics themselves. After all, how the Universe is and behaves must be no less ultimately inexplicable than that it is at all. Might this be how things stand in the relation between (say) sensations and matter? Does a metaphysical gap exist which no science could hope to bridge?

It was in part the aim of Logical Behaviourism, and the Wittgensteinian doctrine of 'criteria', to close gaps of this kind. Then at least in the case of sensory *quales*, such as Locke had in mind, those theories seem unequal to the task. Amongst the criteria for attributing a sensation of blue lies one that is neither behavioural nor situational: a presumption of sameness of constitution. Here the original problem breaks out afresh! And it has to be acknowledged that it is hard to even imagine what could count as a scientific explanation of the emergence of (say) blue. Is it defeatist in spirit to believe that we are in the presence here of a contingency comparable to the great contingencies of existence? I suspect it is, but cannot pretend to know so. Nor do I know whether this line of thought applies to the rest of the mind. My suspicion is that it does. My more or less unrationalized conviction is, that if a system of psychological posits alone make explanatorial sense of certain seemingly behavioural phenomena, explanatorial considerations take the matter out of one's hands and contingency loses its foothold. However, these questions are not my topic.

(2) And so when people speak of 'the mystery of consciousness', they perhaps mean that nothing could explain the appearance of so radical a novelty on the world scene. But it is possible that what they are thinking of is something rather different. It could be that what they have in mind is, that whatever the explanation of consciousness may be, that explanation must be one that is marked by a natural depth which is barely to be plumbed in its entirety. And it is easy to sympathize with such a sentiment. And yet why single out consciousness in this regard? Are we to assume that a comparable attitude is out of place concerning Mentality itself—or even Life? Are not these phenomena marked likewise by depth of this particular type, and in that specific sense of the term by 'mystery' of a kind?

It may seem obscurantist to speak thus of life. Has not vitalism been consigned to a bin reserved for something rather worse than (say) phlogiston? No doubt it is so, but I think we should hesitate before saying that vitality has been 'reduced to physics'. While vital systems are physical systems, and therefore to be physically investigated and at least in part understood in physical terms, the truth of this claim depends on the variety of the reducing, it depends upon the type of the posited explanatory principles. Are vital systems machines? Since no machine is intrinsically a machine, and vitality is both intrinsic and supervenient on physical constitution, they cannot be. But the contentious thesis (improperly) wrapped up in the claim (say) that cells are machines, is probably to the effect that cells might be indistinguishable from a machine concocted by some possible mind: that is, that any particular cell *might have been* a machine, that its causal properties are ambiguous between either interpretation. Now the simplest and most familiar machine-structure is analytical-additive in type: a sequence of input–output situations realized in physical form, in each of which the conditions necessary for a given physical law are exemplified in proper causal isolation, each unit so connected with others as to realize some desired overall input–output situation. Could such an explanatory schema be applicable to vital systems?

I do not think it could. One discovers a clue to vital explanation by recalling something of the character of psychological explanations. Every psychological explanation resembles a battlefield—after the battle. 'It was resolved thus', it seems to say, 'and may for all we know be resolved differently next time.' Similarly in vital

3

systems generally one can more or less never say it will be exactly the same next time. The impact of the system on the particular phenomenon can almost never be wholly ruled out. This suggests a measure of inexactitude in explanation and prediction which is all but irremediable, the inevitable effect of an irreducible systematicity. True, the susceptibility to systemic influence varies from phenomenon to phenomenon, but it is difficult to rule it out completely in all but a few extreme cases. In a word, the most simple and familiar of machine structures is necessarily inapplicable to vital systems, and so I would surmise are all machine explanatory schemas.

Then in its own modest fashion this property corresponds to 'mystery' of a kind. We have every reason to believe that with the passage of time the explanatory gaps will contract, but no one seriously envisages their total closure in the forseeable future. Vital objects are the only material objects in existence which are at once *intrinsically* (or superveniently) and *significantly* much more than (mere) chunks of material stuff. I believe that this logical property corresponds, if not exactly to a new ontology, to a new order of being. After all, the most sublime moments of creative genius equally as much as the humblest processes in the cell are expressions of the life of the organism. That the same property should be manifest in both, carries the implication that the mystery and inexplicability of the one should find an echo in the other.

The point of these observations is merely to question the presumed singularity of consciousness. However close they may be, consciousness is not the same thing as mentality, and if people are impressed by the mystery of the one, it seems to me they have almost as much reason to be struck by that of the other. The closeness of the two phenomena guarantees that it is so.

2. Consciousness

(i) The internal scene

But it is one thing to explain the existence of consciousness, it is another to say what its properties are, what if anything is its constitution, in a word what consciousness *is*. This problem tends to have been neglected by philosophers, owing to an excessive concern with the former question. And yet I think that there is at present a far greater likelihood of progress on questions of character than origins. The tendency of some philosophers to 'jump the gun' scientifically, and engage in what is little more than a form of science fiction, ought not to blind us to the magnitude of the scientific task. Meanwhile, it seems to me that a considerable amount can be learned concerning the character of consciousness. Here it is primarily philosophical elucidation that I have in mind.

Indeed, whatever mystery there may be over the origins of consciousness, I suggest there is no mystery as to what consciousness is. Unlike much in the mind, there is reason for thinking that consciousness is not an indefinable, whether of the type of simple *qualia*, or such as we encounter in some of the fundamental phenomena of the mind like experience, belief, desire. Consciousness has a determinate character of internal type, and there exist logically necessary and sufficient psychological conditions for the presence of this phenomenon. As we shall see in Chapter 2, consciousness is analysable into psychological parts.

Now a cornerstone in the analysis of consciousness is the fact that its presence entails *contemporaneous experience* (a 'stream of consciousness'). This is a transparently clear analytic necessity. And yet plainly consciousness requires more than just experience: after all, dream experience is not merely inconsistent with consciousness, it is logically inconsistent with it. Thus, the experiences entailed by consciousness must be of a certain type: probably not altogether chaotic, possibly not wholly imaginative, certainly not entirely passive, and so on. And consciousness has other internal requirements of a non-experiential kind: for example, in the self-conscious a certain measure of knowledge of the contents of one's own mind is a necessity (as we shall discover in Chapter 3). And so on.

(ii) Connections

But the fact that consciousness is an internal phenomenon, with purely internal determinants, can be misinterpreted. It is not as if consciousness was a totally self-contained item, like a light in a box or some such, sufficient unto itself. A simple comparison helps to make the point. Thus, in a certain sense the black regular marks upon a printed page point beyond themselves to items elsewhere, as the colour or texture of the page do not. Then it seems that consciousness stands in a somewhat comparable relation to Reality. When we speak of consciousness, a determinate relation to the World in which it occurs is necessarily implicit. Indeed, it is doubly implicit. For while the mind as such is World-oriented, consciousness is specifically so. It constantly addresses itself to and in some way actually contacts the World, precisely as the dream merely putatively and invariably ineffectually attempts the same. The unlikeness of dream and waking in this regard makes it clear that in consciousness a special bond with Reality is established. As we say of the waking, they are 'in touch with' Reality as dreamers are not.

This property cannot exist without *knowledge*. The relation to the World realized by consciousness depends on the presence in the mind of suitable items of knowledge. It serves to remind us of the importance of this phenomenon so far as consciousness is concerned. Indeed, despite the fact that the final functional end of consciousness is almost certainly the performing of physical intentional deeds which in some way promote life, I should say that cognition lies closer to the heart of consciousness than does action: the non-accidental ambiguities in the word 'awareness', ranging as they do from knowledge across perception to consciousness itself, strongly suggest that knowledge is the pre-eminent power ushered into being with this phenomenon. Then what I want at this point to emphasize is that the special contact between consciousness and Reality depends in the first place upon the presence of an already existing cognitive base. The following observations show how and why it is so.

That a relation of dependence exists between consciousness and knowledge is evident when we remember the following. The property of intentionality, of being directed or 'about———', which characterizes mental phenomena generally, characterizes the experiences that are analytically necessitated by the state consciousness. This property carries the implication that a conscious subject must know something of the World in which he finds himself. How could a person have experiences with determinate content if he knew nothing of the World towards which they are directed? A self-consciously conscious subject—more, anything that is the bearer of a self-conscious type of mind—must be acquainted with certain general properties of the World: for example, with the character of the overall framework, the rules of individuation and explanation that prevail in that World, together with some kind of awareness of its actual contents. A mind devoid of all such furniture would be unable to sustain determinate experiences, and none of its states could be that of consciousness. In such circumstances, the distinction between conscious and unconscious simply could not be drawn. In terms of what would one do so?

3. Consciousness and Epistemology

(i) Perception

(1) Since knowledge is so closely linked to consciousness, it is natural to assume that a special relation holds between consciousness and epistemology. Indeed, since anyone who is conscious is 'in touch with' Reality and endowed with empirical epistemological powers peculiar to the state, one might naturally suppose that consciousness must involve the functioning of those special powers. But is it in fact so? Now I should emphasize that whereas the knowledge on which sheer mentality, and therefore also consciousness internally depend, might be acquired either innately or at some previous time, what concerns me here is the need for epistemological transactions with the world that are *contemporaneous* with the prevailing state consciousness. More exactly, what I want to discover at this point is whether the internal requirements for consciousness can be satisfied even though the internal scene includes neither epistemological success nor the mere functioning of the naturally appointed empirical epistemological faculty peculiar to the state.

As a preliminary to addressing this question, it helps to take a closer look at consciousness itself. And that is to say, the state of waking consciousness that occurs in a physical being situated in a physical world. At once one phenomenon stands out in experience: perception. Even though perception does not actually fill the conscious mind, it is an overwhelming presence, especially the visual variety. We wake to consciousness every morning, and light floods in upon us as we do, and so long as consciousness endures our surrounds steadily impinge upon us in this concrete

6

sensuous fashion, absorbing much of our attention at the time. And there are good reasons why perception should be thus dominant in conscious experience. For perception is the epistemological bridge conducting us to the phenomenal occupants of the World (with the sole exception of our own self and mind). It is the 'royal road' to physical reality, indeed to the World in its ultimate ontological form. If Physicalism is true then a self-conscious being is a part of physical reality which epistemologically is in touch with a special part of physical reality, namely its own mind. However, such phenomena are experienced by their owner in purely mental guise. Then only in perception does consciousness make epistemological contact with Reality in its true or ultimate (i.e. physical) form. We saw that consciousness is a close and intimate partner to the World, that the conscious are in a familiar sense 'in touch with' Reality. Then in the phenomenon of perception consciousness keeps the appointment and meets that partner as it really is. It is a predestined conjunction. Here the World comes forward to meet it, 'in the flesh' so to say. This suggests that perceptual function must be a centrally important feature of consciousness, indeed almost as important as experience itself.

(2) These observations were preliminary to an investigation of the problem raised above. Namely, how essential to consciousness is this 'overwhelming presence'? Is it a binding necessity? Can consciousness occur if the perceptual attention, not merely is not delivering veridical readings, but is simply inoperative? Can it shut down altogether and consciousness remain intact? The natural presumption must surely be that it cannot: after all, the state 'unconsciousness' is specifically demarcated by the unavailability of the perceptual attention, and in sleep the perceptual attention works at best sporadically. In short, the theory that consciousness necessitates a steadily functioning attention, the unceasing 'radar sweep' we know so well, seems prima facie plausible.

And there are other reasons, of a naturalistic kind, for thinking so. For consciousness is a natural phenomenon which evolved into being, and there can be little doubt that perception played a major part in its evolutionary rationale. It is a truism that when consciousness reigns we are in a position to marshal our main psychological resources as nowhere else, and these notably include the use of cognitive and active powers. For much of the time conscious beings are engaged in a cyclical interactive transaction with the environment, in which perception fuels desire, which leads to the active transformation of what once more causes perception, and so on: a higher-order example of a universal vital cycle. Now the fact that knowledge of one's surrounds is an essential part of this elemental transaction between inner and outer domains, indicates that empirical epistemological function of the kind which can be supplied by perception alone must be part of the very rationale of the existence of consciousness. Then it seems probable that such earthly beginnings will have left their mark upon the concept.

These considerations push one towards the view that perceptual attentive function is a necessity for consciousness. However, such a position involves certain

7

difficulties. For when we come to examine the internal requirements for consciousness—which on the face of it appear to be universal and transcendent of whatever
metaphysics fits the world in which the consciousness in question occurs—we discover that we can assemble a sufficient set which make no mention of a working perceptual faculty. I am thinking of such conditions as an adequate knowledge base, an
unbroken continuity of self-aware experience, a prevailing occurrent condition of
rationality, and so on. Furthermore, even if it were true that perceptual attentive
function is a necessity for consciousness, this can be no simple analyticity of the
kind relating consciousness with experience. Whereas sheer inspection of concepts
reveals that consciousness cannot exist without experience, no comparable analyticity guarantees that those experiences include the perceptual attentive variety. It
does not on the face of it seem possible, merely on the basis of concepts, to outlaw
angelic consciousnesses from the realm of the possible. Metaphysical considerations may do so, the content of a concept cannot. If angelic beings prove to be metaphysically possible, why should not an unbroken continuity of self-aware rationally
structured active experience suffice for consciousness to obtain in them? Are not
these wholly internal phenomena a sufficiency? Then what need of perception on
top of all that? What difference could it make to this already constituted mental
state that outer realities should in principle be able to press in concretely upon the
awareness of these beings? On the face of it, one would say none.

(3) And so we are faced with a conflict. On the one hand purely analytical considerations seem to lend no support to the idea that consciousness necessitates a
working perceptual attention. On the other hand both the identifying tests for the
presence of the state, as well as the relevant functional and evolutionary facts,
suggest that the bond between consciousness and perception must be of a stronger
order than one of mere contingent co-presence. What is the way out of this
difficulty?

I think in the first place we need to state the problem more exactly. For it seems to
me that several distinct attentive situations exist which are easily confused, and that
a failure to distinguish them has led to the present impasse. So to begin, let us be
clear just what it is we are seeking. Plainly, consciousness has no binding need of
steady perceptual success: a person could be conscious when all his senses were
delivering faulty readings. What matters, one might say, is that a reading is taking
place. Indeed, just as the reading in the case of hearing might be that I hear nothing,
so in principle consciousness could survive a situation in which the universal
reading of all 'ports of knowledge' was the null-reading. And yet these latter negative experiential findings ('listen to the silence!') are readings after all. However,
something less than a null-reading is possible in the case of a sense: namely, the
absence of *any* reading. For example, the typical auditory experiential 'count'
of one who has been stone-deaf for many years. And so an even more radical
possibility might be contemplated. Namely, that of a consciousness which exists
in the presence of a universalization of absences of this kind. Is this possible? Could

consciousness exist when, from the point of view of perceptual experience, there are simply *no* readings? Such a situation is consistent with a phenomenon like sleep, but is it consistent with consciousness? I think it is. Why should a man not be awake, unreflectively cognizant of the fact that present experience fails to include perceptual experience of any kind, and his mind be elsewhere engaged? This person would be 'in touch with' the World, know something of its sensuous appearance, know that the environment is not at this moment 'showing itself' to perception, and be preoccupied in thought. While such a state of affairs is vastly atypical of consciousness, and altogether counter to its functional rationale, it seems conceivable.

(ii) 'Transcendence' vs. 'Naturalism'

(1) Then ought we conclude from the above that the state consciousness does not necessitate that the perceptual attention be 'accessible' (or 'on')? But a residual imprecision still dogs this question. It concerns the precise meaning of these expressions. I think we need to pursue this question one final stage further if we are to resolve the conflict that has come to light. This is because the attentive situation has yet to be properly individuated, and the meaning in question fixed. One of the main obstacles to doing so lies in a tendency to conceive of the Attention as a 'faculty'—like sight and hearing (only more so)—something which might be added to or removed from the mind without affecting much else—as the above perfectly natural expressions suggest. As we shall shortly discover, this is a serious misunderstanding. It causes us to pose the above problem in inappropriate terms.

Metaphysically transcendent theories of consciousness conceive of the perceptual attention as something which is *added* to and *inessential* to the state consciousness. According to such doctrines consciousness can be internally determined quite irrespective of whether the attention is accessible or not. And such a theoretical position is eminently understandable, seeing that a set of internal conditions exist which appear to necessitate consciousness yet make no mention of the perceptual attention. Meanwhile the alternative conflicting theory, based upon naturalistic and evidentialist considerations, supposes accessibility of the attention to be among its necessary conditions. In short, the divide between the two theoretical positions is, that whereas metaphysically transcendent theories of consciousness think consciousness can simply lack perceptual attentive power, the naturalist position thinks it can merely fail to use it. One might express the matter this way: if angelic consciousness could exist, it would on this count be seen by the naturalist as necessarily deprived, as 'winged' from the start.

(2) Here I side with naturalism. Despite the fact that consciousness might survive a radical absence of all perceptual readings, whether of positive or negative variety, this is not to say it could survive and the subject be incapable of registering the presence of sensations/immediately-given phenomenal objects. That consciousness might survive a complete drought of attentive experience, does not mean that a conscious subject need not know whether a protracted spell of agonizing

toothache has occurred during the time of his consciousness. Would not all and any conceivable consciousness, no matter where situated and how endowed, find itself in a position to issue definitive reports on such questions? Considerations of this kind convince me that we must be dealing here with a logical necessity.

We could state the position in different terms: namely, through appeal to the principles whereby one individuates states of consciousness. Thus, I do not think any being could be awake and simply—for no other reason than the *kind* of his state of consciousness—lack the power to have and/or notice sensations/immediately-given phenomenal objects. It is true that certain examples of consciousness might be incapable of using those powers, whether because of the inexistence of the required causes of immediate objects, or because of mental impediments to noticing immediate objects generally, but neither property characterizes the prevailing state of consciousness. The first property could not be essential to those consciousnesses, since it could in principle be excised through change elsewhere than within its own precincts. And while the second property has its source within the mind, all such impediments must be mental-causal influences which likewise might in principle be removed. It seems to me that no example of wakeful consciousness can be of such a kind that sensations/immediately-given phenomenal objects could not in principle exist for the conscious mind, nor such that even though they might exist they must of necessity be unnoticeable. If something is the state consciousness, it must in principle be capable of supporting phenomena of this type.

What emerges from this is, that even though consciousness can survive an absence of all attentive readings, whether of positive or null variety, it nonetheless necessitates the *accessibility* of the perceptual attention. And this is transcendent of the metaphysics of Reality. Irrespective of whether angelic consciousness is a metaphysical possibility, if something is the state consciousness then it must be such that, in the first place sensations/immediate objects might in principle occur in or for it, and secondly if they do occur they must lie open to the perceptual attention and be susceptible of noticing. And if it is objected that, since sensations import physical space, such a conclusion is guilty of a form of metaphysical intolerance, in this case of Idealism, let me scale down the claim to the following: any wakeful consciousness must in principle be capable of sustaining events of the type of *noticing*, that is support events in which phenomenal items come as external object to the attention. How could such occurrences not be possible in principle for a wakeful consciousness?

(3) In short, even if for some reason or another a wakeful consciousness could exist in the absence of the capacity to sustain noticing events, it could not be because of the *type* of that wakeful consciousness. We do not individuate *types* of wakeful consciousness through appeal to properties that are at once contingent attributes of wakeful consciousness and discoverable in certain examples of that state. To do so would be to stipulate a contingent property of the state as essential to some supposed type, without designating a type of any kind.

Thus, there are no 'Cro-Magnon consciousnesses' or 'Aryan consciousnesses', there are merely consciousnesses—of Cro-Magnon or Aryan men, each of which might in principle be augmented or depleted in various respects. Just as there are no other possibilities besides rationality or non-rationality of nature, so with consciousness. There are but two types of consciousness, the unselfconscious and self-conscious kind, and a limited few possible states of consciousness. No other kind or state of consciousness can be a priori delimited, nor *a fortiori* guaranteed to lack an accessible perceptual attention. All else is stipulation: the (usual) concept of 'natural kind' being as inapplicable to (wakeful) consciousness as it is to thought or will or sensation (there being no 'twin earth' ('fool's gold') pseudo-examples of these phenomena). I conclude that if a (real) example of (wakeful) consciousness exists wholly without attentive readings, this will in all probability be due to an absence of sensations/immediately-presented objects, though it could stem from mental-causal influences of some schismatic variety. But it cannot be because the attention is 'off' or simply inaccessible. Consciousness necessitates the possession of a perceptual attentive capacity which is accessible there and then. Consciousness of necessity is attentively open to epistemological contact with what lies beyond its own confines. The state unconsciousness necessarily is not, that of consciousness necessarily is.

4. Rationale

(i) The origin of the perceptual power of consciousness

(1) On this reading of the situation, any project of discovering a theory of consciousness which is transcendent of a metaphysics of Reality, must be doomed from the start. If anything, far from leading us in the direction of universality, it is the other way around. For example, the conjectured angelic consciousness, instead of being a metaphysically exotic and alternative variety of a wider consciousness genus, emerges instead as a deprived example of a single unitary kind. This is because, in failing to allow the possible perception of any immediately-given phenomenal item, it fails to utilize a potential built into consciousness from the start. And so, as was suggested earlier, the earthly origins of the one form of consciousness that we know, do indeed leave their stamp upon the concept. The concept we possess arose in relation to a phenomenon which had evolved into being thanks in part to the existence of sensation and perception, and this fact determines a concept which, while it might look to have application in other metaphysical domains where perceptible phenomena are in the nature of things excluded, proves at best to be capable of exemplifying somewhat stunted varieties of the kind in those domains. If consciousness could exist in such metaphysically different worlds, it would be something less than its full self. That 'full self' involves the functioning of the perceptual attention. This is the universality which we should advance in place of a spurious 'metaphysical universality'.

(2) Thus we replace the 'metaphysically universal' theory of consciousness by a merely universal theory. Then if consciousness entails the potential for events of the type 'perceptual experience', how does it come to have this important property? But how could one possibly answer so fundamental a question? Well, I believe this question is susceptible of answer, but before I provide an answer let me review the explanatory situation that obtains in the case of the necessary connection between consciousness and perceptual power just investigated, since this leads to that answer.

It has, I think, to be acknowledged, that this was a somewhat intuitive conclusion, based on a premiss of imaginability and a theory of classification. Namely, the unimaginability of a variety of wakeful consciousness which could not (like uncon-sciousness) even in principle support noticing events, together with the assumption that wakeful consciousness does not admit of internal subclassification into (true) kinds founded on properties of this sort. These arguments are a little stark, and largely unrationalized. Moreover we should remember that the two main varieties of rationale applicable with properties of this type are inapplicable here. Thus the claim cannot be a transparently clear analyticity (like that linking consciousness with experience). Nor is it a logically necessary mental-causal rationalizable deduc-tion from other properties of consciousness (like that linking the rationality of con-sciousness with the impossibility of dreaming). We seem left with the not very satisfactory situation, that upon what look like rather intuitive grounds, we opt for the logical necessity of a proposition which is neither an analyticity nor determined by a priori-given intra-psychic mental-causal necessary connections. It looks as if we shall have to accept that it is a simple inexplicable fact, a blunt truth.

(ii) The realistic commitments of consciousness

(1) But at this point an important property of consciousness sheds light on the problem. Earlier I noted that whereas dreams merely putatively are of Reality, con-sciousness is 'in touch with' Reality. This proposition is necessary, not susceptible of explanation, and transparently evidently true. Now to say of consciousness that it is 'in touch with' Reality, does not mean a conscious subject there and then makes empirical discoveries concerning the sector of the world lying beyond his own mind. As we shall find in Chapter 2, what it rather affirms is that a conscious being is epistemologically empowered, or mentally in a position to make such discoveries. The conscious subject is mentally in a position to detect empirical realities, is a Reality-detector as such, indeed if he is a self-conscious being must already be apprised of some of the main realities in his own mind.

This property of consciousness enables us to resolve the unsatisfactoriness of the above explanatory situation. It is to be accomplished by introducing the property in question as rationale of the necessity. That is, a rationale whereby the proposition that consciousness entails attentive accessibility can with its assistance be seen to follow deductively from other properties of consciousness. Now this rationale is not an intra-psychic mental-causal logically necessary rationale like that linking the rationality of consciousness with the proscription of dreaming. But it is a rationale notwithstanding. It is a rationale which appeals to the fundamental tie between consciousness and Reality, to the necessary truth-orientation of consciousness.

We interpose this property as explanation of the fact that consciousness necessitates accessibility of the attention, in the following way. The point may be expressed through a question. Namely, how is the requirement that consciousness is empowered to receive the imprint of Reality to be realized, when the truths to be discovered have the following character? They are to be temporally aligned phenomena obtaining in the sector of the world lying beyond the subject's mind at the time of consciousness. Then the answer must be, by having the experiential awareness of the subject reliably responsive in epistemologically revealing ways to phenomena impinging upon it from that domain. In a word, by its being perceptually responsive to those phenomena. The rest of the world must impinge in epistemologically revealing perceptual ways upon the contemporaneous experiential life of the mind. How else is Solipsism to be eschewed? Herewith intelligibility appears in this property of consciousness.

(2) The essential concern of consciousness with truth also sheds light upon another important property of consciousness. Namely, the fact that consciousness in the self-conscious necessitates *rationality of state*. Now one might initially think this necessity shared something of the blunt inexplicability that seemed at first to characterize the necessity under discussion. Interestingly in the case of rationality this feature looks from the start to be qualified in its force. Then apart from explaining the necessity of rationality, we shall now see that the truth-orientation of consciousness enables us to understand why the 'bluntness' appeared qualified, and explains in addition why it was that a continuity of rational experience seemed at first blush self-subsistently to determine consciousness in the absence of perceptual function. The reason in either case is because, even if *per impossibile* attentive access could be outlawed from the internal scene, rational experience would ensure discharge of the *interior* cognitive role of consciousness, bearing in mind that a rational consciousness is 'in touch with' inner reality and knows both of and what causes its own beliefs and deeds, etc. And so the rationality of consciousness enables the truth-orientation of consciousness to be expressed in the interior domain—whatever else (hence the above qualification), and makes it at the same time appear self-sufficient.

But in any case the truth-orientation of consciousness manages also to explain the wholly general fact that consciousness necessitates rationality of state. We have just seen that it must be so in the case of the inner domain. However, the entailment linking consciousness and rationality can be seen to be fully rationalized only when one understands, through appeal to the truth-orientation of consciousness, how it is that on pain of Solipsism conscious minds must be mentally in a position to discover what lies outside their own confines. And this potentiality of consciousness depends in turn upon rationality, since it implies the capacity to support phenomenal epistemological links with external reality which are of such a nature as to be of cognitive use only if supplemented with rational interpretation and inference. In short, rationality has internal *and* external work to perform when consciousness reigns. And this completes the rationale determining the necessary rationality of consciousness.

(3) Now I can well imagine the following objection being levelled against the arguments marshalled just recently at the end of (1) in which I linked consciousness and attentive accessibility. If rational experience, in a mind in which the orientation to Reality of consciousness is realized through certain requisite internal and external relations, together constitute sufficient conditions of consciousness, why when the sector of reality under consideration is that lying beyond the mind of the subject, need the sensitivity to the truth of that domain take the form of an attention ready to receive the imprint of extensionally-given phenomenal objects? Might there not in other metaphysical domains, say in an Idealist world, be alternative avenues to the phenomenal truths of the sector of the world beyond one's mind? In short, avenues other than *perception*?

But let us take stock of the main features of the epistemological situation. What we are concerned with is not some form of pure reasoning. It is with experiential epistemological access to temporally aligned contingently present phenomena located in the sector of the world lying beyond a conscious subject's mind. Then while one might, for whatever reason, think of the perceptual as no more than one way amongst others of making epistemological contact with such items, I believe this would be a mistake. If the requisite experiential epistemological phenomena are as stated above, there is reason to think that the epistemological gap between inner and outer has already been closed—by perception. But to see how this is so, we need to take a closer look at the phenomenon of perception.

5. Perception

(i) The nature of perception: a first emendation to received views

(1) If consciousness entails accessibility of the perceptual attention, how does it come to have this property? This question was first raised a little earlier in the discussion. And at first one despairs of ever explaining the existence of so fundamental a property. Nevertheless, an answer proves on reflection to be available, indeed has in effect already been given, as I hope soon to bring out. Now one might perhaps look for an answer in the long-term dependence of mentality generally, and consciousness along with it, upon perception as source of the concepts through which intentionally directed phenomena acquire content. However, this does not really meet our needs, and what I have in mind is something different. For whereas the above answer mentions the *sometime* need of perception, what concerns me here is the necessity *at the time* of consciousness for the attention to be accessible. And

while the long-term dependence is not what one could call a *logical* connection, my aim in the case of perception is to bring to light just such a bond with consciousness. In a word, it is to demonstrate the existence of a contemporaneous logical link between consciousness and perception.

Here at this juncture my comments centre upon perception. It is my belief that, given what I take to be the central facts about consciousness, an analysis of perception suffices to bring to light the logical link between consciousness and perception. Certain somewhat unexpected a priori truths, turning upon what I see as the non-accidental ambiguities in 'awareness', bear this out. More exactly, what comes as something of a surprise is the nature of perception. In my opinion we are in the presence here of a phenomenon of a wholly universal kind, definable in completely general a priori terms. Accordingly, I now at this point address the task of characterizing the relation between perception and consciousness by a delineation of that nature (the actual demonstration of these claims occurring in Part II of this work). It seems to me that we need first to grasp that perception is in certain respects totally unlike the other inhabitants of the 'stream of consciousness'. For one thing whereas they come by their objects with the aid of the thought, perception (along with physical action) relates concretely to its object, which it discovers through physical causality, and in the case of perception (though not with physical action) the phenomenon in question simply consists in an awareness of its object. But to bring out just what it is that is so unusual about perception, it is advisable that I spell out in a little detail what is probably the generally received though unarticulated conception of perception.

Call this doctrine Normal Theory. This theory begins with a characterization of a phenomenon one might easily mistake for consciousness itself, but which is not really the same thing: 'Experiential Consciousness' (as I shall sometimes describe it), by which I mean the 'stream of consciousness' (of literary fame). According to Normal Theory 'experiential consciousness' is populated exclusively by intentionally directed experiences which represent this world (and others) as being a certain way. Amongst these experiences are two which are capable of acquiring in concrete causal manner their naturally aspired-to or putative extensional status, provided suitably related objects exist: one is the bodily will, the other perception. The final element in Normal Theory is the claim that, along with all the other occupants of 'experiential consciousness', and despite the existence of criterial tests for extensional redescriptions, both of these latter phenomena are in themselves distinctive indefinable essentially intentional types: respectively, of 'willing' and 'attentive' character. In sum, 'experiential consciousness' *ab initio* and before all else is a stream of essentially representational distinctive intentional consciousnesses, and bodily action and perception are no more than two concretely engaged sub-varieties.

(2) The following are some of the actual properties of perception which are at loggerheads with this account.

To begin, it is worth remembering that (say) visual experience is putatively an extensional phenomenon ('seem see'), despite falling under intentional descriptions. Then the divergences from Normal Theory cast in these terms begin to appear when we consider the phenomenon of sensation (which is a cornerstone of perception). Thus, since we come to know of our own sensations through noticing them, and this noticing satisfies all tests (non-deviancy, etc.) for being perception, the awareness of sensation rates as a perception. More contentiously, because there is no mental type such that (say) 'notice pain' *redescribes* its instances, ('seem notice pain' being reserved for imaginings), and a fortiori none that do so thanks to its relating suitably causally to pain, the awareness of sensations must be an essentially extensional phenomenon—indifference to (in)existence being no part of its nature (for can one imagine the experience of pain in the absence of pain?) And contentiously again, since the perception of *qualia* in physical objects is through the agency of sensations, since sense-datum theory is true of all perceptions that are mediated by sensible qualities (defended at length in Chapters 17 and 18), all such perceptual experiences must be essentially extensional occurrences (for can one imagine a wholly non-veridical but genuinely visual experience in which *nothing* lies before one?), despite their falling simultaneously under intentional interpretational headings. Finally, it should be noted that the core of all perceptual experiences is 'pre-interpretational': an infant who winces at the light sees light and very likely also its colour, but need see neither *as* 'bright', 'white', 'light', 'out there', indeed *as*—anything. It is around this core that all of our familiar meaningful descriptions, which owe their existence to the close integration of the Perceptual Attention with the Understanding, are ultimately draped.

A word about sensations. Despite Wittgenstein's strictures, the sensation is a mental *object*, indeed the unique example of the kind. And I use the term advisedly, for the sensation unites the property of senselessness, which arises out of its necessarily non-psychological bodily origins, with noticeability or perceivability, which it shares exclusively with physical objects (and with absolutely no other psychological phenomenon). This complex property makes it the potential representer-agency *par excellence* in the mind, a potential which is realized to perfection in sight, thanks to the spatial order and differentiation in the visual field, and ultimately to the omnipresence in the environment of rectilinearly propagated electro-magnetic radiation. Here the physical realm casts its shadow in the mind as nowhere else, and must share with that 'shadow' certain properties in order to do so. Indeed, both in character, and in the logical role which it plays, the sensation reveals a close kinship to matter. Plato allotted a special intermediate role to matter in the scheme of things, and ontologically the sensation (along with the bodily will) seems to occupy a special intermediate position between properly developed mental and merely physical phenomena. The fact that sensations, whether bodily or visual or auditory, are individuated in body-relative physical space, unlike experiences and the remaining occupants of the mind (which are selectively strung along the one-dimensional temporal thread), is some kind of confirmation of this fact.

(3) The conclusion to be drawn from these emendations to the theory of perception and 'experiential consciousness' expounded in 'Normal Theory', is that the doctrine of the intentionality of mental phenomena generally, and of the content of 'experiential consciousness' in particular, has to be restricted: its case is overstated. Intentionality is neither temporally, developmentally, logically, nor causally prior to extensionality: consciousness arises in this world with both kinds of object equally primitively given to it. Sense-datum theory may have a small following, but few can doubt the reality of sensations, and the attentive awareness of sensations is essentially extensionally of its object. While interpretational intentional 'aiming' is a vastly typical feature of experiential life in the conscious, the 'stream of experience' is not *ab initio* and before all else constituted exclusively of essentially intentional consciousnesses: 'experience' at any moment is simply flooded with phenomena which disprove this claim.

Thus, experiential consciousness is not something behind closed doors as it were, pure representation of what lies beyond. Thanks to the phenomenon of perception, essentially extensional consciousnesses of concretely and pre-interpretationally given mental objects are there from the start (and to an abundant degree), side by side with purely interpretational essentially intentional mental phenomena. It is important that we record the unique role of perception in effecting this state of affairs. In particular, the one other experience capable of discovering an extensional object in the concrete mode, namely the bodily will, cannot accomplish so much, seeing that there is no psychic *thing* that is the appointed immediate object of the bodily will, which has instead a perceptually given bodily target-object (e.g. arm) and bodily goal-event (e.g. arm-movement) as its (diverse) immediate objects. Perception is unique in the above regard. Only perception has an extensional essence, and only it has the unique mental object and representer-agency as its appointed object.

(ii) The nature of perception: a second emendation

These emendations lead naturally to a second theory (call it 'Revised Theory') of perception and 'experiential consciousness'. The supposition now is that 'experiential consciousness' in the conscious is occupied by experiences which divide into the essentially intentional (say, thoughts and desires) and the essentially extensional (awarenesses of pains, sounds, etc.). This theory accepts that extensionality is present from the start. And it accepts also that while some experiential consciousnesses acquire their objects abstractly, through the offices of thought and concept, bodily will and perception do so through concrete means and in a form which is at its core pre-conceptual (a fact which is evidenced in the mental life of infants, who need no concepts to feel pain, see light, or kick their legs). Any meaning which is instantiated in the case of these two phenomena is an imposed meaning.

Now an important element in Revised Theory is that it populates 'experiential consciousness' with an array of distinctive *sui generis* idiosyncratic and largely indefinable psychological natures: desire, affect, will, etc. Then it is here that the second amendment occurs: a correction of rather greater moment than the first. I encapsulate the claim in question in the form of a summary characterization of the phenomenon of perception.

To begin, while perception takes different kinds of objects, it is itself the same on each occasion, for there are no *modes* of noticing. This is because perception is pure, bare, ungarnished, extensional consciousness-of some phenomenal reality. For perception is the one experience that is of the type: *experience* of its object. That is, perception is the unique case, amongst the multitude of experiences which might at some time appear in the stream of consciousness, where the species-type under which it becomes determinate and acquires identity, is constituted by a purely formal operation upon the covering genus-type, namely by giving to it merely an extensional object. Thus, uniquely the genus 'experience' can by purely formal means determine a species, and uniquely perception realizes that logical potential of the genus. The conclusion is, that perception must be definable in terms of a priori-given universal concepts: namely, awareness and the concept of taking an extensional object. Perception emerges as a wholly universal and a priori concept.

In sum, perception proves to be an absolutely unique member of the class of experiences which together constitute 'experiential consciousness' in the conscious. It is not the fact that the concept is extensional in kind, and the phenomenon putatively an instance of such. Nor that its extensional object is concrete in nature, and concretely acquired, or that the core of perception is pre-interpretational. All of this is true of bodily action. The first property that is unique is, that it has as immediate material object a concretely given entity which unites the properties of being *the* psychological object and the unique potential *representative* of the physical in the psychological realm. The next rather more interesting property of perception is, that it is essentially extensional in type, at least in the case of all those perceptions mediated by secondary qualities. But far and away the most singular fact about perception is, that it is a universal a priori-given mental concept, wholly devoid of idiosyncrasy, being nothing but the extensional awareness of a phenomenal reality.

What this means is that we must radically adjust the familiar picture of perception as one idiosyncratically distinctive essentially intentional directed experience, set down in a system of other such experiential consciousnesses. Perception is distinctive all right—but its distinctiveness resides in its universality, in its breaking step with all the others, even with bodily action. Uniting the property of being essentially extensionally of a concretely presented mental object, with the fact that the mental object in question stands in a relation of representation to the physical contents of space, and conjoining both with the property of discovering its identifying type or species under the completely universal concept of awareness (so that perception proves to be no more than a bare awareness of a concretely presented phenomenal reality), these three elemental traits justify the image of perception as the one phenomenon in which the mind 'opens its doors' and lets the outside world in. Mere mental things, alongside meaningful mental phenomena, fill awareness from the beginning, and since those mental things attentively represent the objects surrounding us in the environment, their concrete presence to awareness *is* that of those physical objects. The lower-order world of things flows unchecked into the internal and higher-order domain of consciousness, intruding where they might least be expected! Rather like Magritte's locomotive suspended in mid-air before a fireplace in a drawing-rooom, so the environment in experiential perceptual consciousness. Things are everywhere to behold! It is, in Heideggerian terminology, from the very start a case of 'being in the world'—with a vengeance. Here things are present in awareness *qua* concrete object, as 'near' *qua* object as the experiences themselves are 'near' *qua* occupant (for when the experience is perceptual, these 'two' presences are one and the same!). Waking to consciousness, this is the simple character of one great half of experience.

(iii) The significance of the divide in 'experiential consciousness'

(1) Thus, the occurrent system 'experiential consciousness' divides in two. One half consists of essentially intentional experiences of diverse types (thought, desire, emotion, etc.): roughly, the domain of true experiential interiority, where objects are acquired through thought and concept. The other half consists of experiences of a single type (even though directed to diverse objects) where the type is exhaustively characterizable as 'experience of——', and here instead of the interiority of the first half we encounter concrete confrontations with diverse necessarily concrete particular objects. These latter experiences are at once essentially extensionally directed to immediate sensuous objects (colour, pain, sound) and mostly also at the same time intentionally directed to mediated physical objects (people, sky, trees, and the public occurrence of secondary qualities). Thus one half of experiential consciousness is populated by experiences which are at their core essentially intentional, the other by experiences which at their core are essentially extensional. And both halves instantiate a priori-determinable logical structures.

What is the significance of this divide running down the middle of the stream of consciousness? I think it arose in the first place through the need of experiences for objects, and that it persists thereafter through the partial perpetuation of the original situation. This is apparent when we examine the less developed variety of consciousness. The existence of unselfconscious consciousness demonstrates that the 'experiential consciousness' of conscious subjects can be wholly constituted out of experiences which find their objects by means other than thought, and that this must have been the original situation. Then how in fact do experiences acquire their objects in unselfconscious subjects? It is accomplished almost entirely through the agency of contemporaneous perception. The merely animal mind is tied perceptually to its environment somewhat as a goat is tethered to a post, a constraint we have to a large degree shaken off. While in self-consciousness many experiences acquire objects through the thought, and in consequence range far and wide without limit, animal experience does so indexically, concretely, and for the most part perceptually, being anchored in this way to the ground. Behaviourism cannot be far from the truth in their case, and we attribute experiential states largely in terms of local situation and behaviour. In sum, thought being no part of their mental repertoire, unselfconscious conscious experience generally acquires its objects through the agency of perception which links it there and then with its surrounds.

(2) But how do these same perceptions come by their objects? The question is arresting, because at this point the chain of cognitive dependence reaches its final link. Perception acquires its objects differently from all other mental phenomena. It does so through bare awareness-of that object. Here the significance of the *modelessness* of perceptual noticing has purchase. For merely animal consciousness has need of an experience which is at once the provider of content and without need of a provider itself. In short, perception is a unique case amongst experiences, and meets a common need. The other experiences require the presence of an experience which is the port of entry of the local environment into a mind that is steadily involved in its surrounds, and perception answers to this requirement. For perception brings to awareness, and in concrete mode, the environment to which in the unselfconscious the other experiences indexically and concretely relate: perception is mere Reality-registering, the remaining experiences being responses to the Reality thus encountered. In this respect perception might be seen as the founding father of the experiences which fill 'experiential consciousness' in the unselfconscious conscious mind.

Then how could perception be a bare port of entry for objects and also a distinctive presentation of those same objects? For perception is a sheer replication of its objects, and as characterless as such a replica. Its distinction lies in its lack of distinction. It is a phenomenon with as much character and originality as a reflection in a mirror! And yet it is precisely in this way that perception accomplishes the seeming impossibility of enabling a genus-concept to determine a species-concept. It achieves this end through bringing to that genus more or less nothing, by embellishing 'experience' with—nothing: that is, nothing more than a formal development, nothing in the way of distinctive content or character, no scope left for the concept of idiosyncraticity. Determinacy of nature enters through this strange side-door: permitting outer reality to wholly determine what fills 'awareness'. Hence, while almost all the other experiences are indefinable and idiosyncratic, this experience proves to be definable and universal.

Thus, perception is the sheer presence to awareness of extensionally given phenomenal objects. And in unselfconscious subjects such a modeless presentation of objects is obligatory if the other experiences are to find objects. In this way in the unselfconscious a divide appears in 'experiential consciousness' between on the one hand concrete presences, and on the other phenomena which occur through their agency and are directed with their assistance. And this divide is perpetuated throughout all strata of animal kind. Think of the intermeshing of many of our physical acts with the contents of the visual field, phenomena in which the object of manipulation is irreducibly visually individuated. Thus the divide in 'experiential consciousness' persists unaltered into self-consciousness. Even though thought takes over some of the function of perception in giving to many experiences their object, it cannot take it over in entirety, and the original role of perception as provider of objects for multiple experiences remains. Humans live in the here and now, wherever their minds may range. They engage concretely with physical entities in their physical actions and in the sense-perceptions through which those acts discover their objects, so that at any moment 'experiential consciousness' overtly anchors the mind in its physical surrounds. It is for reasons of this kind that the divide which appeared first in the unselfconscious persists into self-consciousness, a mark of our commonality with our non-rational brethren. Indeed, it exhibits in the particular a debt encountered universally, namely that of the mind and (derivatively, also) consciousness to perception as the provider of objects.

6. Consciousness and Perception

(1) The problem that these recent reflections concerning the universal character of perception was intended to illuminate was, why consciousness necessitates accessibility of the perceptual attention. In what way do they take us any nearer to an answer? We have seen we cannot analytically deduce attentive accessibility, as we could the occurrence of experience. Nor can there be a logical deduction from the other mental elements of consciousness, say from the existence of a continuity of rational experience. What rather we should look for are logical connections leading from the concept of consciousness to accessibility of the attention. Then what emerged concerning the nature of perception provides the logical connection that we seek.

But before I spell out that central connection, a preliminary observation. Namely, that the investigation of perception reveals to begin with a fact of some significance. For if what was claimed is correct, it must follow that the concept of perception is derivable by a purely formal operation upon that of the one phenomenon transparently analytically entailed by consciousness, the experience. And this already constitutes a logical link between consciousness and perception: (sheer) awareness leading to (experiential) awareness leading to (sheer extensional) awareness. We take the genus–concept of the experience, and derive the species–concept of perception by assembling a concept out of no more than that of experience and extensional object. That concept is not of an experience taking an extensional object. Rather, it is the concept of *experience* taking such an object. In short, once we assume that the state consciousness is realized, the conceptual raw materials are there from the start, merely waiting to be assembled: the concept of perception grows out of that of the core phenomenon of consciousness. It follows from these considerations that for conscious subjects perception cannot be just one logical possibility amongst others, as holds of sight or hearing. Nor can it be a logical possibility that is founded in part on sheer empirical fact, as the logical possibility of specific faculties like sight and hearing depends upon their empirical reality. It must be one that is conceptually foreseeable. Therefore even if it had been possible for angelic consciousness to exist in the absence of perceptual accessibility, a logical place would have been prepared in advance for perception: an option simply not taken up in this case for reasons of a metaphysical nature. In short, a possibility neglected.

(2) These truths follow upon the analysability of perception into wholly universal a priori-given constituent elements. They are preliminary to, and precursors of, the deductive connection between consciousness and perception which interests me, which I now discuss. Let us start by representing the sector of reality (R) lying outside the subject's own mind (Ψs) as R–Ψs, and consider the epistemological relation in which a conscious subject stands to this outer domain. Then the proposition which I hope soon to deduce from the aformentioned universal character of perception is that the epistemological link to R–Ψs that is guaranteed by the presence of consciousness is constrained by the nature of the situation to be perceptual in type. Now it is an interesting fact that such a claim might well prove acceptable to many if the worlds in question were restricted to physical worlds. It is worth considering why it should be acceptable under those conditions. Is it because we have encountered or can imagine nothing else? But the claim most people would make is surely of a stronger order than one based on the character of their experience or the powers of their imagination. Many would say it was simply *inconceivable* that there be alternative ultimate avenues to physical phenomenal fact. In short, that it is a logical necessity that in a physical world the final court of epistemological appeal, when it comes to discovering purely physical phenomenal fact is, not merely 'the test of experience', it is 'the test of perceptual experience'. What interests me is the reason one is persuaded of this proposition. In my opinion it is because of considerations supporting the universal thesis that is transcendent of the metaphysical character of the world involved: the doctrine that irrespective of the type of the world perception alone meets the conditions necessary for something to count as the ultimate epistemological avenue to outer phenomenal fact that is guaranteed in a mind by the presence of consciousness.

Not everyone will accept a universal theory of the kind envisaged. Why, when the reality under discussion is non-physical and the domain under consideration R–Ψs, need the sensitivity of consciousness to the truth of that domain take the form of an attention ready to receive the imprint of extensionally-given items? Why, in short, need it take the form of *perception*? For example, in an Idealist World what need of such? What need or indeed possibility of sensations, of sensory *quales*, and so forth? May there not exist undreamed-of epistemological avenues to R–Ψs, which make no use of perception or anything remotely like it? To insist that it be perceptual is metaphysically unrealistic (*sic!*), chauvinistic, and so on.

How should one respond to this objection? I think to begin by introducing more precision into the delimitation, both of the (outer) subject-matter consciousness needs to relate with epistemologically, and of the general character of that relation. For example, it is not addressed to (say) the universal metaphysical characteristics of R–Ψs, nor therefore with the marshalling of pure forms of reasoning. Rather, consciousness brings with it at each moment the latent capacity for epistemological contact of an experiential kind with the phenomenal facts of outer Reality. This is because consciousness is itself an occurrent continuous phenomenon that is renewed instant by instant and is 'in touch with'—inner and outer—Reality. What is implicit is the utilization of reliable epistemological avenues to contingently present phenomenal facts and events of R–Ψs; and one might add, given through experiences whose content 'paces' temporally the ongoing state of waking consciousness, data that is temporally aligned with the time of Ψs. Finally, it should be emphasized that I do not presume upon the presence of any perceptual faculty. Thus, I am not suggesting that the epistemological contact in question take any form, for I expressly disavow faculty theories of the Attention. I do not even claim that sensations need act as attentive mediator, let alone the varieties known to us. I am concerned to demonstrate no more than the potential for attentive contact— of some form or another. That is, of steady occurrent latent perceptual power—of some form or another.

(3) In sum, the truth-orientation of consciousness necessitates the latent capacity to make epistemologically well-founded discoveries concerning the contingently present temporally aligned phenomenal occupants of some given sub-sector of R–Ψs. Such a state of affairs implies that the experiential life of consciousness must from moment to moment be ready reliably to respond to select phenomena in R–Ψs, and that a specific foundation for knowledge would thereby be established. And yet if such experience is to be the expression of the latent epistemological contact of consciousness with what lies beyond itself, something more is needed than reliable responsiveness to that beyond. Namely, those experiences must in the final analysis be founded upon experiences in which contents of that outer domain are directly presented to *awareness*. This is because the only conceivable ultimate epistemological avenue leading consciousness beyond itself is *awareness* of what lies beyond. That is, consciousness can go beyond itself cognitively only by breaking out of itself: that is, into awareness of what lies beyond. Only thus in the final analysis can outer Reality be known.

Then this is to say that the experience in question has to be perceptual, for perception is (and is no more than) bare awareness of phenomenal realities. The one experience which combines regular responsiveness to what lies beyond consciousness with the property of being the ultimate and essential expression of the orientation of consciousness towards outer Reality, is perception. It alone unites the necessary evidential and constitutive properties. If an experience has the epistemological significance of reliably evidencing the phenomenal state of a sector of R–Ψs, and has in addition the necessary constitutive property of being putatively an awareness-of that sector under some description which truly fits, it at one and the same time constitutes the requisite epistemological bridge and acquires the status of perception. It follows from these considerations that if the epistemological potential guaranteed in conscious subjects by the truth-orientation of consciousness is realized—no matter in how unutterably different a manner from anything we know or could imagine—it will justify the characterization of the epistemologically significant experiences as 'experiences of (the contacted) x', in a special and familiar extensional sense of the latter expression, the perceptual sense.

Then in using the expression 'experience of——' in the special extensional sense, no mention is made of the specific, highly idiosyncratic, and from the point of view of consciousness wholly contingent, mode in which this special 'experience of——' is realized. This fact can easily 'throw' one, deflecting one from the fundamental truth that, while the mode is wholly contingent so far as consciousness is concerned, that which it is a mode of is not. This completes the deduction.

(4) Now it may even be that implicitly it is metaphysically chauvinistic to affirm that consciousness necessitates the potential for the perception of outer reality. It could be the case that space is a necessary condition of perception of any kind, the 'form of outer sense' of Kant the only conceivable mode in which perception can be realized. My reaction to this suggestion is, if it is true then so be it. I am concerned merely with the necessary connection between consciousness and accessibility of the perceptual attention.

7. The Objects of Perception

(1) And so perception realizes one of the two logically possible structures open to experience: namely, an experience of the specific type 'experience of——' (extensionally). Here we have the means for understanding two salient facts about perception. The first is, the falsity of a 'faculty' account of the phenomenon, the theory that perceptual accessibility relates in a merely additive fashion to the other constituents of consciousness, rather as (say) the faculty of sight does to the other inhabitants of the mind. It makes sense of this fact, since even though perceptual accessibility is not analytically derivable from consciousness, it is nonetheless both entailed by it and the concept of perception constituted through a purely formal operation upon a concept analytically essential to consciousness itself. Thus, it is both necessary and logically prefigured, and cannot be a mere addition to the other constituents of consciousness as sight is. The second significant property of perception that is illuminated by this understanding of perception is this. It becomes readily comprehensible why perception is of necessity the unique ultimate experiential epistemological link between mind and physical phenomenal reality. The reason lies in the fact that if the concept of perception is merely that of extensional experience of a distinct reality, no conceptual space is available for alternative

24

ultimate experiential avenues leading reliably out onto outer reality. The physical case simply exemplifies a universal rule.

(2) On this account of the nature of perception, the way is clear for consciousness to open out concretely in intelligible manner onto the World in which it finds itself, given to awareness in its ultimate ontological form. And in doing so, the phenomenon of perception fills a logical matrix which has been prepared for it in advance by a concept constitutive of consciousness. Then what is the general type of the objects that are thus given to perception? They are *things* (broadly understood). That is to say, concrete things: material objects, events, qualities, relations, and suchlike. And they are not facts about those things. The perceptual objects are concrete realities, not truths about concrete realities—and by 'concrete realities' I mean, merely the realities themselves. Thus, we 'set eyes upon' people, mountains, the Battle of Midway, Naples for the first time, and in general upon objects and phenomena. And we do not 'set eyes upon' truths. We glimpse or 'catch a sight of' or study or scrutinize objects, faces, phenomena, scenes: in short, *visible items*! The Causal Theory of Perception governs the relation between objects and events in the environment and the event in the attention of noticing in which they come to awareness, and the causal relation holds not between a fact in physical nature and a mental event in which that fact comes to awareness, but between the phenomenal particular and the bare awareness of it.

And yet some might insist that the primary unit of perception is the perception that something of a certain kind is present to one. It might be claimed that while we perceive objects, we do so only as elements of perceptions of propositions involving them. That is, that the event of seeing that a state of affairs obtains *involves* the seeing of objects, and this last is an undetachable though deductible element of the whole, being the only way such events occur. As one might deduce 'he saw a smile' from 'he saw a smile on her face', without supposing smiles might be seen without wearers, so in the case of perception. In short, that objects come to the attention only insofar as propositions involving them do. After all, is not the essential function of perception to convey information? In my opinion this theory is to be resisted. This is because the relation between the seeing of objects and facts is causal. We see that it is snowing because we see and recognize snow, and understand the situation (know 'what's what'). The visual recognition of snow is not awareness of the presence of snow: these phenomena are two, and the first is the causal foundation of rather than an undetachable element of the second.

We would be less inclined to suppose the primary content of perceptual experience to be propositional, if we better understood the contribution of the Understanding to perception. The first thing to remember is, that since the function of perception is to lead to cognition, recognitional perception must be the norm. Therefore while we 'set eyes on' things, the claim is with more illumination to be expressed as follows. We 'set eyes on' *structured* entities; and not just *on* them, but in a *structural mode*. For we recognize objects when we not merely see them, but (and with justification) see them *as* the complex entities they are. While perception is of things rather than facts about things, it is not of 'bare particulars'. It involves conceptualization of the contents of (say) the visual field. Now this phenomenon depends in turn upon one's knowledge of certain propositions, and this fact might lead one to substitute a proposition in place of the interpretational content of the perceptual experience. But this would be an error. The conceptual content of the experience is not to be identified with any proposition: after all, the veridical visual field contains nothing but phenomenal items of diverse types, which typically our minds identify in the experience. The imposition of concepts upon the visual data is not to be confused with its 'propositionalization'.[1] An important distinction exists between the conceptual content of, and the cognitive propositional import of, perceptual experience. Much of this becomes clearer when (in Part II of this work) we examine perceptual experiences directed to negative items like silence, darkness, emptiness, absence, and so on.

(3) In my opinion two of the main dangers facing Perception Theory are over-intellectualization and over-interiorization. In perception things come to us 'in the flesh', as 'raw presences' one might say, and this is true of no other experience. Because of this singularity there is a tendency to understand this phenomenon in terms suited instead to the non-perceptual occupants of 'experiential consciousness', so to say in more mental terms. We encountered over-intellectualism just now in the above theory. Thus, while the understanding is involved in perceptual recognition, the content it imposes is of an interpretational rather than propositional order, it is impressed upon a core which owes no such debt to the understanding, and that core is significantly unlike the proposition in not being constituted of concepts. The primitive elements present in the make-up of this developmentally primitive phenomenon are nowhere represented in the doctrine of the propositional type of its objects.

And as I see the matter we encounter over-interiorization in the doctrine that the essence of perception is purely intentional. The position I endorsed earlier was that perceptual experience is essentially extensionally directed to sensory objects, and that typically intentional interpretation is imposed upon that base. This property of perception, taken in conjunction with the concrete nature of its encounter with objects, demonstrates the unlikeness of perception to properly interior experiences like thought and thought-derivatives such as emotion or imagery. Then it is with these issues in mind that in Part II of this work I investigate the main differences between perceptual experience on the one hand, and cognitively significant experiences like those of thought or imagination or discovery on the other. The aim of that enterprise is the distinguishing of perception from its closest experiential neighbours: it is the differential delineation of this elemental event in which the mind comes face to face with the physical world. But it is in the final analysis an attempt to put on display its somewhat blunt and unthinking nature.

---

[1] To use a favourite expression of Prof. John Anderson, of Sydney, and bygone era.

8. The 'Journey Outwards' of the Attention

(1) And so perception realizes one of the two structures open to experience: namely, an experience of the type 'experience of——' (extensionally). Then when a conscious subject fulfils the potential for this experience that is guaranteed by his state of consciousness, he avails himself of a connection which is from a general point of view a lifeline for mind and consciousness, the origin of the content of their 'representations', the very basis of their existence. It is a contact between the experiential core of consciousness and the sector of the world lying beyond the subject's own mind, given concretely in that experience in its ultimate physical form.

Then what goes on as it makes the connection? There are reasons for thinking this cannot happen at one fell stroke. Whereas we 'just' think of whatever happens to engage our interest, we never 'just' perceive anything. More precisely, we never 'just' perceive anything more than the unique mental object, the sensation. Now some may be willing to accept what they take to be the point under consideration by observing that (say) seeing is not hearing or smelling, that the perception of objects must take a specific form, and that in this sense perception is never 'just' perceiving. But that precisely is not what is at issue, for we see after-images and hear 'ringings' in the ears, and in either case 'just' do so. But whereas we 'just' see after-images, we never 'just' see the sunrise or the furniture or anything showing in the physical environment. Between the perceptual experience and the perceived physical object lies a hiatus, which is such that while it is to be closed by the establishing of the necessary mechanistic connection, it nonetheless at the same time requires a 'bridging' of an altogether different kind. It is this particular gap that constitutes the inability to 'just' perceive whatever is given to awareness as physical. It is the necessarily mediate character of all extra-mental perception.

Thus, items non-identical with but somehow 'proxy' for the object have to be perceived before the object itself can be perceived. And this is so, quite irrespective of whether sense-data in particular exist. For sight cannot 'embrace' its object totally and unselectively and immediately, as perhaps the thought does. It has to earn its passage outwards, through the perception of other items which are epistemologically nearer to awareness than is its goal object, before it can arrive at that destination. For example, through perception of the mediating phenomenon of light; or, what is a rather different mediation, through the selective perception of only one side of the object, or maybe instead its profile; or again, what is a different mediation still, through seeing its colour or its brightness or darkness or even its motion. And so on.

This 'journey outwards' of the attention is like the passing of a torch from hand to hand. It is a torch which embodies, not so much truth, as reality, for whereas delusions affirm falsities, illusions present merely seeming realities, and veridical perception puts the attention in contact with what is there and real. It shares much with a comparable 'journey outwards' on the part of the will, which manages to disturb items lying far afield from the mind/body, thanks to the existence of regular causal relations holding between willings and outer events. Then just as the single event of willing acquires multiple objects and characters through this property, so the solitary perceptual event in the attention does the same through identical means. And so it would be a mistake to construe this latter phenomenon as the establishing of a series of linkages between distinct mental events, to interpret the 'passing of the cognitive torch' in such terms. Rather than multiplying the events in the mind to correspond to the multiple perceptions, we multiply instead the objects and the characters of the single perceptual experience. It is in this way that the attention manages to range far beyond its first and original mental object, the sense-datum. The 'journey outwards' of the attention is not from mental event to mental event: it is at one and the same time from external object to external object and from relational character to relational character. Then when we say that we cannot 'just' see physical objects, what we mean is that the single event of perceiving must acquire a *sequence* of characters and of objects before it can acquire the character of perceiving the *physical object*: it can never 'just' possess that character, never 'just' take that object.

(2) Now while the perceptual experience acquires these multiple objects and characters for the most part relationally, and need not in itself reflect their existence, it nonetheless must in general do so. If it did not it would have no way of fulfilling its cognitive function, of 'delivering the epistemological goods'. And so there is reason for believing that the perceptual experience, in its properly developed and fully interpretational form, must incorporate an internal developmental structure in the instant which recapitulates the string of relationally acquired outer objects. In this regard it is strikingly similar to its brother phenomenon, bodily willing, which incorporates more or less instantaneously within its own confines a causally knit developmental sequence which encompasses all the elements of the activated motor-system[2]—with this significant difference, that whereas the perceptual is an a-nomic mental-causal relation, the bodily active is nomic physical-mechanistic causal in character. In short, in non-accidental fashion the typical fully interpretational (say) visual experience incorporates in the instant a causally linked sequence of internal objects, directly reflecting the existence of the outer mediating perceptibles. This property enables it to discharge its epistemological function.

(3) According to me the very first member of the above list of mediators is the sense-datum. I am of the opinion that these contentious entities exist, are perceived, and are 'just' or immediately perceived. I cannot at this point enter into the reasons supporting this doctrine, and refer the reader to the text. However, a preliminary observation is worth making. It seems to me that whereas it is easy enough to take aboard the possibility that the outer reality to which one intentionally relates

---

[2] See *The Will*, Brian O'Shaughnessy, ii: 212–14 and 286, (ix), CUP, 1980.

in experiences like desire and pursuit and imagery may not exist, it is no easy task to convince oneself that when one has an absolutely real and wholly non-veridical visual field, or (if you prefer) when one has a wholly non-veridical but truly visual experience as of (say) red, that simply *nothing* lies there before one. I do not just mean that one cannot have a real visual experience without something *seeming* to be before one, I mean that one cannot have such an experience without something being *there* to be seen, something one could *point* to: in short, something sensuous before one in body-relative physical space. Simple facts of this kind already constitute powerful prima-facie evidence of the existence of sense-data.

The theory of sense-data might be viewed in several different ways. One might think it is of no great moment, one way or the other, whether such items exist: after all, what difference can it make to one's ontology to admit the existence of a mediating sensation in perception? And I endorse this position, with certain reservations which I indicate in a moment. An opposed view, which I cannot share, is that the theory in pernicious fashion interposes items between consciousness and its physical setting, cuts one off epistemologically from the physical world in so doing, and makes of the material object of perception something which lies behind its appearance in some metaphysically unacceptable way—a criticism which fails to notice that the sense-datum is from the start posited as lying in a direction in body-relative physical space (there being no suggestion that it is set in some hermetically sealed so-called 'visual space').

But there is a third and different theoretical position which one might adopt on this question, which I endorse. Namely, that while from the point of view of general ontology it is of no great consequence whether there are such items as sense-data, from the point of view of a philosophy of consciousness it is of genuine significance. It is true that sense-data are contingent presences both in the world and in animals capable of perceiving sectors of that world, and so cannot be necessary for consciousness. Nonetheless, because of the essentially extensional nature of awarenesses of sensibles like colour and sound, sense-data illustrate with beautiful clarity the extent to which it is a misrepresentation of the character of the stream of consciousnes of the conscious to suppose it populated exclusively by essentially intentional awarenesses. They constitute the very best case for demonstrating that experiential consciousness is made up, on the one hand of experiences with purely intentional objects, and on the other hand of a whole range of other experiences in which objects are concretely given to extensional awareness and essentially so.

Indeed, because perception simply *is* awareness-of its object, when perception occurs mere psychic things must on this account be concrete presences in the stream of consciousness in the mode of extensional object. And since those mental objects attentively represent objects in the environment, so too must be the latter. The world flows in through our mental doors, and sense-data are a prime agency in its doing so. Far from cutting us off from our surrounds, sense-data effect a union between experiential consciousness and physical reality, realized within the mind itself. In fact it seems to me that when believers in sense-data are accused of splitting the mind off epistemologically from physical reality, the boot may to some extent be on the other foot. The reluctance to endorse sense-datum theory goes hand in hand with the overemphasis upon intentionality that is so common, and thus with what I would describe as the over-interiorization of perceptual experience—the mind so to say backing away from the raw contact with physical reality which such experience involves.

Finally, it should be noted that the existence of sense-data is an issue of importance from another point of view: that of a philosophy and science of perception, and specifically of the visual variety. A building resting upon shaky foundations is unlikely in the long run to have much of a future, and it seems to me that whether a theory is right or wrong concerning an issue of such central importance as the identity of the very first object given to the perceptual attention, cannot but make a significant difference to any theoretical edifice which is erected upon premises which include a judgement on this matter. In this seemingly simple question we have one of those theoretically fundamental places where science and philosophy overtly overlap.

(4) Prior to the acquisition of a sequence of mediators something which merits the title 'The Visual Given' is presented to consciousness. One is obliged to posit such a 'given' because of the bifurcated causal aetiology of our visual experiences, and above all because of the presence of intra-psychic or *mental causation* in that aetiology. Simple regular psycho-physical causation determines the internal character of the visual field, which in turn in intelligible ways which involve the distribution of the attention and one's cognitive posture of the moment, then generates visual experience. Accordingly, both mind and body must play a significant part in the causal transaction leading to the formation of the visual experience. Indeed, since the mind alone contributes the properties of organization and interpretation, there is reason to suppose that the 'visual given' should be characterized in the piecemeal pointillist terms used by the Empiricists. Absurd as it may sound to some ears, there is good reason to believe that when we monocularly visually experience, this is prompted into being by an array of mere coloured point-values in an ordered two-dimensional sensory continuum. This is at once the triggering agency of, and the object of organization and interpretation within the very bosom of, the visual experience.

Here is where the 'journey' of the attention (of 'Awareness') begins. It ends in physical reality itself. For it is a 'journey' which takes the mind out onto physical reality as a whole. This is the final destination for the attention in a conscious subject, as we shall see when in Chapter 3 we investigate the difference between the realistic perceptions of wakeful beings and the local or circumscribed perceptions of (say) somnambulists or hypnotisees. It is true that in purely particular terms the end of the attentive line is the physical phenomenon set down in three-dimensional physical space and time. However, since this cannot be accomplished in the way reserved for human and self-consciously conscious beings without the simultaneous perception of the containing spatio-temporal setting, coming to the end of this particular road is tantamount to making the perceptual acquaintance of the containing physical world. This receives confirmation when we come to examine just what goes into the constitution of the properly human variety of the perception of material objects. What we discover is a microcosm which reflects a macrocosm. A world in a grain of sand, so to say.

Towards the end of this work I attempt to lay bare something of the above structural framework, the system of concepts through the agency of which are assembled the multiple properties implicit in the typically human perception of material objects. This is carried out mostly with the sense of sight in mind, although touch makes a contribution in this process of perceptually constituting material objects out of their perceptible properties. Then because sensation is a constant element in these procedures, and sensations are individuated in body-relative physical space, the perceptual awareness of our own bodies must be a necessary condition of perceptual acquaintance with the environment: proprioception provides the original spatial framework through which the attention opens onto outer Reality. When this property is conjoined with the fact that proprioception and touch together form a self-sufficient necessary epistemological unit—for if any senses are essential to the animal condition it is these two and they alone—the body-senses assume a significance that far exceeds their overt use as a direct means of discovery. In their absence no experiential epistemology of the physical world would be possible. Their joint role in epistemology is that of a foundation: recessive, scarcely acknowledged, but in the final analysis of overwhelming importance.

9. Recapitulation

(1) At this point I offer a brief résumé, in which I set down something of the general character of what has gone before, and lay out schematically the order of the work which is to follow.

How in the first place does one come to inquire into these two phenomena, consciousness and perception? And why should one be interested in their relation? I think it happens in the following way. Consciousness is as such directed to the World, for the conscious uniquely are 'in touch' with Reality. At the same time perception is our ultimate mode of access to the World. This common bond with the World connects consciousness and perception at a fundamental level, and ensures that perception must be an occurrence of great importance so far as consciousness is concerned. Thus, it provides the concrete setting, both for the acts which probably constitute the evolutionary rationale of the existence of consciousness and generally for the life one leads. Moreover, it is the source of the concepts used in its 'representations' of the World, and upon it depend the processes of internalization which enable the mind to augment itself and grow and consciousness along with it. Indeed, in the sheer absence of perception and perceptually acquired content it is difficult to see how minds and consciousness could so much as exist. Accordingly, perception must have a weighty office to discharge so far as consciousness is concerned. When a conscious person perceives his surrounds, he is availing himself of a channel of communication between the inner and outer world which is part of the foundation upon which consciousness depends for its content and ultimately for its very existence.

How does this fundamental interaction between mind and the outer world become a reality? To answer this question one needs to understand the nature of the elements involved and the relations between them. The interaction in question begins in consciousness. Now consciousness is a purely internal state, and must therefore be internally determined independently of any local causal engagement with the environment. And so one might suppose its relation to perception to be loose and contingent in character. Closer inspection proves it to be otherwise. When we analyse consciousness, and supplement it with an analysis of perception, significant connections appear. For one thing the universality of the concept of perception, and the fact that it realizes an a priori possibility or 'logical moment' of the concept of experience, shows perception can be no mere faculty tacked on to the other psychological constituents of consciousness. But in addition a readiness for perceptual interaction with outer reality proves to be a necessity for consciousness, expressive of its nature as a state which is 'in touch with' Reality.

(2) Then if the occurrence of perception in conscious beings is the exercise of a function which is a condition of both mentality and consciousness as such, if it puts to use a necessarily accessible attentive capacity of consciousness, and if it is the expression of the essential engagement of consciousness with Reality, perception should emerge naturally and intelligibly out of consciousness. Investigation confirms this supposition. Thus it comes out of the experiential core of consciousness, from which in the 'logical moment' the concept arose, for perception is both essentially an experience and the concept exhaustively definable in terms of experience. Furthermore, perception encounters in consciousness an availability of the understanding of such a kind as to enable the mind realistically to interpret the bare data of sense, and help perception to discharge the cognitive function essential to its being.

Then just as naturally as perception emerges from consciousness, so in equally intelligible fashion perception bridges the ontological divide between the inner domain of awareness and outer physical reality. In the work which now follows I investigate the main elements involved in this most fundamental of epistemological interactions. And I do so in the order in which those elements come into play as consciousness moves out onto the physical scene. Thus I begin in Part I by examining the experience, the basic and inscrutable phenomenon which is part of the essence of both perception and consciousness. Thereafter I offer an analysis of consciousness, understood as a unitary phenomenon ranging over the undeveloped unselfconscious and the developed self-conscious forms. I follow this up in Part II with an examination of a phenomenon barely to be distinguished from consciousness itself:

the experiential life of consciousness, the 'stream of consciousness' (so-called) in which perception takes root, viz. the attention. Finally, one of the two structural possibilities open to the attention is that in which it takes an extensional object, which is to say perception. To begin the inquiry into this phenomenon I offer first an analysis of the concept itself, one expressed in universal terms. And then in Parts III and IV I investigate those important varieties of perception in which three-dimensional space is the primary content: namely, sight and the body–related senses of touch and proprioception. Only through an analysis of these senses will one come to know how the mind opens out onto its environment and assembles for itself a representation of outer Reality. And only thus can one know how the gap between the mental and physical domains is closed, and the epistemological basis of mind established.

(3) In tracing out the way consciousness connects in perception with the physical world one is following a trail linking two unutterably different orders of being, a sort of Marco Polo journey to the other end of the world, and yet because it is part of the foundation of mind and consciousness something of an umbilical cord at the same time! It is the delineation of what is at once a necessary condition of mind and consciousness, the unique and indeed the only conceivable ultimate mode of internalization of outer Reality, and an expression of the essence of consciousness. My aim in what follows is to elucidate the relation between these several basic phenomena, and put on display how the epistemological bridge which plays so important a role in this situation becomes a reality. The purpose of this book is to show that, and how it comes to be so, consciousness has from the start an appointment in the concrete with the World in its ultimate physical form, and the manner in which it keeps it.

Part I

Consciousness

I

The Experience

'And I am dumb to tell a weather's wind
How time has ticked a heaven round the stars'

DYLAN THOMAS

'For time is inches
And the heart's changes
Where ghost has haunted
Lost and wanted'

W. H. AUDEN

The entry point into consciousness is the *experience*. That is to say, what is before your mind right now, the most familiar thing in the world: perceptions, thoughts, emotions, images, etc. They are all members of the one tribe. And they continue in a continuous unbroken 'stream' as long as consciousness endures (and beyond). If there is an especial mystery in consciousness, there is as much and probably the identical mystery in the experience, if there is cause for ontological wonder at the one, there is at the other. All that sets the head spinning when one thinks of the emergence of consciousness, somewhere aeons ago in the remote past of this planet, seems to be gathered up in the experience. An eye opened upon the World: here we have a familiar and natural image for this momentous occurrence. It can be no coincidence that the image takes the form of an experience.

And it is not as if these phenomena are things *set apart*: consciousness, and experience. The very word 'conscious' gets pressed into use when we record either. 'The patient is now conscious', 'He was conscious of a sudden impulse to laugh', 'He was conscious of a faint noise': we are not dealing with gross or accidental ambiguities in these cases, these are not mere verbal similarities. The phenomenon of *awareness* lies at the centre of them all. Just what relation exists between these several 'awarenesses' or 'consciousnesses', I shall not for the moment consider, but plainly it is a relation of some intimacy. For one thing, 'consciousness' in the sense of waking, which is a phenomenon that is directed to no object, *entails* the occurrence of 'experiential consciousness': one cannot be awake without having experiences, consciousness encompasses no hiatuses or blackouts. It is possible for one

37

to be asleep, or comatose, or in a trance, without undergoing experience of any kind, but one cannot be conscious and experience nothing.

This is food for thought, as they say. Why the entailment? I do not at present know the answer to this question, but the following consideration is relevant. Why did consciousness evolve into being? What peculiar advantages did it confer upon its possessors? In a word, what is its natural function? That function is surely one which only *experience* can make a reality. Namely, to enable informed physical action upon the environment which makes possible the production of situations favouring survival (etc.). Something along these lines seems certain to be the functional explanation of the emergence of consciousness, indeed of the psychological as such, of mind itself. Then already we have had to mention two varieties of experience: intentional action, and by implication also perception (for where else is local information about the environment to be acquired?). Here we have the beginnings of an answer to the question posed above, even though it fails to explicate the logical character of the bond connecting the two types of 'consciousness'.

Whatever the explanation of the entailment from one 'consciousness' to the other 'consciousness', and the non-accidentality of the usages involving this term, the experience is surely the most striking manifestation of consciousness or wakefulness. It is true that consciousness is not exhausted by experience, else the dreaming would be conscious, whereas they are instead the subject of what one might call 'particular consciousnesses-of' (which is merely to say experiences [with content]). Just what that more is, I investigate in Chapter 2. But somewhat as we reach for the image of an eye opening on the World for consciousness, and thus of a specific experience, so we naturally point to the experience as the most immediate manifestation of the presence of con-sciousness. And both phenomena—consciousness and the experience—are equally fundamental to mind as such. There might be minds without affect, or without thought, or imagination, there might even be minds that are human artefacts of some sort, but there can be no minds in any World devoid of the capacities for consciousness and for experience. If disembodied minds could so much as exist, if the angels were some kind of theoretical possibility, both phenomena would have to inhere in them.

In short, it is clear that we aim at something central to both mentality and consciousness when we turn our sights onto the experience. And yet when we come to look hard at it, at this most familiar of all mental phenomena, it turns out to be inscrutable in the extreme. It says next to nothing about itself: trying to persuade it to give up some of its secrets, is like attempting to wring blood out of the proverbial stone. I do not doubt however that those secrets are there, that there is indeed blood in this stone. I propose not to be put off by the seemingly impenetrable exterior. In what follows, I try to extricate something of what lies behind.

38

1. The Logical Properties of the Concept of an Experience

(a) Indefinability

(1) The problem that concerns me in this chapter is, the characterization of the property of *being an experience*: that is, the property instantiated whenever anything that is an experience occurs. Note that experiencehood is not the same as psychologicality, since many phenomena have the latter trait without the former, such as beliefs and memories, and for the same reason it cannot be equated with intentionality. And in fact no mental constitutive trait analytically singles it out from other mental phenomena. In a word, it is indefinable, like many other fundamental mental concepts. Such a suggestion is scarcely a counsel of despair however. Indefinability in no way prevents us from acquiring this concept, nor from investigating its nature. Then that the concept is *bona fide*, and that we fully understand it, is evident from the fact that we unhesitatingly allocate all mental phenomena into either the class of experiences or its complementary. Thus, mental images and perceivings and shock (etc.) are experiences, while beliefs and intentions and memories (etc.) are not. We have no difficulty in effecting the divide. And we know exactly what we are doing as we sort things in this way.

(2) How do we know these phenomena are experiences? We just do, we have no reason for our judgements. And yet these various mental types have common properties which confirm their experiencehood. For example, when they are occurring we know of their existence. But there is no *explanation* of this cognitive relation—which is simply a brute fact. While each variety of experience is endowed with the properties possessed universally by experiences, they are not members of the genus experience *in virtue of* possessing these properties. Were that how matters stood, it would necessitate an explanation of the genus-species relation holding in these cases. But no such explanation exists. And the reason for this is, that 'experience' is not definable in terms of the properties of experiences.

It is instructive to compare the concept 'affect'. This concept is broader than that of 'emotion', since it ranges over emotions and in addition over shock, amusement, and various conditions no one would describe as emotions. What *justifies* the claim that it applies to these phenomena? Well, what properties have we in mind in roping these various phenomena together under 'affect'? The following could be mentioned: the existence of degree, of non-rationality of type, experientiality, physiognomic, etc. Then is the concept 'affect' actually definable in terms of these traits? Or is it rather that some indefinable reality determines the usage? Or does something else determine it? One test that sheds light on this question is: do we know precisely *which properties* to include in the list? Alternatively: are we certain *which phenomena* count as affective? If the answer to both of these questions is negative, the likelihood is that the concept has no agreed content, and in addition that no single objective indefinable reality determines the use of the word 'affect'. Then I suggest that it is unclear whether we are to include pleasure, and even perhaps excitement as 'affective'. The probable situation is, that we discover in the mind various phenomena which share a number of overlapping properties, and launch a term which is understood to conjoin most of those properties so as to constitute a complex concept. But nothing tells us precisely what we are to put into the list, whether we are to cobble together five or possibly six or maybe more such traits. Nothing seems decided in advance, which is to say that choice rather than an object-ive type determines the concept. The conclusion is, that we have a partially vague and open-ended concept on our hands.

All that we say of the broad concept 'affect', can be affirmed with equal cogency of the narrower 'emotion'. Thus, ought we to make object-directedness a necessary condition of the type? If we say yes, we find ourselves endorsing the paradoxical conclusion that whereas anxiety over a forthcoming exam rates as emotional, free-floating anxiety does not. If we say no, we run the risk of failing to do justice to a regularity pervading phenomena like rage, fear, joy, etc. But are we in any case to class anxiety as an emotion? And what of feeings of love or hate? Here, too, no objective reality exists which can resolve these difficulties. And yet it is not that some of these phenomena do not exhibit a distinctive family of more or less common or overlapping properties which is worthy of linguistic record: the special character of (say) grief and joy must be recognized. It is just that we appear to be in the presence of a shifting sequence of overlapping properties, and of nothing else. In short, such general terms as 'affect' and 'emotion' seem to be assembled *after the event*: they prove to be mere linguistic constructs rather than the *designata* of objective properties. They are merely—useful.

By contrast 'experience' is at once unanalysable and a simple *designatum* of an objective reality. We do not take hold of a set of properties, conjoin them, and arrive thereby at the concept of an experience, and neither do we open-endedly apply the term to an open-ended array of mental phenomena. Two considerations strongly support this account of the matter. On the one hand, we are unable to produce the concepts supposedly constitutive of the concept of an experience. On the other hand, we find no difficulty in sorting the contents of the mind into the two comple-mentary classes: experiences/non-experiences. We simply and unhesitatingly put everything where it belongs. This attests to a decisiveness of sense which owes its existence to an objective unanalysable reality.

(b) An essential property of some individuals and of some types

Being an experience is one of the most fundamental of mental properties. Indeed, in all probability it is an essential property of whatever individual experience pos-sesses it: that is, the individual could not be the entity it is and take non-experience form. But if experiencehood is essential to all *experiences*, it is not essential to all the *types* experiences exemplify, being essential to some types and not others. The types mental imaging and perceiving are, I think, essentially experiential types: 'unexperienced mental image' and 'unexperienced smelling' are surely contradictory expressions. But this is not true of (say) the concept of desire: desire can take experiential form (lust, hunger), and the non-experienced form taken by (say) the long-standing desires which determine our long-term intentions. This difference between psychological types implies that whereas we can specify some experiences by instancing a type, as in 'I had a dream last night' or 'I saw a flash of lightning', in the case of (say) an experience of desire we need to single it out under just such a heading. Finally, some types are essentially non-experiential: for example, believing and intending. There may be an experience of feeling a belief slip through one's fingers, but this is one of insight or awareness rather than of belief itself. There is simply no experience which *is* holding a proposition to be true. And the same holds of intending.

(c) Genus and species

(1) *Qua* type the concept 'experience' is unusual. No other psychological concept functions as it does. The first thing of note is, the *breadth* of its application: it ranges over perceptions, mental and physical actions, affect of all types, etc. It is true that other concepts like 'event', 'process', 'state' have great breadth of application in the mind, but they are not psychological kinds and bear witness to nothing more than the phenomenal character of those mental items. What is interesting about 'experience' is that it is as true a psychological type as 'belief', 'desire', etc., yet ranges far and wide across many distinct psychological types. In short, it functions as a genus-type to numerous psychological species-types. Yet despite being of genus-status, it is as 'original' as any other mental concept. Thus, one identifies experiences *as* experiences as immediately as one identifies beliefs, desires, etc. Indeed, one has *no less* awareness of the experience-status of any psychological item than one has of its ontological status, its psychological type, etc.

(2) It has emerged that 'experience' is a true and unanalysable psychological type, being a wholly objective constituent of the world, exemplified in a broad spectrum of phenomena. Then what type of a type is 'experience'? It has proved to be a genus to the many species of experience which fall under it. This is confirmed in the following important property of experiencehood. Namely, whereas something can be 'just a belief that it is raining', nothing can be 'just an experience' (with a given content). While being a belief will be the final classification of any psychological item that is a belief, meeting the 'sortal'-type need necessary for identity, being an experience is not and never can be. Even though 'experience' is a sub-variety of 'psychological', it is not itself sufficiently determinate to guarantee identity for its instances. Despite the fact that perception is 'just an experience of its object', it is nonetheless of the specific type perception, and so merely a special sub-variety of experience.

Thus, 'experience' is not the kind of kind that can satisfy the need for full determinacy and being. And neither is it the widest or covering genus, as 'psycho-logical' is. Nor is it, like 'psychological', the provider of ontological or categorial status. Meanwhile it has one other property of some significance. It manages to occupy a special place among the sub-varieties of 'psychological', in being a strictly *necessary instance* of that ontological kind. While the realm of the psychological might have lacked the affective type 'amusement', and probably even the broad covering type 'affect' as well, there is no way (no 'World') in which psychologicality could exist and experience not.

(3) In sum, 'experience' is a sub-variety of 'psychological'. However, it is not a true species-concept, being unable to meet the need for full determinacy and being which identity requires. But it is a true genus-concept, ranging over a wide variety of diverse species which do meet that need. It is a reality, which is unanalysable, that is endowed with properties, but not conjunctively constituted out of them. And while it is itself neither an ontological nor categorial status, it is in the peculiar position of being guaranteed reality by the covering category 'psychological'. In short, it is an unanalysable and necessary psychological genus.

2. The Constitution of Experiential Process

(a) The experience and flux

(1) At this point I pass from considering some of the logical properties of the experience, to certain non-logical mostly constitutive traits. In particular, I want now to lay an especial stress upon its occurrent character.

The perceptible world about us, while not essentially in a state of flux, is mutating in our experience for much of the time: leaves on a tree are visibly waving in the breeze, even though the window that frames them advances steadily through time apparently unaltered as it does. And while experience likewise need not change either in type or content, it characteristically also for much of the time is in flux in these several ways: the leaves move in our visual field, one walks across to the window and opens it, feeling the breeze upon one's face as one does. Yet even when experience is not changing in type or content, it still changes in another respect: it is constantly *renewed*, a new sector of itself is there and then *taking place*. This is because experiences are events (glimpsing, picture-painting) or processes (walking, picture-painting), and each momentary new element of any given experience is a further happening or *occurrence* (by contrast with (say) the steady continuation through time of one's knowing that 9 and 5 make 14). Thus, even if I am staring fixedly at some unchanging material object, such staring is not merely a *continuous existent* across time, it is an activity and therefore also a *process*, and thus occurrently renewed in each instant in which it continues to exist. In short, the domain of experience is essentially a domain of occurrences, of processes and events. In this regard we should contrast the domain of experience with the other great half of the mind: the non-experiential half. That is, the sector that encompasses the relatively stable unexperienced mental foundation (e.g. cognitive, evaluative, etc.) upon which experience occurs. While many of the non-experiential contents of this domain could continue in existence when all mental phenomena had frozen in their tracks, say (fancifully) in a being in suspended animation at 0 °Absolute, those in the experiential domain could not. This (fanciful) test—to which I shall often have recourse—is vital equipment when discussing experience.

(2) Accordingly, a few words at this point concerning change in the non-experiential sector of the mind. The first thing to say is, that there is no a priori reason why events of *any* kind should occur in non-experiencing minds. A man might continue to exist when all mental life had come to a halt, say in the above condition of suspended animation. To be sure in many instances of experienceless-ness, for example in the minds of non-dreaming sleepers, memories doubtless dim and fade to a minuscule degree from instant to instant. But there is no a priori need of such change: mentality as such has no binding need of it. Therefore even though the mental world of a non-experiencing being is of necessity an unbroken continuity, that continuity must be non-processive in type. And the proof of this claim is, that such a mind with all its character and contents intact could in principle survive indefinitely at the rock-bottom temperature of 0 °A: all energy vanished from mental and physical systems, all mental change impossible, and yet the conditions for the continuation of existence and identity of mind and its contents satisfied.

An example helps to illustrate this relative independence of time in the non-experiential sector of the mind. Thus, continuation of the knowledge that 9 and 5 makes 14 does not as such necessitate the occurrence of *anything*. To have known for ninety years that 9 and 5 make 14, and for a sudden devastating senility to erase that knowledge, is not for an extended *event* of knowing to have occurred. Rather, a state of knowing endured for that time. By contrast, when a process terminates, an event of the same type is its necessary residue. If I have been looking steadily at a painting for ninety seconds, if for ninety seconds such a processive activity was going on, then at the end of that interval it became true that I had looked at that painting, it became true that an act-event of that type and duration had occurred.

(3) To resume. Characteristically the contents of experience are in flux, and ne-cessarily experience itself is in flux, being essentially occurrent in nature. Then being as such occurrent we can say, not merely that it *continues* in existence from instant to instant, but that it is at each instant *occurrently renewed*. Indeed, the very form of the experiential inner world, of the 'stream of consciousness', is such as to necessitate the occurrence of processes and events at all times. The identity-conditions obtaining are those appropriate to events and processes—in contradis-tinction to those governing states. For it is quite other in the sector of the mind which serves as foundation for these phenomena. While events and processes occur in this part of the mind, such as (say) the essentially unconscious process of forget-ting, the form of the non-experiencing part of the mind is non-processive. We

noted this earlier when we observed that, in the absence of all change, identity-conditions were satisfiable across time for the kinds of psychological items that populate non-experiencing minds. The two parts of the mind have essentially different characters and conditions of identity.

(b) Processes and their constitution

(1) We are trying to chart certain special and non-logical constitutive properties of experiences. Then what that is distinctive in the mind arises with the advent of experience? The following emerged. It is not the mere existence of flux, of event and process, in the case of experience that is distinctive: it is the *necessity* of flux. Then there is one other related novelty which arises with the experience, and it is this which forms the subject matter of the remainder of the present Section 2. Bearing in mind that all that exists in the realm of experience does so in the mode of 'flux', so that whatever endures necessarily does so processively, which is to say that experience across time must be processive, we may say of these processes not merely that they are constituted out of what one might call 'processive instants' ('processive infinitesimals'), we can make the far more controversial claim that they are not and cannot be constituted out of *psychological states*. Indeed, we can make of this property of experiences a fundamental *differentia* of the whole experience genus.

To explain this latter claim, it is advisable that we briefly examine the nature of process itself. Process is one mode adopted by phenomenal continuity; which is to say, that phenomenal continuity is a necessary but insufficient condition of process. A state of solidity endures continuously in a piece of iron without doing so processively: process requires that the continuity be occurrent in nature, and no 'continuing to stay solid' is occurrent from instant to instant. Thus, processes 'go on' or 'continue' occurrently in time, each new instant realizing more of the same as what has gone on so far, and this temporally repeated sameness (dissolving, skidding, rising) is a homogeneity: processes are made up of process-parts the same in type as themselves. Now when a process comes to a halt (at whatever point) an event is at that moment realized (a dissolving, a skid, an ascent), so that we may say at each new instant t_x of an unfolding process that a potential event enduring from t_o—t_x *has occurred* by the time t_x. Then the type of the completed event (a skid, a dissolving, etc.), and of the latter potential events (the same), gives the very type of the process whose ongoing constituted their occurrence. Thus, the process 'lays down' more and more of an event the same in kind as itself, and may in this regard be taken to be the very stuff or phenomenal matter of events the same in kind as itself.

(2) So much for a few general pronouncements on the nature of process. I want now to take a look at the relation between processes and changes of state generally. A familiar example brings out the point which I have in mind. Take a process like moving through space. What are the conditions required for its occurrence? A time

interval; a difference in all the temporally adjacent position-values of an object over that interval; a single continuity in those values; and a match between this continuity and that of times. Provided these four conditions are satisfied, a process of moving must have filled the given time interval: indeed, they are logical equivalences. Moving is therefore shown to be nothing more than a continuity over time of different position-values in a bearer entity. It is not something 'over and above' or supervenient on the latter, it *is* merely a particular continuity of values over time in a bearer entity. Note that at each instant t_x the moving object is *at some position* p_x in space, and is in addition at that same instant *moving* at position p_x. Thus, the state of affairs of being at $p_x t_x$ is a necessary but insufficient condition of moving at $p_x t_x$.

Of what is the process of moving constituted? Is it constituted out of the states, *being at position p_x?* Or is it constituted out of the phenomena, *moving at p_x?* Surely it is constituted out of both. The process of moving over an interval t_A—t_B can be built up out of two (non-distinct, non-rivalrous) ingredients: state-parts, or process-parts. On the one hand we have: a time-interval, position-values, and continuity of temporally adjacent position-values. On the other hand we have: a time-interval, moving process going on at each instant of that interval, and a continuity of spatio-temporally adjacent process-parts. Because *moving* at $p_x t_x$ cannot be going on without *being* at $p_x t_x$, any constituting of a moving process out of process-parts cannot obtain unless a further constituting out of position-values is also possible. But any moving process is a reality only because each new sector of moving process synthesiszs conjunctively with its immediate predecessor sector. In short, constituting a process like moving out of states like being at a position in space at a particular time, is not *in competition with* constituting such a process out of parts the same in kind as itself. Moving-process has state-parts *and* process-parts. It is susceptible of two different analyses, according as different analytical agencies are brought to bear upon it.

(c) The state and processive constitution of non-experiential process

(1) We may therefore say of many processes that they are constituted out of states *and* occurrences: we do not contradict ourselves in expressing the matter thus. Then is this claim true, not merely in the realm of physical nature, but is it in addition true of mental phenomena? Are mental processes likewise analysable in these two non-competing ways?

Let us turn at this point to a part of the mind already mentioned: namely, the sector containing all those psychological items that are non-experiences. Within this region continuities across time of particular mental states obtain which are of such a nature that mental synthesis sufficient to constitute a single instance of a type occurs. An example is, knowing for many years that 9 and 5 make 14. This is an exercise of memory. However, because the knowing involved is not occurring at each instant, it is not what one might call 'occurrent memory'—something which goes on all the time we experience (in 'short-term' form). After all, the above memory might in principle continue at $0\,^\circ$Absolute. Does this imply that psychological processes cannot occur in the non-experiential sector of the mind? By no means. The following phenomena might occur and take non-experiential and processive form: forgetting, coming to understand, deciding. Thus, all of these phenomena could be realized in non-experiencing beings, say either in dreamless sleeping or comatose subjects. Then since such phenomena necessitate change over a period of time, they necessitate actual occurrence; and that is to say, they entail the occurrence of (one, or more) events consisting in the change in time of the state in question. Then it is perfectly possible that the change take processive form. For example, if forgetting occurs it may take continuous form, continuously linking a state of remembering event E well at time t_1 and another state of remembering E less well at t_2—which suffices to ensure that a psychological process of forgetting went on between t_1 and t_2.

Thus, processes are doubtless constantly going on in the non-experiential sector of the mind. And yet having said that, it should be emphasized that while change of mental state in a non-experiencing subject entails the occurrence of one or more *events* realizing the change, and while it allows the *possibility* of processive form for that realization, it does not *entail* the occurrence of process. It remains possible that the change in question be realized by one or more discontinuous events.

(2) Two questions arise: Are non-experiential psychological processes constituted simultaneously out of psychological states *and* process-parts, in the manner we know to be true of physical processes like moving? And are experiential psychological processes likewise constituted out of these twin ingredients?

I shall begin with the first question. The answer to this query is surely in the affirmative. This answer is suggested by the fact that, just as being at position p is one thing and being at p and moving is another, so being in a certain memory-state at time t is one thing and being in that state and forgetting some of that content is another. In each case we begin with the existence of a determinate state, to which we conjoin the fact that no entailment links the obtaining of such a state with the occurrence of the process involving the state. Then in either case all that is needed for the occurrence of the requisite process is a continuity across time of states which stand to one another in some requisite relation. With this in mind I say, that when the non-experiential process of forgetting takes processive form, that process is constituted out of memory-states. However, all processes are necessarily constituted out of *process-parts* the same in kind as themselves, and this is just as true of the forgetting process as it is of any purely physical process. Thus, this process must be simultaneously constituted out of memory-states *and* process-parts.

What of other non-experiential phenomena? For example, cognitive change like coming-to-believe, or practical change like deciding or coming-to-intend? Are we to suppose, when these changes take processive form, that those processes are not constituted out of psychological states of the kind that underwent alteration? I do see how the situation can be any different from that exemplified by forgetting. In all such cases we are able to single out a psychological state which lies at the heart of the process. Indeed, the guiding principle seems to be, that if we are to so much as *specify* a non-experiential psychological process, the way to go about the task is first by specifying a particular psychological state, second positing an event consisting in the change of that state over an interval of time, and finally through positing continuity as the mode in which the change is realized. How else are we to specify non-experiential process? Can one think of a single non-experiential process which is specifiable, not through positing the occurrence of state-change, but simply and irreducibly through itself? I can call none to mind: all the familiar psychological concepts which admit of non-experiential processive instantiation, like 'forget', 'decide', 'comprehend', 'learn', are such that their instantiation entails the occurrence of one or more events consisting in state-change, leaving it open whether those change-events take instantaneous discontinuous form or continuous temporally extended processive form. A particular state always lies at the heart of non-experiential process. I can think of no exception to this rule.

(d)   The purely processive constitution of experiential process

(1) What is the situation in the case of experiences? We have seen that experiences are essentially in a condition of flux. What this means is, that all experiences of necessity 'happen' or 'occur' or 'are going on': in a word, are either events, or processes, or both. No experiences merely obtain or merely exist. No experiences are states. None can be, and of necessity. Thus, suppose we were to bring mental life to a complete standstill, to destroy all mental incident without death, perhaps once more through the imagined total refrigeration. Then while many non-experiential states will persist, all non-experiential process would *cease* and all experiences simply *cease to be* (hence the destruction of mental incident entails the destruction of consciousness). Does not this demonstrate that no experiences are states? In any case, what could count as an example of an experience-state? What is an example of a thing endowed with the following pair of properties: being an experience, and such that a cessation of all mental incident need not destroy it? Intending? But it is not an experience. Desiring? But if it take experiential form, then it will be a kind of 'surge' across time and plainly is occurrent and processive in character. And I can think of no exception to the general rule, that no experiences are states: I know of no experience that can exist without 'happening'.

But if no psychological states are experiences, how can there be a state whose continuous change constitutes an experiential process? What non-experiential psychological state helps constitute what experiential process? None, surely. Then does not this fact show that experiential processes (and events) must differ fundamentally from non-experiential processes (and events)? Does it not demonstrate that, while the latter are of necessity constituted out of psychological states (which could retain being in a complete 'mental freeze'), the latter are not and cannot be (and must destruct in such a 'freeze')? Does it not show that their very constitution is fundamentally dissimilar?

(2) And in fact it proves to be so. Consider a paradigmatic example of an experiential psychological process: activity. The concept of action[1] ('murder', 'theft', 'assault', 'rape', etc.) is an event-concept, and the concept of activity ('murdering', 'assaulting') is a process-concept; and, like any process, activity-phenomena go to constitute the being of a corresponding act-event phenomenon ('a murder', 'an assault'). Thus, if an assaulting-activity was going on for five minutes, and ended at that point, an 'assault' of five minutes duration will have occurred. Now we saw in the case of non-experiential processes like forgetting that, in the first place a relevant psychological state exists, namely a particular condition of the memory; and secondly that the psychological process in question is constituted out of that state (which lies at the heart of all such occurrences). In a word, given any non-experiential process we can discover the constituting state. But what happens when we come to consider the phenomenon: activity? What state 'lies at the heart of' this process? The general thesis propounded above concerning the non-existence of experience-states, implies on purely general grounds that no experience-state can constitute an active process. But it is in any case evident in the case of activity that no state exists that can play that role. Take any activity-process you like, and attend to it at any point in time, and consider the following two questions: what psychological X-state exists at this instant which is such that it is internally necessary but insufficient for this activity? what such X-state merely needs continuity across time for activity to be constituted? We can think of a something (call it Y) which satisfies the latter part of the latter requirement: namely, active process at that instant. But we can discover no such X. What is unique to the experiential process in general, and the activity-process in particular, is that the processive Y-type answer ('listening', 'walking') is the *one and only* answer we can give when it comes to constituting the phenomenon out of parts. We can find here no analogue of the constituting states: position-value in the case of motion, memory-value in the case of forgetting. All we can discover are lesser stretches of, and ultimately quasi-infinitesimals of, the ongoing process itself.

Thus, the very stuff or phenomenal matter of the process, activity, is itself processive, and of the type activity, and it is nothing else. Freeze the mind of an acting subject at a certain instant, and *nothing* of this kind remains: merely a state of intention (part-discharged) and desire (part-fulfilled) and knowledge (of such matters): nothing but the progenitors of action, caught so to say in midstream, but distinct nonetheless from the act they are begetting. Indeed, bring to a halt absolutely all phenomena in some physically acting subject, and what remains? Nothing but the above act-progenitors along with a particular bodily state, such as one's limbs being postured in a certain way. Then while the processive bodily movements

---

[1] The law is specifically interested in act-concepts, albeit of acts of a morally questionable variety. Hence the examples.

are undoubtedly constituted out of such postural states, those bodily processes are not to be identified with the processive physical psychological activities which involve them. Meanwhile the act-progenitor states simply constitute no process of any kind, let alone the active process itself. In short, nothing of an active nature is anywhere to be found in such a situation of 'freeze'. It is clear that the psychological process, striving or acting, is constituted of nothing but striving or acting-parts.

(3) And yet the general thesis may not convince everyone. It might be said that what holds of action need not hold for all experiences. Might not (say) perception be a counter-example? Thus, one is inclined to believe that (say) hearing a sound consists in the obtaining of a relation, that of awareness, between a mind and a sound. Accordingly, one might suppose that there exists an experience which is the realization in time of a state, viz. the relation of awareness between a mind and a sound. This is to strictly model 'He hears the sound' upon 'He touches the wall'. But 'He touches the wall' is ambiguous between an event consisting in the establishing of a relation, and the relation itself. By contrast, 'He hears the sound' exhibits no such ambiguity: it describes an event, and never designates a relation. *A fortiori* the event of hearing a sound does not consist in the realization at or over a time of a relation of hearing the sound. This event occurs at an instant if the sound is instantaneous, and over an interval if the sound is temporally extended; then in the latter case it will need to be renewed instant by succeeding instant, as happens when listening is going on. There is no state 'hearing the sound' at the heart of listening, there is merely the constant renewal of an occurrence, the continuous ongoing or happening of a process of continuous hearing. While it is true that the event of hearing is susceptible of redescription in the light of a relation between a mind and a sound, to wit as 'hearing the sound', this does not imply the existence of an experience-state of 'hearing the sound'. The event is not the relation.

The general conclusion is, that whereas processes in the non-experiential part of the mind are of necessity constituted out of psychological states and process-parts, all experiential processes are of necessarity constituted of nothing but process-parts. This is because there is no such thing as an experience state: the realm of experience is occurrent to the core. Everything experiential is of necessity in flux.

3. Temporal Properties (1): The Present

(1) I move on at this point to consider the temporal properties of experiences. I am convinced that the bond between time and the experience is of great significance. I begin with the relation to the present.

We are experiencing when awake or dreaming or somnambulating, and not experiencing when comatose or stunned or in deep dreamless sleep. Then it seems to me that the experiencing subject stands in a special relation to time not discoverable in those not experiencing. To bring that relation into view, let us begin by asking the question: what, in the way of a relation to time, is inaccessible to non-experiencing subjects? Consider someone in a deep coma. What of a temporal nature does this person miss or forgo? Well, at least he does not experience the passage of time (whatever exactly that is). However, this reply suffers from the defect first of tautologousness, but second and more importantly it fails to pick out any shortfall in *knowledge* (which I suspect is of some significance). So let us at this point pursue the latter question. We shall see that it brings to light a special cognitive relation to the present moment, not accessible to non-experiencers.

Is there anything of a cognitive nature pertaining to time that is inaccessible to the comatose? At first one is inclined to say he cannot know *temporal facts* at all. But he surely still knows the Battle of Waterloo was in 1815. Then one might suppose he cannot know temporal facts *from a temporal point of view*: one might assume that he has no sense of a *present* from which to contemplate such facts. But this likewise is false, for he emerges from coma still knowing that Sampras won Wimbledon in 1999 and that the year 2000 is still to come. But his coma might have endured for an entire decade, and he know nothing of it, so how could he know 2000 is to come? Well, perhaps we should qualify the claim that he knows, and concede that the matter is more complicated. And yet unconsciousness cannot as such delete all temporal perspectival knowledge: after all, dreamless sleepers do not discover which year it is each time they awaken. However, it looks as if sustained deep unconsciousness has a tendency to destroy *knowledge* of one's temporal location. But there is no reason why it should destroy a temporal *point of view*, which is to say *belief* as to the time of 'now'. Even if a subject were to awake from comatose refrigeration in the year 3000, he may well still be entertaining the conviction that 2000 lies in the immediate future. Thus, insofar as 'now' gives the standpoint from which 'then' and 'to come' are descried, an absence of all experience is consistent with belief as to both the existence of a 'now' and of its rough position on the time-scale. In short, a total lack of experience is consistent with a temporal point of view.

Something in one still shies at this last suggestion. And it has to be admitted that the above 'now' was what might be called a 'fat now', extending across many discernibly different instants. But can a 'thin now' of a mere instant mean anything to a comatose being? Well, a man might fall into a sudden dreamless sleep believing the train is now racing through Zermatt station, and awake ten minutes later with the identical belief. It looks therefore as if a belief can be held by a non-experiencing being which is directed to an instantaneous 'now'.

(2) Nevertheless something in the way of 'now' must surely be inaccessible to non-experiencers. What that is, seems to be a direct consequence of their incapacity to experience the passage of time. For we should remember what a waking person knows in this regard. A conscious experiencer knows of any instant that it is the instant it is—even if he has no idea *which instant* it be (whether the first instant

of the third millennium, or the moment of Christ's birth, etc.). But of which instant did the dreamless sleeper believe that 'now the train is passing through Zermatt station'? Undoubtedly, the instant before he fell asleep. Then during the six-hundred-second interval he retained that belief, directed erroneously at each instant to that instant in the past as 'now'. This error is instructive. What a non-experiencing person cannot do is, direct a belief to the same instant as the belief itself, singled out purely as 'now'. If he fell asleep at 6.00 a.m., and awoke at 6.10 a.m., he cannot at 6.05 a.m. entertain a belief about the instant 6.05 a.m. singled out as 'now'. He can at 6.05 a.m. entertain a belief about 6.05 a.m., but he cannot at 6.05 a.m. entertain a belief about 6.05 a.m. singled out purely as 'now'. And he cannot do so, because he cannot do what an experiencer can do: pick out the present as 'now'; and that because a non-experiencer is not conscious of 'now', nor therefore of a continuity of 'now's, which is to say of 'the passage of time' (which is nothing but the continuous non-phenomenal alteration of temporal location).

So far we have considered 'conscious experience', experience in those who are conscious. What of experience in the non-conscious? For example, the experiences of dreamers or somnambulists. Do these subjects have a consciousness of a present instant as the instant 'now'? I think they do. 'At a certain moment in the dream I became conscious of the presence of my grandfather', a dream report goes; and if the report is veridical, if that really happened during the night, dream experience at a certain moment was that 'now grandfather is here', which singles out an instant of time via the use of 'now', implying a consciousness at that time of that instant as 'now'. What of somnambulism? Well, such phenomena are *intentional activities*. This implies that a near future must be aimed at in expressing an attendant origi-nating intention; and this property implies the existence of a match in content between 'now'-is-being-enacted and 'just then'-was-intended-to-be-enacted, which in turn implies a sensitivity-to and awareness-of a present time as 'now'. In short, these experiences seem not to constitute an exception to the rule that self-conscious experiencing beings single out the instant of their experiences at the very least under the heading of 'now'.

The point of the foregoing discussion has been to discover a relation to time, and in particular a cognitive relation to the present instant, guaranteed to an experien-cing subject and guaranteed absent in non-experiencers. We have seen that in the case of non-experiencers no purely indexical knowledge of the reality of the present instant is possible. By contrast, while an experiencing self-conscious subject need not know of 'here' that it is 'here', since he might at some point in time lack any acquaintance with space, a self-conscious subject cannot but know of each instant in which he is experiencing that it then exists. What does this major asymmetry between our spatial and temporal awareness tell us? In my opinion, it reveals just how much more intimate is the relation of consciousness with time than with space. A direct confrontation with time is constitutive of consciousness as such. I hope in what follows to demonstrate that this truth holds equally of the unselfconscious and self-conscious.

4. Temporal Properties (2): The Future

(1) In the present Section 4 I continue the enterprise of characterizing experience through delineating properties directly relating experience and time. The property I now have in mind specifically concerns the future (though it leads naturally to a closely related wider phenomenon). One comes across the property in the following way. Suppose one was a scientist magically transported back to (say) the year 10^9BC, studying the first signs of mind and consciousness on Earth. What phenomena would indicate their presence? Doubtless certain movements on the part of living organisms: indeed, a whole new repertoire of movements-in-situation. Then just what is it these particular movements have that (say) sunflower movements tracking the sun lack?

Consider a plant's movements. These 'actions' or regular responses to stimulus, constitute the activation of local mechanism and in general have survival-value for their 'agent'. Significantly, time enters in no special way into this phenomenon, and would not do so even were the plant's 'actions' to be a teleology across time. Thus, we might say: 'the plant is moving in direction d_1 at p_1 t_1 because it is going to be at p_2 at the later time t_2', so indicating that 'Nature's purpose' lies in a future situation at t_2. Yet all we would mean is, that at t_1 a physical state of the organism exists which is regularly followed by a different state at t_2, and that this is of teleological import. What must be emphasized is, that the physical states out of which the phenomenon is constituted involve in themselves no essential reference to time. Pre-animate teleology towards a future event is constituted out of states which are in this sense a-temporal in character.

Return now to the super-primitive animal, and its structurally novel repertoire of movements (call it $\Sigma\phi$) in situation. This phenomenon cries out for explanation. And the explanation is, that $\Sigma\phi$ manifests the presence of *mentality* and of *conscious experience*. This constitutes an explanatorial revolution. To begin with, it signals the breakdown of pre-animate teleological explanation, since no such laws can explain a $\Sigma\phi$ which is manifestative of consciousness—*ad hoc* clauses mushrooming out of control! But it further involves the invoking of a new ontology and a whole new system of novel entities and types of explanation. It is the 'emergence' of a broad new covering category that is a suitable subject for philosophical inquiry (viz. mind), and with it new types of phenomena (viz. action, perception) and new kinds of explanation (viz. the kind philosophers call 'mental causal', with its attendant singularities), both likewise fit topics for philosophical investigation. We hypothesize such a novel system in explanation of $\Sigma\phi$, and discover that it works, as mere plant teleology does not.

The special property of experience that concerns me is already visible in this super-simple situation. But it is interestingly prefigured in the temporal character of the novel *explanation*. Thus, we say: 'the animal is doing a because it is going to do b.' This can be understood in two ways, one of which exhibits the temporal peculiarity in question. Namely, either as an instance of a *natural regularity* ('Nature's purpose'), or else as the expression of an *intention* (the animal's own particular purpose) (—the nomicity of 'Nature's purposes' to be contrasted with the relative particularity of intention explanation). Then it is the latter form of explanation that is to my mind noteworthy. 'The bee is crossing the garden because it is going to feed on the yellow flower' might be understood in these two ways: either as akin to 'The bird is transporting a twig because it is going to build a nest', or else to 'The dog is crossing the garden because it is going to eat its meal.' Instinctive behaviour like nest-building almost certainly does not express an intention of building a nest, but is instead expressive of many small-range intentions whose expression teleologic-ally happens to result in a nest. The simpler the animal, the more its behaviour is of this kind: the complex ends to which it *appears* to address itself tend to be 'Nature's ends', while the ends which really are *its* ends (i.e. its intentions) tend to be tempor-ally and spatially small-scale. Nature takes care of the grand design, but assigns the details to the agent. In short, the capacity to organize and synthesize, and the closely related capacity to learn from experience, are proportionately smaller as the crea-ture tends towards the primitive. Nonetheless, being animal and therefore the subject of experience, not *all* of its apparent purposes can be 'Nature's purposes'. Intention *must* gain a foothold, bringing with it a quite special relation to the future. Roughly: no animal without action, no action without intention, and no intention without a mental posture directed towards the future (not to be confused with the capacity to *think* about the future).

(2) As noted above, the special temporal property of experience which interests me is already prefigured in the temporal character of the above explanation. Then what is it that is so singular about the intention-explanation from the point of view of time? It lies in the fact that we explain a present phenomenon by reference to a future phenomenon—irreducibly. In the case of plant teleology across time we explain a present phenomenon by reference to a future phenomenon, but in such a way that the reference to time can be 'cashed' in terms of a state and a regularity across time, and the element of time finds no essential representation within that state. And the same can be said of those explanations of animal action which refer to a future event of which the animal knows nothing and which it does not intend, as in (most probably) 'The bird is transporting a twig to make a nest.' But when we invoke an intention—and all intentions necessarily involve reference to the future—there is no way the reference to the future can be 'cashed' in timeless terms. Time lies at the heart of the intention.

To repeat. When the present intentional behaviour is explicable in terms of a future merely hypothetical phenomenon—reducibly (as in nest-building), then the *explanation* is not intentional and the intentions which actually do find expression in the behaviour are simply bypassed in the overall explanation. But when they are not bypassed, as for example in the case of a dog moving in the direction of some food, then we explain a contemporary phenomenon in terms of a merely hypothetical future phenomenon—irreducibly. Here I suggest we have one great novelty appearing with the arise of *experience*. However, this property is explanatory, and thus relational in type, whereas the closely related property which I am at pains to delineate is constitutive. What concerns me is, not so much the unusual character of the *explanation* of $\Sigma\phi$, but the unusual character of the *items* involved in that explanation. In particular, of the acts whose bodily exterior constitute $\Sigma\phi$, and the desires and intentions they express. More specifically still, the irreducible temporal properties of these phenomena. These properties seem to me to be of great moment.

Any intentional action falls under several descriptions, one of which speaks merely of the present, another of the future; and the latter can be invoked in explanation of the former. Thus: 'the dog is running', 'The dog is trying to catch the cat', 'The dog is running *because* it is trying to catch the cat.' It is not just that the dog *experiences* its activity in this way: more to the point is, that the experience itself *is* at once 'trying to run' and 'trying to catch the cat', and irreducibly so. The one activity-experience falls *essentially* and thus irreducibly under two descriptions, one referring to the present and the other to the future. The *very nature* of this phenomenon is such that it refers across a span of time to another time, from an indexically-given temporal point of view, viz. from 'now'. This must be borne in mind in what follows.

(3) Before I finally spell out the special temporal property of experience, it helps to recall some of the earlier observations concerning the constitutive properties of experiences. We noted that they were 'pure flux'; and, if continuous across time, constituted out of process-parts but not state-parts (there being no experience-states). This holds of the processive experience of activity, whereas it is not true of the essentially non-experiential process of forgetting. The process of forgetting is constituted out of process-parts—like any other process; but it is in addition constituted out of state-parts. Then what is especially pertinent to the present discussion is that those state-parts are such that their essential description need not position them on any past/present/future scale: so to say, forgetting does not know itself in temporal terms. The same is true of the merely teleologically directed movements of a plant towards some naturally predestined goal lying in the future: the constituting elements need involve no reference to time. Activity, on the other hand, which is constituted out of nothing but activity-process parts, and in particular out of no psychological states, is as a result constituted to the core of elements essentially positioned on a past/present/future scale. In themselves they point at any instant both present-wards *and* future-wards. It is thus a 'co-presence' in the heart of the phenomenon of present and future.

This ineradicable indexically-given 'co-presence' of another time in a 'now'-present is a feature of absolutely *all* experiences. This is the property which is my special concern. In the above discussion we have seen it relating 'now' and the future. But we shall see in what follows that it holds equally of the past. Then since 'now' is in the present instant given purely indexically, and the latter property essentially connects and contrasts 'now' with its immediate neighbours, any experiencer must be mentally connected to other times as each instant 'happens'. Thus, experience brings with it an awareness of the passage of time. This imports an order which is manifest in our capacity to know of our immediately past experience. It is a mark of the fundamental ordering role of time in the inner world.

5. Temporal Properties (3): The Past

(a) Experience and short-term memory

(1) Intentional action is essentially directed to the future. Indeed, intentional action as such simultaneously takes as object events lying both in the present ('swimming') and the future ('to Calais'). Then bearing in mind that mentality and experience manifest their presence pre-eminently in intentional action, one might easily suppose that the great temporal novelty ushered into being by experience is the 'co-presence' in the experiential instant of *present and future*: orientation to both dimensions of time at each point in experience. However, this would be an error. The great temporal novelty is the irreducible 'co-presence' of the *other two* temporal dimensions in the experiential instant: it is the meeting of past and/or future in the present. In effect, it is the unselfconscious consciousness of the passage of time.

In this present Section 5 I want to show that the relation of experience to the past closely mirrors the relation to the future. I shall do this in two stages: the first taking as topic the phenomenon of short-term memory, the second the perception of change. I begin with memory. Now in self-conscious beings present-tense knowledge-of and short-term memory-of experience function like Wittgensteinian 'criteria' of experience. They are fundamental and generally also decisive tests of its existence. Thus, experiences in the self-conscious must produce contemporaneous knowledge, and mostly also short-term memory, both of themselves and their objects, a knowing and remembering which take phenomenal form. Driving through dense fast-moving traffic, one has some knowledge at the time of one's own experienced acts and perceivings, and some recollection of the traffic that one saw a few seconds ago; and these cognitive recordings actually *occur*, and *mutate*, and for the most part *fade away completely* as new experiences fill consciousness. This constant occurrent turnover of here-and-now and just-then cognitions is characteristic of experience—though it can scarcely be a necessity, partly because one might lose consciousness at any instant, and partly because most animals undergo experience without knowing they do.

(2) It seems to me that we need to discover a non-self-conscious equivalent of these quasi-'criterial' properties of experiences, which is true of *all* conscious beings. After all, experiences are as real in the unselfconscious as in the self-conscious. Then what general trait is it, of which self-knowledge and short-term

memory constitute in the self-conscious a special instance, which can be adduced as a near-'criterial' test of experience in all beings? I suggest that the general trait is, the tendency on the part of experience (and its objects as experientially given) synthetically to unite with their immediate experiential predecessors in such a way as to constitute an occurrent exercise of memory.

Consider the first half of this complex property, viz. the tendency towards *synthesis*. It is a noteworthy fact that, even though discontinuous experience constantly occurs in the mind, experiences tend to form overlapping continuities of determinate type over continuous stretches of time. The onward flow of experience is not like a continuous journey through all the numerical values lying between (say) 1 and 2: a continuity which traverses rationals and irrationals, each wholly independent of its neighbour. Because experience contains event-edifices structured across time, the present has in general to join with its immediate past in such a way as to help realize event-kinds which endure. And the same holds of the objects as given in experience. At any point in time animal experience encompasses event-stages of object-directed events which have duration across time. Characteristically animals at any instant are experiencing experiences and objects whose past is necessary for their present. So much for synthesis.

(3) I turn now to the second element of the above putative criterion, namely memory. An example helps make the point. Thus, a dog chasing a cat continues the chase when the cat disappears around a corner. Then when the cat disappears the dog must in some sense *remember*, not merely the cat which it saw, but also the *act* it was doing. The dog remembers the cat in that it now knows the cat is present because it knew so in the past. However, when we say it remembers what it was doing, we are not speaking of a cognitive state caused by events in the past, and we certainly do not mean the dog has the power to cast its mind back to what it was doing. What we rather mean is that the past action *continues* into the present, so that what the dog now experiences is the identical experiential process it earlier experienced. But why describe this as an exercise of *memory*? The reason is, that had he not been acting thus in the past he would not be acting thus in the present, so that present experience must both unite with and depend upon past experience. This means that the past must in some sense be *co-present with* the present, and such a co-presence is a mode of remembering. Doubtless it is a developmentally early form of memory, to be supplemented later by additional less primitive ways of relating to one's past, notably cognitive modes. What in effect we are concerned with here is the tendency on the part of experience and its given objects to unite across time to form determinate wholes. It is not unlike the property of momentum in a moving object.

And yet all that we have so far noted of experiences must be true also of many non-experiential states, such as knowledge. Many years ago I learned that 9 and 5 make 14, and know so to this day, and the continuity of this one enduring state constitutes a form of memory. Here we have a non-experiential continuity which is also a remembering. And in fact the essence of many psychological phenomena is to be a stage of what endures. Thus, there is no such thing as an instantaneous knowing, or an instantaneous watching, even though there is instantaneous noticing-of or thinking-that. Such a property is a commonplace in the mind, and indeed elsewhere. Then when it is instantiated by a psychological item it mostly constitutes a developmentally first form of remembering. These observations indicate the need of *additional differentia* if we are to hit upon a trait of this type which is a quasi-'criterial' test of experience.

I do not think we should despair of discovering a property along these lines that is distinctive to experience. It will be recalled that in the self-conscious the quasi-criterial property of experience under discussion was, not merely self-knowledge and remembering, but a remembering that was *short-lived and occurrent*. Now we have seen that the concept 'short-term memory' shrinks in the unselfconscious into 'falls essentially under a concept whose instances necessarily have temporal extension', and we noted that this ranges far and wide in the mind across experiences and non-experiences alike. Meanwhile the concept 'occurrent short-term memory', in the form it takes in the unselfconscious, merely adds to the above the qualification that the item thus governed be *occurrent*. Then it is this that is peculiar to experiences. What is distinctive to experiences is that the required synthesis across time is *occurrent memory*—a property which follows from the fact that experiences are of necessity occurrences. The *cognitive* form of occurrent memory evident in self-conscious knowings, remarked upon in someone driving through fast-moving traffic, who inevitably harbours mutating fading knowledge both of the cars he has just seen and his own just elapsed deeds and perceptions, is a special 'higher' case of this universal and distinctive property of experiences.

(b) The perception of change

(1) In short, the immediate experienced past lives on in present experience in the sense that it is in general *constitutive* of what is now experienced. But there is an even stronger sense in which it does: namely, in our steady unflagging capacity to be *concretely aware* in the here and now of the objects *as they were given* to immediately past experience. The perception of change across time is instructive in this regard. Here we encounter a relation to the past as intimate as that linking intention and future, and closely analogous. Accordingly, the question I now pursue is, whether the immediate past of (say) a visible movement is at each instant 'co-present' with its present to the consciousness of a visual perceiver of the movement, and therefore whether visual experience is simultaneously directed to present and past.

We shall see that it is—and again irreducibly. The 'co-presence' of past times and 'now' is beautifully illustrated in a phenomenon which is of great eloquence, and of the first importance for the philosophy of consciousness. I refer to the visual perception of continuous spatial change: say, seeing the parabolic path of a rocket against the night sky. This phenomenon ought to strike wonder into us. It is a truly astonishing fact that one might *show* a person a novel shape, either by drawing it in ink on a page, or else by making a gesture with one's hand! What in the latter case a person is being shown is a structure purely across *space* through being shown a structure across *space and time*! For it is not that the temporal structure of the phenomenon is in this instance *invisible*—which would be the case if one saw at night the path of a nearby tracer bullet—since the viewer can distinguish beginning, middle, and end in his experience of the shape traced out by the hand. What is so puzzling is, that in an important sense the immediate once visible past is *as present* to consciousness as the present, despite being no longer visible (i.e. despite being invisible). The diagram below is a representation of the situation.

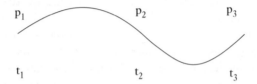

In what precise sense is the invisible past present to visual consciousness? The following are the bare facts of the case: at p_1 t_1 the hand began moving, at some midway time t_2 it passed through point p_2, and at t_3 it came to a halt at p_3. At t_1 the subject saw the beginning of the hand's movement, and at t_3 the end. Then at the midway time t_2 the following obtained:

A. At t_2 he saw the *hand* at p_2.
B. At t_2 he saw the hand *moving* (i.e. the moving process) at p_2.
C. By t_2 he had seen *part of* the movement.
D. By t_2 he had seen *all of* the movement that had occurred by t_2.

But the following did not obtain:

E. At t_2 he saw part of the movement.
F. At t_2 he saw the part of the movement that had occurred by t_2.

Note the following logical relations:
A⇸B (for the movement may be invisible, not in the mode of the tracer bullet, since that contradicts B, but in the mode exemplified by an hour hand, viz. the mode of slowness).
B⟶C (for one cannot see the process continuing at any instant without seeing some measure of it).
C⇸D (for the entire movement [from p_1 to p_2] may be invisible, not in the mode of the tracer bullet—for its parts are visible, nor in the mode of the hour

hand—once again because its parts are visible, but in the mode in which some given extent of the movement of a very large minute hand may be invisible, viz. in being too slow for the mind to be able to bring to bear its synthetic powers and render that extent of its movement visible).

E and F record logical impossibilities. Since E$\longrightarrow$B$\longrightarrow$C$\longrightarrow$one saw the movement over a period of experienced time, and since the assumption of E and F is that 'at t_2' names a single instant of experienced time, we contradict ourselves in affirming E. And the same is true of F.

The puzzle posed by the whole phenomenon is, that D makes it *seem as if* F was true. Thus, at t_2 one sees the object at p_2, and sees it moving at p_2, and one also completes the experience of seeing its ⌒ movement; and since C$\dashv\rightarrow$D we know that the latter third element is additional to the first two, and makes an essential contribution to the experience at t_2. Then a person (Mr X) who at time t_2 completes the experience of seeing ⌒, has at t_2 a different visual experience from one (Mr Y) who at t_2 completes the experience of seeing a merely lesser sector ⌐ of ⌒. They have different visual experiences at the same instant t_2. One is therefore inclined to say that X and Y see something different at t_2. And since we know that X has seen ⌒, while Y has merely seen ⌐, one is inclined to say that at t_2 X must see ⌒ and Y ⌐. But they do not. They have different visual experiences at t_2, but they see the *same thing* at t_2, viz. merely the moving object O. One is inclined to explicate the difference between the two visual experiences at t_2 in terms of a difference of *perceptible object*, and in consequence inclined to squeeze the immediate-past-invisible into that single instant. In effect, this is to model this case upon the situation exemplified by the nearby tracer bullet, wherein past and present are jointly visible in the one instant. The puzzle arises through the difficulty in accommodating in our concept of the perceptual visual experience of the moment, an element other than *what is seen* at that moment. It is the difficulty of coming to terms with the fact that the element of time is in the experience 'equi-original' with any object.

(2) In fact the situation is as follows. The seeing by time t_2 of the ⌒ part of ⌒ is constituted out of experiencing at any instant t_x the completion of the experience of seeing the corresponding $\diagup_x$-part of ⌒ (where the $\diagup_x$'s are a continuity). Then that in turn is constituted out of seeing the object O's moving at any $p_x t_x$ *as* completing the $\diagup_x$-sector of ⌒ (in a truly perceptual sense of 'see as'). Now this latter constituting element *is not* perceiving $\diagup_x$ (since the latter occupies t_1–t_x). And in fact it cannot be explicated any further. And that is to say that we cannot analyse the seeing of ⌒ across the experientially differentiable time-interval t_1–t_2 any further. Thus, an ineradicable reference to other times and places is an essential element of each instant's experience across time of motion. The very essence of the experience of the moment is such that it points determinately backwards in time and elsewhere in space, from an indexically-given 'now' and 'here' spatio-temporal origin-point. The mind constitutes the experience of shape

across time out of *such elements*. It is in this sense that in this experience the past and elsewhere are *as concretely present* as the here and now. This is what is so astonishing about seeing ⌒‿⌒ across time. It is as concretely present to consciousness as ⌒‿ starkly etched in ink upon a page. We are in the presence here of two quite different modes of *direct acquaintance* with spatial diversity. While the latter is doubtless in some sense primary, they are equally concrete modes of making the direct acquaintance of one and the same shape.

What is of particular importance is, that perceptions across time are not constituted out of object-perceptions in the instant: no X-object is such that the perception of ‿‿‿ between t_1 and t_2 is constituted out of (perceiving-some-X-object)-parts: no X is equal to the task. All that we *see* at each instant is O's moving, and out of that constituent alone one will never manage to put together the seeing of ‿‿‿ across time. Yet we *do* see ‿‿‿! And the puzzlement will continue to dog us precisely to the extent that we feel such an X-object must exist. This is to model the seeing of a phenomenon across time upon the seeing across time of a thing. The key to the problem lies in our grasping that more is needed than any variety of *object* can provide, and that the 'more' is already on hand in the very nature of *experience*. The 'more', which comes from the mind itself, consists in what the mind *does* with a suitable object, and is ensconced in the 'as——' which enters the *essential description* of the visual experience of the instant. It is an irreducible element of the experience, and in particular cannot be reduced to the seeing of some variety of object. This mode of acquaintance with a concrete temporal reality is *sui generis*.

6. Consciousness and Change

(1) This direct encounter with the immediate past is *sui generis*, and it is an 'original' element of experience. Thus, it is not as if the perception of material objects appears first in animal experience, and the perception of phenomenal objects across time comes next. And that is to say, not that all perceptions are simultaneously directed to present and past, but that those perceptions whose object is at each moment situated purely in the present, such as the visual perception of a tree or house, are nonetheless for the experiencer sited in a temporal framework which incorporates a past of which he is concretely aware in a way that closely matches the perception of movement. A man staring fixedly at a chair is as directly aware of the perceptual object of a few seconds ago as is the perceiver of a movement across time. The individuation of the perception of any instant requires that it be so.

Indeed one might at first suppose that, since the function of perception is to inform us of phenomena in a changing world, all perception must be of change across time. However, this is no more true than the reverse supposition. Each of these extremes is an abstraction from reality. Perceptual worlds populated exclusively by change across time, or exclusively by unchanging objects, are scarcely imaginable: so to say pure manic Heracliteanism, or depressive Parmenideanism!

Consider the latter: a sort of graveyard of immobilized entities, all frozen in their tracks. And in fact such a scene would be a world, not in reality of changelessness, but of persistence and change in which the change is presented to consciousness in the mode of the hour hand. It is conceivable that all visual perception took this form, though since intentional bodily action depends internally on proprioception, and physical action is fundamental to the animal condition, rather less than conceivable that absolutely all perception might be of an 'hour-hand world'. Meanwhile the Heraclitean alternative presents even greater problems for the imagination, bearing in mind that change is always relative to an unchanging 'ground'. But the point to be emphasized here is, that we can experience one type of object (unchanging desert, the 'fixed stars') only if we can experience the other (earthquake, a rocket-path). In a word, they are 'equi-original'.

(2) And yet considered from the point of view of experience, the symmetry vanishes. In the very nature of things there is a sort of natural bias towards the perception of change. Even in the situation of total lack of change in the objects of perception, change continues—within. (It is a direct manifestation of the *life* of the subject, as indeed is experience itself: they exemplify the 'ticking over' that is in a general sense essential to life.) However frozen the perceptible world may in fact be, the 'internal clock' of consciousness ticks on, and all that can stop it is oblivion. Heracliteanism is true of the domain of experience.

In the light of this fact it seems to me that the perception of the shape of movement might with some justice be proposed as a fitting image for consciousness. While the perceptibility of change in one's environment is a necessity merely *qua* contrast with the perceptibility of stasis, in the case of the phenomenon of *experience* the necessity for awareness of continuous occurrence across time is internal to the phenomenon itself—a necessity which is encountered equally as directly in intentional action as here. One could put the matter this way: that consciousness is possible only if it is akin all the time to the perception of shape across time. In this image we import the direct encounter with temporal change, the sheer awareness of the passage of time, that we know to be essential to consciousness. The proper image for experiential consciousness is, seeing the gesture across time, or reading the luminous ticker-tape sentence, and it is not seeing the hour hand of the clock, or the immobile Pyramids. More exactly, it is seeing the gesture across time in seeing the hand that moves, or seeing the hand that moves in seeing the gesture across time. Consciousness at any instant encompasses more than the instant.

(3) This 'co-presence' of times is a constitutive property. It is this which the image of the visible gesture emphasizes: it drives home the message that, despite being divisible into 'now'-parts, the nature of experience is temporally *in extenso* from the temporal standpoint of that 'now'. It is almost as if at each instant one saw *more than* the instant, as if one were equipped with a sort of prism facing in both temporal directions, whereby one simultaneously witnessed both 'elsewhere' and 'here' in time, given miraculously in their appropriate temporal locations. This

misleading image has the virtue of situating the decisive property non-relationally within the experience itself. That property is best captured by reaffirming the claim that the *essential description* of any experience of the moment contains an irreducible reference to the immediate past/future of the experience, given from the temporal vantage-point of 'now'. The experience of the instant is never given, and cannot as such be given, merely as 'now'.

Close up the past, wall off the future, and you cover over the present too. For there is simply no such thing as 'the solipsistic fruits of the instant'. Just as I cannot see motion at any instant unless I now see what I also witnessed elsewhere in time, namely the movement-phenomenon that reaches up to this very instant; just as I cannot be going anywhere unless I am coming from somewhere, or coming from somewhere if I am going nowhere, indeed can be doing *nothing* in the absence of either!; so it is right across the spectrum of experience. The experience is in its very constitution embedded at a determinate point in a concretely given temporal continuity, and not just *known to be* sited in some determinate way. While dream experience has odd temporal characteristics (as will emerge in Chapter 2), the sheer narratability of the dream demonstrates that the property of temporal 'co-presence' is not peculiar merely to experience in the conscious. It is true of experience as such.

(4) Time is the form, not as such of the psychological, and not merely of the experience: it is rather to be characterized as the form of any properly developed mental psychological phenomenon. Thus, time cannot be the form as such of the psychological, since two qualitatively indistinguishable pains might simultaneously exist in one's two thumbs, thanks to the proprioceptive perception of the body, and ultimately to the long-term body image. Therefore space, or more exactly the experienced space of the body, must be the form of the psychological primitive, sensation. But time cannot just be the form uniquely of experience either, since we individuate mental states generally across time. For example, one cannot from t_1 to t_2 hold two enduring distinct beliefs directed to the same proposition, any more than one can from t_1 to t_2 support two active thinking experiences with identical content.

Then time with determinations appropriate to the temporal mapping of experienced process must be the specific form of experiential consciousness. It is not just that we individuate experiences, and most significantly internally indistinguishable experiences, by positioning them on the ultimate differentiating one-dimensional co-ordinate system—time. In addition, an experiencing subject is one who experiences the passage of time. Experiences not just are, and are not just known to be, they are *experienced as* 'simultaneous with' or 'just after' or 'a continuation in time of' or 'leading towards' particular existent experiences; and this is a universal structural characteristic specifically of the realm of experience. A conscious animal inhabits time just as concretely as it does space. To awaken is to discover oneself in both.

62

The supposition that all movement might have been as the hour-hand's and invisible, indeed that absolutely all perception might have been as if of a sort of Parmenidean graveyard of immutability, such theoretical possibilities must not deflect us from the central point. Namely, that experience itself cannot be of this kind. Even the unchanging perception of a fixed immobilized world conceals a processive continuity, that of the perceiving itself, which is occurrently renewed in each instant, defining itself through that change as it proceeds. And this is how it is with experience as such. That is why I say that the proper image for conscious experience is, not the seeing of the hour-hand, nor of a close at hand tracer bullet, nor even of the very large visibly-moving minute hand: it is the sight of a swallow in flight, or of a meteor crossing the night sky.

7. Summary and Conclusion

(a) Summary

(1) We have managed to assemble a set of properties of the experience, beginning with four logical properties. Thus, experience is:

   A. An indefinable.
   B. An essential property of all experience-individuals, and of some types which take experience form.
   C. A genus kind, not a species kind, and hence incapable of satisfying the type-condition necessary for identity and being.
   D. A non-contingent or necessarily actualized genus of the category, psychological.

These four logical properties were then augmented by the following non-logical properties. The experience is:

   E. Occurrent in type: it is event/processive in character, and not of the type state.
   F. If an experience is temporally extended, its constitution is purely processive and non-state in type.
   G. There are no experience states.

And:

   H. When experiences across time synthesize to constitute instances of experiential types, they are exhibiting the developmentally first form of occurrent memory.

And:

   I. Experiences are veridically and indexically given to self-conscious subjects as temporally sited 'now'.

J. And the experiential instant essentially relates to neighbouring other times.

K. So that an experiencing subject must be aware of the passage of time.

And I suppose we should add the following celebrated property:

L. In many cases (e.g. feeling nausea, seeing vermilion, being amused) there is something that is 'what it is like' to have the experience.

(2) Despite the formidableness of this list of properties, experiencehood is unanalysable, being an 'original' constituent of the mind. This is evidenced in the fact that our capacity to identify instances of the property outstrips our capacity to quote a justifying rationale. Does not our certainty that (say) some mental image is an experience, *precede* our ability to invoke a rationale? (A rationale that is inevitably open-ended.) And in any case numerous psychological indefinables, like belief/striving/sensation/etc., have known constitutive properties. Thus: belief is directed to propositions, strivings are experiences, sensations exhibit degree, etc. The existence of such properties can be no indicator of definability. And, one might ask, definability in terms of—*what*? Of more of the same ilk as itself? This suggestion carries within itself the seeds of its own destruction. A principle to the effect that necessary constitutive properties must help constitute a definition of the covering concept, would defeat the whole idea of the mind as a system of diverse psychological types. Mental substance would drain away at a trice. Like Baron Münchausen's horse the mind would support its own weight! If necessary constitutive properties led automatically to definition, everything in the mind would be defined in terms of everything else, and all content vanish into thin air. Something must provide that content: presumably, indefinables of the like of belief and striving. Why not experience also?

(b) Conclusion

(1) I have spoken of the non-experiential sector of the mind: that is, all that holds and happens in a mind of non-experiential type. The multiple unbroken lines of memory running back through the mind to early childhood typify this relatively stable corpus. If anything merits the title 'substance of the mind', this must be its site, for all that gives to a mind a determinate character is non-experiential, since whatever mental characteristics one's mental history attests to finds its place here. Indeed, it may even be that we discover in this sector of the mind the grounds of its very identity. Can a mind exist that has no mental character whatsoever, a mental *tabula rasa* without even the properties of wax or the 'virgin page'? But whatever the truth on this matter, and on the need for a measure of stability, this domain can scarcely be 'Parmenidean', for it harbours continual change. And yet this sub-sector of the mind is like the rest of the World inasmuch as those changes are of states. And that in effect is to say, that events in this part of the mind are founded on what has no need of change or incident to be. This is borne out by the fact that the mind and

this sub-sector could in principle survive in complete stasis. All manifestations of mental life could cease, and they continue unscathed.

It is upon such a base that experience arises or 'appears'. Here the picture is truly Heraclitean, all fire and motion with nothing with the potential for stasis in it, no states in the middle of the movement, no matter that burns so to say. Experience appears in flux on the surface of the mind, upon the relatively stable corpus without which it could not so much as exist. And while the quasi-substantival ground of experience continues in a steady necessarily unbroken line, experience comes and goes like the weather, being unable to exist without constant agitation. This is because each experiential instant looks beyond itself temporally, is like a window opening out onto both temporal corridors. And this in turn must be what renders unavailable to experience the type of autonomy that states necessitate and import. Thus, at any moment in time the experience is temporally both elsewhere and here in its content, for it cannot exist without progression, incident, movement. In this sense it is generally in advance of itself (though not in dreams), and more or less inevitably behind itself also, since experiences synthesize across time to realize the developmentally first form of occurrent short-term memory. There is no repose within consciousness. It either 'goes on', or destructs.

(2) Since occurrence is the stuff of experience, being all event and process in the absence of states, time enters constitutively into its make-up: the content of each experiential instant necessarily includes temporal properties. But in addition certain fundamental relations with time are realized uniquely for experiencing subjects. In particular, experience guarantees a direct confrontation with the passage of time, and in a sense that applies as much to the unselfconscious as the self-conscious.

This direct encounter with time was apparent in the two main temporal properties noted during the preceding discussion. I briefly repeat them here, the first in terms fitting only the self-conscious. Thus, we saw firstly that experiencing subjects know of each instant that it is the instant it is, at the very least in the indexical form of 'now', and that such knowledge is unavailable to non-experiencing beings. And secondly experiences proved to be of such a nature that the experiential instant essentially refers to other times—as the example of the rocket at night beautifully illustrates (or the equally convincing case of intentional action). In this sense the experiential instant is temporally given both for what it is itself, and in relation to neighbouring times. And in this way the passage of time is accessible uniquely to those who are experiencing.

What is the unselfconscious equivalent of these confrontations with time? Any experiencing animal has an awareness of the present, insofar as it has the capacity to distinguish one moment from another. We encounter this power in the most rudimentary of creatures. Thus, an insect might respond to a mating signal that took the form of three identical repeated brief emissions of light, the cue being to act *at and upon* receipt of the third light. This creature perceives and acts selectively across time, and that alone is sufficient for it to be credited with temporal recognition. (And it is neither here nor there that its behaviour is instinctive.) The point is, that the creature here finds its way through time exactly as it does though space.

This is knowing the present instant when it 'appears'—unselfconsciously. However, each instant is what it is, and is not its temporal neighbours. And so the capacity to recognize the present cannot be the same thing as what I have been calling the 'co-presence' of other times in the experiential instant. But this latter capacity also finds its unselfconscious form. We have merely to remember the importance to animal life of perceptually identifying continuities across time like mating dances or the movement-patterns of prey or predator. More centrally still, one could instance purposeful activity. In this experience we discover a relation to the future closely akin to that to the past in the above examples. While a dog crossing the garden to dig up its bone is doubtless not actually thinking of that forthcoming event—unlike a human gourmet approaching some famous Parisian restaurant, he is not to be likened to an animal on a treadmill either. The mind of this creature is occupied by active processes which irreducibly point towards future events.

(3) A noteworthy absentee from this account of experience is space. Time seems to be centre-stage in the theory, space nowhere to be found. And there can be no doubt that time is the unique dimension upon which experiences are strung. Indeed, it seems to me that investigating consciousness reveals that time is closer to our essential nature than is space. An elucidation of the concept of experience looks at first blush as if it could proceed almost as if the mind had no essential need of space—perhaps illusorily. We sometimes think we just might be able to imagine a World containing consciousnesses without matter or space, even if we reject the idea on consideration. But we entertain no such ideas in the case of time. We simply know forthwith that we could not imagine consciousnesses without time. We know at once.

And it is experience that puts us *in touch* with time. I do not mean in the 'what it is is like'-mode of '*quales*'. Rather, it does so in the sense that in experience we directly confront time in the several ways revealed in the discussion, which are tantamount to an awareness of the passage of time. After all, one cannot have knowledge of the reality of time without an awareness of its mutations. Finally, we saw that experiences do not just *inhabit* time, take up positions in time—which is true of absolutely all events (or for that matter states): time is their very *stuff*, insofar as they are constituted of the essentially temporal constituents, process and event, and of nothing else—being pure 'flux'. Their development is not a mutation in time from something a-temporal in nature to something else a-temporal, it is uniquely from process-stage to process-stage, and thus it is not so much change as *sheer* incident. Experience may even be described as an 'emergent' or 'higher' kind of process, a 'higher fire' that can burn without fuel or substance. Where else in nature do we discover process in the absence of state?

This necessary agitation I have suggested is a direct manifestation of the vitality of the organism. It is an example of the 'ticking over' that is in a general sense essential to life. The mind, and the body, can in principle mimic death, at least in hypothetical states of suspended animation. But the realm of experience is necessarily incapable of such pretence, and so too *a fortiori* is consciousness itself. The forces of life are nakedly on display in this domain.

2

The Anatomy of Consciousness

I turn from the unanalysable elemental phenomenon of experience to an examination of the closely associated phenomenon that is thought by many to be the most
fundamental and important factor in the lives of humans, and indeed of animals
generally: namely, consciousness itself. At once a whole set of problems confront us.
What we mean when we speak of 'consciousness'. What the character of the phenomenon is, considered both from a general classificatory and from an analytical
point of view. And so on. It is with these considerations in mind that I have divided
the present chapter into three parts. The first part is devoted to a discussion of the
type and general status of consciousness; the second to an examination of the characteristics of consciousness; and the third part consists in an elaboration of the main
conclusions of the preceding discussion.

A. TYPE AND STATUS

1. States of Consciousness

(1) Some might take the problem of consciousness to be the elucidation of the
nature of the *experience*. Others might take it to be the elucidation of the category of
the *mental*. My concern here is with something different again. It is with the vastly
familiar light that appears in the head when a person surfaces from sleep or anaesthetic or dream. In other words with the state we call 'waking', which I shall mostly
refer to as 'consciousness'. Then perhaps the first question to settle about consciousness is, whether it is a variety of a wider kind, or instead a kind all on its own
(rather as livingness is). Then the natural presumption is, that it is a variety of the
kind, state of consciousness. Whether or not this is so, depends upon the reality of
'states of consciousness'. This I shall try to demonstrate.

Might consciousness be to the animal what life is? That is, of the essence? It may
not. The evident existence of events that are *losses* or *regainings* of consciousness
demonstrates that consciousness cannot be necessarily coextensive with vitality
(and thus with sheer existence or being) in animals. Something can be a living
animal and not conscious. This entails that an animal can be in one or other of the
two conditions, conscious or not-conscious; and that might look like the contrast

THE ANATOMY OF CONSCIOUSNESS

needed to establish the existence of the covering type, state of consciousness. However, this is an illusion: the contrast is incapable of demonstrating the reality of the type. To accomplish this task we need to show more. Namely, that the non-conscious animal must be in a state which is a variety of a kind of which consciousness is another variety; that is, rule out the possibility that the non-conscious animal is merely one such that none of its states happen to be consciousness: that is, merely one in whom consciousness is absent. We need to show that there exist distinct states which are gathered together under the same umbrella with, and in opposition to, waking. We must show that some states are *specifically marked out* for the characterization 'not-consciousnesses'.

Then I think it plain that there are such states. A man who is not awake is either asleep, stunned, comatose, or some such, and these states are from the start specifically marked out as 'not-consciousness'. It is not merely a property of sleep that it is not waking: because it goes some way to telling us what sleep *actually is*, it is part of its essence that it is not waking. Thus, an animal must either be conscious, or in a state which has the necessary and indeed essential property of not being awake. This strongly suggests that whatever that alternate state might be, it and waking must be varieties of some one covering kind.

(2) However, it does not actually prove it. The existence of a given state, together with the existence of some other state which is essentially opposed to that state, still leaves it open that these two states are not different varieties of some one encompassing kind. Instead they may be no more than a state and another state that essentially consists in the absence of that first state. Are living and dead different varieties of some one encompassing kind? I think not. It seems to me that they are merely the two opposed possibilities in a single line of business. We are not here opposing one property and some distinct other, but a single property and its absence.

Then could it be that the states that are essentially marked out for the property of not being consciousnesses, are so for the unsurprising reason that they essentially and exhaustively *are*—the absence of consciousness? That is, is consciousness to the animal what life is to the animal body (or to a cell, or vegetable, and so forth)? While a dead animal is almost certainly a non-existent being, a dead body or dead plant is a real existent. Then as an animal body is either alive or dead, might it be that the animal is either conscious or else in a second determinate state which simply *is* the lack of consciousness? Just as 'dead' does not have application to a whole range of conditions which have in common that they are not states of livingness, but singles out instead one unique state of absence of life in the vital, could it be that there exists a single state which just *is* the lack of consciousness in beings with minds? Is 'life'/'death' a valid model for understanding the situation?

Let me express the same question in different terms. Is the state of sleep (say) merely a special instance of a state which has the following property: that the concept under which it is individuated as a state is a *contradictory* rather than *contrary* of the concept under which consciousness is individuated? This position will be false if sleep is one type of state, and the state ('unconsciousness') that happens to be induced by (say) chloroform necessarily a different state; for in that case the three terms 'conscious' 'sleep' 'unconscious' will relate as contraries rather than contradictories. Then a preliminary indication that 'life'/'death' cannot provide the correct logical model for understanding the relation between 'conscious'/'asleep'/'unconscious', is the simple fact that the former list is of two terms whereas the latter is of three.

But in any case the following considerations confirm that the model is inapplicable. Because death simply and exhaustively *is* absence of life in the vital, there are not *ways* of being dead—any more than a cupboard can be variously empty of food. Now this is not because death has the property of being an absence of life: it is because death *exhausts its nature* in this property. Thus, even though disease is an absence of health in the vital, any particular disease has some sort of determinate real essence; and this is so because it is an inessential property of any disease that it is a disease, no disease being global, which ensures that no disease *is* simply and exhaustively lack of health. Hence it comes about that there are ways of being unhealthy, as there are not ways of being dead, for death is global and has no real essence. By contrast, it seems certain that there are ways of not being conscious: say, by being asleep, or comatose. There are ways of dying as there are ways of losing consciousness, but whereas the paths to death lead to the monolithic state of death, the paths leading away from consciousness conduct one in different directions towards diverse states. This looks like a proof that the logical model of 'life'/'death' is inapplicable.

(3) Thus, one state is consciousness, and another is sleep, and a third and different state again is the one we call 'unconsciousness', and the three covering concepts relate as contraries rather than contradictories. And that is to say that the concept of the state of consciousness is vindicated: it singles out a genuine reality. This tells us a little about consciousness itself. Namely, that while it is not of the essence for an animal to be conscious; or conscious *or* in a state that simply *is* the absence of consciousness; it is of the essence for an animal to be in a state of which consciousness is a sub-variety. That is, it is of the essence for it to be in a *state of consciousness*. Necessarily, every animal is in some state of consciousness. Indeed, necessarily every animal is in some single (i.e. unique) state of consciousness.

Now the existence of a covering kind, ranging over these several states, together with the existence of at least three sub-varieties of the kind, suggests that a proper logical model for state-of-consciousness terms might be a genus-species terminology like colour or animal terms. But if this were correct, there ought in principle to exist novel states of consciousness. Indeed, as the actual colours might in principle be swelled with new colours beyond our experience and imagination, so the list of possible states of consciousness might be expanded to include a limitless array of other states beyond our experience and imagination.

There is something evidently the matter with this suggestion. This is because it is inconsistent with the pre-eminence of consciousness amongst states of consciousness—at least. The very term 'state of consciousness' should halt us in our tracks! Developmentally consciousness must come first, and the others states derive from it. Consciousness has I think to be part of the innate repertoire of anything that is an animal, indeed of anything that has a mind merely in the sense of having the capacity to support psychological phenomena. And yet it cannot be quite true to say that all the other states of consciousness develop out of the state consciousness. Because the presence of consciousness never constitutes the presence of life, it must always in principle be possible in animals for the state of life to inhere in the absence of consciousness. Now at the same time it must in principle be possible for any animal to exist when all vital function has been suspended, and that surely is a sufficient condition for the inherence of a state of sheer unconsciousness. It follows from these two considerations that the potential for the state of unconsciousness must be as essential to the animal condition as the capacity for consciousness itself. The emergence in creation of consciousness inevitably casts such a shadow.[1]

If that is how matters stand, it is not so much that consciousness comes first and the other states of consciousness develop out of it, as that consciousness and its inevitable derivative co-possibility unconsciousness appear simultaneously at the lowest rung of the developmental ladder. And yet even though consciousness may not be *temporally* prior to unconsciousness, it is nonetheless prior in providing the *content* for the deprived state that necessarily exists as its companion possibility. Then these two states look at first blush as if they might initially relate in the manner of life and death. In the developmentally super-simple case, consciousness and unconsciousness exhaust all the possibilities, in a way reminiscent of life and death. And yet it is mere appearance. While the only alternative to death is modes of life, there can always in principle exist alternatives to unconsciousness which are not modes of waking (e.g. sleep or trance). It remains to be seen what constraints are to be exerted upon these alternatives.

It is for such reasons as are advanced above that the logical model of genus-species fails, along with that of life/death. The various varieties of the kind, state of consciousness, are not on an equal footing as 'lion'/'giraffe'/'buffalo' are one as good as the other. In an important sense the state of consciousness that we call 'consciousness' comes first, and with it as inevitable derivative accompaniment the state of unconsciousness; and any other states that there might be, arise with them already present as background repertoire. Now if the logical model of life and death had been correct, the nature of the concept of a state of consciousness would in a certain sense be unproblematic. As the concept of vital condition allows for only two contradictory possibilities, life and its absence death, so it would be here. Because life is not the absence of death, whereas death is the absence of life, we can say that the content of the concept of vital condition is that of life. Similarly we would be able to say that the content of the concept of a state of consciousness

[1] Cf. 'Beginning with doom in the bulb', 'The womb drives in a death as life leaks out' (Dylan Thomas).

would be consciousness. But if matters are different from this, if there exist genuine third possibilities like sleep, the situation looks more obscure. All the more so when the existence of an order of priorities shows that the model of genus-species must fail.

2. The Individuation of States of Consciousness

(1) My concern has been to discover if consciousness is a sub-variety of a wider kind; and if so, the identity and logical character of that kind. This is perhaps the very first thing that we ought to know about the phenomenon. It emerged that any-thing endowed with a mind must be in a type of state which is such that conscious-ness is the pre-eminent and parent sub-variety. The very expression 'state of consciousness' points the way, and the 'all or nothing' model of life and death, together with the genus-species model of (say) colours or mammals, prove to be inapplicable.

At this juncture we must grasp the nettle, the individuation of states of con-sciousness. How do we recognize and distinguish one state from another? Now it is natural to attempt this task through a mere citing of state-properties; that is, through doing no more than draw up a set of distinctive concatenative lists. However, such a procedure works in the dark until we understand the significance of those typifying properties. Then I suggest that state-of-consciousness properties do not contingently and at a remove signal the hidden presence of a real essence in the manner of familiar natural-kinds. They are something closer to the matter than mere epistemological 'pointers'. An example shows this. Thus, while the state con-sciousness has various typifying properties, it can be simply individuated by a priori-given necessary and sufficient conditions: namely, by the obtaining in the self-conscious of a rational state in which experience is occurring. Accordingly, consciousness has no empirically hidden core, and wears its heart upon its sleeve. The same is true of unconsciousness, which in the self-conscious is logically equivalent to the obtaining of a non-rational state—by which I mean a state such that belief is typically non-rationally caused—in which the perceptual attention is categorically unavailable. In either case it is impossible to imagine analogues of 'twin earth' natural-kinds. If on some 'twin earth' a being supports either of the above two constellations of properties, such a being must be in the same state of consciousness as his counterpart on earth—and there can be no two ways about the matter. The familiar epistemological ambiguity encountered in the case of (say) water is not encountered in the case of states of consciousness.

(2) I mention the problem of individuation to enable me to complete the task of delineating the logical character of the covering kind or genus under which the concept of (waking) consciousness falls. We have just noted that we are not here dealing with real essences. Moreover, we know that states of consciousness are a priori individuatable. Both facts suggest interpretations of the role of the typifying properties (as we shall see). The other data relevant to answering this question is

provided by the phenomenon of *degree*. Thus, while one can be absolutely or vividly awake, one can neither be more and more nor limitlessly awake, whereas one can by contrast be either more profoundly asleep or more deeply unconscious. This is not surprising, and turns upon the variable which determines degree in these latter two phenomena: in the case of sleep the availability of the intuitional attention, in the case of unconsciousness the possibility of dream or other experiences and ultimately of mental life in any form. The rationale is fully transparent and a priori. The concept of deepest unconsciousness is as a result perfectly precise a priori: namely, the total suspension of psychological events and processes in beings with minds. (What would be a 'twin earth' to that?)

Then bearing in mind the property of degree, the fact that we are concerned here with a priori-determinable rather than with real essences, and the failure of the aforementioned two models, the following theory concerning the covering concept of *state of consciousness* recommends itself. Namely, that the concept is such that all possible alternatives to the state consciousness are privations in relation to that state. They are not diminutions of the state, not faint or impoverished versions of consciousness, since they are not examples of consciousness: they are *privative derivatives*. Instead of merely negating consciousness as death merely negates life, those states stand to consciousness in a relation which bears some resemblance to negation, and accounts for the attractiveness of the life/death model: they whittle away at it. Hence it comes about that there are not a potentially limitless array of states of consciousness as there are of colours or mammals. Conceptually we begin with consciousness and privatively derive the others by denuding it of powers. The state of waking marshals our central mental powers—to experience, sense-perceive, think, and reason, to cogently and actively manipulate the environment with a view to fulfilling our needs—and all other states of consciousness are noteworthy for the absence of some or even all of the above. All the other individuating constellations of properties are marked by the absence of a power that is a near essential part of the armoury of a self-conscious being.

So of what kind of a kind is consciousness a kind? A kind that is essential to its owner's very being: a kind such that it has a pre-eminent sub-variety; in relation to which the others are privative derivatives, modes of not being it rather than pure absences of it. Consciousness pre-eminently instantiates such an essential kind. This progeny is parent to its own logical family.

3. The Relation between States of Consciousness and their Properties

(1) We have spoken of states of consciousness as if they were realities. Why? It is one thing to establish the existence of a covering concept through demonstrating that the terms are contraries with contrary content, but why believe that they single out real existents? Why believe that there are wakings and sleepings and suchlike? Certainly the syndromes of properties seem to show so. But if as we have argued

these constellations are not epistemological 'pointers' of underlying real essences, why believe there is anything *more than* the properties themselves? Four considerations point that way. First, the existence of necessary and sufficient conditions for the states. Second, the fact that the states explain the properties, e.g. the state unconsciousness explains the absence of sense-perception in one concussed. Third, the fact that there exist agreed techniques for causing and removing the various states, e.g. concussion, smelling salts. And finally fourth, that the properties cannot exist in isolation of their fellows, but travel of necessity in groups. As a result I cannot bring myself to doubt, either the reality of states of consciousness, or the usual taxonomical carve-up.

Then how do these states relate to the syndromes of properties that ensure their presence and whose presence they explain? Might they be *constituted* of them? In that case the explanatory function of the states of consciousness would not be causal. Or are they instead the distinct and necessary *cause* of the syndrome? This is a substantive issue. The question is: does concussion *just* knock out sense-perception? or does it instead knock it out *by* knocking in unconsciousness which then causes attentive shut-down? or is there some other as yet unformulated third alternative? One vitally important fact to remember is, that techniques for manipulating presence or removal of any one member of any state-of-consciousness syndrome, address themselves not so much directly to the particular phenomenon itself as to the state of consciousness which guarantees or proscribes it. Thus, to delete the phenomenon of attentive-function one does not attempt directly to expunge it from the mind, but rather wreaks *such* change that many other alterations in the mind occur along with the phenomenon one sought to produce, alterations such that a change of state of consciousness cannot but be effected along with it. And it is not that we lack techniques of sufficient finesse to remove the phenomenon on its own, and have perforce in our clumsiness to resort to the equivalent of a club: there is no remedy even in principle for such 'crudeness'. This 'technical holism' (as one might call it) should be borne in mind when we come to adjudicate between the two rival theoretical positions on the issue of constitution.

(2) Neither position looks attractive. It is difficult to believe that states of consciousness are complex mental states made up out of other mental states. Mental Chemistry and suchlike seem near universal impossibilities. Again, a state like consciousness is as elemental a mental phenomenon as any, and it is hard to believe that it could depend for its being upon other presumably more fundamental mental phenomena. Further, we have just noted that we never manipulate the supposed constituent properties on their own, but inevitably alter the state of consciousness in the process. It must be a strange kind of constitutive assembly when the putative constituents necessarily travel in packets which inevitably realize wholes!

So much for the first theory. When we turn to the second theory, we find something that looks if anything even less palatable. I mean, the theory that states of consciousness are the distinct and necessary cause of the properties which attest to their presence. The claim that unconsciousness *causes* attentive shut-down rings hollow to my way of thinking, if only because the former is inconceivable without the latter. And what is the evidence of distinctness? The explanatory role of the state? But explanatory force would be preserved, albeit of a constitutive rather than causal variety, if distinctness was discounted. Again, the rejection of distinctness would obviate the need to postulate necessary causation between distinct existents. These considerations push one towards the view that in *some* undetermined sense, the state of unconsciousness must actually *involve* attention-closure. That is, towards the constitutive theory in some shape or form. But towards *which* theory exactly? And how to avoid the difficulties facing the constitutive theory?

What is the resolution of this problem? I think we must begin by endorsing the above theoretical intuition. That is, by rejecting the second theory, that states of consciousness are the distinct necessary cause of their properties. Next, we note a measure of holism in the situation. It is true that some syndrome properties do not entail their brethren properties: for example, the non-rationality of unconsciousness does not entail attention-closure, since sleep realizes the former without fully realizing the latter. Nevertheless, others do, and all are consistent with only *some* states of consciousness. In other words, they each necessarily occur in sets, each of which realize a unique state of consciousness.

Accordingly, the following account recommends itself. We accept that states of consciousness are assembled out of mental phenomena, but reject the supposition that the constituents have a fully autonomous existence. Because everything with a mind is in some *one* unique state of consciousness, which is logically rather than indexically individuated by its properties, each such property must be as dependent upon the state it helps constitute as is the latter upon it. In this sense the constituting of states of consciousness, while a real constituting out of real parts, is not additive in nature. The parts cannot even in principle exist prior to the kind of item which they succeed in constituting. Therefore concussion neither *just* knocks out sense-perception; nor knocks it out *by* knocking in unconsciousness which then causes attentive shut-down: it *just* knocks out sense-perception *in* knocking in unconsciousness. Here we have a third alternative to two intolerable positions.

(3) The theory that states of consciousness are logically rather than indexically individuated by their properties smacks at first of a kind of conventionalism, rather as if we cobbled together an arbitrary mental construct out of given parts. This would rob the constituted whole of a nature in any serious sense. (A lack that Real Essences would make good in convincing fashion.) However, the remaining elements of the theory reveal this account to be a misrepresentation. The dependence of the constituting states upon the constituted state of consciousness, together with the fact that they travel of necessity in constellations of properties which instantiate some one unique state of consciousness, stand in the way of such an interpre-

tation. These considerations disprove the additive theory, through placing constraints upon which part can join which in constituting a state, and by limiting the number and type of such constituted states.

4. The Psychologicality of Consciousness

(1) Consciousness involves experience, and is a phenomenon in which intuitional attending occurs. This suggests that consciousness must be a psychological phenomenon; indeed it might seem obvious it is. However, something like an antinomy threatens this doctrine, which I will shortly explain. But first a word about psychologicality. When I use this term I am speaking of the property common to undirected phenomena like sensations and intentionally directed phenomena like thoughts. Just what the property is I shall not attempt to say, and doubt whether there is anything to say of an explanatory nature. Then in a way it seems obvious that consciousness is a psychological state. After all, it has essential properties which are psychological: for example, it entails the occurrence of experience in the bearer. And yet the living brain is not a psychological being, and necessitates psychological states in its owner. Could that be how matters stand? Might consciousness be a non-psychological brain state with psychological properties? But consciousness actually *involves* psychological phenomena like experience. How can it avoid being psychological in type? And it should be remembered that one immediately knows one is conscious when one is: Cartesian-type self-knowledge holds here. Is this likely in the case of a brain state that is not a psychological state? While it is true we also immediately know of our own existence, and we are no 'psychological being', the cognitive immediacy linking us to consciousness seems almost certain to derive from its mental character. In short, it is an occurrent psychological phenomenon.

(2) But with this conclusion, antinomy threatens. If consciousness is psychological in status, so too must be the covering kind of which it is a variety. That is, states of consciousness must as such be psychological states. But coma, and indeed the deepest conceivable depth of unconsciousness in which all mental life is suspended, are states of consciousness. Yet can the latter nadir of unawareness be a psychological state? (What price 'privileged access' here!) This supposedly unacceptable conclusion follows from the psychologicality of consciousness, and might seem to amount to antinomy. Can it be resisted? I think it can. For what are the objec-tions to adjudging profoundest unconsciousness psychological in character? Two spring to mind: first that it is inconsistent with experience of any kind, second that it is a wholly negative condition. Consider them in order.

It is true that profoundest unconsciousness is inconsistent with experience, being inconsistent with mental vital process as such. However, it is not merely consistent with, it actually necessitates life. Then the life resident in the suspended organism manifests its presence precisely in the continuing inherence of non-experiential psychological phenomena like cognitive states and character traits. (And this

76

too is a necessity.) Why should not unconsciousness join their ranks? After all, psychologicality *is not* experienceability. And even though waking consciousness manifests its existence in experience, it is not itself an experience. Why should not a psychological state like deepest unconsciousness manifest its existence in the impossibility of experience?

So much for the first objection. The second, more interesting objection, claims of profoundest unconsciousness that it is a wholly negative condition and *therefore* that it cannot be psychological in character. The 'therefore' is in order: were this condition nothing but the absence of a state, it could not lay claim to an order of being. The emptiness of food of a cupboard has not the ontological character of physical space, or material object, or material stuff, or indeed of anything else. However, what must be contested is the claim that profoundest unconsciousness is thus wholly negative. It is worth recalling that consciousness relates to the other states as contrary rather than contradictory. Had it been the case that for a state of consciousness *not* to be consciousness *was* for it to *be* sheer not-consciousness, the claim would be correct and the argument valid. Had matters stood thus however, the psychologicality of consciousness could not entail the psychologicality of its contradictory alternative. On the contrary: the latter would precisely be the absence of the former, and would in consequence lack any order of being. Accordingly, one could conserve the psychologicality of consciousness, while dispensing with that of the alternative.

The failure of these objections is a consequence of the aforementioned fact that there exists an encompassing kind which embraces the states of sleep, consciousness, and unconsciousness, viz. state of consciousness. Even in the theoretically limiting case (the 'nadir') in which the privative alternatives to consciousness find maximum negative realization, the kind itself doggedly lingers and refuses to vanish. This anchors that extremest of negative states in an order of being, despite the vanishing of all of the properties manifestative of the consciousness-ness of consciousness—such as attentive-function, rationality of state, and so forth. In the limiting case the privative kind alone lingers; but it is enough to guarantee to its instances an ontological status identical with that of the plenitude in relation to which it is thus privative: namely, with consciousness itself. I mean: psychologicality. Accordingly, I see the existence of deepest unconsciousness as no serious embarrassment for the relatively obvious doctrine of the psychologicality of consciousness.

(3) Not only is consciousness a psychological state, in a good sense it is *the* psychological state. It is not merely that the alternative states of consciousness are privative in relation to it, and not just that consciousness has to be a real potential in any being with a mind. One other consideration points towards the same conclusion, and provides a significant clue as to the character and function of consciousness itself. This emerges when we adopt a verificationist standpoint and ask the question: how would we verify the presence of *psychologicality* in a wholly novel object? The

answer is general and simple. We would look for bodily phenomena, situated in determinate settings, which were indicative of an integrated battery of intelligibly linked psychological phenomena: namely, perception of sectors of that setting, cognitive attitudes concerning the latter, together with desires and intentions and intentional physical willings directed towards precisely those same sectors of the environment.

Two things are especially interesting about the above psychological network. First, it is nothing less than the use of the central typifying mental powers of animals as such. Second, it is indicative of the inherence of a full state of consciousness. Thus, we would find it behaviourally all but impossible to detect the presence of psychologicality in a Rip van Winkle species that scarcely ever emerged from sleep or hibernation. The occasional change of posture, the odd stray grimace of discomfort, would in an entirely novel animal be on their own insufficient to establish mentality of any sort. This conclusion strongly suggests that consciousness has the function of enabling the central mental powers to arise and work together. It suggests that consciousness is the psychological foundation of our normal mental life. This would accord it a position of absolute pre-eminence in the mind.

B. PROPERTIES

So much for type and status. I turn now to an examination of the characteristics of consciousness. Oddly enough, these seem to divide into what might be termed 'negative' and 'positive' characteristics. I begin with the negative, the most noteworthy of which come to light when we consider the issue of the object of consciousness.

5. Negative Properties

(a) The object of consciousness

(1) It is natural to describe consciousness as a state of awareness. But of what? Of the World—of Reality? It may well be so. But what sort of awareness is that? It is not, I think, an awareness of an *object*. Indeed, the state consciousness is simply not a directed phenomenon. The following considerations bring this out.

'Conscious' is put to different uses in 'he was conscious' and 'he was conscious of a faint rustling': the former is the state-of-consciousness use, the latter the directed-consciousness or experiential use. Then the doctrine that the state of waking is a directed awareness ignores this distinction, and generates a regress in doing so. This is because particular consciousnesses-of or experiences are *permitted by* the prevailing state of consciousness. For example, dreaming consciousnesses-of are permitted by sleep and light unconsciousness and proscribed by both waking and profoundest unconsciousness, just as perceptual consciousnesses-of are permitted by waking and trance but not by unconsciousness. Then if consciousness was directed, it would require a permissive consciousness-state matrix; while if that in turn was directed, a further permissive matrix would be required; and so on. In short, the supposition that consciousness is a directed phenomenon leads to regress, the reason being that directed consciousnesses are not psychologically self-sustaining and must take root in some single supportive state of consciousness. The stream of consciousness flows so to say upon a sustaining psychological bed, or better it flows within a containing permissive psychological setting. An occurrent undirected psychological phenomenon which is not itself an experience, makes possible a contemporaneous complex of directed experiences. Reducing the former to the latter neglects this concealed intra-psychic dependence, and leads inevitably to regress.

Thus, consciousness cannot be an experience of the World. This same conclusion may be reached by another route. Namely, via the proposition that consciousness is neither a perception nor putative-perception: a fact that is evident when one remembers that we do not *redescribe* any state as 'consciousness' in the light of its discovering some object. And this last is so because it is absolutely *internal to consciousness* that it is consciousness: not because it is a particular experience—for it is not an experience; and not so to say purely idiosyncratically in the manner of a *quale*; but because it is constitutively and intelligibly determined as consciousness. What makes a state the state of consciousness is precisely the inhering of certain conditions in the inner world. Then if there is no such thing as consciousness finding a perceptual or intuitional object, there can be no such thing as its aspiring to find such an object. In short, consciousness is neither a perception nor putative-perception.

(2) This latter fact demonstrates that consciousness cannot be an experience of the World. But it has the further virtue of providing us with another proof of the more general claim that consciousness is not an intentionally directed phenomenon. Thus, if consciousness were intentionally directed, it is clear it would have to be of the type, putative-perception. If consciousness is not of the type awareness-of, of what directed type is it? None other is conceivable. Then this more general conclusion to the effect that the state consciousness is not an intentionally directed phenomenon, can be readily generalized to states of consciousness generally. States of consciousness as such—which are wholly internally determined—are object-less. Like consciousness itself they lack intentional content.

Thus, in its own strange way consciousness and indeed states of consciousness generally join such psychological primitives as sensations in being at once psychological and lacking in intentional directedness. Like them it has no content, is 'about' nothing. And yet it is natural to say that one who wakes surfaces to an awareness of the World. Evidently, this is no intuition, nor is it any mode of contacting an object. Provisionally, let us say that one who is conscious is 'in touch with' Reality: meaning, that he is in a position to discover how the World is. This union of contentlessness and a readiness to follow the way of truth, makes the image of the empty canvas or virgin page a valuable one for the state consciousness. But it is really only an image.

(b) Origins and meanings

(1) We have just noted that consciousness possesses the important negative trait of lacking intentional content. A second negative property seems to me of equal moment. It pertains to meaning or sense. This particular property owes its existence to the *type of the origins* of the state consciousness. Then first a word about the latter. The origins of consciousness are as such wholly and merely bodily, i.e. cerebral non-psychological. And the same holds of the state unconsciousness; though not (say) of hypnotic trance, which is mentally determined. It follows (trivially) that consciousness must negatively depend upon the absence of (say) trance-inducing mental factors. However, this negative dependence can in nowise be reduced to a positive dependence. Consciousness is the product of nothing psychological: necessarily it is built on the solitary rock—cerebral state.

This cannot be said of many psychological phenomena, and once more lines consciousness up with that primitive psychological mediator, the sensation. These undirected contentless phenomena are the *recessive psychological groundwork* of the 'tapestry' of experience. They depend immediately and necessarily upon the brain alone, and they make possible in their own distinctive ways the experiences which fill consciousness.

Then because consciousness has immediate physical origins, the same must be true of the stream of consciousness of the conscious. Thus, consciousness explicitly founds the stream of consciousness in the flesh: it explicitly reveals a necessary and causally immediate dependence of conscious experience upon the body. At the same time the occurrence of such experience is mediated by consciousness, since it is clear that we are thus experiencing only because we are conscious. However, this mediation is of a non-causal order. Thus, consciousness is not the causally sufficient condition of those experiences, and is rather the logically necessary and sufficient condition of experience of the distinctive type that is encountered uniquely in consciousness. Accordingly, the mediation by consciousness must instead be deemed systemic in character. This strange situation is determined by the fact that the 'holism' of consciousness necessitates a corresponding causal or technical 'holism'. Now the dependence of consciousness upon the flesh takes regular form. The science of Anaesthetics informs us of regular physical conditions for the removal and reinstatement of consciousness, and thereby reminds us that psycho-physical law governs the existence even though not the content of the stream of consciousness of the state consciousness. Then the multi-determining mental source of content provides a foothold for rationality and the will, while the sheer bodily and nomic origin of experience, and of such a character, makes of such phenomena a necessity. Thus, we have our own individual say over what particular content the stream of consciousness shall encompass, but we have no immediate say whatsoever that it shall or shall not be, or that it shall or shall not be of the kind unique to consciousness.

(2) These origin-characteristics are responsible for the negative property of consciousness that pertains to meaning. Let me now spell out the rationale governing that property, prior to spelling out the property itself. Thus, consciousness has proved to be wholly without psychological cause. *A fortiori* without immediately known psychological cause. *A fortiori* there can be no 'my reasons' for consciousness, let alone 'my good reasons'. Accordingly, consciousness cannot in this sense be accounted a rational phenomenon, and we have no direct accountability for it. Rather, consciousness *is* the state wherein rational determination is the general rule: it *is* the rational state. But it comes or goes as the brain decrees. We and our judgement are simply not consulted in this transaction. Then because consciousness lacks mental origins, consciousness cannot be susceptible of redescriptive interpretation in the light of its origins. Thus, no meaning can be assigned to this phenomenon, it fits into no meaning-conferring wider holistic network, it simply falls outside the 'meaning-circle'. (More precisely, it falls under.) This is the negative property referred to above. Consciousness is at once without direction, without content, without significance.

(c) Inexperienceability

I come to the last negative characteristic: inexperienceability. Consciousness is neither an experience nor the immediate object of an experience. It is thus not in any proper sense *introspectible.* This is in a way surprising: probably because consciousness necessitates the occurrence of experiences from which it is not distinct, perhaps because coming-to or losing-of consciousness can be experiences, and probably also because one who is conscious knows so in the immediate way he knows of his own experience (which is psychological) and his own existence (which is not!) The fact remains, consciousness is neither experienced, nor is it immediately attendable to; and the most one can do along these lines is, think about this immediately known psychological state as it persists. Accordingly, consciousness has no *quale*, no 'feel', and there is nothing that is 'what it is like' to be conscious—though there *is* what it is like to be *experiencing* what one who is conscious *must* be experiencing, viz. a rationally ordered stream of consciousness. However, we must distinguish the stream of experience and the state of consciousness, since we are having such experience only because we are conscious, and whereas the experiences change with the passage of time the state remains one and the same. This occurrent psychological phenomenal continuity, of whose existence one is immediately apprised, functions as an internally necessary non-distinct condition of experience, without itself being an experience. When this property is conjoined with the aforementioned negative properties, consciousness begins to look like a sort of psychological nothing. Devoid of experiential character as such, wholly without direction and content, lacking all sense or meaning, one wonders how it can corner any kind of reality within its confines.

6. Positive Properties

(a) Experience and attention

(1) Until now consciousness has proved noteworthy largely for what it is not. Yet it is worth recalling the little positive about it that has emerged during the course of the discussion.

Thus, it is an occurrent phenomenal continuity; it is constituted out of the occurrent utilization of integrated powers; it is psychological in order of being; a variety of the kind, state of consciousness: to wit, the parent variety—consciousness. And because it is the pre-eminent variety and the other states are privative in relation to it, the normal genus-species schema proves inapplicable to the kind of which it is the core case. Finally, while consciousness is constituted out of various constituents, such as rationality in the self-conscious, these constituents fall short of full autonomy in the sense that they are not independent of the state they together constitute, and of necessity occur in constellations of properties which instantiate one unique state of consciousness.

If the above account is correct, consciousness cannot be construed as some kind of psychological atom which reveals its distinctive character merely through its causal properties. It proves instead to be a complex mental condition (a psychological totality) in which certain requisite parts are encompassed and appropriately synthesized. I am reminded of the self-conscious condition as such—in which rationality of nature, language-possession, the capacity to think, knowledge of truth and falsity, of the modalities of actual and possible and might have been, indeed of the World itself, are simultaneously realized and mutually necessitating. These characteristics are not generated by some inscrutable psychic atom; neither are they the autonomous independent parts of a unified whole, like the parts of a machine; and yet they are indubitably different one from another; and all that is required for self-consciousness to crystallize is that the whole charmed circle arise into being. This seems to me to be the correct model for the state consciousness that is under discussion.

I propose at this juncture to start filling in the picture presented by that state. That is, delineate the constituent phenomena themselves. I begin with the intimate connection between consciousness and experience. It is not just that these two phenomena normally appear together: consciousness actually *entails* experience at whatever instant it exists, and is the only state of consciousness that does. Now while this claim is analytic it is not a trivial analyticity, precisely because we do not *begin* with experience and assemble consciousness out of it; and this because every experience depends necessarily upon the prevailing state of consciousness. This is evident enough in dream experience, where the very type of the experience demands a state other than consciousness; but it is a general necessity. Accordingly, the fact that consciousness necessitates experience is 'substantial'; and that it does in fact do so is clear when one recalls that one detects 'blackout' or loss of consciousness in the midst of an ongoing state of consciousness, precisely by detecting an hiatus in or absence of experience.

It must be a matter of colossal importance so far as consciousness is concerned that it entails contemporaneous experience. What can be the explanation of this binding need? Now the kind of explanation for which we may legitimately search is systemic rather than causal, and is at the same time functional in type. Then my preliminary intuition is that the constituents of consciousness *so* constitute the state that it acquires through their presence the capacity to accomplish certain fundamental tasks essential to its being. That consciousness is no psychic atom which reveals its nature exclusively causally, does not entail that it lack powers: it leaves it open that it is a psychic structure with essential functional[2] powers. The preliminary suggestion which I propose is that experience is essential to consciousness because it is a necessary condition of consciousness managing to do what is its primary function to do. What that function is we must now investigate.

(2) We approach closer to that function when we turn to the related phenomenon of the *attention*. This concept shuttles between the concepts of 'experiential space' (roughly) and 'intuition' (perception). Thus, we say 'my attention was taken up with thinking about something', but also 'a bright light caught my attention'. A man inwardly ratiocinating 'spends' attention thereby without his attention taking an intuitional object, and yet there are noticings and attendings which clearly do take intuitional objects. How do these two kinds of phenomena relate? Evidently, intimately. For the more attention is expended in the one, the less is available for the other; and, attention being a kind of mental life-blood, the more the very existence of the other is threatened. Thus, the concept is quantitative in nature, and the amount limited: experientially a mind can concern itself with *so much* and no more at any instant: it can drink in or give forth or simply contain to that extent only. These considerations suggest that we are dealing with a unitary phenomenon which takes diverse forms.

Conceived broadly as experiential space, the attention has no peculiar bond with consciousness, as the phenomenon of dreaming shows. However, when understood more narrowly as the faculty of intuition or perception, it plainly does. Indeed,

---

[2] My use of 'function' is stipulative. When I say 'the function of psychological item X is to cause Y', I mean that X tends typically to cause Y, and that its doing so is in general contributory to the working/surviving of the mental system and/or living system in which these events occur. Then sometimes it is unclear whether an item has a function, e.g. dreams; though often enough clear that it has, e.g. act-desire. Since many general causal properties of psychological items are essential, many of these 'functional properties' are a priori-given, e.g. act-desire's function of causing willing, or limb-movement-willing's of causally leading to the non-psychological event of limb-movement. However, many may not be. For example, dreams may have the psychological function of preserving sleep, or reordering one's beliefs, etc. These, if true, are a posteriori.

83

states of consciousness precisely divide on this count. Unconsciousness is a state in which the faculty shuts down, sleep a state in which it is accessible but generally not recording, consciousness one in which it is accessible and typically recording. And yet full consciousness is consistent with wholly null intuitional recordings: darkness, silence, and something the far side of total numbness: not a trace of the physical world in view. How can this possibility be accomodated by a doctrine which closely links the state consciousness and the occurrence of intuition? Well, a recording of null is not a null of a recording: it is the limiting intuitional reading of zero. But in any case a null of all recordings is possible in consciousness, whether positive or negative in type: one can imagine a subject lost in thought in the absence of all intuitional experience. Yet still the capacity for intuitional contact with the environment will be operative. No matter how lost in an experience, a man could scarcely be conscious if he did not know whether his eyes had just now been dazzled or his ears inundated by cacophony or his body racked with pain. How tight is this necessity? If angelic consciousnesses existed they might lack a faculty of intuition—but the concept of a soul-substance in a Kingdom of Spirits is so burdened by difficulties as to be near discountable. Nevertheless, the connection between attentive accessibility and consciousness is not, I think, *transparently* necessary. For this reason the intuitional attentive element in the typical complex picture presented by consciousness must be accounted of a different order of necessity from that exemplified by the elements, rationality of state and (above all) occurrence of experience (which is no less than analytic).

In sum, consciousness entails present experience, which is such as necessarily to involve a measure of putative intuitional contact with the physical world, whether of positive or null or merely counterfactual-conditional variety. For some reason as yet undivined, tuning out intuitionally on the physical world is tantamount to tuning out on Reality; that is, on the voice of Reason—which keeps track of Truth. Indeed, inasmuch as the (broadly conceived) attention is *occupied* in one thus (narrowly, intuitionally) wholly disengaged, it is tantamount to being occupied with *Unreality*, viz. with the unreal world of the dream. It is as if such a withdrawal of the intuitional attention from physical reality within an ongoing stream of experience inevitably substituted a replacement World which necessarily does not exist; and that is to say, that Reality cannot be twin. Whatever the reason, our (animal) consciousness (anyway) obliges that our (obligatory) experience in part be constituted out of putative intuitional contact with the physical world. It seems that the function of consciousness must be to link us attentively to the physical world that contains us. That, at least.

(b) Verification and belief-formation

(1) Further light is shed on the constitutive requirements for consciousness by returning to the verification of the presence of consciousness in an ideal case already mentioned: the perfectly simple animal. We noted earlier that the

verification in question coincided with the verification of the synthesized presence of those few psychological phenomena that are essential to animality as we know it, viz. action, perception, etc. Then I think these phenomena provide a clue to the constitution of consciousness, for the following reason. Whatever the *necessary* psychological conditions for consciousness, they ought to obtain in this simplest animal as it generates such bodily phenomena as evidence consciousness to a third person. Then my surmise is that this simplest case is one in which the mind is stripped down to its essentials, so that each mental kind present in that mind will be at once operative and essential to the whole. Accordingly, my guess is that each such elemental kind must be a necessity for consciousness *in general*. The self-conscious variety of consciousness, while vastly more developed and structurally novel, will not I suspect break free of the rules binding in this simplest case: it will merely obey them in its own peculiarly elevated way. So, at any rate, I surmise.

The requirements for consciousness are wholly internal and constitutive. Accordingly, it must be inessential that the exemplar simple consciousness be verifiable in any particular case, and inessential that its perceptual and motor-systems be in good order. The working principle which I therefore propose is to inspect the *purely internal* phenomena that are operative as this ideally simple mind reveals its presence to outside view in normal motor-perceptual interaction with the environment. This should give a lead to the constitutive requirements for consciousness. Then it is certain that *intuitional attentive experience* will occur. And certain that it will take outer-directed *interpretational form*. Equally important is what this intuition accomplishes in the mental system: namely, that it generates *belief concerning the environs*—and in the right way. A significant and well-formed cognitive response is the end-point in this sector of the causal sequence.

(2) I think this last is a universal property of consciousness. Whatever the value of the ideally simple case as test, I suspect that we can on this count generalize from that case to all others.

It is not that one need entertain beliefs concerning the present environment, nor that those beliefs need stem from present intuition, if consciousness is to exist. Rather, a cognitive sensitivity to perceptual experience must inhere, and of the right kind. This cognitive sensitivity, and the mode of belief-formation concerning environmental realities, are I suggest intrinsic to consciousness, which requires in general that beliefs be well-formed, and in the manner appropriate to the species; indeed, should normally lead their owner to Reality. Thus, in the conscious the mode of belief-formation out of veridical perception should be such as normally to make *knowledge* of that belief. For example, desire will in general switch off as a significant causal force in the determination of belief (whereas by contrast in dreams it may well not). And what one knows about the look of things will generally mediate the formation of environmental belief out of visual experience, and in the right way. And so on.

A word about 'the right way'. This takes different form in the super-simple (e.g. bees), the medium-complex (e.g. cats), and man. The super-simple arrive in the world heavily prepared, learn little from experience, and innate factors significantly mediate the formation of beliefs from perceptual experience; yet because they evolved in matching environments, those well-formed beliefs tend to be knowings of the environment (in super-simple impoverished terms, e.g. 'moving', 'near', 'here'). The medium-complex are advertisements for Humean theory: regularities in experience tend, without comprehension, to trigger believings out of perceivings; yet because the beliefs of those beings are a reliable guide to the reality of the physical situation, since Nature selected beings whose belief-formation mimicked Nature's regular ways, these well-formed beliefs tend likewise to be knowledge. Reason enters the picture late, but it too is no more than a superior 'right way'. Reason is after all the *very best* instrument for discovering Reality and Truth (missing until now); but nonetheless has the same role to play as the innate tendencies of the insect or the slavish dependence upon experience of the average animal: namely, it is a mode of access to Reality.

In place of innate predispositions, and an uncomprehended history of regular experience, we discover in man a system of beliefs which is his internal Representation of Reality. Consciousness requires that this swing into play, and in the right or rational way, in the genesis of present environmental belief out of present perceptual experience. This is a way of saying that one is 'in touch with Reality' at the time. Yet there is no guarantee that Reality will match the portrait; indeed, just as there are insane portraits of people so certain belief-systems insanely misrepresent the World. Nevertheless, they *aim* at the World, and this suffices for an actual, even if disturbed state of consciousness. The rational animal, however mad, will when awake tend to form his beliefs through rational appeal to his World-Picture, even though madness in the mad will doubtless stand revealed as the full content of his beliefs is spelled out. Thus, a madman believes he is being offered tea because he seems to see tea being offered, but believes he is being offered poisoned tea because in his belief-system there exists a firm cognitive commitment to the omnipresence of poison-feeders. In a word, there is method in his madness, and sufficient of it to ensure consciousness. Unless his thought-processes are fragmented to an extent that matches 'word salad'—which is more or less enough to bring consciousness to its knees—reason and consciousness are in this being simultaneously ensconced.

The gist of this is, that in the conscious the mode of belief-formation presently operative is such that perceptual experience generates belief in a way that tends in the proper setting to make knowings of these believings. Here we see a prime function of the state consciousness. It puts us *in a position* to know about the present state of the World. It is not itself a perception of the World, but is an empowerment so to perceive. Consciousness is an empty canvas, ready to receive the imprint of Reality. Better, a clear window onto the World; precisely because it is itself devoid of content and inexperienceable, yet expressly dedicated to revelation. Or like

Tolstoy's perfect prose, which fits its subject-matter to the point of invisibility. Consciousness seems to be all potential or fertility. Hence the importance of discussing its negative properties first.

7. Activity

(a) The bodily will

(1) But life is more than cognition, we have scarcely lived if we have not acted, and consciousness is a high point of life development. This should put one on guard against assuming it is exhausted by its cognitive function, and alert us to a certain dynamism in the condition. Once again it is instructive to recall the mental state of the ideally simple animal as it revealed its conscious state to outside view, and significant that it was a state of *activity*. I follow this lead, and wish to suggest that a certain use of the will is constitutive of consciousness. What that use is, emerges during the ensuing discussion.

Typically one who is conscious engages in *two* ontologically heterogeneous varieties of action: bodily and mental. A word first about the former. While absolute bodily stillness can be intentionally willed, this condition sometimes obtains in the conscious thanks to sheer absence of will. Thus, the bodily will can in the conscious take the occasional complete rest. It follows that bodily willing cannot be constitutive of consciousness. Then might *availability* of the bodily will be thus constitutive? After all, whereas the bodily will is unavailable to the unconscious, it seems invariably to be available to conscious beings. But this theory encounters a difficulty. For bodily willing rests on a substratum of proprioceptive body-awareness, and it could happen to the conscious that their body *not* seem thus present, so that it must in principle be possible to be conscious and for the bodily will to be simply unavailable. One could be fully conscious, and unable to even *try* to move one's body— which just did not seem to be there! While not a paralysis, this condition is a loss, not merely of active motility, but of the bodily will itself! Therefore availability of the bodily will cannot be constitutive of consciousness either.

(2) So neither actual bodily willing, nor availability of the bodily will, are essential to consciousness. However, something just a little less than the latter is surely essential. Thus, whereas the bodily will is unavailable to the unconscious, in the state consciousness it is both conditionally and normally available, and this property seems necessary for animal consciousness. And yet this property cannot be *peculiar* to consciousness, since sleep is a state in which bodily awareness and the capacity for bodily will persist. Then what I think we should at this point be seeking is, a property pertaining to bodily will which is both necessary and peculiar to consciousness. I say so because it seems intuitively apparent that such a trait exists. Are not wakeful beings intimately linked to bodily action in a way that is unique to the state? Whence the power of Behaviourism and its more sophisticated derivatives if this was not so? We must look for a feature distinctive to waking.

87

Perhaps the following property answers to the need. One important respect in which consciousness and sleep differ, is in the origin and type of the bodily act-desires finding expression in bodily willing. Typically in sleep what occur are idle bodily act-inclinations, which find expression in simple basic bodily willings making next to no demands on one's belief and concept systems. Matters are very different in consciousness. Here perceptually informed fully conceptualized beliefs concerning the environment continually elicit active meaningful physical interactions with it. Despite the existence of phenomena like somnambulism which demonstrate that perceptually derived beliefs can in sleep do something of the same, there is surely a parting of the ways on this count between sleep and waking. In waking life the cognitive system links with the motor system in highly structured transactions in a manner that is all but unique to the state. These links and occurrence are automatically actualized when a person wakes to full consciousness.

In the light of these observations we may say that in the conscious the following bodily-act mental phenomena and/or linkages are part of the normal picture. A conditional availability of the bodily will is a necessity. And the following are generally operative: bodily act-desires, bodily willings, and the suitable determination of those bodily act-desires and willings at the hands of that novel sector of the belief-system which derives from present perceptions. All this is typical at least. The onset of consciousness *is* in part the onset of such internal capacities and such mental linkages. For animal consciousness is a state such that the seeming presence of the needed and actively manipulable tends to evoke the *desire* to perform such physical manipulations, which in turn tends to generate *bodily willings* to that end. When conscious beings confront a seemingly inviting environment, the bodily act-system comes to life, whereas by contrast comparable cognitive phenomena in dreamers might call forth anything—or nothing. Such dynamic responsiveness in such regions of the mind to such beliefs seems to be internal to animal consciousness. Animal consciousness is a condition of practical involvement in physical nature. The reason must lie surely in the obvious functional advantages of the active satisfaction of vital need. In any case, animal consciousness is such that the bodily will is automatically engaged in these ways.

(b) The mental will

We have here spelled out certain mental capacities and causal linkages which are essential to animal consciousness, and several experienced active psychological occurrences which are at least typical of the state, all relating to the bodily will. Then while the former are actualities, the latter active experiences are no more than highly likely conditional realities. Animal consciousness is consistent with complete quiescence of the bodily will. No *experience* utilizing the bodily will is essential to consciousness.

However, there exists one psychological phenomenon which is at once an experience, of the type willing, processive, and categorically necessary for consciousness.

I refer to the other ontological variety of will: mental will. I do not mean that consciousness itself is a mental activity. Clearly it is not, if only because this continuous psychological state is neither process nor experience. Rather, the mind of one who is conscious is necessarily a mind actively governing the movement of its own attentive and thinking processes. We get an inkling of this necessity in the following. It is an astonishing fact that we humans when conscious and open-eyed scarcely know, not just how not to *see*, but how not to *look*! More or less inevitably we occupy ourselves in looking activities for much of the time, and strangely enough do not experience this necessity as in the least alienating. Then so it is with the mind itself. In general the direction taken by our thoughts and attention is in the conscious actively self-determined. And it has to be: we have no choice in the matter. And this likewise is no alienation. The inactiveness of a state (viz. consciousness) which internally involves activeness (viz. of mind), generates the paradox that the conscious find themselves in the grip of a *necessity* to freely choose their own occupations of thought and attention. You might even say that we awake in this World in midstream, swimming for our own dear lives!

Consciousness, which is not a perception, but which is perceptive in so priming the mind and so linking us to our Cognitive Representation of the World that we are in a position to augment that Representation, simultaneously involves *mental activeness*. Thus, the present state of a sector of the World can be revealed only to a being which takes active charge of his own thoughts and attendings. I do not mean actively determines their *content*, which would be at once omnipotent, barren, self-refuting, and logically impossible; but selects the direction of their movement, which is to say the content of the governing enterprise.

And so it seems clear that a measure of self-determination is a necessary condition of a proper cognitive contact with a sector of Reality. What is less obvious is why it is so. Why is it that the seventeenth-century image of consciousness as a quiescent internal reflector is so far from the truth? This explanatory problem is, to my mind, the main issue at this point. In effect, the problem is to discover how the property of activeness of mind necessitates or is necessitated by the other equally essential properties of the state consciousness. As rationality of nature, the capacity for thought, and knowledge of one's own mind, form a tight circle of essentially self-conscious characteristics, so my assumption is that the active self-regulatory character of the conscious (i.e. wakeful) self-conscious mind forms a circle with the rationality of that state, and certain other properties like epistemological power. The problem is, to trace out the *rationale*. Why should a mind that is in a position to augment its present Representation of Reality be one that actively takes charge of its own thinking and attentive function?

(c) Time and the dream

(1) We find an important lead in the *temporal properties* of conscious experience. Consciousness necessitates a certain simultaneous orientation towards past,

present, and future. Significantly this is absent in the experience of the dream, as we shall see. Why? My suspicion is, that the inactiveness of the mind of the dreamer is a determinant. In any case I propose to discuss the temporal properties of dream experience, partly because it reveals how such temporal structures essentially connect with the character of the prevailing inner life, but above all because it puts us in a position to demonstrate how the necessarily active nature of conscious experience guarantees the relation to time essential to the state consciousness. This constitutes a rationale of the active character of consciousness.

What are the temporal properties of dream experience? What is the nature of the dreamer's encounter with time? It is visible in the distinctive character of dream experience, which is in turn not independent of its origins. And in fact the question is best approached through a consideration of origins, for much is determined by this salient property. Then what is noteworthy is, how little say the dreamer has in the occurrence of his own dream. He is the inactive and wholly unconsulted recipient of dream experience. He is inactive because dreaming is not an activity, and he is unconsulted because he neither knows why he dreams at all, nor why he dreams what he does dream. Accordingly, while the *dream present* is undoubtedly a reality for the dreamer, it is a reality that merely happens to him: it simply comes to him out of the blue. This fact has significant implications so far as the other two temporal dimensions are concerned.

(2) It has repercussions concerning the *dream future*. Thus, not only does the dreamer not know what the dream's future contains, he does not even adopt cognitive attitudes towards it. He neither expects nor hopes it contains one thing rather than another. By contrast, a waking phantasizer expects his present well-rehearsed familiar phantasy to contain the next actively projected phantasized element, and this is distinct from his phantasizing expectation on his own part; so that expectation can occur both without and within a phantasy. Actively running through his well-worn roulette-phantasy, the phantasizer at time t_1 comes to the point where he stakes his all upon the number 7, whereupon he then proceeds to phantasize that he is wildly agog with the expectation of seeing 7 (since he phantasizes that he has bribed the croupier!); so that at the time t_1 he is both phantasy-expecting seeing 7 *and* actual-expecting phantasy-seeing of 7 (at t_2)—for that happens to be the next stage of this well-worn phantasy 'track'. To repeat: when engaged in phantasizing, we can both phantasize expectation and simultaneously expect later elements of that phantasy. That is, expectation can occur within and without phantasy.

But this is not true of dreams, since nothing answers to expectation from without. We entertain no expectations about succeeding dream stages, precisely because we are unable to think about those phenomena, and this because we are in no position to single them out under headings which distinguish dream from reality. While a dreamer can entertain expectations within a dream, the object of expectation is nonetheless drawn from Reality rather than from the dream. Why, if I dream

I am to be shot at dawn, should the object of my expectation be a dream shooting? And surely it is not. My relief upon waking is because the real World contains no such prognosticated horror. What makes the wakeful phantasizer's expectations of phantasizing true is subsequent phantasy; whereas nothing makes his phantasized expectations true, precisely because they are not expectations. The situation is exactly reversed in the dream. If I wake to discover a coincidental imminent shooting hanging over my head, then my dream-expectation was prophetic and true; but if I subsequently merely dream of a shooting, it was not. Thus, so far as the dreamer is concerned, the future of the dream does not even exist, being at once out of sight and out of mind. It is because the dreamer confuses the dream World with the real World, that the dream World eludes detection and cognitive attitudes towards it cannot get off the ground. In dreaming one aims one's intentional arrows, which either miss their mark or discover it in the World. Strangely enough, they never find it in the dream—self-consciousness being at a low ebb at this moment. The dream never manages to refer to itself.

(3) The *dream past* presents a different picture again. Whether one is awake or dreaming one recollectively retains the past of a dream: *qua* past of a dream if awake, *qua* past merely of one's experience if dreaming. Yet these recollections form no part of the dream, they appear at no point in its description, so that what makes them true is the actuality of the recollected dream experience. I recollect next morning that 'I seemed to see a swan', and what makes this true is, not that in reality I saw a swan, but that in reality I had such an experience. The successful reference to the inner imaginative life is made possible by the fact that the waking recollection is no part of that imaginative life. So much for a relation to the dream past *from without*.

What of the past *within the dream*? How does the dream event that is now in the past relate within the dream to the dreamed present? It has not completely vanished from view, seeing that the dream present can continue what *was*. I *was* dreaming that I was singing a song, and I *am still* dreaming that I am singing the very same song. The dream, after all, is conceptualizable or describable. Nevertheless, each instant disengages in certain significant ways from its predecessor instants. You could say that the dream present lacks modes of solidarity with, or responsibility to, its past. The disengagement is at once cognitive and constitutive. Whereas when awake I believe I am half-way through an enterprise like (say) swimming the Hellespont in part *because* I believe the past contains my swimming the first half, when dreaming I *simply* believe I am thus half-way through some enterprise—and certainly not *because* I believe the past contains the first half of that deed. In dreams I believe what I believe for no reason, good or bad, and not even for the piffling reason of its seeming so (which at best acts as mere unreasoning cause). So much for cognitive disengagement.

The other variety of disengagement is even more radical. It suggests an absence of persisting identities. It shows in the fact that I can be dreaming of *anything* in one instant and *anything* in the next. In a sense therefore the dream is created anew in each instant: not to the point where narrative disintegrates into unsynthesizable fragments, but insofar as the character of present experience necessitates neither a past nor a cognitive attitude to a past. It is an important feature of dreams that they arise out of nothing, appear in experiential mid-air so to speak: a fact which must surely reveal something comparable in the case of each subsequent instant. In a sense each instant of the dream sprouts like an orchid out of thin air. This is because it is continuity of content, rather than persistence of contents, that unifies the dream.

These facts demonstrate that in dreams neither the dreamed past, which is to say the actual past sectors of our dream, nor our attitude to that dreamed past, meaning dream elements specifically referring to earlier elements of the dream, play any constitutive role in determining present dream experience. A dream present is consistent with absolutely any dream past and any dreamed cognitive attitude towards that past. Despite the constraint imposed by the narrative, the past is all but lost as we dream.

(d) Time and consciousness

Thus, the dream present is a sort of Time Island. First in its failure to have internal or constitutive connections with its own past; second in having neither an actively projected nor a merely expected future—for dreams as they unfold neither surprise nor conform to expectation.

Such a relation to time is inconsistent with consciousness. This is because consciousness requires that we be in a position to perceive *events across time*: which is to say, not merely events which themselves cross time, but the very profile across time of the event itself. It is in this manner that we perceive temporally diversified phenomena like bodily gestures, a meaningful utterance, a particular melody, which may in this regard be taken as *prototype objects* for consciousness. Then such perception is possible only if we retain cognitive links with our internal past, and an open but real cognitive connection with an anticipated internal future. How, midway through hearing a sentence, could I know what I was hearing if I did not entertain views as to what I had already heard and as to what I might next hear? Then it is certain that intentional internal action is an experience which internally fuses the necessary three temporal axes. It manages to unite a projection from a present of a determinate future, and a partial constitution at the hands of a determinate past of a determinate present.

This is particularly evident in the case of orientation towards the future. For example, listening is intentionally directed not just to *what I have heard*—in the sense that the present object of listening is something with a part which I have already heard (say) a few moments ago—the auditory object avowedly stretching like a *thing* back into the past. It is also a listening to what I *will hear*—in that the object of listening is equally something with a part that I will hear: it extends analogously into the future. Thus, I listen from . . . to. . . . This listening-for, this craning the neck to gain a glimpse of the future, typifies human or self-conscious consciousness as such. When in certain fatigued states of mind the phenomenon of listening tends to fall away from itself in the direction of mere inactive hearing, it tends *pari passu* towards a condition of degeneration. The purely inactive perceptual recipient who merely hears, tends towards the condition in which he neither individuates the parts of the temporal continuity, nor structures the perceived phenomenal particulars across time. What would be the epistemological fruit of one who related in this way to a protracted utterance or melody? A blindness to order and sense seem to be the inevitable outcome: loss of the very objects of perception.

Then what is true of listening to utterance or melody is in this regard true of all consciousness. Whatever entity that we perceive, it is as such not stationary in time. No matter how frozen and stationary in space, it is from the point of view of time like the prow of a boat imperceptibly cutting through infinitely glassy water. It is essential to consciousness that this quasi-motion be captured: without it we will not even manage to perceive that which immutably proceeds through time, viz. the fixed or unchanging material object itself. In short, the World of which we are conscious is not the Spatial World, it is the Spatio-Temporal World. Consciousness necessitates that the mind open out onto the latter. Indeed, consciousness is of such a nature that awareness of the former can be accomplished only through awareness of the latter.

Then my suggestion is that we will not achieve the above if we do not relate cognitively and experientially to the past and future of the objects of awareness; and we will not relate thus to their past and future if we do not relate thus to our own internal past and future; and that this last is something that is manifestly accomplished in intentional internal action, in all probability uniquely so. It alone seems to provide a unified temporal structure in which each present point explicitly grows out of its past and essentially points to and develops towards its own future. It seems therefore that the inner world of the conscious must in some overall or superintending respect be intentionally active: an activity which explicitly is *from* (in the past) *to* (in the future) in form. This provides us with a temporal framework adequate for awareness of the contents of the physical world. Then since it is essential to consciousness that it put us in a position to enlarge our present Representation of Reality, it seems that for this reason alone the mind of the conscious must be intentionally active.

C. CONCLUSION

I will bring this chapter to a close by reviewing, and in certain places embellishing, the main findings concerning the nature of consciousness uncovered in the foregoing discussion. I set these out under the headings (α1)—(α6). I begin with a short account of the place of consciousness in its owner's nature.

(α1) Essence and function

One might at first think consciousness was as essential to its owner as life itself. The truth falls only a little short of this. It is the *state of consciousness*, a type of which consciousness is pre-eminent parent variety, that is thus necessary. Vitality and mentality are of the essence, consciousness something near. And yet if the state of consciousness is a necessity, the potential for the pre-eminent parent variety must be equally necessary. That is, the potential for consciousness must be as essential to animality as life itself.

Now there exist in nature orders of development that in pyramid fashion are necessary structures of their owner's being. Consciousness is such a thing: it is a 'high point' in that nature, for it depends upon much else in the nature which had already evolved into being (say, its vitality). This is reflected in the elevatedness of its function. For consciousness is the condition of a double revelation: of the essential nature of the subject through acts in the World, and of the World through perception to that acting subject. Only if consciousness inheres in a being can these twin revelations be realized. At one stroke consciousness helps to reveal through action what is there *in* the conscious, and through perception what is there *to* the conscious. Thus, it brings about a situation in which active cognitive interaction with the environment becomes possible. The effecting of such interaction is its peculiar function. Consciousness enables the expression of the full animal essence.

These functional considerations help to clarify why it is that the remaining states of consciousness are privative in relation to consciousness. That is, why consciousness is pre-eminent among states of consciousness, and why there can be no rival forms of consciousness. It is because no alternative Reality is rendered accessible through those other states, if only because they cannot marshal the internal wherewithal to represent a second Reality. For example, the necessary temporal co-ordinates are not available. The required elements of any such representation simply fade away or fall apart, and what remains is merely an exposed remnant of the machinery for accomplishing a single unique end, viz. the two-way interaction with the World. As there is only one Reality, so there is only one fully autonomous state amongst states of consciousness. Therefore the alternative states cannot have their own distinctive necessary function. Thus, it cannot be the a priori-given function of sleep to reveal the (so-called) 'World of the dream', even if it is a posteriori so. The only state with a priori-given function is consciousness, the potential for which is as essential to its owner as life itself. Man's essence is to be in active cognitive interaction with the World.

(α2) Global character and analysability

So much for the significance of consciousness. And yet when we come to look at what consciousness itself is, we encounter a strange dearth of properties. Indeed, it seems almost to be nothing. Paradoxically this first and pre-eminent of all mental phenomena proves to be a glaring exception to the rule according to which the mental is to be defined in terms of intentionality. For consciousness is wholly devoid of intentional content. More, it is completely without phenomenological character. Indeed, it is not even an experience or an immediate object of experience. And it finds no place within the meaning circle of mental phenomena.

And yet the poverty of nature is an illusion—produced by looking in the wrong direction. Far from being an outcast to the meaning circle of the mental, consciousness finds no place within the circle of conscious experience precisely because it supports that circle. And if, illusorily, it appears like some kind of psychological nothing, it is not because it is a mere psychological atom which is somehow endowed with a distinctive set of causal properties. If it looks so, it is because we approach the phenomenon of consciousness armed with differentia drawn from too narrow a mental taxonomy. We take it to be yet another particular and unanalysable mental phenomenon, alongside fundamentals like desire and will and belief. We fail to note its global or systemic character.

For consciousness is a system. Now it is precisely this feature which makes it ineligible for the familiar differentia of phenomenology and intentional content. For the intentionally directed for the most part take particular realities as putative object. How could consciousness restrict itself in this fashion? Either it takes the World as object, or it takes nothing, and since the World is not a perceptible, it must take nothing. Then consciousness is in two significant respects unlike other occupants of the mind. First in making possible an entire mental scene and as a result falling outside that scene, second in lacking all mental explanation. For consciousness is sited at the end of a particular line of mental dependence. It is a line which begins within the stream of consciousness: this experience (e.g. action) depending on that experience (e.g. cognitive), which in turn depends thus upon another (e.g. visual), and so on: the whole stream of experience depending finally and internally upon consciousness itself. Here mental explanation comes to an end, and openly gives way to purely cerebral and causal explanation. While the *properties* of consciousness (e.g. its epistemological powers) are susceptible of mental explanation which is cast in terms of the mental constituents of consciousness, the *existence* of consciousness is not. And the same must be true of those constituents themselves. Consciousness and its constituent parts arise simultaneously together poised on the one purely physical base.

And so an intra-psychic non-causal relation of dependence exists between the stream of experience and its non-distinct psychological contemporary, consciousness. Ultimately, this is because of the property we described earlier as 'technical holism', which in turn derives from the fact that consciousness is itself a 'holistic' totality. For the only conceivable path into existence for a stream of experience of the type encountered in consciousness, is through the purely cerebral phenomenon which is the absolutely immediate and simultaneous cause of the state consciousness. Since there is not even in principle a differentiation of causal roles within that cerebral cause, since it produces the entire totality at one stroke (including such a stream of experience), we say that this experiential stream owes its existence to consciousness. And we mean, not that consciousness is its cause: rather, that in the absence of consciousness, and thus also of the cerebral cause of consciousness, the stream of consciousness could not exist. 'He is experiencing because he is conscious' affirms such a truth.

Now we saw that consciousness is not a naturally hidden nature like the familiar natural-kinds of the physical sciences. And neither is it an idiosyncratic atomic mystery which is inexplicably blessed with a few distinctive causal properties—as if idiosyncrasy was the only alternative to pure emptiness of being. In fact consciousness is constitutively analysable a priori, and its properties are as a result explicable—non-reductively. Thus, the state consciousness has parts. But these are parts 'with a difference', being neither more nor less autonomous than each other, or indeed than consciousness itself. They each together, and the totality which jointly they constitute, arise of necessity simultaneously out of one and the same immediate bodily cause. Their diversity is beyond dispute, but so too is the interdependence present in all directions. The parts depend for identity on the whole precisely to the extent that it constitutively depends upon them. While experience can occur without consciousness, whereas the reverse is not possible, the experiences of the conscious cannot do the same. In a word, the interdependence of consciousness and its constituents is mutual and total.

(α3) Category

If consciousness was an experience, it would be of the type event or process. But it cannot be an experience, for there is more to consciousness than experience: for example, rationality of mental state and knowledge of one's own mind are constituents of self-conscious consciousness. Then what can be its general category? Is it an event or process or state, or none of these? Now for what it is worth, we *speak* of consciousness as a state, and class it as the pre-eminent sub-variety of the kind we *call* 'state of consciousness'. But how seriously should we take such terminology?

Whatever its general category, consciousness is essentially occurrent in type, for each further instant of consciousness is an occurrent renewal of what has been 'going on' from instant to instant. Thus, consciousness can no more 'mark time' than can experience. This is because all that goes to make it up takes occurrent form. For example, when we include rationality in its analysis, we are not referring to the mere presence of the capacity which distinguishes man from other animals. Rather, we mean its actual employment in each instant in which consciousness continues. Indeed, what would it be for rationality (or its absence) to characterize (say) coma? When we speak of the rationality or non-rationality of a mental state it is invariably in the context of experience, whether waking or dreaming. It is an essentially occurrent rationality. And the same is true of the knowledge which is part of the same complex mental picture in the conscious. While a conscious person knows his own mind, that knowledge is contemporaneous with its mental objects, which are in turn singled out under purely indexical temporal headings, directly manifestative of our awareness of the passage of time.

And so despite describing it as a 'state', it seems to me that what we have in mind in speaking of consciousness is a complex set of occurrent mental phenomena, going on from instant to instant: presumably, events and processes. As we remarked above, consciousness can no more 'mark time' than can experience. Like a travelling circus or band of nomads, the 'whole show' is essentially on the move.

(α4) Cognition

The constituents of consciousness help to determine its function. They therefore play their part in making possible whatever it is that consciousness specifically equips its possessor to accomplish. To wit: transact in a certain way with Reality, and most especially concretely with contemporaneous Physical Reality. This is consistent with the fact that the unconditional occurrence of *experience* is the first necessity of consciousness. And alongside that, at least in animate consciousness—as opposed to what other rarefied possibilities?—the continuing availability of the *intuitional attention*—even if it deliver mere null readings like 'silence'—or less. How could one transact in the concrete with the environment if these conditions were not met? Because of its problematicity I shall say nothing about the genesis of the perceptual impressions made possible by the attention, except to note a characteristic accord between their content and one's system of beliefs. But I must say a little about the *mode of formation of belief* concerning present empirical Reality that is distinctive to the conscious. Thus, the conscious show a natural tendency to believe in the reality of what they seemingly perceive. They share this property with dreamers, but differ in that in the conscious perceptual-seemings *cause* rather than merely accompany belief. The mode of belief-formation, and doubtless also of impression-formation, is such that when the subject is in the proper environment, let us say that of evolutionary ancestry, the beliefs *tend* towards knowledge. The sub-system: experience—intuition—perceptual impression— empirical belief, has in the conscious the function of leading to empirical knowledge of one's environs.

But the function is more specific than this. It is not enough as a general rule that the conscious form a belief with local empirical content like (say) 'there is a door at the end of this passage'. This could after all be the discovery of a somnambulist. The element of indexicality ought to be replaceable by something universal, and at the same time capable of supplement. Let me illustrate what I mean by elaborating the example. Thus, 'this passage' should be replaceable by (say) 'the passage in the middle of the Hotel Imperial in Marienbad in mid-June 1960'; while 'this passage' should be supplementable with (say) 'in which I, Mr N., now stand'. The typical end-effect of the working of the cognitive sub-system within the state consciousness, is knowledge that locates the known in its widest setting, and in relation to the subject. This requires that something in animal belief-formation play a role (primitively) analogous to that of the belief-system in human belief-formation: roughly, a knowledge of region and of one's place in it. A cognitive perspectival effect is necessary. The conscious subject is an oriented being, and this includes cognitive and spatio-temporal orientation. It is true that consciousness can survive the loss of orientation of this kind. Even then the tendency persists in the form of the thought 'whenever and wherever it may be'—and discomfort. The knowledge, and indeed the scarcely noticed shadowlike accompanying *propositional feeling*, of being sited where one is in space and time, is the norm even if not the necessity. Normally, we *feel* that we are where we are! Were one transported effortlessly to the moon in ten seconds flat, or discontinuously projected a century hence through sudden refrigeration and subsequent thaw, one would dramatically discover what that feeling was—by its absence! The rational conscious generally are endowed with cognitive and affective orientation.

The sub-system: experience—intuition—Region/World map—perceptual impression—belief, is functioning successfully when it is throwing up such oriented knowledge. By contrast, the states constituting alternative states of consciousness do not form sub-systems which have functions within those states. For example, the states constitutive of sleep can causally interlock, but they might lead to any of sheer quiescence, dream experience, behavioural response to a sensation, even to somnambulism—but no specific function is being discharged when a somnambulist acquires his tunnel-vision beliefs or performs his bizarre tunnel-vision tasks. The causally engaged states do not constitute a sub-system with the express functional purpose of effecting somnambulist seeings, believings, and doings. All we have here is a truncated version of a genuine sub-system that works in the state consciousness towards a genuine end.

(α5) The bodily will

The cognitive sub-system in consciousness tends to effect knowledge of the environment under headings which locate it in Regional/World space-time and relate it indexically to the subject. Consciousness, though devoid of phenomenology and intentional content; harbours within itself machinery with this express function. Knowledge is an essential aim of this inexperienceable contentless state. Hence the attractions of such images as empty canvas and virgin page. As noted earlier, this was the sevententh-century conception of consciousness. One thinks of all those paintings by Descartes' contemporaries of people standing by windows flooded by light. They inhabited a mental climate of such a kind that epistemology took pride of place in their understanding of mind, doubtless because of the early triumphs of the physical sciences. Light was of obsessive interest to them precisely because it was a mediator to *knowledge*, just as it proved to be of great importance to a later generation of painters because it was a mediator and thus closer to *subjectivity*. For the significance of the mediator is double. It conducts the mind outwards to Nature, yet crops up between Nature and the mind. Which significance is to the fore, depends upon one's interest.

This cognitive sub-system does not suffice to constitute consciousness. If it did, knowledge would reign supreme in our lives. When Heidegger wrote that 'dasein is *fascinated by* the World', he was thinking of something more than cognition. And ought there not in any case to be a function for knowledge? Knowledge is not a feasible final end for living matter, and must be presumed to have some natural purpose. Thus, why *such interest* in knowing how one is physically placed here and now? This fragment of data is of absolutely no consequence in itself. It can scarcely be doubted that the evolutionary function of knowlege must have been to assist in the satisfaction of vital need through intentional action. Indeed, that the function of knowledge is thus dynamic is evident on other grounds. When Schopenhauer claimed that knowledge was originally a servant of the will, when Freud asserted that the ego differentiated out of the id, they were of this mind, and for diverse reasons. But in any case to suppose that consciousness has discharged its function when it strands us with situational knowledge of a region, is to overlook something which emerged earlier. Namely, that when consciousness is manifesting what it can accomplish in its bearer, a significant double revelation is occurring at that moment: of the World through perception to the subject, and of the subject's powers through active expression to the outside. So far we have spoken as if justice needed to be done merely to the first phenomenon.

The other phenomenon is active, and bodily active at that. Animate consciousness encompasses a *special availability* of the bodily-act system. With this in mind I will try briefly to characterize the causal sensitivity of the bodily-act system to present perceptual cognition that exists in the conscious. Thus, if the above functional claim is correct, several such causal bridge-formations should inhere in that state. Then attempting to determine their nature is procedurally equivalent to asking the following concrete question: what particular causal sensitivities of the bodily-act system to perceptual cognition *come into being* as (let us say) a dreaming subject wakes? What such sensitivities are *absent* in (say) a dreamer and present in the waking?

The novel states of affairs involving the bodily-act system that the onset of consciousness ushers into being are several, and they occur at very fundamental levels. Thus, it is not just that the conscious tend to *do* what they desire to do. (Which is true and important—for it is not true (say) of the dreaming—but not the most fundamental fact.) It is not even that they *desire* to do what they desire to be so. (Which is also true and important, though once again not absolute bedrock.) The whole edifice of the bodily will rests upon something even more elemental than these propensities. It depends on the upsurge and unmotivated active expression of a *set of basic physical inclinations* taking place when one comes face to face perceptually and cognitively with Physical Nature. The propensity for the arise and expression of mere inclinatory bodily act-desire, when confronted with the situational disclosures of consciousness, is as essential to animal nature as the epistemological apparatus which fathers it. It is the very starting point of willing.

Thus, it typifies the conscious that when confronted by the actively accessible—that, typically, and in fact, is necessary to their own or to Life's systems—*they tend to experience certain inclinatory bodily act-desires upon which they tend to act*. Often enough they do not in the case of a particular such item, yet often enough they do, and in general they express thereby one of a stable repertoire of simple natural inclinations, which together constitute a kind of base upon which arises a generally desiring attitude towards the environment that is universally pervasive in the conscious. Most of us sometimes feel like drinking water or running, few of us feel like eating parrot feed or coal, and all of us want to do something or another of a physical nature for most of our waking lives. This gives a picture of how the bodily-act system responds in the conscious to perceptual cognition. Animal consciousness is as such actively, and in the first place through inclinatory bodily act-desire, anchored in its surroundings. While the link need not be manifest in each instant, it is nonetheless a continuing reality.

(α6) The mental will

What of the mental will? Its functioning is a categorically necessary condition of consciousness, at the very least in the self-conscious. It is not that order requires it, as dreaming demonstrates. And neither does self-knowledge. However, rationality does. And the internal temporal framework which is necessary for the satisfaction of consciousness's cognitive function seems possible only if the mental will is operative. And so we say that *experience*, which is necessary for consciousness, and which must in part take *intuitional attentive* form (for that too is necessary), must in addition take overall *active* form. Consciousness is such that these *three experiential conditions* have to be categorically satisfied as long as it exists. It can tolerate neither pure emptiness, total inwardness, sheer drift.

How do the two ontological varieties of willing relate? How does the internal active process relate to the bodily active phenomena which we have taken it to be the function of consciousness to produce? Is it simply a second parallel functional goal? Or is it, on account of its ontological 'superiority', perhaps the overarching goal?

It seems to me that it is not. Animal consciousness provides a lead here. Whether or not it too necessitates mental willing, it is I think significant that perceptual activity is the only mental activity which animals perform, and that it is *subordinated* activity. Thus, watching, listening, smelling, all of which are *internal* phenomena, and all modes of *active* attention. Then these activities do not as a general rule occur independently of the phenomena occurring when consciousness is manifesting its presence in informed intentional physical action. Rather, they tend to *sustain* it. Think how an animal that is pursuing its quarry will actively train its perceptual attention upon it. I suggest that this instantiates a general tendency. In an extremely wide sense, ranging over such simple practical cases and the most inward and intellectual self-conscious mental activities, subordination of the mental to the bodily will is the general rule and presumably the natural function of the mental will.

I will try to explain how this can be so. It is not just that we show a general tendency to write or talk or paint or perform whatever actively transpires within. Certain considerations reveal the connection to be closer. Thus, internal activities are for the most part subordinated to what might be described as 'the life', taking the term stipulatively to stand for that totality of phenomena in terms of which we compute the overall qualities of a man. Then these last are mostly of a physical order. Think how one might ruminate for days in making a vital decision that issues in a simple but momentous act of signing one's name. Then it is the outcome in the *public physical world* that ultimately matters to one's life. More: it is the *active* outcome. A life is something which is almost in its entirety assessed in terms of physical action in situation. Man may not actually *be* the sum total of his intentional physical deeds: not much slips through the net however. But the mental will, through thinking, plots the course of that life. It therefore determines, without actually constituting, the final functional end of mind and consciousness, which is to say the general character of a whole constituted largely of physical deeds. It is in this roundabout way that the mental will comes paradoxically to be subordinated to the bodily will. And we can see how the mental will manages nonetheless to find for itself a role consonant with its dignity. Thanks to the almost limitless weight of meanings that bodily movements and artefacts can bear, the mental will discovers an avenue of expression in the physical realm that amounts to nothing less than the appearance in Physical Nature of an entirely new dimension of meaning. But the intentional bodily will that is (so to say) 'stand-in' or proxy in Physical Nature for these ontologically 'superior' phenomena in the inner life of the conscious, remains the end of the functional line for consciousness. This is because its history largely constitutes the life, and it is the life that is the end of that line.

Let me emphasize that I do not intend this conclusion as a mindless paean to the glories of sheer physical willing. Far from it. The end of the functional line for consciousness is not frenetic bodily action spurred somehow into being by the onset of cognition. It is informed intentional action dedicated to the transformation of that which is the subject-matter of the causative cognitions, viz. the containing environment. Likewise it is not the mere shifting of matter prompted somehow by internal active process. It is far-ranging informed bodily action which seeks to realize ends which were brought to light only through internal enterprise. Therefore even though bodily action is the functional end-point of consciousness, it does not *transcend* or put behind it that to which it owes its existence. Those progenitive sources are integrated into the act. This natural unity is an immediate reflection of the unity holding between the constituent sub-systems of the state consciousness.

3

Self-Consciousness and Self-Knowledge

(1) In the previous chapter I put forward an a priori analysis of consciousness. I suggested that a particular group of mental phenomena were constitutive of the state of waking consciousness, which I assumed to be an analysable psychological complex or totality. This account was cast in terms which have application across the wide spectrum of animal kind, such as the property of supporting experience, of being mentally in a position to 'read' the environment, etc. In short, I attempted to dismantle the phenomenon of consciousness, understood as embracing both the unselfconscious and self-conscious varieties.

This chapter is concerned with elucidating the latter 'higher' more developed form of consciousness. Indeed, that is the aim of the remainder of Part I of this work, extending from the present Chapter 3 through to Chapter 6. Then since Chapter 2 was entitled 'The Anatomy of Consciousness', these ensuing few chapters might with justice be called 'The Physiology of Self-Consciousness'. Thus, in the course of these chapters I try to bring out the functional part played in the constitution of self-conscious consciousness by certain fundamental elements of the state. I shall contend that, while important novel phenomena appear at this 'higher' stage which find no place in merely animal consciousness, the very items which make for consciousness in unthinking animals, do the same in the present case, only in more developed form. Now among the major novelties arising with self-consciousness are self-awareness, self-determination, rationality, and thought. The present chapter focuses on the first of these: self-awareness—by which I mean knowledge of one's own existence and the contents of one's own mind. I hope to shed light on the part that this novel mental characteristic plays in making self-consciousness a reality: that is, show how it helps make possible other equally fundamental elements in the 'higher' phenomenon which they together realize. This charting of functional roles has an analogy with physiology.

Before I embark on this enterprise, a preliminary word on the relation between 'self-consciousness consciousnesses' and self-consciousness consciousness. It is a common practice to refer to those beings who are uniquely capable of supporting the latter state by an expression referring to that state—rather as one might speak (say) of 'depressives'. The reason seems evident enough. It consists in the fact that the properties which single out the distinctive bearers of the state are themselves involved in the constituting of the state itself. When we speak of 'persons' we have in mind beings endowed with a distinctive set of properties, consisting mostly in capacities such as for thought and reasoning, but also in the knowledge of certain fundamentals like self, world, time, truth. These properties are necessary conditions of one another, and in some cases are related by bonds of mutual entailment. Thus, a being with the capacity for thought or a knowledge of truth is necessarily one with the capacity to grasp and be determined by rational relations, and vice versa. In short, the properties in question form a relatively tight circle which, over the course of evolution and/or early prehistory, must have come into existence as a single unified whole. Then even though creatures of this developed kind are capable of being in deprived states of consciousness in which few elements in the circle are put to use, the state of full waking consciousness is such as to both enable and call upon one's central mental powers: for example, that of rationality. And so rationality both characterizes 'self-consciousness consciousnesses' *and* the developed (i.e. waking) state in which their capacities for awareness are fully realized. Facts of this kind must underlie the choice of the description of 'persons' as 'self-consciousness consciousnesses'.

(2) Amongst the circle of properties distinctive of the self-conscious state is that of self-awareness. Then let me explain why I begin my exposition of self-consciousness with an account of this property. One reason is historical: the importance people have attached to the concepts, Cartesian 'translucence' and Freudian 'unconscious', attest to the significance of self-knowledge. But there is another reason also. Prior to the onset of the more developed ('higher') form of consciousness, one great sector of Reality lay outside the scope, not of experience, but of the cognition of conscious beings: namely, their own minds. Then as a correlate of this lack, the full reality of the psychological life of other beings must along with it also have been inaccessible to cognition. In short, with the advent of self-awareness, the entire realm of the mental must for the first time have become an object of knowledge. There must be some good reason why the opening up of a whole new realm to cognition came into being. One of those reasons is surely mental-causal in character. For despite the fact that the circle of properties of self-consciousness is tight and self-sustaining, some of these fundamental characteristics make possible others as not vice versa. For example, while rationality does not make possible self-knowledge, self-knowledge is a functionally active necessary condition of both rationality and self-determination or 'freedom'. In short, I surmise that self-knowledge operates causally at a relatively deep level in the setting up of the circle of developed traits. In any case, since we designate the state in question by mentioning this property, it seems fitting that we accord it pride of place in an exposition of the nature of self-conscious consciousness.

The chapter falls into three main parts: A, B, and C. The first A is concerned to spell out a modified Cartesian thesis of self-knowledge. The second B attempts to demonstrate that self-knowledge and consciousness keep close company, through investigating four different mental states in which shortfall or absence in one is closely reflected in the other. The final section C offers a summary and provisional characterization of self-consciousness in the light of the preceding discussion.

PART A. INSIGHT

1. A Cartesian Thesis

(a) Introduction

While men sometimes wonder concerning their own motivation, they do not usually wonder (say) whether they are in pain, whether they know their own name, why they think someone is now at the front door, etc. Short of the introduction of the special circumstance of mental derangement, or trivialities like linguistic ignorance, we barely comprehend the suggestion that a man might be unaware of the existence of his present experiences, or, indeed, of much else besides that is presently true of his own mind. Yet nothing is more natural—and without the supposition of derangement and the like—than sheer ungarnished ignorance concerning these matters in the third-person situation. This asymmetry is of the utmost importance. Upon it hinges the very concept of personhood. If we are to do justice to the insights of Freud and others, it must not be at the expense of those of Descartes. Indeed, Freud could with some justice be represented as a sort of latter-day Cartesian: after all, he hypothesized failures in Cartesian 'translucence' to be coextensive with and causative of impediments to mental maturation and the full realization of individuality. Accordingly, I see possibilities of a dialectical reconciliation between these two apparently opposed epistemologies of the mind. In short, to grasp the insights of Freud we must first understand the precise nature of those of Descartes, and it is to the latter task that I now address myself.

I hope to demonstrate that self-knowledge is the natural condition for the self-conscious, a self-knowledge that is absolutely immediate in type. More exactly, I hope to show that such an awareness is the natural condition for the self-conscious *conscious*. For we do not suppose that natural insight into one's own present state of mind must obtain in states of consciousness other than the fundamental sub-variety: *consciousness*. That a man under general anaesthetic is ignorant of his present condition of unconsciousness, is no sort of qualification of the claim I am advancing. However, it reminds us that the property of which we speak obtains necessarily only in consciousness. Indeed, the claim must be understood as characterizing the very essence of self-conscious consciousness. And so the claim in question is: that *consciousness in the self-conscious* is a state such that immediate self-knowledge obtains in its owner. Just under which conditions this power is manifest, and what the precise content of the knowledge is, are matters which we must investigate prior to formulating an exact thesis of natural insight. Then because the thesis propounds as essential to self-conscious consciousness an insight that is immediate and more or less guaranteed, it seems proper to characterize it as Cartesian in spirit.

(b) Self-conscious knowing is in no way, and is not an experience

(1) Very occasionally we discover what is here and now occurring in our own minds through inference and appeal to experience. For example, we might take seriously the suggestion of a friend that our present motivation is other than we might have supposed. But before all else and for most of our waking lives we are absolutely immediately aware of a great slice of the present contents of our own minds. That is, we know of a great many such items 'just like that' or no-how. And it could not be otherwise. How could a child learn what passes in his own mind from his elders first, and only secondarily graduate to immediate self-knowledge of such phenomena? What kind of a mind would it be that could discover from other people about its own thoughts and desires and intentions, but was unable to immediately know of such items in its own mind? It defies comprehension. There can be no doubt that imme- diate self-knowledge is an essential element of human mentality. Such natural insight governs our knowledge both of present experiences like thought and affect, of unexperienced mental states like belief, of the mental sources of many of our acts and beliefs and desires, and so on. Thus, I know that I am now thinking of this, I know I now believe that, I know that I do so because I just now observed such and such, immediately and automatically and as a complete matter of course. This property has to be realized as soon as a mind is a reality. More exactly, as soon as a human or self-conscious type of mind is a reality.

(2) And so mankind is typically apprised of much of what inhabits his mind at any instant, and there exists no cognitive path via which this knowledge is reached. In particular, there exists no quasi-perceptual faculty of 'inner sense' through which we come to know such facts; and that is to say, that knowledge of outer and inner phenomena must arise in *wholly dissimilar* ways. If 'inner sense' is understood to be the natural quasi-perceptual means through which we come to know our own minds, then 'inner sense' is a myth! And what a strange involuted mirror of a mind it would need to be, in which its own experiences and cognitive states were disclosed to its owner through the deliverances of a quasi-sense! For amongst the present contents of that mind one would have to find a place for the distinctive experience of disclosure of those contents to the subject—generating an obvious regress. In order to avoid this infinite multiplication of mental contents, the mirror-in-the- mirror illusion, we have no choice but to accept that the knowledge of present ex- periences and cognitive states and much else besides cannot in general be through a quasi-perceptual or experienced avenue of knowledge.

Accordingly, the epistemological situations with regard to 'outer' and (a whole range of) 'inner' phenomena must be grossly dissimilar. Compare the cognitive relation to some ('outer') *perceived event* with the cognitive relation to an ('inner') *present experience*, beginning with the former. Let us suppose that at time t I become aware of a flash of lightning. Then we distinguish *three* events occurring in that instant. Thus, 'at time t there was a flash of lightning' and 'at time t I saw a flash of lightning' report two distinct causally related events, while 'at time t I learned that there was a flash of lightning' reports a distinct third event caused by the seeing. Now the event of seeing lightning *is* the event of noticing a visual sensation which meets certain causal requirements: a phenomenon whose occurrence necessitates no specific cognitive attitudes, and whose distinctness from its cognitive mental effect is thus guaranteed. Then it is the existence of the latter two distinct events, seeing-of and coming to know-of the existence of a flash of lightning, together with the causal relation between the two, that enables us to say that here sight was the *avenue* of knowledge of the perceived event. Seeing was *how* we learned of the 'outer' event.

The situation is entirely different in the case of knowledge of one's own present experiences. 'At time t I thought "my train leaves in five minutes"' and 'at time t I came to know that I had at t such a thought', report respectively an experience-event of type thinking-that and a simultaneous event consisting in the onset of a state of knowledge of that experience. But there occurs no third event that is analogous to the noticing of visual sensations, distinct both from the thought-event and the learning of its existence, caused by the former and cause of the latter. This unlikeness to the perceptual situation shows there was here no experienced avenue of knowledge.

(3) The above event of knowledge-onset, which comes into being through no mediating experience, leaves no memory of itself. And the reason it does not is, that this cognitive event is not an *experience*. And in general it could not be otherwise. We have seen that self-conscious consciousness necessitates a measure of knowledge of the present contents of one's own mind, but if this in turn necessitated experiences of knowledge-onset, a second regress would be set in train. Thus, the above measure of knowledge of the mind must arise otherwise than in the mode of experience, it must so to say be a *silent or non-conscious partner* to much else in the mind, and leave no residue in event-memory. Indeed, we can have no *natural insight* into the occurrence of this cognitive event, whose existence is instead to be inferred.

In sum, we know of our present experiences and cognitions and much else besides *through* no experience, *in* no experience, and *absolutely immediately*. This continuous silent immediate 'cognitive print out' of present mental content is a cornerstone of the self-conscious mind. Then the above rather complex epistemological claim brings us nearer to the final statement of Cartesian 'insight' towards which we are gradually working. However, there are several important additional variables which need to be added to that statement before it is complete.

(c) A Cartesian principle of insight

(1) Thus, the knowledge of our own experiences enters the mind at the same time as the experience, and lodges in the mind thereafter in the form of memory. And

while the onset of that knowledge is a mental event, it is not an experienced mental event, nor one of whose existence we are immediately apprised. Rather, it consists in change located *elsewhere in the mind* than in the stream of consciousness. After all, much more can at any moment be attributed to a mind than a stream of conscious-nesses, and change must be possible in those other sectors of that mind. It is in this way that the silent event of augmenting the knowledge-system, which happens simultaneously with experience, manages itself not to be a further experience. And it is this fact which enables us to avoid an endless multiplication of ex-periences.

Now this immediate knowledge that we have of present experiences and of much else, is far from being an outré or occult divination of phenomena. It is the *natural accessibility* of a whole slice of the present life of the mind to the subject. And yet it is not so for all subjects, nor all of the time for any subject. It may not be true of the radically insane, and while dreamers know at the time that they seem to see this or that, they mostly fail to know that those experiences are imaginings. Thus in this latter situation occurring during sleep, insight in the self-conscious proves to be only partial. And in deep unconsciousness occurrent insight of any kind is simply non-existent. Then precisely what do self-conscious beings achieve in the way of insight? and when does it happen? What we need at this point in the spelling out of a Cartesian principle of insight is something not as yet accomplished. Namely, a statement of the *content* and *conditions* of this natural insight.

Such insight occurs very imperfectly in sleep, and even less in unconsciousness. It takes place in its properly developed form only when one is awake. Then it seems to me that the dreamer's ignorance of his own mind is instructive concerning the content of natural insight. For exactly what does a dreamer not know? At least two properties of his dream escape him (properties which are normally accessible in waking consciousness). The dreamer is ignorant of the *ultimate character* of certain experiences he undoubtedly knows of—under narrower headings; for while he knows of his present dream 'seeing', he does not know it is imagining. And it is in addition an ignorance of *mental origins*, for the dreamer lacks all knowledge of the origins of his dream experiences and beliefs. Now these two failures of insight during sleep suggest the following more exact thesis concerning natural insight. Namely, that a wakeful self-conscious state of consciousness is such that it involves an immediate knowledge of present mental contents under ultimate or adequate headings, where 'mental content' is allowed to range over experiences, cognitive attitudes, and certain mental origins. In the ensuing discussion I will endeavour to demonstrate a truth which takes account of these additional variables.

(2) But I have still some distance to go to complete the statement of self-conscious insight. Then it takes us significantly nearer that goal if we now distin-guish (α) the kind, (β) condition, and (γ) state of consciousness, as follows. (α) The consciousness of man is a self-conscious consciousness, whereas that of 'dumb beasts' is different in kind. Both man and beast are conscious in the same sense of

that term—for 'he was stunned' or 'he regained consciousness' mean the same of man or fish—but the kinds of their consciousness are different. (β) While a mentally normal-ish man and an occurrently deluded psychotic instance the self-conscious kind of consciousness, the condition of waking consciousness in the latter radically disturbed subject is not (as we shall later discover) quite that of normal waking consciousness. A grossly deluded psychotic who 'sees' angels in the supermarket, or a consumer of LSD with comparable experiences, are probably *imperfectly* (rather than 'dimly', 'half', 'marginally', etc.) conscious, being in states which have something in common with dreams. Finally, (γ) the state of consciousness of a wakeful person, of one deeply unconscious, or of a sleeper, are all different states of consciousness.

Given these distinctions I now re-formulate a thesis of self-knowledge, in which certain novel conditions are introduced. Thus: a *properly formed state of waking self-conscious consciousness* is such that the wakeful person cannot be significantly ignorant of the present contents of his own mind, where 'present contents' ranges over experiences, cognitions, certain mental origins, etc.; and he must know of these phenomena under adequate headings, absolutely immediately, and 'silently'. This brings us close to a final statement of the claim I hope to establish in the ensuing discussion. It affirms what is an a priori principle and a necessity. It is the statement of a principle of near-infallible access: a principle in the spirit of Descartes, a conditional Cartesian thesis of self-knowledge. This necessary proposition characterizes the essence of self-conscious consciousness.

2. Consciousness and Normality in the Mind

(a) Self-awareness and normality

(1) The above principle might be thought circular. It might be claimed that the received concept of a normal-ish condition of wakeful self-conscious consciousness is such as to exclude sustained ignorance of the existence, character, and content of mental processes of the kind of (say) thinking and imagining. In consequence, the above thesis might be seen as a mere statement of a stipulation. This threatens to trivialize a claim which is surely not trivial. For the position is not merely that sometimes (or mostly) the wakeful person knows the truth of his present mental processes, and sometimes (or rarely) not, and we choose to bless the first, but not the second, with the title 'minimally normal example of consciousness'. This statistical concept of normal mental functioning is not the only possible, and certainly not the most interesting concept. If it were, we would in effect be putting forward a triviality, linking self-awareness with a construct called 'mental normality', as a supposed Cartesian insight.

How shall we restore its rightful substance to a modified or conditional Cartesianism? The concept of normality, in the case of living organisms, is something more than that of a mere counting of heads. In fact, it is close to the concept of *health*. Now a physically healthy animal is in such a state as to physically permit the exercise of its physical powers: a formulation resting upon the presumption that the animal is endowed with a *nature*, which it can more completely or less completely *realize*, and that there can be *better or worse* physical conditions of the animal. Analogously, I shall take a mental disease to be an inherent condition of the mind, that is at least such as to interfere with the capacity of the person to realize his generic and individual mental potential—a narrower concept than that of a mental disorder (which might be a temporary condition produced by a drug). Then when I speak of insight as natural to the state of waking self-consciousness, I must be understood to be expressing my claim in terms of the wider concept of 'normality'.

(2) As already intimated, insight in a conscious or wakeful subject is sometimes significantly flawed in serious mental 'disturbance'. For example, Macbeth did not know he merely imagined Banquo at the feast. Then at first glance this might seem to disprove the Cartesian thesis of near-infallible access. And in fact it does disprove a particularly optimistic statement of Cartesianism: namely, that consciousness necessitates relatively full insight into one's own mind. It demonstrates that self-conscious consciousness can coexist with significant failures of insight. Now this simple fact might incline us to abandon the Cartesian thesis forthwith. But in my opinion that would be to misunderstand the Cartesian claim. Thus, it fails to grasp that the Cartesian doctrine precisely characterizes the *nature* of self-conscious consciousness, and that being part of a nature is not the same thing as being *invariably exemplified*. The concept of a vital nature makes allowance for *malformed* examples of the kind: items which instantiate the type, but in a way that falls short of a norm; and Macbeth surely exemplified such a thing. It was to this concept that I appealed in an attempt to adequately characterize self-consciousness. It led me to formulate what is in my opinion a true necessity, involving certain conditions of validity, which is universally exemplified. Namely, that a properly wakeful self-conscious mind knows its own present mental contents. This statement is logically equivalent to the following 'nature statement': immediate self-knowledge is of the essence of self-conscious consciousness.

Thus, in order to salvage the Cartesian doctrine in such a way as to retain content or substance, I had recourse to the concept of 'mental normality', understood not in a statistical sense, but in a sense which recognizes that we are speaking of items endowed with natures and functions. That sense is 'well formedness', which in the vital is close to 'health'. The amended claim is, that a properly functioning wakeful self-conscious mind must adequately know itself. This is the thesis which I have taken upon myself to demonstrate. Now it is clear that most examples of waking consciousness meet this requirement. My claim must therefore be, that the exceptions to the rule are faulty examples of the kind—as opposed to (say) mere borderline cases. What I need therefore to demonstrate is, that a wakeful self-conscious subject who is in substantial error concerning his own central mental states and processes, must be in a malformed or mentally malfunctioning state of consciousness. That is, an example of consciousness in which *something is wrong*, in which the *scheme of nature* has gone awry, and doubtless such that the state in question cannot discharge its *normal functions*. And I need to explain how it is that this is so.

(b) Self-awareness and truth

And so we shall fill in the concept of a 'well-formed'/'ill-formed' state of waking consciousness, in part by noting the constituents of the state and their modes of interrelation; but we shall detect their presence above all *functionally*. Consciousness has a task to perform—like a liver or a kidney, and can do it well or badly. I intend to demonstrate how impairment in self-knowledge in a wakeful person leads inevitably to *malfunctioning* of the state of waking. If insight is an essential property of self-conscious waking, when impaired self-knowledge obtains in that state, malformation ought inevitably to occur in the state—leading to malfunction. Malformation in one should 'track' malformation in the other, and malformation in performance should 'track' both.

If we are to make out the case for the necessity of the link between waking-consciousness and insight, we will have to investigate the type of consciousness obtaining in the wakeful mentally 'disturbed' whose insight is impaired, and substantiate the claim that it is malformed, and provide the operative rationale. This is because such cases seem on the face of it to disprove the Cartesian thesis. Then that project requires that we have a preliminary understanding of self-consciousness itself. Indeed, it helps to more exactly formulate the Cartesian rule of special access, if we can say a little more concerning this state. Now one species-potential of humans is awareness of the environment—and this might be realized by (say) a human who has lived his life amongst (say) wolves, scarcely developing the capacity to think. But another 'higher' potential is the potential—common to all rational humans but possibly irrecoverably lost to this being—for a full and human consciousness; and that is to say, for an awareness of the world as it is *under the aspect of truth*: something which can be realized only by those with the capacity for *thought*. This introduces a new variable into the situation.

Then the principle which I hope to establish in this chapter can be better expressed in these terms. Namely, that when the truth of the inner world is not apparent to the conscious subject, when in the wakeful there occurs substantial error concerning the truth of inner reality, then there occurs an *impaired* realization of the potential for consciousness of the world under the aspect of truth. Therefore to begin I must show that there exist conditions of consciousness which are not so much diminishings or fadings, as occur (say) when one is approaching sleep or unconsciousness, as *defective examples* of consciousness, and I must secondly demonstrate that those conditions can owe their existence to the above defect in a truth-aware insight. Then consciousness, like health, will stand revealed both as an actuality and an ideal, for there can be more and less and better and worse of it. We shall restore substance to Cartesianism by showing that in the wakeful substantial error concerning the truth of the present mind entails, in a personal or self-conscious consciousness, an improper consciousness, a defective awareness of the world, an imperfect sense of reality. And we shall in so doing defend the claim that self-knowledge is essential to self-conscious consciousness.

(c) The functional role of truth

(1) Before I complete the present part of the discussion, I want to make more explicit the special relation to truth that is constitutive uniquely of self-conscious consciousness. In particular, I want to say something concerning the *functional utility* of that relation. The significance of this lies in the fact that deficiencies in self-knowledge under the aspect of truth lead to failure in accomplishing what such knowledge normally makes possible. That is, to functional failure.

Self-awareness necessitates awareness of truth. Thus, a child who regularly makes the sound 'hungry' as a way of getting food, only thereby manifests self-consciousness and knowledge of the fact of its hunger, when it knows the *sense* of 'I am hungry', which consists in knowing when *it is true*. In short, knowing he is hungry is knowing it is true that he is hungry. Indeed, for any thinking language-user to know any proposition p, is for it to know that 'p' is true. Self-consciousness requires that all knowledge, including that of the inner world, be for the self-conscious creature *under the aspect of truth*.

Meanwhile (merely) animal consciousness, while it relates cognitively to the world, has nothing to do with truth. Or perhaps better expressed: animals know truths, but not their truth. A dog knowing it is about to be fed, does not know it is true it is about to be fed. It could do so only if it could *compare the thought* 'I am about to be fed' with the reality that makes it true (for truth arises out of the matching of thought and reality). And this in turn requires the knowledge that one has that thought, together with the capacity to contemplate its denial as a possibility that is here in fact not realized. But because 'animal thought' (if one may call it that) is essentially categorical-practical, animals cannot relate in this way to their 'thoughts', which are essentially modes of practical involvement in their surrounds (so that behaviourism must be nearer to the truth in the case of non-rational animals). In this special sense animals may be said to be *immersed* in the world in a way thinking beings are not. And for the same reason, animals have no autonomous inner life.

One important consequence of the above account of animal mental life is that there can in their case be no *working towards* a belief, no believing through *cogitation*, no form of *responsibility* for belief, and in consequence no kind of *mental freedom*. This is because cogitation entertains propositions under the heading 'not yet to be used' or 'may be rejected', it 'puts them on ice for the time being', whereas the 'practical-immersion' (as one might dub it) of animals only entertains propositions as 'to be used here and now'. Thus, the animal merely *has* its beliefs, which are produced in it through sense, regularities in experience, desire, innate factors, etc. It does not know it has them, it had no hand in their installation, and it cannot compare them to the world. All it can do is harbour them and act upon them.

Transcending the condition of 'animal-immersion' is achieved through the linguistically assisted capacity to think in the modalities of the possible and the hypothetical, which is an exercise of imaginative power. This means that to know that p, I must reject the possible match of the denial-thought (not-p) and reality, I must know that not-p might have been true but is in fact false. And in self-conscious beings this is manifest in precisely the internal freedom that is absent in the unselfconscious. Alongside the momentous development of rationality, of which incidentally it is a necessary condition, one of the primary uses of self-awareness in thinking creatures is in self-determination and mental freedom. This consists in effecting a concordance between acts and beliefs, etc., and the *values* (evidential, moral, prudential, aesthetic) without which self-awareness would never have appeared upon the face of the earth. The evolutionary advantages of this mutation in our inner lives are considerable. We come to know the world through rational means, and to act in rational ways which put that knowledge to use. We are aware of our own minds in order to rationally govern our existences in a rationally disclosed world. This must be the prime function of self-knowledge. We shall discover in what follows how it is that significant deficiencies in self-awareness affect via this route the prevailing state of consciousness whose function it is to make possible just such a way of being.

(2) Then here, in terms informed by the foregoing discussion, is a final statement of the Cartesian thesis of privileged access. Thus: a properly wakeful self-conscious being must have a suitable measure of absolutely immediate knowledge, under the aspect of truth and adequate headings, of present mental content (ranging over experiences, cognitive attitudes, certain mental origins, etc.). And insofar as he falls significantly short of this norm of insight, there must be something amiss with, some disturbance in the state of waking consciousness. More simply, if a wakeful person is significantly lacking in self-knowledge of the kind specified above, an impairment must exist in the prevailing state of waking. That is to say, in the state we call 'consciousness'.

(d) A review of the argument

At this point I briefly review the foregoing argument. The wakeful and self-conscious—as opposed to the non-wakeful and/or to 'dumb beasts'—know their own minds, silently and absolutely immediately. This proposition is not a statistical truth, but an a priori principle of Cartesian-type infallible access. And yet an apparent exception exists to the above claim. Thus, some mentally 'disturbed' yet wakeful people seem to be grossly ignorant of certain phenomena in their own minds which it is normal to know. Does not this disprove the rule? Or could it be that it is the exception that proves the rule? Or is it possible that neither claim is correct?

The rule in question—that the wakeful self-conscious know their own present minds—can be variously understood. It might be taken to affirm the unconditional necessity: $\Box$ (x)[(wakeful & self-conscious)x → ~ ($\exists$y){(mental item drawn from a familiar array of mental items, viz. experiences, cognitions, certain mental origins, . . .)y & (ignorant of y)x}]. That is, 'no self-conscious waking being is significantly ignorant of phenomena in his own mind.' Then if this is how the rule is understood, the example of ignorance of one's own mind on the part of some mentally 'disturbed' beings decisively disproves the claim.

But it seems to me that this is not how we should understand the Cartesian claim that 'the wakeful self-conscious know their own minds'. Rather, the above claim is akin to assertions like 'the eye is the organ of sight'. It is a 'nature statement', a statement which is a partial revelation of the nature of the items involved in the claim, and of their functional role in the whole. This assertion appeals to the concept of being 'well formed', as applied to wakefulness. Surely this can be 'well formed', just as much as a sane mind is mentally well formed and a healthy liver physically well formed. When consciousness comes into being, various mental powers and phenomena swing into play in mutually supportive fashion, constituting a working unity, and flaws can appear in and variously mar this occurrent system. Accordingly, a genuine necessity can be assembled which admits of no exceptions, through appeal to the concept of normality in that system. Thus: $\Box$ (x)[(self-conscious & normally conscious)x → ~ ($\exists$y){(mental item drawn from . . .)y & (ignorant of y)x}]. That is, 'No self-conscious being who is in a state of normal (well formed, etc.) waking consciousness, is significantly ignorant of his own mind.'

In sum: my aim is to demonstrate that 'a well-formed state of self-conscious wakefulness is such that the present contents of that mind must be insightfully given to its owner', through demonstrating that 'a wakeful subject significantly self-ignorant must be improperly conscious or awake'. I do so through investigating four different states in which insight is diminished and consciousness absent or impaired: sleep, trance, intoxication, psychosis. And that concludes the first Part A of this chapter, which was devoted to assembling a thesis of 'Conditional Cartesianism'. The ensuing Part B addresses itself to the latter enterprise.

PART B: DIMINUTIONS OF INSIGHT AND CONSCIOUSNESS

3. Consciousness

For the moment I put the topic of self-knowledge to one side. As observed at the beginning of the present chapter, the overall aim of the discussion in the first

Section of this work is broader in scope: it is the elucidation of the self-conscious state of consciousness. The present chapter is no more than a significant part of that enterprise. It addresses itself to one vital strand in the edifice of self-conscious consciousness, the property of self-knowledge, an element which I suspect to be causally more primitive than some others in the unified circle of constituting properties, helping in its own way to make possible certain other essentials. Then if I am to proceed in this enterprise I need to look more closely at consciousness itself. After all, the claim under examination is that a close link exists between defects in that state and defects in self-knowledge. Accordingly, I must discover tests for proper examples of consciousness. Now waking consciousness is one instance of a broad covering type or genus, 'state of consciousness'. It seems desirable therefore that as a preliminary we should have some understanding of that covering type. While we have already examined this concept in Chapter 2, I need at this point to express some of those findings in terms which are specifically relevant to the present inquiry into self-knowledge.

(a) States of consciousness

What is a 'state of consciousness'? We are inclined to postulate a rigid connection between states of consciousness and particular episodes of consciousness ('consciousnesses-of'). Thus, we are inclined to say that if a creature at some time t is aware-of something, if it is so much as *experiencing,* then it must for that reason be in a state of consciousness. And so indeed it must be, but not for the reason that it is experientially conscious of something at t, but simply because it is alive and an example of a conscious type of creature. Thus, it is a cat and not a mollusc. Any sentient being is *always* in a state of consciousness. Necessarily it is in such a state, and necessarily it is in *but one* such state.

But is not a person who is (say) dreaming under nitrous oxide in a state of consciousness as (say) a deeply refrigerated space-traveller is not? Since he is now experiencing an episode of consciousness as the other is not, must he not now be conscious in a sense the other is not? Well, it is doubtless true that he alone now supports and has the capacity to support events of type awarenesses-of or consciousnesses-of. Nevertheless, the icy astronaut is also in a state of consciousness, indeed in the same broad state of consciousness. It is simply that differences exist between those examples of the state. Thus, they are both in the state of consciousness, unconsciousness: in this respect they agree. Where they differ is in the degree or depth of their unconsciousness: one being a light unconsciousness, the other as deep perhaps as it is possible to be; and the latter condition may be characterized by the fact that it is physically impossible for anyone in that state to be aware of anything. And yet, not being death, it remains a state of consciousness. In a word, the phenomenon of 'state of consciousness' is something other than one's being in a state which supports episodes of awareness or consciousness. As we saw in Chapter 2, it is to be explicated rather in terms of consciousness itself.

(b) Consciousnsss and the world

Then what *is* consciousness? Here, too, I restate a few of the conclusions of the previous chapter in a terminology which bears directly on the problem under investigation: notably, one cast in terms of 'domains' or 'worlds'.

Now we can at this preliminary stage go some little way towards giving an account of consciousness in such terms. Thus, consciousness is awareness of the world. And what is that? It is a state only to be found in entities of a certain kind: to wit, animals. Ostensively, it is the state that necessarily ceases when one is asleep or stunned. This state is not an awareness of any particular item or totality, even though it is an awareness of the world. For animals, as for the seeing eye, the centre of this awareness drops out of the world of which the animal is cognitively aware, but for thinking creatures it does not. Thus, for man consciousness of the world, waking consciousness, involves awareness both of that part of the world that consists in his own mental life, the 'inner world', and of all else that remains of the world, which we might call 'the outer world'. The outer world includes both one's own body and all the phenomena occurring in other minds and objects, and it would prejudice too many issues to call this 'the physical world'. Waking consciousness involves awareness of the here-and-now reality or presence of this 'outer' domain lying beyond one's mind.

Then notice that whereas we distinguish between 'awareness of the outer world' and 'awareness of the present specific contents of the outer world', the two concepts coalesce in the case of the inner world. There is simply no such thing as a consciousness of present inner reality in the absence of present empirical knowledge of occurrent contents, even though there is such a thing in the case of outer reality. At this point I shall content myself merely with drawing attention to the existence of this major asymmetry.

Then the contentious Cartesian-inspired theory which I recently proposed, can be cast in these terms. Thus: in self-conscious creatures consciousness of the world itself, including consciousness of the outer world, is possible only if consciousness of the inner world exists, under the aspect of truth, under adequate headings (where 'inner world' ranges over present experiences, cognitive attitudes, certain mental origins, etc.). More exactly, consciousness of the present specific phenomenal contents of the inner world, is a necessary condition of awareness both of the world itself, and of awareness of the outer world, which is to say of the domain lying beyond our own minds. And it must therefore also be a necessary condition of the making of limited empirical discovery, from the perspectival vantage point of oneself here and now, concerning the present specific phenomenal state of the outer world: what one might call 'the present state of the outer world' (from a limited egocentric vantage point).

A stronger claim, for which I shall not at present argue, is that adequate consciousness of the present specific phenomenal contents of the inner world is a *sufficient* condition of awareness of the world itself, including the outer world. My suspicion is that this interiorist theory is true: that adequate consciousness of the inner world in an experiencing subject is a logically necessary and sufficient condition of consciousness as such. That is, a proper cognitive consciousness of the inner world in an experiencing subject is logically equivalent to the obtaining of consciousness. While there are reasons for endorsing this theory, I shall not pursue them at this point. However, before I leave this topic, I must emphasize that this contentious theory is to be clearly distinguished from the relatively uncontentious doctrine that the determinants of consciousness are *wholly internal*. Whereas the contentious theory offers a *cognitive guarantee* for consciousness, the latter offers a *constitutive characterization*.

(c) A mental-structural account of consciousness of the world

I now offer a short structural account of self-conscious waking or consciousness of the world, hereafter referred to as 'w-consciousness', in which I put to use the above concepts and considerations.

My aim in setting out the issue in these terms is to prepare the way for the main enterprise of the present chapter: namely, displaying in functional terms the essential connection between impairment of self-awareness and impairment of w-consciousness. This analytical enterprise will involve me in reference to certain non-experiential sectors of the mind: to the knowledge-system, the value-system, properties and capacities which might be generic to the species (such as the capacity to see) or specific to the individual (such as having a visual history). A structural account anatomizes the mind into essentially interdependent parts, and indicates the relation between these parts and their contribution to the working of the mind in normal wakefulness. Then the relevance of this is, that it should reveal something of what goes into the constituting of self-conscious consciousness, and in particular the part played by self-knowledge.

What, in such structural terms, can one say of w-consciousness? W-consciousness is not an *unanalysable simple*, as one might think if one took it to be a distinctive idiosyncratic mental item akin (say) to a *quale*. Neither is it an empirically *deep* phenomenon, accessible only to scientific investigation. And it is not the *perception* of the world. It is an analysable mental state, a specific condition of the mind, for it must be emphasized that consciousness is an autonomous self-contained *interior phenomenon*. Roughly speaking, for persons but not for non-persons, w-consciousness is full and proper only if the mind is at once experiencing and in a properly rational state. This implies that it is a moment-by-moment condition of an experiencing mind in which (say) one's cognitive attitudes, one's desires and actions (etc.), are as a general rule rationally determined by one's sensory-system/knowledge-system/value-system/etc. (It will emerge in due course that the latter feature necessitates the additional property of 'insight', together with that of active mental self-direction or freedom).

Thus, w-consciousness is not the perception, through perceiving a local sector of it, of the world—as if the world was a special universal object. For one thing, perceptual contact with the environment is an insufficient condition of w-consciousness. But it is not a necessary condition either. W-consciousness cannot be the perception of reality, since it is consistent with complete unawareness of the present state of the outer world. Absolutely faulty sense-organs, total uncertainty concerning time and place, even complete ignorance as to one's identity, are consistent with perfect mental health and acute w-consciousness. Thus, w-consciousness is consistent with complete unawareness of the present state of the outer world. Then the (less) contentious theory which I am proposing (so far without demonstration) is, that there is one sector of the world, a domain which one cannot conceivably perceive, harbouring phenomena which are *in* the world, suitable awareness of which is a logically necessary condition of awareness of the world—and that is one's *inner world*! Now we have already commented on this matter a few pages back. If the claim is true, it reveals a significant Cartesian bias in the facts: indeed, a momentous asymmetry. The claim is that to be properly conscious of the outer world one must be properly conscious of the *present specific contents* of the inner world, but to be properly conscious of the inner world requires no veridical awareness of any of the present specific contents of outer reality. It is almost as if inner reality was all that mattered!

(d) Consciousness and epistemology

Let me now express the theory of consciousness just advanced in terms which for the moment lay an especial emphasis upon epistemology. I do so partly because the epistemological powers of consciousness are of great functional importance, but largely because the immediately ensuing discussion of the states of consciousness, sleep and trance, is concerned primarily with the epistemological properties of those two states. Then perhaps the first thing to emphasize is that consciousness is not a mode of epistemological success—as if the world was an object. Rather, consciousness is *correct epistemological posture* on the part of an experiencing subject. The conscious mind, even though it may discern nothing, listens *for* the truth of the outer, and indeed the inner world as well. The true nature of the outer and inner world is its ultimate commitment, its unfailing and genuine concern, a condition of mind involving a blind submission to the world in the determination of cognitive attitudes. In this state the mind bows down before reality. All of one's cognitive attitudes aim to conform to the one great and unique archetype: the world—an end that is accessible only via the path of reason.

However, we ought not to overemphasize the cognitive properties of consciousness at the expense of the property of self-determination. Far from being in opposition, these two traits depend upon one another. We have seen that consciousness instantiates a circle of mutually necessitating properties. It follows from this fact that other valid characterizations of consciousness must exist besides one cast in terms of epistemology. Thus, activeness of mind is part of the necessary picture: consciousness cannot be realized in sheer mental passivity, let us say of the kind encountered in dreaming. Consciousness, which is the correct epistemological posture on the part of an experiencing subject, is at the same time the condition of a rational creature actively engaged in thinking; and that in turn is the obtaining within of an overall condition of mental self-determination or mental freedom—which is a further necessary condition of present rationality. In short, w-consciousness consists in having a certain type of inner life: a continuity of (partially, but nonetheless overall) active experience such that the inner life at that point is suitably (i.e. rationally) responsive to reality. Then here in this formulation we have a summary statement of what it is for a self-conscious being to be conscious. And so, as we earlier observed, the criteria of consciousness prove to be wholly internal in character. W-consciousness, which is awareness of reality—it is a useful truism to affirm—is a (purely) psychological and (completely) internally validated state with a (merely) physical cause.

That concludes this short summary account of the state, consciousness. It was undertaken as a preliminary to the ensuing study of certain diverse states of consciousness. The epistemological properties of consciousness which we have just noted prove to be especially relevant to understanding what is going on in these several conditions.

4. Sleep and Trance, and the Cognitive Map of Reality

(a) The normal epistemological awareness of the outer world

At this point I offer an account of two related states of consciousness. I attempt to discover what is distinctive to sleep and hypnotic trance. I choose these two phenomena because investigation of them sheds light on the *specific cognitive powers* of waking consciousness, most especially upon its capacity to reveal what one might call 'the present state of the outer world'. Thus, neither of those states is identical with consciousness, and yet they cannot be all that far off: for example, they are each closer than the various forms of unconsciousness. Then it is illuminating to discover the respects in which they fall short of consciousness on a cognitive count. One feature of the mind which comes into prominence in this discussion, is the vital role played in the constitution of consciousness by one's belief/knowledge-system: what one might call our 'cognitive map of Reality'. This concept proves to be essential equipment when we come in the subsequent Sections 5–8 to examine two malformed examples of waking consciousness.

Common to both sleep and trance, and in contrast with the state unconsciousness, say coma or general anaesthesia, is that in each case the subject is not completely sealed off experientially from his surrounds. We have seen provisionally that epistemological posture is all-important to wakeful consciousness. Then in sleep and trance experiential epistemological links to the outer world still exist: the subject is capable of awareness of items in the environs. More, cognitive links of a limited sort remain. However, they are surely not of the kind that occur in waking.

What is missing? The answer to this question is the aim of the ensuing discussion. What is so special about a wakeful man's awareness of objects in the outer world? What sort of cognitive events occur in the conscious mind at such times?

It seems to me that something along the following lines takes place. We know that waking consciousness is consistent with the perceptual awareness of *absolutely nothing* in the ('outer' sector of) [the real] world. Nevertheless, such a perceptually empty consciousness, since it is awareness of the *world*, continually *orients* to the world: it carries the real world with it all the time, as the framework within which to site anything it happens perceptually to encounter. Waking consciousness continually has this framework 'at the ready' to receive any 'newcomer' from the 'outside': this is an essential property of waking consciousness; and should the perceptual drought be broken, that precisely is what will happen to the perceived particular. In a word, the item will be *realistically perceived*. Such a perceiving is realized, as will shortly emerge, through the distinctive use of one's cognitive map or representation of the world. And that is to say, through one's belief/knowledge-system of the moment. It is above all this perceptual phenomenon whose nature I hope to elucidate in what follows. I do so by the study of two contrasting conditions, states of consciousness in which matters are very different from the above, viz. sleep and trance.

Thus, in those few other states of consciousness in which it is possible to perceptually encounter items in the world—and notably the two states we are about to examine—one has no such realistic framework mentally at hand. Even if we manage to be perceptually aware of items in the world when in these states, our minds do not embed such phenomena in the real world. We either locate them in unreal worlds, or in something even less. For example, in the unreal imagined world of the dream or the unreal imagined world of the hypnotisee, or we might instead site such particulars in a mere locale or region, as perhaps happens to the perceptibles observed by somnambulists. We should try now to understand the cognitive and experiential properties of these perceptual encounters with items in the environment when we are in these non-wakeful states. This should bring us closer to discovering what more needs to be added to perceptual discovery of the environs if consciousness is to be realized. Thus, it should clarify what is the *natural epistemological harvest* of the 'correct epistemological posture' in relation to the outer world: that is, whatever naturally comes to cognition when consciousness avails itself of its essential capacity to reveal the present state of the outer world.

(b) The marks of sleep

(1) What is it about sleep that makes it the state it is? It cannot be that it is a state in which the subject is incapable of experience: the phenomenon of dreaming shows this. And neither can it be that a sleeper is incapable of perceptually experiencing items in the environment. The following makes that clear. One vital differentia of sleep is that it is a state of non-consciousness such that the sleeper is readily

rousable to consciousness through intensity of experience. Thus, a sleeper can experience sensations or emotions in a dream, and either experience has a tendency to cause waking that is proportional to its intensity. It follows that an openness to experience must be essential to sleep; and since loud noises often wake sleepers, it follows also that the experience might be of public phenomenal objects. Therefore sleepers are not as such cut off epistemologically from their environment. Here we have a major differentia between sleep and unconsciousness. Sleep unites non-consciousness with susceptibility to outer 'stimuli'. The functional advantages are obvious. It enables the system to shut down, yet be responsive to emergencies.

Now while sleep is consistent with the occurrence of experience and perception, it can occur in their complete absence. Sleep is a non-rational state in which the mind ceases to direct itself, indeed in which any inner life is almost entirely inactive and imaginative. And yet this cannot be altogether true. For we know that perception can occur during sleep, and that it can occasionally be active, say in somnambulism. Finally, we should note that it is possible that (largely unexperienced) sensation persists throughout sleep. In any case it seems certain that while for the most part the perceptual attention 'retreats into its shell', it can be contacted exceptionally by strong sensory 'stimuli' like (say) loud noises, which in turn show a propensity abruptly to terminate the state.

(2) What are the *cognitive powers* of sleepers? More specifically, what does a sleeper *discover* when he perceives items in his environment? A sleeper who screws up his eyes because of the light, is in shallow sleep and simultaneously aware of a light. One is inclined to add: but he is not aware of it *as* a light. But this could be false, for he might in a dream be aware of it as a light, indeed may even coincidentally be aware of it as the very light L that is now shining on him. Then what would he *discover* as a result of this perception? He cannot but know he now seemingly experiences L, since we know of our dreams at the time—under narrow headings. And it would be true also that he now experiences L. And yet it seems that he will not *discover* this truth. During sleep perceptions do not as a general rule instruct their owners about the environment. And so it can seem to a sleeper true that there is a light before him, and there can truly be a light before him, and he can both be aware of it and *as* what and when and where it is—and he will nonetheless generally not discover anything through these means about that light. Whereas this sleeper made both the *attentive and interpretational leap* from mind to objects in the environment, he did not through present perception make the additional *cognitive leap*. While this is not true of somnambulists, who make limited regional discoveries, it is true of most sleepers. Cognitively they are sealed off from their surrounds, as not experientially.

Notice how this cognitive isolation comes about. We know that the senses are not automatic avenues to truth: partly because of their sheer fallibility, but also because sense-perception is informative only when backed with *knowledge*. By itself sense-experience is cognitively barren. Then how is a sleeper to make the transition from sense-experience to knowledge? Well, it occasionally happens, though always with limitations. Yet even then it must take rational form. Whereas unselfconscious beings make the jump from perception to their peculiar brand of knowledge, largely because they are unthinking natural instruments for cognitively reading their ancestral environment, with the self-conscious the transition can only be accomplished rationally (when we are in a position to credit the evidence of our senses). Then generally both reason and the necessary fund of knowledge fail to come to the assistance of sleepers, and do not enable the inference. While a limited availability of both must be operative in somnambulists, who manage to discover merely local fact, nothing like this holds of most sleepers. It is in these ways that knowledge generally fails to follow upon the heels of sense-experience during sleep.

(3) Even though a sleeper occasionally perceives 'outer' phenomena for what they are, he is nonetheless for the most part cognitively cut off from his environs. But he is invariably epistemologically cut off from empirical reality or *the world itself*. His epistemological posture is unsuitable for discovering the present state of the world. The only world he is capable of constituting, the only world therefore of which he can be aware, is one assembled by his imagination, the unreal world of the dream. Two closely related features of his state of consciousness ensure this cognitive incapacity: lack of 'insight', and absence of rationality. Lack of 'insight' is apparent in his relation to dream experience, for although he knows when he dreams that he experiences, he fails to know he imagines, and while he knows in his dream what he believes, he has no idea why he does so believe. In short, an experiencing sleeper neither properly identifies, nor knows the origins of his experiences, nor has any hand in their occurrence. Such a relation to present experience is inconsistent with rationality. But non-rationality of state guarantees ignorance of empirical reality: it is not the epistemological posture of one attuned to the world: only the rational are in this condition. Thus, it cannot be the state of consciousness we call 'consciousness'. Then since he is not oriented to the world, he cannot bring the world as framework within which to embed whatever perceptions he may undergo in this state. And so his perceptions cannot be what we described as 'realistic perceptions'.

Then what goes to constitute an 'awareness of the present state of the world'? In particular, what part do one's normal cognitive capacities plays in its constitution? The hypnotic trance proves to be instructive in this regard. In negative manner it manages to point up something of what goes to make up the vastly familiar situation in which our cognitive and perceptual powers are normally at work. And it sheds significant light on the nature of 'realistic perception'.

(c) Hypnotic consciousness is a merely regional consciousness

As with the sleeper, we might at first suppose that a deeply hypnotized person cannot be aware of objects in his environment, and here too we would be wrong: he is not attentively sealed off from his surrounds. A person in an hypnotic trance is perhaps continuously conscious of the hypnotizer, and is certainly continually perceptually conscious of his voice. Indeed, unlike most sleepers an hypnotisee is not wholly sealed off cognitively from his environment. Thus, he makes perceptual discoveries concerning occupants of that sector of the world: for example, learns that the hypnotizer is saying to him of the table that it is an automobile. More, unlike most sleepers he embeds the environmental objects of which he is perceptually aware in a putative domain or world. And yet that world cannot be the real world, since it has been assembled merely by his imagination at the behest of a 'voice'— even though its occupants are probably set down in real physical space; for like the sleeper the hypnotizee is not conscious of the world, since he too is not awake. His consciousness of those real objects in the real world, a consciousness of them under the aspect of truth, must be a limited or merely regional or (as one might say) 'non-connective' consciousness. This fact ensures that it cannot be a *realistic consciousness* of those objects. The following makes this clear.

Now the ordinary waking or realistic consciousness of objects may be described as 'connective' in the following sense. It is consciousness of its object as falling under a limitless number of headings which are drawn from one's knowledge-system. Consider a normal waking perceptual consciousness of some item in the environmment. The whole fabric of the knowledge-system at one stroke *makes possible*, and *assimilates* as a further strand in that knowledge-system, the knowledge conveyed by the sense-data encountered on this occasion. Thus, while 'orientation knowledge' (of one's situation in space and time, etc.) is necessary for the acquisition of knowledge from perception, it is itself impossible without further knowledge, such as knowledge of places, which in turn requires knowledge of other matters, and so on. And so the new knowledge must be ensconced in the knowledge-system with the assistance of whole sectors of that system, and it is this assimilation that situates the new object of consciousness under an infinite set of accessible headings. For example, when I see St Peter's Cathedral I see a sense-datum, and generally know I am experiencing a veridical sight of St Peter's; and simultaneously know that I see what is (say) remote from the star Sirius, even though I may never before, and not even at that moment, have had the thought. And there is *no end* to the number of such realistic headings under which I may be said to see St Peter's on any such occasion. And this is to say that I see St Peter's, related in a known way to an orientation-standpoint of which I am aware, as embedded in a reality of which I and any other self-conscious creature know an infinite amount. With self-consciousness, the region mentally containing the object of awareness expands to infinity.

But the hypnotizee, in being conscious of the voice as of the hypnotizer, is not conscious of that voice *as of* one person amongst others, located at just this time and place, in a domain more or less without limit. Indeed, that the sound is heard as of the hypnotizer is in a sense the *ultimate heading* under which it is experienced. In effect, for the hypnotizee ultimate reality at that moment lies in the personality of another. Then since that other mind is not Reality, the subject must be in a trance. The *whole fabric of reality* as normally understood by the hypnotizee, which is to say his *knowledge-system*, is not at that moment brought into cognitive connection with the experience, so that his experience of a voice and of a person cannot be realistic awarenesses, it is not an experience of them as sited in the real world. Instead, both voice and person are in his mind embedded in a seeming reality of the voice's own devising, albeit one a stage closer to reality than that of sleepers, since physical space and real objects are generally identified and used in the constitution of that world.

Thus, for the hypnotizee the world is for-the-hypnotizer, since for the hypnotizee the character, and indeed the very existence of the items in the world of which he is seemingly aware, are directly determined by the utterances of the hypnotizer, who almost commands them into being. And therefore the hypnotizer must be the essential mediator linking the hypnotizee with the world of which he is putatively conscious. While the hypnotizee possesses a knowledge-system, whose contents are largely inaccessible at that moment, that which his knowledge-system represents, which is the real world, he now takes to be as the hypnotizer's utterances say they are. He takes reality to be as he is told that it is. This totally non-rational determination of cognitive attitudes proves the hypnotizee cannot be conscious of the world. And therefore he is not awake. But he cannot be asleep either: for sleep is such that the sleeper can be returned to consciousness through intensity of experience, whereas the hypnotizee resumes the normal epistemological posture only through the *meaning* conveyed by certain select auditory sensations, say through a command. Thus, he is in a trance.

(d) Deductions regarding the cognitive requirements of consciousness

(1) So much for the moment for the delimitation and characterization of these two states of consciousness. What may we deduce concerning consciousness itself from these observations? Thus, what of an occurrent phenomenal nature do we require if we are to ensure the presence of consciousness in a subject? Present experience is a necessity; but bearing in mind the experiences of dreamers and hypnotizees, it must be an insufficiency. Present sense-perceptual experience cannot be necessary—although the *possibility* of such is surely necessary; but that too must be insufficient, when one remembers the perceptions of hypnotizees, somnambulists, and sleepers. Again, the perception of present physical realities *as* what they are, is likewise insufficient. Indeed, perception that non-accidentally identifies its object and apprises one of its existence, is also not enough, as both somnambulist and hypnotizee demonstrate. Finally, perception that achieves all of the above, and manages veridically to site its object in a continuous sector of spatio-temporal reality which in turn it also perceives and identifies, is still insufficient; and once again the

example of somnambulism is instructive. Something more than all of the above is required if we are to ensure the presence of the state in question. And so something more if we are to be credited with contact with the outer world, and with perceptual experience which reflects that contact.

(2) While perception is not necessary for consciousness, when it occurs in consciousness it has a character which suffices to ensure the presence of the supporting state of consciousness. Thus, it must in the first place be capable of generating knowledge of the reality of its object, under the aspect of truth. And it must be an awareness that sites its object *in a world*. More to the point and centrally, it must site its object in the *one real world*, in contrast to the worlds of dreamers or hypnotizees. Then this property implies that typically the object will find itself related in a limitless number of ways to multitudinous other objects, in accordance with the capacity of the knowledge-system to generate an infinite number of headings which are true of the object of knowledge and known by the subject to be so. In conscious minds links of this kind are set up between the knowledge-system and the objects of perception.

Now the belief/knowledge-system operative in the conscious normally possesses the further vitally important property of *internal consistency*. While the cognitive system need not be a *true* representation of the world, it usually for the most part is consistent in character: that is, it does not normally exhibit the kind of gross internal contradictions found in the organized delusional worlds of the drastically insane. The world cannot but be consistent with itself, and *bona fide* ('well-formed') representations seek to reproduce this property. In short, the cognitive portrait of the world that one harbours in one's mind, whether correct or incorrect, must in general at least be a *viable representation*.

The cognitive representation need not be accurate. It is consistent with consciousness that the belief/knowledge-system be flawed in all sorts of major ways. However, three basic conditions of consciousness, involving the belief/knowledge-system, are necessities. The first is, the *very existence* of a belief-system: without some kind of a cognitive map of the world, however simple, intentionality could not inhere in a mind, and in its absence consciousness is an impossibility. The second is, that the cognitive representation inherent in the mind must truly aim at the real world, whether or not it is itself true; and in general this requires that it be in large measure pervaded by the aforementioned features of rationality and consistency. And this in addition thirdly implies that the principle of admission for novel beliefs must be rational in type; which is to say, one of rational consistency with the present contents of the belief-system.

The second and third of the above features were absent in the two states of consciousness discussed above. They must have been part of the reason why those states fell short of wakeful consciousness. And they were in addition part of the reason why the consciousness of particular items in the environment was in those states not a 'realistic consciousness', and so not part of a consciousness of 'the present phenomenal state of the outer world'. Thus, the objects given in perception to a sleeper or hypnotizee are not automatically brought by the subject's mind into rational connection with his cognitive map of reality. We look to find these features in wakeful consciousness.

(3) The discussion of these two states, neither of which exemplify consciousness nor *a fortiori* deformed examples of that phenomenon, nor *a fortiori* also the connection between such deformation and failure of 'insight', was undertaken with a view to bringing into prominence the cognitive equipment which is put to use in consciousness, and in particular when we make intuitional contact with the 'outer world'. There can be no doubt that the epistemological function of consciousness is of central importance to the state, and that this function is especially manifest in our empirical perceptual transactions with the environment. When we return now at this point to the central topic of this chapter, namely the close connection between 'insight' and consciousness, we will find that these cognitive characteristics loom large.

5. Disturbed Consciousness (α): Drunken Consciousness

I come now to an enterprise directly bearing upon the central thesis of this chapter. Namely, the attempt to connect the character of wakeful consciousness with the character of the 'insight' prevailing at the time. I have chosen to discuss two states which reveal disturbances in both, and in each case hope to explain the correspondence. I select these two states because they exemplify the positive and negative modes of impairment. I begin by examining the mind of one in a state of relatively extreme drunkenness.

It will emerge in the course of the ensuing discussion that drunkenness must be a less than fully rational state, that it involves deficiencies in 'insight', and that the prevailing consciousness is inevitably impaired to a degree which matches those deficiencies and the intoxication which is their cause. The impairment in question is of the kind *atrophy*, and it stems from a feature which typifies drunkenness: namely, *omission of the relevant (requisite, pertinent)*. Thus, the malformation of consciousness is born neither of mental confusion, nor of delusive imaginings; it does not arise out of mental fragmentation, or loss of mental structures; its source, we shall see, is of a more negative character. Roughly, it comes into being through the subject's failing to utilize his mental resources. This obtains in the determination of both cognitive attitudes and actions, both from the point of view of evidence and valuation. The upshot in the extreme is that rational determination and self-awareness decline, along with much else. The nadir of drunkenness is a state in which the cognitive-system, indeed mental meanings themselves, have all but evaporated from the mind! This extreme phenomenon highlights some of the features that consciousness normally involves—through omission. It seems to me that a study of the modes of atrophy manifest in this extreme case sheds light on the situation obtaining in a properly conscious mind.

(a) The mental mechanics of drunken unintentional action

(1) Let us begin by examining the determination of cognitive attitudes and acts in the drunken state. Now we sometimes say of people, in a more or less serious sense which characterizes a *state of mind*, that they 'do not know what they are doing': a description which questions both the rationality and state of consciousness of some agent-subject. For example, the hypnotizee agent, the somnambulist, the psychotic assassin, and perhaps in addition the very drunken subject. This already suggests the possibility that drunkenness interferes with consciousness.

It is clarifying first of all to set down a relatively harmless sense in which the intoxicated are ignorant of what they are doing. Thus, drunkards perform more than their share of unintentional acts, and this fact determines a rather uninteresting sense in which they 'do not know what they are doing'. Such a characteristic is compatible with full rational self-determination, imputes no unawareness of intentional acts, and leaves consciousness unscathed. Drunken unintentional acts derive primarily from drunken omissions, such as the failure to think, remember, or notice. For example, the drunkard fails to remember to turn off the tap, and unintentionally floods the bathroom. Or fails to notice that his sleeve, as he reaches for the whisky, is contacting a row of exquisite coffee cups, and so fails to notice that he is knocking over the cups, spilling the coffee, and smashing priceless objects.

(2) Let us attempt to lay bare the mental mechanics of these unintentional acts. We shall see that they arise out of nothing more untoward than a breakdown in the normal accessibility of items in the knowledge-system. But what *is* that normal cognitive accessibility? It is, I think, advisable that we answer this question before attempting to give an account of cognition in minds in a state of inebriation. So at this point I shall try to say what of a cognitive nature would in all probability happen in the mind of a sober person who finds himself in the very same setting as our intoxicated protagonist (say, a particular drawing-room in London in 1900). This should help us to characterize the latter's cognitive processes.

We shall assume that lodged somewhere in the sober subject's knowledge-system lies the general item of knowledge (k) that in any drawing-room whose description and setting *matches* that of this drawing-room, precious objects are prone to stand on *just such a table* as that on which the whisky now rests. As a result of this general knowledge, upon arriving in that room the subject doubtless at that very moment acquires the additional indexical knowledge (k′) that precious objects are prone to stand *on this very table*.

How does this happen? Now much of our knowledge-system is expressible in tensed location-sentences which refer to times and places variously close to here and now, e.g. 'Napoleon stood on those very heights on 2 December 1805.' In addition, some recently acquired cognitions—'I arrived by cab a moment ago', 'Yesterday I was let out of prison'—make direct use of ('orientational') knowledge (call it k″) of our *present* situation in space and time. But one other cognition actually *is* that very k″, e.g. 'I am now in a room in Mayfair, at point p_1 and time t_1, in the year 1900.' Then in the present case the acquisition of the indexical knowledge k′ (concerning the properties of the table and objects before one) was *made possible* in the sober mind through the *accessibility* of the two independent items, k and k″, lodged at that moment in the subject's knowledge-system: the knowledge k″ of one's present situation managing to give to the quite general knowledge k a point of application to the world. But k′ was *made actual* through the mind's *mentally linking* k and k″.

What is this 'linking'? Is it an inference? Is it an event? Because, from the point of view of sheer content, k & k″ → k′, it might seem to be both; but it is difficult to see how it could be. The problem is, that we are threatened with an unending multiplication of events, and I am reminded of nothing so much as the multiplication of images in a kaleidoscope—on the occasion of a single physical change! What happens in the present situation is, that the general knowledge k manages to find application to the world through the offices of the specific orientational indexical k″, so that one now acquires the present indexical k′ through acquiring k″, in the context of a recollected k. Then I suggest that the acquisition of orientational k″ is the *very same event* as the acquisition of k′, indeed is the same event as acquiring knowledge with multiple object-contents. This automatic multiplication of the objects of knowledge is what I am calling 'linkage'—and is the same property as that already encountered in the discussion of hypnotic trance and dubbed 'the connect-ive character of conscious awarenesses'. Thus, learning that one is in a Mayfair drawing-room usually *is*, for those who know Mayfair drawing-rooms in the year 1900, learning that one is in a room prone to harbour select and costly objects. It need not be so, but when it is, it is through 'linkage'; which is to say through taking the present object to fall under a certain complex characterization (fed by the knowledge-system). Then this discovery cannot be distinct from one's awareness of the situational object, else we should need to suppose that a massive splintering in our awareness of objects was part of the order of nature.

This account of the acquisition of k′ is forced upon us. Since each event of knowledge-acquisition can hardly be accompanied by a simultaneous infinity of distinct events of knowledge-acquisition, even though an infinity of novel descrip-tions apply, there either was *no* event of k′-acquisition or that event *was* the acquisi-tion of k″. But there *must* be an event of k′-acquisition, since the acquisition of k′ was a change that happened in time. And therefore the description of this k′ must, in a mind in a suitably sober state, be given by a permissible redescribing of k″. Therefore it is possible, indeed it is usual, that k″ occurring in one for whom k is accessible, *is* k′ occurring in that mind. Thus, no inference occurs, and the acqui-sition of each new item of knowledge cannot be the acquisition of infinitely many new items of knowledge. And yet an infinity of different descriptions is available, owing to the existence, accessibility, and 'linkedness' of the knowledge-system.

But for the drunkard, who we shall assume to have momentarily *forgotten* k, k″

was installed in the absence of k'. And so he failed to expect the presence of nearby precious possibly fragile objects. Consequently, it was with coarse vigour that he reached for the whisky, and unintentionally smashed a precious array of objects. This brief description has shown how drunken unintentional acts, acts one does not know one is doing, arise out of the mind losing its normal contact with certain relevant items in the knowledge-system. It was not that this subject drew the wrong inferences, that his reasoning powers were at fault: it was rather that a particular item of knowledge lodged in his mind proved to be inaccessible. Then despite the fact that his state of consciousness is so far more or less unimpaired, his sense of reality is already visibly under siege. The world begins to close in around the seriously inebriated.

(b) The mental mechanics of sense-impression and belief formation

(1) While k is temporarily forgotten, thanks to the alcohol in the blood continuously coursing through his brain, much in his knowledge-system remains accessible, including new arrivals. Now at any particular moment it is primarily through perception that knowledge of physical reality is acquired, and these events of knowledge-acquisition are themselves conditioned by the knowledge-system. Accordingly, we should I think complement the above account of the processing that new knowledge (such as k″) normally receives at the hands of the knowledge-system (e.g. by k), with a short account of the determination of new cognitive attitudes through sense-experience, as it occurs in both normal and drunken consciousness. This is because my main concern at this point is the characterization of drunken epistemology. I hope to reveal the type of the depletions in this fundamental power of consciousness which are to be found in this state.

The sense of sight, in providing visual sensations for the drunkard, seems to him to present the spectacle of a flask of whisky, and correctly and with justice he takes it do so. But *why* do those patches of colour in the visual field seem to present a decanter and not a laboratory container? Why does he not seem to see a *rhinoceros*? In part this is determined by his knowledge of the relative distribution of these objects in London rooms, in part by his previous experience of these and other such items, in part by the internal character of his visual field, and perhaps also through innate factors. In some mysterious way which I shall not here explore a visual impression arises out of all this.

One thing of note is, that even though mental causation is involved in the genesis of the experience, those mental agencies cannot function as *one's reasons*, for one bears no responsibility for how-it-looks-to-one-as-if, and one has no immediate insight into the origins of one's visual impression. Nevertheless, knowledge of appearances and of distribution undoubtedly plays a part in this transaction: after all, with a wholly different cognitive background, the experience would be different. Then for the drunkard, for whom sectors of the knowledge-system are unavailable, this can result in his gaining the *wrong* visual impression. Think of the character in E. A. Poe's story who, upon seeing what was in fact an insect close to his eye on the window pane, seemed to see a dragon coming up the valley! Here we see how the influence of an inappropriate cognitive posture might lead to the wrong visual impression.

(2) How do we manage to pass from perceptual impression to belief? And how from belief to knowledge? The question, 'Why does he think he sees what he seems to see?', is always legitimate, and can never be brushed aside, however obvious the answer. In suitable circumstances, which are at once proper viewing conditions and plausible containers of the seemingly seen, we *credit the evidence of our senses* (as English revealingly puts it). That is, we identify what it looks to us as if we see and what we think we see. Yet there is no binding necessity for any example of seeing to import knowledge, and it does so only when we are and think we are in a position to trust the evidence of our senses. Of course, this is pretty standardly. But we have always to take due account of the relevant ocular and extra-bodily circumstances when we say 'I see and therefore I know'. We must *know* we are in a situation where we can trust the sense of sight, if, on top of seeing, we are to both know that we see and know what is there. And this is not difficult. But it depends upon one's knowing one is not placed in a truly exceptional situation. In a situation where one can rely on nothing, the senses of necessity fail to convey knowledge. Knowledge is the necessary soil out of which empirical knowledge is bred.

(c) A general account of drunken epistemology

(1) In sum, our 'drunk' enters a Mayfair drawing-room, and generally misunderstands and misbehaves. His eyes are doubtless open as he staggers into the room, and his consciousness is flooded with sense-experience. A non-temporal developmental hierarchy from (1) sensation to impression, (2) impression to orientational cognitive attitude (k″), (3) from k″ and k through linkage to k′, k′ being an embellishment upon k″—all this is the norm. But in the drunken state each stage is prone to misfire, due to nothing more faulty in the general working of the mind than the inaccessibility at that moment of certain items of knowledge. The hierarchy in question takes the following form, to each stage of which we append the corresponding drunken aberration.

(1) The path from sensation to impression is non-inferential, since the reasons for a thing's looking a certain way are not one's *own*. Yet items in the knowledge-system play a part in the determination of the impression out of sensation. Then the inaccessibility of some of those items of knowledge can lead the subject to form the wrong impression, e.g. he sees a flask of water as gin-filled. (2) The path from impression to orientational cognitive attitude (k″) is inferential. Thus, he knows he is now in a room because he knows he now sees a room, which in turn he knows through knowing the character of his impression in known circumstances, and so on. Whole sectors of the knowledge-system cooperate in making possible this novel item of perceptual knowledge, which simultaneously they incorporate. Then the

inaccessibility of certain items of knowledge can lead one to make the wrong deduction, e.g. he thinks he is in his own quarters. (3) Finally, the immediate orientational knowledge (k″), itself made possible by the assimilating knowlege-system, is in normal assimilation linked with the whole of the knowledge-system, and this brings into existence a limitless array of descriptions of that orientational knowledge. Then this state of affairs can be obstructed through the inaccessibility of certain items in the knowledge-system; and what that implies is that, although k″ comes into being, k′ may well not. He experiences the setting as utterly commonplace and plebeian.

(2) And that concludes my discussion of drunken epistemology. A word now concerning the relevance of that discussion. My aim in discussing the state of drunkenness is to support the general contention that failure of self-knowledge in the conscious is coextensive with deformation in consciousness, and because I believe that drunkenness exemplifies this truth in one significant mode, viz. that of negativity. Then the first thing to do is show how consciousness suffers in this state. Accordingly, I chose to examine an area of mental life in which one's state of consciousness tends to be readily manifest, namely epistemology. After all, we have characterized consciousness as 'correct epistemological posture in an experiencing subject'. Then in the discussion of drunken epistemology we can see at close quarters how the world-representation suffers in drunkenness, and thus how consciousness is already 'under siege': we see consciousness begin to 'shrink' from the inside, we see the distinctive mode in which deformation is realized, viz. atrophy. But in addition we discover in those epistemological peculiarities the distinctive path via which this deformation is realized: namely, through the negative means of dis-use of the mental resources necessary for the instantiation of consciousness. Here we have the special interest of the state drunkenness. It lies in the distinctive type of the deformation, and the special way in which it is realized. And the overall interest resides in what this tells us about normal consciousness: it confirms in the concrete our earlier very general characterization of consciousness as a state which marshalls the central powers of the mind. Filling in the depletions, we gain a picture of the plenitude.

(d) The behaviour of the drunkard in the light of his value-system

(1) There is a different non-cognitive road leading to the same destination as the above: that is, to a state wherein consciousness is malformed in the mode of atrophy through the mental effects of inebriation. Thus, one measure of consciousness in an experiencing subject is the extent to which *rationality* holds sway in the mind. Now a decline of rationality manifests its presence, not just in epistemology and the formation of cognitive attitudes generally, but practically in the way one carries on in the world. Drunkenness is an obvious exemplification of this truth. Its expression in action is patently flawed from a prudential, and sometimes also a moral point of view.

And so for the moment I leave drunken epistemology, and look instead at the practical drunken response to its cognitive findings, and drunken behaviour generally. Here irrationality is evident. One has only to think of the non-rational behaviour so characteristic of this state. As a general rule, a man who is drunk is less inhibited than usual: the forces both of caution and self-control tend to be in retreat. Now ordinarily self-control is exercised either prudentially in the interest of desired goals, or else in the name of certain *values*. Then why do acts which are counter to one's values occur more readily in the intoxicated? In part perhaps through the intensity of certain liberated desires, in part through unawareness of external constraints, but frequently it is through an act's no longer seeming objectionable. This shift in 'moral colour' can stem from the temporary espousal of novel values, but characteristically it results from the *temporary inaccessibility* of one's actual values. That is, the act is no longer seen under the proscriptive heading which those values normally impose, so that in this state the normal linkage between the value-system and one's judgement tends temporarily to be severed—with predictable consequences in one's behaviour.

An example illustrates this loss. Thus, some may wish to say, of some very violent and very drunken man, that 'he does not know what he is doing'. What they might mean is: the man we all know this person to be is one who abhors such acts, and that man does not know that he himself is behaving in this fashion. However, this claim is patently false. There is no cognitive or *identifying heading* fitting this act of which this subject is ignorant, and all one could legitimately mean is that there exists an *evaluative heading*, say 'act that I abhor', which fits this act and eludes its agent. This is indeed an ignorance, one typical of extreme drunkenness, but scarcely an ignorance of *what* he is doing. He need harbour no delusions on empirical matters of fact. The ignorance in question arises through his failing to apply his system of values at their point of application. Then if such behaviour can be deemed irrational, it seems that through the drunken trait of omission on a moral count a person can find himself launched into non-rational action. Here we see how a failure to utilize a basic mental resource, one's 'table of values', can push a person towards irrationality. In sum, when it comes to the determination of action, the state of drunkenness shows a tendency to lead to irrationality along paths which match the characterization of drunkenness as involving the failure to utilize one's mental resources: in the present case, one's moral and prudential values.

(2) But the origins of the irrationality of drunken behaviour range farther afield. An example illustrates what I have in mind. Thus, it is clear that a state in which one drives cars as drunkards do, can hardly be fully rational. Then as we have just noted, this is in part because the gathering inaccessibility of one's mental resources makes its presence felt on issues of value and prudence. However, we know also that in the normal course of events *self-control* is exercised in the name of these standards, and requires the capacity merely in thought to contemplate one's projected behaviour and freely to choose whether it shall see the light of day. And such a capacity is

surely also in decline in drunkenness. The typical self-conscious power of standing over oneself, of making oneself an object in thought for oneself, and relating to that being as a judicial force, seems in this state to be in partial abeyance. The powers of self-determination, and thus of freedom, are in partial abeyance.

In sum, the act of driving in the typical drunken manner proves to be non-rational through two forms of neglect. Not in flying defiantly in the face of reason, but merely in failing to be performed in a spirit of due evaluative self-consciousness: the agent failing to see it under certain normative aspects, so that it seems neither dangerous nor harmless, neither wise nor foolish. But the neglect is more extensive than this. It embraces in addition the use of the power of free choice and self-control: the subject failing to mentally stand back self-consciously and distance himself from the deed. The internal division of the self, into agent and self-supervisor, here grows a trifle blurred, and this is what one would expect when a subject's values are in recession. On both counts the sway of reason is lessened; and, since reason and consciousness keep close company, consciousness suffers.

(e) The end of the road

So much for the moral and prudential mode of realizing the generally non-rational character of intoxication. But the cognitive and epistemological aberrations already investigated lead in the end to a similar condition. For it would be an error to suppose that irrationality is confined to moral and prudential valuation, and that the mere inaccessibility of elements of the knowledge-system in epistemology ('mere forgetfulness') cannot disrupt rational processes of thought. To be prone to forget blindingly relevant facts concerning empirical matters of fact, is to ensure that one is less aware of the true character of one's environment, and less able to 'think straight' on such questions. Moreover, the inaccessibility of values spreads beyond moral and prudential issues to standards of empirical evidence, and laxity intrudes. As a result, a drunken subject's cognitive attitudes towards factual matters tend increasingly to be non-rationally determined. Rather, they are marked increasingly by 'subjectivity': the wish or need tending to be father to the belief.

Then with the general decline in rationality consciousness inevitably suffers in the way we glimpsed in incipient form in the epistemological processes which take place in common or garden examples of drunkenness. If one extrapolates from that situation to an absolute extreme of the state, the deformation becomes marked and undeniable. It is not that drunken consciousness tends towards the condition of mere animal consciousness. For one thing that is an impossibility in any being who has transcended the merely animal state, and in any case a drunkard's cognitive representation of the world is in recess. And neither does the drunken mind support a limited regional consciousness, of the kind occurring in somnambulism, for he either sees objects as set down in boundless space and time, or else in more extreme states scarcely individuates them at all. Finally, this state does not involve a turning away from the world to some other phantastic world assembled by his imagination.

The deformation of consciousness that it involves is different from all of the above. What rather the drunken condition sets in motion is a drift in a wholly different direction. Now we know that the absolutely fundamental feature of mental meaning or intentionality could not so much as exist without a cognitive representation of the world, for in that case the mental realm would have nothing to 'aim at'. Then the more inebriated one is the more that representation is inaccessible, being part of a general condition of forgetfulness. Accordingly, the drunker a subject, the less he can be conscious of the world. And so the drift must be towards an almost wholly impoverished state of consciousness which barely differs from sheer unconsciousness. He must tend towards a drunken near-unawareness of the world, and so towards a drunken near-unconsciousness: the absolutely extreme condition of drunken stupor ('*stupor extremis*'). (This is not the same as 'passing out'.) So much for the deformations of consciousness attendant upon the state.

(f) Summary

(1) I draw this part of the discussion to a close with a summary account. The claim is that severe drunkenness is a less than fully rational state, that this entails impairment in the state of consciousness, and that closely associated with both conditions is the characteristic upon which I have concentrated much attention, impairment in self-knowledge.

The impairment in consciousness is of the form atrophy, and arises through a property of drunken mental life which increases in degree as the extent of intoxication waxes. Namely, the failure to employ one's mental resources. My suggestion has been that the phenomenon of dis-use, a sort of 'fleecing' of the mind of its assets, culminates in a state of stupor in which next to no mental resources are utilized and next to no consciousness realized. The theory I have been advancing is that the drunken impairment of consciousness arises not out of confusion, not out of delusion, not through misuse of the imagination, not through the destructuring of structural relations constitutive of consciousness, but through purely negative means: the failure to employ one's powers. Consciousness, which makes possible the marshalling of the central powers of the mind, depends simultaneously upon the accessibility and utilization of certain mental powers. In the state under consideration this is significantly under-realized.

It is worth noting how these various omissions come about. Some failures are 'original' to the state (like aberrations of memory), while others are derivatives therefrom (such as the incapacity to execute complex intentional action). Thus, intentional action necessitates beliefs concerning the arena of action, and it is along this avenue that the drunken tendency to forget impedes the capacity to intentionally act. It is not that the will is paralysed in the grossly inebriated. Rather, the intentional will tends to be *blinded*. The condition of drunken *extremis* is one in which, while the will may be available, it is given nothing to accomplish; indeed, knows of no *status quo* or point of embarkation. While the realities of space tend in this extremity to be obscured in forgetfulness, the even more important realities of past and future prove equally inaccessible. Accordingly, mere sub-intentional action, so to say senseless fidgeting, is all that is open to the will: active experience in the absence of all meaning. And a comparable loss of cognition leads in *extremis* towards uninterpreted sense-experience: sheer sense without intentionality, perceptual impressions that travel no farther than 'lights and colours' (Berkeley's 'proper and immediate objects'). If I am right, the most extreme of drunken stupors is a state in which experience, sensation, and perhaps also action persist, in the absence of meaning: a small pool of awareness in which nothing can be discerned, a circle pointing nowhere beyond itself! This must be on the edge of sheer unconsciousness.

The dissimilarities to sleep and hypnotic trance are significant. Whereas experience without meaning and order is the asymptotic end of drunken consciousness, the state of sleep is such that experience, which might be in total suspension, is equally capable of taking the meaningful and structured form of dreaming. One could express the matter thus: that whereas the dreamer is 'lost in his dream', the mind of the grossly intoxicated is simply 'nowhere', for the imagination which might construct such an escape from reality is in this state incapacitated along with much else, and the mind is incapable of representing a world of any kind. Meanwhile the hypnotizee—who as naturally supports experience as he does not, and in whom imagination and intentionality are accessible—passively permits his imagination to be utilized by another as a tool in the arbitrary construction of a world that is noteworthy for its impoverishment and unreality. Yet despite these flaws, here too sense and order persist.

(2) What of insight, which was after all the topic? Plainly, it does not obtain in *stupor extremis*: not because misreading of one's mind is in the ascendant at such a point, but because the decline of interiority is so wholesale that mental causation barely has a subject-matter to govern. However, this nadir is the limiting situation in a steady impairment of both consciousness and insight. On the way to this extreme, rationality inevitably declines as the processes of atrophy progress, in part because of the inaccessibility of one's standards of behaviour as well as those governing empirical judgement (determination by inclination being increasingly the rule). This eclipsing of reason is invariably accompanied by failure in insight. Irrational belief never wears either its character or origin upon its sleeve, nor for that matter does irrational action, which often enough wallows in self-justification. And so one must be ignorant of the true mental determinants of these less than rational phenomena. Then in all these cases the failure of insight takes the simple and negative form of *omission*, rather like that sector of the mind described by Freud which is not so much 'repressed' as circumvented or never 'visited' by consciousness: the drunken person relating in a similar fashion to the determinants of his

beliefs and deeds. In any case, insight into one's own mind declines along with con-sciousness. Thus, extreme drunkenness leads to impaired consciousness and impaired self-awareness.

6. Disturbed Consciousness (β)(1): Insane Consciousness and Freedom

(a) Introduction

The extremity of drunken consciousness is the negative mode of failed insight and impaired consciousness, the degenerative case whose motto might be 'nothing venture nothing gain', awareness of reality draining away out of the mind through the failure to utilize its resources. I turn now to the positive mode: the state in which the impairment of awareness of reality arises out of mental malfunction. That is, through misuse rather than dis-use of mental powers. My interest in this phenom-enon, as in the other examples, is as a lead to understanding what obtains in a prop-erly formed state of self-conscious consciousness or waking. The close association between well-formedness and insight provides a clue to the functional situation prevailing in the minds of the conscious. In particular, the specific way things go wrong when insight is faulty, helps to elucidate the nature of the contribution made by insight to the inherence of the state. My suspicion is, that it makes its contribu-tion at a relatively deep level.

The kind of disturbance of consciousness of which I am thinking is to be found in certain psychotic or drug-induced conditions (whose specific features I delineate in due course). These conditions determine a state of waking in which certain important mental capacities fail to be properly operative: notably, the capacities for self-knowledge, rationality, and the power of self-determination. Such failings cannot but lead to a deformation in the prevailing state of waking consciousness. Now unlike in drunken consciousness we do not in these aberrant phenomena encounter a dearth of mental meanings, gross breakdown of access to the knowledge-system, the fading away of the capacity for intentional action, etc.: by and large, these are intact. Rather, what seems to happen is that the pro-ducts of the imagination tend to invade the experienced world. Not, of course, wholly, as happens in the dream, else we would be faced with a *loss* rather than *impairment* of consciousness, but to a significant degree. Indeed, it is almost as if the subject inhabits and acts within his own dream—as one 'possessed', almost as if reality mutated there and then into something phantastic. In a word, misuse of the imagination is at least part of the trouble: it leads to a disturbed state of waking consciousness in which (as we say) the subject 'does not know what he is doing'.

It is interesting that we characterize a disturbed state of awareness in terms of *action* and our *ignorance* in relation to action. Why? I can only surmise as to the answer. But the following considerations seem to me relevant. A disturbed state of waking consciousness remains, for all its flaws, a state of waking consciousness. Now consciousness is a condition in which the mind of the subject is necessarily active, and the body at least 'on active alert' (even if supine in a hammock). Indeed, the natural 'output' of a mind in this condition is action, including typically physical action of some kind or another: pure inertia of the physical will being somewhat unusual in waking consciousness. Thus the aforementioned characterization of the impaired state of awareness is cast in terms of an ignorance of what must be the *natural expression* and probably also the *functional goal* of consciousness. It is given in terms of a *failure of natural insight* in relation to this pivotal phenomenon. It seems likely that this is no accident. We have been able to demonstrate a close connection between loss of insight and impairment of consciousness. What more natural than that the ignorance should extend to the functional goal of the state? In any case, my immediate concern is to discover what precisely the ignorance is, in relation to one's own actions, that obtains when one is in this 'positive mode' of disturbed consciousness. What failure of insight exists on this count when consciousness is something less than itself in this way?

(b) The state of 'not knowing what one is doing'

(1) What does it mean to say of a person that his mental state is such that he 'does not know what he is doing'? It cannot mean what literally it might appear to mean. Absolutely anyone might perform acts whose character is in part hidden from themselves, either because what they do has unknown unintended effects, or because the arena of action is not what they took it to be. In both situations there is an intended act which the subject knows he performs, and an unintended act of which he knows nothing, but in neither situation does the latter fact warrant the *mental-state description*, 'he does not know what he is doing'. Anyone, mad or sane, drunk or sober, might find themselves engaged in deeds with these properties. Such ignorance of one's own actions implies nothing about one's state of mind. The state of 'not knowing what one is doing' must be something more than a state such that one does not know of something that one is doing.

But if an insane man (let us call him X) were to be discovered earnestly addressing a herd of cows browsing in a meadow as 'you bright seraphim', in an eloquent, coherent, but bizarre speech that begins with the words 'I am alpha and omega', there can be little doubt that he is in the *mental state* of 'not knowing what he is doing'. Why do we say so? Could we mean what we might naturally be taken to mean? Namely, that he is ignorant, not merely of unintended properties of his own 'doings', but of the very movement of the will itself. Could it be that he is so cut off from his own mind that he is ignorant of his own willings? Can a mind be *so* divided? Has schism *no* limits?

(2) There are considerations which strongly point to a negative answer to these questions. That is, reasons for believing that one cannot be thus 'out of touch' with

the intentional will. Return to X addressing 'the seraphim' in an insane speech. We shall suppose him to be three-quarters through uttering a complex sentence 'abcd'; indeed, three-quarters of the way towards *completing the activity* of formulating the difficult and original thought abcd. Must he not *know* that he has just now passed through 'a'? But cannot he utter the words 'abcd' 'as one possessed'? Unquestionably he could have done so, but X was by contrast engaged in *formulating the thought* abcd, and just as a man cannot intentionally be walking from A to D without knowing where he stood and stands, so one occupied in such a mental activity cannot but know something of the stages he has passed through. But a man can walk from A to D without intending to go from A to D, so cannot a man formulate a thought abcd without intending to do so? Indeed he can, for 'd' might be the very last brick in an edifice that was difficult to construct and impossible to forsee from afar. Nonetheless, he was engaged in the single unified activity of *attempting to formulate a thought*: a directed, intentional, and active phenomenon with a beginning, middle, and completion; and the final sentence 'abcd' puts its achievement on record. Such activity requires that the agent takes 'bearings' on the way. In short, know where he stands at each point.

And this is the general character of intentional act situations. The intention cannot propel one into action in the manner of a kick: 'kick-start' one as it were, and then disengage as the intentional deed gets under way. The intention must stay with the act throughout its course, mutating continuously as its own stages find continuous expression in the unfolding stages of the intended act. It follows that understanding that one stands at a certain point on the beginning/middle/completion scale, is an essential condition of a self-conscious being engaging in intentional action. One must understand oneself to stand in a certain relation to a past and future *within* the intentional act: it is internal to the intentional process itself. Therefore—at least under some description or another—one must be apprised of the intentional active contents of one's own mind. Intentional action and knowledge of one's action cannot in the self-conscious be prised apart. If there are such phenomena as unconscious intentional actions, this must be because there is also unconscious knowledge: that is, they will continue to keep each other company—in the 'unconscious'. After all, knowledge can be lodged in the mind but inaccessible, rather as ancient memories can be present in the memory though temporarily forgotten.

(c) What is the ignorance appertaining to one's own actions?

The above considerations prove that whatever the state of 'not knowing what one is doing' may be, and whatever ignorance of one's own mind obtains in that state, the ignorance cannot be a simple ungarnished ignorance of the intentional will. Nor can it be a mere ignorance of the character of one's own acts: first because the drunkard who unawares spills coffee is not in the state of 'not knowing what he is doing', and second because the man addressing 'the seraphim' was engaged in speaking and aware of doing so. And yet it has to be admitted that he was not aware of his activity under the broad veridical heading, 'addressing imaginary beings': a heading which puts its real character on display. Can this be what we mean in speaking of 'not knowing what one is doing'? Do we mean he is 'out of touch' with the real character of his behaviour? In fact, so 'out of touch' with reality that he *has* to be 'out of touch' with the true character of his deeds?

Something along these lines seems right. And yet we cannot in attributing this state simply mean that his acts are the work of a mind that has *lost its grip on reality*. The following makes this clear. A madman (let us call this second individual Y) who brushes his teeth one morning may know that he brushes his teeth, and know he brushes them in a room set in a building surrounded by meadows; but just because he is mad, simply through the cognitive disorders which are part of that condition, he must be ready to endorse descriptions of his act that reveal both falsity and delusion. Thus, this man thinks he brushes his teeth in a room set in a building surrounded by meadows—that are close to the Nile. (For he believes he is Amenemhet III!) This description reveals that while in a *regional sense* he knows where he is, he does not *really know* where he is. It puts on display his loss of a sense of reality, through displaying some of the delusive contents of his belief-system, and revealing thereby the unreality of the world that he takes himself to inhabit. And yet it is consistent with his knowing what he is doing in the special state-sense that is our present concern. He cheerfully says, 'I am brushing my teeth this morning, over by the window', and so he is. He may be 'out of touch' with much at that moment, but he is not 'out of touch' with his own present deeds.

Evidently the state-sense of 'not knowing what one is doing' is exemplified by the madman (X) addressing 'angels', but not by the madman (Y) brushing his teeth. Then what is peculiar to the former case? Plainly *some sort of ignorance* in relation to one's own actions is necessary, and clearly also it must betray *mental aberration* of a kind. Thus, while X is aware of addressing conscious beings and unaware of addressing cows, and the drunkard was aware of pouring out a colourless fluid and unaware of pouring out water, a significant difference between the two is that X's ignorance is expressive of his *state of mind*. And yet it seems that something more must be operative in X. After all, some perfectly sane self-deceiver might satisfy tests along these lines. Then as remarked above what we must add is that the act is initiated by a mind *in no fit state* to know its true character. It must be for some such reason that we employ the sentence 'he does not know what he is doing' to describe this state. Not to know what one is doing, seems at the very least to be performing a deed in a state of mind such that one is in no fit state to register its true character. Macbeth's invocation to Banquo's ghost, the psychotic assassin who strikes down a 'satanic' head of state, the somnambulist walking upon a roof, even the sleeper who engages in a brief snatch of conversation, are each a case in point.

Now the man (Y) who was brushing his teeth that morning was precisely not in this state. We have assumed him to be insane, but loss of sanity and reality-sense are insufficient for the state in question: we need above all *occurrent delusion* for it to be realized, and it is a serious error to suppose that the condition of insanity necessitates *constant occurrent delusion*. A mad person can know what he is doing, both in the literal sense, and in the state-sense under discussion, and it is clear that the aforementioned act of teeth-brushing exemplifies both. Plainly, this is not a mad act. Meanwhile the cognitive disorders to which he (Y) is prey, which lead to our saying of him that he is 'out of touch with reality', could be openly displayed in suitably endorsed first-person descriptions of *all* of his acts, whether mad or not, e.g. 'brushing my teeth by the Nile', 'Amenemhet III's toilet', and suchlike. And this is true of anyone who is insane, whether occurrently deluded or not. It is true therefore of the occurrently deluded man (X) as he performs the insane deed of addressing a herd of cows. We may therefore say of X that he fails on the one hand to act as he both intends and supposes that he acts, as a result of occurrent delusive processes which interfere with his awareness of his surroundings. But we can in addition impute to him a failure to act under self-appointed headings which reveal the contamination running through his entire cognitive representation of the world. For example: 'Napoleon's address to the seraphim.' His is at once a mad act, and an act performed by a madman; Y's was merely the latter.

(d) Mental freedom in the insane

(1) We assume that the state of 'not knowing what one is doing' must, unlike the conditions induced by coma or concussion, be a state of the mind in which certain actions are performed, acts which usually require a measure of awareness of one's surrounds. We have provisionally characterized that state as *at least* such that its bearer is in no fit condition to know the character of those acts. But just what *is* the state itself? And precisely of *what* is this person ignorant? In what does his lack of self-knowledge consist? Where does insight break down? It seems to me that the ignorance referred to in the description of the state is not merely of the character of his own actions, and not merely of the setting containing them. It is in my opinion in an area of the mind where self-knowledge is of crucial importance, and typical of the human condition as such.

When in general parlance we reach for the sentence 'he does not know what he is doing', it is usually to absolve someone from culpability for the performing of a questionable deed. As already noted, we do so not merely through imputing ignorance of the occurrence of a deed of such a character, and in my view not even on the wider grounds of not being in a mental state where such knowledge could be assumed to obtain. I believe it is on still wider grounds. I think we are implicitly singling out what *lies behind* the latter epistemological incapacity, and claiming absolution on that count. While we imply that at the time of the deed he was 'not himself', and impute a major diminution of responsibility, we do so on the grounds not just of his internal state, but on account of his ignorance of the prevailing *internal dynamics* which determined the act. Thus, we imply a serious diminution in the capacity to *self-determine* his own actions: one that keeps close company with his general irrationality and loss of insight. When we say of someone that 'he does not know what he is doing', we mean that this man is performing a deed in a state of mind inconsistent with full self-determination. I suggest that the state-sense of 'not know what one is doing' singles out the state of mind of such an agent. And the ignorance referred to in the description of the state—the breakdown of natural insight—is of the real determinants of his own actions (and by implication, of their wider character or signification). Failure of insight, and loss of freedom, converge in this phenomenon.

(2) The occurrently deluded man (X) who addressed 'the seraphim' was in the state of 'not knowing what he was doing'. This state is marked by a lack of mental freedom. What is mental freedom? Typically, it is exercised when we freely choose our own actions, though it plays a vital part in the formation of belief as well; indeed, these twin freedoms work together in the self-determination of free action. Thus, self-conscious beings have the power to distance themselves in thought from their contemplated deeds, to stand back from the projected act like a second and 'higher' person in the same skin, imaginatively confront it at the level of thought and in the modality of the possible, and either endorse or reject it for reasons which persuade them. Then it seems to me that X at the moment of his speech was suffering from a significant loss of such power. Meanwhile, I can discover no reason for saying the same of the insane man (Y) who is merely brushing his teeth one morning 'by the Nile'. How to bring out the difference?

It is no doubt possible that X decided to address 'the angels', and it may even have been for reasons which at the time seemed cogent enough. But underlying this behaviour lies the *belief* that he is in the presence of angels. How did such a belief enter this man's mind? Since the belief is insane in character, it is likely to be a product of the systematized delusions which have taken root in and spread far and wide in his belief/knowledge-system. As we shall shortly see, such a property implies that the belief cannot have been freely installed in that system, so that the act it engendered must have arisen out of what was lodged in the mind without the knowledge and thus also without the free assent of its owner. Then how could such an act be free? One cannot disengage free action from free belief, construing it a sort of *acte gratuit*, a senseless midair leap! And even if this belief was acquired only after apparently 'mature consideration', there is every reason for supposing that at some point in its origin lie considerations at once irrational and not freely endorsed. But freedom is as strong as its weakest link! It follows that the belief that he was in the presence of angels cannot have been embraced in all freedom by this subject.

The decisive point is that delusive beliefs are installed as alien or foreign bodies in the mind, and take possession of it. They constitute an enslavement as can occur in no animal; for they are not cognitive representatives of the person, being installed without consultation with him and altogether outside his 'ken'. They rise up in his mind like apparitions out of the depths, unmediated by the judgement, and being *beliefs* and therefore that which it is impossible for him to *disregard*, he is chained to them. This is because the real reasons for the belief, which is to say the real causes, work non-rationally and in the dark, and his belief is such as to be insensitive to rational considerations. He either has no 'say', or else too much and the wrong sort of 'say', over which beliefs take root in his mind: he either has no freedom, or else the hubristic pseudo-freedom of omnipotence! That neglected topic, *freedom in believing*, no less important than the related *freedom of the will*, constitutes one aspect of a general problem of freedom, since we do not when free act simply 'out of the blue'. Both freedoms are equally central to properly human status, and are each threatened by the same things: brainwashing, group pressures, fear of individuation, neurosis, etc.

It is essential to belief being free, which typically it is in man, that one freely give *inner assent* to the proposition in question. And this can be accomplished only when one genuinely purports to relate that proposition in coherent rational fashion with the knowledge-system. That is, when one is in a position rationally to think about, judge, and endorse it, and thus mentally to be *active* in relation to that belief in the course of a process of assessment. Therefore self-deceptive belief is free though irrational; for a self-deceiver will continue to pay absolute homage to reason whenever this is due—hence the binding need for rationalization! This crucial phenomenon of inner assent, which finds external expression in utterances like 'On the basis of the evidence I decided that it must be true that——', is to be opposed to the hubristic demented 'I decided that it should be true that——'! Then it follows from the fact that a belief was installed without inner assent, that the act engendered by that belief must have emerged out of what was embedded in the mind like an alien object to which the person was chained, and thus cannot be free action. As observed above, freedom is as strong as its weakest link. And so we may say that, while the subject who was putatively addressing 'the seraphim' knew what he was trying to do, his enterprise lacked the quality of freedom. That is, while a form of self-consciousness is encountered in X at that moment, it is not such as to exemplify freedom. Standard human self-determination cannot have been exemplified in X's act of speech-making. It arose in a situation of self-ignorance: namely, of mental causes which were of such a kind that the freedom which depends both upon our knowing of and assenting to their efficacy cannot have been exercised.

What we have traced out here is a rationale linking failure of insight and loss of freedom, in a situation where a subject is 'unaware of what he is doing' in a sense which carries the implication that the prevailing consciousness is imperfect in type. And in elaborating this rationale we can see how it comes to be the case that self-knowledge functions at a causally deeper level than some of the other essential ingredients of the structured phenomenon, self-conscious consciousness. Facts of this kind must have much to do with our choice of terminology ('self-conscious consciousness'), and the importance we attach to the property itself.

7. Disturbed Consciousness (β)(2): Insane Consciousness and (continued) the Belief-System

(a) The belief/knowledge-system in normal consciousness

(1) To resume. We characterize the positive mode of impaired consciousness as a state marked by a failure of natural insight concerning the natural output of consciousness, viz. intentional action. Thus, we say of the subject X who is addressing cows in the meadow that he is in the *mental state* of 'not knowing what he is doing'. We do so, not because he performs acts he knows nothing of, not because he is ignorant of his intentional will (for he cannot be), not because he is insane, and not even because his mental state is such that he is cognitively cut off from his acts under their widest heading. Rather, it is at the very least because he is in no fit state to register the true character of his actions (for he is the victim of occurrent delusions). But ultimately we say 'he does not know what he is doing' because at that moment his state of mind is such that he has no idea *why* he is doing what he is now doing: he acts as one '*possessed*', his acts are those of a *mentally enslaved* being. If a self-deceiver can be said in this regard to be his own slave, this madman is the slave of forces lying beyond his awareness and outside his control.

Now we know that consciousness is a condition in which one more or less fully assumes one's naturally appointed psychological powers, including pre-eminently one's epistemological powers. It is clear that the capacity to acquire fresh knowledge of the present state of the world is all-important to consciousness. It seems to me therefore that we should uncover the role played by *knowledge* in a mind in the imperfect state of consciousness just described. Intuitively it is apparent that cognitive function is at fault there, and I think we should discover in what respect. But first it is advisable that we clarify the role played by knowledge in normal waking consciousness.

We noted earlier that a belief/knowledge-system (hereafter called 'B-Syst.' or 'K-Syst.') is a necessary condition of meaningful intentional experience, and thus of waking consciousness. And yet what precisely does B-Syst. accomplish for consciousness? As we have already noted, it must at the least provide raw material for experiential content (as it does for an imagination engaged in constructing dreams and novels, etc.). But it plainly contributes more. My present concern is to understand that further role, and then discover to what extent it discharges that office in the positive mode of consciousness-impairment. In short, what now follows is something in the way of a necessary 'aside' in the present inquiry into the connection between insight and consciousness.

(2) With this end in view, I now set out what I take to be the normal role of B-Syst. in consciousness-formation. The normal subject's B-Syst. is a cognitive representation of the world, perspectively from 'here', 'now', 'me', expressible

through countless spatio-temporally ordered claims, including spatio-temporal and causal relations. Despite its perspectivalism the world thus represented is the same world as that known to Tutankhamen and Shakespeare, since there is but one; but the particular system of propositions (B-Syst.) clearly shows that it is a representation on the part of an individual living (say) in London in 1999. This portrait of the world reveals the subject in two ways: in being from the standpoint of a single mind, and in manifesting the idiosyncratic character of that mind—as a portrait by Van Gogh reveals as much of Van Gogh as his sitter. Now since the world is internally consistent, so too must be any veridical portrait, so that any properly formed B-Syst. will aspire to the property of rational consistency under the aspect of truth. Then despite the inevitable presence of error and inconsistency, the normal and average B-Syst. is for the most part true and rationally consistent.

Are there any limits, not to consistency, but *falsehood*? Well, it seems that a suitably originated B-Syst. could absorb into itself an entire army of errors without necessarily destroying the capacity for present consciousness. Provided rational consistency inheres, and the experiencing mind is in such a state that the principle of admission is as it should be, consciousness surely obtains. To this extent the state consciousness is wholly autonomous and interior. While the gross errors in the B-Syst. must prevent such a consciousness from discharging its epistemological function, they do not irremediably maim that latent power. We can reasonably assume that the aforementioned largely non-veridical B-Syst. has within itself the resources through which that function could be restored, since this B-Syst. is in principle properly correctable. It may be via such an escape-route that normal consciousness remains as real a possibility in a mind in this cognitively incapacitated state as in any other mind. But I have in any case little doubt that it does.

(3) When experience occurs the B-Syst. mutates and for the most part expands, and in waking consciousness does so overtly and systematically. Thus, while dreams augment the B-Syst., that increment is no part of the dream, since the past within a dream vanishes without trace as the dream advances to its next stage; but in waking consciousness the continually occurring cognitive novelties constrain subsequent cognitions, since much that is now learned depends internally on recent knowledge with which it *integrates*. Whereas memory has no structural role in dream experience, it is internal to consciousness. I can dream it is now midday *whatever* I have just dreamed, but I cannot when awake learn that it is midday if I have just discovered it is midnight. And so the B-Syst. in the normally wakeful subject is continually expanding, systematically and consciously; continually engendering and assimilating more elements, all according to the *modus operandi* of rational consistency; and, under the aspect of truth, is a perspectival, fallible, roughly correct, cognitive portrait of the world.

What does this tell us about consciousness? Clearly the B–Syst. plays a central part in the constitution of consciousness. We know that without it intentionality could not exist, and it is evident also that without a B–Syst. (that is in addition a K–Syst.) consciousness could not fulfil its essential cognitive function of revealing the present state of the outer world. Now the world that epistemologically unfolds across time to a conscious mind containing a B–Syst. is such as to be rationally consistent with that B–Syst., and in this sense the world of which we become aware is a *mirror* of the B–Syst. But in addition for a mind that is conscious the already revealed world has to be continually revealing more of itself as time passes: it is simply inconceivable that the world be contemplated *sub speciae aeternitatis.* Thus, a central function of consciousness is precisely to create *unceasing novelties* in B–Syst. It is therefore in a way a case of 'new wine in old bottles': the known character of the revealed world persists in the mind, and enables us to enrich the very characterization which we continually bring to bear in the enriching process.

It is not that the conscious must be thinking of elements in the B–Syst. It is not even that B–Syst. need be generating knowledge of the outer world (though we cannot extend such 'charity' to the inner world). But if we are to be conscious, we must harbour a B–Syst. which (at the very least) might so interpret experience as to lead to knowledge of *the* (or at the very least *some*) outer world. Since the only access to reality available to self-conscious beings is that provided by *reason*, the B–Syst. of the conscious must on the whole be internally rationally consistent, and the experiencing mind such that the presently operative *principle of admission* to B–Syst. that of rational consistency with B–Syst. This gives us some idea of the role of B–Syst. in the constitution of normal waking consciousness. It is a cognitive *key* to some world or another: probably of necessity to this world alone—even if this world is in many regards not as B–Syst. represents it—possibly merely of necessity to some world or another. And it is a key which is available only to the wakeful conscious.

(b) Impairments in the belief/ knowledge-system

These observations have been made with a view to understanding the cognitive disturbances going on in the course of the positive mode of consciousness-impairment. Accordingly, what we need at this point is a better understanding of the cognitive systems of the delusionally insane, for it is clear that they must play a decisive part in such interference with normal cognitive function. I begin by considering a familiar related phenomenon.

Aberrations of a relatively serious kind sometimes occur in a person's B–Syst. One such is the well-known isolated 'pocket' of insane delusions: for example, the small system of beliefs accruing around the highly secret but profound conviction that one is the illegitimate offspring of royalty. What makes a particular belief insane? One is inclined to say that origin does, rather than content or truth-value. And there can be no doubt that insane beliefs must have irrational origins. However, the following consideration suggests that truth-value and above all consistency may also be determinants. While the average cognitive system can easily enough accommodate false and self-deceptive beliefs, say a belief in one's own abundant generosity, how could it accommodate the belief that one is Napoleon? If it includes the belief that Napoleon died in 1821, that one lives but once, and that it is now (say) 1999, how could it be a viable system? This suggests that insane beliefs cannot be brought into consistency relations with a veridical cognitive portrait of the world: that the way the world actually is must in some *fundamental respect* clash with those beliefs (which typically concern elemental reference-points, such as those of identity and time and place). And that in turn suggests that if an insane belief is not *isolated* in the mind, it will put in jeopardy the entire world-representation. It seems to me that a mad belief must be one that, if it is not effectively contained within a localized sector of the mind, would succeed in destroying one's sense of reality. It is a sort of lethal threat to that effect!

If this account of mad belief is correct, we can see why certain insane 'pockets' inhabit only the 'east wing' of some otherwise sane minds, and why they are so rarely 'visited'. Open the doors, and you open the floodgates! And this is what can easily enough happen in a B-Syst. that is already genuinely insane. Frequently there is a central cluster of delusions in such a mind; but what is of crucial importance, and determines the presence of insanity, is that those core beliefs must at some point in its history have managed to generate in systematic fashion a network of additional corroborative beliefs and succeeded in drastically contaminating the entire cognitive-system. Such widespread systematized delusions are liable to appear in the middle of everyday life to an alarming degree, and may well include dramatic and extensive revisions of perspectival standpoint (space, time, identity). When an extreme cognitive condition of this kind is reached, the subject is likely to be seriously incapacitated, since gross and crippling falsehoods tend to determine his actions, and his life inevitably suffers.

Two notable properties of these grossly damaged cognitive-systems should be emphasized. The first is the presence of inconsistency of a kind that has no remedy, that cannot be temporarily repaired by stop-gaps of the kind invoked to justify our familiar self-deceivings. This carries the vital implication that the B-Syst. in question could not conceivably enable or faciliate a reliable 'reading' of the world. Then even though this property of an insane B-Syst. is of great moment, it may be that the second property ought to be emphasized even more, if only because it is so much less frequently noted. It is that the cognitive contamination of the B-Syst. is never total: a vast amount of everyday knowledge remains which is accessible to its owner. And I am thinking not merely of knowledge of particular entities and their specific ways of working, but of everyday sub-perspectives within some grand perspective which may already have carried away the very world itself! For example, within the arrogant perspective of being God, Napoleon, or Caesar, the humbler perspective of standing in a meadow some short distance away from creatures that one approached a few moments ago by means of a rural path—such small-scale orientational facts show a tendency to be conserved.

(c) The belief / knowledge-system in the dream

The positive mode of consciousness-impairment occurs when the imagination 'exceeds its office', and intrudes illicitly in cognitive areas in such a way as to obstruct the normal processes of rational epistemology. Now it is illuminating to compare the dream in these same respects, since here too the imagination non-rationally determines putatively cognitive phenomena, only in a different manner that sheds light upon the present case. Then not only does dreaming imagining not occur in waking consciousness, it is a *logically sufficient* condition of its absence. To anyone seriously perplexed over the nature of consciousness, this simple fact ought to come as an illumination, indeed should open doors in the mind. For how can it be that the bond is *logical?* The answer is, I think, simple: it is because in dreaming the replacement of reason by imagination in determining belief is almost total. This fact alone entails that the prevailing state of consciousness cannot be consciousness.

The importance of the hegemony of the imagination in dreaming lies in the fact that for the self-conscious reason is the only avenue to the real: to 'track' the true we must follow the path of reason. Then since this is impossible in dreams, and since consciousness must facilitate the 'reading' of suitable epistemological data, dreaming cannot be the experience of conscious beings. While the dream calls upon the B-Syst., it does so merely as a source of raw material for the imagination to work upon, somewhat in the way a novel depends strictly on knowledge of the ways of the world. In particular, B-Syst. does not in the dream function as *evidential base* for cognition. If there is such a thing as a 'Principle of Admission' for new beliefs when dreaming, it must be altogether different from that of waking. Reason is simply not consulted, and the claims of consistency are ignored.

It is interesting that none of this counts as a *misuse* of the imagination. In dreaming the imagination does not intervene where it has no place: it obstructs no natural mental process, it stays on its own ground. With this in mind one can say, that there is nothing malformed about dreaming: it has a nature of its own which by and large it realizes through the rule of the imagination; and if it has a function, it must be to accomplish something quite other than the epistemological goals of consciousness. Therefore dreaming does not illicitly intrude in the province of consciousness (in the sense in which the hallucination precisely does encroach upon the territory of perception). Hence a dreaming subject does not instantiate an *impaired* or *ill-formed* or *unhealthy* condition of consciousness. His dreaming is made possible by an *absence* of consciousness which is consistent with an imagining which involves firmly committed cognitive attitudes like belief and certainty.

(d) The belief / knowledge-system in impaired waking-consciousness

So much for generalities spelling out, first the role of the B-Syst. in the constitution of consciousness in normal consciousness, and then secondly the character of the deformations in the B-Syst. liable to be encountered in the delusive insane. Now the aim of this discussion has been to help us understand the impairment of cognitive function which I hypothesized as contributory to the positive mode of disturbance of consciousness.

Interestingly, such impairment in a B–Syst. need not as such damage consciousness. Then what we need to discover is, what additional factors are necessary for it to do so, and the manner in which they effect that transformation. A case in point is the subject (Y) engaged in brushing his teeth one morning in a room by green fields (which he would say were by the Nile). The B–Syst. of this person we have assumed to be mad, and therefore to suffer from the systematized and uncontained presence of mad beliefs—beliefs which it is impossible to bring into intelligible relations of consistency with a myriad of other beliefs. In a word, he harbours a cognitive-system which cannot conceivably 'unlock' the world to its owner. Nevertheless, we say of this man that he knows what he is doing, and that his state of consciousness is one of more or less unimpaired waking. How can this be? Causally, I think the answer lies in the fact that neither his core delusions, nor their many cognitive off-spring, happen to be 'touched' by the humdrum incidents occurring that morning in his bathroom. Constitutively, the answer is that within the limited circle of his present experiences and actions, the rule of reason is more or less total. The gross inconsistencies running through his B–Syst. need not, indeed in general cannot, contaminate absolutely everything in that system. Then until they 'touch' his present cognitions, the subject Y remains a 'sound piece of epistemological apparatus' (as one might say) for reading the state of his environs. Just how long this fragile state of affairs persists will doubtless depend upon the vagaries of his inner and outer life.

Thus, let someone enter dressed in the garb worn in Egypt in the year 2000 BC, let them utter certain greetings suitable for a monarch of that era, then my assumption is that in all probability these experiences will generate two kinds of aberrative and closely related phenomena. On the one hand occurrent delusions, fuelled by his imagination; on the other hand a disturbance in the state of waking that had pre-vailed up until that moment. And yet how can mere delusions 'dim the light' of awareness? This question betrays a misunderstanding of the nature of consciousness. They modify consciousness, not by diminishing sensation or the intensity of experience, but by altering the Principle of Admission for novel beliefs. Namely, by replacing one that followed the path of reason, by one following in part that of the imagination. This cannot but damage the capacity of the subject epistemologically to 'read' his environs. Thus, it cannot but impair consciousness itself.

Once again, we must emphasize that the impairment is unlikely to be total. Once again, we should remember that while this man Y may, in the midst of the above sudden irrational disturbance, begin to speak of a world different from that which contains him, he may yet continue to navigate his surrounds with ease. Once more we need to take note of the fact that reason retains significant scope even in this highly disturbed mind: for example, in correctly interpreting much of the present data of visual perception. We have seen that the products of the imagination illicitly and inevitably intrude into experience when the Principle of Admission for novel beliefs undergoes the aforementioned alteration (whereby the rule of reason is seriously compromised). But only when they do so in entirety, and in so doing constitute something of the nature of a dream, would it be true to say that the damage to consciousness was total.

(e) The B-Syst. and impairment in self-knowledge

Since I am approaching the end of this examination of the constitution of the positive mode of disturbed consciousness, I will remind the reader of the theory which the above analysis was supposed to support. While the overall goal of the discussion is the functional elucidation of self-conscious consciousness or waking—what one might call 'the physiology of self-conscious consciousness'—the theory under examination in the present chapter is more specific in character. Namely, that in the self-conscious, impairment in self-knowledge and impairment in waking-consciousness entail one another. Or as one might express it: failure of self-awareness, and deformation of consciousness in the self-conscious, are logically equivalences.

But what do we mean by 'failure of self-knowledge'? This question ought to be settled before we conclude this discussion. Well, we imply at the very least a lack of knowledge of some of the contents of one's own mind. But we must mean more, for much happens in our minds ignorance of which cannot be accounted failure, as the following demonstrates. Thus, it goes without saying that the mood with which one awakes in the morning is something whose *origins* are at least in part a mystery. Indeed, a mind completely in touch with the sources of its own moods would be a mind lacking in all resonance and depth: not merely not worth the having, but frankly unbelievable! For rather as one might 'just feel like whistling', so one can very easily 'just be in a good mood', and in either case it is completely natural, indeed it is an inevitability, to be ignorant of its full mental determinants. It is therefore a mistake to represent ignorance of the mental source of a mental phenomena as a failure *as such* of self-awareness. When we speak of impaired self-consciousness, we must be thinking of ignorance where knowledge is some kind of norm.

Knowledge of mental source is not a norm in the case of moods, nor in the case of simple inclinatory desires. But it is for most of the desires that determine the course of our lives. And it is above all in the case of *belief*—which contrasts significantly in this regard with both of the above phenomena. This is because there simply is no such thing as a *merely natural* non-rational belief: no analogue of sheer inclination: nothing that is a 'just believing'. The reason for this is clear, of great moment, and already familiar. Belief, in the self-conscious, aims at the true, and the self-conscious have only one way of discovering truth, namely to follow the path of reason. Thus, belief aims in addition at the rational. In short, in the self-conscious belief as such aims at the *true and rational*! More exactly: belief in the self-conscious posits its propositional content as both true and rationally consistent with the world. By contrast, the unselfconscious, not overtly aiming at the true, have Nature alone as their unconscious guide: their constitution (reflecting their evolutionary ancestry), and physical situation, tend at the instigation of perceptual stimuli to generate beliefs whose content tends to be true. Such beings 'just believe'. We never do. Then this is how it comes about that self-knowledge concerning origins is a norm for belief. Rationality is a norm in the case of the beliefs of self-conscious beings, and rational origins are almost invariably accessible to their owner.

8. Disturbed Consciousness (β)(3): Impaired Consciousness (concluded) of outer Reality

(a) Failure of self-consciousness in impaired waking-consciousness

(1) The theory under examination in this chapter is that failure of self-awareness in the self-conscious conscious, and impairment in the prevailing state of consciousness, mutually entail one another. Let me now summarily set out the facts which emerged that support this doctrine. This consists in marshalling evidences of the occurrence of these two states of affairs. I begin with failures of self-awareness. The example that I select might equally be the subject X addressing the 'seraphim', or subject Y when his fragile state of cognitive contact with the world had been rudely shattered by the appearance of a 'high priest' clad in the garb of ancient Egypt! Alternatively, it could just as well be a perfectly sane person, with an intact B-Syst., temporarily under the influence of LSD. The failures of self-knowledge encountered in these cases have already been noted. They encompass errors pertaining to origin and character.

A. Ignorance of mental origins

(i) *Of beliefs*:

While these 'disturbed' subjects may be assumed to know (say) why they believe that green grass is nearby, they must in general be unaware of the origins of their occurrent delusions. Thus, even if they could manage to trace convincing deductions from certain premises to some delusive belief, the inevitable irrationality of those premises guarantees ignorance of the real sources of the belief. For it must be emphasized that in the case of putatively rational phenomena like belief, rationality of origin and knowledge of origin are intimately linked phenomena, and conversely that irrationality of origin and ignorance of origin keep equally close company.

(ii) *Of actions*:

The insane activity of addressing the 'seraphim', which might like the delusive belief be traced to known premises, ultimately derives from opaque mental sources. Since the real origin of the delusive belief is hidden, so must be the real mental source of the acts it elicits. Action is as rational as the least rational of its premisses, and irrationality invariably wears a mask.

B. Ignorance of the character of present mental phenomena

(i) *Of experiences*:
The subject X does not know that some of his present seeming visual experiences are visual hallucinatory imaginings and not visual experiences.

(ii) *Of beliefs*:
X does not know that his delusive though real believings are mere imaginings-that, precisely in the manner of a dreamer, and in contradistinction to a novelist, who knows that his quasi-believings are no more than examples of imagining-that.

(iii) *Of states of consciousness*:
X does not know his state of consciousness is an impaired waking-consciousness.

(iv) *Of states of mind*:
And X is ignorant of the fact that he has lost contact with reality, he does not know he is 'not himself'.

(2) One other possible failure of self-awareness seems to me worthy of mention, even though it rests upon a debatable theory. It sets out with the observation that, when in a B-Syst. delusions are introduced, those beliefs need not supplant logical contraries.[1] For example, the belief 'I am Amenemhet III' need not automatically cancel out the belief 'I am Mr Y'. Since consistency is no longer a binding constraint in a mind in the disturbed state of Y's mind, it seems possible that Y might harbour somewhere in his mind, even though inaccessibly, a relatively consistent and true enough B-Syst., upon which are *superimposed* beliefs which are logically inconsistent with it.

That this is possible is scarcely open to dispute. What is decidedly contentious is the further claim that this *has to be* the original, and indeed the present, path along which delusions enter a mind. That is, that just as the imagination necessarily feeds off knowledge, so being 'out of touch' with reality depends upon the capacity to be 'in touch'. More exactly, an insane mind which embraces insane delusive beliefs which are irremediably inconsistent, must be a mind which harbours a relatively consistent B-Syst. And that is in effect to say that insanity arises upon the ground of sanity: the inherently impossible cognitive representation of the world must be a distortion of an already acquired viable representation: 'loss of a sense of reality' must be just that—*loss*! Then the failure of self-awareness which I am supposing this state of affairs to exemplify, consists in the inaccessibility of the viable B-Syst. upon which are imposed the products of an unreasoning imagination: it is the inaccessibility of a veridical internal representation of reality. In the jargon, the subject is 'out of touch with the sane part of himself'. The suggestion is, that there *has to be*

[1] At a certain moving point in Gogol's *Diary of a Madman* it dawns upon the diarist, in a moment of great illumination, that 'Russia *is* Spain!' This blinding revelation, which is tantamount to the undoing of one of the structural pegs holding up the very fabric which makes thought possible, is an example of the inconsistencies which I have in mind.

such a 'sane part'. The only alternatives are: having, or losing. There is no never having had, on the part of the insane. There is merely lack of access to what one presently possesses.

I cannot enter into a serious defence of this claim. It is true that full-blown schizophrenia tends to be an illness of early adulthood, which lends it a little support. However, I do not wish to contest the existence of childhood psychosis. Nor the theoretical possibility of being unable to develop to the point where one can speak a language and properly think. But just as a person cannot develop a pathology in his use of language without at some point having made the acquaintance of that complex holistic entity, so likewise I suggest that a coherent holistic cognitive picture of the world is a precondition of a delusive world-system. What I therefore doubt is, that the mental impairment in insanity can take a form—not of *mere rudimentariness*—which is in any case scarcely insanity—but a form in which a *different world* is conjured up by the imagination—without depending upon the possession of the capacity to know the real world under the aspect of truth: that is, without the subject being able properly to *think*. What I would surmise is that such beings must have 'made the grade' in conceptualizing and contacting reality, perilously and not very convincingly, but slipped back—perhaps as the strains mounted. In a word, I suspect that *collapse* is essential: mental tragedy. The expulsion from the Garden of Eden might be a fitting myth for the insane. Somewhere in their minds the insane must know what they have lost. So, at any rate, I suspect, and would instance the loss in question as a further failure of self-awareness in the 'positive mode' of impaired waking-consciousness.

(b) Impaired consciousness of outer reality (following upon insight loss)

(1) Throughout this chapter I have supported a theory which attaches great significance to the (human, personal) capacity for self-knowledge. Then as a preliminary to setting out that theory I began with the assumption that awareness of the world, which is waking consciousness, has two constituents: awareness of the outer, and awareness of the inner world. Then the theory in question is, that awareness of the outer world, which is awareness of that part of the world that is other than one's own mind, *necessitates* awareness of the (specific contents of the) inner world under the aspect of truth and under adequate headings (where the inner world is understood to consist in present mental content of the kind of experiences, cognitive attitudes, certain mental origins, etc.).

A more ambitious claim is that it is *necessary and sufficient* for consciousness that an experiencing subject be aware of the present specific contents of his inner world. If this theory were true, the latter awareness would in addition be necessary and sufficient for an awareness, not of course of the present phenomenal contents of the outer world, but simply of the *outer world*. Then so far I have done no more than argue for the less ambitious theory: that is, that awareness of the outer world necessitates awareness of the specific contents of the inner world. The defence of that theory has been through an account of an extreme of mental 'disturbance'. I now summarily expound that defence.

What the claim amounts to, in the present discussion of occurrent mental disturbance in the 'visionary' Mr X, is this. That there exists a necessary impairment in awareness of the outer world on the part of one—here, Mr X—who suffers from a (radically) impaired awareness of the inner world. Then let me now in what follows try to bring out this dependence through characterizing two *contrasting* states: first a normal awareness of the outer world, second the imperfect awareness of the outer world that existed in X as he addressed 'the seraphim'. We shall, I think, discover that the latter flawed state is not distinct from the flaws in self-awareness noted recently in the review of X's relation to his own mind. It is in this way that I hope to reveal a necessary connection between adequate awareness of the present specific contents of one's own mind and consciousness itself. And that is to say, the fact that it is a necessary condition of consciousness.

(2) Accordingly, awareness of the outer world becomes the topic for the moment. Now 'awareness of the outer world' does not mean awareness of the present facts of the environment. A man could suddenly surface from deep unconsciousness to an alert wide-awakeness in which all is black and silent and devoid of 'feel' of any kind, and his mind at that instant be straining beyond itself in an effort to epistemologically make contact with his surroundings. Is he not conscious at that moment of the presence of the reality lying beyond his own mind? (As a dreamer is not.) Yet while he perceives nothing of that reality, he must at least be in a state 'apt-for' closing the epistemological gap. Now as we have seen, this requires the harbouring of steady mental 'property' of the type of a well-formed B-Syst. Then a full and proper awareness of the outer world will typically be dependent firstly upon a B-Syst. endowed with the following fundamental elements. (1) Knowledge of the existence of certain objects, events, states of affairs, (2) places and times, (3) and natural laws of various kinds, (4) from the standpoint of here-and-now-and-self, (5) such knowledge being cast into spatio-temporal and causal order, and (6) the whole pervaded by the property of rational consistency.

And secondly (7) *occurrently the subject finds himself in such a state that* his occurrent cognitive attitudes are rationally determined by the relevant parts of the above belief-system, (8) a determination under the aspect of truth, (9) via the rational employment of laws and particularities embedded in that system, (10) through the use of orientation-knowledge taken in conjunction with present sense-intake. If all of this is fulfilled then a full and proper awareness of the outer world, and so also a wakeful consciousness, must obtain (irrespective of whether or not a complete sensory and perceptual 'blindness' reigns within).

Here we have a statement of the conditions needed for a 'full and proper awareness of the outer world'. Let us now take a look at what is going on in the mind of the occurrently deluded X as he addresses the herd of cows in the meadow. The situation is this. (a) He knows some experiences under true minimal descriptions, e.g.

'I now seem to see angels', (b) but not under adequate classificatory descriptions, e.g. 'I now hallucinatorially seem to see angels', (c) he is occurrently deluded, e.g. believes he is God the Father, (d) thanks to processes in his mind of which he is unaware and over which he has no say, (e) a non-rational determination of cognitive attitudes which is unresponsive to relevant data lying within his B-Syst. and/or impinging from without, e.g. he knows he is Mr X, that he is devoutly atheistic, and that he can hear a close friend urging upon him that he is 'not himself today', (f) he is unable freely to determine his (unchosen) beliefs and (chosen) acts. Etc. Etc. Etc.

It is evident that X's mental state cannot meet the requirements for a 'full and proper consciousness of outer reality'. While it is possible he harbours within a B-Syst. which is 'well-formed', and certain that his mind is possessed by uncontained systematized insane beliefs, both his access to a veridical B-Syst., and his mode of utilizing belief in determining cognitive attitudes towards outer reality, fail to meet the requirements necessary for a full and proper awareness of the outer world. Then how can it be that he manages nonetheless to be conscious of the outer world? (For he *is* awake, and he *is* aware of his environs.) Well, he perceives much in the world, say the lowing of cows (albeit *as* the music of the spheres), the grass as grass (albeit *as* heavenly sward), and the wind merely as wind. Thus, he is responsive to sensation and knows much that comes to him from the senses; for, when their content is brought under reduced descriptive headings, as in 'I hear a low crooning noise', many of his cognitive attitudes prove to that extent rationally determined, and many others are in any case under any description rational. Therefore we must say that even though his is a merely faulty openness to reality, an impaired waking consciousness, a consciousness that is malformed, it is nonetheless real.

PART C: CONCLUSION

9. The Nature of Self-Conscious Consciousness

So much for the 'phenomenological facts of the case'. And that brings to a conclusion the main enterprise of this chapter, which was to investigate the nature of the intimate tie between consciousness and self-knowledge, and ultimately to grasp something of what goes into the constitution of the special 'higher' form of consciousness that (significantly) we describe as 'self-consciousness'.

The thesis which I have defended is in some ways puzzling. Why should the opening out to cognition—during the gradual and drawn out process in which self-consciousness came to birth upon our planet—of a wholly novel sector of the world, namely the present specific contents of the subject's own mind, be of such importance to consciousness? And how can it be a necessary condition for consciousness of a world which is very largely constituted of outer reality? To my way of thinking what this fact points to is an essential tie between consciousness and the outer world which must be present from the very start. In what follows I shall say a little more on this topic in Section 9(e).

In any case what emerged in the foregoing discussion lends its support to, and helps explain, the central thesis linking self-knowledge with consciousness. The procedure followed consisted in dismantling four different states of consciousness into their constituent functional elements. These are each states in which experience of the environment occurs—so they cannot be all that remote from waking consciousness, and yet common to all is that consciousness is either absent or an imperfect example of the kind. It seemed to me that if we could understand what it was that ensured this 'shortfall', we would be better placed to grasp what takes place in the mind when consciousness normally occurs. In proceeding in this fashion I follow a well-worn scientific tradition, in which the study of wayward examples of some given natural type is undertaken in order to shed light upon the norm. At this point I set out some of the conclusions arising out of that inquiry.

(a) Cartesianism

I now spell out the theory of consciousness that emerged. The theory is uniquely of the consciousness of thinking beings or 'persons': self-consciousness (so-called). This is the developed variety of a type that has of necesssity but one other variety, that of non-thinking beings ('dumb beasts'): mere consciousness one might call it. There can be no doubt that thinking and non-thinking creatures are conscious in the same sense of the term. 'He was stunned' says the same of man and beast.

Consciousness, waking consciousness, is awareness of the world, of reality. This state has two necessary parts: awareness of the 'inner world'—one's own mind, and awareness of the 'outer world'—everything but one's mind. Then I proposed a somewhat Cartesian theory concerning the relation between those parts. Namely, that awareness of the present specific contents of the inner world is a necessary condition of awareness of the outer world, of the present specific contents of the outer world, and of consciousness itself. By contrast, awareness of the specific contents of outer reality is not a necessary condition of awareness either of outer or inner reality, nor is it a necessity for consciousness.

A stronger thesis, for which I have not really argued, is that awareness of the inner world is also sufficient for consciousness. And yet, bearing in mind the sheer internality of consciousness, and the fact that suitable awareness of the inner world involves awareness of origins (where awareness is, as with belief, the norm) and type (say, being a seeing rather than dream-'seeing'), the case in favour of the theory is surely formidable. After all, what more needs to be added to this internal scene if one is to be aware of the present reality of the rest of the world? If this theory is true, adequate awareness of the present specific contents of an experiencing inner world must be both necessary and sufficient for consciousness, which might exist therefore in the complete absence of awareness of the present specific contents of the outer world. This has an even stronger Cartesian flavour.

These theories serve to emphasize the psychologicality of consciousness. And they remind us that, being neither a perception, nor putative perception, nor indeed putative anything, consciousness is an interior phenomenon sufficient unto itself. Whereas seem-seeing aspires to seeing, belief to knowledge, and trying to acting, consciousness aspires to no type or character. Even though consciousness fulfils its natural function when the conscious subject is suitably or rationally aware of a sector of the outer world, it acquires no confirmatory type when that goal is realized. While this theory is scarcely 'individualistic', for it is consistent with this view that epistemological potential is essential to consciousness, it nonetheless affirms that the determinants of consciousness are wholly interior in type. The state is at once psychological and autonomously so.

(b) Epistemology

Consciousness has several functions, the prime of which is in my view epistemological, viz. that of putting one in a position to discover the specific contents of the phenomenal world, from the vantage point of a mind which knows itself. In any case, epistemological function is the central element in the account of consciousness which follows. That function can be exercised only when consciousness of the outer world (ow-Cs) fulfils its own specific function of enabling the interpreting of epistemological data that are revelatory of outer reality. The phenomenon of ow-Cs—the awareness of the domain peopled by all phenomenal items other than the contents of one's own mind—is not the *perception* of anything, and in particular is not the perception of the contents of that domain. Rather, it *precedes*, and enables where possible, the perceptual and cognitive '*reading*' of the data indicative of those contents. When this occurs, waking consciousness has fulfilled one great half of its epistemological function (which extends both inwards to the mind and outwards).

Consciousness can exist when its outer epistemological function is not being discharged. It is consistent with an outer epistemological 'harvest' of—nil! But of course this is exceptional. Typically when awake we are aware of particulars in a physical setting, and through the use of reason discover their existence. Then what is so *distinctive* about the familiar wakeful awareness of items in our environment, to which we each of us 'surface' every morning? I ask, because it seems intuitively apparent that something distinguishes such awareness. Well, we know that it is perceptual, identificatory, cognitively fruitful. However, these properties proved to be insufficient for delineating the character of the awareness of particulars that occurs in conscious beings. Something else obtains, which the example of hypnotic trance brought to our notice. Namely, that the awareness in question is (what I dubbed) a 'realistic awareness'.

By that I mean an awareness of existing particulars as embedded, not just in a region, nor merely putatively in the real world (remembering the possibility of experiencing a real light as part of the unreal world of a dream), but as *actually* set in the real world. Here we have an awareness in which the fact that waking is awareness of reality *directly manifests its validity*. It does this through the mind's imposing a realistically-oriented cognitive framework on the particular—something not found in the unrealistic awarenesses which fill our dreams. The presence of the containing real world shows in the systematized network of possible descriptions under which we are ready to bring each perceived item (and for these reasons I described such a 'realistic awareness' of particulars as 'linked' or 'connective'). In a non-perceptual sense of 'perceive as' we perceive those items as falling under these descriptions: in a non-occurrent sense of 'think' we think of them in such multiple terms. At the moment of perception we site the item in our mental landscape, somewhat as one might locate a city on a map of the world. This is the character of the experience of particulars that occurs in waking consciousness. The object of perception brings an entire world with it, as mental 'back drop'. Then here in this phenomenon we make the acquaintance of a fundamentally important ingredient of self-conscious consciousness. Namely, the system of beliefs present in the mind at the moment of consciousness.

(c) The cognitive map

The source of the multiple descriptions is the belief-system. The world, as we take it to be, is given by the belief/knowledge-system (B-Syst. or K-Syst.) of the moment: the totality of our cognitive attitudes, a systematized unity marked by the character of perspectivalism. This constantly mutating cognitive 'picture of the world from here and now and myself', which we all carry within us, is of overwhelming importance to consciousness, and specifically to the fulfilment of its epistemological function. How is one to 'read' the epistemological data if one has no idea what to look for? But quite apart from epistemology, B-Syst. is of primitive importance to consciousness, indeed to mentality as such, as the provider of content for intentionality, for meaning within the mind, for the capacity to refer beyond itself.

As we have already observed, such is the interiority of consciousness that, while the B-Syst. has the function of making possible the 'reading' of perceptual data, it need not itself be at all accurate in character. It could in principle harbour all manner of errors even as consciousness persists undimmed. Indeed, the B-Syst. of the moment might be completely incapable of carrying out its epistemological function in relation to the outer world, even though a perfectly wide awake state of consciousness exists! To be sure, certain constraints have to be met before this strange state of affairs can be realized. Thus, the B-Syst. must on the whole be rationally consistent—though the phenomenon of a wide awake Mr Y brushing his teeth one morning 'by the Nile' reminds us that this claim should be qualified. That example demonstrated that it is the presently operative sub-section of B-Syst. that must be rationally consistent if the example of consciousness is to be well-formed. But the general truth remains: that consciousness necessitates that the B-Syst. be internally rationally consistent.

The other requirement if consciousness is to be possible with a grossly inaccurate B-Syst.—in fact, a requirement for *any* example of consciousness—is that the

B-Syst. be suitably originated or 'well-born'. That is, it must have such a history that the concepts which provide its basic raw material are so grounded in realities as to encapsulate genuine content. And here we have a fact which should act as a corrective to any overweening Cartesian-ish misinterpretation of the interior nature of consciousness.

Then under these circumstances—in which gross inaccuracy in a B-Syst. is combined with consistency and a suitable history—consciousness could exist, and wellformedly so, even though it was totally incapable of fulfilling its epistemological function. Indeed, it could exist in a perfectly well-formed state even if the senses were in addition altogether 'blind'. (So to say: not only a terrible dictionary, but no text to read either!) One could I suggest be wide awake, despite this double epistemological liability. While this is a little perplexing, we should always remember that in such cases epistemological function is at all times in principle capable of being restored. Thus, the senses might resume their function, and the distorted but 'well-born' B-Syst. might be corrected and proceed to 'unlock' the veridical incoming data, whereupon the Physical World will stand forth in all its glory!

(d) Rationality

'Unlocking' occurs when the B-Syst. is for the most part a veridical K-Syst. which is internally rationally consistent, when sense-intake is veridical, and the experiencing subject in a state such that the principle of admission for novel members of the B-Syst. which is operative at that moment is that the putative novel member is rationally consistent with incoming data and the prevailing B-Syst. Then we can see from this that reason plays a decisive part in the fulfilment of epistemological function, and thus in the constituting of consciousness.

Now I have repeatedly emphasized that for the self-conscious the only access to Reality is to *truth*, to the true *as* true, and that the only access to the true *as* true is the path of *reason*. Self-conscious belief posits its content as *true and rationally grounded*. The unselfconscious may be led by Nature and experience to beliefs whose content is true, and in that sense to truths, but they are never led to the property of truth, since reason is the unique guide to that property. Indeed, they cannot be led to truths which are delineated via the systems of concepts accessible only to thinking language-users—witness the impossibility of a *preferential* description of the content of animal belief—that is, the necessity of *non*-preferential descriptions of the content of those beliefs. Then to reiterate: reason alone leads to the truth of truths; and I would add that it alone leads to truths whose content is expressed in terms of the concepts given to rational or language-using thinking beings. That is, to the Reality accessible uniquely to self-conscious subjects.

We have seen that this requires a well-formed (i.e. rationally consistent) and wellderived ('well-born') B-Syst., operating in conjunction with a suitable principle of admission, viz. a rational principle. Provided the subject is experiencing, this state of affairs suffices for consciousness—even though it is no more than a necessary condition of the fulfilment of outer epistemological function—which requires in addition that the B-Syst. be a K-Syst., together with veridical sense-intake. Accordingly, the subject must be in a *rational state*. That is, a state in which for the most part one's beliefs and judgements, and so also one's acts and much else, are rational phenomena. That is, causally determined by *considerations* acting *qua* considerations, in which the relation of 'being a good reason for' is steadily causally efficacious. One believes *precisely because* one 'understands', 'grasps', 'sees' the instantiation of this special relation: one so to say detects the presence of 'why-ness'. Something that no animal eyes can 'see' ('why' simply failing to cross their mental horizon!).

We have seen how much of the above can be conserved in relatively disastrous mental settings. Even the occurrently deluded psychotic, harbouring an insane and grossly inconsistent B-Syst., is the locus of much that satisfies this requirement. And this is hardly surprising, when one remembers that insanity only occurs in the rational! It is a risk endemic to the very type. Insofar as one's mind assembles a world, together with the attendant element of infinity (whose analogy we discover in the unending constructibility of sentences), rather than a region of the kind constituted by non-rational minds, the danger always exists of coming to stand in such a relation to this rational construct that one can no longer put it to use in finding one's way around what it cognitively represents, viz. Reality. We call this condition 'being out of touch with Reality'. The familiar and somewhat hackneyed expression 'losing one's reason' puts its finger on the cause.

Despite the existence of malformations produced in consciousness by failures of reason, of the kind noted in Mr X as he addressed 'the seraphim', those malformations are precisely that—malformations, not destructions. Consciousness survives in misshapen form in these circumstances. Thus, the general rule remains inviolate: that only insofar as reason governs in the self-conscious, can consciousness obtain. And the explanation I shall once again repeat. It is because consciousness has the centrally important function of putting us in a position to contact the real, which is to say the truth of the true, and that this contact can become a reality only through reason. Reason lies at the heart of human consciousness.

(e) The question of interiority

(1) One might wonder how adequate (etc.) awareness of the specific contents of one's own inner world can be necessary and sufficient for the state consciousness, while at the same time consciousness is awareness of a world which encompasses inner *and* outer reality. Leaving aside any suggestions of solipsism, does not such a theoretical position imply that consciousness must in essence be directed uniquely to a mental domain, and only secondarily and inessentially to physical reality?

The facts bear no such interpretation. In the first place consciousness is a complex psychological phenomenon, indeed it is a complex *internal* psychological phenomenon in that its a priori necessary conditions include no specific physical properties (unlike physical actions). In the second place no psychological state finds itself *redescribed* as 'consciousness' in the light of its causal properties. Then from these two simple facts we may legitimately deduce that the determinants of being a state of consciousness must be wholly internal—a scarcely surprising conclusion. And from such a proposition nothing of any great moment can follow concerning the objects given to the experience that is necessitated by its occurrence.

It should be remembered that the account offered of consciousness lists as essential properties (i) the epistemological power to apprise us of the specific contents of the inner world and 'unlock' the cognitive significance of the data coming to us from the rest of the world, (ii) a B–Syst. which is both (relatively) consistent and 'well-born' at the hands of a world which includes the outer world, and (iii) the property of intentionality. These facts are simply inconsistent with any such idealistic interpretation of the interior character of consciousness.

(2) And yet is it not strange that adequate (etc.) knowledge of the specific contents of one's mind should guarantee consciousness of, indeed should guarantee therefore the very existence of, the domain lying beyond that mind? (Is this a bizarre variant on the Ontological Argument?) A subject in some extreme epistemological situation, attending to the prevailing silence and darkness, to the unremitting absence of signs of physical realities of any kind, straining for data from 'outside', does it not seem odd that the mere internal situation could ensure awareness of the presence of that 'outer' realm? More, guarantee its very existence! But the theoretical suggestion is not that the internal situation ensures a perceptual awareness of the contents of, let alone that it actually creates!, that domain. Rather, it is that a being equipped with an intentionally directed B–Syst. whose concepts and contents are drawn largely from outer reality, and finding himself in a certain optimal condition of consciousness, should be directly apprised of the here and now concrete existence of outer reality. I see nothing especially problematic in this idea. Perhaps the nub of the matter lies in the latter clause: namely, that the 'outer' world is the source of the bulk of the contents that populate the inner world of this conscious subject.

(f) Freedom

(1) I now summarize the conclusions reached concerning mental freedom and its relation to consciousness. They follow closely on the heels of the discussion dedicated to establishing the centrality of self-knowledge to consciousness. In my opinion both self-knowledge and mental freedom are necessary, indeed surely also sufficient conditions, of the state of self-conscious consciousness in an experiencing subject. I would like at this point briefly to trace out the rationale underlying these few claims.

During the discussion I proposed two slogan-like definitions or characterizations of consciousness: 'consciousness *is* correct epistemological posture—when experiencing'/'consciousness *is* rationality of state—when experiencing.' These definitions are not in competition. Since reason is the unique avenue to reality, it goes without saying that the correct epistemological posture is rational. Then while the rationality of one's mental state manifests itself in a variety of mental phenomena, ranging from cognitive attitudes to desires and actions, it above all governs *belief*. Indeed, the rationality of most other mental phenomena originates from this source. For example, the desire to turn a particular door key is rational only because the instrumental belief that it expresses is rational, and the same is true of the act which gives expression to both. Without such a foundation the act and desire would be either idle and inclinatory, or compulsive and irrational: a case of 'I just *feel like*', or one of 'I just *must!*': reason either bypassed, or defied.

The phenomenon of rational belief proves therefore to lie at the heart of consciousness. Earlier we contrasted normal run-of-the-mill rational beliefs, such as the example provided above, which are legion, with the less common self-deceptive irrational delusive beliefs ('I am naturally a very generous person, but at present financially embarrassed'), and the even less common insane irrational delusive beliefs ('I am Amenemhet III *and* Napoleon I'). Concerning the latter two varieties of irrational belief, the following difference emerged.

(2) One is responsible for self-deceptive belief, but somehow 'out of touch' with this fact: the belief serving certain ends, with which again one may be 'out of touch'. But one can imagine how, faced with shock and pressing necessities, one might 'snap out of it' and acknowledge to oneself that one had until now held such an irrational self-delusive belief for the reasons mentioned. Thus, the origins are at once purposive and concealed: responsibility, alongside misuse of one's responsible capacities, coexisting side by side. And the concealment is essential. For the underlying reasoning in self-deception cannot bear the light of day. It would be rather as if a juror were to say the absolutely unsayable: 'we all know that if we go on like this we will miss the football match, so I suggest we find the man not guilty, even though we know our judgement has no more likelihood of being true than false, and even though it defeats the point of the entire enterprise, and is in any case highly delinquent.' It is somewhat *as if* this went on in the mind, only to disappear from view, leaving the bare judgement as its residue. The mental mechanics of self-deceptive belief are 'unsayable', precisely because irrationality cannot be the banner under which one consciously functions. Thus, 'I believe p for the bad reason q' at the very least has a touch of lunacy about it, and if understood as the fruit of immediate 'insight' is precisely non-explanatory. As we have repeatedly insisted, belief is putatively of the true and rational. Accordingly, since bad reasons cannot rationally explain, they cannot therefore explain *qua* reasons.

Nothing like the above is conceivable in the case of the insane delusion that one instantiates the double identity of an ancient Egyptian monarch and a French emperor of the last century. This is why I asserted of such beliefs that they rise up like apparitions, or appear in the mind as alien invaders. And since they are beliefs, and precisely commitments on our part concerning the character of reality—not being that which can be shrugged off—as we shrug off mere feelings like the *déjà vu*—they enslave their host. No responsibility of the kind misused in self-deception, and used properly for much of the time in the formation of most belief, is in evidence here. If it exists and is operative, it is completely inaccessible.

(3) What is 'normal responsibility' in the case of belief? I described it as 'inner assent'. The expression is valuable, though perhaps misleading in suggesting that coming-to-believe is active. In fact 'inner assent' consists in forming a belief for reasons. Not only is this event not an act, it need not be the fruit of an act of cogitation: for example, I engaged in none such when I just now discovered that it was sunny. What we require is, that the belief be caused by reasons. That is, by 'considerations': say, empirical facts which have the status of evidence. And yet this characterization still strikes me as inadequate as it stands: to my way of thinking it has an unacceptable flavour of *impersonal objectivity* about it. We do not mean merely that that which *is* a consideration caused the belief. We do not merely mean: $(\exists x)$(consideration, x & causative-of-belief, x). If we really did mean no more, it would be the 'consideration' that appeared in the mind like an alien apparition! We require in addition that it act *qua* consideration—upon *us*! We need it to be the case that *our* reason was appealed to, and effectively engaged, in the causal transaction. The important locution 'my reason for believing' reminds us that the transaction is an individual or personal one. A conversion precisely of *ourselves* took place.

I suggested that the actual nature of the process of rational belief-formation is best given in the utterance: 'In the light of the evidence, I have decided that ——'. It is not that doubt must have its foot in the door, as the word 'decide' may suggest. What one rather means is, that one *judged* it so: that is, *one's* judgement concurred. Considerations do not cause beliefs in the way that sudden noises cause shock: they act through appeal to one's reason. Whereas the causation by shock exemplifies a near-nomic regularity, when reasons cause beliefs they obey no mental regularity. Then this absence of natural necessity opens up a vitally important 'loophole' for the processes of self-determination. While the event of conversion is precisely not voluntary—belief being putatively of the objectively real and true—the voluntaristic term 'assent' somehow finds a natural use. How can this be so?

The explanation is dialectical. Thus, somewhere in the remote past something which is unknown in animal cognition arose at a certain stage in human development, viz. a particular type of mental phenomenon. This novel dialectical development—which we find instantiated in the aforesaid 'conversion' to the truth of 'p'—manages to unite absence of choice *that p*, with the fact that always lurking in the background is the (real) possibility of an active process of deliberation on (a re-opening of) '*p*?' The latter hypothetical deliberative process would find itself terminated in a special way, not by an act, and not by an analogue of a mere 'brute' psychic occurrence like shock, but by a pellucid event of conversion to a state such that the freedom to question this very conversion—*once more appears*! Between insane hubristic choosing what shall be fact, and alienating invasiveness by fact, lies the possibility of freely coming to terms with fact. One absorbs fact into one's being in a way which confirms one's individuality, thanks to the power of rational judgement. It is, as we say, 'free'. The permanent possibility of active thinking, where one deems it necessary, is central to the speech form 'my reasons for believing ——'. It fills in what is meant by 'responsibility for belief'.

(4) The personal character of rational believing is such that it requires *knowledge* of what converted one's judgement. How could one's judgement have been engaged without one being aware of the rational pressures being brought to bear upon it? That is, upon *oneself*? And how could one have been directly implicated in the outcome without knowing so? Then this is how it is that rationality demands awareness of the mental forces which carried the day in one's own mind. And, since rationality of belief-formation is the *sine qua non* of the rational discovery of the state of the world, and so of enabling consciousness to fulfil its prime epistemological function, it is in this way that self-knowledge proves to be essential to the self-conscious variety of consciousness. Here we see the rationale linking self-knowledge and self-conscious consciousness.

(g) Self-knowledge

(1) However, we need to be be more specific concerning the self-knowledge that is necessary. Certain metaphysical positions on this issue are relevant. Thus, the Spinozist Deity knew and determined Himself completely, so that mental contingency and mental inexplicability were inexistent in Him. And insofar as I understand the claims of Hegel, something closely akin is said to occur developmentally when the spirit/nature ('slumbering spirit') opposition is finally overcome by spirit knowing and determining itself completely and thus in pure freedom. Even the Freudian dictum, 'where id was, ego shall be', might be read in an Hegelian sense— though it would surely be a misunderstanding: that self-knowledge promotes (say) self-individuation carries no such implication; and in any case we have no choice but to accept contingency in the human mind. A certain kinship exists in this regard between Freud and Schopenhauer. The belief of Schopenhauer that the Will constitutes our individual essence, and is an inexplicable contingency, being the noumenal reality of each being, led him to make the following policy statement: he deemed it advisable that we came through (often bitter) experience to understand our essential and unchangeable mental nature, and act as best we could in the light of that knowledge of ourselves, developing instead a (superimposed) 'acquired character'. But he expressly ruled out the possibility of our coming to understand in mental or indeed any other terms *why* these mental drives were as they were: they constituted the rock-bottom essence of the individual mind harbouring them! (As soon understand *why* the Laws of Physics are what they are! And as soon change either!)

(2) I mention these metaphysical doctrines to dispel misunderstanding of what I mean in claiming that self-knowledge is a necessary condition of self-conscious consciousness. I am not advancing an absurdity like, 'only if one knows the mental

origins of all mental phenomena in oneself can one be conscious.' Nor do I suppose that one will grow more conscious if one comes to understand oneself better. Somewhat as rationality in man is an unqualified reality, for all our imperfections, so it is in the case of consciousness.

It was something of a different order that emerged in the discussion. Namely, that a significant change in the normal mental *status quo* occurs with the appearance of occurrent delusions of the kind exemplified in Mr X as he addressed 'the seraphim'. At that precise moment his consciousness became deformed as no sane person's consciousness can be deformed. As each human is without qualification a rational being, so likewise in the case of waking consciousness. Thus, it is an 'oil and water' situation, rather than one of degree: increased self-knowledge brings no heightening of consciousness in its train. And we know in any case that normal human consciousness is consistent with self-ignorance of the kind that is an inevitability in us all. Earlier I instanced in this regard moods and mere inclinations, but I might have added much else: the hidden origins of many of our affective states, of visual impressions, and so on. It goes without saying that perfectly well-formed instances of self-conscious consciousness occur in minds ignorant of much that goes on in themselves. It is precisely the norm.

But we cannot extend this toleration all the way: at a certain point we must draw a vitally important line. What we say of moods and inclinations, we cannot say of beliefs. Belief, the holding of a proposition to be true, is the central case for the theory being advanced. As we earlier observed, we cannot 'just believe' as we can 'just feel like playing tennis', precisely because belief in man is putatively of the true and rationally disclosed or consistent. In general belief cannot in the self-consciously conscious have hidden mental origins. While belief in dreams almost invariably exhibits this property, it takes place of necessity in the absence of consciousness. And what holds of belief, holds also of its immediate cognitive and active derivatives. The reason for all this is by now obvious, and has been much reiterated. Namely: that rationality and consciousness are our access to reality, and rationality involves the responsible conversion of our judgement. Since we are personally implicated in these transactions to the point of culpability, we cannot cognitively wash our hands of them. Freedom of belief, in the sense spelled out, is a necessary and sufficient condition of consciousness in an experiencing subject. And that is to say, that self-knowledge in the sense spelled out earlier in the chapter, must in a self-conscious experiencing subject be necessary and sufficient for consciousness.

4

'Translucence'

We have seen that insight into the existence of a whole range of mental phenomena is normal to the state consciousness in self-conscious beings. And yet it is more to be expected with some phenomena than others. For example, it is more natural in the case of belief and action than with motives or the mental sources of affect generally. Then might there exist some mental phenomena in which it is simply out of the question, indeed necessarily impossible? Are there limits beyond which insight cannot go? This question forms the main topic of the present chapter. I hope in the course of the discussion to uncover certain principles governing insight, to which we may appeal in considering such a question. I doubt whether rules alone can help one to answer the question in fully general terms, but I believe they can act as a constraint upon what we should entertain as possible. Then it is with such a project in mind that I divide the chapter into three parts: Part A spells out the nature of the problem; Part B addresses itself to the task of discovering whatever rules there might be; while Part C examines a centrally relevant example. For the most part I take 'insight' to signify the brand of mentalistically-immediate knowledge of phenomena in our own minds with which we are all familiar and sometimes refer to as 'translucence'.

PART A: THE QUESTION OF LIMITS

1. The Primacy of Consciousness and Experience in the Mind

(a) Preliminary considerations

(1) The Cartesian theory of mind is in contrast with those theories which locate the essence of mentality in certain developmentally primitive psychological phenomena which are posited as having no essential connection either with experience or consciousness. And it is different again from theories in which it is a sheer matter of indifference to being of mental status that an item be in principle immediately accessible to the awareness of a conscious experiencing subject. Cartesian theory has of course to come to terms with the existence of states like coma, in which the mind continues to exist in the absence of consciousness and experience, as well as with the natural tendency of certain mental phenomena to resist detection: say,

whatever shameful motivation happens to be driving someone in some dishon-
ourable project persisted in with stubborn determination. But a plausible enough
doctrine—in the spirit of Cartesianism and in direct opposition to the above kinds
of theories—is the claim that being of mental status entails being in principle
immediately accessible to the awareness of an experiencing subject, a doctrine
defended by John Searle in his book *The Rediscovery of the Mind*.[1] Broadly conceived, this is the type of theory I shall be examining in the ensuing discussion.

Before I address myself to this topic I would like to consider a significant fact
which underlies the Cartesian theory of access. Namely, the closeness of the connection between sheer mentality on the one hand, and the absolutely fundamental
phenomena of consciousness and experience on the other. The question I want to
consider is, what is the reason for this closeness? While the existence of these close
ties is not the same thing as immediate epistemological accessibility, the primacy of
the phenomena of experience and consciousness in the mind undoubtedly determines the doctrine of universal accessibility.

(2) Whatever one's views on the contentious issue of the extent of our powers of
insight, no one can seriously question that the occurrence of mentality is closely
bound up with that of consciousness and experience. But why is it so? This problem
is no doubt too large to pursue very far, but I offer a few comments by way of a
partial answer.

I begin by setting out more exactly the nature of the bond holding between the
three fundamental phenomena (viz. mind, wakefulness, experience) which stands
in need of explanation. The following claim seems likely to be true: in any world
in which psychological phenomena of absolutely any kind exist, there exists the
possibility of experience and the state consciousness. And considerations of a
verificationist and developmental order lend support to this claim. For what are the
phenomena which would indicate to a third-person the presence of rudimentary
mental life in a living entity? The most natural answer cites bodily events in situation, which are the outer sectors of bodily actions that have been prompted into
being in a conscious subject by perceptual experiences of its environment. And so
at one stroke both the state consciousness, and perceptual and active experience, are
invoked in the interpretation of the physical events. It is difficult to imagine what of
a pre-scientific order could constitute evidence of mentality in some wholly novel
living object, let us say in a different life-system, which did not in this way simultaneously invoke the presence of the state consciousness and the occurrence of
experience.

Then we want to know why it is so, what is the reason for the tightness of the bond
between sheer mentality and these two fundamental phenomena? One possible
response to this question is to appeal to considerations of function. Thus, we know
that the state consciousness is such that one's central mental resources are available
for use in that state: notably, the power to perceive, discover, think, reason, and act.

---

[1] *The Rediscovery of the Mind*, MIT Press: 1994.

And we know too that their coordinated activation enables intentional action upon one's environment which tends to further the life of individual and/or species. Since such powers and coordination are possible only in states of full and proper consciousness, and since many of the resources put to use are experiential in character, it seems that psychologicality could find itself in a position to realize the peculiar advantages conferred by its arise upon individual and species, only if consciousness and experience are there to enable it to do so. Then might it be the case that this property of consciousness constitutes the rationale for the closeness of its bond with mentality and experience?

(b) Intentionality

(1) It seems to me not. The appeal to function does not on the face of it appear either absolutely or sufficiently fundamental. While some mental functions are a priori-given, such as that of act-desire to lead to intention and action, it is difficult to know whether intentional action is a priori-given as a function of consciousness. True, in making possible the coordinated use of one's central mental powers, consciousness makes possible informed intentional action which might further the main projects of one's life. But it enables much else, including self-destructive projects. True, furthering the main projects of one's life is part of the very process of self-realization, of more becoming whatever of a truly enhancing kind it lies within one to become, and this might be thought to typify human existence at its best and most distinctive. But it is far from obvious that it is so, and we should remember that non-rational and rational animals are conscious in precisely the same sense. Meanwhile it has to be said that the appeal to evolutionary advantage cannot be construed philosophically without the support of certain additional assumptions.

(2) A more promising policy is to stand back and consider the nature of mind itself. Now in some ways the mind resembles a stage-set upon which occur 'shadows' of the 'Outside World'. Thus, the mind is not a realm of mere *sui generis* and self-subsistent existents, a sort of exotic herbarium of ontologically novel forms. Rather, it is peopled by phenomena which almost invariably either represent or explicitly refer to the containing World of which it is part, and more or less exhaust their nature in so doing. It is not that it is a duplicate world in the sense in which one might so describe a novel, which merely re-models our own world. Nonetheless, to an overwhelming extent the mind encompasses phenomena which relate in this way to Reality. For example, the belief-system, which typically also is a knowledge-system, a map of Reality; or the interpretational content of our perceptual experiences, which generally posits a slice of physical Reality; etc. The most succinct way of stating the point is to affirm the generally intentional character of mental phenomena, indeed merely the property of possessing content, of being 'about'. And yet it is not simply that it is 'about' something or other, for the content of mental phenomena is not as a general rule directed to some bizarre metaphysical domain. Typically, and surely also originally, it is directed to items in *Reality*. Purely

fictional novels, even fairy stories and myths, merely suppose our world to be different: they do not represent some other metaphysical realm. They talk of real things, of London and Paris, and humans, and animals—however monstrous in type, etc. What else? And how else to be delineated in the first place than in terms of what already we know?

Then it is significant that in the absence of such content there is no way we could delimit any one state of consciousness rather than any other. While experience and rationality constitute sufficient conditions of consciousness, rational projects require intentional content in the form of determinate goals, and experiences generally likewise demand a content, and without content neither phenomenon could exist. This is a way of confirming the truth of the above claim that in the absence of intentional objects there could be no way of specifying the state waking consciousness (as opposed to, say, sleep, trance, unconsciousness, etc.). So here we have a close tie between consciousness and intentionality, and since mentality is inconceivable without representational content, an equally close tie must exist between mentality and intentionality. Minds without the potential for sustaining phenomena with representational content are inconceivable.

(3) Where is this content to be found? How is it to be acquired? Now a certain measure of innate knowledge and capacity is to be credited to minds generally. Indeed, in all probability it is a necessity; for just as the adage tells us that 'out of nothing, nothing comes', so we might add that 'onto nothing, nothing can be built'. Mentally speaking we need already to be, and to know something, if we are to become and learn more. However, it is a mark of rudimentariness in a mental system to be largely populated by innate knowledge and capacities. And so there can be little doubt that if the content in question is to develop, the mind must acquire a suitably endowed belief and concept-system through empirical and largely perceptual means. And not just through the occurrence merely of perception, but perception occurring in a mind in a state fit for interpreting the essentially ambiguous objects given thus to perception. In short, in a conscious mind. That is, in a mind in which the twin phenomena of consciousness and experience are realized.

Thus, the sheer need of mentality to internalize Reality and variously to represent it in diverse mental modes, in believing this or desiring or fearing or regretting some other thing, points to the absolutely general connection between mentality or psychologicality on the one hand, and the state consciousness and the phenomenon experience on the other. The primacy of consciousness and experience for mentality as such, discovers a rationale in the property of intentionality.

(c) Summary

We know that simple minds can exist in which many mental phenomena are incapable of occurring. Thus, since rationality is a necessary condition of much that occurs in our minds, all those creatures that are non-rational in type must be unable to support a multitude of familiar mental phenomena: guilt, humour, 'insight', reasoning, and so forth. Meanwhile we know that minds can in principle exist in conditions of profoundest unconsciousness where virtually all mental life has ground to a standstill, including it goes without saying consciousness and experience of any kind. And we know too that some people believe that machines will very likely at some point in the future be constructed which can think and experience. We also know that some people of great intelligence have at some time believed in the existence of angelic minds, and thus of immaterial and presumably also non-living minds. In short, the range of states of, and the variety of conjectured examples of minds, is considerable. But I suggest that common to absolutely all of these minds, whether real or else merely as understood, whether simple and rudimentary or sophisticated and intelligent, lies the potential for both consciousness and experience. The potential may be lost, indeed in cases of severe brain damage irretrievably lost, but that which was lost was once either possessed or at least a potential. No mind could exist in which the potential for consciousness and experience was no part of the natural repertoire. The potential for consciousness and experience is an essential property of mind as such.

2. The Clear Image

No other psychological phenomenon—not even action and perception—stand in so close a relation to mentality as do consciousness and experience. This fundamental truth finds a natural reflection in an *epistemology of the mind*. Thus, both consciousness and experience are phenomena that are necessarily immediately accessible to a self-conscious subject: a wakeful person knows he is awake, and knows he is experiencing, with an immediacy that has no parallel outside the mind: indeed, we cannot even imagine what it would be to set about discovering whether these phenomena exist at the time of their occurrence, so immediately accessible are they. These very general facts about the mind must surely have been felt by Descartes when he put forward his theory of mind, including the doctrine of 'translucence'.

The time at which he proposed that theory was one in which important changes were taking place. At that moment in history, through the agency of the science of physics, the absolute autonomy and full intelligibility of physical reality must have impressed itself very powerfully upon many. The mental impact of the triumphantly successful advance of a science endowed with the formidable characteristics and high aspirations of physics must have been considerable. I am thinking of the combination of an almost limitless exactitude with a profoundly mathematical character, together with a working ideal of ultimate covering laws of complete universality: so to say timelessly and spacelessly true, true of anything physical anywhere anytime. The type of the rationale of the physical realm, and its majestically universal character, was probably laid bare for the very first time in this way. The steady success of the subject physics was a sort of proof in the concrete of the ultimate self-subsistent character of physical reality.

It seems likely that Cartesianism was at least in part stimulated into existence by this colossal development in human thought. In any case Descartes proposed a theory of mind in which a comparable autonomy and intelligibility were claimed for the domain of mind, which was posited as a region of being wholly distinct from the physical realm. Three phenomena were accorded pride of place in this theory of mind: the state consciousness, the phenomenon of experience, and 'translucence'—the capacity of self-consciousness to know with absolute immediacy and near-infallibility the present contents of its own mind. In this picture of the mind nothing in the way of screens or impediments to vision were countenanced: no *mental things* could obscure the 'view': everything of its very nature lay open to consciousness. The image was one of peering into a deep but infinitely clear lake, each pebble on the bottom as visible as if it were a few inches from one's face in bright broad daylight.

There is an element of divinity in such a conception. In this theory the mind of man is cast in the divine mould, in the image of God. Even though it is merely finite as against His infinitude, it shares nonetheless certain of His perfections. Now there are various ways in which the divinity of the Deity has traditionally been said to reveal itself, including the familiar traits of infinite power, knowledge, and goodness. Three other properties interest me at this point. The first is that of being actuated by, indeed of harbouring nothing but, the sentiment of love: an influence which in general tends to promote synthesis and unity. Another is the absence of matter (St Thomas Aquinas: 'That in God there is no matter').[2] And the third characteristic is the capacity for perfect self-knowledge, a property ensuring the possibility of total self-determination and absolute freedom. These latter two perfections are claimed for the mind of man, though not of course the first, since the human soul is said to be subject to demonic assault along with divine assistance. And those two attained perfections are closely related. Thus, Cartesian mental theory eschewed 'Mental Physics', and banished from the mind along with it all analogues of matter and material objects. Then as we have just remarked, one epistemological consequence of the wholly immaterial character of mental phenomena is, that there can be no such thing as senseless mind-objects or quasi-physical opacities generally which might stand between a conscious subject and the contents of his own mind.

The latter doctrine is surely correct. Indeed, it is a simple momentous truth about the mind. It is evident that if there exist impediments to mental self-knowledge, they must be more complex, meaningful, and 'sophisticated' in character than the above, and such as in some way to implicate the subject in a role for which in many cases he bears a measure of responsibility. The schismatic possibilities in consciousness of the kind charted by Dostoevsky in *Notes from the Underground* and *The Double* (1870s), in the Freudian Unconscious (1890s), in Heideggerian 'inauthenticity' (1927), and Sartrean 'bad faith' (1943), preoccupied European thinkers of this era. And it has in any case to be acknowledged that so far

---

[2] *Summa Contra Gentiles*, 17.

as some mental phenomena are concerned, the very idea of mental–epistemological error is puzzling in the extreme, threatening us with propositions which seem to verge upon contradiction. Plainly, there is no analogue of this in the epistemology of the physical environment. The epistemological situation obtaining in the self-conscious mind must be without precedent in nature.

3. Naturalization: Muddying the Pool

(1) We begin with the image of a translucent pool in which the contents of the conscious mind are infinitely visible to their owner. Schismatic situations, deriving from the logical structure of self-consciousness, from its double and almost duplicituous character, constitute a first blemish in this perfect picture. But they do not *muddy* the pool, else the factor of responsibility would be simply inexistent. However, certain other properties of the mind threaten to do just that. In particular, those which emerged in the course of the *naturalization* of the mind that followed upon the advent of Physics: a process which accelerated rapidly with the romantic movement, and continues to this day—now in a quite different and altogether non-romantic spirit. These naturalistic developments threaten self-consciousness with an almost ignominious expulsion from the original Eden-like epistemological paradise, the lucidity clouded as a result of the assimilation into the theory of mind of certain natural features of the human condition. In particular, the two main determinants of this alteration in the earlier picture of the human mind seem to have been the attempt to come to terms, first with man's *vitality*, second with his sheer *physicality*.

(2) Consider the first of these. The Darwinian ape which haunted Victorians appeared in mental form in the shape of the mental processes of 'Mr Hyde', locked up raging in the (primitive) basement-cellar of the mind—rather than the (more schizoid) 'east wing' of Jane Eyre (also raging!)—both outcasts manifestations of the violence done to human mental nature by the 'high-mindedness' of that era: their very rage understood as the torments of the (justifiably) damned! More precisely, I am thinking of the introduction into the theory of mind not just of the phenomenon of instinct, but of an instinctual *substratum* which was posited as its very foundation. Schopenhauerian Will and Freudian Life-Instinct are mental representatives of the continuing need of life for the fuel, both physical and psychological in type, which drives its essentially occurrent processive way of being. Each of these theories conceives of instinct as the *foundation* of the mind ('at a certain point in time the will kindled a light for itself' (Schopenhauer), 'where id was ego shall be' (Freud)), and by implication posited it as its actual essence. And such a theoretical position is consistent with the radically developmentalist character of the doctrines.

These theories are probably closer to the facts than predecessor doctrines, corresponding to an enlarged and more realistic conception of the human mind. Nevertheless, they have their attendant risks. Apart from the ever-present danger of a destructive Reductionism, they show a tendency to *split* the mind. And this is what one should expect from theories which found intellectual and executive function upon a *developmentally prior* instinctual base. For this is a view which implies that the latter might in principle exist in the complete absence of the former. Such a concept, of a psychological force operating without representation of any kind, strikes me as suspect, and we shall see that it carries with it certain significant and to my mind implausible epistemological implications.

Schopenhauer attempted to demonstrate that the will had no absolute need of knowledge, indeed ultimately no need as such of the intellect, in an argument based upon the nature of instinctual behaviour. The example chosen was the nest-building behaviour of birds, who he assumed had no conception of the nests for which they laboured. However, his argument was certainly invalid. Thus in it he illicitly transferred the *teleological goal* (i.e. a nest) of many intentional acts (say, of many acts of twig-moving) into the content of some *supposed single willing* (of a nest) expressed in and presumably also uniting those multiple separate acts. But the only conceivable justification for positing a willing with such unitary content would be the presence and efficacy of a comprehensive desire and *intention*, and that would necessitate belief-in and awareness-of that final goal, which contradicts his thesis. Freud made comparable claims. Thus, he assumed that, just as the superego must have developed out of the ego, so the ego in turn must have developed out of the id (1923); and at an earlier point in his career proposed an hydraulic model for the 'libido': a claim which finds a precise echo in Schopenhauer's assertion that the will always wills the same thing, viz. life. Freud argued with some cogency for the hydraulic model, largely on the grounds of what he described as 'the mobility of the libido', the tendency for sexual impulse to rapidly switch its objects; while Schopenhauer supported his claim with the similar observation that, no sooner have our most cherished and long-term desires found their ultimate fulfilment, than new desires rapidly spring up to take their place.

Thus, both men believed in the existence of mental forces which were only secondarily directed to the objects discovered in the world through cognitive intellectual powers. They believed in drives which were in essence directed without cognitive assistance, and presumably also without use of representational function, towards a unitary primal goal. And it was in such a force, so conceived, that the mind was said to discover its essence: a proposition which is explicitly affirmed in Schopenhauer's account of the Noumenal Character, whose content is exclusively made up of a set of postures of the will (e.g. generosity, love of failure, concupiscence, etc.); and, at least by implication, in the Freudian stratified theory of mental development. Accordingly, on these interpretations man's essence must lie in non-rational mental forces. At bottom man emerges as non-rational in character.

The mental-epistemological significance of these theories is this. Since they posit the existence of mental forces which can operate independently of knowledge and intellect, they allow for primitive mental phenomena which of their nature lie outside the scope of immediate first-person awareness or 'insight'. At one point Schopenhauer writes: 'The intellect gets to know the conclusions of the will only *a*

171

posteriori and empirically. Accordingly, when a choice is presented to it, it has no datum as to how the will is going to decide', and a little later adds 'This distinct unfolding of the motives on both sides is all that the intellect can do in connection with the choice. It awaits the real decision just as passively and with the same excited curiosity as it would that of a foreign will.'[3] And in Freud's *The Ego and the Id* (1923) the topology of the mind is such that, whereas parts of the ego and superego are said to be conscious and other parts not, the id in its entirety is as such and necessarily deemed to be unconscious. The clear Cartesian waters of the mind seem irremediably to be muddied in these doctrines which seek to assimilate instinct into the theory of mind. In my view, the fault in these theories lay not in the project of assimilation, but in the extremity of the variety of developmentalism through which it was accomplished. Their basic fault was a neglect of the unity ('holism') of the mind.

(3) Thus, the vitality and animality of the human mind find representation in the science and philosophy of mind in these doctrines which seek to accord due weight to instinctive forces in the life of the mind. Here we have a major project of naturalization. But the other (more latter-day) project of naturalization is even more comprehensive. It tries to come to terms with the fact that man is not merely a part of the 'animal kingdom', but a part of physical nature, a part of the physical world. It hopes to draw out the full implications for the mind of the fact that these self-conscious beings are physical systems like the rest of the vital world. Then the relatively recent arise of such sciences as neuropsychology, cognitive science, etc., pose in more or less concrete form the problems which we must consider.

Once again certain dangers attend the project. For example, not so much the abomination 'Mental Physics' as the abominable 'Eliminationism'. And a variety of other aberrations, at least as I see it, threaten us and common good sense. Theory-laden and as yet unwarranted terminology, such as the expression 'folk psychology', are hoist upon us without serious argument. And so on. However, these matters are not my concern here—which at the present point is no more than mental epistemology. More exactly, it is the extent of the range of, or the scope of Cartesian 'translucence'.

(4) A phenomenon like visual experience is instructive in this regard. The meaningfulness of this phenomenon suggests that its causal conditions must be at least partly psychological in kind, and such as in some way to utilize the intellect. Then it is a notable fact about perceptual experience, not merely that we have no immediate insight into its origins, but that insight is as such inconceivable. It looks therefore as if cognitive factors might be playing a part in causal transactions which forever lie outside the range of the kind of 'translucent' insight emphasized by Descartes. Now the formation of the visual experience is precisely the type of phenomenon investigated by neuropsychologists and cognitive scientists. Cases of this kind raise the possibility that purely cerebral investigations might bring to light causal

[3] *The World as Will and Representation*, i. bk. 4: 55, trans. by E. F. J. Payne, Dover, 1969.

transactions going on between mental phenomena which are not even in principle accessible to insight. It suggests the existence of a whole mental domain in which it might be so, and thus the possibility of an even more radical corrective to the Cartesian epistemological position than was provided by the Freudian 'unconscious': a domain which in this regard is on a footing with Schopenhauerian Will and the Freudian Id.

How much ground should Cartesian 'translucence' yield in the face of these developments? Ought one to abandon all hope of the mind's being moulded in the Divine Image from the point of view of mental epistemology? So one might naturally believe. However, the fundamentality of the link between mentality and conscious experience, the deformations in waking consciousness attendant upon certain major failures of insight, and the unacceptability of the Schopenhauer–Freud thesis of primal mental forces which developmentally precede the acquisition of intellectual-representational function—these considerations should cause us to treat the theory of the necessarily unconscious cognitive sector of the mind with caution. It seems to me that we need to look more closely at what goes on when insight occurs generally, and the kinds of the phenomena for which it is a norm. But to accomplish this we need in the first place to sort mental phenomena into a few fundamental categories. Since this classification is applicable both within and without the mind, it is advisable that we begin this second part of the discussion by considering physical phenomena in these terms.

PART B: THE SEARCH FOR PRINCIPLES OF INSIGHT

4. Event, Process, and State Types in the Mind

(a) Events and processes in physical nature

(1) Most events and processes in physical nature consist in change at or over times, although some do not. Movement is change of place, blushing is change of colour, but a whistle and a sensation do not at least transparently consist in change, and even though electromagnetic radiation is a form of energy and 'goes on in time' it can scarcely consist in change: while the radiation may change its position, it is not itself change in any bearer. But are these latter phenomena events and processes, or are they instead of some other category, say 'phenomena'? Well, the Conservation of Energy does not assert that energy is incapable of adopting event form—think of kinetic energy, and I can see no reason why whistles and sensations and radiant energy should not be classed as event/processive in character. After all, they of necessity occur at and over times. However, these questions of classification are not really my present concern, and I mention them merely as a preliminary to singling out the most familiar sub-variety of event. Thus, for the most part I shall be confining the discussion to unproblematic change-events like movement and blushing.

173

The changes of which I am thinking are of such things as position, colour, the amount of sugar in solution in a given body of water, and so on. Now these are the kinds of items whose existence would in no way be threatened if all incident were to cease for a time in their sector of the universe: everything at 0°Absolute in that region, all events and phenomena grinding to a halt, nothing 'going on' (as we well say).[4] The intelligibility of the concept of an item which measures up to these specifications, is part of the reason I feel confidence in supposing that the concept of a 'state' is something more than of a mere receptacle for all those items which fail to fit into the other well-known pigeon-holes of event, process, material object, etc. Thus, blushing is change in the colour-state, from a pinkish white to a decided pink, in an animal (etc.). The changes that constitute a vast array of physical events and processes in physical nature are in most cases *changes of state.* Even the concept of acceleration is that of change of rate of change of position-state. And so on. Change-events like blushing are analysable, exhaustively and without remainder, in terms of state-change and time, as radiant energy is not. We precisely can say what blushing is, as we can scarcely do in the case of radiant energy.

Now amongst change-events, and most especially amongst change-processes, we draw a distinction between those phenomena which have a destination and thus also a completion, and those which do not. For example, between the dissolving of a piece of sugar in a cup of tea and the skid of a car: both processes are constituted out of continuities of states, both are analysable in terms of change, but whereas the process of dissolving has an end and a completion, that of skidding has merely an end. I mention this distinction, because it proves later to be relevant to a special variety of mental process which I examine.[5]

(2) The linguistic means by which we single out events and processes vary, and in ways which need find no direct reflection in the phenomena they designate. Thus, we sometimes single out change-events by terms which unambiguously designate events. Examples are: 'skid', 'earthquake', 'meltdown', 'death', 'birth'. The existence of such pure event-terms is perfectly consistent with the fact that the concept of the event in question may be analysable into state concepts, often not themselves thus analysable. Then let us note in passing that movement and other *spatial events* have the following special characteristic: they are in the first place analysable, but secondly and significantly that into which they are analysable is itself a priori known and not further analysable. Accordingly, we may say of such events—and of few

---

[4] The state liquidity needs energy, so this can scarcely be true as stated. But I use this test merely as a rough confirmation in certain cases of the fact that some given concept is not constituted out of the concepts of change or happening or process. And it functions as a sufficient rather than necessary test.

[5] 'Peace process' must be a misnomer, and convicted doubly on a charge of optimism. There is no processive X such that more of X terminates eventually in the completion state, the reign of peace. Nor is there any processive Y going on, of nature (say) 'peace-ing', such that at the end 'a peace' will have happened. However, the process referred to under the misnomer is real enough and its description indubitable, viz. 'the process of trying to produce the state of peace'. The tainted terminology betrays a familiar failing: the incapacity to wait, the need of instantaneous fulfilment.

others—that they are transparent to the core. Contrast in this regard the concept of acceleration with that of radiation.

But it often happens that change-events are singled out differently from the above. That is, otherwise than through the use of a term which unambiguously singles out an event. Consider the claim: 'Over the centuries the Rembrandt darkened.' Does this speak of an event? While it could be used to do so, as it stands it does not. It simply affirms that the lightness-value of the painting altered in a certain way between (say) 1650 and 1999: it records a difference in a state-property between two times—no more. Then given the nature of the subject-matter, such a difference *entails* the occurrence of at least one event of darkening. However, it leaves it completely open whether or not (say) n events of darkening and m of lightening might have been the bridging occurrences by means of which this alteration of state came into being: it so to say expresses no opinion on this matter. Then when we make use of such an expression as 'the Rembrandt darkened' to pick out an *event*, this fact will generally be *pragmatically* conveyed, as happens in most uses of (say) 'the sugar dissolved'. But sometimes the ambiguity will be resolved by the use of the definite or indefinite article, as in 'the dissolving of the sugar' and 'a dissolving of the sugar'. And sometimes it will be fully resoluble only through a direct appeal to the category in question, as in 'an event of colour-change occurred' or 'a process of dissolving was going on'.

(3) So much for the moment for the sorting of physical phenomena into their respective categories. This was undertaken as a preliminary to classifying psychological phenomena under the same headings. And my reason for wanting to effect such a classification is, that it seemed to me that the mental epistemological properties of psychological phenomena vary in ways which are determined by their categorial type. Accordingly, I pass on at this point to the classifying of psychological phenomena. Because of what emerged in Chapter I concerning their somewhat unusual categorial properties, I begin by examining experiences.

(b) Experiences

(1) In the earlier discussion of the concept of the experience, it emerged that there is no such thing as an experience-state. And in fact, experiences must be occurrent to the core—literally! For there can be no psychological core phenomenon, which is not an event or process, lying constitutively at the heart of an experience. In particular, none such that the experience is constituted out of it in the mode of change-in that core. As one might say, it is non-rhetorically true that experiences are occurrent to the core.

Now experiences are either merely events, or else both process and event. That is, experiences take the form either of events which are not processive in constitution, or processes which are such that as they advance they lay down or realize a potential event which is actualized by the termination of the process. The first kind of item one might describe as a 'discontinuous event'—for the reasons just given, the second as a continuous process which at first merely potentially and then actually constitutes a 'continuous event'. Examples of the first are noticing the traffic-lights change colour or having a thought flash through one's head, while examples of the second are listening to a spoken sentence or dreaming a dream.

Let me elaborate on these claims, beginning with 'discontinuous events'. Thus, there is no experiential process, indeed no psychological phenomenon of any kind, which is constitutive of the experience of seeing the red traffic-light appear: in this respect the experience is a 'simple'. The situation in the case of experiential processes is a little more complicated. For one thing, complex structures are possible. An experience like active ratiocinative thinking is a process whose advance can be internally assisted by discontinuous experience-events like flashes of insight, which need not halt the activity-process but would mostly form part of its developmental history. And even a relatively homogeneous active process like listening reveals certain complexities. For example, listening to an utterance goes to constitute the continuous act-event of *having listened* to it, and both entails and involves the non-identical non-act continuous-event of *having heard* the utterance. Then since the process of listening encompasses an hearing component, we may say first that listening is constituted wholly out of lesser stretches of listening-process, but secondly that it nonetheless is at the same time part-constituted out of lesser stretches of a continuous experiential hearing-process.[6]

(2) Since there are no experience-states, experiences cannot be constituted of experience-states. Indeed, there are no psychological states such that any experience can be constituted of them. *A fortiori* no experience can be constituted out of change in a psychological state. In fact, with the possible exception of experience-change like 'getting angrier'—which may or may not be an experience (not to be confused with anger itself), and where in any case the core is experiential—experiences are never constituted out of change in anything psychological. In any case, experiences can at best be made of nothing but experiences.

And so, like the concepts of much else in the mind, such as the concepts of belief and sensation and intention, many experience-concepts prove to be mental 'originals'. That is, many are what one might call '1st-order mental concepts', by which I mean explicable or definable in no other mental terms. While those other few ('2nd-order') experience-concepts which are thus explicable, are at once definable in terms of, and instantiations of, indefinable experience-concepts of the first kind. For example, an experience like striving-to-hear might achieve the success-status of 'act' and 'listening-to', so that the concepts of will and awareness must be prior to that of listening-to; but we can travel no further along this road, since the act of listening exemplifies the indefinable concept of striving. All experience concepts are either indefinable, or definable in terms of other indefinable experience-concepts.

In sum, experiences are never definable in terms of states, and are either indefinable or definable uniquely in terms of indefinable experience-concepts. One

---

[6] As emerges in Ch. 14.

consequence of this dual property is, that experiences are almost invariably singled out by terms which are pure event/process terms: 'noticed', 'saw', 'dreamed——', 'listened to——', 'tried to——', 'raged at——'. In this regard they are comparable to non-psychological terms like 'lurch', 'skid', 'wobble', which also designate nothing but events. And yet in actual fact they must be fundamentally dissimilar from these latter, for it is so to say mere chance that such unambiguously event-terms as 'wobble' and 'skid' exist, for they are definable in terms of state-concepts and concepts of change. The physical event in question might very well have been designated instead by expressions analogous to expressions like 'darkening', which are ambiguous as to categorial status. By contrast, in the case of experiences we almost invariably pick out the item in question through the use of terms which are reserved for events and processes, such as 'notice', 'see', 'listen', 'pursue'. As a general rule, experiences are singled out by words which are pure event and process terms. It is difficult to think of a single experience which finds itself designated through analogues of terms like 'darkening'.

(c) Non-experiences

(1) Turn now to all those fundamental psychological phenomenal types which are neither experiences nor occurrences: cognitive attitudes like belief, affective attitudes like love, long-term desires, intentions, memories, etc. These non-experiential types are neither events nor processes. Instead, they must be classed as mental states, since their existence and persistence does not depend internally upon occurrence of any kind. And as confirmation of this simple truth, we once again note that they could in principle continue to exist if all cerebral and psychological occurrence were to grind to a complete halt in their owner.

Let us consider a paradigm example of the genus: belief. Here we have a mental state which is ontologically on all fours with the '1st-order' experiential event-types listed earlier, such as trying etc. And belief has like them to be counted amongst the 'originals' in the mind, for it is like them in that it is neither constituted out of, nor is the concept of belief explicable in terms of, any other psychological phenomenon: that is, it too must be what we have called a '1st-order concept', exactly as is the experiential concept of trying. Then just as experiences are almost invariably singled out by terms which are pure event/process terms, like 'saw——', 'dreamed——', 'raged at——', 'tried to——', so also these fundamental 1st-order mental non-experiential mental phenomena are almost invariably singled out by terms which are pure state terms, like 'believe', 'intend', 'disapprove', 'admire'. Then to this list of states we can add those '2nd-order' states which are not '1st-order', but are definable in terms of other mental phenomena: for example 'know'. And I think we can in general say of non-experiential states that they are either indefinable, or else if definable it is in terms of other indefinable states with which they are identical. Here, too, these states almost invariably are singled out by terms which unambiguously are state terms, such as 'know'.

(2) The above array of non-experiential types consist of nothing but state types. Nonetheless, it must now at this point be emphasized that being a state is not a condition of *rigor mortis*: states are not essentially immutable. Rather, they are a kind of thing for which mutation is no more than a possibility. States change: ice melts and water freezes; and mental states are no exception. The fact that all fundamental non-experiential types are state-types, does not stand in the way of there existing psychological changes in the non-experiential sector of the mind. And so it can in no way prevent there being such things as non-experiential mental *events*. I can go to bed believing it would be a good idea to buy a particular house, and wake next morning with the conviction that it would be rash to do so. During the night, and outside all experience, change occurred in the contents of my mind: a belief went out of existence, and another took its place. In short, mental events occurred which one did not experience. And it may well be that mental *processes* in addition went on which again one did not experience. For example, I go to bed convinced it would be a good idea to buy the house, and wake with the conviction that it would be a tremendously good idea to do so; and if during the night these two cognitive conditions were spanned by a steady continuous increment in approval of the idea, then a mental process must have been going on outside of my experience.

And in fact such processes are in all probability going on all the time, 'out of sight' but not 'out of mind'. Consider the familiar fact that one might now remember some past experience less well than one once did: say, a wonderful party one attended many years ago. Here we can single out two mental states: namely, at time t_1 remembering the party very well, and at some later t_2 remembering it less well. Then provided these two states are spanned by an unflagging continuity of lessening or 'fading', a process of forgetting will have been going on all the time between t_1 and t_2—not unlike the slow fading over the decades taking place in some old sepia photographs in a family album in the attic.

(3) Is this process intentional? One is at first inclined to suppose it cannot be, on the grounds (as one might express it) that forgetting processes do not know themselves *as* forgettings: that is, they go on externally to the memory-states, and so (as one might suppose) must be able to intend nothing. But here I think we may well be confusing the 'destination' of a 'destination-process', such as we encounter in dissolving and fading processes, with an intentional-content. And it seems that, just as remembering has to be remembering something, and just as the state can exist even if nothing answers to that content, so too there cannot be a forgetting without these same properties. Then whereas an essentially forward-looking process like listening to statement xyz tries to bring it about that xyz will have been heard, so that here something processive is going on that is essentially directed towards its own completion, certain other varieties of 'destination-process' do not possess this property: for example, processes like fading—or forgetting. In this sense the parts of the latter two processes relate merely additively to one another, despite having in either case a destination or completion. In short, in this important respect forgetting is unlike

listening: it lacks an intentional content which is *at the same time* the completion of the process of forgetting. However, to lack such forward-looking intentional content is not to lack intentional content, and it is clear that forgetting does not. In a word, non-experiential mental processes occur, and some at least are intentional.

(4) How do we designate events and processes of the kind just discussed: namely, changes to mental states like believing and intending which occur outside experience? This question immediately suggests two closely related questions, which I shall answer immediately after addressing the above. Thus, are the concepts under which these latter events and processes fall '1st-order' mental concepts? And are the terms under which we single them out pure event and process terms, as are terms like 'notice' and 'listen'?

To begin with the question of designation. Consider a term like 'forgot'. This can be used to single out an event, but can equally well be used to designate a change of state. It is true that such change entails the occurrence of an event of forgetting, but it fails to entail the unique existence of any event of that kind: rather, it entails that *at least* one event-realization of the state-change occurred, and leaves it open just how many such events took place. And so the event of forgetting is singled out by a term exhibiting the same ambiguity as to status noted in such physical-event designators as 'darkened', 'dissolved', etc. It is not that there are not events and processes of forgetting, nor that the terms 'forgot' and 'forgetting' may not be used to designate them, indeed it is not that there could not be terms which did so unambiguously, as 'skid' and 'skidding' unambiguously single out event and process. However, if we are to pick out these occurrences in the first place, it must be by appeal to the concept of (change of) memory-state, to which we need to append the expressions 'an event of——' or 'a process of——', just as we do in the case of merely physical events and processes like darkening and dissolving.

Now this is so for the same kind of reason as held in the case of the latter phenomena: namely, that the event in question *consists in* change of state. Accordingly, the answers to the remaining two questions must be, first that these events and processes cannot be 'originals' or '1st-order' mental concepts in the sense experience-events like strivings and non-experience states like believing are; and secondly, the terms under which we single them out will in the first place naturally exemplify mere change-concepts like that of darkening, although event and process terms may be stipulated out of such material. In these two respects such events are to be contrasted with the experiential events singled out by terms like 'notice' and 'listen'.

(d) Generalities concerning non-experiential psychological phenomena

(1) That concludes the enterprise of sorting out the phenomena of the mind into their broad categorial types. Then because *non-experiential* psychological phenomena have certain interesting epistemological properties, the following summary

conclusions drawn from the preceding discussion will be confined to phenomena of that type.

Assume that our present concern is nothing but (absolutely all of) the familiar known types of human psychology: acts, beliefs, emotions, intentions, perceptions, memories, expectations, forgettings, desires, love, etc. Then the following general truths have emerged concerning non-experiential psychological phenomenal types. The first set of truths pertain exclusively to *non-experiential psychological states.*

(i) There exist a set of non-experiential state types which are explicable in terms of no other psychological type: we have called them '1st-order' types. (Examples are: belief, intention.)

(ii) All non-experiential 1st-order psychological types are state-types. (Examples are: belief, intention.)

(iii) The other definable ('2nd-order') non-experiential state types are definable in terms of the '1st-order' state types, with which (perhaps invariably) they are identical. (Examples are: knowledge, memory.)

(iv) All of the above non-experiential state types are naturally singled out by terms which unambiguously are state terms. (Examples are: 'believe', 'intend', 'remember', 'know'.)

(2) Meanwhile the following emerged concerning *non-experiential psychological events and processes.*

(v) There are no non-experiential 1st-order event types or process types.

(vi) All non-experiential events and processes are explicable in terms of change in non-experiential 1st-order psychological states. (Examples are: forgetting, ceasing to intend, coming to understand.)

(vii) As a result they are in the first place singled out by terms which are structurally ambiguous (like 'forget'), although they might then be picked out under pure event or process terms which have been stipulatively defined in terms of the latter.

(viii) They are bona fide intentional psychological phenomena.

5. The Varieties of Insight

I am trying to discover principles governing insight into the contents of one's own mind. My intuition is that the epistemological properties of mental phenomena vary according to their general kind or category: in particular, upon whether they are events or states, and experiences or not. It was with this in view that I began the second part (Section B) of this chapter by inspecting the make-up of events generally. It emerged that most, but not all, are constituted out of changes of state at or over times. This fact tends to determine the way the event is designated, for if it is a change-event and definable in terms of state-change, the name of the state-change tends to find itself adapted to event-uses—even though pure event terms like 'skid' can be defined into existence out of such material.

Turning then to the mind we noted that experiences are occurrent to the core, and as a result are almost invariably singled out by terms reserved uniquely for events—there being no non-event psychological phenomenal constituent core whose change-designator could occur in diverse uses. However, my main concern is the non-experiential sector of the mind. Then we saw that all 1st-order ('original') non-experiential concepts are of states, and, being indefinable, those states almost invariably are singled out by state terms. Meanwhile non-experiential event/ processes occur of which these states are the constituent core phenomenon. And so they must be definable in terms of these states: none can be 1st-order 'originals'; and as a result almost invariably will be designated in the way merely physical change-events like darkening are designated, viz. by adapting state-change concepts to event-use.

I return now to the central topic of 1st-person mental epistemology. More specifically, to the attempt to discover principles determining the range of operation of immediate awareness or 'insight'. We shall see that insight is possible in the case of most of the above categories of psychological phenomena. Then since the epistemological situation obtaining in each of those categories is dissimilar, I offer below a characterization of those few situations. In most cases a distinctive variety and extent of failure of insight forms part of the mental epistemological picture, alongside the modes and extent of insight. Those categories are (a) Experiences, (b) States, (c) State-change, and (d) Relations.

(a) Experience

(1) In a certain respect this category of item is infallibly known. There are simply no such things as 'unconscious experiences', for merely through being an experience the item in question has (more or less) arrived already at 'cognitive headquarters' (as one might express it). Thus, it is already part of the 'stream of consciousness', and sheer ignorance of the presence of an experience, whether singled out under correct or incorrect description, is something it is difficult to make head or tail of. It is noteworthy that Freud never posited the existence of unconscious emotions: what rather he thought might sometimes lie outside consciousness was their 'ideational content'.

Then the variety of failure of insight encountered with experiences tends to concern *type* rather than experientiality or intentional content. We see this in the experience of dreaming. Thus, while a dreamer is doubtless aware he is experiencing, his cognitive powers can let him down over their type. Indeed, the *norm* is to be in error on this count when the content of the dream experience is of the two main 'psycho-physical types', bodily action and perception—as we shall see. Accordingly, insight into experience must be mental-state dependent and phenomenal-type dependent. Meanwhile we have immediate and unconditional access to the *content* of our dream experiences. And yet insight can fail here too. For example, in the case of emotional experience, whether it be in a dream or elsewhere, here as in any other experience, indeed any other mental phenomenon, the existence of such phenomena as self-deception ensure that this must be a possibility. However, it is a matter of some interest that since error as to kind is actually the norm in the case of dreams of the two 'psycho-physical types', such error cannot be the work of self-deception. (*Pace* J. P. Sartre who claimed that in dreams we are 'in bad faith').[7] It is an inevitable effect of one's state of consciousness.

Note that the error concerning experiential type can be serious, for it can be over experiential essence. It is not just that the experience has to earn its credentials through its causal connections, and one erroneously experiences it as having done so: say, experiences seeing an after-image on a wall as the seeing of green paint. Such a subject correctly identifies the essence of his experience as visual experience. However, more serious classificatory error is encountered in dreams in the case of the two 'psycho-physical types'. While dream emotions and thoughts are usually as they seem—emotions and thoughts—so that their essence is accessible even in such a state, the essence of those experiences in which we putatively concretely interact with the environment is almost invariably concealed from those in whom the imagination is in the ascendant. The apparent bodily volitions of dreamers are mythical and imagined, as are the apparent perceptual experiences of dreamers and hallucinators. The experience is correctly and essentially identified as experience, but substantively and essentially misidentified as being of the type imagined.

(2) It remains merely to summarily observe that gross and substantive error concerning present experience generally necessitates conditions in which the imagination is in the ascendant, whether as in dream or drug or insane experience. For the most part experiences in the waking mentally normal-ish are experienced with near-infallibility as what and of what they are. Then such ways of experiencing experiences wholly immediately and altogether 'silently' generate beliefs as to their existence and character and content which in normal waking life are examples of knowledge. It goes on all the time, automatically and out of sight. When I have an experience, I usually immediately and no-how know so; and if I am questioned as to whether I have such an experience, I can if I wish put that knowledge to use in answering in the affirmative. And I do nothing to be able to do so.

(b) States

(1) The second important category to be examined from the point of view of first-person epistemology consists in those non-experiential mental items listed earlier under 'states'. For example: cognitive attitudes, memories, intentions to act, and so forth. These states are hidden realities. Thus, they do not just spring into existence when one thinks about the state, or puts the state to use. They are continuous residents of the mind, and ontologically on all fours with experiences.

What we must now ask is, whether 'insight' or mentalistically-immediate knowledge obtains in the case of these states. More exactly: is it a norm? That is, is

---

[7] *Being and Nothingness*, Methuen, 1957: 68.

it encountered (say) typically in the waking life of more or less any mentally normal-ish person? Is it normal that one knows one believes p, intends doing Φ, loves X, wants to dine tonight at the Ritz, etc.? Surely it is. These states seem to be no less immediately cognitively accessible than one's experiences. Suppose I intend visiting Australia in June 2000, and now in February 2000 decide as a result not to book a concert scheduled for 15 June. Then here I make use of knowledge of a firm intention to travel: knowledge that was lodged in my mind from the moment I formed the intention, the instantaneous and immediate effect of that intention. And this is a norm in human existence, for we plot our lives from cognitive stand- points which encompass such inroads into the future. Then whereas knowledge of sensations occurs only if the means noticing-of are utilized, and knowledge of present experiences is an immediate co-present occurrent effect which lingers in short-term and often also in long-term memory, the knowledge of states like inten- tions is a silent and steadily effected presence, persisting along with the states themselves. In short, 'insight' in the sense stipulated exists in relation to this intention-state, irrespective of whether at the time it crosses the horizon of one's experience.

(2) How does this insight manifest its presence? A minor complication exists here. Thus, if I believe it is raining, I can answer both 'Is it raining?' and 'Do you believe it is raining?' And these twin capacities exemplify one and the same insight. When I volunteer 'It is raining' with as much alacrity as 'I believe it is raining', we should not suppose the situation to be that I am insightfully related to *two* phenom- ena: the internalization of a proposition, and belief in that proposition. For while I make a meteorological rather than psychological claim in 'It is raining', so that if I volunteer 'It is raining' with equal assurance to 'I believe it is raining' it must be an assurance founded upon meteorology rather than psychology, nevertheless it is mediated by a cognitive attitude towards the fact. For these are not *opposed*—any more than are seeing and seeing from a standpoint. Just as I cannot see a material object otherwise than from a direction, so while I am not speaking of my mind in saying 'It is raining' I yet give expression to a belief, adopting a cognitive standpoint towards the fact, and overtly purport to do just that.

I mention these matters because frequently when we speak of 'insight' into a mental state, we are thinking of conscious experiential situations in which we openly affirm either *the presence of the mental state* or else just as readily *the truth of its content*. Now these latter are not the same thing, but in the case of some states— intentions for example, and most especially beliefs—we more or less strictly imply the presence of the state merely by affirming its content. I might say 'I believe it is raining', but could equally well have said 'It is raining', conveying and consciously intending to, that this is my belief, so that the very institution of fact-stating rests on the presumption that a person knows his own beliefs. Somewhat similarly I might say 'I intend doing Φ', implying that I know of this state, but I might instead simply convey my intention by predicting my action, as in 'I will soon do Φ'.

Thus, in the case of beliefs and intentions there is a propositional content, which one might simply affirm in giving expression to the state, and this might make it seem that 'insight' into the content is one thing and 'insight' into the state another. But this is an illusion. And in the case of numerous other states there either is no propositional content—for example when one loves someone X, or else there is no assumption that an affirmation of content conveys the state—say if one desires that something p be the case. In these situations self-knowledge will be manifest, not by one's saying 'X!' or 'p!' in special tones of voice, but by simple avowals that the state inheres. But in this regard they really are no different from those other states, such as belief and intention, where it might at first seem as if we could split off the content from the state.

(c) State-change

(1) The third phenomenon to be assessed from the point of view of mental episte-mology is non-experiential occurrence. Then whereas experiences are occurrent to the core, no non-experiential phenomenon is of this kind. This is because all non-experiential occurrences consist in changes of state. That is, the section of the mind falling under 'non-experiential occurrences' must be one and the same as that falling under 'mutations in mental states'. Then the following epistemological gen-erality emerges concerning that region of the mind: a conclusion which is at log-gerheads with a thesis of universal 'translucence'. Namely, that there can be no such thing as immediate epistemological access to mental events of this kind. Now when it is viewed from one standpoint, this conclusion seems of very limited significance. However, when it is considered from another aspect, it proves to be of somewhat greater interest.

(2) Why it seems of limited significance is that the phenomena which it governs are of the familiar aforementioned kind: forgetting, coming to intend, and so on. And nobody is going to feel that if insight is barred to such phenomena, a Cartesian thesis of 'translucence' has suffered much of a setback. After all, that out of which these occurrences are constituted, namely states of memory and intentions, are immediately accessible. Accordingly, we have no need to have recourse to the depth-findings of (say) scientists if we are to discover whether these events have occurred: we can work it out for ourselves through inference from change of state.

None of this can be denied. And yet it is worth recalling a few of the properties of the events and processes to which insight is thus barred. The first is, that these occurrences are not mere constructs: they are real mental phenomena, and exem-plify known mental types. The second is, that despite one's initial misgivings on the matter, they prove to be intentional in type, indeed essentially so. A process of forgetting is as essentially an intentional process of forgetting as is a process of moving essentially one of moving. The next property of note is, the extent of the epistemological 'blindness'—which is considerable. Thus, it obtains uncondition-ally and universally, holding no matter what the type of the occurrence or the

184

mental conditions prevailing at the time. And it is not merely of the occurrence under some preferred description. One simply has no insight into the process and/or event under any description: into its existence, its duration, how many may have occurred, and so on.

This is surely not nothing. Finally, one might add that, even though the examples quoted are all constituted out of insightable states, the principle of the inaccessibility of non-experiential occurrence seems to rest on its own merits. Despite the fact that insight into non-experiential states is the norm, insight into non-experiential occurrence looks to be a general impossibility. And such occurrences are anything but rare: not only are states generally not a condition of rigor mortis, mental states almost unfailingly mutate. Intentions are necessarily time-sensitive, and empirical beliefs are usually from a standpoint which is determinate as to the place, time, and identity of their owner. Then it is surely of some importance that this entire 'underworld' of incessant incident is epistemologically accessible only through the indirect methods of inference. We can never get at it directly.

(3) The character of non-experiential occurrences shows in the fact that they are designated by terms reserved initially for state-change, such as 'forget'. Thus, all events in the non-experiential sector of the mind are change-events, and all processes what I have termed 'destination processes'. We have seen that in the realm of the purely physical there are processes such as (say) moving which are constituted out of state-change without being destination processes. However, because the states out of which non-experiential processes are constituted are 1st-order states, the processes have to be definable in developmental and thus in 'destination' terms.

(d) Relations

What should we take to be the natural 'catchment area' for mental epistemology? So far I have spoken of nothing but mental phenomena: of events, processes, and states; and subdivided these phenomena into experiential and non-experiential categories; and duly recorded their epistemological character. But immediate epistemological access is possible not just into select examples of the above, but in addition into some of the relations holding between them. Interestingly, the relations I am thinking of are not in themselves specifically mental in character, since they are exemplified in precisely the same sense both within and without the mind. In particular, this is true of the all-important temporal and causal relations.

Temporal relations are immediately accessible in many cases in the mind. And this is scarcely surprising, in view of the structural role of time in the inner world. Such relations are unconditionally immediately accessible when the relata are also immediately accessible, and invariably inaccessible when they are not. Likewise causal relations are often accessible to immediate insight, whether one is thinking of rational causal relations as in the determination of many beliefs and actions, or non-rational relations as in the sources of a whole range of affective phenomena.

However, while one cannot be conscious of such a causal relation when one is not insightfully related to the relata, the reverse is possible. It is possible for one to be immediately aware of causally related phenomena without being immediately aware of that relation. Mental association provides many examples: say, when one is ignorant as to whether hearing some name caused one to visualize a certain face, or uncertain whether a particular thought caused a sudden impulse. While sometimes one is immediately aware of such causal relations, as when one reports 'your saying abc made me think of xyz', just as often one is not. There is no necessity, one way or the other.

But in the case of some other phenomena one can be mentalistically immediately aware of both the phenomenon and its cause, and it be simply *inconceivable* that one be similarly related to the relation. The most important example is the perceptual, and especially the visual experience. Here one is immediately conscious of the sense-datum cause (under physical object-oriented descriptions), and in the mode of extensional object, and simultaneously immediately aware of the visual experience it engenders, merely *qua* experience. The two are causally related, but there is simply no such thing as an immediate awareness of that relation. Whereas I can just know that hearing that bang caused my state of shock, or that tasting this beer caused my pleasure, I cannot immediately know that seeing this mosaic of colours is causing me to see it as I do. I merely surmise on theoretical grounds that it must be so.

This is the strongest example of epistemological inaccessibility into a causal relation holding between immediately accessible relata. But there are many other cases where mental phenomena cause conscious mental phenomena, which are such that it is near certain that we will be uninsightfully related either to the phenomenal cause or to the relation. The full source of one's moods is one familiar example. But so too is the origin of many of one's simple inclinations. Frequently they have internal determinants, but in some cases it is difficult to even imagine what insight into either cause or relation would be.

(e) Adjusting the stipulated sense of 'insight'

(1) That concludes my assessment of the epistemological properties of the main mental categories. However, before I attempt to draw a few general conclusions from this data, a word on the concept of 'insight'. There are reasons for thinking that the stipulation whereby 'insight' is taken to be mentalistically immediate knowledge, ought to be adjusted to accommodate a further property which is normally expected of situations of insight. Certain considerations help to bring this to light.

The first consideration is, that *mental phenomena* generally manifest their existence variously: there are many evidences accessible to both first and third person of mental phenomena. The second consideration is, that the *knowledge* of those mental phenomena must also manifest its presence in multiple ways. Then how do these 'two' 'manifestations' relate? Consider the belief that it is raining, and let us ask how it reveals its existence. In some pre-eminent regard this belief manifests its presence in the set of largely linguistic acts examined in (b) (above): in saying 'it is raining', 'I think it is raining', 'raining' (in response to a question), in thinking about it to oneself, and so on. However, such a belief also manifests its presence in other ways: for example, in the act of taking an umbrella as I go out of doors, in my expecting the sight of rain as I look outside, etc. Then while the first set of phenomena self-consciously concern themselves with the existence of the belief, the second set simply make use of it. So much for the belief. Let us now pass on to considering one's knowledge of that belief.

(2) What I think we shall see is, that just those phenomena which evidence *belief* also manifest *knowledge* of the belief.

Consider first the self-conscious variety of evidential phenomena. When I say 'it is raining'—which evidences the presence of my belief—I imply as I speak the inherence in me of such a belief (as Moore's Paradox emphasizes). That is, I intend to convey a belief of mine, and that communicative intention is *rationally based* upon knowledge of that belief. Likewise when I self-consciously avow that 'I believe it is raining'—and once again give evidence of a belief—I act once again out of an intention that is rationally based on knowledge of the belief. In short, these somehow pre-eminent self-conscious manifestations of a belief are at once evidence both of the belief *and* of 'insightful' knowledge of its existence.

But what about the other kind of manifestation of belief: say, grabbing an umbrella as I rush out of doors? Might not this act manifest (i.e. evidence, be caused by, etc.) the belief, without manifesting knowledge of that belief? This idea is surely implausible. It suggests that taking the umbrella relates *merely* causally to the belief it is raining, rather as shock relates merely causally to hearing a sudden bang. But the act in question is at once rational and intentional, and the intention arose as a *rational product* of a belief and desire. Then just as intentional actions necessitate knowledge of both act and intention, for one must know how far one has progressed in an intentional act and what remains to be done, so too do the reasons for intentional action necessitate knowledge of those reasons—amongst which occur in this case the fact that I believe it is raining. For the act to be rational, I need to be able to quote a belief in justification.

So let us assume that manifestations of the presence of non-experiential mental states—beliefs, intentions, act-desires, etc.—are at the same time manifestations of knowledge of those states. This seems plausible in the case of all rational manifestations, which in the case of humans tends to encompass almost all of the evidentially all-important *active manifestations* of the state. That is, self-conscious knowledge of these states causally mediates their rational expression in our lives. And they mediate, not merely self-conscious avowals, but an act like the grabbing of an umbrella, and an expectation of the sight of rain, and a decision not to book a concert, and so on.

(3) Then if self-conscious knowledge invariably inserts itself between the state and its expression, what could it be for insight to be *inexistent* in relation to the state? After all, the states under discussion are just the kind of item one expects on occasion to be lodged in the Freudian 'unconscious', which tends to be peopled by unconscious desires and beliefs and intentions, etc. How can 'insight' *be* self-conscious knowledge if this is so? So what in the light of this consideration should be the proper characterization of those situations in which we would say that insight into a state is missing? Well, it seems to me that such situations must be those involving the absence of that special variety of evidence which consists in self-conscious avowals of the kind just discussed, even as conflicting evidence of a different and somewhat decisive kind points strongly to the presence of the state. Failure of insight must consist in the complex epistemological situation these evidences reveal.

Let us take the stock kind of example. A devoutly religious general in a situation of haste sends his troops across a bridge many believe unsafe, but fails somehow to send either himself or his family or close friends across with them. Later, and after the debacle, he avows with apparent great sincerity, to his confessor and even to his highly secret diary, that he never for a moment doubted the safety of the bridge. And so on, and so forth: the standard situation suggestive of gross self-deception. What is the correct characterization of this case?

One theory might be, that he believed the bridge unsafe but did not know he did: that he lacked 'insight' (in the stipulated sense of the term). The evidence that he believed it unsafe was his conduct concerning people whose welfare was of overwhelming importance to him, taken in the context of his well-known contempt for his troops. Meanwhile, the evidence that he did not know of the belief was his avowals to trusted confidants. However, in the light of the above conclusion that knowledge of mental states mediates most of their active expression in our lives, and especially when the act is rational in type, it becomes increasingly difficult to say that he did not know of his belief. Wherever there is 'method in the madness', so to say, we should be on the lookout for this possibility. Then do we not impute 'method' in the implicit calculation that should the bridge collapse those he most loves in this world—himself, his family—might go to their doom? Must not reasons that are *his* be involved, and will they not necessitate *knowledge* of themselves and thus of the belief?

And if we are inclined to say that 'in part of his mind he knows and in part he does not know' (jargon-wise), we openly (and impossibly) split the mind and person in two, and contradict ourselves. Since only people and animals can know things, and parts of minds cannot, if he knows 'in part of his mind' then necessarily he knows, while if 'in some other part of his mind' he does not know, necessarily he is ignorant. And since he cannot know and not know, we must resist such a characterization. Then might it be the case that he knows and at the same time believes the opposite? Since we attach great weight naturally to evidence concerning those he loves, this strikes me as unlikely. However, the answer to this question is not really my concern—and I set the problem to one side. The purpose of the discussion has been to bring to our notice the need for adjustment to the stipulation concerning the sense of 'insight'.

(4) Thus, if the general really believed the bridge was unsafe, and if ('somewhere') he knew he did, as seems evidenced in the calculatedness of his behaviour regarding his family, how can we stipulate that 'insight' is mentalistically-immediate knowledge of one's mind? After all, the above looks like a classic case of self-deception: a defining example of 'loss of insight'. If it really was true that this man was aware of his belief that the bridge was unsafe, it seems clear that we need to stipulate a different sense for 'insight'. Now it is an important fact that we would say both of this knowledge of the belief, along with the belief itself, that they are inaccessible phenomena, not something he can call up into his mind and think about, and as a result that the belief cannot be cogently reviewed and so rated as fully rational. His calculated behaviour concerning his family, while displaying something more than the intelligence of a fox in that it involves the use of *considerations*, must be adjudged something less than fully rational. It is intentional, and performed out of reasons which are his own, but those reasons were neither acquired nor filtered through a process of thinking and assessment. Accordingly, it seems natural to say that the concept of 'insight' ought to be reserved for those cases of mentalistically-immediate knowledge that are thus accessible and thinkable-about by their owner.

One last comment before I take the search for principles of insight a stage further. It is that what this recent discussion concerning stipulation shows is that, somewhat as an educated adult cannot traverse the most primaeval jungles without mentally transporting with him the imprints of a millennium of civilization, so we cannot banish a meaningful mental phenomenon like intentional action into deep unawareness without transporting along with it the mental setting without which it could not be what it is. No mere 'bleeding chunks' can be thus 'repressed' all on their own into the 'unconscious'. In a word, any form of deep unconsciousness necessitates schisms of a kind in at least part of the containing mental framework.

6. Principles of Insight

(a) Aims

My present aim is to discover rules governing insight and its absence. I entertain no illusions as to what this can accomplish: in particular, I do not suppose one is going to unearth a key which will unlock all doors. The most one can hope for are a few principles with a priori-given universality—such as that of the insightability of experiences; and in addition, rules which seem to apply universally to the psychological phenomenal types known to mankind. This search for regularities was undertaken with a view on the one hand to assessing theses of 'translucence', whether it be an improbable universalist thesis of insight, or the claim made by John Searle under the title 'Connection Principle', viz. that to be mental is to be the sort of thing that is or could be conscious. But it is also carried out to help in the assessment of antithetical theories, in which the tie between mentality and consciousness is significantly loosened.

A word at this point about the Connection Principle. Searle advances ontological arguments in support of this principle, which are based on his views concerning the nature of mentality. I have to say, I do not find those arguments convincing. For one thing, despite the intimacy of the bond between mind and intentionality, the property of psychologicality is indefinable: there is simply no saying what that is common to (say) sensations, bodily willings, and thoughts makes them all of the same clan. But neither can I accept the argument based on the supposition that the ontological status of non-conscious (i.e. non-experiential) mental states like (say) belief is different from that of experiences. Both phenomena are essentially intentional psychological phenomena, and, if Physicalism is true, must be at once psychological *and* physical in character. Experiential and non-experiential psychological phenomena are surely ontologically on all fours. Indeed, it is not just that the arguments are unconvincing: I doubt whether a proof of the Connection Principle is possible, even if the principle happened to be true of the familiar phenomenal types of human psychology. But in any case it is false—strictly speaking, as the example of state-mutations demonstrated. And even if the 'spirit' of the principle is true, I suspect it is beyond demonstration. In my opinion Searle is right in assuming that any proof would have to be based upon considerations concerning the nature of mentality, but wrong in supposing that such a proof exists. However, these are merely 'hunches'.

(b) Conditions and the status of the rules

(1) A reminder concerning the classification adopted above. There exist a number of mental phenomena, experiential events like trying and states like belief, which are indefinable, which I dubbed '1st-order'. And there exist a number of mental phenomena, experiential events like action and states like knowledge, which are at once definable (being 'success'-types) and identical with 1st-order phenomena, and I dubbed them '2nd-order'. Meanwhile, there exist phenomena which are definable in terms of 1st-order phenomena without being identical with them, being instead constituted uniquely out of them, and I suppose we could call them '3rd-order'— though the only examples I can discover are event/processes of the kind of (say) forgetting. So far as I can tell, such a classification accommodates all the familiar known types of human psychology.

(2) Most rules of insight are conditional both upon the type and property of the phenomenon, and on the prevailing state of consciousness. Thus, we saw in the case of experience that, while the range of insight is high, whether or not insight is a norm depends on the property of the experience and one's state of consciousness. This tends to be obscured by the fact that in waking life experiences wear their heart upon their sleeve. However, if the state of consciousness is of the kind (say) of sleep,

only some experiential properties are immediately given to awareness. Indeed, substantial error concerning essential type is a norm for those dream experiences which putatively relate us concretely with the merely physical domain. But if the type is restricted to purely thought-mediated internal phenomena like affect, desire, belief, and suchlike, then insight into essential type is the norm, both in waking and in the non-rational state of dreamers, and perhaps generally.

In short, rules of insight do not aspire to universality, or purport to invariably guarantee states of insight. They affirm conditions of type of phenomenon and of state of consciousness, such that accessible mentalistically-immediate knowledge of the object is normally guaranteed. For example, I normally stand in such a relation to my mental images, knowing their content with the mentalistic brand of immediacy—to be contrasted with that of (say) proprioception (where gross error is readily and unproblematically imaginable). Note that this norm is in no way invalidated by the fact that a person might sometimes deceive himself as to image-content. Thus, I am not suggesting that where insight is a norm it invariably prevails: rather, that where it is a norm and does not prevail something must be responsible. Nothing normally explains why images cause accessible immediate knowledge of their content, but shame might cause one to deceive oneself.

(3) This last is a point of some importance, and should be borne in mind in what follows, since it clarifies the status of the rules. The claim is that in certain cases accessible immediate knowledge of a psychological phenomenon is the 'norm'. This property is to be distinguished from the immediacy of the causal transaction—though they go together. Immediacy here consists in the fact that no causal agency mediates the causation of knowledge by its mental object, whereas 'norm'-ality implies that it stands in no need of explanation that it does so cause such knowledge or that the knowledge in question is accessible. Now the phenomenon of self-consciousness internally requires immediate self-knowledge in a whole host of cases, and notably with rational phenomena and thought. And that is to say that the very setting which makes possible items like thoughts depends internally upon the fact that self-conscious beings have immediate knowledge of them. Therefore it cannot be a contingent fact that self-conscious beings know the content of their thoughts: it is *normal to the system*. Accordingly, it generally needs and has no explanation in any particular case that one knows the content of one's thoughts: at best one might invoke the absence of obstructive factors, which might render the knowledge inaccessible.

Now it follows from the above that when insight fails to obtain in the case of a norm, some mental X must be responsible. Hence we come to talk of 'self-deception', or 'repression', or 'projection', or 'splitting off', and suchlike. These are something more than the soporificity of opium, and designate realities. Modes of mental pain, characterological sources of an intolerance of particular mental pains, these also are realities, and they play a causal role in deflecting their owner from a norm in specific ways which we capture through the above well-worn concepts.

Common to all these cases is that we are recognizing the need of mental explanation, in a way we do not with normal phenomena.

(4) The generalities which emerge from the foregoing inspection of the facts bring together a few universal rules, and in such terms as to connect the rule with our manner of specifying and/or designating the phenomenon involved. A few simple truths emerge. One is that almost all the mental phenomena of which we are apprised are normally insightable in a state of proper consciousness. Another is that the only phenomenon which defies the rule proves to be constituted out of insight-ables: more, that the only way we have of specifying the type which is guaranteed to be thus inaccessible, is through appeal to the concept of an insightable. Finally, causal relations prove to be a different story altogether.

(c) Principles

(1) I now state in summary form the generalities which have emerged. Before I do, I make two provisos. The first is that despite the foregoing comments on conditions, I propose to drop this factor from the statement of rules, since the conditions are satisfied in proper consciousness, and that suffices for the insightability of a phe-nomenal type. The second proviso is that I restrict the phenomena under discussion to those of known human psychology. Whether the long-term future of the human race will throw up types which defy these rules, or whether our own minds or other psychologies in other parts of the universe already do, is not my present concern.

(2) I begin with *principles of insight*:
A. All experiences are insightable.
B. All psychological phenomenal state types are insightable.
C. All 1st-order psychological phenomena are insightable.
D. All 2nd-order psychological phenomena are insightable.
E. The origins of rational phenomena are insightable, as are the origins of many non-rational phenomena, such as select varieties of affect.
F. The temporal relations of insightable phenomena are insightable.

The following are *principles of inaccessibility*:
G. All non-experiential occurrences are uninsightable.
H. The origin of all perceptual experiences which are at once momentary phe-nomena and interpretational in kind, are uninsightable.
I. The origin of mere inclinations and moods are never wholly insightable.
J. The temporal relations of uninsightables are themselves uninsightable.

And so on.

(3) The following 'rules of thumb' concern our manner of either specifying and/or designating psychological types.

A′. 1st/2nd-order psychological types are generally singled out by terms which are pure event/process terms or pure state terms, as the case may be.

B'. Non-experiential occurrences are invariably initially singled out under a terminology of state-change.

And so on.

(d) Comments

Two things are notable about these rules. First, nowhere do we encounter a 1st/2nd-order phenomenon which is necessarily inaccessible. Second, the one phenomenal kind which is necessarily inaccessible is constituted out of, and simultaneously delimited in terms of, an accessible phenomenon. The following question naturally arises. Namely, whether one might go beyond the latter limitation, and in so doing likewise transcend the former. I mean, discover in the mind a 1st-order type, a type therefore not explicable in terms of any psychological type and *a fortiori* in terms of one already known and insightable, which is as such necessarily uninsightable. An alternative question contemplates a possibility only a little less radical. That is, whether one might discover special examples of a known—and usually insightable—type, which are such that insight into their existence is simply inconceivable. What follows in Part C is an attempt to clarify the issues involved, through examining a specific phenomenon in which the main factors appear.

PART C: A PROBLEMATIC EXAMPLE

7. The Formation of the Visual Experience

(a) The causal relation and the causal relata

(1) It seems to me that the Cartesian position on the question of insight survives the challenge posed by Schopenhauerian metaphysics of the mind and by Freud's final theory of the instincts. However, cognitive science raises the problem afresh: roughly, the possibility that there might exist cognitive analogues of 'Will' and 'Id'. In short, phenomenal states or event/processes which of necessity are inaccessible to insight. That is, inaccessible phenomenal types rather than inaccessible causal relations. As we have already seen, it is beyond dispute that causal relations exist between some mental phenomena which are necessarily inaccessible.

It is clear that visual experience must arise out of causes which at least in part are mental. Thus, if sense-data exist they must cause the impression in which is inscribed their own interpretation. While if sense-data do not exist, the fact that the mind almost invariably goes beyond the given of coloured expanses in two or three dimensions, implies that the less interpretational impression causally develops into its final more interpretational form at the prompting of its earlier stages[8] (somewhat similarly to the psycho-physical causal development taking place constitutively within the bodily action).[9] Either way, causation from mental event

---

[8] See Ch. 20, §6. [9] See B. O'Shaughnessy, *The Will*, ii. 212–14 and 286 (ix), CUP, 1980.

to mental event occurs, irrespective of whether it is assisted by cerebral non-psychological agencies.

(2) What can we say about the *causal relation* and the *causal relata* in this transaction? A word to begin about the relation. As we have already observed, the causal relation between the sense-datum (and any other mental agency) and the visual experience is necessarily inaccessible. Now this cannot be because there is no such thing as 'one's reasons' for the experience being as it is, since many non-rational mental causal relations are immediately accessible, as in the genesis of shock or pleasure or affect. And I have to say I simply do not know the reason for this inaccessibility. What about insight into the causal relata? Well, one is aware of the *experience* so to say in the experiential mode, and aware of the *sense-datum* qua extensional object of that experience, and in either case the awareness is mentalistically-immediate (even though different in kind). And, one is inclined to add—*that is that!* For one seems to be aware of no other mental causal determinants of the visual experience. And yet how does one know that this is so? Indeed, after a little reflection it becomes evident that one cannot know such a thing.

It is true that one is aware of no other experiential phenomena which might have helped cause the impression. But why should not the impression have non-experiential mental causes? And why should one not be conscious of them? Since we have no insight into the origin of the impression, we have no insight as to whether or not a mental item is causally implicated. Such a state of affairs is consistent with the possibility that one might be conscious of some or even all of any additional mental causal factors. In a word, we are in no position to claim to know that the only causal relata of which we are aware are visual experience and sense-datum.

(b) The mental causes of the impression

(1) Then why might one suppose that visual experiences have other mental causes besides the sense-datum? Certain considerations suggest it might be so. The meaningfulness of the phenomenon, the fact that interpretation of the sense-datum normally occurs, constitutes one reason. No visual field of objects can be of necessity of one unique rather than a variety of other possible visibilia: perceptual data is essentially ambiguous. Strictly speaking we are given no more than a continuum of colour point values lying in two or three dimensions.[10] Then what else but mental determinants could explain the fact that such a datum seems to present to view (say) a roomful of familiar faces? And it seems near certain that one's knowledge of the visual appearance of types and individuals must play a part in ensuring that one's mind 'goes beyond the given' in one rather than another way. And plausible also to suppose that one's knowledge of the character of the situation in which one finds oneself, very broadly conceived (in a dense crowd, underwater, in outer space), and of the probability of encountering one type of object (say, hippopotami) rather than another (say, electrodes), likewise plays a part. And yet these are merely

---

[10] See Ch. 20, §1 and §2.

surmises—for one has no insight to act as a guide, and it is conceivable one could be mistaken on at least some of the above counts. In this regard the Julesz figures are highly instructive, demonstrating the existence of a surprising independence from content in the formation of binocular visual experience.

(2) Then there are reasons for thinking, not merely that cognitive mental states roughly along the lines of the above must assist the sense-datum in the formation of the visual experience, but that *intellectual factors* involving the understanding must be playing a part in that transaction. The considerations pushing one towards this view are of two kinds.

The first begins with the observation that normally what we seem to encounter in the visual field breeds 'contentment' in the understanding—unlike the 'impossible figures' of psychologists. It 'all hangs together': chairs are distributed in space, do not come in wildly disparate sizes, and subtend at the eye angles inversely proportional to their apparent distance, and so on. More, the objects which figure in the content O of the visual experience VE(O), in conjunction with the nomicity governing the transmission of light and the retinal determination of visual fields, causally explain the sense-datum. Furthermore, the following causal claim is usually true. Given [the present sense-datum, the distinctive visual appearances of things generally, the rectilinear propagation of light, one's knowledge of the broad character of one's situation, and the distribution-probabilities of objects in such settings], then the O-content of one's VE(O) is almost invariably identical with the O it would be most reasonable for one to hypothesize as cause of the sense-datum. In short, the solution to a causal problem is given to one in concrete form. Thus, the visual experience seems like a rational judgement incarnate!

(3) All this suggests that the *intellect* is at work. But so also does a different line of thought. For if mental factors like sense-datum, knowledge of individual appearances and present situation, are jointly at work in the formation of the impression, *by what means* do they lead to such an end-product? They can scarcely do it 'just like that', somehow additively, rather as if one threw them in together and 'let them sort it out themselves'. One looks for some *intelligible* mental means. One feels there must be some kind of mental rationale whereby they can be seen to lead to the content of the impression, some mental 'logos' must be at work. No merely additive 'chemistry of the mind' or 'parallelogram of mental forces' seem either intelligible in themselves or capable of generating internal consistency (etc.)

Thus, the apparent intellectual accomplishments of sight, in conjunction with the need for a rationale whereby the undoubted mental causal factors might be seen to lead intelligibly to their end-product (which is 'agreeable' to the understanding), make it natural to hypothesize a sort of 'uniting thread':
a mental phenomenon of some kind stitching together the disparate mental causal influences in a way which calls upon the intellect. It is thus natural to hypothesize the occurrence of a mental intel-

lectual process which plays such a role, leading in the end to a visual experience with object-content O, viz. VE(O). (A necessarily hidden non-experiential process, it should be noted.)

(c) Problems facing the postulation of hidden intellectual processes

(1) However, there are difficulties in positing such an intellectual process. For the only intellectual process we know of which can lead us from a set of evidentially significant fragments of data to the conclusion they warrant, is that of reasoning. But the supposition that reasoning is going on is unacceptable on a number of counts. The first is that the visual impression is a necessarily non-rational phenomenon (like hunger, moods, pain, and unlike knowledge). The second is that reasoning is a form of thinking, and thinking is an activity and experience, and experiences are immediately accessible to consciousness. The third absolutely decisive consideration lies in the fact that (say) visual depth-experience occurs in non-rational creatures, indeed in many cases to an enhanced degree—as in eagles, and such beings are incapable of thought, of thinking, and reasoning. While if we say that unconscious computation goes on in their minds, we are by implication saying that thinking and reasoning are going on! Computation cannot be all that far removed from arithmetic, algebra, the propositional calculus, and no eagle can engage in these procedures. While if it is said that computation is nonetheless going on in their brains, the supposition must be that brain rather than animal is doing it, and that it is not reasoning. The only reasoning beings, indeed the only reasoning things that we know of at the present moment, are humans.

(2) A different difficulty lies in the fact that there is no non-rational analogue of the process of reasoning, encountered in enhanced form in foxes and other intelligent animals and culminating in non-rational but quasi-rational end-points like a correct expectation or a veridical impression. Reasoning is a phenomenon of the inner life, it is an active experiential process conducting us inferentially from one proposition to another, and there is no less developed experiential process in the mental life of animals which mutated into reasoning as rationality appeared in the course of evolution. Unselfconscious consciousness mutated into the self-conscious variety, but which mental processive 'what' in their inner life changed its spots and turned into reasoning? What is its name? While certain learning or cognitive phenomena doubtless were precursors of reasoning, no mental processive experiential type answers to the above specification. But since the visual spatial accomplishments of non-rational animals can be considerable, we should expect there to be such a phenomenon if a mental intellectual process constituted the rationale leading from mental causes to visual experience.

At this point one might have recourse to what strikes me as a desperate expedient. Namely, to posit a wholly novel mental intellectual kind. To be sure, there is nothing the matter with such a suggestion—if one can justify it. But it is something of an extreme, as the following makes clear. There is a serious difficulty facing any project of defining a novel kind in terms of its end-product: say, as 'the whatever intellectual process culminates in the fully interpretational visual impression'. The difficulty is that such an end-point is consistent with more than one contributory causal agency. This is in sharp contrast with the definition of the forgetting process in terms of the concept of memory-states: a definition precisely without remainder. There is simply no way of knowing whether a recipe in terms of end-point has singled out one or many processes. In short, the causal recipe cannot launch a novel concept.

Finally, there is a very simple obstacle to positing intellectual processes of *any* kind determining the visual impression, in rational and non-rational subjects alike. Processes are never instantaneous, and intellectual processes must one assumes occupy time of experienceable dimensions, as opposed (say) to a duration of 10^{-8} seconds. But the visual impression springs fully formed into consciousness: no sooner does one open one's eyes than it all stands before one.

(d) The possible sources of 'understanding-syntonicity'

(1) We abandon the theory of a necessarily unconscious psychological intellectual processive thread across time, intelligibly relating the supposed disparate mental causes of the visual impression. What remains that might act as a 'logos'? What that is instantaneous in character? Bearing in mind the non-rational character of perceptual experience generally, as well as the visual acuity of non-rational animals like eagles, the relation of inference is a non-starter. And remembering the visual accomplishments of some newly born creatures like foals, it seems improbable that regular non-rational mental links of the kind of association can explain sight's primary spatial achievements. Even though empirically acquired knowlege of type and individual appearances must causally contribute to the impression, it is rather less likely that the delimitation of contours and surfaces, or the determination of depth, can have such origins.

And so we are searching for a way of accounting for the fact that the arrival of sense-data in a mind in a certain attentive and cognitive state, leads instantaneously and non-rationally to the formation of a content which is at once 'agreeable' to the understanding and the solution to a causal problem which might be posed in the form of a question. Thus: given [one's present sense-datum, and the rectilinear propagation of light, and (etc.)], what is the most likely cause of that sense-datum? Nothing in the way of present experience can be invoked as *explanatory mediator*, indeed nothing of which one has immediate awareness is capable of playing such an explanatory role: rational relations generally are proscribed in the causal history of the impression, and association seems at best capable of determining knowledge of individual appearances. Where is one to turn if one is to bring 'rhyme and reason' into this mental scene? How is one to explain the understanding-syntonicity of visual experience?

(2) Meanwhile in the visual field all looks as we know that it precisely is: there is no gap between what we see and what is. Then might just that veridicality of normal visual content be the source of understanding-syntonicity? After all, the shadows on a wall cast by the setting sun are projectively explained by their object owners—which is 'agreeable' to the understanding: why should it be any different within and without the mind? Could it be that the link between sense-datum and impression is largely cerebral, that the mind automatically individuates surfaces and contours in the visual field, upon which are belatedly imposed interpretations utilizing one's knowledge of the appearance of types and individuals—and little more? Is the 'agreeableness' to the understanding largely the fact that the visual field is generally veridical, and Reality is internally consistent with itself? After all, that is just the kind of thing understandings are sensitive to!

If this is how matters stand, we will have been the victims of an *intellectual illusion*: namely, that the understanding-syntonicity of visual experience must be the result of causal relations of an intellectual mental order. Then at the very least this is a suggestion which we must take seriously. Prima facie the above hypothesis seems more acceptable than positing intellectual relations and/or phenomena of a kind one is unable to characterize.

(e) Requirements of a satisfactory theory of visual experience-formation

(1) In the light of the extended discussion concerning visual perception which follows later on in this work,[11] it seems to me that certain facts about visual experience should be borne in mind when we are considering the theory that necessarily unconscious mental phenomena play a part in the determination of that experience. Any satisfactory theory of visual formation should take into account the following:

1. The sense-datum, and attentive-posture, cause the visual experience.
2. We 'see by inheritance'[12] (witness the visual accomplishments of foals).
3. We 'see by experience'[13] (just as one's [largely innately determined] body-image can eventually assimilate [even unexpected] novelties [like a hump or vast corpulence], so one's visual experience can [within limits] be responsive to surprising novel regularities in experience which overturn known established regularities).[14]
4. The visual experience is at once constituted out of and completes an instantaneous mental causal sequence internal to itself[15] (rather as the bodily action at once encompasses all of, and [normally] realizes the natural terminus of, a motor-mechanistic causal development which simultaneously falls under the psychological concept of will).[16]

[11] See Chs. 15–22.　[12] See Ch. 20, §6.　[13] Ibid.　[14] See Ch. 20, §4.
[15] See Ch. 20, §6.　[16] See B. O'Shaughnessy, *The Will*, ii. 212–14, 286 (ix), CUP, 1980.

5. Unlike the motor action the internal visual experiential sequence does not exemplify a nomic regularity: it can be affected by repeated experience, as bodily action not. (Hence the slogan 'we see by experience'.)

6. Each stage of development of the visual experience is accessible to consciousness, and appears in the onion-structure of increasingly ambitious descriptions under which the (one) experience is given to its owner (e.g. 'seem to see a round red patch', 'seem to see a red hemisphere', 'seem to see a red hemispherical side', 'seem to see a balloon', etc.). How these last relate to the so-called 'primal sketch' of David Marr[17] (etc.) is unclear. No description is so unambitious as to match the 'raw primal sketch', but maybe others correspond. When they do, they imply the psychologicality of the 'sketch' and its accessibility to consciousness. Where not, this technical concept at best designates cerebral phenomena.

7. The first stage in this causally bonded sequence of events, which is like its successor-stages in being an event in the attention, is a noticing wherein spatial synthesis is a reality and interpretation absent.

8. Why the sense-datum causes such an initial noticing may well be for the most part innately determined.

(2) These facts make no mention of necessarily unconscious *psychological phenomena* amongst the causes of visual experience: unconscious causal relations certainly (as ubiquitously elsewhere in the mind), but phenomena not. Short of continuing the present discussion of visual formation to an inappropriate degree, I must at this point rest with the view that nothing that has come to light in the discussion supports the claim that any general theory of consciousness which is cast in the spirit of Cartesian 'translucence' is decisively disproved by the phenomenal situation encountered in the determination of visual experience. I see no evidence here of a 'Cognitive Unconscious' in any interesting sense. All mental processes are in principle accessible to their owner, whether immediately *qua* experience or inferentially through their constituting state.

[17] David Marr, *Vision*, W. H. Freeman & Co., 1982.

5

Consciousness and the Mental Will

It has emerged that one condition of consciousness in self-conscious subjects is a measure of self-knowledge of the kind set out in Chapters 3 and 4. In its absence an occurrent state of rationality, and as a result consciousness along with it, simply cannot be realized. Then since rationality of state does not play a symmetrical causal role in the ensuring of self-knowledge, self-knowledge must be a relatively more deep-seated mental causal condition of consciousness than some other constituent elements of consciousness. Now it seems to me that self-knowledge is not the only mental phenomenon with this property. There are reasons for believing that mental action, and above all the mental activity of thinking, play a comparable causally central role in the constituting of consciousness: indeed, there are reasons for supposing that the active process of thinking underlies the whole edifice of rationality and thus also of consciousness. The present Chapter 5 is concerned to spell out the nature of the generally active condition, while the succeeding Chapter 6 considers the specifically active condition of thinking.

1. Introduction

(a) Activeness

(1) One interesting fact about the conscious is, that their experiential life is *active* in character. I do not just mean that it is eventful, I mean that it is actively or intentionally or willingly eventful. Despite the fact that many experiences in the conscious are not chosen, the flow of experience seems nonetheless to be active as a whole. Precisely what this assertion comes down to must at some point be spelled out, though for the present we might settle for the rather vague claim that the main processive constituents of the stream of consciousness of the conscious are intentionally active phenomena. Note that we cannot say the same of consciousness itself, since waking is not an active phenomenon. This continuous occurrent phenomenon is neither an ongoing activity nor an immediately willed phenomenon, and very likely does not even take processive form (which would be enough to guarantee it is not an activity). And the 'stream of consciousness' is no different in these respects from consciousness. Nevertheless, the flow of experience in those who are conscious presents us with an array of closely knit active processes and an activeness

which is in some way central to the state. As one might express it, when one is awake one is 'master in one's own mental house'—a fact which is in no serious conflict with the unceasing spontaneity of thought, the continuing unanticipatedness of one's next thought. After all, to be master in one's own mental house is not the same thing as being tyrant! It is my contention that, even though a conscious person is at each moment infinitely dependent upon the proper functioning of his own mental resources for his consciousness, he remains nonetheless at that moment actively in charge of his own experience.

It is a strange fact that consciousness should necessitate activeness of the mind. We know that action arises out of desire, and typically out of need. The conclusion forced upon us is, not that consciousness arises from desire, but that for it to appear at all desire must appear with it. Now it seems natural to conceive of consciousness as akin in ways to awareness, as something with a predominantly cognitive stamp. Then is it not odd that desire should have anything to do with it, that the conscious must harbour desire on sheer pain of loss of the state of awareness? And yet there can be no doubt that they must—if it is true that the mind of the conscious is an active mind.

The aim of this chapter is to *substantiate and rationalize* the latter claim. Alternatively, it is to say *why* the stream of consciousness of the conscious is an active flow. More exactly, it is to discover *what contribution* the activeness of the stream of consciousness of the conscious makes to the obtaining of that state of consciousness. Negatively but illuminatingly expressed, it is to find out *what it is* about an inactive stream of consciousness that ensures that its owner cannot be conscious.

(2) Let me at this point emphasize that in making these claims I am not proposing to elevate activeness to a position of pre-eminence within consciousness, say by supposing either that we create or are responsible for our own condition of consciousness. For one thing, I am convinced that rationality of mind is more central to the nature of consciousness than is activeness of experience. But in addition I recognize that the mind can be *possessed* by action in such a manner as to render consciousness impossible: witness the mind of a somnambulist or of one conversing during sleep. In short, I am not suggesting that activenesss of the stream of experience is a *sufficient* condition of consciousness. My claim rather is that it is a *necessary* condition. And my prime concern is to bring out the *significance* of this property—since I cannot believe that it is 'epiphenomenal' from the point of view of mental function—a mere by-product of the situation holding in the mind of the conscious. Thus, I hope to uncover perspicuous links between the activeness of the stream of consciousness in the conscious, and the inherence of some of the centrally important properties of the state consciousness.

(b) Procedure

For the most part I will be concerned to spell out the specific contribution of activeness of the mind to consciousness. Then even to take the first steps on this path

requires, not merely that we entertain plausible views concerning the main properties of consciousness, but that we be actually aware of some of those properties. If
consciousness was an impenetrable mystery to us, we should be without any method
of detecting the existence of a connection between the presence of consciousness
and the activeness of the stream of experience, we would have no way of knowing *in
virtue of what property* of consciousness an inactiveness of that stream ensures the
absence of the state. In short, if we are to make inroads into this question, we must
already possess information about the nature of consciousness. We must know some
of the central characteristics of the state. Then what mental powers do we expect to
find functioning in a wide-awake person? Something like the following, surely. The
occurrence of experience, which is mostly self-directed; the mental capacity to perceive (irrespective of whether the senses are working), and so to learn about the
environment; a functioning rationality; and the knowledge of one's inner life,
together with the power of self-determination. This much surely.

Let us assume that when a condition of self-conscious wakefulness exists, most
of the above obtain. Then my aim is to demonstrate a dependence on the part of
some at least of these traits upon activeness of mind. Alternatively, a clash between
mental inactiveness and some of these traits. Which traits precisely? Two are automatically excluded: for obvious reasons activeness in the stream of consciousness,
and because dream experience is largely inactive and occurs outside waking I disqualify experience also. Accordingly, I suggest that any one or more of the following
list of properties is worth considering. Being mentally in a position to discharge
normal epistemological function; rationality of mental state; and self-knowledge
and self-determination. Tracing out significant relations between activeness in the
flow of experience and the inherence of one or more of these attributes of consciousness, and in that way bringing to light the rationale underlying the dependence where such dependence exists, will be my chosen method of answering the
question posed at the beginning of this chapter. Namely: what contribution does
activeness in the stream of consciousness in a conscious subject make to the occurrence of the state? Alternatively, it is my way of answering: why is inactiveness of
experience inconsistent with consciousness?

(c) A procedural question

A procedural difficulty arises. It stems from the fact that the recently enunciated set
of fundamental properties of consciousness form a 'holistic' complex of interdependent items. Now 'holistic' interdependences are often compared to the 'holism'
discoverable in linguistic totalities, and in some cases are actually traced back to
such origins. There is good reason for resisting any such aetiological account in the
present case. In my opinion the interdependence in question is with more illumination to be likened to that relating the 'faculties' of the mind—something
which holds irrespective of whether we are thinking of pre-linguistic non-rational
minds or the self-conscious minds of humans. As an example, the relation of

interdependence between executive and cognitive function, which surely holds throughout animal nature. And in fact a relation of interdependence holds in general between the fundamental properties of the state of consciousness. Such a relation cannot be traced back to the linguistic powers of self-conscious minds (indeed, the reverse must surely be closer to the truth!).

This interdependence, which is occurrent, is not to be confused with the closely related interdependence of the fundamental properties of self-conscious minds as such, which is an interdependence of capacities. Here I am thinking of such traits as the capacity to experience, to think, employ language, to grasp and make use of the concept of truth, to appreciate the modalities of necessary and possible. These properties would subsist, in relations of interdependence, in a deeply unconscious person. The relations of interdependence to which I am drawing attention hold only of the waking, even though they are no more than exercisings of the above capacities.

This occurrent interdependence has procedural implications for the present project. This is because the connections traceable between activeness within the stream of consciousness and some of the fundamental properties of consciousness, are analogously interdependent. The procedural implications are that there can be no *absolute priority* when it comes to setting out the several essential contributions made by the activeness of conscious minds to the embracing state of consciousness. A certain arbitrariness must characterize our choice of where to dive into the select circle of fundamental phenomena. All we can reasonably do is proceed piecemeal, acting on the understanding that we are neither delineating independent relations nor following any absolute order. Then I propose to begin by examining what may well be the least contentious feature of consciousness. Namely, the property of being mentally in a position to carry out the epistemological functions of consciousness, and above all that of coming by empirical means to know about the environment. In the ensuing discussion I intend to bring to light some of the relations between this capacity and the mental will.

2. Mental Will and Perceptual Function

My point of departure is the following question: what contribution does mental action make to the fulfilment of the epistemological function of consciousness? I begin by making a few observations concerning that function.

Evidently, knowledge here begins in *experience*, which is typically the means by which most knowledge manifestative of a present state of waking consciousness is acquired. Now the experiences occurring in waking jointly constitute what people casually refer to as '*the stream of consciousness*'. Then of the several main varieties of experience making up that 'stream'—thinking, affective, perceptual, motor—perceptual experience is the variety most obviously dedicated to epistemological function, and I devote the present Section 2 to considering it. We shall see how the mental will makes decisive contributions to perceptual function, through enabling its objects to incorporate *three* main characteristics which are essential to the fulfilment of that function: structure, intelligibility, and what one might call 'perspective'. Those three properties form the topic of the ensuing three sub-sections.

(a) Structure

(1) My limited initial enterprise is to consider the contribution made by mental activeness to the cognition that is gained through perceptual experience when one is conscious. Then the most obvious property imported by activeness into perceptual experience is *structure*. Consider the following example. Let us suppose that two people are seated in a bus, right up in the front by the driver, with a vivid wide-angled view of the unfolding scene, and assume that the bus is just beginning to enter a famous and somewhat exotic city which neither of these people have ever set eyes upon. And suppose that at that very moment a violent and sordid argument suddenly erupts between them, more or less over nothing, which endures for about twenty minutes—by which time the bus is slowly wheeling to a halt in the majestic square at the heart of this splendid old town. The question I want to consider is: what would be the epistemological fruit of their no doubt vivid and multifarious visual experiences during those highly unpleasant twenty minutes? Obviously not nothing—even though those sights passed by like apparitions in a dream! Many fragments linger, a church here, a doorway there, a policeman in strange garb holding up his hand, etc. And not merely fragments, but something of a time-order too, albeit a little unreliable in places: thus, memory sites the policeman as later than the church with the shining dome, but is a little uncertain as to where in time to set down the unobtrusive green doorway which for some reason caught the attention in the midst of this phantasmagoria.

What is noteworthy for its absence is structure: structure across space (that is revealed across time). And the reason for this absence is obvious enough. It is not so much the absence of *mental activity*, since it is likely that these demented arguers continued looking spasmodically in mindless distracted fashion as the sights swam by. Rather, it is the absence of *suitable internal objects* for those mental activities. It is the inexistence of perceptual projects with an *extensive spatial content* that accounts for the lack of spatial structure both in the resultant perceptual experience and in the knowledge gleaned therefrom. For example, these particular viewers had no interest in discovering what lay around the next corner, in noticing whether they were travelling towards those two unusual gothic towers visible at one point behind some aged apartment blocks, in seeing whether they were moving roughly in a straight line, or in any such structural issues. Their interests were altogether more fragmentary.

(2) *Structure 1.* In perception the adage 'as ye sow so shall ye reap' has force. This is because of two factors, which I now examine in turn.

First, it is because any intentional project whatsoever is a cognitively synthesizing force: it unites as one acts the multiple changing cognitions acquired during action. The commitment across time, both past and future, which is internal to intentional action, guarantees the retention in memory of the fruits of the cognitive synthesizing capacities put to use during the course of action: it guarantees to the agent a knowledge of his experienced active past. After all, a self-conscious being cannot be engaged in intentional action if he harbours absolutely no knowledge of his immediate active past. Think of the disastrous effect upon agency of a radical breakdown of short-term memory: it is a recipe for a special mental variety of paralysis (which extends to the physical *and* mental will)! What this rule implies is, that in the midst of intentional action one must retain a cognitive grip both on the past of the deed and of its objects. Now this principle is just as true of intentionally active *perceivings* like looking and listening as anywhere else. Merely to engage actively in perceiving is sufficient to ensure a cognitive hold upon the past of act and object. Earlier sectors both of the perceiving process, and of its outer perceived objects as well, must in some measure be retained for later cognition.

This claim needs to be couched more differentially if we are to adequately delimit the property I have in mind, as the following consideration reveals. Thus, it is evident that a measure of retention of the past of an experience is a necessity for *experience* as such: it is not merely a necessity for intentional action. For example, I cannot be hearing a continuous sound if at each instant I retain *nothing* of its past. It is certain that a radical breakdown of short-term memory would constitute a crisis for more than intentional action: it would stanch the flow of most experience!

If this is true, why single out intentional action for special mention? It is picked out for a very good reason. It is because the intention is unique in the mind in conferring upon us the power to determine the content and temporal properties of an experienced future which will become part of our recollected past. No other mental phenomenon has this property. Whereas the mere experientiality of absolutely any experience ensures a measure of short-term recall, we have in the intention the means of choosing part of our own internal history. In plotting an experienced future that we are entering upon, we implicitly plot a past which we will carry forward with us in memory. Thus, the intention is a cognitively synthesizing agency which can be used like an instrument, enabling us to take a hand in the construction of the changing cognitive map by which we live.

This special property of the intention stems from the unique encounter with time which is internal to intentional action. It is a consequence of the following fact. Namely, that any occurrent intentional willing at any moment of its existence takes as its internal-object an active event with sectors given as determinately located in past and future. In intentional action we relate self-consciously to an event-edifice structured across time in which we posit at each point a determinate past and a specific projected future: indeed, we do so 'on the move'—temporally! Where else do we encounter such a thing? Here a subject self-consciously creates a single temporally structured active experience, in which he explicitly posits a constantly mutating and determinate past and future as he himself moves temporally within and down that very experience. Now this is as valid of perceptual activities like looking and listening as of any other activity. Therefore if one engages intentionally in actively perceiving some temporally extensive object X, this generally suffices to ensure that earlier stages both of the perceptual process *and* the corresponding outer perceived X will be retained in awareness for cognition.

We see this property clearly when the perceptual activity is *expressly individuative* in aim. That is, in those vastly common situations in which in actively perceiving one is concerned to single out some structured individual perceptible, rather than mere continuity or process. For example, in listening to certain sounds I may intend to hear a melody or a statement through to its end. In such cases retention of the past acquires individuative import, and issues of extent and structure loom large. And this is true of absolutely any intentional activity which takes an individuated item as object. And the range involved can be great, opening up extensive and organized tracts of space and time. Think of the cognitive 'underpinning' needed for an intentional enterprise like sailing solo around the globe. Temporally ambitious projects both require *and* bequeath corresponding cognitions. Then in the case of the intentional perceptual activities of listening and looking this will be true both of the inner (perceptual) and the outer (perceived) reality. The net effect being that the objects retained for cognition are at once chosen, and endowed with properties of organization and comprehensiveness they would have lacked without mental activity.

(3) *Structure 2.* Thus, the intentional project acts as a synthesizing agency in the formation both of its cognitive presuppositions and its cognitive residue. But simultaneously the intention introduces synthesis and structuring of a quite different kind. For it acts also as a synthesizing agency in relation to its *active experiential expression*, effecting unity thererein: it unites experiences, and the objects of experience along with them. Here we have the second determinant of the fact that richer perceptual objects tend to accrue to richer perceptual projects.

What I have in mind is the fact that intentional projects do not just require and bequeath knowledge of future and past during action, they also *conjoin experiences* that will occur in the future and those already in the past as parts of one comprehensive experience. Thereby they enlarge and structure experience. The intentional act of uttering the sentence 'I want another cup of coffee' is a complex act-experience which comprehends the six distinct act-experiences of uttering those six words. A welding together of separate experiences as parts of a single active experience is therewith accomplished. Then this capacity for experiential synthesis proves to be of great significance when the project happens to be perceptual, for it extends onto the *objects of perception*. Thanks to it the objects which we perceptually experience can be assembled for the attention as parts of one complex perceived object. For example, the intentional activity of watching a dancer execute a rapid manœuvre consisting of six steps, is a complex and synthesized experience which involves the visual experience of *individuatively seeing* a six-step long dance phenomenon. In the absence of this intention, one may merely have perceived step after step after step—no more.

In the special case of perception this synthetic power depends upon a special property of the active perceptual attention. More exactly, on the causal properties of intentional perceptual willings. Thus, the internal object of active perceptual projects has an *attractive power*: it tends to draw forth, out of a perceptual field, and to absorb into awareness, the very object it seeks. If you are listening for the sound of the oboe in an orchestral chord, that precisely is what you are likely to hear; if you are looking to see the six-step dance manœuvre, here too this complex phenomenon is liable to come to your notice. In a special active attentive mental process that is not unlike the exertion of suction, the mind creates within the attention something of the ilk of a vacuum or matrix to receive what it causes to impact upon itself: it produces producing (from without). In short, what we are concerned with here is one of the main causal determinants of the objects of the perceptual attention. Because of it a process of looking can synthesize parts of a visible phenomenon which might instead have been experienced as mere fragments. Indeed, it is because of this property that looking can so much as exist. So much for the two modes of active structuring.

(4) *Structure as a whole.* Then in the case of the two arguing travellers there was neither a laying down in memory of extensive (mental, perceptual) act-stage parts, nor a laying down in memory of corresponding extensive object-stage (perceived) parts, nor the exercising of the attractive power of spatially extensive internal objects of active perceptual enterprises. The net effect of these neglects is, the phantasmagoric march past of the mostly disordered fragments of a large and ill-perceived object (to wit a section of a city), received into minds which at that time fail to bring forward any large-scale spatial structures to contain those parts, or any temporal thread upon which contiguously to site them. Mere islands of data, whose interrelations in space and time are as vaguely given as were the drifting continents upon ancient maps of the World.

All of this flowed from derelictions of the will. For we should remember that the enlargement and structuring of the internal objects of activities like looking has an *explanatory* as well as causal role to play. After all, it would be something of a *mental miracle* if these arguers had managed to gather significant information about the layout in space of the unfolding city—let us say of the kind disclosed to the consciousness of the ardent professional mapper who we shall suppose was seated next to them. There is simply no automatic registering of such data as the mapper acquired. Whereas the two-dimensional shape of an object like a drawing can instantaneously be apprehended without perceptual activity, those shapes (and much else besides) that are revealed to awareness only across time are for the most part perceptible only to subjects who intentionally harness the attractive power of the internal object of an active perceptual enterprise. While this is not true of simple shapes which are revealed over a few seconds (like the path of a rocket at night), it is true of almost all else. How could one hear a speech as a single entity, properly interpreting the sound masses and suitably individuating the speech from other residents of the sound world, in the absence of a process of listening?

What we do and do not manage to perceive over time, in the absence of the two active forms of mental causal control sketched above, is a relatively unpredictable matter. All manner of items and structures might be experienced, for all manner of reasons. Disorder, and a general dearth of meaning, is liable to be found in the experiential haul of the net which gets drawn in after perceptual consciousness has been left passively at the mercy of forces outside our control: a 'rag-bag' of odds and ends. This fact drives home the message that, in bringing the attentive will into play in our perceptual enterprises, and above all in choosing for those enterprises internal objects in which meaningful structures across space and time are introduced, we import a measure of sense and order whose appearance would otherwise be something of a mental miracle. The mental will alone is capable of such feats.

(b) Intelligibility

(1) In sum, the syntheses needed if across time we are to discover through perception the structures pertinent to the individuation and identification of a whole class of perceptible items, can be realized only if the necessary multiple temporally spaced perceptions take place within an *active perceptual project*. Now those perceptions occur in the course of a project which is driven by desires in which *knowledge and judgement* find representation. Then what I want at this juncture to suggest is, that it is under the wing of intentional perceptual activity that *reason and the understanding*, acting in conjunction with one's given fund of knowledge, manage to bear directly upon the processes of perception when they involve recognition across time, culminating in the constituting of an intelligible object.

We walk around a sculpture which interests us, again and again from many directions, and think in the end that we have some sort of knowledge of what the object looks like, that we could recognize a 'look-alike' or 'visual double'. In short, we experience its appearance. For as befits beings who conduct their lives in a space of three dimensions, the appearance of this object is experienced within those same three dimensions. Then even though perception is not a rational event, this epistemological procedure is a rational process. It is an activity driven by knowledge of the right perceptual means for a chosen perceptual end: a procedure which expressly brings the understanding into play, since we seek at each stage in looking at the object to grasp how it thus far 'all hangs together', and must put to use knowledge of our physical situation as we do. Indeed, without such a rational enterprise as this special example of *looking to see a shape*, this complex event of perception could not have seen the light of day. Knowledge breeds, not just more *knowledge* with the aid of new perceptions, but more *perceptions* with the aid of activity in which reason and the understanding are engaged.

The result is, the coming to consciousness of *internally intelligible* objects. Any object of which perceptually we apprise ourselves in this way, is given in the process as intelligible in character: the parts of the whole that we see and understand it to be, hang together in the mind in a set of consistent relations. When perceptual synthesis has to be accomplished over time through a set of multiple perceptions, activity (perceptual, and sometimes also ambulatory) is the necessary path by which this goal is reached. That is, perceptual activity through which reason and understanding are given scope in the process across time of assembling a single complex object for the perceptual attention.

(2) This lies outside the reach of non-rational animals as such. It should be clearly distinguished from something else that can be inaccessible to a non-rational animal: namely, a non-rational perceptual individuation that is (say) too complex. Thus, some non-rational animals simply lack the mental wherewithal to constitute a single item for perception out of the perceptible parts of some given object. The simpler an animal mind, the less its attention can assemble and the more impoverished its perceptual world. While absolutely *any* living creature with eyes can set them upon *anything* that is visible, in the case of each visible item only *some* beings will be capable of harbouring a veridical visual experience whose internal object encompasses parts of that external object in such a way as to constitute a *recognition and individuation* of it. Can a bee visually individuate a chair or a spoon?

Here we have one limiting factor. The other, which emerged above, was of a wholly different order. For whatever any non-rational creature may or may not be able perceptually to accomplish, those perceivings must of necessity be qualitatively different from the processes in humans of the kind recently described. In short, among perceptions there exist significant differentia on *two* different counts: on the count of complexity, and on that of intelligiblity—together with corresponding limitations. It may well be the case that bees are incapable of visually singling out chairs and spoons. Meanwhile, we have just noted that no non-rational animal can perceptually assemble intelligible structures, items which are accessible only to the rational. The following is an obvious example of the kind.

(3) If (say, in an elevator) one (correctly) hears the four sounds 'please' 'close' 'the' 'door' as issuing from a single unifying intention, that hearing of the complex outer phenomenon veridically synthesizes those sounds in one's awareness as parts of the one meaningful auditory whole. Simultaneously it unifies the four hearing experiences as parts of one hearing experience, namely the perception of that audible totality. An essential condition of such accomplishments is that one understand those parts to stand to one another in certain specific relations (something which is as true of seeing in the round as of meaningful wholes). Here we have a very simple example. However, spectacularly complex syntheses are common enough. It is a remarkable, though everyday experience, to have heard 'Die Meistersinger von Nürnberg', and much else of that ilk, in just this way.

To repeat, it is not just intelligible objects of the type of utterances and operas that are perceptually synthesizable only with the aid of reason. What of a visual nature goes on in consciousness when we take a proper look at (say) the Venus de

Milo is the same. Even though sculptures are rarely designed for aerial viewing, they are intended nonetheless to be viewed 'in the round': that is, in such a way as to reveal their three-dimensional virtues. Properties like sphericity are intended, not merely to be inferrable from visible contours and aspects, they are meant to be *seen*. And this is a 'higher-order' occurrence than one might suppose. It necessitates synthetic processes in the understanding which call upon one's rational powers. When the self-conscious experience the three-dimensional appearance of objects, this is what transpires within. Rational processes reveal intelligible objects.

Matters are qualitatively different with non-rational perceivers. When prolonged motor-perceptual exposure to some complex perceptible object leads to their being able to identify and act appropriately towards it, the relations of rational consistency that hold within our own representation of an object find no counterpart in their case. It is not an *intelligible object* their minds assemble. The World is, and cannot but be, consistent with itself, and the only consistency discoverable in non-rational internalizations of objects is a simple derivative of this fact. A fox who masters the oddities of a chicken-coop which was designed to outwit him, is merely a creature whose mind rapidly fashions cognitions whose contents match the outer object. While this is 'grasp' of a kind, the mind of this fox has not represented an internally intelligible object. Even though we correctly speak of understanding and intelligence being exercised here, the fox remains unacquainted with rational relations: it is a *non-rational* understanding that he brings to bear upon the problem. He learns rapidly what it is difficult or impossible for some other animals to learn. No more.

(c) 'Perspective'

(1) Thus, mental activeness imports intelligibility into much perceptual experience, since the perceptual projects are rational phenomena. It thereby enlarges the range of objects open to us. But it introduces one other important element into the epistemological 'yield' of waking consciousness: what I shall call 'perspective'.

I shall introduce this concept by noting that when in the normal course of our life we look about us at the world, we see much that fails to engage our practical interest: large-scale slices of the environment are irrelevant. Then it seems to me that simple facts like this can lead us to treat cognition as rather more of an end in itself than it can actually be. Think by contrast of the following example. Suppose that a racing driver travelling at something like 150 m.p.h. sees a few hundred yards down the track what looks suspiciously like a puddle of oil. Such a perception concentrates the mind marvellously—to adapt Dr Johnson's remark. It ushers into being an active attentive situation in which practical priorities overshadow all else. More exactly, one so structures the visual attention that one comes to discover details of the anticipated scene which enable the satisfactory completion of a somewhat perilous intentional instrumental activity. Now this is entirely the work of the mental will. It intentionally enmeshes two intentional activities, one motor and the other visual, producing thereby a measure of *internal experiential unity*. And such a state of affairs has matching cognitive repercussions. The history of these acts and their settings leaves a residue in the mind in which this internal unification is manifest. A spatio-temporal slice is cut out of the outer world for cognition in which one's practical involvement in the environment, and the active structuring of the attention its successful performance necessitates, are indirectly visible.

Then what I want to emphasize is that this example is no more than an hyperbolic instance of what holds to a degree of much perceptual experience. It is responsible for the World's wearing a look which is an objectification of our practical involvement in it. As a general rule the phenomena of the inner and outer world of consciousness tend not to relate as 'ships in the night' (consciousness not being so schismatic). Indeed, typically a measure of natural unity is present across the main sectors of the stream of consiousness, both between the voluntary practical and the perceptual cognitive, and it extends onto the cognitive 'yield' of consciousness.

What these observations remind us is, that the epistemological function of consciousness is not to construct a universal veridical cognitive portrait of the World, so to say *sub specie aeternitatis*. It is to assemble a mutating, perspectival, practically oriented, limited portrait, in which the enduring large-scale features of Reality recede into the background, and the immediacies of present life are to the fore. These features have implications from the point of view of experiential content and cognitive 'yield'. The selective slice of the environment given over an interval of time to cognition tends to be evidence of a mind at work (one's own), rather like the disarray left behind by Goldilocks or like Man Friday's footstep. This data indirectly reveals that *someone has been there* (indeed, is still present!). One inherits from the past a spatio-temporal slice of the World which has been relevant to the practical needs of some conscious being, and gains from the present a cognitive shadow of oneself! And behind most of this lies choice and mental action, without which a vastly different, more impoverished, and depersonalized cognitive 'yield' would result.

(2) Let me sum up what has emerged so far in the course of this disussion concerning the contribution of mental action to the discharge of the perceptual function of consciousness.

Through the use of the mental will we enlarge the momentary perception by extending it across space as well as through time, into the past and towards the immediate expected future, reaping correspondingly enhanced objects of cognition. And we extend it by making the objects of perception internally intelligible. In addition, we choose where in space we shall site ourselves, and so determine the field from which the objects of perception are to be drawn. And we tend attentively to select perceptible items relevant to the enterprises of the moment. Thus, we so act internally within our attention that the several cognitively significant strands of experience—the thinking, perceptual, and physically active—tend to a degree to bear a relation of partial integration to one another (so that what one perceives in the environment partially reflects what occurs within). And all this occurs as a result of mental activity.

What would it be for consciousness to be without those epistemologically oriented mental volitions? In any particular case it would emerge unscathed, since we can be conscious while perceiving nothing. But if we are speaking from a general standpoint, if we suppose that consciousness might in general be without these powers, we in effect hypothesize a consciousness as such incapable of fulfilling its prime epistemological function. That may not be possible.

3. Mental Will and the Distinctive Character of Consciousness

In the remainder of this chapter I advance a second distinct argument in support of the claim that a working mental will is a necessary condition of waking consciousness. Now whereas the first argument was directed to the epistemological properties of consciousness, the present argument is concerned initially neither with its epistemological nor even its functional properties. Rather, it addresses itself to the constitutive character of the state: more specifically, to those of the stream of consciousness of the conscious. However, the argument has direct epistemological implications, and this fact has guided me in my choice of topic and argument. In short, epistemology remains the theme, even though at first only indirectly. Just in what way it does becomes clearer towards the end of the chapter.

(a) The distinctive character of conscious experience

(1) The experience of the environment which enters the awareness of those who are conscious has something of the following character. Thanks to the appearance of a sector of the world close to one's body, to the presence of items relevant to one's interests, and to an awareness of structures in space determined by one's activities, one is *implicated* in the cognitive data. Thus, one is not unlike H. G. Wells's 'invisible man' seeing his own footsteps appearing in the snow! Somewhat as we are visually aware of physical objects through experiencing parts of our own mental machinery, to wit visual sense-data, indeed through experiencing our own brain according to Russell, so at each moment outer reality is disclosed to consciousness through awareness of sectors of the world closely indicative of one's present (and recent, and even impending!) presence. And it more or less has to be this way. It is not that the world is a pure wilderness which is knowable only if order is imposed upon its chaos. It is rather that there is no *one objective order*, so that if it is to come to awareness it must be through a chosen and indeed personal mapping, one's 'lifeline' cutting out the stencil so to say.

If this is what tends to come to us from 'without' when conscious, what of the internal scene? What do we discover when we look within? Well, it seems to me that a special *inner life* is necessary for consciousness, one involving specific modes of thought, feeling, and imagination. Indeed, it seems that the inner world of the conscious is both distinctive and inimitable. After all, consciousness is a self-vali-dating phenomenon, in the sense that phenomena external to the state can have no bearing upon its being the state: consciousness. Thus, waking consciousness is a mental state, and can exist when all occurrent interactive causal links to the envir-onment have been severed: one can be fully conscious in complete darkness, silence, and total sensory-motor failure. Yet whereas one can stand in any old occurrent causal relation to one's surrounds and preserve the state of consciousness, we cannot extend a comparable licence to the interior phenomena themselves. Decisive constraints operate within. And not merely in the mind as such, but specifically in the inner life or awareness of the subject, which is to say in the *stream of conscious-ness*. And that is to say that the stream of consciousness of the conscious is both dis-tinctive and inimitable.

(2) These considerations suggest a completely different (and non-functional) argument for the theory that consciousness internally depends on a working mental will: one based on the distinctive character of the experiential inner life of the con-scious, rather than on the epistemological uses or cognitive accomplishments of consciousness. Thus, one might try to demonstrate such a dependence upon the will through appeal in the first place to the special character of some *cognitively significant* element of the stream of consciousness of the conscious (as opposed, say, to the affective). Then if an inner life endowed with this special cognitive property is necessary for the state, might it not in the second place be the case that this special property depends for its existence upon a working mental will? Along such lines an argument might be assembled to the effect that mental action is an essential to the constituting of an experiential stream of consciousness that is both necessary and sufficient for consciousness.

Such an argument must take the form of demonstrating that the streams of con-sciousness of the conscious have a certain *pivotal* and at the same time *openly evident* property, which can exist only if the mental will is at work. Accordingly, if we are to assemble a constitutive argument along these lines, we must discover such a prop-erty. Earlier I noted a certain arbitrariness in our choice of which characteristic of consciousness to attempt to link to the will, seeing that the constitutive properties of consciousness form a tight circle—whereupon I decided to break into that circle at what is perhaps its least contentious point, viz. its epistemological powers. Here I look elsewhere, although (as remarked above) the property we in fact choose stands in close relation to epistemology. The question we must now consider is, which property of the stream of consciousness of the conscious meets the above specifications?

(b) Choosing a property of conscious experience which depends on mental willing

One avenue by which one might come upon such a property is through considering a highly familiar (and flawed) objection to *any* argument for the activity thesis which is founded upon the supposed 'distinctive and inimitable' character of the stream of consciousness of the conscious. Namely, a 'dream objection' of the kind advanced by Descartes in the *Meditations*. To wit: if character rather than causal interaction with the environment determined consciousness, all that is relevant in that character ought to be reproducible in a dream—in the absence of consciousness and the mental will. After all, the dreaming seem to themselves precisely to be awake, and the principle that whatever can be consciously experienced can be dreamed seems inviolable. The conclusion we are invited to draw being, that even if consciousness happens to necessitate a working mental will, the reason cannot lie in the character of the stream of consciousness of the conscious.

Now so far as I can see the only validity dream-arguments of this kind possess, is in demonstrating that *content* cannot be the differentia of the streams of consciousness of the conscious. Such arguments cannot prove that the stream of consciousness of the conscious is not 'inimitable', indeed cannot even prove that the *constituent experiences* of that 'stream' are not 'inimitable'. And yet in the present context this 'dream objection' has one signal virtue—which is the reason I cite it. Namely, it brings to our notice a—non-contentual, non-experiential—constituent of the 'stream' which one might otherwise overlook, viz. the type of the rationale governing its progression through time. It is illuminating to compare the stream of experience in the conscious with that of the dream on this count. My suggestion is that in waking consciousness a different *explanatory principle* is at work from in dreaming, one that bears a significant relation to the mental will. This brings to light what is probably the most fundamental flaw in the 'dream objection'.

How does one come by this response to the 'dream objection'? I think along these lines. One begins by endorsing the principle that whatever is consciously experienceable is dreamable. Thus, suppose I dream I am the 'mapper', seated up in the front of a bus next to two embarrassing arguers, watching a narrow street curve around into a grand avenue which I can see leads after a few hundred yards into a large square, thinking as I do such thoughts as 'I wonder if there is accommodation nearby?' All this is the kind of thing a conscious 'mapper' might have experienced: it is a reproduction in dream form of what might occupy the consciousness of a wakeful being. But what about the *explanatory links* between those various experiences, what about the *causal powers* whereby one element in a real 'mapper' 's conscious experience gives way to another? Are these determining factors likewise reproducible in dream form? I suggest they are not even reproduced if (fantastically) one were to dream they were reproduced! Reproducing the *contents* of waking experience cannot reproduce the *causal rationale* of waking experience. And in fact not only is the rationale different, it is of a wholly different order. And what this difference shows is, that the flow of experience must be a radically different kind of phenomenon in the two cases. This is what I shall argue and elaborate.

4. Mental Will and the Causal Rationale of Conscious Experience

Then it is this property which I will take as a yardstick of consciousness. And to start with it leads me into an examination of the dream from an explanatorial point of view. For here in the dream we have the contrasting case with which to begin the substantiation of the thesis that the rationale of conscious experience is distinctive to the state. Thereafter I concentrate my attention upon the stream of consciousness of the conscious, once again with explanation as the theme. This project involves an examination of the several cognitively significant processive streams that are to be found in the conscious mind. In short, it leads into a study of consciousness from a different angle from any so far attempted in this work. Thus, whereas in Chapter 2 I attempted to delineate the 'anatomy of consciousness', and in Chapter 3 characterized what one might call the 'cognitive physiology' of the state, the ensuing discussion takes us into a different terrain altogether. Namely, into an examination of the character across time of the cognitively significant processive constituents of the stream of consciousness of the conscious: in particular, the type of the prevailing 'logos'.

(a) The rationale of the dreaming stream of consciousness

Accordingly, I now begin the comparison between dream and waking experience with this property in mind. I start by considering causation in the dream. We will see that whatever causal principle leads from any one dream element α to its successor element β, it can be neither rational, nor purely cerebral, nor 'associative' in type. Consider these possibilities in turn, starting with the suggestion that rational causation might link α to β.

When does rational causation occur in the mind? For the most part when we believe or desire (etc.) for good reason. All important is the capacity to grasp rational relations like that of being evidence, and for such 'grasp' to have the power to determine psychological phenomena, immediately and exhaustively. One mark of such rational origins, one necessary though insufficient mark, is their immediate accessibility to their owner. Then how could anything of this order hold in the case of dreaming? For dreams are in general wholly inscrutable from the point of view of origins to the dreaming subject. In short, it is obvious that rational forces cannot be what propel the dream forwards.

Then there is reason to think that dream causation must be partly mental, and so not purely cerebral in character. One consideration is to be found in the fact that dreams are narratable phenomena: no 'word-salad' or mass of mental fragments, but a continuous experiential process in which items retain their identity across time. The latter feature is evidenced in our capacity to refer back to earlier occupants of a dream in recounting it. For example, 'I saw an apple on a table and walked over and picked it up.' Such a capacity for persistence and reappearance on the part of the *dramatis personae* of dreams suggests the likely hypothesis that the first appearance of the apple was causally contributory to its subsequent appearances. How could identity across time be preserved within a dream if this was not so? While this is scarcely a decisive proof, it finds support in the fact that the experiences of the day frequently reverberate within a dream, thus implicating memory and with it mental causation on at least some occasions.

The third type of causation, the variety of mental causation we call 'associative', is plainly not the causal key to the dream. 'Mental association' links strings of images, self-indulgent trains of thought, stray enterprises like the parts of a meandering daydream, and various other 'freewheeling' mental phenomena, and is frequently traceable to connections in one's experiential history. Nothing like this holds of dreaming. If 'association' really did govern this phenomenon, it ought to be relatively obvious that it was so. Then it is interesting that as close a student of dreams as Freud could feel free at one point in his career to postulate 'wish fulfilment' as the governing causal principle, and then many years later to retract the hypothesis in the face of difficulties posed by anxiety dreams. This underlines the point.

The upshot of these considerations is, that from the natural standpoint of subjectivity, as opposed to that of science, it is a matter of some obscurity why one dream element is followed by its successor. One simply has no natural insight as to why one dreams what one does. Indeed, as a general rule one has next to no intuitions on the matter, more or less irrespective of how sensitive or perspicacious one may be. Here and there one notes an echo from waking life, now and then one surmises that these imaginings cohere with such and such a personality trait or give expression to some impulse or wish, and these observations may be shrewd enough, but natural insight has little or no scope with dreams. We exercise this latter capacity when we explain the origins of our beliefs and desires and actions and intentions. I can think of nothing remotely comparable in the case of dreams. Here 'natural insight' is 'out of its depth'. Plainly it is 'out of its depth' in the formation of perceptual impressions. Here we have another phenomenon with the same property.

So what is the principle of progression in the case of the dreaming stream of consciousness? Short of theoretical speculation, no principle is known or knowable. Whether or not the type of causation exemplified is mental causation, as at least in part it seems likely to be, the origins remain hidden from view.

(b) The rationale of the stream of consciousness in the conscious (1): idle active drift

(1) Earlier I claimed that if we were to assemble a constitutive argument in favour of the thesis that consciousness necessitates a working mental will, we should have first of all to discover a pivotal cognitively significant and readily demonstrable constitutive property of the stream of consciousness of the conscious, and then secondly show that this property depends upon the mental will. The property I chose to examine was the distinctive character of the rationale governing the progression of the experiential processes with cognitive representational content that occur in the minds of the conscious. More exactly, its pellucidity. Then the argument that is built around that supposed property takes the following form. It first attempts to

demonstrate the existence of the aforesaid pellucidity, and then secondly tries to show how this property depends upon a working mental will. So the first thing we need to do is establish the first part of this dual assertion. It leads me to examine the explanatory situation prevailing in experiential processes in the conscious. We shall see that it is grossly dissimilar to that encountered in dreaming.

Accordingly, I turn at this point from dreaming experience to the stream of consciousness in the conscious. Roughly, this is divisible into two broad categories of experience: the inner life of thought and affect, and the intuitional awareness of objects. The phenomena I now examine, drawn from these two categories, are chosen with a view to delineating the explanatorial situations obtaining with cognitively significant experiences in the conscious. They are daydreaming, controlled phantasy, active perceiving, and ratiocination. The aim is to uncover the principles governing the progression through time of these experiential processes in conscious subjects. Then I shall begin by examining those phenomena which might be thought to pose the greatest difficulty for any thesis positing pellucidity of rationale.

(2) So let us start by considering those loose-knit conscious experiential processes that are nearest in type to the phenomenon just discussed (viz. the dream). The daydream is the most obvious example, but there are other comparable phenomena. One of these is an activity that one might describe as 'directionless soliloquy'. Molly Bloom's monologue in *Ulysses* is a case in point. We all know people who, as one might express it, 'free-associate in public', who 'natter away', uttering 'the first thing that comes into their head', and Molly Bloom's monologue is nothing but a silent internal example of such. This phenomenon has interesting properties. To begin, it is a case of 'talking to oneself', and being talking cannot but be intentionally active. Now these particular intentions stand to one another in a rather special relation. For here each intention is continually giving way to a successor intention, yet without their expressing themselves in discrete stages, and without their realizing any single comprehensive intention as they do. After all, this phenomenon is rarely chosen, and what one might call 'will power' has no scope here. Thus, such an activity simply cannot be done with *determination*. One can no more do with determination what Molly Bloom was doing, than one can day-dream with 'grit'. This is because the connective tissue of these rapidly changing intentions is mere association and inclination. As one word-project is approaching its termination, another is already welling up into place through the operation of such mental causes as that 'it made me think of . . .' and 'it gives me pleasure to go over . . .', etc.

This phenomenon provides us with a model for the daydream. In daydreaming we encounter a similar intention-situation. Now when I speak of 'daydreaming', I am thinking mostly of non-verbal reminiscence or idle phantasy, and once again of determination by inclination and mental association. A daydream unfolding is not unlike a young child wandering slowly across a field, his mind and its intentions drifting almost like a raft at the mercy of stray currents. Yet why suppose intentions operate *at all*? After all, one can scarcely so much as intend to daydream, mostly one simply slips into the state and discovers oneself adrift in the process a little later. Well, it certainly follows from this that the process cannot be intentional under 'daydream'. Nonetheless the mind remains intentionally active under other headings at each point in that process. Thus, the immediate future is already prefigured in descriptions like 'I was remembering the time we visited X . . .', and this strongly suggests the existence of a foreknowledge conferred by intentions. What seems to be peculiar to the daydream is the steady deflecting of intentional and mostly nonverbal inclinatory imaginings at the hands of factors like association and inclination. A certain frame of mind seems to be needed if this is to occur. It is difficult to daydream with anxiety.

(3) My present topic is 'idle active drift' in the experience of the conscious. Then it is worth briefly considering the wonderfully interesting phenomenon of presleep phantasy (that from which one sometimes 'awakes' with a start!). When this phase of the inner life looms up, the intentions have all but petered out, the objects of phantasy have acquired something of a life of their own, and it is less than clear why one imagined item gives way to its successor. While association and inclination may still be operative, a spectrum of cases probably exists, one end nearer to dreaming from an explanatorial point of view, the other closer to the daydream. When Freud said: 'Here we catch the censor red-handed', what I think he had in mind was the fact that in this state we sometimes actually experience one thing as 'being' or 'standing for' or 'changing into' another. This suggests the operation of a different 'logic'.

One way of bringing out the full significance of this state is by describing the novelties occurring at the less self-aware end of the above spectrum. Here the future shows a tendency to simply descend upon one, and correlatively what is happening is (as one might say) 'news' to the subject. In a somewhat divided state of mind, perhaps in a temporary fluctuation in wakefulness, one can find oneself marvelling at what one has just found oneself thinking, at the sudden loss of grip upon reality, at the sheer oddity of the mental content. Such a cognitively receptive frame of mind is a sure mark of the lessening of the sway of the intention and generally of active self-command within one's own mind, and goes as we have just noticed with a diminution of self-understanding. Now these observations show how a phenomenon of this kind can lend support to the theory that consciousness and transparency of rationale keep close company. After all, the unselfconscious end of the 'spectrum' verges upon sleep.

That concludes my discussion of what are probably the three most notable examples of idle active drift in the conscious: 'mere directionless soliloquy', daydreaming, and the earlier or more self-aware varieties of pre-sleep phantasy. A summary statement of the explanatory situation obtaining in these examples of mental spontaneity is, that the rationale from moment to moment of the progression is openly accessible to one, seeing that the advance is intentionally active. However, just why these rather than those intentions arose as the process advanced is a matter upon which one may lack authority or insight.

(c) The rationale of the stream of consciousness in the conscious (2): active perceptual processes

So much for the explanatorial situation in the case of those experiential processes in the conscious that are closest in character to the dream. These are phenomena in which, while the rule of intention is constant, it is far from comprehensive or over-arching. The other examples of experiential process in the conscious that I examine are noteworthy for 'single-mindedness', for the presence of a single unifying intention binding the parts together. The first of these is, active perceptual processes like listening and looking (where self-determination might appear to be qualified by the encounter with outer phenomena). I now proceed to examine such phenomena. Thereafter in Section (d) I investigate those active thinking sectors of the stream of consciousness whose intentional objects are at once comprehensive and fully individuated. We will see that comparable explanatory situations obtain in all of these cases.

Suppose one is listening to a speech. This experiential phenomenon is perpetuated across time thanks to an intention and act-desire, and ultimately for certain reasons. Does this mean that mental phenomena completely determine the character of the process? By no means. Audible events over which the listener has no control inevitably also play a decisive part. Thus, that one is at time t listening to some sentence s, requires a joint and concurrent explanation in terms both of the (mental) sources of a voluntary activity *and* (non-mental) impinging air-waves. In the absence of either of these two disparate factors, listening could not occur. Ought we to conclude that the explanation of the progression of this substream of the stream of consciousness is only *partly* internal? I doubt it. In order to see how this can be so, contrast the above situation with one in which the speech is punctuated here and there by the sound of nearby fireworks—which one hears.

One heard those fireworks both because one was listening to the speech (as opposed, say, to being lost in a daydream) *and also* because of their loudness: these two independent causal agencies proved sufficient. Likewise one heard the sentence because one was listening *and* the sounds impinged on one's auditory apparatus. Now these explanations are palpably dissimilar in type. For the objects of hearing are disparately acquired. Thus, to *what* was one listening? One did not *merely* listen, nor do so merely *prior* to hearing, so to say writing a blank cheque in the attention. Listening is not like flinging the doors wide open in a welcoming gesture, and waiting for arrivals! The inner and outer objects pace one another to a nicety throughout the process. One was at each instant listening precisely to what one was hearing: the internal object of listening gathering *exactly as* the perceived object crystallized. Therefore determinacy of object is not conferred from without—

which lessens the motivation for positing split causes. While we do not want to embrace the absurdity that an inner process might invent its outer objects, we go the wrong way about avoiding it if we suppose that listening and sound act independently. The very existence of such an activity as listening depends upon the strange confluence of inner and outer factors. They are indeed two agencies, and distinct existences, yet *listening* cannot occur unless more than the mind determines what occurs within listening. It remains an unqualified truth that listening is pure mental activity, with purely mental origins.

The conclusion is, that the explanatory translucence of the progression of listening is in no degree 'muddied' by the fact that this process encompasses as part of itself hearings in which are encountered events its owner neither willed nor even expected. In such situations a sort of dialectical transcending of the opposition of the creative will and the sheer recalcitrant 'otherness' of physical reality is effected: a developmental accomplishment of the first order. What *is* listening but such a thing? These irremediable openings out onto the environment in no way compromise the self-determination of the process. So much for directed inner process which is at the mercy of the 'outside'.

(d) The rationale of the stream of consciousness in the conscious (3): directed active interiority

(1) Something similar is found in the active thinking sector of the stream of experience, in what one might call the true realm of interiority. I examine two sharply opposed examples of the kind. On the one hand a rehearsed phantasizing of the Walter Mitty kind, on the other hand a process of intensive ratiocinative exploratory thinking (where one seems to be at the mercy of the 'inside'). I begin with the former.

We shall suppose that a well-worn phantasy occurs, commencing with Mitty entering the casino at Monte Carlo and culminating a few minutes later in his breaking the bank. As with listening the onset and perpetuation of this process owe their existence to intention and desire, and ultimately to reasons. However, this process differs significantly from listening in that all that occurs in the course of its development is typically forseeable in advance. No problem arises of bringing interior and exterior, or rational and non-rational, dual causal forces into an intelligible and quasi-dialectical relation. No oil and water explanatory structure threatens. All that occurs in the ongoing continuous process emerges, not merely out of the resources of the mind, but from the mental will pure and simple, driven often enough by rational forces.

(2) The other example of directed active interior process, namely intensive exploratory thinking, looks on the face of it very different from the above, and in many way akin to listening. Thus, in neither case is the future already prefigured, so to say coiled up like a carpet in the subject's mind, merely awaiting the signal to unroll. And explanatorily also it seems structurally similar to listening, despite the

fact that it does not lay itself open causally to the environment. My suggestion is that they are indeed closely akin, but that their unlikeness to rehearsed intentional phantasy is less significant than one might think. Ratiocinative exploratory thought shares this much with fishing, that one is in either case dependent upon whether anything of value lies within a given region and on whether any such item is accessible. In each case one engages in an activity in the hope that a desired entity 'surface' to cap one's efforts, something which is to this degree determined in advance: that it is singled out from the start under a definite description which unites the specificity of some given desirable trait with an openness as to realization, in such a way as to leave scope for the unknown. Just as listening to a speech prepares a mental matrix for the reception of intelligible sentences relating intelligibly to those preceding it, without either anticipating the sentences in advance *or* being wide enough to accommodate the noise of fireworks; and rather as fishing leaves space for this or that variety of fish, but scarcely for old boots; so exploratory thinking imposes restrictions such that some astonishing mental occurrences will be accounted continuations of the ratiocinative process, whereas some others—such as a stray memory of a cricket match—will not. This restriction of scope has explanatorial repercussions which align listening and ratiocinating more closely with intentional phantasy than one might suppose.

Thus, in ratiocination the resources of the mind play a role comparable to that occupied by the outer world in listening. In neither case is explanation in terms of mental purposes deflected. Even though unknown resources of the mind play an essential part in throwing up into consciousness the relevant thought θ as one puzzled over xyz, and despite the fact that the functioning of those resources is not one's thinking, it remains an unqualified truth that thought θ entered the mind because one was thinking about xyz. What sort of a thing would thinking be otherwise? How is thinking so much as possible in the very first place if not through the stirring up of such mental machinery? Whereas the bodily will eschews positing willing and mechanistic-functioning as joint contributory agencies through the device of *identification*, the mental will avoids the identical pitfall through the quite different means of *self-transformation*, the immediate production of the production of change in its own being. In short, we should not suppose we are in the putatively fortunate position where two distinct causal agencies coincidentally contribute to the generation of the one effect. Rather, one causal agency is of such a kind that it internally involves the activation of a non-identical agency. We have already encountered this causal structure in listening. Listening both involves and causally explains hearing through being the active production of a mental attractive force which immediately causes the causing by air waves of the hearing it involves: it draws hearing into being and itself.

The net effect of these unusual explanatory situations is, that despite the fact that the cooperation of mental resources is not the same as thinking, any more than the impinging of shock waves on the auditory apparatus is listening, thought θ entered the mind because we were thinking about xyz, and we heard a certain passage in the speech because we were listening to the speech. Both phenomena realize a state of affairs in which the line of rationality is perpetuated despite the impact of external causal agencies. As we expressed it, a dialectical overcoming of the opposition of the will's creativity and the 'brute otherness' of phenomena external to the will is effected in the phenomenon. Rational explanation can hold sway despite the fact that the mental events in question owe their existence to unchosen phenomena. And it can do so without qualification. It was for this reason that I earlier claimed that listening and ratiocination are less dissimilar explanatorily from rehearsed intentional phantasy than one might think. Despite the inevitable impact on the mind of phenomena external to the will, the line of progression of this sector of the stream of consciousness is capable of wholly rational determination. Ratiocinative thinking and listening to a speech are rational activities. This type of situation typifies the whole of our encounter with Nature when in the state consciousness.

5. The Mental Will and Explanatory Translucence

That concludes my survey of the explanatory situation obtaining in the main varieties of experiential process. I now want to interpret those findings, to bring out what they reveal concerning the explanatory properties of these processes. The thesis I shall defend is, that activeness of character and pellucidity of developmental rationale go together. Now it is clear that the greatest difficulty for this thesis is presented by *imaginings*. Accordingly, I begin by reviewing what emerged on this count.

(a) Imaginings: diverse explanatorial situations in dream and waking experience

I began with the explanatorial situation in dreaming. The first property we noted was narratability, each instant flowing intelligibly into the next. The characters in a dream are sufficiently preserved amidst flux to permit reference across time within the dream. This limited retention of identity suggests that each sector of the dream helps produce its succeeding sectors. However, the rationale underlying that progression is inaccessible to first-person insight. The overall picture we are left with is this. Either on the one hand that each element α draws into existence its immediate successor element β, according to an opaque rationale. Alternatively, that α simply arises and β simply follows for reasons wholly unknowable pre-scientifically.

I then contrasted the explanatorial situation holding in a process in waking consciousness which shares imaginative status with the dream: namely, an intentionally individuated phantasy of the Mitty kind. At first one might assume that certain significant causal similarities existed. It might at first seem as if each element of phantasy assisted in the production of its successor element, helping to draw it into being, so that (for example) the phantasy of hearing the croupier intone '*les jeux sont faits*' might seem as if it helped produce a seeing in the 'mind's eye' of a spinning roulette wheel, which in turn engendered one's 'seeing' a ball roll into a slot on a wheel. And yet we know it is not so. Just as a dishonest mind might be actively determining what happens to an actual ball on a real roulette wheel, so in the Mitty phantasy a controlling mind lurks behind the events happening in the imagination and pulls the mental strings. It is this mind, not the elements of the phantasy, that is responsible for the development of the mental sequence. It is the mind of the owner of the mental 'establishment'!

Note the causal agencies at work in this case. It might superficially look as if an image of a croupier closing bets, and one of a ball rolling into a slot, are what should concern us. But in fact what is going on is of a completely different order. At the bottom of it all lies *desire*: act-desire, and doubtless also propositional-desire. Out of this base is spawned an intention: to 'run through' a well-worn internal film, which in turn engenders a striving to imagine certain gratifying events, which somehow leads to the occurrence of these imaginings. All of this is extra-visual, and extra-dramatic within the mind. It is, so to say, off-stage, the working of a stage-manager or director or puppeteer; for the actors themselves have no life of their own, being wholly animated from elsewhere. This is, after all, not just a case of mental causation operating within or across a mind. We are in the presence here of a very special mental-causal line, one such that the subject can take responsibility for and identify with it: the line of the will. The mental causation that culminates in action has this special character.

Let me now summarily compare the explanatorial situation in these two processes in the imagination, beginning with the dream. This phenomenon is a mere mental happening arising opaquely in the mind, a piece of mental Nature as one might say, with no further identity conferred upon it through 'higher' ulterior meaning-endowing origins. By contrast, the intentionally individuated phantasy possesses an individuating structure and overall character: it has a beginning, a mid-point, and a completion point, being an artefact of the mind. Such an origin in intention and will lifts this phenomenon into an altogether different explanatorial league from the dream. This phantasy is at once literally the work of a mind and explanatorially out in the open: it wears its explanatorial heart upon its sleeve. Act-desire and belief give rise to intention, intention and indexical time-orientation in turn engender willing, and they do so without remainder.

(b) Daydreaming and the universal thesis

(1) How widespread is this latter complex property, in which are united activeness of character with transparency of explanation? Well, not every process in the consciousness of the wakeful is active in type or pellucid in rationale: for example, affective processes like the development of grief. To be sure, these phenomena are without representational cognitive content. Yet even if we restrict processes in the stream of consciousness to phenomena with cognitive content, a problem is posed for any universal thesis by loose-knit processes like daydreaming. Here it seems more plausible to suppose that each sector of the experience might draw into being

its immediate successor, and for reasons partly opaque to the subject. 'Association' and inclination tend to be hypothesized in these cases, along with imponderables, and it is often unclear what rationale governs the development of the process. Then how can such an account of daydreaming be squared with the universal thesis, according to which all experiential processes with cognitive content that are occurring in conscious beings are said to unite explanatorial pellucity with an activeness of status that is its source?

(2) Well, while it may be that the daydream follows an *overall path* that is determined by association (etc.), it is a serious mistake to suppose each point in the process draws its successor point into being associatively (etc.). This is because behind each incident in a daydream lies an intention, and it is these intentions which determine the immediately succeeding phases of the process. In short, once again it is the active subject himself. Accordingly, it cannot be that in daydreaming image breeds image for reasons unknown, as happens with dreams. Rather, while occupation breeds occupation for whatever reason, each phase in the process leads to its successor phase through the mediation of an intention. In short, through the practical commitment of the agent-subject.

Then it is an additional question just why it is that any one such occupation leads into another, why one occupation gives rise to a new inclination, to a new intention, and therewith to a succeeding occupation. Doubtless it is often in part through 'association'. Nonetheless *at each point* behind the scene lies an intention and its expression in the will. That causally active intention is at that very moment determining the next stage of the process, and so playing an explanatory role in relation to the advance of the process. And that is to say, that the subject himself is 'behind' it all. He is still in charge of the 'newsreel' as one might express it, even if a little sleepy on this occasion!

(c) The general explanatorial situation of experiential processes in the conscious

(1) The summary situation concerning imaginings as a whole is this. Both the character of the phenomenon, and the type of its explanation, significantly alters as we pass from controlled phantasy, to daydreaming, to pre-sleep phantasy, to dreaming. The imagining of controlled phantasy is active and intentional, that of daydreaming is the same (in wayward fashion), dreaming is simply inactive, and in pre-sleep phantasy a spectrum of possibilities bridge the latter two cases (with matching explanatorial properties). In short, there is more than meets the 'mind's eye' in these imaginings. Behind the string of phantasies lies a very different explanatory story in these several phenomena. In two cases at least a mind lurks behind these processes, not just in that the workings of a mind mediate the transition from element to element, but in that a person intentionally 'pulls the strings'. This is not true of dreaming, but holds of the Mitty phantasy, and, though differently, is true of daydreaming. It is this person, rather than the elements of the phantasizing (let alone the 'phantasy X's'), that possesses the power responsible for the onward movement

of this mental phenomenon. At each instant desire and intention propel a striving by a subject. And that precisely is not to assert that each *stage* of the active process causes its successor active stage (let alone claim that the '*phantom objects*' generate one another!)

I have confined the present discussion concerning the rationale governing the movement or progression of experiential processes to imaginative phenomena. This is because of the difficulties they present for the thesis of explanatorial pellucidity. What emerged is that when those experiences occur in the conscious, they are exercisings of the mental will, and thus the product of desire and intention-commitment. Then as a result of these origins, a pellucid developmental rationale exists. While this is not true of dreaming, it holds of all conscious imaginings. Nowhere do we encounter phenomena which clash with the rule linking translucency of rationale and activeness of the mental will.

(2) Then it remains only to recall the earlier discussion of active perceptual processes like listening, and thinking processes like exploratory ratiocination, to grasp how comprehensive must be the sway of this rule in those processive experiences with cognitive representational content which populate the stream of consciousness of the conscious. We saw how phenomena like listening and thinking were in part determined by events lying outside our control, yet in such a manner as to in no way deflect the developmental line projected by the originating intention. It remains as true as in any other activity that listening advances these further few steps because of whatever mental forces persuaded one to listen in the first place and continue listening now. In this way the explanatory lucidity that enters the mental scene with the appearance of the will extends to these phenomena in which the mind is, so to say, buffeted from without. Thus, despite the essential unpredictability of one's next thought, intelligibility is instantiated in exploratory ratiocination just as much as in the example of Mitty's controlled imaginings. While affective experiences occur in dreaming and waking and differ from these phenomena in this respect, those experiential processes that are endowed with cognitive representational content must in waking subjects exhibit the dual properties of activeness of character and explanatorial pellucidity.

(d) Explanatorial pellucidity

I should say a little at this point about what I have called 'explanatorial pellucidity'. It is clear this concept must go well beyond that of knowledge of mental origins, as well as that of mentally-immediate knowledge of mental origins. That I know that I now see a landscape because my visual field is presently inhabited by coloured patches, leaves a million questions unanswered. And that I know I just now got a fright because of that gun's being fired onstage, which is a 'because' that is an immediate mental datum, again leaves much unresolved. My tranquil neighbour did not bat an eyelid, and it is a matter for investigation which might transport one back into the farther reaches of evolutionary history as to why the 'because' was actualized in me in the first place. That is, I need not know *why* I got a fright *because of* that noise. Indeed, it is difficult to imagine anything that could conclusively patch up this explanatory gap. The same qualifications apply to some other cases, less primitive in nature, and more open to mental explanation, where the object of experience actually includes its own rationale. Thus, I know I am frightened of this large evilly snarling dog on account of it looks very much as if it might hurl itself violently at my shins. Yet not everybody would be aquake in this situation. Odd, and even unnatural as it may seem, some people might stay as cool as a cucumber were they in my shoes. These divergences in response reveal the existence of unknown operative causal agencies.

In speaking of explanatorial pellucidity we must have something stronger in mind than the above. Not just mental causes which are immediately known, nor those which bring their own rationale, but those which close up the kind of gap these cases reveal—if that is a real possibility. While rationality might seem to point the way to such a thing, one must make two caveats. An explanation is rational only if reasons both immediately and exhaustively explain the explicandum. Accordingly, rationality looks to be an *ideal,* so that while many beliefs count as rational, we have realistically to accept that it is never possible to completely weed out all non-rational influences like desire. Nevertheless, insofar as those reasons act explanatorially as rational causes, they do so exhaustively. The other caveat is, that the explanatorial pellucidity that concerns me in this chapter pertains specifically to reason. But in fact the concept of pellucidity has a wider application than reason. I elucidate this claim in the ensuing discussion concerning the special properties of action.

6. The Special Nature of Action

(a) Action and lucidity

The problem is to discover the contribution made to consciousness, not by the bodily will (for we can be fully conscious though supine in a hammock, and even if totally paralysed), but by the mental will (which cannot in the conscious be analogously incapacitated, or indeed wholly idle). What is under present scrutiny is what insomniacs experience as a compulsion they would dearly be without: the treadmill-imperative!

One central idea has informed my thinking in the second half of this chapter, and it received support in the foregoing discussion in which we compared the explanatorial properties and activity-status of experiential processes in conscious and non-conscious subjects. It is that the mental will imports internal intelligibility into the processive advance of the stream of consciousness, and that in the self-conscious it does so through enabling reason to determine that advance. It seems that the only experiential processes that are rational progressions are active in character, and that only through rationality, and so through rational agency, can internal intelligibility enter experiential processes in the self-conscious. Only a mind steering its own cognitive path through a wider cognitive scene, a self-causing which is furthered by rational steps, can introduce pellucidity into the flow of experience. While a string of mental states, such as beliefs or long-term desires or intentions, can rationally support one another without exercise of the mental will, I can think of no analogue among experiential processes.

(b) Action and reason

(1) These singularities are closely related to some of the special properties of action. It seems to me that what is so interesting about the will is not so much its kinship to force, as its managing to effect a union of this property with several others of significance. The first of these properties is one which might on the face of it appear somewhat antithetical in character to force: namely, a marked sensitivity to the promptings of reason. Then to this strangely married pair of properties I conjoin a third, which is encountered in bodily willing and is a direct derivative of the essential dependence of physical action upon the eliciting of mechanistic cooperation. This is the property of realizing the *only* tight inner-to-outer projective system in existence; so that the wholly interior event of (say) deciding to move a hand from left to right in a straight line, finds its appointed expression in just such an outer event. These three properties in conjunction determine much. They have much to do with the evidential pre-eminence of bodily action for mental phenomena, so that for example Wittgensteinian 'outer criteria' tend to be active-situational in type. And they enable reason and meaning to objectify themselves, to appear in physical actions, and thus also in our surroundings, and so in inscriptions, in entities like roads and frontiers, and indeed in artefacts generally. In short, they give to reason the opportunity of objectifying itself across space and time in physical nature. And while the inner terrain of the mind is such that tight mechanistic law cannot be properly instantiated, the mental realm nonetheless incorporates mechanisms which ensure that the mental will stands a non-negligible chance of accomplishing its mental ends. Here also meaning and reason appear in phenomena as a result of their origins: as an example, a fruitful thought arising in the course of ratiocinative process.

(2) Just why the will should stand in such close relation to reason is a little mysterious. But it is a notable fact, insufficiently remarked as it seems to me, that every one of the relatively few mental items capable of rationality (and irrationality, and insanity) finds a place in the 'conative' system: action itself, and all of its causal antecedents, ranging over willings, act-desires, intentions, decisions, together with cognitive phenomena of the kind of belief and knowledge. Indeed, it is a necessary condition of an immediate rationality in a mental phenomenon that the type can occur at some point along the causal line which culminates in action. Whatever the explanation may be of the existence of this

rule, the rule itself is surely indicative of the closest of ties between action and reason.

One consideration strikes me as highly relevant to that explanation. My suggestion in this chapter has been that the mental will introduces pellucidity into processive experiential phenomena through importing rationality. But it is likely that a comparable explanatorial pellucidity involving the will *antedated* the emergence of rationality in nature. And it seems probable that the origin of this wider property must lie in the character of the antecedents of action, whether rational or not. Thus, each of those antecedents is essentially geared to causality. The causal properties of act-desires, of act-intentions, and willings, are a priori given, and those properties come close to exhausting the content of the phenomenon. It is of the essence of act-desire that it tends to cause act-intention and willing and wholly expresses itself in so doing; and of the essence of act-intention that it arises out of belief and act-desire, that it naturally causes willing, and must do so if its time-determination is self-consciously and indexically given as this present instant; and so on. These properties of the antecedents of action make possible an explanatorial lucidity not discoverable in inactive experiential processive advance. And they give a foothold to rationality when it appears at some point in evolutionary history. It is true that not all of the actions of self-conscious beings are rational. Nevertheless, intentionally active processes like thinking and listening (etc.) are of such a nature as to ensure that in such phenomena the wider property—namely, the explanatorial lucidity made possible by the special character of the antecedents of action—can take the specific and more developed form that is realized in the wholly transparent explanations of rational action.

One might express the matter in these terms. That rationality when it evolved into being availed itself of a particular well-worn explanatorily open pathway: namely, the channel which in the non-rational connects perception with well-formed belief and thereby with appropriate action. What is the evolutionary precursor of rationality? Better expressed, which pre-human phenomena are of such a character that their natural extrapolative extension would lead to rationality? It must surely be those phenomena in which animal intelligence and understanding find employment, since these psychological traits take both a more primitive form *and* the relatively transcendent form of rationality. Well-formedness of belief, and its expression in appropriate action, are what one naturally thinks of. Thus, a cat hears a voice calling it to dinner and scuttles in through a 'cat flap', thereby manifesting its capacity to learn from the world's regular ways and satisfy its pressing desires. The pre-eminent importance of action for the animal mind—what I described as the greater plausibility of Behaviourism in their case—must in the final analysis be the reason that the natural developmental antecedents of rationality take largely active form. Then the explanatorial pellucidity that flows from the predominantly causal character of the causal antecedents of action, provides a foothold for rationality (which shares this property).

7. Epistemology and the Rationale of Experience

While the overall problem under discussion in this chapter is the contribution of the mental will to consciousness, the more specific aim has been to reveal the part played by the mental will in enabling the discharge of the epistemological function of consciousness. The first half of the chapter tried to show the extent of the contribution of the will to perceptual, and in that way to epistemological function. Then although the latter half concentrated instead upon certain internal constitutive properties of the stream of consciousness of the conscious and their dependence on mental action, and to that extent cut itself adrift from epistemological questions, those conclusions have a direct bearing upon epistemology. Accordingly, at this point I would like to bring out the relevance of what has emerged concerning explanatorial rationale in conscious experience, to the epistemological powers of consciousness.

(a) The stream of consciousness

I have been investigating the stream of consciousness that occurs in the wakeful self-conscious. This phenomenon is continuous in character, but it is not a process, and is perhaps misdescribed even metaphorically as a 'stream'. Then I think the facts of the matter are best set out in the following terms. If one is conscious one is experiencing; and consciousness is an occurrent continuity; and the experiences of the conscious are describable in a narrative whose subject-matter extends continuously across time. Taken together, these properties guarantee the existence of experiential continuity, indeed of experiential processes, in a conscious subject. A continuity of experience occurs in the conscious, which is analysable into discrete processes of various types, some standing in relations of unity (say, looking and painting), some not (say, walking and reminiscing), together with discontinuous experiential phenomena (say, a passing thought or a perception), the whole marked by certain additional properties which I shall not discuss. As we have just now observed, those multiple experiences do not together constitute a single complex process. While it may well be that 'the stream of consciousness' stands for a particular mental system, it names no experiential process.

What happens if one imposes a 'will freeze' on this scene? (A 'will freeze' is not to be confused with an 'experiential freeze', which is tantamount to 'experiential annihilation': experience has to 'tick over' merely to exist, even if it does no more than 'mark time' or 'keep running to stay in the same spot': even if the contemplated scene is as obdurate and fixed in its ways as the Pyramids of Egypt, the scene within is an Heracleitian flux.) Then my suggestion has been, that with the imposition of a 'will freeze' upon conscious experience, one cannot but replace the prevailing state of consciousness, waking, by another state of consciousness, perhaps sleep. Yet how to prove it? I have deliberately avoided simple devastatingly final answers, such as an answer cast in terms of the implicit relation to time, or one addressing the possibilities open to thinking. My reason for doing so was that I wished to explore the explanatory situation entailed by such a 'will freeze'. And my overall purpose in doing that was to discover the impact of mental inaction upon normal epistemological function, which is in effect to discover the normal contribution of the mental will to that function, and thus to consciousness itself.

(b) Epistemology

(1) What are the epistemological powers of those in whom the mental will is *inoperative*? The following emerged. If mental willing is absent and a stream of consciousness exists, neither rationality nor explanatorial pellucidity can characterize the experiential processes constituting that 'stream'. And that is to say, that all processive experiential advance with cognitive representational content must to a degree be explanatorily opaque to its owner. In addition, no consciousness in such a state can harbour those mental events—investigated at length in this chapter—which are at once internal to, a continuation of, the intelligible fruit of an encompassing rational process, and yet not represented in the determining intention: for example, no occurrences like a hearing which integrates into a listening that engendered it, nor a flash of insight that relates similarly to ratiocinative exploration. In short, an entire range of internally intelligible events, alongside intelligible processes themselves, must in this condition be presumed absent from experience. Given these restrictions, what epistemological scope is there for the owner of a consciousness in this state?

Consider the scene within. What epistemological scope obtains in the first-person mental sector of the world under these circumstances? What knowledge of present psychological reality may one expect in an experiencing mind which is altogether inactive? Certainly not nothing, since experience inevitably engenders knowledge of itself. And yet we know that one will be unaware of the rationale governing processive development. And other deficiencies come to light, apparent in dreams and elsewhere. Thus, while dreamers know of their own experiences, their knowledge is variously blemished: first in being under less than adequate classificatory headings, second in being presented in false cognitive clothing. And these cognitive failings are compounded by a total ignorance of the sources of the experiences. In short, one great slice of the world must in a number of significant respects be epistemologically blanketed, not merely to dreamers but to all in whom the mental will is static.

(2) In effect, I have been drawing out the epistemological consequences within the mind of a 'will freeze' (amongst which occurs the opacity of the developmental rationale of experiential process). But my main concern is the impact of such a 'freeze' upon what must be the developmentally prior, and probably also the more fundamental, element of normal epistemological function. That is, upon our capacity to discover through perceptual means the state of the physical environment.

What this question comes down to is this. When internal epistemology is so blighted, can one come to know in rational manner empirical facts of the familiar environmental kind, through the normal epistemological channels? But can one so much as *acquire a belief* rationally in these impoverished circumstances? Well, dreamers occasionally acquire beliefs for good reasons, for example in drawing some inference, so it cannot be altogether out of the question. On the other hand, dreamers are not in a rational state, since their beliefs characteristically arise non-rationally, and even their few rare rational beliefs are incapable of being rationally reviewed and assessed. And this property is *general* to the condition being discussed, since active rational process is *ex hypothesi* proscribed, including ratiocinative thinking. In short, while dreams might seem to point the way to a limited scope for rational discovery, that possibility is so hemmed in by restrictions as to be useless.

(c) Constituting an outer world

Might one in the absence of rational experiential process acquire a belief as a rational consequence of a perception? I do not really propose to discuss this question, and shall sidestep it. Instead, I will approach the problem differently. Namely, in terms of the concepts of phenomenal continuity (such as the continuing liquidity of water) and of process (say, melting or dissolving). The question is: whether one might discover in the outer world phenomena of these latter two genera in the absence of active rational experiential process? But first we need to consider a closely related preliminary question: namely, whether one could *comprehend* the developmental rationale uniting sectors of outer process or outer phenomenal continuity, in the absence of a rational and comprehending 'tracking' within? Might one banish rationale from view in the internal continuity, yet bring it to view and discern it in the outer phenomenon? Can a person whose inner processes are non-pellucidly and non-rationally perpetuated, pellucidly detect explanatorial and rational structures 'without'?

Here it is helpful to recall the earlier discussion of the process of perceiving 'in the round', in which the three-dimensionality of one's body enters internally into the process of intuitionally encountering the three-dimensional properties of the perceptual object. The nature of this process is of such a kind as to lend support to a slogan which one might express in the words: 'No *what* without *why*.' The world is threaded with intelligibility, and the process of constituting the object of visual perception 'in the round' brought home how knowledgeable acquaintance with a material object cannot in general be acquired in the absence of a process of coming to comprehend how the object constitutes an intelligible whole. It seems to me that this bears out the relatively obvious answer which one must give to the above questions. In the absence of a rationally structured stream of consciousness, the detecting of outer physical phenomenal continuity and process must in general be impossible. In short, outer epistemology would suffer irremediable damage. Thus, what is probably the most central function allotted to consciousness would be unrealizable. Here, I think, we can see one of the essential contributions that the mental will makes to the constituting of consciousness. And one can see how it comes to do so.

6

Interiority and Thinking

I pass at this point from considering the causal contribution of the relatively deep-seated factor of mental activeness in the constituting of consciousness to what is undoubtedly the most important example of mental action, namely the active process of thinking. In what follows I attempt to delineate something of the pivotal part which this phenomenon plays in the constituting of consciousness. However, before I do so I shall try to set out briefly what emerged in the previous Chapter 5.

1. Introduction

(a) Résumé of previous chapter

(1) In Chapter 5 I asked: why does consciousness necessitate mental willing? The answer given was predominantly epistemological. Thus, the first reason advanced was that the perceptual part of the normal epistemological function of consciousness could not be properly discharged by a mind in which the will was immobilized. However, the other reasons were not wholly epistemological. In fact, the second half of the chapter addressed itself only indirectly to issues of knowledge, indeed only indirectly to issues of function. It was concerned instead with the distinctive character of the stream of consciousness of conscious subjects. Here the relation to epistemology was merely implicit.

In that later discussion I advanced two claims linking the character of experience in the conscious with consciousness. The first claim was that the occurrence of a phenomenon with the distinctive character of the stream of consciousness of the conscious, is a necessary and sufficient condition of consciousness. And this is a truly substantive thesis. Of no other state of consciousness can any of the following be said: (i) that it necessitates a stream of consciousness, (ii) that it necessitates a certain kind of stream, (iii) that a certain kind of stream suffices for it. This is evident when one remembers that all non-waking states of consciousness can occur without experience, and that each variety of non-conscious experience occurs in more than one state of consciousness. For example, dreaming occurs in sleep *and* light unconsciousness, somnambulistic experience occurs in sleep *and* hypnotic trance, and so on. My suggestion was that waking provides a dramatic contrast on all counts, that each of these three assertions is true of waking consciousness. The proposition being advanced is, that the character of the stream of consciousness wholly determines the presence of waking consciousness.

This was the first claim concerning the experiential character of consciousness. But the problem being investigated was the role of the *mental will* in the constituting of consciousness. With this in mind I made a second more contentious claim concerning the experiential character of consciousness: namely, that this distinctive character includes essential properties which depend on a working mental will. Then if both of these claims are true, the conjunction of the two propositions would provide me with a second—and non-functional and non-epistemological—argument for the theory that mental activeness is a necessity for consciousness: an argument based on the character of the wakeful stream of consciousness.

How was one to prove that activeness of mind is essential to that character? Not simply by sheer inspection of the stream of conscious experience, but by showing that a readily detectable and pivotal property of conscious experience owes its existence to the mental will. Thus, I opted for the method of demonstrating that the mental will imports an *explanatorial pellucidity* into the stream of consciousness which is unique to that experiential continuity, and that it does so through introducing a rational principle of development. Now this was the second argument for the necessity of mental action for consciousness. Then one can see upon reflection that such explanatorial pellucidity must be a necessary condition of understanding one's environment, and thus of identifying its occupants, and therefore of epistemological effectiveness. So here again, by implication, we link the presence of a mental will with epistemological function. Thus, the non-functional and non-epistemological claim concerning the necessity of mental willing to waking that appeals to experiential character, helps in this way to constitute a second epistemological argument for the same conclusion. So much for the line of argument of the previous chapter.

(b) Dreams and meaning

It helps to introduce the subject-matter of the present chapter to single out one element in the discussion of experiential character in Chapter 5. At one point I compared dreaming and waking experience, since the unlikenesses of these phenomena are illuminating. The first respect which interested me was the rationale governing the progression through time of these experiential continuities. I showed in the discussion just how different this was in dream and waking, thereby confirming the obvious enough fact that dream and waking experiential streams are intrinsically and not merely relationally dissimilar. Evidently there is more to a stream of experience than the *content* of those experiences. For one thing, there is the question whether the 'seemings' are the *experiences* they 'seem'. But as the above discussion demonstrated, there is also the question as to the type of the *genetic link* binding each experience to its successor, since this plainly differs in the case of waking and dreaming.

234

However, there is a further dissimilarity between waking and dreaming streams of consciousness—and it is this which leads me into the topic of the present chapter. It concerns the phenomenon of *meaning*. Dreams differ from waking experience in lacking meaning in a quite central sense of that protean term. One might say of dreams that each element is linked to its successor merely by an 'and', that no further significance accrues to those elements as they come together, that the content of the dream is what it is and nothing in addition. In short, the dream seems to be a mere 'piece of Nature'. When we turn to experience in the conscious, matters prove to be very different. While the conscious mind is a natural phenomenon, it introduces into the stream of experience important novel elements which are closely linked to sense and interpretation. Thus, wherever we look in our conscious experience we encounter wide encompassing projects and the destinations imported by intentions, totalities which confer meaning upon their constituents, and running through the whole some form of pervasive unity of which the subject is aware. It is natural to characterize this as the presence of meaningfulness in the stream of experience. Then the questions which interest me, and form the subject matter of the ensuing discussion, are these: what is the sense in which dreams do not and waking experience does have meaning? and what is the relevance of such meaning to the need by consciousness for a working mental will? The chapter is divided into three parts under the following headings: A (Meaning), B (Thinking), and C (Interiority).

PART A: MEANING

2. Meaning in Experience

(a) The relevant variety of meaning

(1) I begin with a few words on 'meaning'. One might say of some α that it 'means' β, in various senses. 'Red sky at sunset means a fine day tomorrow' invokes the familiar sense of being a *natural sign* of something. This is one sense of the term. But when Freud spoke of the meaning of neurotic symptoms, of paralysis in an arm meaning a parental prohibition, he surely meant that it 'stood for' such a thing in a different sense. In all probability this is the sense in which one might say of some religious icon or image that, to the devout, it stands for a saint: they pray to this physical image, not literally and grossly primitively, but to the saint through the mediation of this *concrete proxy* for the saint. I suspect that this is the sense in which Freud spoke of the meaning of dreams. Dreaming of a landscape might in this sense be interpreted as 'being' dreaming of 'the mother': it represents her in a special proxy sense akin to that applicable to icons and 'keepsakes': one so to say retains contact with this primary being as one's interests radiate out into the world.

Neither of the above two senses is the experiential sense I have in mind. When I claim that dreams lack meaning, the somewhat stronger sense of meaning to which I am appealing incorporates the following characteristics—at least.

(i) The meaningful item α must be susceptible of a redescription which links it *interpretatively* to the meant item β. (Cf. A rash is redescribable as a symptom of measles.)

(ii) The interpretative redescription must be substantive in the strong sense that it confirms the acquisition of its *nature* on the part of the α item. (Cf. The act of hitting a gavel on a table has the nature of *making an item sold*.)

(iii) It is an *essential* property of the meaningful α that it means and is a β. (Cf. The act of hitting a gavel on a table falls under the essential description: 'trying to declare an item sold'.)

(2) It may or may not be that the above properties suffice to delimit the sense of 'meaning' that has impressed itself upon me. But for the moment I shall suppose it does. Then it is plain that dreams lack meaning in this sense. And it is clear that a process in consciousness like listening to a speech is endowed with it. Listening to a sequence of sounds at some point in a party political speech might fall under the further *interpretative descriptions*: 'listening to the words "unemployment has by now reached . . ."', 'listening to an early stage in the speaker's indictment of his political opponents', and so on: descriptions which are informed by the *understanding* of the listener. And these properties are essential or internal attributes of each sector-stage of the listening process. Thus, they embody meaningfulness in the sense delineated.

How does such 'meaningfulness' come about? If these phenomena satisfy a set of interpretational descriptions which reveal their essential nature, indeed a nested sequence of interdependent characters which reveal the complexity of that nature, what is the source of this property? Well, we have been here before. In the last chapter we noted that a mind *lies behind* some mental phenomena and not others: not in the sense that mental causality links those items, but in that a self-aware mind is in certain cases determining the overall character of what is happening within its own precincts. Now this quite evidently is lacking in a phenomenon like dreaming. When one dreams nothing of this sort lies behind these experiences: one simply *has* them, without their possessing any further essential interpretational character deriving from the work of some inner agency. As one might express it, each point in the dreaming process is what it is and is nothing else. No redescriptions reveal additional and essential natures in the case of those experiential stages. (And irrespective of Freudian signification, one might add.)

This precisely is how matters do not stand in the case of most waking experience. In the normal course of waking consciousness, behind (say) our perceptual and motor experiences there occurs *something else* of a mental nature which confers an essential nature upon those experiences, embedding them meaningfully in wider mental wholes: so to say a second tier in the mind. Speaking generally and non-specifically, it is the interiority of the experiencing subject—an X which is evidently closely linked to the mental will. It is this factor that I hope to identify in the ensuing discussion. This mental accompaniment seems to be the source of the meaning to be found in waking perceptual and motor experience. By contrast, in dreaming we are simply *immersed* in our experience without any second interior realm of meaning-giving. Then for what it is worth, this is the largely intuitive picture which impresses itself upon me as I begin the discussion. And to repeat: my goal is the identification of the supposed internal meaning-conferring X, which I take to be a necessity for consciousness.

(b) Action and meaning

When the mental meaning which I suspect to be peculiar to consciousness is instantiated, mental act-intention seems on the face of it its most likely source. And yet if intentional activeness of mind is the *sole* source of mental meaning, a difficulty arises. This is because intentional mental willing occurs in states other than consciousness. This fact poses a problem for any account of consciousness in which meaning is central to the state. Either we simply abandon the theory that meaning in the strong sense spelled out is necessary for consciousness. Or else we must supplement it with the theory that an even stronger variety of meaning is needed. Let me try to show how this dilemma arises. I will do so by depicting certain *active situations* in which varying *degrees of interiority* obtain.

Consider the following examples of action:

(i) Driving across a vast flat empty landscape, with great relaxation, casually watching the scene, thinking idle thoughts as one goes, concentrating on nothing.

(ii) The much discussed case of the long-distance truck-driver, who 'comes to' at a certain point after driving through the night for a few miles in complete silence and in seemingly automatic fashion, with little memory of what has been going on.

(iii) A soldier in a platoon marching long-distance at night 'comes to' and seems to himself to have been asleep and even to have been dreaming a little.

(iv) A sleeper with his eyes wide open engages in somnambulistic walking along a dangerous parapet in bright moonlight.

In all these situations motor activities are taking place, and in at least three of them closely integrated mental activities of the kind of looking as well. Now these latter perceptual activities are essentially intentional, there being no such thing as a looking that is not intentional under some description. Then the interesting conclusion which this forces upon us is that, as in example (iv) which characterizes a state other than waking consciousness, intentional mental willing can be occurring in a mind in the absence of consciousness. After all, the man who is walking along the parapet scarcely 'intuits' his way. He cannot fail to be looking where he is going. There is at least that much method in his madness!

In the light of this fact we must say: intentional mental activity cannot be enough for consciousness. It may be a necessity, but it cannot be a sufficiency. What more is required? It is not open to us to say that *meaning* in the sense so far spelled out is the answer. There can be doubt that the activities of the non-conscious sleepwalker precisely satisfy the given requirements for the strong variety of meaning delineated above. Thus, even if this man fails to know his ultimate destination, he cannot but know his mutating short-term immediate goals as he proceeds on his way: merely being intentional guarantees this much. And that suffices to endow the mental process of looking with the strong kind of meaning to which I have so far appealed. Therefore something more than this strong kind of meaning must be necessary for consciousness. What can it be? This is the difficulty.

(c) Interiority

(1) Return to the above examples of action. What is it that is *on the wane* as we progress from cases (i) to (iv)? The natural reply is: interiority (in a sense of that term which it is my task to discover). But of what kind? We discover a clue in the example of the long-distance driver. What are we to say of this man's state of mind? That while his consciousness is surely imperfect, it is yet real. After all, he is not in a trance, even though he may have progressed a little on the way towards one. While he fails to record much, he at least knows he has been driving along a road, that he has been looking at that road, and possibly also some such fact as that he swerved to avoid something or another that was in his way. All of this attests to the presence of consciousness, even if it is a poorly formed example of the kind.

Note the respects in which the truck-driver's consciousness falls short of the waking norm. While this man might have been 'miles away', lost in thoughts and memories, that is not the situation we chose to discuss. Instead, we selected a case of pseudo-trance which manages to fall the waking side of examples like the somnambulist and surely also of the exhausted soldier. What we are assuming is a *radical emptiness of mind* on the part of a waking person. Thus, this man engages in a simple looking procedure, and a simple instrumental activity to which that looking is wholly subordinated, and his experiential life is more or less exhausted by these two occupations. He recollects little of his recent past and anticipates a merely rudimentary and immediate future, so that the temporal arena containing him must have contracted drastically during this episode. Nothing like thinking or even feeling appear to be going on within him. And yet it seems likely, were a driving crisis to loom up suddenly in his path, that he would 'come to' with a shock and struggle to cope with it. Thus, while his consciousness is undoubtedly imperfect, it must nonetheless be intact. His understanding has not 'closed down' altogether. It 'ticks over'—recessively.

(2) This subject inhabits a shrunken temporal scene, and simultaneously his behaviour has something of the character of automatism: he is simply 'going through the motions', as one might say. These features are clear indicators of a

dearth of the meaningfulness characteristic of normal consciousness. Then what specific factor has diminished it, and what would make good that loss? Something vital is on the wane in the case of this driver that is surely of the type of self-awareness. But precisely what does that involve? Possible answers are: the activity of *thinking*, the knowledge that he is doing what he is doing under *some description* or other, the knowledge that he is doing what he is doing under its *widest or fully realistic description*, the knowledge of *why* he is doing what he is doing, a general *rationality* of state. After all, most of these traits are either absent or imperfectly realized in the case of this mindless 'automatized' driver. For the moment I shall concentrate on the first answer: thinking. How does thinking relate to consciousness? Is it a necessity if consciousness is to exist?

Why should we single out thinking for special attention? There are several reasons for doing so. For one thing it alone of the above phenomena is an exercise of the mental will, and the natural suspicion is that the mental will in some form lies behind the meaningfulness of conscious experience. Now we saw in the previous chapter how the mental will imported a measure of explanatorial pellucidity into conscious experience. And yet this property on its own proved to be insufficient for full intelligibility. But the one active experiential line that carries its own rationale is that of thinking. For thinking is a mental willing which *par excellence* knows where it is going, since it is above all thinking that lies behind our typically human destinations. Indeed, thinking has all the look of being the meaning-giver *par excellence* in the mind: after all, it has especially close connections with the thought, the capacity to mentally journey beyond the here and now into the realm of possibility—where goals are shaped and meaning born. It is for reasons of this kind that I choose at this point to examine the hypothesis that it is above all the process of thinking that is deficient in the mind of the long-distance driver who is in a pseudo-trance. That is, that the 'interiority' of which we have spoken, which is so plainly diminished in this man, takes such specific experiential form.

PART B: THINKING

3. The Nature of Thinking

(1) But first we must know what it is that we are talking of. We must discover what thinking is. Thus, what principles govern the classification of a mental phenomenon as an example of thinking? The following pre-reflectively apparent facts serve as pointers to those rules.

  (i) Thinking is a mental process.
  (ii) Thinking is an experience.
  (iii) Thinking is active, it is an exercise of the mental will.
  (iv) Those mentally active experiential processes that are perceptual—say, looking and listening—are not thinking (unless it is comprehendingly to words).

239

(v) Thinking is not causally interactive with the environment in the regular manner of perception or physical action.

(vi) Thinking is in this sense 'detached', not bound to concrete actuality, being able to range over counterfactual possibilities, etc.

(vii) A necessary condition of thinking is the capacity to entertain thoughts.

(viii) And thus to be acquainted with negation and truth.

(ix) This capacity is internally involved, indeed constitutively so, in the process of thinking (thoughts being in a sense the stuff of thinking).

(x) Thinking necessitates rationality of nature.

(xi) Thinking is possible only for language-users.

(xii) Thinking has cognitive content.

(xiii) Dreaming is not thinking.

(xiv) Continuously experienced affect is not thinking.

(xv) Trying to remember a name counts as thinking.

(xvi) Much thinking—at the very least—can be carried out in or through the 'public' perceptible using of words: the internal process of thinking can be objectified or expressed in the physical acts of speaking or writing.

(xvii) Whereas one can simultaneously see X and hear Y (which are highly disparate items), and register both X and Y under independent headings, one cannot simultaneously entertain two unrelated thoughts [thinking p & thinking q ≠ thinking (p & q)].

(xviii) Whereas one can be continuously watching some 'outer' physical event and at the same time occupied in thinking of something altogether unrelated, one cannot simultaneously be continuously engaged in entertaining mental-imagery (say, of a tennis rally) and thinking about something unrelated (say, Pythagoras' Theorem).

(xix) The latter suggests that, when one is awake and continuously imagining something, imagining is the form then adopted by one's thinking.

(xx) If an animal could voluntarily imagine, it would be thinking: *ergo*, the non-voluntary forms of imagining—hallucinations, dreams, etc.—are the only imaginings open to non-rational beings.

(2) What are natural hypotheses as to the nature of thinking, in the light of these 'pointers'? Each of the following three theories strikes me as plausible:

A. Thinking is trying to construct a thought.
B. Thinking is trying to produce or construct a thought.
C. Thinking is trying to produce or construct a thought or engage in an imagining.

It is worth remembering that if it is indeed true that thinking is an active internal process, it must be an intentional active process and must therefore have determinate *aims*. What can those aims be? What may we be assumed to be trying to accomplish when thinking? It goes without saying that one tries to be engaging in a process that counts as thinking. But is there nothing else, nothing that is more specific yet of a general nature, which one can indicate by way of answer? It is considerations of this sort that make each of the theories A–C (above) attractive: they meet the need expressed above in ways that are plausible.

In the light of the 'clues' (i)–(xx), I tentatively propose the following set of properties as a definition of thinking. Namely, that thinking is:

(1) An experiential psychological process.
(2) An intentional activity that is an exercise of the mental will.
(3) It is the activity of trying either to assemble or else to produce a thought or imagined sequence.

And we might add as a rider the following two properties:

(4) Thinking is internally dependent on the capacity to entertain thoughts, and thus upon knowledge of a language.
(5) And is perhaps constitutively dependent on the use of one or both of these powers.

4. Thinking and Language

(a) Wittgenstein's views on thinking and language

(1) Language looms large in this account of thinking. Then the validity or not of the proposed definition ought to become clearer if we can better understand the relation between thinking and the use of language. Wittgenstein pointed the way on this important question, both in his earlier startling pronouncements on the nature of thinking in *The Blue Book* (1934), and in his later remarks (1945–9). During the intervening period he changed his mind on several fundamental points. Thus, we find him in 1934 making the following claims:

(α1) No experiential understanding process accompanies speaking.
(β1) No process of thinking is independent of using words.
(γ1) Thinking is essentially the activity of operating with signs.
(δ1) Meaning, which is given by the use of a term, is not a psychic thing.
(ϵ1) No mental object determines its own interpretation.

It is α1—γ1 that are the focus of my discussion (however important the claims δ1 and ϵ1 may be to the theory of thinking which they embody).

Meanwhile during the period 1945–9, Wittgenstein expressed the following views—several of which amount to a correction of some of the above.

(α2) Thinking is not speaking aloud—which is a bodily activity: the concepts are categorially different.
(β2) Thinking is not an accompaniment of speaking.
(γ2) Thinking cannot proceed on its own unaccompanied by speech.
(δ2) Language is thought's instrument.

(2) The changes of mind seem to me judicious. However, β2 is surely unacceptable: it seems certain that processes in the understanding accompany the saying out aloud of one's thoughts when one is 'thinking aloud', and that these are internal to the activity of thinking. Thus, one is immediately in contact with a developing thought as one is speaking in the course of (say) ratiocination. One knows one has formulated *so much* of a thought and not all, and that the partially indeterminate thought stands in need of completion and thus of full determinacy. One grasps all this as one proceeds, knows directly of one's own internal efforts, indeed grasps it all with an immediacy that is absolute and mentalistic in type. In short, there can be no doubt that α1 / β2 must be incorrect. And it seems certain that γ1 ought therefore to be withdrawn—as Wittgenstein in effect does in α2.

(b) Ratiocination and language: the necessity of symbols

The problem being considered is how thinking relates to the use of language. Let us approach this question by examining ratiocinative thinking. We could equally well have chosen recollective thinking (e.g. thinking of last night's party) or enumerative thinking (e.g. listing primes below 50), but opt for ratiocination since it is surely paradigmatic of the kind. Then in all these cases we are trying to produce a thought in our own minds. And we do not merely strain indeterminately at this task, somehow attempting vaguely to blow away the mental mist concealing a dimly divined thought, we try by the *specific methods* of inference or recollection, etc.—for the activity of thinking takes *specific form*. We try in specific ways to engender determinate entities. Thus, the logical form of the thought produced by ratiocination is $p \longrightarrow q$, by recollection and enumeration is $p \& q \& \longrightarrow$, etc. In short, ratiocination is a search by means of inference for a thought of the form $p \longrightarrow q$ which one's mind has yet to entertain.

Then the very first and major point to make on the relation between thinking and language is, that there simply is *no such thing* as 'just thinking about the problem—
—', no such thing as thinking without using words. While there is 'just talking' without thought, as in sheer 'parrot speech', the reverse is no more possible than is 'just opening a door'. Somewhat as all door-openings have to be by actively altering one's body/mind, so all thinkings about problems have to be *through* the aid of or *by* the use of words (as Wittgenstein observed (β1/γ2)). Much of the philosophical problem facing us at this point consists in elucidating this 'by': that is, in determining the relation between thinking about some problem (which I hereafter designate as 'S(θ)' or 'striving to arrive at the thought θ') and the using of words or symbols (hereafter called 'S(say θ)' or 'striving to state in words the goal thought θ').

Without prejudice as to their identity-relations, I shall describe these 'two' phenomena as 'two'—which leaves it open that they might be one and the same activity (as Wittgenstein thought in 1934). However that may be, we must not lose sight of the fact that exploratory reasoning is the attempt to arrive at a *thought*, it is not the attempt to arrive at the *formulation* of a thought. In a word, the desire to S(θ) must be the progenitor of it all. It fathers the desire and intention to S(say θ), and does so because $S(\theta)$ cannot proceed on its way unless an $S(\text{say } \theta)$ does the same. For to repeat: there is *no such thing* as 'just thinking about the problem — '.

Note that the thoughts referred to in $S(\theta)$ and $S(\text{say } \theta)$ are one and the same. Then because of the exploratory nature of the ratiocinative $S(\theta)$ under discussion, the intention $I[S(\theta)]$ finding expression can never be directed to all determinations of the intentional act it will eventually generate: $I[S(\theta)]$ must undergo a developmental history—of $I[S(\theta)]_1$, $I[S(\theta)]_2$, . . . —complete only when θ is complete. Then how can $S(\theta)$ even so much as begin? It can begin because θ is already singled out *under a definite description*. Thus, it might be singled out as (say) 'the answer to the question: why is the crescent new moon on the moon's right?' In a certain sense θ must already be dimly perceived—else one would have no direction to follow as one begins thinking.

Now we have seen that there necessarily is no such thing as 'just $S(\theta)$', exactly as there can be no 'just opening the door'. Just as it is a necessity that the latter *under-describes* an act, whose full description must be of the form 'opening the door by ϕ-ing' (where ϕ is a bodily or mental act of some kind), so '$S(\theta)$' underdescribes an act, which of necessity falls essentially and intentionally under '$S(\theta)$ by/through/etc. $S(\text{say/write/etc. } \theta)$'. This is a matter of some consequence. It is the first major point to be emphasized in this discussion concerning the relation of thinking and the use of language.

(c) Identity relations

(1) In sum, the activity of exploratory ratiocination $S(\theta)$ is, in some way that we have yet to understand, to be accomplished by articulating words and ultimately a complex sentence. How do these 'two' activities relate? Might they in fact be one and the same phenomenon?

A valuable lead is given on this absolutely fundamental issue when we reflect on the question: what form or mode is taken by the use of words or symbols? Now so far as the enabling of $S(\theta)$ is concerned, it is a matter of complete indifference whether $S(\text{say } \theta)$ takes the form of speaking or writing or hand signalling—or talking silently to oneself. This simple fact tells us much. First, it shows that the ontological status of the verbal enterprise is irrelevant to the occurrence of $S(\theta)$. Then let us for argument's sake assume that the articulation happens to be an exercise of the bodily will, say the activity of handwriting. Turn now to the $S(\theta)$ co-present with this process. What is its ontological status? There can be no doubt that it is an exercise of the mental will, that it is an 'interior' phenomenon as writing precisely is not. Its epistemological properties ensure this (quite apart from the fact that the thought, the most paradigmatically 'interior' of all psychological phenomena, is surely on an ontological level with thinking itself). Thus, one knows one has been thinking, and knows the point to which that thinking has arrived, in each case with the mentalistic immediacy and certainty encountered with experiences generally. In a word, $S(\theta)$ is *essentially* 'interior'. By contrast $S(\text{say } \theta)$ is not, since it can adopt either the 'interior' form of soliloquy or the non-'interior' form of handwriting.

The conclusion must be, that S(θ) ≠ S(say θ). Necessarily, there occur two activities when we engage in thinking and articulating simultaneously. Then how do these two activities relate from the point of view of boundaries or identity? Might they be distinct? Or might one include the other? Or might they overlap? These are the questions we must now settle.

(2) Because the full description of S(θ) is 'S(θ) by/through/etc. S(say θ)', it is a natural initial presumption that these activities must be non-distinct. However, there are reasons for resisting this inference. Remember that S(θ) is *essentially* 'interior', while S(say θ) can as readily adopt the form of bodily willing as of mental willing. Accordingly, let us once again for argument's sake assume that it takes the form of bodily willing, say handwriting. Then what common territory can there be between S(θ) and such an S(say θ)? Then why assume that there must be common ground if S(say θ) takes the 'interior' form of silent soliloquy?

The natural conclusion is that S(θ) and S(say θ) are not merely two, but are in addition distinct. And yet it is clear that their relation must be intimately close. After all, the full description of S(θ) involves reference to S(say θ), and *this* S(θ) could not have occurred without *some* S(say θ). Conversely, *this* occurrence of S(say θ) could not have occurred without *this* S(θ). The reason for the latter dependence is noteworthy: it is because S(θ) *informs* S(say θ), for what one says in the course of ratiocination one says *because of* events in the S(θ) process, which is to say because of what one grasps or understands as one proceeds in S(θ). Indeed, the properly full description of S(say θ) is: 'say that which is contributory to the statement of the θ which is arising out of S(θ).' After all, S(θ) and S(say θ) are concerned with the same token θ. Necessarily, this S(say θ) is prompted by this S(θ).

(d) The causal situation in the case of thinking and articulation

(1) We have noted that S(θ) cannot so much as get under way without an S(say θ) doing the same. Then is this dependence of S(θ) upon S(say θ) causal? Once again, it is natural to resist such a claim, thinking of the fact that we underdescribe the former activity if we omit reference to the latter. And yet we are speaking here of *distinct existences*, neither of which could have occurred in the absence of the other. Prima facie it is difficult to avoid the conclusion that each is a causally necessary condition of the other.

Then let us take a closer look at the causal situation. The relation of S(say θ) to S(θ), that of being informed-by, seems to me less puzzling than the reverse, which is one of 'enabling' in some ill-understood sense of the term. Now we say that S(θ) *necessitates* the occurrence of S(say θ). What kind of necessitation can this be? Plainly not that of means for an end, for we do not suppose that saying is the *means* one adopts in order to arrive at the end thinking. This is impossible, since all that one says is informed by and grossly dependent on the inner $S(\theta)$ process.

What looks like a more promising theory begins with the following familiar observation. Namely, that there is a striking similarity between 'There is no such thing as "just thinking about problem X"', and 'There is no such thing as "just opening the door"'. Consider the latter claim, which records a necessity. From what does it derive? It has an ontological basis: necessarily, all acts are *either* mental *or* bodily (since all acts are the production of change in their owner's being). Accordingly, door-opening must either be a mental phenomenon of the ontological type of (say) imagining, or else a psychological phenomenon of the ontological type of (say) trying to move a limb. This imposes a necessity, that of adopting a mental or bodily form. Then one might naturally suppose that the necessity whereby thinking must make use of speaking or writing (etc.) is comparable: that thinking must adopt some concrete symbol-using form if it is to so much as exist. However, it is clear on reflection that this must be an error. If it were true, the relation between $S(\theta)$ and $S(\text{say } \theta)$ would be one of identity. Just as giving a kick is both the form adopted by and identical with the act of opening the door, so it would be in the case of thinking and speaking.

(2) So the promising answer, that the 'enabling' of $S(\text{say } \theta)$ for $S(\theta)$ is that of providing a necessary form, must be rejected. It seems that we are in the presence of a very special relation, perhaps without precedent in the mind, between two distinct activities which of necessity spring up together. Neither activity can occur without the other, they share no part in common, and they are each causally necessary conditions of the other! And yet despite being causally necessary conditions, neither can properly be described as *the cause of* or as *part of the cause of* the other. I say so because, since they are both activities, each must arise immediately out of the usual obligatory sources of action, viz. act-desire and intention. I see no contradiction in making these disparate causal claims. Doubtless it is a causally necessary condition of thinking that a road drill not be operating a few feet away, and a causally necessary condition of handwriting that one's hand be free to move, and yet each activity arises of necessity from the usual progenitors of action.

Before I leave the topic of causation, a word about the intentions which causally underlie these two activities. Thus, if the acts of thinking and speaking of necessity spring up together, does the same hold of the intentions that they express? The intention-situation seems to me to be a little different from that prevailing with action. For the whole intellectual exercise must all begin with a desire and an intention, not to think *and* to articulate, but simply to *think*: $D[S(\theta)]$ and $I[S(\theta)]$. However, if these mental items are to find expression, they cannot but engender an $I[S(\theta)$ with the aid of articulation], and so an $I[S(\text{say } \theta)]$. Therefore while two intentions must be finding expression whenever thinking gets under way, the intention of thinking founds the other $I[S(\text{say } \theta)]$.

5. The Essential Dependence of Thinking Upon Language

(a) A statement of the problem

(1) We have still to resolve the central problem of identifying the type of the necessity whereby thinking has to find expression in linguistic form. We have seen that it is neither the necessity of discovering a *means for an end*, nor of *adopting a determinate form*. What other possibilities exist? I think we shall discover that the initiation of processes in the understanding which are directed to word-structures, is the essential task of thinking. This would explain the necessary dependence upon the use of words. But we need to understand how this is so.

What exactly is going on when the ratiocinative process sets off in tandem with a process of articulation? What is it that the articulation provides that is so necessary if thinking is to even take its first steps? Let us begin with an intuitive 'stab in the dark', a preliminary assay at an answer. Thus: it seems that thinking can harness the specific concepts necessary for its advance through mental space towards the thought, only if specific words signifying the concepts put to use in the thought are actively employed in the construction of the sentential statement of the thought. More exactly, the harnessing of the concepts and logical form used in the internal constituting of conceptual structures, can occur only if words signifying those concepts and form are actually employed.

These intuitive statements probably capture between them the point that needs developing if we are to explain the dependence of thinking upon speech. They state a partial explanation, which itself stands in need of explanation: namely, that the constituting concepts and form can be harnessed only through one's concretely using the words corresponding to both. But why is it so? It is not so when a thought using the identical concepts passes through one's mind. Then why is it so when one actively assembles a thought? Let us take a closer look at the relation between these two processes, thinking and saying. What is going on?

(2) The first thing to note is, that S(say θ) is not a simple *objectification in words* of S(θ). Thus, S(say θ) does not *describe* S(θ). And neither does S(say θ) describe all that is *requisite for* the progression of S(θ): for example, S(say θ) does not articulate a fertile thought θ' which passes through one's mind during thinking. S(say θ) does not take the form: 'I am thinking my way towards the thought θ' (given by a definite description) 'and have just reached stage——, and I suddenly think θ', and I am now changing direction thuswise——.' Nothing like this gets articulated. Rather, all that is uttered entirely pertains to θ. The words used in S(say θ) gradually express the gathering goal of the inner process, they express the developing thought θ that is being created piecemeal as one goes—and no more. Thus, in informing S(say θ) what to say, the inner process S(θ) of trying to arrive at thought θ must be continuously stirring up the mental machinery, and as a result continually throwing up into the mind a whole sequence of intentions—to S(say a), to S(say b),

etc.—as it goes. And the ultimate object of that saying is a statement of the thought θ that is the goal of S(θ). Here we have a rough account of what is going on.

(3) However, these facts take us no nearer to answering the central question. Why the dependence of S(θ) upon S(say θ)? Let me now express this question in more specific terms, and see if that brings us any nearer to a resolution of the problem. After all, S(θ) is not just active thinking, it is either the asserting of a novel proposition or the asking of a novel question or suchlike. Accordingly, the general question can more accurately be stated as the more particular: why cannot one ask oneself a question without using words? Or: why cannot one assert a proposition to oneself without using words?

It may seem to be cheating to assume that S(θ) must be (say) an asserting or a questioning. Are not such phenomena *already* linguistic? In my opinion, not. However, let me restate the problem. Let us describe the active inner process of thinking as one of producing in one's mind a proposition in the affirmative or inter-rogative (etc.) mode. Then note that experiential acquaintance with a proposition, whether in affirmative or interrogative mode, does not entail experience with words. If it did, the 'central' question would indeed circularly answer itself. And that it does not, is clear from the fact that ideas and questions are continually entering one's mind instantaneously and wordlessly. To be sure, that the proposition in question is the proposition it is, doubtless involves the harnessing within one's mind of specific concepts and logical structures. But it does not entail the experiencing of *words*. Thus, one can *variously*, and yet perfectly *accurately*, verbally express the one thought which one has when an idea crosses one's mind. To be sure once again, the concepts involved in the constitution of the thought will be those embodied in the language one speaks, and this can be no coincidence. But that does not entail that words are experienced when thoughts pass through one's mind.

Once again one may suspect cheating. And it has to be agreed that there is a very little substance to the charge. This is because of the latter feature: namely, that the concepts put to use in the constitution of thoughts, whether with active or inactive verbal assistance or not, are those embodied in one's language (the innate capacity to learn language not being the same thing as the possession of the system of concepts bequeathed by particular languages). In short, the gap between mental processes with content and the utilization of language, cannot be all that great from the very beginning! Here we have the grain of truth to the charge of cheating. A simple example like the relatively arbitrary 'carve up' of the spectrum into its constituent colours, makes the point in an obvious way: it is clearly thanks to contingently existing *words* that we can have such thoughts as 'yellow has little in common with magenta', 'there is some yellow in scarlet', 'the moon is orange near the horizon', and so on. How otherwise?

(4) Why cannot one mentally put together a question or an assertion without using words? This we have deemed the 'central question'. Note that we are speaking here of an *activity*, that of thinking, and thus of a process extending

experientially *across time*. In the light of these observations, I now put forward a final statement of the problem. Why is it that the (language-derived) constituting concepts and logical form of a question or an affirmation (etc.) can be harnessed for use when one is actively constructing a thought of that kind, only if one employs words corresponding to both? It is a not so when a thought using the identical concepts and logical structure passes through one's mind. Why is it so when one actively constructs that thought across time? Might there not be other ways of constructing a thought which utilize our capacity for wordless acquaintance with thought? What in effect we want to know is: what would it be like, actively and across experiential time, to frame a question or assemble a proposition in the affirmative mode that uses the concepts of one's language, without employing language? What would it be like simply to 'think one's way' to such a thought-destination?

(b) Unanalysable complex experiences and thought-experiences

(1) We shall see in what follows that the difficulty stems, not so much from the activeness of the process of thinking, as from the necessary temporal extensiveness of any process, active or not. Thus, the problem seems to be that posed by the need when thinking to experience a thought across time, whether actively encountered or not. And the difficulty in doing so seems to derive from the fact that thoughts do not lend themselves to certain familiar modes of analysis. The puzzle seems to turn upon the problem as to how experientially one might constitute a thought across time. What principles of assembly are viable?

Thus, while a thought can enter one's mind, what are we to understand by 'part of a thought entering one's mind'? Indeed, what is one to understand by 'a non-propositional part of a thought'? Various senses might be stipulated for this expression, but none such that experiencing a thought is made up out of a sequential assemblage of experiences of 'non-propositional parts of a thought'. For example, what would it be for the contribution made by the word 'the' in 'the cat is on the mat' to enter one's mind all on its own? Since there is no such thing as 'experiencing the sense of a word', there can be no such thing as 'the sense of each word of a sentence passing wordlessly before one's mind and thereby bringing the thought or sense of the sentence to mind.'

(2) But might there not be *other ways* of experiencing a thought across time? Might there not be ways of doing so, in which we both detach ourselves from words *and* manage to traverse the thought over time without traversing 'non-propositional parts of a thought'? The following considerations suggest that there might be such a thing.

Not everything that can be experienced across space or time has parts (in fact or in experience), i.e. is amenable to analysis (in fact or in experience). How might one dismantle a smile? Or an ironical expression on a face? One can dismantle a smiling face, and one can single out those parts of the face which determine the presence of the smile. And yet are narrowed eyes to be accounted 'part of a smile'? The smile extends across the face, and the region ranges over the eyes, and the narrowed eyes make their contribution to the existence of the smile, but that scarcely makes the eyes part of it. Expressions on faces are simply not in the same line of business as eyes or their shape. Then what of 'that part of the smile which is visible at the eyes'? But what kind of a thing can that be? What is its type or order of being? And what would it be to concentrate one's attention upon such a thing and bring it into an enhanced awareness or visibility? But if one relates thus selectively, one loses the whole of which it is a supposed part! But to lose such a whole is to lose the supposed part, for this part has no existence outside of the whole! Indeed, this supposed 'part' must be *essentially* sustained by the 'whole' it supposedly constitutes! Then what sort of a *part* can it be? The parts of melodies are notes, of living animals are cells, but the 'parts of an ironical look' seem to be no kind of thing. They cannot be of the type of an *expression*. For while eyes and mouths have looks of their own, such looks cannot be 'expression-parts of the ironical expression': there is no 'calculus of looks'! And in fact the 'ironical look' is something which either comes 'as a whole' or simply comes not at all. I know of no analysis of it—in fact or in experience. And I suggest that the spatial analysability of the area over which a facial expression shows, constitutes insufficient ground for positing a comparable analysability in the expression itself. Analysis gets no grip on such an item.

(3) Now this is just an example, and its 'all or nothing' character proves it cannnot be a model for thought. Nonetheless, it shows one can experience items across differentiable expanses of space/time without being able to experience parts of those items corresponding to those of space/time. Paradoxically, this opens up the possibility of experiencing a thought across time. It is at first natural to suppose this impossible, since it is natural to assume experiencing a thought across time must involve experiencing a sequential array of non-propositional parts of the thought as we proceed through the thought, and nothing seems to answer to that specification. However, the example of facial expressions shows that this need not be how matters stand. Other structural possibilities exist, some of which differ from that exemplified by facial expressions, and amongst these must be found the structure realized in thinking. For it is clear on reflection that we can in fact experience thoughts across time, indeed that this must be the most familiar of phenomena! For we do so whenever the activity of thinking, $S(\theta)$, reaches a successful conclusion! Even though this is accomplished only through the use of language, it demonstrates the truth of two important principles.

First, that there really is such a thing as experiencing a thought across time. Second, that there exist other methods of experiencing thoughts across time than the method of additive analytical constituting. The question now arises: might not such a different method make possible the wordless experience of a thought across time? And does not that open up the possibility of actively and wordlessly 'thinking one's way across a thought'? However, before we can answer this question we must discover what the method in fact is when we make use of language. If we are to make progress on this issue, we must acquire a clearer picture of how θ comes to mind during S(θ) and S(say θ).

6. Listening and Speaking

(a) Listening with understanding to an articulating thinker

(1) How is it that one actively and across time manages to experience thought θ? For that precisely is what is accomplished by the activity of S(θ) when with articulation we succeed in arriving at θ. It seems to me that considerable illumination can be gained on this matter if we examine what takes place in the course of a closely related phenomenon: namely, listening with understanding to a thinking being who is articulating aloud a thought θ which is gradually gathering in his mind. Then it will help to uncover what is going on if we suppose that the articulation proceeds at a snail's pace. Thus, the 'thinker' slowly utters the words: 'If all cats are black and . . . .' What exactly is going on in the mind of the listener?

What has happened in the mind of the listener by the time he hears the word 'and'? The following, as it seems to me. A particular logical form will have been understood to have been launched by the speaker: p & . . . $\longrightarrow$q . . . .It is also understood at that point that numerous options as to the sense of the θ being articulated still remain open to the speaker, and that some few have already been closed off. Let us now melodramatically suppose that gangsters arrive and shoot the speaker with the word 'and' still in his mouth! Then the listener would report what had thus far occurred in something like the following terms: 'he was trying to affirm *a proposition which involved a deduction from the supposed blackness of all cats and something else.*' And there is nothing problematic in that. Here we imply the existence of a determinate state in the *understanding* in some listener's mind, a state whose fully determinate content is such as to refer to and partially to characterize an as yet undetermined proposition. While the proposition thus characterized had not yet been specified, the process in the understanding was moving towards that destination. And such a phenomenon of understanding is not to be construed as acquaintance already with a thought. While thoughts doubtless cross the mind of the listener as all this is happening, they are distinct from the phenomenon in his understanding.

Then we have merely to imagine that the speaker wondrously revives from his wounds, and continues his complex sentence on to its conclusion: 'if all cats are black and some swans are white, then possibly some swans are black and no cats are white': [{(x)(Cat x $\longrightarrow$ black x) & (∃y)(swan y & white y)} $\longrightarrow$ ◇ {. . .}]. By that time a determinate thought will have been brought to the mind of the hearer. Then note that he approached this thought in stages, not through *thought-stages*, but through the *understanding of specification-stages*: developments occurred in the understanding of a single developing sentential specification. Only when that specification was complete did a thought shine through the specification. And it did not shine through like a beacon at the end of a tunnel! For it was not an event over and above the phenomena taking place in the understanding. The experiencing of the thought, and the completion of the process in the understanding, were one and the same phenomenon.

(2) Note what happened when one heard the simple sentence 'All cats are black' with understanding. Let us once again assume that the phenomenon was slow and spread out over (say) ten seconds. Note particularly what went on when one heard 'all'. What is it to hear this word with understanding? Plainly, we did not experience a *particular thought* that is the sense of 'all'. Indeed, there is *no* experience that is the experiencing of the *sense* of 'all'. However, there is an experience of hearing 'all' *as* endowed with its usual sense, and one of hearing 'all' as endowed with that sense at the beginning of a *statement*. The latter experience involves hearing 'all' as express-ing an intention, and as beginning in a well-known manner to lay down the logical structure of a sentence which has yet to be enunciated. We do not as yet know that logical structure, nor therefore the sense of the sentence of which 'all' is the opening—any more than we know the shape of the building (say, Chartres Cathedral) containing the small slice of flying buttress that we can thus far see as we walk down a high narrow street in the direction of the cathedral. In either case we keep an open mind concerning what lies for the moment beyond our ken, leaving open certain doors in our mind and shutting some others, on this journey with understanding from a determinate beginning towards an unknown but equally determinate end.

Then what must be emphasized is that somewhat as our experience of the physical part is *as of* some whole material object, so in a different mode the hypothe-ses which we entertain as we hear the unfolding sentence with understanding happens in fact to be directed towards the logical form and sense of a *whole sentence*. In this sense the understanding in such experiences may be said to be 'totalistic' in its objects and never 'atomistic'. 'All' is not understood as denoting a merely atom-istic self-contained sense. And the process of hearing culminates, intelligibly and without one's positing an assemblage of such atomistic elements, in one's grasping a sense or thought over time in the course of an intentional activity of listening to the articulation of a thought. Had the activity been one of listening to the articula-tion of (say) a definite description, it would have progressed differently. Either way the intention driving the listening internally conditions the experience of hearing both word and word-sequences.

(b) What would a pure 'thinking one's way across a thought' be like?

(1) To repeat: the understanding of the listener entertains hypotheses as to the logical form and content of the sentence being articulated by the thinking speaker. And as the speaker proceeds, more determinations are registered by that listener. Now this sequential process in the understanding of a hearer must find an analogue in the understanding of the speaker. It is true he does not entertain hypotheses

concerning the logical form of what he is going to have said. However, as he progresses he understands that certain possibilities are closed off at each stage of $S(\theta)$ and $S(\text{say } \theta)$ while certain others remain open, exactly as happens in the mind of the listener. After all, the developing word-structures being articulated mean the same to speaker and hearer, and both assume so as the twin activities of articulating and listening proceed. Each therefore harbour identical states in the understanding directed to identical word-structures.

Then how is a thinker to actively effect in his understanding a developmental sequence of just such understanding-states, without having recourse to words and sentences? For example, the word 'all' is generally highly functional in the constituting of the logical form of its containing sentences. Then how could one capture the closing off of certain possibilities and the leaving open of others which 'all' involves, without the use of symbolism? And how to do so merely by 'thinking'? True, one might wordlessly and inactively think the sense of 'All cats are black'—in an instant. But if there existed a wordless and inactive thinking of the sense of this sentence across (say) ten seconds, we should need to 'think' the closing off of certain possibilities and leaving open of others as we proceed. But what occurs in the understanding, when one suitably hears or says 'All' at the beginning of a sentence, is not of the nature of a thought.

(2) What this tells us is, that the experiential process occurring in one's mind as one engages in $S(\theta)$ does not take either of the following forms. First, it does not involve one's having a sequence of experiences of the supposed parts of a thought, thereby managing in the end to have had a temporally extensive experience of a 'whole' thought. Second, it does not involve one's experiencing a determinate thought which proceeds to mutate at verbally spaced intervals in step sequences into successively more complex thoughts. That is, the way in which the understanding manages across time to acquire a proposition as thought-object, is not like the assembling of a jigsaw picture out of its discrete parts. And neither is it comparable to the situation in which a painter progresses through a series of preliminary sketches to his final work.

Rather, the process passes through a series of stages, in each of which the understanding gains further specificatory information about an as yet unspecified proposition. Accordingly, it takes a succession of meta-objects of the ilk of 'a proposition involving a deduction from the supposed blackness of all cats *and* something else' (approaching that proposition so to say 'from above'). And each succeeding stage acquires a more determinate specification as object: for example, 'a proposition involving a deduction from the supposed blackness of all cats *and* the supposed whiteness of some swans *and* maybe something else.' These meta-objects are not propositions, having no truth-value. They are increasingly determinate specifications of an as yet unspecified proposition. In short, the transition to the acquisition of a proposition object is not of the type of assembly, nor that of increasing exactitude. It is a meta-process cast in terms of symbolism, marked by a steady increase of determinacy to the point of identity. At that precise moment, a thought will have appeared before the mind.

This experience of a thought was temporally extensive, since the acquaintance with the proposition began as one enunciated the first word and ended with the last. Then the 'stuff' of that experience was not *thought*: it was one's *understanding* of the vehicle of thought—the developing word and sentence-structures. Here we have an actively engineered experience of, and the simultaneous creation of, a thought; the truly creative processes being those phenomena taking place within the depths of the mind which continued to throw up the part-intentions continually finding expression as S(θ) and S(say θ) progressed. The whole procedure necessitated the use of language because, since activities have experiential temporal extent and there is no experience of 'thinking a word-sense', the process in the understanding that culminates in one's having experienced a thought-sense across time must be the non-additive crystallization in the understanding of a determinate sentence-sense out of open possibilities which are gradually closed off.

(3) Thus, the experience of the thought across time has parts (unlike the momentary experience of the thought), but to be *part of an experience* of an item is not to be the *experiencing of a part* of that item. Then what has emerged out of this discussion is that the activity of thinking consists in constructing, by such specific means as (say) inference, a proposition of specific logical form such as p $\longrightarrow$ q, which is constituted out of the concepts embodied in one of the languages the 'thinker' understands. Then the only way those concepts can be assembled to constitute such a thought is, not by 'thinking' each concept side by side in time—there being no such thing—but by assembling across time with understanding a verbal structure employing the symbolism which culminates in the determinate specification of the thought. Thinking is an active process of engendering phenomena in one's understanding, whose object is a changing entity expressed in the symbolism which encapsulates thought. It is precisely not the active process of engendering, either thought-parts which go to constitute a thought, nor interim-thoughts which culminate in a final thought.

PART C: INTERIORITY

7. Consciousness and Meaning

(1) I return to the relation between thinking and consciousness. But before I pursue this question I must try and resolve the problem of meaning. I claimed earlier that experiences in conscious subjects exhibit meaning of a kind not encountered in the non-conscious. Then while that meaning may in part have its source in mental act-intentions, the mere fact that mental act-intentions can be operative in non-conscious beings shows they cannot be the *sole* source of that meaning. Thus, the active occupations of a somnambulist exhibit a strong variety of meaning stemming

from the intention, and yet are not meaningful in the sense consciousness requires. It was with this problem in mind that I listed a series of situations (the relaxed car-driver, the long-distance driver, . . .) in which *mental activity* persisted as *consciousness* diminished or faded away. Whatever is going on in these minds as consciousness lessens, it must have much to do with the meaning in question. If there really is a variety of meaning present in conscious minds, and a 'meaning-giver' agency at work in those minds, they must both be in retreat as we move through these several states towards the condition of unconsciousness. Inspecting these states with such considerations in view, should uncover the phenomena in question. Those particular states should be noteworthy for the relative decline or sheer absence of such items.

The most revealing case is the long-distance driver who has drifted into a near trance out of the sheer repetitiousness of his occupations and the resultant near-emptiness of his mind. What kind of meaning is *on the wane* in his case? The answer to this question ought to reveal the sense that we seek. Let us call meaning in the sense 'natural sign of': meaning$_1$. And the sense 'concrete proxy for': meaning$_2$. And the sense imported by intentional action, whereby items find their essential nature under interpretational redescriptions: meaning$_3$. Then my supposition is that there exists a further variety of meaning, which I shall call meaning$_4$, which is what consciousness uniquely exhibits, and that this is already on the wane in the mind of the long-distance driver. It is this sense of 'meaning' that is invoked when we apply the epithet 'senseless' to the actions of a somnambulist. For while there remains much of 'sense' in his experiences, since his mind is filled by integrated purposive intentional acts which import meaning$_3$ into the stream of experience, there plainly exists a sense in which the intentional activities of somnambulists rate as 'senseless'. Determining what that sense is, should uncover the meaning we seek.

What do we have in mind in applying this term to a somnambulist? Not that he does not have a *purpose* in what he is doing: after all, his walkings and lookings are intentional acts (whatever else). And not that he does not know *what* he is doing (for the same reason). And not even that he does not know why he does it (ditto). I think we mean that he does not fully or really know *why* he is doing what he is doing. He may know he walks because he wants to walk, but he neither knows why he so *wants* nor why he *does* what he wants. It is true that when conscious we frequently perform mere inclinatory acts out of no ulterior motive. Nevertheless, we invariably engage in such deeds on the tacit understanding that no serious impediment proscribes them: in this sense they are performed self-consciously with our consent or 'blessing'. Nothing of this kind holds of somnambulistic action, where desire simply has its way 'unvetted'. This bluntly non-rational feature—which we discover again in acts arising out of post-hypnotic suggestion—makes the agent in our eyes not unlike a piece of clockwork which has been wound up and set in motion. Somewhere down the line mental forces are in operation over which he has no control and concerning whose existence he is wholly ignorant. He simply fails to know why he is doing what he is doing. This act really does occur 'without rhyme or reason'! It falls to his lot to perform it as hunger or toothache might descend upon one.

(2) The somnambulist's visual and motor activities exhibit meaning$_3$, since an intending mind lies behind them such that they admit interpretative redescription which reveals their essential nature, say as 'looking for what lies ahead' or 'walking ahead'. Nevertheless they rate as 'senseless' in another sense. This sense resembles that in which the repeated efforts of an insect to scale a glassy incline strike one as senseless. I have dubbed this meaning$_4$. From the example of somnambulism, I think we can say what it is. Meaning$_4$ meets the requirements of meaning$_3$, but introduces an additional element such that whenever meaning$_4$ inheres in experience, it is the subject himself—rather than some alien force with which he cannot identify—that determines that experience: in a word, the element of self-determination. This suffices for the inherence of precisely the sense that is absent from the clockwork-like movements of somnambulists.

While it would be false to say that the mind of the long-distance driver is in anything like the state of a somnambulist, it is nonetheless moving in that direction. As he drives along the highway with little or no thought, it becomes increasingly unnatural to speak of self-determination. That is, to say of him that the intentions presently activating his will are freely albeit tacitly endorsed in his mind from moment to moment: increasingly it is as if earlier stages of his mental life are the locus of the causal forces which 'wound him up' and set him doing what he now does. While it would be literally incorrect to say so, the state in which he finds himself is such that were it to wax or develop or deepen those characterizations would begin to find a point of application.

Now because the acts of the non-conscious have origins with which the subject cannot identify, the redescriptive meaning$_3$-descriptions under which they fall exhibit a narrowness or parochiality, indicative of the fact that it is a *sector* of the mind rather than the owner of that mind that is their ultimate determinant. And so it is as if to lack meaning$_4$ is to lack a special limiting or even transcendent form of meaning$_3$: namely, one such that the parochiality in question gives way to the widest possible redescription, in which the comprehensive standpoint of *the subject* is engaged both in his conception of his own act and so also in its determination. Thus, it might be said that in these circumstances the two characterizations, one in terms of meaning$_3$ and the other of meaning$_4$, coincide. This happens when rationality holds sway in the mind.

Then what is meaning$_4$? It is all that meaning$_3$ is, but must in addition be such that the property of internal intelligibility, discussed at length in Chapter 5, is manifest in whatever phenomena exhibit the trait. It is an intelligibility deriving from self-determination, and ultimately from the rationality which in general underlies it. This reinstates the 'rhyme or reason' so evidently missing in somnambulism. A man walking to buy a newspaper finds his consciousness occupied by visual and motor experiences which exhibit an intelligibility that is not discoverable in the experiences of somnambulists. It is not just that an intending mind lies behind these experiences, it is that a mind lies at the bottom of it all. The pyramid of explanations rests upon a point where the subject gives his mental consent.

8. Thinking and Consciousness

(a) Introduction

I return to the topic of interiority. It was out of an interest in interiority that I examined the nature of thinking. The question prompting that inquiry was: is thinking a necessity for consciousness in self-conscious beings? What suggested to me that it might be so was this. Despite the fact that dreaming is a phenomenon of the inner world, dreamers lack interiority in an important respect. Which precisely? At first one is inclined to say that what they lack is meaning$_3$. Yet while this is true, phenomena like somnambulism decisively demonstrate that the lack runs deeper still. At the very least dream experience lacks meaning$_4$ as well. Now we know that the self-determination requisite for meaning$_4$ and thinking keep close company. After all, in thinking we actively take a hand in the installation of our own (generally) rational beliefs: this inner process helps to ensure the rationality of one's mental state during the state consciousness. Thus, it seems as if it might be the origin of meaning$_4$. Then could it be that what is missing in an experiencing imagining sleeper is thinking? Is this the source of the loss of interiority? Are thinking and interiority one and the same?

Once again the example of the long-distance driver proves illuminating. Even though this man instantiates meaning$_3$ in his experiences, and probably also some form of meaning$_4$ as well, his state of mind is plainly deficient both from the point of view of meaningfulness$_4$ and interiority generally. And it is deficient also in thinking. The long-distance driver has to a degree been *possessed* by his occupations, which seem to be performed without due processes of thought. Then it is evident that self-possession and full intelligibility would return with thinking. This suggests a particular theory of consciousness: a theory in which we bring together the phenomenon of thinking, the property of meaning$_4$, and the general thesis concerning the mental will. It is a theory in which they are brought into intelligible relation with one another.

The theory is that the variety of meaning presumed sufficient for waking consciousness, meaning$_4$, is a *special sub-variety* of meaning$_3$: namely, the meaning that is realized when the mental willing that enables meaning$_3$, and that is as we have seen essential to consciousness, assumes the form of *thinking*. After all, thinking is an exercise of the mental will which we know to be endowed with certain vitally important properties conducive to rationality, and we know also that rationality of mental state is a necessary and sufficient condition of consciousness in experiencing subjects. Along such lines one might come to the conclusion that in the self-conscious thinking lies at the heart of consciousness, that it is both necessary and sufficient for the condition. In this way, interiority and thinking would prove to be coincident.

(b) The special properties of thinking

(1) The suggestion that thinking is essential to consciousness can be easily misconstrued. There is a tendency to understand the theory in obscurantist *idiosyncratic* terms. Thus, we might seem to be claiming that there exists a distinctive mental experiential thread running through the mind, whose sheer idiosyncratic presence somehow ensures consciousness. But in fact if thinking is necessary and sufficient for consciousness, it cannot be on account of any such properties.

Let me explain why. We know that the thought is constitutive of thinking. Then to speak of the *quale* or 'what it is like'-ness of thought, evidences a misunderstanding of the vital distinction between the concept of an experience and that of the 'what it is like'-ness of an experience. These are not the same: in particular, the latter concept has more limited application. Thus, the distinction between knowledge by acquaintance and description has genuine purchase with experiences of sound or nausea or déjà vu: a single experience of the item will generally open the eyes of the unacquainted to what it is people have been talking of all along. But the distinction is absolutely inapplicable to two vastly familiar experiences of elemental import: the infinitely primitive experience of striving to move a limb, and the infinitely developed experience of thought. In neither case is there conceptual space for talk of *quale*. This is because the type and content of the experience exhaust its being. It is not that these experiences are ineffable—it is precisely the opposite: words go the *entire way* in capturing what is there. In the thought a proposition enters experience, in the bodily will a psychological force for the production of limb movement does the same, and that is all there is to say. The concept of *variety* of type, which works so strenuously and well in the case of affect and sensation, has nothing to accomplish here. Type and object do all.

(2) What is of import in thinking is not to be found in some supposed special *quale* or 'what it is like'-ness. It lies in certain other mental properties. Namely, in its activeness, in its being susceptible of rational determination, but above all in the fact that it is directed to the production of thoughts and along such a special avenue to the installation of belief. Thinking is a process whereby we can take direct responsibility for our beliefs, and for their rationality. It is these properties which confer upon thinking its central position in the mind. If thinking is a necessity for consciousness, it must be on account of them.

To remind ourselves of the special assets of thinking, it is salutary to remember what the arrival of the thought on the evolutionary scene brought in its train. The capacity for thought is in part a capacity for a form of mental *liberty*. He who can think can wrench his mind away from the here and now and concretely present (in a way not open to 'dumb beasts'). He can direct his mind to other times and places, to hypotheticals, counterfactual possibilities, and so on. In the thought everything before the mind is so to say 'on ice', not as yet entertained in the form of a cognitive attitude. This almost aristocratic luxury allows one to stage the equivalent of experiments in the mind, mock-ups or 'war-games' through which we can test our beliefs and plot our intentions. And this province of thinking is a mode of imagining. The imagination enables us to take off into the realm of the hypothetical, and in that way assess putative determinants of possible beliefs and plans. Here we can see how it is that imagination is essential for rationality of belief-formation and action, and thus for rationality itself.

This capacity for detachment from present concrete actualities and for contact with mere possibility, determines the superintending role of thinking in the mind. It enables it to monitor present and contemplated beliefs and actions, and confirm or adjust them according to the demands of rationality. Then what I must now consider is whether these assets stand in some unique relation to consciousness. That is, whether mental activeness, the potential for rationality that is attendant upon the will, and above all the production by such means of thoughts and by that special avenue also beliefs, introduce into the mental scene features which are jointly essential to consciousness and found only in thinking. More particularly—since rationality in the experiencing subject is necessary and sufficient for consciousness—whether they constitute the unique and 'royal road' to rationality.

(c) Are there properly formed examples of consciousness without thinking?

(1) The theory to be discussed is that in the self-conscious thinking lies at the heart of consciousness, that it is necessary and sufficient for the state, in all probability through enabling rationality. Now amongst the phenomena which thinking might take as its subject-matter when one is conscious, no doubt in some form of monitoring or overseeing role, are our own present active involvements with the environment. Indeed, if the above theory is correct it must be essential to consciousness that it do so upon those occasions. Such a theory has to face a difficulty posed by the existence of certain examples of waking consciousness which are anything but imperfect—in the way the long-distance driver's consciousness was undoubtedly flawed—in which thinking looks as if it may simply be absent. These rather special cases tend to be practical situations in which one's involvement with the environment is intense and total and often dramatically brief. Consider the following examples:

   (i) Leaping at full stretch for a slip catch in cricket.
   (ii) A racing driver travelling at 150 m.p.h. sees a puddle of oil a few hundred yards down the track—and circumnavigates it—all in the space of three seconds.
   (iii) Crossing Niagara Falls on a tightrope.
   (iv) Four top-class tennis doubles players all at the net are involved in a high-speed volleying exchange of (say) a dozen strokes.

Participants in such occupations are prone to say that thinking is something to be avoided. How true is this statement? And what measure of interiority exists on such occasions?

(2) The man on the tightrope might insist that thinking is to be avoided. On the other hand he might instead say something with a different flavour: namely, that it is fatal to let one's mind 'wander' (—but a 'captive' mind may be a *needed* mind!) Thus, one might claim that thinking comes to a halt, but one might instead say that what is fatal is to permit one's thinking to be anything but *wholly subordinated* to the task in hand. Whichever of these two accounts we accept, it is important that we first distinguish thinking that is subordinated to a task from thinking that is free to wander. If the tightrope walker were to allow his mind to range far and wide, to fully avail himself of its libertarian powers, he would surely plunge to his doom. But why must his thinking take such untrammelled form on so perilous an occasion? Accordingly, the problem may be restated. Does thinking continue during episodes of intense practical involvement with the environment? Is it the case that it occurs but is wholly subordinated to the occupation? Or is it rather that for the moment one simply gives up thinking and gets on with the task? Is it unwise to let it 'wander', or unwise to even let it 'work'?

It seems to me certain that in at least some of these situations thinking is taking place. For example, the racing driver may be muttering to himself admonitions like: 'give the oil a wide berth, but don't graze the barrier', or 'more to the right! more! not *too* much!' Likewise the tightrope walker may be muttering: 'don't listen to those sounds: watch the next stretch of rope and *nothing else*!', and so forth. These are undoubtedly situations in which thinking is occurring. Indeed, far from being a distraction from the task, it seems to be an essential to concentration and successful performance. While it is true that the thinking is simple and repetitive in content, we should not confuse simplicity and repetitiousness with sheer non-existence. Every new step on the tightrope presents the identical practical problem—afresh, for there can be no resting upon one's laurels in such situations! The purpose of thinking here may not be to chart 'the great unknown': rather, to guide oneself with an iron hand, to stand over oneself. But it surely *exists*. In fact a man in these situations might even say: 'never was my mind more active!'

(d) Thinking and attending

(1) Is thinking essential for consciousness? The above examples of *intense practical involvement* with the environment seemed at first to pose a difficulty for this theory. However, on closer inspection they proved not to do so. Provided we restrict the scope of the thinking, 'clip its wings' and subordinate it wholly to the task in hand, it emerges in such situations as a reality and indeed as essential to success. Then what of situations of *practical disengagement*? What goes on in the mind of a man who is (say) sitting immobile in a chair for the space of something like ten minutes? What of thinking here? It seems to me beyond dispute that this man would

automatically be taken to be engaged in thinking of some kind or another. And it is surely a matter of some theoretical importance that we make this assumption *absolutely unhesitatingly* and as a complete matter of course. And it is surely of the greatest significance that to fail to do so would be to assume the presence of some kind of daze or blackout. The intimacy of the link between thinking and consciousness comes clearly to view in so simple an example.

The summary situation is that when a conscious person is intensely engaged with his environment he thinks about what he is doing, and when he is disengaged he thinks about whatever he pleases. He does the first so that rationality and success should characterize his behaviour, and the second for whatever reason. Accordingly, it seems that the only occasions when thinking might conceivably be absent from consciousness, are those humdrum situations in which a subject is practically involved with the physical environment with something short of passionate fervour: say, in brushing one's teeth or crossing a road. We must now discover whether thought is necessary on these occasions as well. The rule which suggests itself is, that the more routine the act the more it approximates to the situation of practical disengagement, the less routine the more to that of intense involvement. Either way thinking proves to be obligatory: tooth-brushing is often a moment for vague introspection (as in some early Bergman films), road-crossing a time for wide-awakeness of attention and intellect.

(2) A simple preliminary distinction needs to be drawn between two ways the mind can be involved in action. 'Keeping one's mind on what one is doing' generally means, ensuring that what one is doing absorbs one's attention. But it is sometimes used in the sense, thinking about what one is doing. Then even though these two activities often go together, they are distinct: the first is *concentrating*, the second *thinking*. Indeed, the first is not in general an act *additional to* what one is doing, the second is. While the first is a property of what one is doing, the second is an internal active process which takes that very act as its object. A good racing driver will usually engage in both simultaneously for most of a race. He should drive with concentration, and with thought ('intelligently').

Then it goes without saying that intentional actions absorb a measure of attention. But do they necessitate thought? A tennis champion plays a backhand straight down the line without the least strain. Did he think as he stroked the ball? Plainly the act absorbed some attention—in the mode of *occupant* of awareness. And the muscular events involved doubtless absorbed some attention—in the mode of *object* of awareness. But he may not have had to think about how he played his backhand, so well 'grooved' was the stroke. And yet in sending the ball down the line he was carrying out an intention for which he had a reason, acquired it may be when he saw his opponent outmanœuvred on the far side of the court. Then did he at that moment *think*? Or did the automaticity of the deed suffice to wipe his mind clean of thought? It seems to me that it cannot have done so, and that the occurrent acquisition of reasons for behaviour have to take the form of thought-events. Automaticity of stroke production is not automaticity of mind. However, in order to generalize this judgement, it is necessary that we examine a little more closely what rationality of behaviour as such requires.

(e) The requirements of rationality

(1) We require of conscious active beings that they know what they are doing, and why. Can this requirement be met without thought? Now the rationality of consciousness typically demands (say) the entertaining of beliefs for good reasons. And being in this latter state requires, not merely that somewhere in the past one acquired reasons for these beliefs, but that those reasons be *perpetuated* into the present. After all, one cannot dump one's cognitive responsibilities upon one's past self: it is not like signing a document in law! Now this 'perpetuation' need not, and indeed in general could not, take the form of present cogitation, else nothing rational could ever be actualized. But it must persist, and be such that if stopped in one's tracks one would be in a position to justify one's beliefs. Moreover, we saw in Chapter 3 that the possession of reasons involved what might be called a *personal 'conversion'* of oneself. I quote from that chapter:

What we require is, that the belief be caused by reasons. And by 'reasons' we mean 'considerations': say, empirical facts which have the status of evidence. And yet this account still strikes me as inadequate as it stands: to my way of thinking it has an unacceptable flavour of *impersonal objectivity* about it. We do not mean merely that that which *is* a consideration caused the belief. We do not merely mean: (∃x)(consideration, x & causative-of-belief, x). If we really did mean no more, it would be the 'consideration' that appeared in the mind like an alien apparition! We require in addition that it act *qua* consideration—upon *us*! We need it to be the case that *our* reason was appealed to, and effectively engaged, in the causal transaction. The important locution 'my reason for believing' reminds us that the transaction is an individual or personal one. A conversion precisely of *ourselves* took place.

(2) Thus, rationality requires that a personal 'conversion' of oneself be a reality that is not relegated to the past. The 'conversion' must be a reality which is continuously with us. We require therefore the constant possibility, indeed the constant readiness in one's mind, to review one's beliefs *should occasion demand*. And this implies that there exists a present (here and now) awareness of the rationality-status of one's (here and now) beliefs. And thus that there exists a constant readiness to recognize that occasion does in fact demand here and now! Then can this be accomplished in the absence of thought? Can there exist an occurrent immediate awareness of the sources of, and validity of, our present changing cognitive attitudes, without the occurrence of thought? On the face of it, one would say not: do not these occurrent awarenesses amount precisely to thoughts? Indeed, do not they form a continuity which, in being active, precisely constitute the process of thinking? To see how this can be, let us examine a practical situation involving such occurrences.

We shall suppose we are crossing a busy road, say Hyde Park Corner. We assume we are looking where we are going. Assume also that one knows at each point in time why at that moment one believes whatever one does believe on these constantly changing highly practical matters. And all of this is actually going on there and then in one's mind as one manœuvres one's way through the maze of swirling traffic. Then can the *occurrent reasons* determining those shifting beliefs be given to immediate self-knowledge in their role as rational cause, but the *rational events* of inferential type leading from reasons to present beliefs be taking place nonetheless outside experience? Can these inferential step be occurring without thought? I do not see how they could.

Consider a particular incident. One sees a nearby truck bearing down fast, experiences it as threatening, and at that moment knows why one does. Then must not a *thought-event* have occurred in one's consciousness as one saw the truck and recognized it as a threat? Did not the occurrent rationale determining one's novel belief necessitate an experience of *inferential thought*? Thus, it seems to me that we would report the situation in these terms: 'I saw the truck, and knew at once that it was a danger.' Here we report an experience of coming to know, which in being given *as* for this or that reason, must at the same time be accounted an *experience of inference*. Now these are typical *thought-events*. And this is what *continuously* goes on in one's mind as one is threading a path through the traffic. For it is assumed one threads a rational path, rather than an obsessional-neurotic, or paranoid-psychotic, or merely animal trail. Those ongoing and continuing thoughts form something more than a chaotic 'thought-salad'. But whence the order in the succession? May we not conclude that the mind itself is ordering them in an exercise of the mental will: namely, in the activity of thinking?

(f) The necessity of thinking

I can discover no example of consciousness without thinking. It seems that thinking is a necessity if consciousness is to exist in the self-conscious. But we know in any case from the earlier discussion that the stream of consciousness has to be a rational progression if consciousness is to occur, and how is that rationality to be maintained in the absence of thought? More specifically, how is it to be guaranteed in the absence of a steady process of thinking which continuously transcends the present concrete situation and brings the special powers of thought to bear upon it? The practical situation just examined drives home in concrete fashion the message that the mental willing necessary for consciousness has to adopt the form of thinking if rationality is to prevail. It is in this way that we manage to take responsibility for the rationality-status of our beliefs.

Let me express the matter thus. If rationality is to be preserved throughout our experiences, it is necessary that a guiding hand be continuously determining that thoughts relevant to one's present concerns be continually entering one's mind. Those thoughts may be questions, decisions, inferences, and so on, but they must be of such a nature that the rationality-status of one's mental, and especially one's active processes, is constantly maintained. This cannot happen haphazardly, simply of its own accord: it must be the work of a self-aware mind which knows where it is going and takes a hand in determining that direction. The unceasing process that ensures this constant undercurrent to our experience of the world is thinking. It is thinking which introduces that distance between self and self which *is* interiority.

Meanwhile, the following simple intuitive consideration confirms the belief that thinking is necessary if consciousness is to occur in the self-conscious. It returns me to an earlier topic. I asked whether it would be possible for a normally conscious man who is sitting in a chair, let us say idly looking around at the furniture, to be thinking of absolutely nothing over an extended period like ten minutes? Could he be fully conscious for ten minutes and this be the complete and whole story? *Just* looking around—and thinking *nothing*! Why is it that this description seems so definitively a recipe for some kind of daze or trance? The case strikes me as eloquent in the extreme, despite its simplicity, and even though its force is 'intuitive' and unrationalized. Why does it seem so certain that this person must be actively thinking if he is to be properly awake? The obvious answer is that it merely exposes to view in the particular what is a completely general necessity.

9. The Multiple Determinants of Consciousness

We know that the various traits constitutive of being a self-conscious type of creature form a tight closely-knit circle of mutually entailing properties. I am thinking of such characteristics as rationality of nature, the capacity to think, the knowledge of language, an awareness of truth and negation, of the passage of time, of the world itself, as well as of one's own existence and mind or inner world. And so on.

Then it is similarly so in the case of the several traits which emerged in the discussion as constitutive of waking consciousness. We saw that ($\alpha 1$) present occurrent experience, and ($\alpha 2$) exercise of the mental will, are each necessary though insufficient conditions of consciousness. However, logically sufficient conditions for that state are realized when we conjoin with the above two phenomena any one of the following necessary conditions (various logically equivalent sets of sufficient conditions for the existence of consciousness being thereby constituted):

($\alpha 3$) Rationality of mental state.
($\alpha 4$) The occurrence of thinking.
($\alpha 5$) And thus of interiority.
($\alpha 6$) The obtaining of meaning$_4$ (of internal intelligibility) in the stream of consciousness.
($\alpha 7$) Mental freedom or self-determination.
($\alpha 8$) A proper self-knowledge concerning those mental phenomena for which self-knowledge is the rational norm.

Then waking consciousness is the state that is realized when the whole complex circle of mutually necessitating phenomena is fully complete. No property or phenomenon is in advance of any other, and the state is essentially complex. It pre-cisely constitutes a marshalling of the central powers of one's mind. What they knit to form is none other than consciousness itself.

The role of thinking is central to the whole structure. In the final analysis it is because thinking is active and thinking is essential to consciousness that mental action is a necessary condition of consciousness: the general necessity discovers its rationale in this particular necessity. Thus thinking is at once the custodian of rationality, being the appointed means of ensuring its continuing operational pres-ence in the mind, it is the source of the interiority necessary to consciousness, and it is that through which the vital element of cognitive and active self-determination are introduced into the mind in this state, for it is above all in this phenomenon that we take charge of what happens in our own minds.

Part II
The Attention and Perception

Introduction to Part II

1. The Constitution of Consciousness

(1) In Part I I 'anatomized' consciousness in the self-conscious into a group of mental elements which together constitute the state. First, and transparently analytically so, a continuous 'stream of experience' must be 'flowing', just exactly so long as consciousness endures. Second, the prevailing state of mind must be rational, so that in general the beliefs and actions of the conscious take place in that state for reasons and not just causes. Third, a general mental activeness needs for the most part to characterize the onward flow of one's cognitively significant experiences, and in particular and pre-eminently an active process of thinking must be going on continuously, ensuring through its special powers the rationality of the progression of experience and ultimately the presence of the properties of interiority and self-determination. Fourth, a specific measure of occurrent self-knowledge is obligatory. Fifth, the attention must be open to perceptual contact with outer phenomena.

These constituent elements of consciousness fall into three groups:

A. Experience.
B. Rationality of state, a specific measure of self-knowledge, thinking, self-determination, etc.
C. Availability of the perceptual attention.

How do these elements relate logically to one another? Before I consider this question, I will make a brief comment on the relations holding between the properties gathered together under B (which I shall describe as 'The Apparatus of Rationality'). What we discover here is mutual entailment right across the board. For example, it is not possible to be in a rational state in the absence in general of knowledge of the origins of one's beliefs (an ignorance which is the norm in dreams). Nor can one be rational unless one's beliefs have causes which persuade one personally, which is to say in the absence of a form of inner assent, cognitive self-determination. This in turn depends upon the constant active superintending process of thinking, which is the custodial agency responsible for the continuing state of rationality. One fact of some significance emerges from these considerations. Namely, that self-knowledge and the active process of thinking are conditions

267

of the other elements of the apparatus of rationality. These two phenomena must be of pivotal importance in the constituting of self-conscious consciousness.

The circle of mutually entailing properties collected under B arises into existence fully complete. The properties are non-identical, mutually supportive, and are parts both of the occurrent apparatus of rationality and the prevailing state of consciousness. They are to be described as parts because together they entail the presence of the apparatus of rationality, and when conjoined with A (Experience) and C (Attentive accessibility) entail that of Consciousness. But while they relate additively with A and C, they do not relate additively with one another. There is no situation in which the state consciousness cannot as yet exist because, while most of the above circle of rational self-conscious properties are present, those of (say) thinking and self-determination are still missing, requiring merely to be added to the already present properties to realize consciousness. In short, while these properties are parts of the occurrent state of consciousness, they are not *individual* parts: it is the totality B which is added to A, not they individually.

(2) To return to the question asked above: what logical relations hold between (A) experience, (B) the apparatus of rationality, and (C) attentive accessibility? The following are evident: A—|>B, because (say) dream experience occurs in sleep and shallow unconsciousness, and A—|>C because dreams occur in shallow unconsciousness. Likewise A & C—|>B, since sleep is consistent with perceptual experience. Again since consciousness is an occurrent phenomenon, and (say) thinking is an experience, it is clear that B—→A. The problematic issue is the question discussed at length in the Introduction: namely, the relation of B to C, which is to say that of A & B to C. In the Introduction I argued that A & B—→C, on the grounds that A & B entail consciousness, which in turn entails C in virtue of the fact that the conscious are aware of Outer Reality and mentally in a position to discover temporally aligned outer phenomenal truth.

The summary situation is as follows:

(i) A—|>B.
(ii) A—|>C.
(iii) A & C—|>B.
(iv) B—→A.
(v) A & B—→C.
(vi) A & B—→Consciousness.
(vii) A & B & C—→Consciousness.

(3) Then although A & B —→ C because A & B —→ Consciousness, cannot one say that A & B —→ C without needing to invoke consciousness? The truth is that one can, but it is simultaneously only because A & B together ensure consciousness that the entailment holds. Matters are clarified by considering the situation in the case of the unself-conscious consciousness of non-rational creatures. The constituent elements of that less developed variety of the state consciousness are:

A'. Experience.

B'. The occurrent presence of the naturally appointed means for generating empirical knowledge out of perceptual experience.

C'. Attentive accessibility.

Consider what B' involves. It includes the tendency to interpret sense-data in terms of innate and experience-acquired knowledge of the appearance of phenomenal objects; the tendency to believe in the presence of objects O, where O is the content of present sense-perceptual experience; and the tendency to form further beliefs, caused in turn by belief in the presence of such O's together with innate and experience-acquired propensities, regarding unperceived phenomena. Examples of this last are: a fledgling bird expects attack on sighting a hawk-profile, a dog expects a kick on recognizing its brutal owner. This constellation of properties constitutes a mental apparatus which leads in general to perspectival knowledge of some of the present contents of the local environment, and comes into existence as consciousness arises.

There are two points of interest emerging from these latter observations. The first is, that the 'apparatus of rationality' (B) of self-conscious beings must be a higher form of the B' invoked in the unself-conscious case (what one might describe as 'the mental apparatus of empirical epistemology'). The second is, that the apparatuses in question are specifically directed towards the discovery of empirical truth on the basis of perceptual experience. Then if this is an essential property of both B and B', of both the 'apparatus of rationality' and the 'mental apparatus of empirical epistemology' of unself-conscious beings, why should we not directly deduce C (attentive accessibility) from A and B in the case of self-conscious consciousness simply through filling in with greater exactitude the precise character of the B-property necessitated by the state? Thus, what we mean by 'the apparatus of rationality' (B) is not a faculty for making timeless deductions of logical and mathematical truth, but a faculty for making contemporaneous empirical epistemological discovery—whatever else it may accomplish in the realm of the a priori. The fact that consciousness is an occurrent ongoing state, renewed instant by instant, and that property B is entailed by the orientation of consciousness to contemporaneous outer empirical truth, implies that B must take such a specific form. Since one cannot imagine these occurrent phenomena in the absence of present attentive accessibility, it seems to me that we may legitimately infer C from A and B.

(4) The upshot is, that consciousness is constituted additively out of A and B and C, even though the concept of additiveness lacks application once we dismantle B into parts which are also parts of consciousness. Now that more or less concludes what I have to say about the constitutive make-up of the state of (wakeful) consciousness. It provides my answer to the question: What is consciousness? As observed at the beginning of this work, there is no mystery as to what consciousness is, whatever mystery there may be concerning its appearance in the world, which is to say over its origin. In particular, while one may marvel

at the core ingredient of consciousness, the experience, perhaps because of its indefinability or maybe on account of its irreducibility, it is no more of an ontological novelty or an indefinable than is the phenomenon of belief. Each of these phenomena have properties, neither are definable in terms of them, and they are both irreducible novel or 'emergent' phenomena. Why should not Reality come to contain items which have no precedent in the past? Is Creation so shackled to its infancy? Is it so *barren*? It is futile to attempt to transmute these items into what they are not. In the language of G. E. Moore: the experience is what it is and is not another thing, and the same holds of belief and desire and will and much else.

2. Consciousness and Perception

(1) Here I review certain issues raised already in the Introduction, only now in somewhat different terms. My aim at this point is to bring out how the analysis of consciousness just accomplished in Part I provides the means for understanding what occurs in the conscious mind when a subject makes perceptual contact with his environment, and something of the wider significance of this event. Now this significance can escape one. For it is easy to think of consciousness as self-sufficient in a way it is not. After all, consciousness is internally determined, being entirely constituted out of mental phenomena. In particular, despite its obvious links to cognition, consciousness is not the perception of anything: no state finds itself redescribed as 'consciousness' in virtue of its standing in some requisite perceptual relation to outer phenomena. In fact not only is consciousness not the perception of anything, it is simply not directed to objects of any kind. Whereas hearing a sound is a consciousness of a sound, consciousness is nothing but—consciousness. In this respect it is indeed self-sufficient.

This fact can cause misunderstanding. Consciousness is directed to no object because it is directed to what transcends all objects, the World. Thus, consciousness is directed to the World, but not in the mode of object. The conscious are aware of the World as dreamers merely putatively are: as we say, the conscious are 'in touch' with Reality as dreamers are not. What this implies is that empirical truth, and indeed truth in general, is the goal of the cognitive processes of the conscious, and that they are mentally empowered or in a position to arrive at such truth. It may be and probably is the case that the evolutionary rationale of mind and consciousness consists in the performing of intentional action which promotes life, but there can be no doubt that the acquisition of the cognitive basis of such informed intentional action is an a priori-given function of consciousness. The empirical cognitive power of consciousness is part of its essence. It is an epistemological power which finds expression first in the realistic perceptual experiences typical of consciousness, in which the full resources of the K/B-Syst. are put to use, embedding the objects encountered in perception in a universal cognitive context, and it is completed when the apparatus of rationality leads the mind through this avenue to empirical knowledge cast in such universal terms as to merit the description 'cognitive contact with outer reality'.

(2) When the epistemological power of consciousness is exercised by means of perception, consciousness fulfils one of its major functions. In fact, considered from a wider standpoint this perceptual epistemological phenomenon proves to be of even greater moment. For one thing the processes of cognitive internalization which begin in perception help the mind to grow and develop in substance, indeed enable its owner to so much as lead a life! But there is an even wider significance to the event. Namely, that of introducing into the mind the content without which it could not in general exist. For consciousness is simply not possible in a mind devoid of a K/B-Syst. What kind of 'representations' could occur in such a vacuum? In the absence of a cognitive system, however rudimentary, the distinction between the various states of consciousness could not be drawn, nor the states themselves individuated. Thus, despite being internally determined by its mental constituents, consciousness fulfils its nature and renews a contact upon which it ultimately depends, when it goes beyond or outside of itself and puts to use its epistemological power, making cognitive contact with outer reality. It is a predestined conjunction that is thus realized between these two realms, first in that it is the expression of an essential function of consciousness, second insofar as such cognitive interaction between consciousness and the World is when considered generally a condition of its very being, but also third as we shall discover in Part II in that consciousness already prepares the way logically for this interaction.

(3) To repeat, consciousness fulfils its nature when it puts to use its epistemological power and makes epistemological contact with outer reality. And this is true whatever the metaphysical character of the world in which consciousness arises. On pain of solipsism, consciousness must be capable of going beyond itself cognitively into the remaining sector of the world. Then one might at first think it a matter of indifference so far as consciousness was concerned how it fulfilled its epistemological destiny and made contact with outer reality. Provided it gave expression to its cognitive power, and enabled the mind to internalize sectors of outer reality, it might seem to be neither here nor there that the epistemological contact in question took the form of perception rather than some other equally accredited avenue of access to outer reality. Accordingly, the prospect seems to arise of a theory of consciousness which is transcendent of the metaphysical status of the world. The situation that is in fact realized by our own consciousnesses, set in a physical world which we encounter epistemologically by means of perception, would on this understanding of the facts be no more than one possibility amongst others.

Closer inspection proves it to be otherwise, and this thesis discovers its justification in the discussion which now follows in Part II. The epistemological contact with outer reality that expresses the functional nature of consciousness, renews the substance of the mind, and in the final analysis helps make both it and consciousness possible, is constrained by certain elements of the situation to be perceptual in character. Perception is the 'royal road' to outer reality: it alone gives expression to the property of consciousness that we characterized as its being 'in touch' with outer reality. Indeed, it is the only conceivable ultimate path to outer reality, and all the more obviously when the discussion is confined to physical worlds. What we shall see in the course of Part II is how it comes to be the case that perception is not just one way of learning about outer reality, but is from an ultimate standpoint the only conceivable way. Moreover, it is not just an avenue leading mind and consciousness attentively out onto outer reality. In perception we encounter physical reality *as it is*, for in perception we encounter physical phenomena in their ultimate *physical guise*. We do not experience them as (say) psychological phenomena, but as material objects and physical events and spatial properties and so forth.

A summary statement of the situation which has emerged concerning the nature of the relation between consciousness and perception, goes like this. The mind, and consciousness along with it, is born of the World, inasmuch as neither phenomenon could exist without the function of representation. Accordingly, in the experience of perception consciousness meets its maker, concretely or 'in the flesh', and in its ultimate (i.e. physical) ontological form. It renews its substance at that point, augmenting the content upon which intentionality depends, siting its own events in temporal relation with those 'without', and simultaneously executes a fundamental a priori-determined essential function without which it could not in general exist, a function which in all probability constitutes one half of the functional rationale determining its very existence.

3. Experience

(1) And so consciousness stands ready, poised so to say to go beyond itself in perceptual, and through those means also informed active encounter with physical reality. Its internal constitution encompasses an occurrent readiness for such a concrete encounter, together with an accessible cognitive portrait of the World in the form of a K/B–Syst. which is put to use in those experiences, assisted by the occurrently functioning apparatus of rationality necessary for the interpretation of the data received in perceptual experience.

Thus the predestined meeting of inner and outer begins in *experience*. That is to say, in what is the phenomenal core of consciousness. Now a momentous occurrence, so far as animal kind is concerned, took place with the emergence into existence of the experience: a direct encounter with Time. If *per impossibile* minds could exist in the absence of experience, time would not have crossed their horizon. This is not to say that we encounter time through undergoing a distinctive experience of time. Rather, it states that simply through experiencing anything one experiences the passage of time, and that in no other way can one encounter the reality of time, whatever might exist in the way of innate knowledge. The direct encounter with time which takes place in experience occurs because the conscious in experiencing have an irreducible awareness-of the just-elapsed, and an immediate directedness-towards the intended future: the necessity of short-term memory and of mental activity guarantee these properties in consciousness. The objects of experience at each instant are therefore experienced not just *as* momentary slices of phenomenal items, they are experienced *as* (momentary slices of) objects with a determinate recent history and an expected impending future. And it could not be otherwise. The constant embedding of the instant in a mutating determinate temporal setting is internal to experience itself: delete from awareness the containing context in which flux is continual and one erases the present with it! Thus, the experience brings with it the awareness of the passage of time. For beings with minds, the experience is the bearer of time.

Now experience is entailed by, and is naturally described as the core of, consciousness. In this way time lies at the heart of consciousness—as space not. Merely to be conscious is to be aware of the passage of time, whereas no comparable encounter with space is guaranteed as consciousness arises and experience unfolds. Accordingly, time must be adjudged closer than space to the mental essence of animal and human kind. Within our minds we are temporal beings before all else.

(2) These experiences in the conscious do not occur as isolated fragments, as is perhaps true of the momentary uninterpreted perceptual experiences of sleepers, say when they wince at the light or start at a sound: they occur in the presence of a colony of other experiences. And in fact consciousness entails an entire system of contemporaneous experiences, the 'Stream of Consciousness'. This gives rise to a familiar sense of the word 'Consciousness', what one might call 'Experiential Consciousness', the sense invoked in utterances like 'At that moment his consciousness could contain no more' or 'At that moment his entire consciousness was focused on one thing'. It is to be distinguished from the central (i.e. waking) sense of the term, which designates the phenomenon which is the main topic of the present work. However, I do not wish in any way to suggest they are things apart—far from it! After all, 'Experiential Consciousness' is at once part of *and* the prime phenomenal manifestation of consciousness. Indeed, one might wonder what more there could be to wakefulness than the stream of consciousness of the wakeful. Nevertheless, certain elements which appeared in the 'anatomization' carried out in Part I, such as the requirements of an occurrent rationality and self-knowledge, are no part of the stream of consciousness. And they, too, are essential. Taken in conjunction these several phenomena realize the state consciousness, the stream of consciousness being the visible or experiential face of the continuous occurrent complex whole.

(3) Then in this phenomenon, and in the experience which is its 'stuff', we discover the means for strengthening the claim that consciousness fulfils its destiny when a conscious subject perceptually encounters the physical world. I hope in the ensuing discussion to show how perception arises in the midst of the stream of consciousness, and the relation in which it stands to that phenomenal framework. Above all, I endeavour by providing a general theory of the nature of perception to make clear just how *naturally* it appears in this context: I seek to effect a strong

273

synthesis between perception and Experiential Consciousness. One of the broad aims of the present work is to explicate the nature of the transition as the mind flows out onto the physical world in the concrete way that is unique to perception, and demonstrate how it is the fulfilment of a destiny or predestined role. It is to provide an intelligible account of the bridge phenomena leading from the interior experiential core of consciousness out onto the domain of things which is its appointed goal, and show just how it happens to be thus 'appointed'. This enterprise involves my studying the starting point of the transition, namely the perceptual experience. My project at this point is that of providing a completely general theory of the nature of this phenomenon, which is itself cast in universal terms. This is now undertaken in Part II.

The theory which I expound concerns the nature of perception as such. Thus, I hope in Chapters 7–9 to demonstrate that a universality lies concealed behind the particularity of the various modes of perception. Indeed, one such that perception emerges as an a priori concept, to be analysed in terms of the fundamental and indefinable concept of the experience (and therefore also in terms of the attention). The concept of perception proves to be a sort of logical 'moment' in the development of the concept of the experience. It is through this fact that the experience provides means for strengthening the claim that consciousness fulfils its destiny in the perceptual encounter with the World.

7

The Attention

It seems to me that the attention, a phenomenon which stands in close relation to perception, has been insufficiently studied by philosophers. Now it is clear that the attention is closely linked also to consciousness. Then I hope in the course of the ensuing discussion in Part II of this work, by tracing out some of the connections between these three phenomena, to shed light upon the essential nature of perception, and in particular to show how it is that perception exemplifies one of the two major functions of consciousness. I aim in this way to reveal its central status in the mind. In the present chapter I confine the discussion to an examination of the attention itself.

1. The Attention as Container

(a) The non-cognitive function of the attention

There is a sense of the word 'perception' in which one who grasps a truth has a perception. Plainly, the sense of 'perception' in the expression 'sense-perception' is different. In this sense of the term, which is that exemplified in (say) the seeing and hearing of phenomena, a perception is a *noticing*. That is, it is an event in the attention, which is such that some phenomenal reality is the object of that attentive event. As we express it, perception is making attentive contact with some actual existent.

What do we mean in talking of 'The Attention'? Are we referring to a *particular faculty*? In particular, do we mean the capacity to harbour certain idiosyncratic phenomena which link one in a pre-eminent fashion cognitively with the environment? I do not think we do. Such a characterization of attention fits the capacity for *sense*, which is to say the capacity to support the special arrays of sensation that are capable of being put to use in sense-perceptual experience. However, there are reasons for doubting whether it is an adequate characterization of either perception or the attention. One reason consists in the fact that the attention has a use or function in mental life which is distinctively different from its use in perceptual cases.

A notable example of the latter occurs in act-situations. Thus, it is certain that intentional action makes demands of some kind upon the attention—whatever precisely those demands may be. Think of remarks like: 'Because I was attending so closely to my driving, I had little attention left for the conversation.' In my opinion the role allotted here to the attention is neither simply, nor primarily perceptual.

Some people will disagree with this claim. They might argue that in such cases attending is synonymous with perceiving, and interpret the above remark as a statement of the familiar fact that perception is a faculty with limited capacity. As I cannot hear much of a symphony and of a conversation simultaneously, so I cannot suitably listen to a complex conversation and at the same time direct a reasonable amount of perceptual attention onto dense traffic, gear lever, steering wheel, and the limb movements that I make as I drive. Who can quarrel with this last claim? And it must be admitted that it is at least consistent with a perceptual interpretation of the need for attention in action. Thus, it is clear that intentional physical action necessitates continuous ongoing knowledge of the physical progress of one's act as one acts. And it is evident also that this cognitive need has to be met perceptually. The conjunction of the latter two perfectly valid claims might seem to support the theory that in the case of physical intentional action, the function of the attention at such a time is uniquely that of perceiving the act and its objects. Indeed, it is natural to extend the theory to absolutely *all* cases of intentional action. For we know that intentional action *as such* necessitates knowledge of the progress of one's act, and that intentional action necessitates the use of the attention. What more natural than to suppose that the latter attending exists in order to meet the former cognitive need through perception?

Well, natural it may or may not be. But it would be a serious mistake to do so. A simple consideration decisively demonstrates the point. Thus, it is certain that *mental* or *internal* intentional actions (like ratiocination, or internal speech) likewise necessitate both knowledge of the progress of one's act and the use of the attention—and it is obvious that this cognitive need cannot in these cases be met by perceptual means. In short, the attention is needed here, but for non-perceptual purposes. And it is so in absolutely all cases of intentional action. Even when the attention is called upon for perceptual purposes, as it undoubtedly is in physical acts like driving a car, it is at the same time called upon for reasons of a wider scope than that of perception, indeed for reasons of wider scope even than that of cognition.

(b) Attention as psychic space of a certain kind

(1) The truth of this claim becomes apparent when we remember that a whole host of mental phenomena have need of attention, and that some of these mental phenomena are more or less independent of cognition. Emotion is such a case. Admittedly we do not emote with concentration, but it is a fact nevertheless that emotional experience makes demands upon the attention. Think of the extremes of emotion, which in certain cases are sufficiently intense to blot out most other experience, including perceptual attentive experience of all kinds. It is not the disturbance of

rationality that interferes with other mental life in cases of this sort, it is before all else the sheer *intensity* of the experience. Then it is clear from such an example that the attention must have a wider function than that of supporting perception or facilitating cognition. Many phenomena—including affect, perception, action, desire—necessitate a measure of attention if they are to so much as *exist*, and it is above all *this* function that determines the need for attention in intentional action and those multifarious other cases. Attention ultimately functions as a sort of life-blood for a whole range of mental phenomena; or perhaps better expressed, as a kind of psychic space. It is true that we need to employ the attention perceptually in certain cases, such as intentional physical action. But both in this and all other cases of intentional action, along with emotion and thought and many other internal phenomena, we need attention for the wider reason of providing psychic space of a certain kind, which is a necessary condition of their very existence. Just what this psychic space is, and how it relates to perception, must now be considered.

(2) Once again intentional action gives a lead. Thus, in what precise way does intentional action make demands on the attention? We have seen that one way it can call for attention is the cognitive-perceptual way: for example, we need to perceive our own physical acts in order to execute them with control. And it is clear anyway that the order 'Attend to your action' has a perfectly familiar use that is purely perceptual. We encounter this use when a tennis coach says to a pupil: 'Play the stroke again, and notice what you do.' However, we saw that this is not the only use for the attention. Indeed, such a procedure of self-observation, if carried to extremes, would draw the mind away from the stroke, would be a rival further occupation, and might in the end manage to drain the act of the attention that—in the *second* quite distinct mode—it needs if it is to so much as exist. For to repeat: the attention has another altogether different and non-perceptual role to play, in which it functions like life-blood or living-space for certain mental phenomena, including action.

The latter central role is invoked in the more familiar use of 'Attend to what you are doing', which amounts to 'Concentrate on what you are doing'. In effect, this order asks us to bring the action *into the forefront of consciousness*. And this, far from being a rival act which is in competition for attention, addresses itself precisely to the task of enlarging the hold which the act has upon the attention. Thus, 'Attend more to your driving' means, *not* 'Drive more cautiously', *not* 'Perceive better what you are doing as you drive', *but* 'Let your driving occupy a more central place in your attention'. And this is something that one can actively do—and not by doing something *in addition* to driving, such as bringing into play some efficacious inner technique of one kind or another. Rather, we obey the order in question merely by intentionally engaging in a driving which is endowed with *new and chosen properties* of an attentive nature. Attending to driving in this central sense involves, not just an increase in visual and proprioceptive perception, not just an increase in information

277

feedback and resultant forming of responsive differential intentions, but first and above all an increase in the extent to which the act itself is centre-stage in awareness. The difference between this present active occasion, and the active occasion immediately preceding it, is what is actively effected in obeying the order to 'Attend more to your driving'. It is an increase in 'awareness of action' in a *non-perceptual* sense of that expression.

Now here in this particular example we put on display the nature of the need which intentional action *as such* has for the attention. What we find as we attend more in this way to what we are doing is, that all parts of and all necessary addenda to the act loom larger in consciousness, and correlatively that certain other mental phenomena tend at the same time to recede. Thus, the psychic space that the attention provides for action and a whole range of other mental phenomena, is a space of *awareness* or *consciousness*. We need attention for intentional action, ultimately for the reason that intentional action must be a content of consciousness. Intentional action may or may not be given to consciousness *qua* object of a perceptual awareness, but it has more or less of necessity to be given to consciousness *qua* content of consciousness. This property it shares with emotion, imagery, and—it must be added—with perception itself.

(c) The attentive system

The above discussion appeals to a concept of the attention in which items can be given to the attention, not just in the role of object, but in that of occupant. The attention, we say, is occupied or taken up by emotion, thought, intentional action, and perception. We have identified the attention so conceived as awareness or consciousness, in some sense of the term. However, it is evident that this claim stands in need of elucidation. Just what 'awareness' or 'consciousness' are we talking of?

Before I address myself to this question, we should note that the items which occupy the attention are all *experiences*—a phenomenon about which I do not propose to say a great deal at this point. But we can at least say this much about experiences that is pertinent to the discussion. That they are those psychological phenomena of which at any moment we are conscious, that experiences are what fill the attention, and that they are that out of which the whatever-it-be that we describe as 'the stream of consciousness' is constituted. Suppose we take a cross-section of the stream of consciousness at any instant. What is the nature of the revealed item? It is a set of simultaneous experiences, standing to one another in certain relations which are characteristic of the prevailing state of consciousness, such as distinctive causal and referential relations: a set of experiences which in all probability constitutes a system. We refer to this set or system in common speech, in somewhat offhand manner, as 'the experience of the moment'. For example, we might say: 'At that moment experience was focused on one thing', or 'was almost suspended', or 'was chaotic'. Then whatever it is that we are singling out here, which we call

'Consciousness' or 'Experience' in this sense, seems to be the attention that is occupied by and distributed between experiences, whether they be active or emotive or perceptual.

The reality of this centrally important phenomenon, 'The Attention', which is what we mean in speaking of 'Experience' in the special possibly systemic sense explained above, is the reason why it is not sufficient to describe perception as the exercise of a faculty which consists in the capacity to harbour phenomena that link one in some pre-eminent fashion cognitively with the environment. Plainly, the very same attention which is involved in perception performs in addition tasks of a quite different order.

2. The Attention and Quantity

(a) In what sense is attention necessary for experience?

(1) I return to the question with which we began the discussion. Namely, of what do we speak in talking of 'The Attention'? Why the definite article? Is it just a manner of speaking? Or are we perhaps referring to an entity, such as a particular system? When I raised this question originally, I stressed the fact that if (say) emotion or thought or perception are to so much as *exist*, attention needs to be available. The conclusion which forced itself upon me was, that in speaking of 'The Attention' we are referring to an experiential mental space, an experiential space which it was natural to describe as 'Consciousness' or 'Awareness' or 'Experience' (in a sense of these terms that still stands in need of eludication). Meanwhile it has to be admitted that it is also unclear just what one is claiming when one affirms that attention *needs to be available* if (say) emotion (etc.) are to so much as exist. What kind of need are we talking of? I intend at this juncture to pursue the latter question, in the hope of shedding light upon the former problem. That is, of gaining a better understanding of 'the space of awareness', which is to say of the attention itself. The phenomenon of attentive-need looks as if it might provide a clue to the nature of the 'awareness'. After all, it is a direct manifestation of the limited extent of that 'awareness'.

One possible reading of the claim that attention or awareness is needed if experience is to occur is that the particular state of consciousness that we call 'consciousness' (or 'waking') is necessary if (say) emotion is to exist. However, this interpretation can be rejected forthwith, bearing in mind that dreams involve experiences. The most we can say along these lines is that the prevailing state of consciousness must be such as to *permit* either *experience as such* and/or the *particular experience* in question. Thus, deepest unconsciousness permits no experience of any kind, and waking does not permit dream experience. But in any case it is clear that we are not talking of a prevailing state of consciousness when we observe (say) that 'attention is necessary if one is to drive a car, or listen to a conversation, or even to feel a surge of emotion'. This mental space must be something that is occupied by the experiences of the moment. In sum, emotion needs not just a state of consciousness that *permits* experience, it needs more than that. And because emotions occur in dreams which occur in sleep, it needs something less than the unique state of consciousness that actually *guarantees* experience, viz. the state of waking consciousness. Clearly the requirement in question must be expressed in terms other than those of states of consciousness.

(2) What emotion rather needs is something that is actually utilized by the occurrent experiences of the moment. Then might it be that the need is merely one in a *tautologous* sense? After all, such familiar emotional phenomena as getting into a sudden rage, as opposed to what one might call mere attitudinal emotions, are without doubt experiences, so it goes without saying that if an emotional feeling is to occur at some point in time, contemporaneous occurrent experience must be a reality at that moment. But are we really saying something trivially circular in saying: 'Car driving needs attention to be available if it is to occur'? It seems to me that we are not. The sense in which we say 'Experience needs attentional space if it is to occur', is that in which we say 'The experience in question could not occur because the attention was wholly taken up by experiences xyz', and it is clear that the latter remark is dissimilar in kind from a tautological claim like 'The experience in question could not occur at time t because no experience was occurring at t.' Perhaps we can express the sense of 'Experience needs attentional space if it is to occur' through the following binary claim. If an emotional experience E is to occur at some time t, then the following must be true at t:

A. Experience must be occurring at t.
B. The sum total of the experiences at t that do *not* include emotion E, must not completely crowd the canvas of the mind (to put the point figuratively). For example, let them not include searing toothache, or vastly absorbing intentional action, or a set of distinct perceptions that is almost unbelievably large in number, etc.

This formulation unites a tautologous claim (A), with a causal clause (B). If A is false at t, then logically necessarily emotional experience is not occurring at t—for circular reasons; while if B is false at t, then for non-circular causal reasons emotion is almost certainly not occurring at t. Since A is a precondition of B, we have a right to regard A and B as the two parts of a single claim that is causal in character. The significance of that assertion, its bearing upon the question of the precise nature of the 'awareness' of the attention, must now be investigated.

(b) The quantitative properties of the attention

The above analysis of 'Emotion needs awareness if it is to exist' brings to the surface a familiar quantitative theory. The imagery that presses itself upon one is of the canvas of the mind, or of the stage of the mind, or perhaps of a mind-room—images in which we conceive of consciousness as a container. Common to all these conceptions is the idea of a quotum of experiential space, and the existence of such a thing as a *quantitative ceiling*: that beyond which the mind cannot go in absorptive capacity, on pain of snuffing out potential additional occupants (in a sort of experiential Black Hole of Calcutta).

The question arises: is there in reality such a ceiling? Perhaps even more important for our present purposes: what if anything is the connection between the Quantitative Theory of Awareness, and the supposition that by 'The Attention' we mean a form of mental or experiential space, what I earlier referred to as 'Experience' (in the sense, the system at any instant of present occurrent experience)?

The theory that there is a more or less fixed amount of experience that the mind can hold, I shall call the Theory of Limitation. It goes hand in hand with, but is not necessarily identical with, a theory that I shall call the Principle of Distribution. This is the familiar enough truism that the attention finds itself variously distributed between its various occupants; or perhaps better expressed, that the various occupants of the attention can at any time take up or utilize various amounts of attention (a phenomenon which is subject to the will). Normally this kind of claim will be expressed in very rough *fractional* terms, as when we say that a particular experience absorbed *most* of one's attention. Such an assertion inevitably links the two theories, for it expresses a claim concerning distribution in terms which assume the truth of Limitation Theory. Thus, there is in the mind a sort of Law of Distribution, to the effect that the more attention is absorbed by a particular experiential item, the more there is a tendency for other experiential items to lose it. The very word 'absorbed', which expresses a concept quite other than that of intensity, indicates that we are assuming the truth of Limitation Theory in formulating this law. No great harm, one might say, since Limitation Theory in some form or another looks pretty certainly to be true. Nevertheless, it is not absolutely obvious that the Law of Distribution rigorously implies the truth of Limitation Theory, and one could perhaps imagine minds in which things were different.

But it is one thing to speculate how minds might conceivably be, it is another to describe how in fact they are. Then as things stand, Limitation Theory more or less has to be true. We seem to be dealing here with a natural constant, akin to that invoked in claims like 'No human can run a mile in a minute.' It is true that training may alter what attentively can be accommodated, just as it can alter what athletically can be accomplished, though within pretty rigid limits in either case, and in any event the significance of the results of such training requires at all times to be carefully assessed. For example, it is certain that the acquisition of a measure of *act-automaticity*—such as occurs when one learns to tie one's tie or drive a car—is the acquisition of the capacity to perform identical deeds with a significant diminution in the amount of attention that those acts occupy, and this fact should act as a curb upon any supposed empirical demonstration of the theoretically limitless extent of the attention. Provided we relativize to time and to individual, a very rough Principle of Distribution holds to the following effect: If at a certain point in time Q is the quotum of attention available to some individual, and if some item x absorbs amount A, then Q – A is available for all other experiences. These so-called laws and principles are, it seems to me, little more than truisms.

(c) The relation of attention and experience in the light of quantity

(1) Thus, the attention of which *in fact* we speak is such that it can be variously distributed, and such that there is so much to go around and no more. The latter quantitative truth, and the interchangeability of the items that use and need parts of the quotum, show that we are dealing with a unitary phenomenon. I have suggested that the phenomenon is the system of contemporaneous experiences at any instant. It has emerged, not surprisingly, that the system is of *limited extent*—being constituted of limited numbers and/or limited intensities of items. (A property it shares with various other psychological systems, e.g. those of bodily sensation, of body-image, of visual sensation, of belief, etc.)

The question this feature raises is, to what extent if any the theory of the attention as the System of Present Experience is dependent upon Limitation Theory and Distribution Theory. Thus, I am concerned with the relation between the following kinds of truths: 'Thoughts and emotions are consciousness-fillers', 'The attention gets variously distributed between its occupants', 'There is a finite quantity of attention to go around at any instant.' In particular, does the truth of a proposition like 'Thoughts and emotions are consciousness-fillers' depend upon the truth of the theory of Limitation? Now the phenomena of Distribution and Limitation jointly evidence the existence of some something—akin in ways to a space of canvas, or the space of a stage, or even in ways to a sort of fuel—which can variously be occupied or used up. It is all in certain respects reminiscent of Caloric Theory,[1] and laws reminiscent of a Conservation Principle, and even in ways of (say) Conductivity Theory, seem as if they might in some crude fashion govern the phenomena of the attention. The question to which we must now address ourselves is: what is left of the idea of attentive or experiential space if the analogue of a Conservation Principle is simply dropped?

(2) Let us for argument sake suppose *per impossibile* that there was at any moment absolutely no limit to the amount of attention available to our minds. Thus, instead of saying 'I was concentrating on reading' or 'I was absorbed in reading' and suchlike, we would now say: 'I was reading with great intensity' or 'I was reading with much more intensity than I was experiencing anything else'; even though we might instead have added 'but I was listening with even greater intensity to Mozart's "Requiem"'; and cap it with 'and I was reaching with maniacal urgency for a precious vase which was in the process of falling to its destruction.' I shall not really

---

[1] And of (early) Freudian Libido Theory. Freud spoke at various times of a 'reservoir of libido'; and of 'the mobility of the libido', the capacity of a single quotum of sheer amorous impulse to be redirected from object to object; and at the same time (though later not) conceived of anxiety as 'transformed libido'. Common to this conception and our everyday conception of attention are, the properties of conservation and distribution.

explore this phantasy very far, but it has to be said that it is not transparently obviously unintelligible. However, the consequences of these strange mental economics are decidedly bizarre. Thus, the fact that the attention is, not so much trained on, but directed onto or occupied in part by some item x, would go with *no* tendency for the attention to be less occupied by other items abc. Nor would the measure of the intensity with which x engaged awareness go with any such inverse tendency. Nor perhaps would the concept of a focal point of the attention have much purchase. And so on.

Let us say of this possibility that it is possibly possible. But let us suppose for argument's sake that it is actuality. What would be left of what we have been calling 'The Attention'? Do these infinite experiential spaces now lying open for experience, nullify the very concept of experiential space? It is clear that they do not. It is conceivable that certain unities that are essential to the mind *as such* are by implication jettisoned in this thought-experiment—in which case the conjectured possibility must be inconsistent with absolutely *all* mental phenomena. But until it can be shown that this is the position, I think we should conclude that the theory of attention as Experiential Space is completely independent of Limitation Theory. 'Awareness exists at t' says that 'experience exists at t', and surely experience can exist at t whether or not there exists an upper limit to how much or how intense that experience can be.

(3) The thought-experiment demonstrates this independence. But it has another virtue. It brings to light an ambiguity in 'Experiences need experiential space if they are to exist' that can cause us to mythologize the attention—as will emerge as we follow the phantasy through.

Thus, what would happen to Distribution under the above imagined extreme circumstances? The image of a quasi-caloric substance which gets variously distributed would be abandoned. We would not *transfer* attention so much as *alter* its objects and the intensity of the attention given to them. The concept of Distribution would be replaced by one of mere fluctuation. And the concept of *not having enough attention available* for some experience, would be wholly inapplicable. So what would be left of the sense of the utterance which began this discussion: namely, 'Emotion has need of attention if it is to so much as exist'? What, if these strange mental economics obtained, would be left of the complex elucidatory claim that, if some emotional experience E is to so much as exist at a given time t, then

A. Experience must be occurring at t, and
B. The sum total of the experiences occurring at t that do not include emotion E, must not completely 'crowd the canvas of the mind' (i.e. let it not be a case of searing toothache etc.)?

In the extreme circumstances that we have envisaged, the claim that 'emotion needs attention if it is to so much as exist', would simply collapse into tautology.

It would then merely assert: if an experience E of emotion is to occur at time t, experience must be occurring at time t. However, it must be emphasized that this latter observation in no way demonstrates that the real core of the actually true claim that 'emotion needs attention if it is to so much as exist' is tautological in character. After all, the possibly possible possibility is limitlessly counterfactual. Indeed, it seems evident from the above that 'emotion needs attention if it is to so much as exist' acquires its actual content from the conservational or limited character of awareness.

(4) Accordingly, if the extreme counterfactual possibility was realized, 'Emotion needs attention to exist' would change its very sense. The claim would mutate from being something like 'There must be space available in a painting if it is to accommodate a certain image', to 'A figure in a painting must occupy space in that painting.' The concept of need would cease to be operative in the assertion, we would make do with no more than the concept of experience, and a synthetic utterance would give way to one that was merely circular in character. Here we encounter an ambiguity in the sense of 'Experiences need attention if they are to exist', which is prone to lead to serious confusion, as we shall now see.

3. A Mythology of the Attention

(1) At this point I would like to draw together several strands of the foregoing discussion, with the aim of bringing into view a somewhat seductive but erroneous theory of attentive consciousness, which in my opinion derives largely from the phenomenon of Limitation. I return to the very beginning. I began by asking: What is the attention? Is it a specific faculty, viz. the capacity to harbour events (say, the noticing of colour) which link one pre-eminently cognitively with the environment? I rejected this theory, on the grounds that items come to the attention both as occupants and objects. Besides perceptual function, the attention has the further function of providing a form of mental space within which experiences can exist. But what kind of mental space? The example of car-driving shed light on this matter: it showed that the space must be one of *awareness*—though of some as yet undetermined kind.

Just what kind of awareness it is, became the main problem. Now we could say if we knew *which* 'awareness' experiences need if they are to so much as exist. What kind of 'awareness' can that be? It cannot be a state-of-consciousness awareness, for we mean neither that experiences require a state that *guarantees* experience—which is false, nor one that merely *permits* experience—which is true but not what we have in mind. Then is the need a merely tautologous one of the kind expressed in: if an experience-awareness is to occur at t, experience-awareness must be occurring at t? On the face of it one would say not, since we illustrate the fact that the attention has the function of providing mental space by instancing non-circular claims like 'car-driving needs attention to be available if it is to occur'. Plainly, the latter need is substantive.

(2) This phenomenon, which exemplifies 'Limitation', makes it appear as if there exists some mental something, of type awareness, and limited quantity Q, which is variously used up or occupied by experiences. An imagery of the attention comes naturally to us: of a mental 'life blood', but above all of a sort of mental 'space' of awareness present in the mind, which is occupied exclusively by the experiences it enables to exist. This imagery is a way of recording genuine truths, and it is in itself both natural and harmless—provided we understand just which facts it describes or represents. However, the imagery which comes so naturally to us can easily be misinterpreted, leading to a mythology about the nature of 'Experiential Consciousness'. It can thereby plunge us into total incomprehension of the true character of the attention.

The myth in question takes the following form. It is of a mental existent (which I shall call S), a particular mental 'space' that is of type awareness (in some sense), which coexists with and is distinct from contemporaneous experiences. Those experiences relate to that awareness-space, not as its objects, but as its occupants, and that property enables them to exist. Then already we have made the fatal mistake and succumbed to the illusion. It consists in implicitly endorsing a relational analysis of the awareness of one's own experience. Let me explain how this is.

The fact that experiences need awareness-space if they are to exist, makes it seem that the awareness which takes experiences as occupant is one thing, and the experiences which occupy it something different. Then we are already enmeshed in the myth. We find ourselves supposing that awareness of experience is a relation holding between two distinct existences, awareness and experience. And because 'he was highly aware of his driving as he drove' describes a *different experience* from 'he was marginally aware of his driving as he drove', the awareness of which we speak must itself be an experience. Accordingly, this theory must suppose that one's awareness of one's experiences is a contingent relational and experiential addendum to those experiences, rather than an in-itself or intrinsic necessary property.

Since an experiential relation to awareness is posited in this analysis of experiential awareness of one's experience—meaning, that which (say) waxes and wanes during the course of long-distance car-driving—the theory leads inevitably to regress. It thereby teaches us the fundamental truth that the experiential awareness of one's experiences must begin and end with the experience: it simply *is* the experience itself. Meanwhile a relation of (a wholly different kind of) awareness to experiences does actually exist. Here I am thinking of the *cognitive relation* in which we stand to experiences. Thus, we *know* of our experiences as they occur. And it is of the first importance that this relation does not lead to regress, that no principle exists to the effect that knowing of one's experience necessitates a distinct knowing of that knowledge, *ad infinitum*.

(3) Note what is central to this mythological account of the attention. It first of all consists in the theory that the attention is a space of awareness that is distinct from its experiential occupants: a sort of mental 'hole', which is of necessity fit only to contain experiential occupants. Second, in the assumption that the experiential non-cognitive awareness of one's own experiences—that which waxes and wanes during long-distance driving—consists in the existence of a relation holding between two distinct mental existents: to wit, the above supposed awareness space and the experiences themselves. It conceives of experiential consciousness as a form of internal or introspective awareness of limited capacity, which somehow is occupied by and directed onto immaterial experience-objects. Thus, it by implication abolishes the distinction between the two functions of the attention, and inevitably generates regress.

What might lead one to embrace this relationalist mythology? What factors could lead one to detach 'awareness of experience' from 'experience'? One determinant is the existence of the above cognitive relational variety of 'awareness of experience'.[2] Another source lies in the fact that the attention is a reality, endowed with properties which overlap with those of the mythical S (as we shall later see). But the main source lies in what we have called 'Limitation'. Then it seems to me important that we try to understand the role played by Limitation in generating this myth. The reason is, that it helps to lead us to the correct theory of the attention.

(4) Limitation reveals its existence in such familiar phenomena as there being insufficient attention available to permit one effectively to drive a narrow alpine pass and engage simultaneously in serious discussion. Then note that the *entire evidential foundation* underlying the concept of Limitation consists in causal relations between simultaneous experiences. If you concentrate on the hairpin bend you fail to register the cogent point made by your companion, if you leap excitedly for a volley in tennis you will hear few of your doubles-partner's admonitions, etc. And that is absolutely all there is evidentially to go on. There is no other verification, and none that is independent of, or better than, or more direct than, these causal interactions between simultaneous experiences. Limitation is simply an 'inter-experiential' concept. In particular, there is no such thing as a direct or confrontational encounter with a supposed distinct 'space of awareness' (the mythical S) and a mechanism generating the phenomena of Limitation.

---

[2] The experiential awareness of our own experiences is none other than the 'pre-reflective' or 'non-positional' consciousness of Sartre (see *Being and Nothingness*, pp. l–lvi, Methuen, 1957). That is, it is an immediate consciousness of an experience X, which is such that X is not the intentional object of that consciousness. We encounter mention of such 'awareness' in 'For some of the time, as he drove on through the night, the driver was only marginally aware of his driving.' These are the cases, noted earlier in the present chapter, in which an item comes to consciousness, not as its object, but as an occupant. In his (understandable) anxiety to distinguish this phenomenon from cognition, Sartre (as it seems to me) makes the mistake of denying the existence of cognitive awareness of our own experiences as they occur.

Thus, Limitation and the fixed quotum Q of possible experience cannot be causal properties of a mental agency of the kind of S. The phenomena manifesting Limitation are not *three-way* causal interactions between a present mental phenomenon akin to S, the sum total of present experience ΣE_x, and a prospective possible experience E (whose pre-attentive causal antecedents are satisfied). The exclusion or toleration of E is not an *effect* of interaction between ΣE_x and some S. Indeed, the hypothesis of a separately existing S is precisely that the phenomenon of Limitation is such an effect, the theory being that through Limitation we casually and indirectly detect the presence of a separate mental agency S. In sum, this myth hypostatizes a merely causal-behavioural property of ΣE_x as an entity S, supposes mental causal interaction to occur between that S and ΣE_x by way of explanation of the phenomena of Limitation, and confers the extent (Q) of the real phenomenon of Limitation on the unreal entity in question.

(5) The thought-experiment of imagining Limitation inexistent showed that what normally we affirm by 'experiences need awareness-space to exist' cannot be that there exists a distinct space of awareness of which experiences have need. Subtracting Limitation exposed the inexistence of any awareness-space causing Limitation. If that space is distinct from its effects, it ought to survive the demise of Limitation. But in the absence of Limitation, 'Experiences need awareness-space' collapses into tautology, and the supposed space vanishes from view. If there were such a space, then even if the space of awareness were of unlimited extent, experiences would still need some of it, just as material objects have need of physical space, despite its largesse. And therefore 'Experiences need awareness-space to exist' should in those extreme circumstances retain its sense (though lose its point). However, in fact the utterance changes sense and affirms a mere tautology. This shows that what 'Experiences need awareness-space to exist' normally asserts is, that simultaneous experiences must be such as to permit coexistence. Thus, it records an inter-experiential state of affairs—almost a Darwinian struggle for existence! Deleting the struggle from the scene deletes the apparent space which appeared to be the object of struggle. Thereby the space is revealed as mythical.

In whatever sense experiences really do need experiential space to be, it must apply irrespective of shortage or excess. Accordingly, that sense should be exemplified in situations of unlimited availablity. Indeed, since situations of shortage show a tendency to generate a mythology, the space that is actually needed ought to be laid open to view in the unrestricted situation. Then that sense proved to be the tautological sense in which experiences provide their own space (and we know that there is a limited amount of that to go around). In short, experiences provide their own space, and there is a natural limit to its extent. The tautological need which survives the coming and going of Limitation, exposes to view the real awareness-space which experiences occupy. Then if it is true that experiences together constitute their own space, those experiences must occupy that space somewhat in the way in which jigsaw pieces inhabit or occupy the limited space of a jigsaw picture, rather than the way a painting occupies a frame. Now all of this is a rather misleading way of saying that the only psychological phenomena that occur in the way of experiential awareness, are the experiences themselves. The awareness-space that we call 'The Attention' simply consists in the experiences of the moment. It is what we mean by 'The Stream of Consciousness' or 'Experiential Consciousness'. 'Consciousness', in this specific sense of the term, *is* the Attention.

4. The Attention: A System

(1) All of the items which occupy the attention are experiences. As noted above, they are that out of which the stream of consciousness is constituted, a cross-section of which reveals a set of simultaneous experiences, which is a phenomenon that in common speech we sometimes off-handedly refer to as 'the experience of the moment'. Now this is what we have in mind in speaking of 'The Attention'. It is nothing less than Experiential Consciousness itself. And it is something decidedly elemental and infinitely familiar. It is what goes vague-ish or soft at the centre as sleep begins insidiously to fall (though it reappears as dreams!). Figuratively, it is the analogue of all that meets the eye and ear as a film gets under way. To repeat, it is what we frequently refer to as 'the stream of consciousness'.

My concern in this discussion has been with 'Awareness', taken in this sense. That to which these several expressions refer is something that is closely akin to a psychic space. And yet as we have just seen in the recent discussion of the mythical S, it cannot be something that, like the space of a canvas or stage, precedes and outlives its occupants. Rather, it is exhaustively constituted by those occupants, almost in the manner of a jigsaw picture—a picture which is bounded in extent. Thus, it emerged that the space the experiences in fact occupy is merely that provided by themselves. Each experience occupies attention, indeed each individual experience occupies a sector of the *very same* something as is occupies by its fellow experiences, even though the something in question cannot be distinct from those experiences. Then since that 'something' is neither a distinct space, nor merely the space of each individual experience, what can it be but a system of those experiences?

(2) What is a 'mental system'? It is more than a figure of speech. For example, a man's beliefs form a system, for the following reasons. Beliefs cannot exist in isolation, indeed expressly they cannot exist in isolation of other beliefs, since beliefs strictly necessitate more of their own kind, defining themselves in relation to those others; and they generally stand to those others in relations of consistency, and in a limited few varieties of causal relations distinctive to their kind; and so on. Similarly, the visual sensations of the moment constitute a field of visual sensations, and while not all of the above properties occur in their case, many do. In particular, if there exist two simultaneous visual sensations and they are not parts of separate visual fields, a determinate spatial sensuous relation must hold between those sen-

sations, which implies that they are individuated in relation to one another, and in general the visual sensations of the moment stand to one another in the relations appropriate to the system they form. Then note that when mental items come together to form systems, they are not conjoining to constitute a single enlarged example of their own kind. Thus, the system of our present beliefs is not one belief with vast conjunctive content—which is simply beyond our powers! No more than do the bodily sensations of the moment form one extensive bodily sensation, for it is necessary that we be able sensuously to differentiate sectors of the sense-system which together they constitute.

(3) Then the discussion of Limitation tends to confirm the surmise that the experiences of the moment form a system (which is to say that the Attention is a system). It adds its weight to an already impressive list of synthesizing properties. Thus, it is not just that those experiences are simultaneous and of the same broad experiential type or genus—which theoretically is consistent with their passing each other by like ships in the night. Other synthesizing factors obtain. For example, the very *character* of those experiences is significantly constrained by the type of the prevailing state of consciousness: if the prevailing state is (say) sleep, the experience will in all probability be dreamlike and imaginative in nature. And the same holds of the *relations* holding between those experiences: thus, if the state is waking and the experiences visual and motor, a relation of rational causation may well be instantiated between them. And the experiences of the moment in a particular mind have a tendency to *refer* to one another, indeed to do so in indissoluble manner, as happens when the object of the above motor-action is given to its owner in terms which are in part, and irreducibly so, visual-indexical in type. And therefore the experiences in question must individuate themselves in relation to one another. And so on.

Then not least amongst these system-determining properties is the fact that all the experiences of any moment share the common property of *Limitation*, according to which there exists a natural quantitative ceiling measured roughly by the product of the number-of with the intensity-of experiential items. All experiences share this property, and all contemporary experiences share its very measure. It is rather as if each of those experiences knew of the existence of its fellows; and it is in any case certain that they exert a causal constraint upon the intensity, and indeed existence of one another, which is mediated by the measure of the moment. This constraint completely bypasses non-experiential phenomena like beliefs and memories and moral values (say), which simply fall outside the scope of the Limitation in question, but strictly governs motor and perceptual and emotive (and etc.) experience.

All of this fleshes out the claim that the experiences of the moment form a system. Denuded of the above array of properties, they would be like so many psychological atoms wandering in a void. Endowed with them, they constitute a continuous ongoing phenomenon which is a sort of circle or centre of awareness. This awareness is the Attention. And it is to this Attention that perceived existents come. Such items enter this circle—as object. They do so when they come, not just to the circle itself, but to a select subclass of its occupants. Namely, to those that are noticings.

8

The Attention and Perception (1)

In the previous chapter I advanced a theory of the attention, in which I interpreted this phenomenon as the system of experiences present in the mind at any moment (or across time): 'Experiential Consciousness' as one might call it, 'Consciousness' in one sense of the word, none other than the 'Stream of Consciousness' of literary fame. Now we know at the same time that the attention is intimately linked with perception. In the course of the ensuing discussion I hope to shed light on the essential nature of perception through tracing out some of those links, which is to say through relating perception with Experiential Consciousness. In particular, I hope to make clear how it is that perception exemplifies one of the two major functions of Experiential Consciousness. I aim in this way to reveal its central status in the mind.

1. The Dual Functions of the Attention

Let me first of all review some of the main findings of the previous chapter. I began by noting that the sense of 'perception' in the expression 'sense-perception' is something other than that of insight or 'grasp'. Roughly, it is coming face to face with Reality rather than Truth. After all, sense-perceptual experiences have no truth-value (as we shall see in Chapter 10). Perception is an event in the attention, which is such that some real phenomenal item is the object of that attentive event. As we express it, perceiving is making attentive contact with an actual existent.

At a certain point I asked a question which bears upon an issue of some importance—a question prompted by an awareness of the cognitive power of perception and the closeness of the relation between perception and the attention. Namely, whether in speaking of 'The Attention' we are referring to a *particular faculty*, viz. the capacity to harbour distinctive idiosyncratic phenomena which link one in some pre-eminent way cognitively with the environment. I suggested that there was reason for doubting whether this was an adequate characterization of either perception or the attention. The remainder of the discussion centred upon giving reasons why it was an inadequate account of the attention. It emerged that the attention has a function in mental life which is quite other than its use in perceptual situations. Attention proves to be a necessity, both in non-perceptual cases and perceptual alike, and for reasons of wider scope than those of cognition, as a provider of a form of mental space. Many phenomena, whether of cognitive or non-cognitive import, require a measure of attention if they are to so much as *exist*, a need which is consistent with but not reducible to the fact that the attention has a further role to play in which in perception physical items come as object to it.

The above theoretical account appeals to a concept of the attention in which items come to the attention, not just as its objects—as happens in the case of perception—but as its occupants as well. The attention, we say, is occupied or taken up by emotion, thought, intentional action, *and* by perception. Now these occupants are all of them *experiences*: an indefinable genus, whose typifying properties are nonetheless familiar and well known. And the experiences of the moment seemed to me to constitute a system, a system which is I suggest the attention itself (or 'Experiential Consciousness'). It is to this sense of 'consciousness'—not to be confused with the fundamental state-sense ('waking')—that we appeal when we speak of the 'stream of consciousness'. Then the claim which I made, and intend in the ensuing discussion to elaborate further, is that it is to this system that perceived objects come as object. More exactly (and contentiously): that that is all there is to it.

The reality of the phenomenon 'The Attention', understood in the above systemic sense, provides us with the means for explaining why it is not sufficient to describe perception simply as the exercise of a faculty which consists in the capacity to harbour idiosyncratic phenomena that link one in some pre-eminent fashion cognitively with the environment. Perception is all of this—give or take a little leeway in the term 'idiosyncratic'. And yet it is something more. The claim which I shall defend in this chapter is as follows. Perception is the unique case amongst the various phenomena which constitute or fill experiential consciousness or the attention, in which a phenomenon manages to find a real phenomenal object such that the occupant of awareness is at the same time *merely* an awareness of that object. Its specific identifying type is—awareness, and it is of a real phenomenal object. No more. Idiosyncrasy plays no part in its characterization. It is the only experience that *is* an experience of something. You might even say that it is idiosyncratic in being devoid of idiosyncrasy! These formulations are an attempt to restore to perception something of the pre-eminent status that the narrow idiosyncratic rendering of the concept robs it of.

2. Perception and Idiosyncrasy

(a) A theory of perception

Perception is an attentive event, such that a phenomenal reality is object of that attentive event: it is the attention finding an object. Meanwhile the attention has the further function of providing for experiences a psychic space of awareness, taken in a sense that means: the system of present (etc.) experiences (what one might call 'Experiential Consciousness').

Now these two functions—that of providing psychic space for certain select mental phenomena, and of bringing certain phenomenal existents to consciousness—do not appear to be the diverse functions of diverse phenomena. They are rather to be understood as diverse functions of a unitary phenomenon. After all, perception is an event in which the attention acquires an object and is *at the same time* an event that calls upon or uses attention, and the extent to which the attention is engaged is identical in either case. For example, if a particular sound looms large in my awareness, then the hearing-experience absorbs just such a considerable measure of my awareness (for they are one and the same phenomenon). We might sum up this unifying theory in a formula. Namely: that the whatever-it-be that perception is the coming of some existent as object *to*, must be the very same whatever-it-be that emotion, thought, action, and perception *occupy or use*. In short, 'attention' refers to the same thing in 'The perceived object comes to the attention' and 'Intentional action needs attention if it is to so much as exist'. 'The Attention' in this way acquires the wider signification of experiential consciousness. And it has this wider signification, irrespective of whether we are thinking of experiencing in general or perception in particular.

In sum, when we say that 'in perception the physical object comes to the attention', we must be understood simply as saying that 'it comes as object to awareness'—and no more. Accordingly, we cannot be speaking of an idiosyncratic capacity when we characterize perception as an existent becoming object for the attention, for this characterization is cast purely and exhaustively in terms of the central psychological phenomenon of *awareness*. It baldly claims: perception simply *is* some phenomenal reality becoming object for awareness. Perception simply *is* consciousness or experience of an existent object. Idiosyncrasy goes out the window, and perception emerges as one of the two central possibilities or functions of that central phenomenon of animal mental life: awareness. This is the theory that I am concerned to advance. Call it the departicularizing, or the centralizing of perception.

(b) A difficulty for this theory of perception

(1) This theory has to face a serious difficulty. If attention is experiential consciousness or the system of experience at any instant, and perception is experience having a phenomenal reality as object, why should not any intentionally directed experience which happens to be directed onto a phenomenal reality count as a perception of that existent? For example, why should not a mental image which is of St Peter's Rome count as a perception of St Peter's? After all, it does not merely purport to be of that object: it really is of *it*. Yet plainly it is not a perception. So how can we accept the definition?

I shall now set out this objection in a little more detail. It begins by reiterating the argument that was supposed to establish the broad understanding of perception. We described perception as *awareness acquiring an object*, on the grounds that the attention which takes some phenomenal existent item as object was the very same as the awareness which provided experiential space for action, emotion, and so on; and this was supposed to departicularize perception. But how exactly are we to understand 'awareness acquiring an object' as it occurs in this account? A perfectly natural reading of the expression is this: 'An occupant of awareness acquiring an existent item as its object.' Now there can be no reason why the mental image of St Peter's should not be accounted 'an occupant of awareness acquiring an existent item as its object', and therefore on this 'natural reading' no reason why the mental image should not be a case of 'awareness acquiring an object'. But this latter conception was supposed to be an explication of the broad, as opposed to idiosyncratic understanding of the phenomenon of perception. Therefore either the mental image is a perception, or the argument in favour of the broad conception fails. But we know the mental image is not a perception. Therefore the argument fails. So far the objection.

However valid or invalid this objection, it brings to light one fact of importance. Namely, that if an occupant of awareness is to be a perception, it needs something more than a phenomenal existent as object. Therefore the justification for characterizing perception as awareness acquiring some existent item as object, cannot be that perception takes an existent item as object and is itself an occupant of awareness.

(2) To suppose that the justification might be of this kind, would in effect be to equivocate on the expression 'awareness'. I can bring this equivocation out in the form of a dilemma.

Is a mental image of St Peter's an awareness of St Peter's in the sense a seeing of St Peter's is? If we say that *it is*, then to say that perception is an existent object coming as object to awareness, is merely to affirm that perception is an intentionally directed experience with an existent item as object; and that is perfectly consistent with an idiosyncratic reading of the concept: for we have yet to spell out the unique differentia which singles it out from its fellow occupants of awareness. If on the other hand we say that *it is not*, then how can we justify the claim that the sense of 'awareness' is unitary in 'Perception is awareness of some existent object' and 'Emotions and mental imagery and intentional actions occupy awareness'? How, in other words, can we justify the aforementioned formula to the effect that 'the whatever-it-be that perception is the coming of some existent object as direct-object *to*, *is* the very same whatever-it-be that emotion, imagery, action, and perception occupy or *use*?' Thus, the sense of 'awareness' threatens to split into a broad and a narrow idiosyncratic pair of meanings, whereupon we find ourselves forced back into the idiosyncratic or particularized account of perception as the functioning of a special faculty.

(3) Let me at this point develop this latter line of thought, for it seems to put its finger on something of importance. That is, attempt in slightly different terms to explain how it is that the fact that 'awareness of St Peter's' looks to have different senses in 'A thought of St Peter's is an awareness of St Peter's' and 'A perception of St Peter's is an awareness of St Peter's', seems to drive one back into the arms of the idiosyncratic theory.

We noted above that something more must be asked of an intentionally directed experience that has an existent object, if that experience is to count as a perception. And there can be no doubt as to what that additional requirement is. It is something very simple. It is that the intentionally directed event be attentive in type. Then this latter requirement seems to put seriously in jeopardy the whole project of departi-cularizing the supposed faculty of perception. For if the requirement is that an attentive-type event occur, it is in effect that a distinctive one out of a whole gamut of possible experiential events occur. And that is to say, that the brand of awareness that has to obtain must be other than that available to the other denizens of the stream of consciousness: that is, to all of the other occupants of awareness. Presumably therefore it must be an awareness in some special or particular sense. What price universality here?

3. Resolving the Problem

(a) The form of the resolution of the problem

(1) I think the resolution of this problem must take the following form. We have to accept that perception has to be an attentive event, and that it is not enough to be an attentive event that an event be an occupant of the attention: after all, most occupants of the attention are not attentive events. And we have in addition to accept that a perception is an awareness of an existent object in a sense of the expression 'awareness of an object' that is unique and *sui generis*. On both counts, we must accept that we are dealing with a singular or distinctive occupant of consciousness. Nevertheless, and in the teeth of these apparent concessions, I think that we should reject the idiosyncratic theory of perception. Thus, we should not allow these truths to lead us to abandon the doctrine that perception simply *is* an existent object becoming object for awareness.

How can this be achieved? Let us pause for a moment and consider the situation. The example of mental imagery pointed up a need which has yet to be met in this discussion: a need for exactitude in exposition. Namely, to spell out the distinctive sense of 'awareness acquiring an object' appealed to in the universalist definition of perception. The mental image showed that we cannot intend the expression in the sense 'intentionally directed experience whose object is a phenomenal reality'. Accordingly, the sense invoked in the definition becomes at this point an issue of central importance. And there are strong pressures towards an idiosyncratic reading of that sense, in which case perception—like most of the other contents of the stream of consciousness—would prove to have an ultimately *indefinable* character. Then how can the theory be defended against such criticism? Two methods suggest themselves. Either to offer an analysis of the sense invoked: the assumption being that the correct analysis cannot but produce acceptance of the universalist doctrine. Alternatively, to bring forward considerations of such a kind that it becomes intuitively apparent that the sense of 'awareness acquiring an object' appealed to in the definition is universalist or non-idiosyncratic in type. In the next Chapter 9 I follow the former course. In the remainder of the present chapter I opt for the latter.

(2) I believe that the departicularization of perception—which is to say, the validation of the universalist reading of 'Perception is awareness of an existent object'—can be accomplished by establishing a particular thesis about meanings or senses. Namely, by demonstrating in the first place that 'aware of' has the same sense in 'Perception is awareness of an existent object' and 'We are aware of the occupants of the attention': for example, that 'aware of' has the same sense in 'He was aware of a strange smell' and 'He was aware of a multitude of emotions at that moment'; or 'He was aware of something in the middle of his visual field' and 'He was aware of a sudden impulse to do something outrageous'; or 'He became aware of an insistent knocking' and 'He became aware of a nagging lust'. And by demonstrating in the second place that 'aware of' has a different sense in the claim 'A mental image of a real existent is an awareness of that existent', or in the claim 'A thought of tomorrow's sunrise is an awareness of that sunrise', or in 'An hallucination of Banquo is an awareness of Banquo'.

Demonstrating that 'aware of' has the same sense in 'We are aware of the objects of perception' and 'We are aware of our own experiences', which amounts to a repudiation of the doctrine of ambiguity, amounts also to a reinstatement of the principle that 'the whatever-it-be that perception is the coming of some existent as direct-object *to, is* the very same whatever-it-be that emotion, thought, action, and perception occupy or use.' And it demonstrates at the same time the failure of an idiosyncratic analysis. After all, what more central occurrence of 'aware of' can there be than its application to experiences?

The claim therefore is, that our experiences are awarenesses in the sense of being given to awareness or consciousness, without (mostly) being awarenesses in that same sense of any existent object. All except one: namely, perceptual experience. It is idiosyncratic therefore in being singular, in being a special case; but it is idiosyncratic in no other sense. Indeed, its specialness is not that of idiosyncrasy at all: on the contrary, it instantiates a very general a priori concept. Namely, that of an object-taking awareness of an existent. Perception is special in being the unique case in which, amidst all the awarenesses that populate the stream of consciousness, a particular awareness occurs that is in the very same sense simply an awareness of an existent item. Thus, it is a unique double instantiation of the concept of awareness: it is a double awareness. We are conscious of this fact when we remember that the perceptual experience is an awareness which is at once (reflexively) of itself *and* of its objects. The objects of perception in a certain sense mimic the occupants of the attention: mere things appear to jostle around in the stream of consciousness alongside thoughts and emotions, just as concretely given to the subject of experience as they: so to say, cuckoos in the nest of consciousness!

(b) Expressing the above in term of the concept of experience

Let me at this point express the above contentious claims, which have so far been cast in terms of 'awareness', briefly and simply in terms of the fundamental (and in this context, synonymous) concept of *experience*. Thus: we experience sounds and we experience anxiety, in a sense in which we do not experience the objects of memory or imagination, or for that matter events lying in the future. Note that this theory involves the supposition that, while 'experience——' has a unitary sense in 'He experienced a sound' and 'He experienced a strange yearning', in one case experience takes an external object, in the other case it lacks such an object and we are concerned with a purely reflexive use of the word 'experience'. As an example of the latter, consider the empty yet unexceptionable 'We experience our experiences'. This reflexive utterance is a tautology, but can on occasion prove to be an illuminating truth notwithstanding. It is worth saying that we experience dreams and mental images and moods, but do not experience intentions or beliefs or merely attitudinal emotions. And so we might explain the very essence or nature of perception as: the experiencing of phenomenal existents given non-reflexively or objectively, where 'experience——' has the sense it has in (say) 'Fish and birds do not, and apes and humans do, experience dreams'. What we encounter in the case of perception is a genus term working for once as a species term! This is a measure of the universality of the phenomenon of perception.

4. Arguments Pro the Departicularization Theory of Perception

I am attempting to cope with the difficulty posed by the fact that (say) mental imagery of phenomenal existents rates (in some sense) as 'experience finding a phenomenal existent as object' without at the same time being a perception, simply by reaffirming the claim that in what I have claimed to be the central sense of 'awareness of', perception *is* and imagery *is not* awareness of its object. And I am supporting this assertion through the claim that 'awareness of' has the identical (and central) sense in both perceptual *and* reflexive experiential occurrences. In Section 4(a) (below) I assemble several considerations favouring this meaning-thesis, and cap them with a cognitive argument in 4(b). In effect, I am advancing this meaning-thesis in support of the universalist theory of perception. (As noted earlier, arguments in support of that doctrine which take the form of an *analysis* of the perceptual sense of 'awareness of an object' are set out in the next Chapter 9.)

(a) Four considerations favouring the univocality of 'aware of'

The theory in dispute is: that 'aware of' is univocal in 'We are aware of our experiences' (dreams, sudden impulses, emotions) and 'We are aware of what we notice' (sounds, tickles, lights); but that it has a different sense both in 'We are aware of the objects of memory' (last week's party, one's first day at school, one's greatgrandfather), and in 'We are aware of the objects of imagination' (of Banquo as one hallucinates him, Napoleon as one reads *War and Peace*, the Eiffel Tower as one visualizes the Eiffel Tower). The implication is that we only experience or are aware of the past when we see astronomically distant events in the heavens, and that we never experience or are aware of the future. An image or thought of tomorrow's sunrise is neither an awareness of, nor an experience of that event. Or if we say that it is, it must be so in a quite different, and indeed of necessity in a *stipulated* sense. So the theory which I am affirming claims.

This theory stands in need of argumentative support. Accordingly, I offer the following four preliminary considerations (A–D) in its favour:

A. The first consideration is little more than an intuitive appeal to the meaning-doctrine being advanced. Thus, there exist unmistakable ambiguities in the expression 'aware of', which seem to confirm the theory. A first occurrence of 'aware of' is in 'Everyone is aware of his own name', and here 'aware of' means 'know of'. A second occurrence is in 'A thought of tomorrow's sunrise is an awareness of tomorrow's sunrise', and here 'aware of' has the meaning 'is an experience that is intentionally directed onto'. And a third and obviously different occurrence is in 'We are aware of our own experiences'—and I have to add that I can detect no difference in the sense of 'aware of' in 'We are aware of what we perceive or notice'. My claim is that 'aware of' preserves the one sense in the latter two sentences, even though 'of' is put therein to two different uses: a merely reflexive, and an object-taking use. But I am unable to say what 'aware' *means* in these two fundamental occurrences, and am convinced the concept is unanalysable. Notice by the way that I am not suggesting that noticing or *perceiving* is an unanalysable concept. Far from it! The departicularization thesis is first and foremost a theory of analysability—in a domain where unanalysability is the nearly invariable rule. If my account is correct, the concept of perception is that of an awareness of a real phenomenal object. It is analysable therefore in terms of the unanalysable concept of experience or awareness. We simply take hold of the concept of an experience, and give it a non-reflexive extensional object. The concept of perception is therefore a kind of *first derivative* from the fundamental concept of an experience. This is what I had in mind at the beginning of this chapter in saying of perception that it exemplifies one of the two major functions of experiential consciousness.

B. The second consideration begins with the observation that the perceptual use of 'aware of' is extensional, since it fails to exhibit indifference to existence, and what we perceive is independent of the aspects under which it is perceived. Likewise the reflexive experiential use of 'aware of' is extensional, for I cannot experientially be aware of a non-existent dream. By contrast, the use of 'aware of' in 'Hallucinatees are aware of hallucinated objects' or 'Humans are aware of the future' is purely intentional.

C. Perceptual awareness is concrete and precognitive. It is concrete because it is the bearer of interpretations, and it is precognitive because it is no more than a natural foundation for knowledge. Then it is surely of some significance that experiential awareness of experiences is the same. Thus, it is concrete because nothing conceptual mediates one's relation to one's own experiences, and it is precognitive since we know of our present and recent experiences precisely because they are experiences. But nothing is the bearer of interpretation in a merely intentional awareness, which is constituted out of concepts in the very first place; and intentional awareness as such depends upon a fund of knowledge.

D. The perceptual sense of 'P is an awareness of x' is given in the following analysis. P is (i) an experience, (ii) which is extensionally and non-reflexively of x, and (iii) that is all that it is. Now this is not to say that (i) and (ii) are its analysis, since to say (i) & (ii) & (iii) (i.e. enough!), is not the same as saying: (i) & (ii)—and that is enough. The point is, that while we insert a property after (i) and (ii), we do not insert a new *contentual* property: on the contrary, that precisely would be 'idiosyncratization'!: we insert the novelty, that that is *all* there is to the concept. We put in a new property, that of being no more than. And this is what I earlier meant, when I claimed that perception is idiosyncratic merely in being devoid of idiosyncrasy. Then a comparable analysis applies in the case of the awareness of experiences. Thus, the sense of 'A is an awareness of an experience x' is given in: A is (i) an experience, (ii) which is extensionally and reflexively of the experience x, and (iii) that is all that it is.

(b) Considerations based upon cognition

(1) These considerations lend support to the idea that 'whatever objects in perception come as object *to*, *is* the very same whatever that thoughts and perceptions (etc.) occupy or *use*, viz. awareness or consciousness or attention.' I turn now to considerations based upon cognition, which in my opinion point to the same conclusion. Accordingly, a few words at this juncture on the cognitive properties of the two main phenomena under examination: perception, and experience.

In perception an existent item comes as object to the attention or consciousness. Now perception has cognitive properties which mark it off from absolutely all other experiences, and this feature reflects the fact that certain regular causal connections, travelling in the direction from outer to inner, rather than just concepts alone, link the perceptual experience to its object. Thus, a perceiver is in a position to know both of the existence and perceptible properties of the perceived object, and these external realities normally form part of the content of his short-term memory and so also of the corresponding short-term latent cognitions. Then to repeat, these cognitive powers are unique amongst experiences.

A few words now on the concept of the experience. As I have repeatedly asserted, I think this concept is unanalysable. That is, I think we cannot even in principle say *what it is* that makes an emotion or an attempt to recollect or a dream an experience. Nevertheless, experiences have certain typifying properties. In particular, they are closely linked to contemporaneous occurrent knowledge of themselves and to persistence in short-term memory—provided we are speaking of self-conscious beings. Normally I know, not everything that went on in my mind ten seconds ago, but the experiences of that recent moment. Normally one carries with one an ongoing continually mutating short-term memory whose content precisely is of one's recent experiences (*and* the outer objects of perceptual experience!). This property functions, hardly as a defining test, but as a test nonetheless of experience. (That it is neither defining nor necessary is obvious when one reflects on the existence of animal experience and discontinuous consciousness-loss, e.g. 'blackout'.)

(2) We have just seen that the content of short-term memory is of one's recent experience *and* the outer objects of perceptual experience. This observation highlights a point of some interest. Namely, that there exists a significant similarity between the cognitive relations in which we stand to *experiences in general*, and the cognitive relations in which we stand to the *outer objects given in perceptual experience*. Now we know that, precisely because the majority of intentionally directed experiences are not (simply, as such) experiences of some outer reality, they are of little outer or epistemological cognitive significance—and that perception is unique in contravening this rule. While most experiences lead cognitively to contemporaneous knowledge of themselves, and to short-term memory of themselves, they tell us nothing about any answering outer object that happens to be their content, e.g. a mental image of St Peter's will as a general rule be uninformative to one about that object. But in the unique case of perceptual experience we are led cognitively both to contemporaneous knowledge of the experience *and* its outer external object, and to short-term memory that is likewise both of the experience *and* the outer external object.

Thus, from the point of view of cognition, the object of perception finds itself in a position that closely resembles that occupied by experience as such, and it is perhaps this feature that makes one want to say that the objects of perception jostle around in the stream of consciousness, like cuckoos in the nest, so to say disguised as experiences. (For we awake in the World with outer perceptibles as near to us experientially as our very own thoughts!) In any case, I wish to suggest that the mirror-like cognitive relation holding between perceptual object and experience, helps to justify the extension of the univocal word 'experience' into a *new use* in which it takes a non-intentional non-reflexive object (constituting thereby a bona fide novel psychological kind). We conjoin this cognitive similarity to the aforementioned shared properties of extensionality and concreteness (etc.), and offer them in support of the intuition to the effect that what material objects come to when we perceive *is* what perceptions occupy or use, viz. experiential consciousness.

9

The Attention and Perception (2):
Assembling the Concept

I am pursuing the problem, raised in the previous chapter, of justifying the proposed analysis of the concept of perception. My claim there was, that this concept is susceptible of a very simple definition, one cast exhaustively in terms of the fundamental a priori-given concept of the experience. The suggestion being, that perception is nothing but awareness or experience of a phenomenal reality. If this analysis if correct, the concept of perception must equally be classed as an a priori concept.

A difficulty was then raised. Namely, that the above expression 'awareness of a phenomenal existent' has application in non-perceptual, and not just in perceptual situations. Whether or not this is true, the difficulty is in any case admitted. There can be no doubt that the expression 'awareness of a phenomenal existent' stands in need of investigation. It might perhaps on the one hand be understood by some to mean the following: an occupant of awareness that is intentionally directed to a phenomenal existent. Meanwhile, there unquestionably exists a second and highly familiar sense of that expression, viz. the sense invoked by me in the 'universalist' analysis of perception. It is this latter sense which is the topic of the ensuing discussion.

The discussion which follows addresses itself to the task of spelling out the latter—perceptual—sense. It does so through employing resources of an *analytical* kind. In undertaking this task, I hope by such means to bolster the argument of the previous chapter, which, in appealing in rather blunt fashion to meanings, might have struck a discordant note with some. In short, I aim to produce acceptance of the contentious theory of perception by analytically revealing precisely what is being asserted in saying of perception that it is 'awareness' or 'experience' taking a phenomenal reality as object. The assumption on my part being that, once that meaning is laid out for inspection, the theory will convince. Then it will help us to appreciate what goes into the meaning in question if we begin by examining the sense from which it is to be *distinguished*. That is, the supposed intentional use of 'experience of object O', to which appeal is made by anyone claiming that there exists a non-perceptual purely intentional sense in which one can have experience of phenomenal existents (say, when one visualizes the Venus de Milo).

1. Intentionally Directed Experiences in General

(a) The properties of intentionally directed experiences

(1) Does 'An experience occurred which was intentionally directed to object O' entail 'An experience of O occurred'? If it does, then since we can think of tomorrow's sunrise, we must be able to have an experience of the future. It is because I do not think this last is a real possibility, that I am reluctant to endorse the supposed entailment. After all, we cannot stipulate our way to actual possibilities. However, I do not wish to make heavy weather of the issue, and am prepared for the sake of argument to assume for the moment that an accredited usage of 'experience of' exists in which we can have an experience of the future.

Then it is desirable that we put on record the sense that is being attributed to 'experience of O' in this unnatural usage (a sense incidentally that is independent of O's existence). In fact it is no more than a way of saying of something that it is an experience *and* that the experience in question is intentionally directed to some item O. In this sense of 'experience of O' we can have experiences not merely of sounds and sensations, but of events in the future and the remote past. Indeed, we can even have experiences of counterfactual entities like Wagner's opera 'Die Sieger' and Napoleon's victory at Waterloo! We should even be capable of having experiences of abstract entities like universals and metaphysical putatives like transcendental egos!

(2) Does the endorsement of such an unnatural usage affect the sense of the word 'experience'? It is clear some new uses of old terms do constitute shifts in meaning. For example, in 'see with the mind's eye', the word 'see' is put to so special a use that it ceases to have its usual sense. After all, this event precisely *is not* a seeing, and seeing is no part of its truth-conditions. Nevertheless, this 'seeing' is *necessarily linked* to seeing. For whereas the use of the word 'see' in 'I see the point of the argument' is a merely contingent derivative from visual 'see', the use and sense given to 'see' in 'see with the mind's eye' is *essentially* a development from visual 'see'. That is, it is a development of a sense which is essentially founded upon the normal visual sense as base. This is because 'see with the mind's eye' is essentially a quasi-seeing.

Matters are different from both of these latter situations in the case of the word 'experience' in the special intentional use of 'experience of' which we have stipulated above—a use which I shall from now on refer to either as 'experience$_1$ of O' or else as 'E$_1$ of O'. Thus, if 'experience$_1$ of O' means 'experience with O as internal object', the term 'experience' must in this expression retain its normal sense. After all, whereas a seeing with the mind's eye is precisely and necessarily not a seeing, an experiencing$_1$ of an object is necessarily an experience. Accordingly, we may be said to be putting the word 'experience', taken in its usual sense, to a particular intentional use in 'experience$_1$

of O'. We begin by making use of the word to pick out what normally it denotes, and then proceed to offer part of the analytical characterization of the item thereby singled out. This puts on display the logical form involved, and the univocality in question.

(3) Let us at this point set down some of the characteristics of an experience$_i$ of object O. In the first place it does not entail the existence of O. That is, no intentionally directed experience entails the existence of its intended object.

Secondly and much more important for our purposes is, that if O does exist and the experience$_i$ really is of that O, the experience$_i$ of O does not thereby acquire some *type* to which it naturally aspires. Whereas a seeming to see O proves to be a seeing of O if O exists and certain other conditions obtain, a seeming to see O acquires no further type if O is real and the seem-seeing really is intentionally directed to it. And this is true of *all* experiences. Thus, a mental image that is said to be of St Peter's Rome acquires no further type if the said St Peter's proves to be real and the mental image really is of that very reality. It begins and ends its life as a mental image, just as a thought about the proof of Fermat's last theorem is never anything more than a thought, quite independently of whether such a proof is mathematically possible. In short, experiences$_i$ acquire no further type through being really directed onto real objects, even though some intentionally directed experiences manage to acquire a type to which they aspire (i.e. putatively exemplify) if they link non-deviantly (and etc.) with some real object. Seeing is an example of this latter kind, mental imagery and thought are not.

(b) Being and the intentionality of experience

Closely connected with this latter property, though of even greater importance from our point of view, is the fact that being an experience$_i$ of an object O is insufficient for identity or *being* for that experience. To be an experience$_i$ of O is not as yet to be in possession of what is required if adequate determinacy is to obtain. The experience is as yet insufficiently determinate to be. It needs to be some *type* of experience for it to be *anything*. Even though being an E$_i$ of O partially analyses, and indeed partially constitutes the essence of the experience, it leaves the essence undetermined. This is because full determinacy and being can be realized only with the acquisition of a specific type. Thus, if an experience$_i$ that is intentionally directed to some O is to be a reality, it must be an image consciousness, or an affective consciousness, or a perceptual consciousness, etc. It is not enough for reality that it be an experience with an object O as part of its intentional content. In short, if the experience is to have identity or being, there must exist such a thing as the *specific mode of presentation* of its intentional object. The object must be affectively or perceptually or imaginatively or conatively presented to awareness. It cannot *just* be intentionally given. A consciousness that is of some something must take specific form.

2. The Special Case of Perception

(a) A different use of 'experience of——'

Amongst these instances of experience₁ of some object O occurs one experience that is special in an important regard. Here I am thinking of perception. The contentious proposition that I wish to suggest is the following. That this particular experience, which falls under 'experience₁ of O', falls at the same time under a concept and expression 'experience of O' taken now in a quite different (and non-intentional) sense. This constitutes a different use of the term 'experience', understood once more in its usual sense, and I shall dub this use of that term with normal sense 'experience₂ of O' or 'E₂ of O'. And I say that it employs the word 'experience' in its usual sense for the same reasons as were advanced earlier—namely, that the instantiation of an experience₂ *is* the occurrence of an experience—as 'seeing with the mind's eye' precisely *is not* the occurrence of a seeing. In applying the expression 'experience of O' in this second sense, we as before begin by singling out an experience, and thereupon proceed to predicate a specific property of it.

Let me now attempt to justify the above (so far, unargued) claim that the perception of an object is an experiencing of the object, taken now in a non-intentional sense. I begin by instancing a contentious but illuminating example of this second perceptual variety of 'experiencing of——'. If a man *'feels* his pain' (as we say) then he *experiences* it,[1] and that is to say that the sensation comes to his attention or is *noticed* (something which is by no means a necessity, as the phenomenon of 'taking his mind off his pain' makes clear). Then that experience of noticing is, I suggest, the very same thing as the perceiving of the sensation, for does not this experience of awareness lead quite naturally to knowledge of its sensation object? And would not the knowledge be inexistent without the awareness? Here it seems to me we can see very clearly how perception is the experiencing of its object in a special extensional sense of the expression. But is it not in any case evident from other less contentious examples? Is not the hearing of a sound an experiencing of it? And must not the sound exist? And would we not say the same of the seeing of a red after-image? Or of a rising sun? All of these perceivings are experiencings of their actually existing and wholly distinct object in a non-intentional sense. Whether or not that is *all* that they are—which is the very point at issue in this discussion—they are at least this much.

(b) Some of the properties of experiences₂ of their object O

(1) I shall now at this point list some of the main characteristics of the property which we attribute to an event in describing it as an experience₂ of some object O:

---

[1] Degrees of *awareness* of sensations surely exist. And they in no way entail the existence of, or correspond to, degrees of *reality* in their sensation object. Indeed, is anything at all singled out by the latter characterization? What is a 'partly real' sensation of contact?

that is, in the perceptual sense of 'experience of——'. This is undertaken, in part to justify the claim that there exists such a use of 'experience of——', and partly to spell out some of the singularities of experiences$_2$ of objects.

I begin with two properties that are of relatively marginal interest so far as this discussion is concerned (even though of considerable importance to the philosophy of perception). First, if an experience falls simultaneously under 'E_1 of O_1' and 'E_2 of O_2', the two Os need not be the same. Thus, I can seem to see a red balloon when in fact I am having a visual experience of a setting sun. On the other hand and secondly, if the experience really is to fall under 'E_2 of O_2', if one really is to be perceptually experiencing that object O_2, then there must exist *reduced descriptions* of the two objects of the one experience—of O_1 and O_2—such that those objects coincide. As all or most actions are intentional under *some* description or another, so all genuine perceptions must under *some* description be of what *seemingly* we perceive. I can seem to see a red balloon in seeing a setting sun, but I can hardly see a setting sun if I do not seem to see something or another, whether it be a round red outline or a round outline or redness or mere brightness in some visual locale, which truly holds of the setting sun. The sun must under some lowest-order characterization appear to one's mind as it is. Crudely expressed, one must get some minimal perceptual something *right* if one is to make perceptual *contact* with an appearing object. While a whole sequence of interpretations can all miss their mark, that upon which they are in the first place imposed cannot in its entirety also mismatch one's putative experience of it. At the very beginning point inner and outer must in some regard non-accidentally and wholly reflect one another. What would be nomically linked if they did not?

(2) Before I continue, I would like in passing to put it on record that this E_2-use of 'experience of O', the perceptual use of the expression, seems to be as natural as the E_1-use is unnatural. As unnatural as it is to speak of an experience of the future or of an experience of such counterfactual entities as Napoleon's victory at Waterloo, so it is natural to speak of an experiencing of what is here and now present and real and given directly to the senses.

The remaining few properties which I list are rather more pertinent to the present project of distinguishing the two uses of 'experience of O', and spelling out the singularities of E_2 of O. The first is, that E_2 of O entails both the reality of O, together with the obtaining of such conditions as help to ensure that the proper perceptual contact with or relation to O is established. Deviant causal chains and suchlike need to be ruled out if we are to know (say) that in seemingly experiencing a reddish gleam as between some leaves, I really am experiencing the sun. This extensional contact with some outer phenomenal object cannot be conjured into existence by mere conceptual means. It needs to earn its way in the real world. Hence the importance of causal considerations and content-match.

(3) The next property of the experience$_2$ of O is of special interest, to my way of thinking. Namely, that being a perceptual or E_2-type experience of some object O is

a sufficient condition of being or identity for an event. Now it is true that we perceive phenomenal items in the environment through various sensory modalities, and the existence of such modalities might seem to constitute a difficulty for the above thesis, since it might seem that event identity is discovered through those modes, rather than under 'experience$_2$ of——'. However, the difficulty vanishes when we remember that immediacy invariably lurks beneath the mediation of sensory modes. Whenever a perceptual experience adopts a specific mode of acquaintance with some given object O, as it does in the case of the seeing of material objects, it also falls essentially under descriptions in which a modeless acquaintance is realized—in the present case with (say) colour. Thus, whereas we may perceive an object through noticing its colour, we merely notice that colour. Such a modeless acquaintance or merely perceptual experiencing-of that immediate object suffices for identity on the part of the experience. It needs no more.

Thus, being an E$_2$ of O is a sufficient condition of being or identity as the property of being an E$_1$ of O is not. And yet it can hardly be a necessary condition, seeing that it is an inessential property of the E$_2$ event. The essence or identity-conferring property is not, being an E$_1$ of O, and neither is it being an E$_2$ of O: it is being a seeming E$_2$ of some O or other. However, what matters so far as this present discussion is concerned is, that the property of being an E$_2$ of O is a *sufficient guarantor* of identity or being, since it entails the instantiation of the essence of the event, viz. being a seeming E$_2$ of some O or other. That property suffices for identity (the instantiation of the essence being a necessary and sufficient condition of being)—and that is the nub of the matter. This is plainly true of an awareness of an immediate object like a sensation, which clearly has all that it needs to be, but it is true generally. In short, to know of an event that it is an E$_2$ of O is to know the mode in which the full determinacy necessary for identity is realized. To know of an event that it is an E$_1$ of O is to know no such thing.

That concludes the enterprise of differentially characterizing the second use of 'experience of O', and in effect of justifying the claim that there exists such a use. I turn to a closely related but distinct task.

3. Constituting Piecemeal the Property of Being an E$_2$ of O

At this point I address myself to the main project of the present chapter, the constituting of the concept of perception. The purpose of the ensuing procedure is at once elucidatory and argumentative, as the following considerations make clear.

(a) First requirements of being an experience$_2$ of some object O

(1) The reality of the above vitally important characteristic of the property E$_2$-ness—namely, that of being a sufficient condition of identity or being—which is clearly a contentious issue—can be brought out revealingly and in my view

convincingly in very different terms from those so far employed. To accomplish this end, I embark at this point upon an attempt to constitute the specific property that we attribute to an E_2 of O. What goes to make up E_2-ness? What are we affirming of an experience when we say that it is a perceptual experience of a sound? or of a pain? or of the sun? What goes to make up a perceiving of O?

A word first about procedure. My aim here is to analytically assemble the complex property that we predicate of an event when we classify it as a perceiving. The process of assembly which I follow proceeds piecemeal, and the property assembled gathers in complexity as the process advances. We shall first of all assume that we are presented with some individual event, and begin by predicating of it some first property (call it P_1), and ask whether that suffices to ensure that the event is a perceiving. And we will then move on to a more complex P_2, and ask the same question. And continue this process until we arrive at such a P_n that we can give an affirmative answer to the original question. Naturally, such a long-term aim conditions the choice of properties which are inserted into the gathering predicate P_x. The ultimate goal of the above procedure is to show that the concept of perceiving is no more than that of experiencing its object (in the extensional sense of the expression).

(2) We begin with the property of being an E_1 of O: that is, of being an experience which is intentionally directed to some specific object content O_1. Then to this first condition we might be inclined to add the further condition that O_1 really exists, and such additional conditions as will ensure that this experience manages to really be an E_1-type experience of that real object O_1. (For example, really is a seeming to see an object that is a reality, say the Venus de Milo.) However, these latter conditions turn out to be unnecessary—at least as they are stated. I say so because in really seeing something, it is neither here nor there that what I seem to see is real, or that I make intentional contact with such a reality: I can seem to see what is mythical in actually seeing a reality. On the other hand we saw earlier that there must exist (reduced) descriptions under which O_1 and O_2 coincide if perceptual contact is to be established with some object: for example, 'being red and having a round profile' might be the coinciding values in a particular example of seeing the setting sun. So let us suppose that thus far the event is an experience standing in an E_1-type relation to some object O_1 that is a reality.

We shall now make a second assumption. Namely, that the type T which this E_1-of-O exemplifies is what one might call a 'putative type', in the sense in which seeing and acting are 'putative types' (and emoting and visualizing are not): that is, a type such that they are realized only when 'aspiring' forms (seem-to-see, strive-to-act) manage to 'make the grade'. Thus, T must be a type that is putatively 'of' some object in an extensional sense.

(3) Now let us add a third very important property to the above (in the attempt piecemeal to constitute E_2-ness). This familiar enough property is exemplified by perceiving—at the very least, and is realized in part through the conjunction of a

requisite nomicity and the reality of some object O_2. It consists in acquiring the extensional object-taking type to which by nature the phenomenon aspires. More precisely, this property (which we know to be exhibited by perceptual E_2's) is such that the E_1 experience passes from being a merely putative example of a given type T to being a genuine example of T, where T is a type that necessarily is directed to some object in an extensional sense. In sum, what we have thus far put together is the following complex property. Namely: that of being an experience that is intentionally directed in some (aspiring) mode to a reality, which manages at the same time to (fulfil its aspiration and) be of such a type as to necessitate that it be of some real object in an extensional use of 'of'.

Then it is of great importance that the complex property thus far assembled cannot manage to realize adequate determinacy and thus confer identity and being upon the experience in question. It confers upon an experience which we know to be intentionally directed to some object in some (as yet undetermined T-ish) mode or another, the further property of being of a kind (T, again) such that the bearer has to be of some real object in a special extensional use of 'of'. But the point that I wish repeatedly to emphasize is, that until the 'T' in question is given a *specific value*, nothing determinate can be singled out by the complex specification or property which we have spelled out. We do not as yet know which phenomenon we might be talking of.

(b) Comparing physical action and perception

This is evident when one takes note of the fact that *two* very different phenomena measure up to the specification thus far provided. Namely, physical action and perception. Both of these phenomena are intentionally directed events which realize an 'aspiration' in finding an extensional object. Both therefore satisfy the above complex predicate. Therefore the predicate cannot as yet have managed to single out a real or specific or determinate phenomenon.

Then what more needs to be added to the above complex property, if we are to ensure determinacy of character and thus a nature for the event to which we are predicating the increasingly complex predicate we are assembling? Well, what more would be required if our project consisted in assembling a predicate which sufficed for identity, not on the part of a perception, but of the other phenomenal type which satisfies the above complex predicate, namely physical action? I suggest that the more we would need is that the event—known already to be an experience that is intentionally directed to some real existent as object content O_1 *and* to exemplify an event-type whose instantiation necessitates that the experience in question be of some real object O_2 in a special extensional use of 'of'—be *active* in type. In short, to ensure the property of determinacy in the case of an event of this kind, we would have here to appeal to the concept of a *distinctive type of experience*. That is, we have need of a further experiential concept. This is because the concept of a bodily action is that of an *active* event which relates in a certain required manner to some real bodily occurrence. It is the concept of the *willing* of a real bodily event, in the special extensional use of 'of'.

Turn now to the other phenomenon that is extensionally 'of' some real existent in this same way: namely, perception. What more do we need to add to the complex property of being an experience intentionally directed to a reality, which instantiates a kind which has to be 'of' some real existent in a special extensional use of 'of'—if we are to ensure determinacy of nature and identity—when the experience under consideration happens to be perception? Do we have to appeal to the special concept of a distinctive type of experience? Do we need to import some novel experiential concept? In my opinion we do not. I suggest that we have here all the conceptual equipment that we require. All we need do is to make use of the concept of an experience and embed it in a particular structure. When we conjoin the concept of experience with the special extensional use of 'of', we succeed in defining the phenomenon under consideration. Herewith, at a single stroke, the enterprise of constituting the concept of perception is summarily concluded.

(c) Recap of the defining procedure

The above conceptual operations have brought us to our destination of analytically assembling a definition of the phenomenon of perception. I will now go over the stages by which I arrived at the definition.

I began by assuming that there exists an event with the following array of properties:

1. It is an E_1 of O_1 in some as yet undetermined T-ish mode: that is, it is an experience that is in some T-mode intentionally directed to some object O_1.
2. The T in question is putative in type. (As seeing and acting are 'putative', and as emoting and imagining are not.)
3. An O_2 exists which is such that O_1 and O_2 fall under the same description, e.g. 'round red something' or 'arm movement'.
4. Attendant nomic (etc.) conditions obtain such that E_1 falls under a type (T, again)—which is 'of' its objects in the special extensional sense adumbrated—and of O_2.

At this point I laid great stress on the fact that more is still needed if we are to succeed in specifying something actual, and *a fortiori* if we are to specify perceptual experience of an object. Thus, (1)–(4) are satisfied by physical action *and* perception, both being intentionally directed experiences which instantiate a type that necessarily is 'of' some existent in the special extensional sense of 'of'. Now if we were to be engaged in constituting the phenomenon as *physical action*, if we were assembling a property which would guarantee both full determinacy and identity for such a phenomenon, we would have need of a further fifth clause in which we invoked the novel and distinctive concept of will. But if we are to constitute the phenomenon as *perception*, we require a fifth clause in which we do no more than appeal to the already invoked concept of experience. We simply conjoin that concept with the special use of 'of' and arrive at the T which here applies—which simply *is* an experiencing *of* a physical reality. Whereas the willing of O is not an experience of O in the non-intentional sense under consideration, the perception of O is and is no more than just that. While the willing of O is *an* experience and is extensionally of its object, the perception of O simply *is* experience extensionally of its object. As remarked earlier, it is the unique case in which the genus 'experience' functions as a species!

(d) Perception is unique amongst experiences in discovering its identity under 'experience——'

We may therefore say, that whereas being an E_1 of O is insufficient to confer an identity upon an experience, and satisfying (1)–(4) is likewise an insufficient condition, being an E_2 of O_2 is a sufficient (though non-necessary) condition of identity. Even though it is an inessential property of E_2 of O_2, it nonetheless determines the essence of E_2 of O_2 as: putatively E_2 of some O or other. Thus, perception simply *is* an experience of some object O in such a use of 'of' and such a sense of 'experience of O' as to entail the reality of O. And so the specific identity-type of perception is, being an experience$_2$ of its object. By contrast, the specific identity-type of physical action is not being an experience$_2$ of its object—indeed, it is no such thing at any time! Rather, it is that of being a willing of its object in the same use of 'of' as that in which perception simply is an experience of its object. We might sum up this whole situation in the following formula: As physical action *is* a willing of its object, perception *is* an experiencing of its object.

This last is the central point of the entire discussion. Accordingly, what is special about perception is not that it is an intentionally directed experience that really is directed onto an object that is real—all of which is true of a mental image of St Peter's—and which need not be true of perception. And it is not that it is an intentionally directed experience that is of *such a type* as to necessitate its being extensionally 'of' some real existent. The special feature is, that the latter type is exhaustively constituted out of the concept of experience. For to repeat, as arm raising *is* the willing of arm rise so perception *is* the experiencing of its object. It is the unique experience with this property. It is the unique experience that is the experiencing of its object in the sense arm raising *is* the willing of arm rise. Whereas no experience finds its identity in being an E_1 of its object, for we always have to ask '*Which* experience?' if we are to constitute a reality, perception finds full determinacy and identity in being the E_2 of its object. It is the only experience that finds its identity under the concept of *experience*. This is what is so special about perception.

(e) The mode-less-ness of perceptual acquaintance

(1) This has significant implications concerning the perceptual mode of encountering its object. We can bring this out by comparing perception once more with

physical action. If this latter phenomenon, which is at the least an example of an experience₁ of some object, is to achieve determinacy of nature and being, a specific variety of experience must be exemplified, namely that of *willing* experience. Thus, striving (Sφ) to produce limb movement (φ) is a specific and *active mode* of (intentionally) experiencing₁ its object φ (an experience that happens as a general rule to be accompanied by a perceptual experiencing₂ of proprioceptive kind of this same φ). That is, the active consciousness experiences₁ its object in *active presentation*—a pure example of which is encountered when Sφ completely fails and proprioceptive experience of φ is wholly absent. Turn now to the related case of perception. The special status of this phenomenon shows in the fact that there is simply *no* mode of presentation of its object. When we experience a pain or a sound, everything distinctive in the experience comes from the *object* of the experience, it precisely does not reside in the *mode* of experiencing the sound or pain—there being no such thing. All that is distinctive in the experience derives from the distinctive character of its object: it is a *sheer* experiencing of a distinctive object. The perceptual consciousness is wholly devoid of character: it is *mere* experiencing.

Only one experience gets its distinctive character, not through the mode of experiencing its object, but via the character of its object. Perception therefore is idiosyncratic, or rather special or unique, merely in being the one unidiosyncratic experience. Its essence is not revealed in the mode in which its object is given to it, which is to say in the mode of presentation of the object to the experiencing subject, but in the *absence* of any mode of presentation.

(2) These last observations support the claim which we earlier made that the objects of perception concretely enter the stream of consciousness, so to say mimicking the experiences which constitute that stream ('cuckoos in the nest of consciousness'). In the place of concrete presence as *occupants of*, what we have in the case of perception is concrete presence as *objects of.* This property is a direct derivative of the fact that the identity-conferring type for perception is no more than 'experience of' and is such that here experience takes a concrete real object. Since that is all there is to perception, bearing in mind that perception is no more than the case in which objects are concretely given as objects to experience, the objects of perception appear directly in the stream of consciousness—as objects! They uniquely join the experiences *qua* concrete presences. An 'ontological snob' might say of them that they insolently jostle around in that privileged milieu with their ontological 'betters'!

4. Summary: The Two Arguments—of Chapters 8 and 9—Restated in Terms of Object-Type

(1) That concludes the analytical argument. Then in the light of this discussion, I now offer a brief summary of the two arguments—the one just used, and the argument employed in the previous Chapter 8—in favour of the universalized or a priori

theory of perception. In this summary statement I avail myself of the several concepts of object-type that have appeared in the course of the recent constituting process.

We have thus far noted two uses of 'experience of', the problematic (and probably stipulated) purely intentional use as in 'experience of tomorrow's sunrise', and the familiar and well-established perceptual extensional use as in 'experience of today's sunrise'. Now we saw earlier in Chapter 8 how it helped explicate this latter use to liken it in certain respects with a *second* extensional use of 'experience of'—a use that might naturally be described as 'reflexive'—in which we do no more than *identify* the experience concerned. We encounter this particular use in such everyday utterances as 'many people have experiences of anxiety on such occasions' or 'he was suddenly overcome by an experience of shame'. I shall distinguish these two extensional uses under the following nomenclature. I will dub the perceptual use 'E_{2a} of O', and the reflexive use 'E_{2b} of O'. Examples of the above three uses of 'experience of' are as follows:

E_1. 'An experience of tomorrow's sunrise.' For example, an affective experience: say, an experience of dread over its impending occurrence.

E_{2a}. 'An experience of today's sunrise.' For example, a visual perceptual experience: say, gazing upon it.

E_{2b}. 'An experience of anxiety.' For example, just feeling anxious.

Meanwhile the diverse and distinguishing logical properties of these three uses of 'experience of' are as follows:

$$E_1 \text{ of } O \nrightarrow O, \text{ and } E_1 \text{ of } O \longrightarrow \Diamond \sim(E = O).$$
$$E_{2a} \text{ of } O \longrightarrow O \; \& \; \Diamond \sim(E = O).$$
$$E_{2b} \text{ of } O \longrightarrow O \; \& \; \Box \, (E = O).$$

(2) It seems to me natural to assume that E_{2a} and E_{2b} are two sub-varieties of the one extensional type. Is it not intuitively apparent that we can experience sounds and anxiety as we cannot a Napoleonic victory at Waterloo or Wagner's opera 'Die Sieger'? Even though one phenomenon appears as object and the other as occupant, both concretely appear in the stream of consciousness.

If this is how matters stand, we ought to be able to explicate and support the central thesis of this and the previous chapter—namely, the contentious universalist or a priori-ist analysis of the concept of perception—in two different ways, using the above two expressions and employing either the *analytical* argument of the present Chapter 9 or else the argument from *meanings* of the previous Chapter 8.

Thus, we might do so by appeal to the concept of *physical action* in explicating 'experience$_2$ of——' (as we have done in the present chapter). Alternatively, we might turn to certain *actual experiential phenomena* in explicating 'experience$_2$ ——' (as in Chapter 8). We could say either of the following:

A. As arm raising *is* the willing of arm rise, so perception *is* the experiencing of its object.

OR

B. We often enough (perceptually) experience lights and sounds as we often enough (non-perceptually) experience emotions like joy and rage, and as we never and indeed never could experience either the future or such counterfactual entities as Napoleon's victory at Waterloo.

(3) I think that either (A) or (B) might be offered in explication of, and in support for the claim that perception simply *is* the experiencing of a real object. In any case, I shall conclude this present part of the discussion with a brief comment on the significance of the second claim (B). It leads me to reiterate my recent observations concerning the phenomenon of 'concrete presence'.

It may perhaps be that claim (B) amounts to the following. The strained intentional sense in which we might be said to experience counterfactual events is, 'an experience whose intentional object content is that event'. By contrast, the reflexive sense in which we experience experiences is, 'an experience occurring in the stream of consciousness'; and here we affirm the concrete and not merely thought-mediated presence of the item in that phenomenal system. Meanwhile, the perceptual sense in which we experience (say) visibles is, 'an object concretely presenting itself in the stream of consciousness'. Thus, *concrete presence* in that phenomenal system, a presence which is not realized through the mediation of thought, obtains in each case, even though in two different modalities: namely, as occupant-of and as object-of. Then the common property of concrete presence may be what we affirm of each phenomenon in saying that 'we experience lights and sounds *as* we do joy and grief'. This may be the rationale whereby we seem free to explicate the contentious claim concerning the nature of perception in these terms.

5. A Cardinal Flaw in the Objection: Pseudo-Extensionality

(1) At this point I want to outline one further failing in the main objection—voiced in Chapter 8—to the proposed universalist definition of perception. But in order to lead up to that topic, which concerns extensionality, I must first briefly review the discussion.

The aim in the present Chapter 9 has been to define perception. More specifically, the enterprise has been one of *concept-building*, with a view to arriving at the correct analyis of the concept. Thus, I hoped to constitute the concept of perception out of other concepts. Indeed, my central claim has been that this can be accomplished through recourse to nothing but universal concepts which are a priori to any form of mind. That is, without appeal to a posteriori empirical psychological concepts (as the concept of amusement is a posteriori) or even to wide-ranging but scarcely universal psychological concepts (like that of emotion). The suggestion is,

314

that it can be carried out in terms of the concept of *experience*, together with that of *object*. No more.

Yet what exactly are we saying when we define perception as experience *taking an object*? In what sense do we intend 'taking an object'? Doubtless we mean that the object is extensional in type rather than intentional, but is that *all* that we mean in making such a claim? I ask, because it emerged that if perception and willing are to find their objects, they must possess a property unique to them among extensionally related items. If these psychological items are to be extensionally of their object O, not merely must O exist, but they themselves *ab initio* must be *putative instances* of the kind that is realized in part through the reality of O. That is, in discovering their object they must satisfy their own inherent aspiration to type. Thus, a 'seem see' must prove to be a 'see', a 'try to act' must be an 'act'. The question this raises is, whether it implies that will and perception take objects in a sense which includes, but is more *comprehensive* than that of extensionality? Might idiosyncrasy enter the scene in the form of certain additional requirements? Does a special sense of 'object' come into play in these two cases?

It seems to me that it does not, and that the special requirements for the discovery of an object in the case of these phenomena are those of finding an extensional object—in *their* case. Surely, as we can only possess or lose a chair that is real, so in the very same sense we can only paint or see a chair that is real. In a word, the aforementioned specialness must stem from the nature of willing and perception: it does not come from the character of their objects. It concerns the special requirements for the acquisition of an extensional object when the contendor for that object is of the type either of *will* or *perception*.

(2) This brings me to the main topic of the present section. Thus, a difficulty for the proposed universalist definition of perception, cast in terms of the concept of extensionality, was raised in the previous Chapter 8. If perception is experience taking an object, an object that is extensionally given and thus a phenomenal reality, why should not a mental image of St Peter's also rate as a perception? Is it not an experience, and is it not likewise directed onto a phenomenal reality? In effect, this objection addresses itself to issues of *meaning*. In effect, it says: if the sense of 'experience of——' in the definition is an extensional sense, why cannot 'experience of——' be intended extensionally in the case of a mental image that is known to be truly directed onto a phenomenal reality? Why is not this also 'an experience of——' in an extensional sense? But if it is, it must on the definition be classed as a perception. However, we know that it cannot be a perception. Therefore perception must be *more than* 'an experience of——' in the extensional sense of that expression. Therefore the latter cannot give the definition of perception, and we are obliged to invoke a further distinctive experiential concept if we are adequately to characterize it, and thus opt for idiosyncrasy in the theory. So far the objection.

In Chapter 8 I answered this objection by a rather blunt denial that the meaning of 'experience taking an object' is preserved across (say) examples of imagery of realities and perceptual cases. A more exact answer was then assembled in the present Chapter 9, using analytical means. That analytical reply was in two parts. It first of all noted that 'experience taking an object' might be understood either as '*an* experience taking an object' or else as '*experience* taking an object'—where the latter is understood to state not merely what something *has*, but what it *is*. This reply then went on to point out that the definition of perception is to be construed in the latter sense. 'Perception is experience taking an object' asserts, not merely that perception is an experience that has the property of taking an object, it claims that that is *all that it is*. And for that to be so the defining type of the phenomenon must be given under the concept of 'experience'. This vital property holds of perception, indeed it does so uniquely, but it does not hold of mental imagery (whether or not of phenomenal realities). Accordingly, mental imagery *as such* is incapable of satisfying the definition, and the objection fails. Perception is unique amongst experiences in being nothing but an awareness of a phenomenal reality. To notice such an item *is* to perceive it. That is all perception is.

(3) One fatal flaw in this objection lay in its underlying theoretical assumptions concerning the acquisition of extensional objects. It is a matter of the first importance that some mental phenomena simply cannot take extensional objects. Some mental phenomena simply cannot manage to be 'of' an object in the sense in which (say) a touching or burning is 'of' something. Those mental phenomena which discover their object through the offices of the thought, seem invariably to be of this type. And it is of no account either way that the object intended may be a phenomenal reality, or that it may be known by all concerned to be so. The mind here posits but one object in one mode.

The imagination provides us with exemplary instances of the kind in question. Thus, describing something as 'a mental image of St Peter's' can *never* be the specification of an extensional object of an imagining. Even though pragmatic factors, the publicly known obtaining of certain contexts, might inform all interlocutors of the reality of the object being imagined and spoken of, no *logical deduction* from 'he had a mental image of X' to 'X exists' can ever be valid. No context can accomplish so much. Now it was claimed (above) by the 'objector' that 'experience of——' might be intended extensionally in the case of mental images we all know to be directed onto phenomenal realities. How does that claim fare in the light of the above consideration? It plainly cannot survive. The experience in question is simply of such a type as to be incapable of sustaining the property of extensionality. While a speaker might even take himself to intend the expression in an extensional sense, and while the expression has extensional applications elsewhere, that is far from its being extensionally applicable here. When the experience in question is a visual imagining—whether of Napoleon or St Peter's Rome or Beelzebub or whatever— it is never applicable.

Here we have a second decisive counter to the above objection to the proposed definition of perception. Thus, the mental image of St Peter's fails to satisfy the definition on two distinct counts. First, it could at best be no more than *one experience amongst others* that is extensionally directed onto an object: it cannot itself simply *be* the experiencing of an extensionally given object. But secondly, it in any case cannot be directed *extensionally*, it simply cannot be 'of' its object in the sense visual perception might be 'of' (say) the rising sun or willing 'of' (say) arm movement or a burning 'of' a bush. The most that can be accomplished along such lines is that considerations of context, though not of content, might communicate to interlocutors that the object intended in the experience is a phenomenal reality. However, that is not the same thing as taking an extensional object.

(4) The proposed definition of perception is that perception is merely *experience taking an object*. This definition reveals perception to be a central element of mentality as such. It shows that perceiving is one of the *two* possible roles open to experiential consciousness: on the one hand to encompass experiences, on the other to take extensional objects. Then since consciousness and experience are universal to any account of mind—what sort of a mind would it be that lacked the potential for either?—perception on this account moves into a position of absolute centrality in the mind, and centre-stage in the philosophy of consciousness. I have labelled this doctrine the 'departicularizing of perception'.

IO

Perception and Truth

The present chapter is concerned with the phenomenon of perception as understood in terms of the theory just sketched, and therefore ultimately in terms of consciousness. The aim at this point is to gain a more complete understanding of this phenomenon, to bring to light some of its more important properties. One way of going about this task is by adequately distinguishing perception from its closest mental neighbours. Now a perception or intuition is an episode of consciousness, it is an experience, and it is of cognitive significance. Accordingly, the task of differential delineation leads naturally to an examination—not (say) of affective experience (which lacks cognitive import)—but of two closely related experiences which share with the intuition the property of being of cognitive significance. The first is, what one might describe as the perceptual discovery-experience: by which I mean, the sort of phenomenon that occurs when one *sees that* the traffic lights are green. The second is the thought-experience: that is, the kind of phenomenon that one reports when one informs someone that 'the moment I saw the green light I had the thought "the lights must have changed some time ago!"'. The discussion that follows addresses itself to distinguishing perception from these two varieties of experience. Now it seems to me of some interest that both of these cognitively significant experiences involve a close relation to propositions and to truth. For these reasons, and in any case because of the inherent importance of these relations, I propose to investigate perceptual experience with them in view. Above all, I aim to discover how perception stands in relation to truth.

1. Distinguishing Intuition and Perceiving-That (1): Theories of Perceiving-That

(a) A statement of the theories

Can perceptions occur that have propositional content? On the face of it, yes. Such phenomena seem to occur all the time. Do we not continually perceive that this or that is the case? We certainly *say so*, and therefore at least *in some sense* do so. But we must understand what it means to say such a thing. What, precisely, is the nature of the phenomenon that we call a 'perceiving-that'? Could it be that it is (α) an atten-

318

tive event—with a propositional object—which is *not* a cognitive phenomenon of the type of (say) believing? Or might it be instead (β) an attentive event—with a propositional object—which *is* simultaneously a cognitive phenomenon like believing? Or is it simply (γ) a perceptually engendered cognitive phenomenon like believing?

I will argue in favour of the latter (γ)-analysis. One fact is worth bearing in mind before we begin this inquiry: namely, that whenever a person perceives-that p, he both believes that p and perceives something which is relevant to p's truth-value. For example, one believes that the traffic lights are green, and sees the greenness of the traffic lights. Then let us consider an even simpler example, and investigate theories of perceiving-that cast in terms of that simple case. Thus, let us suppose that we suddenly hear a familiar and distinctive sound, viz. a whistle. Then this hearing of the whistle is co-present, both with hearing that a whistle occurs, and with believing that a whistle occurs. This suggests the possiblity that *three* enumerable phenomena might all be occurring on such an occasion, viz. a hearing-of, a hearing-that, and a believing-that. But is that really true? It is clear that the answer to this question must depend upon the constitution of the phenomenon that we call a 'hearing-that'. Then the following is a more or less exhaustive list of possible theories as to the nature of this occurrence. *Hearing-that the whistle occurs* might be:

A. Hearing the whistle (*as* a whistle).
B. Believing that a whistle occurs (as a result of a contemporaneous event of A-type).
C. A complex event, constituted of hearing the whistle *and* believing that a whistle occurs.
D. An attentive event of type hearing—not to be confused with any sort of believing—whose (propositional) object is, that a whistle occurs.
E. An attentive event of type hearing (not to be confused with a believing) whose (propositional) object is, that a whistle occurs—of which the attentive event, hearing the whistle (*as* a whistle), is part.

It is difficult to think of any serious alternatives to the above five theories. I propose at this point to examine them in order, beginning with Theory A.

(b) Assessing the theories of perceiving-that

(1) Theory A identifies hearing-that a whistle occurs with hearing the whistle *as* a whistle. Then against this theory are ranged a number of more or less decisive considerations. First, that a logically necessary condition of hearing-that a whistle occurs is, a belief that a whistle occurs—which is surely a distinct existent from the event of hearing a whistle. As well as the following facts. That it is not possible to *redescribe* the direct whistle-object of hearing *as* the proposition 'that a whistle occurs': a whistle cannot be experienced as a truth about itself. That we indexically

and concretely individuate or single out the *object-referent* of hearing-that a whistle occurs *as*, a something that is *already given* in the contemporaneous perception of the sound. That some perceivings-that are indubitably cognitions which are caused by contemporaneous perceivings: say, seeing that it rained last night (on catching sight of wet streets). Finally, that some perceivings-of might very well occur in the absence of any perceiving-that: say, an infant screwing up its eyes at the light, who certainly sees light but need not see-that anything occurs or is the case.

Against Theory C is first of all its inherent implausibility. And why in any case should perceiving-of and believing-that unite to constitute a third complex event? What principle of unification is at work here? All I can discover is the existence of an immediately given causal tie. But that surely is insufficient, otherwise complex events would be springing up all over the place in the mind! For example, images would unite with their precipitating thoughts, acts would join up with their originating act-desires and intentions, and so on. These considerations, together with Ockham's razor, permit us to reject Theory C.

(2) Theory D is interesting, as Theories A and C are not, but like them it has unacceptable implications. Thus, it implies that *two* attentive perceptual events occur when we hear a whistle—hearing-of the whistle and hearing that-the-whistle-occurs—both of which are sharply to be distinguished both from one another *and* from the co-present cognitive phenomenon of believing that the whistle occurs. Now there can be no doubt that a hearing-of the whistle occurs, a hearing-of which is a hearing-of *as* a whistle. Nor any doubt that a believing phenomenon occurs, with propositional object. However, I can see no reason for postulating a third distinct attentive non-cognitive event also with propositional content. What justification is there for such a hypothesis? Nothing comes to mind. The hypothesized event seems mythical.

Explanatorial considerations support this reading of the situation. Thus, *why* does one believe that a whistle is occurring when it is? Surely, because we hear a whistle, in a situation in which we trust the deliverances of our senses. In short, the situation is not that *hearing-that* a whistle is occurring causes one to believe that a whistle is occurring. Rather, *hearing* a whistle causes one to believe that a whistle is occurring. If one hears a whistle as a whistle, and knows one's hearing is reliable, one believes simply for those reasons. They are enough.

And functional considerations likewise support this theory. For what would be the function of this supposed third event? Is not hearing a whistle *as* a whistle sufficient in normal circumstances to engender the knowledge, namely that a whistle occurs, that it is the function of such a perception to engender? The function of the object-content of the phenomenon of perceiving-x-as-X, the causal role of the X-interpretation imposed upon the bare givens of sense, is the engendering—not of some intervening second awareness-event, viz. perceiving-that something (here and now, etc.) is X—(but) of knowledge that something (here and now, etc.) is X. The interpretational content leads normally and with absolute pellucidity to contemporaneous knowledge with identical object. I conclude that we can dispense with Theory D.

In favour of Theory E is, that hearing-that a whistle occurs and hearing a whistle *as* a whistle almost always occur together. But I can see nothing else in its favour. How can noticing an individual phenomenal something be *part of* noticing that *it is true that* the phenomenal something occurs? And once again, functional considerations support this position, bearing in mind that hearing a whistle *as* a whistle is a sufficient ground for the generation of the belief such perceptions typically effect. What can be the function of this supposed complex container event? And Ockham's razor lends support to the rejection of the latter: why multiply entities when functional office can be accomplished in their absence? In short, Theory E looks to be even more implausible than Theory C.

(3) When we remember that at least *some* cases of perceiving-that are indubitably believings—such as seeing that it rained (or *did not* rain!) last night; and when we consider the obvious weakness of the Theories A, C, and E, together with the difficulties facing Theory D; we seem to have a strong case in favour of Theory B. That is, in favour of the view that seeing-that (say) an individual like a material object or a physical event exists, or that a quality like colour or shape inhere, consists in the belief attendant-upon and concordant-with the *content* of the simultaneous perceptual experience: a belief, it should be added, that is both immediately and overtly caused by that indexically individuated content.

It is, I think, important that we spell out precisely what the content of this perceiving-that belief is, since it reveals something of interest. For example, hearing that (say) a miaow sounds, will generally be a believing that *that (present, audible) miaow* sounds, and this belief will be directly given to its possessor *as* immediately caused by the awareness of the very miaow it refers to. Then the latter more precise characterization of the phenomenon of perceiving-that, helps to bring to light a further feature of the relation between intuition and perceiving-that. Thus, it is evident from the above formulation that this example of perceiving-that—and, indeed, perceiving-that as such—finds its content (or topic) only through the *agency* of the distinct contemporaneous perception. It indexically singles out the object of the belief *as* what is there and then experienced in the contemporaneous perception: it discovers a referent so to say *on the back of* the intuitional awareness of the object. In a word, perceiving-that owes a double debt to the intuition. It causally owes its very existence, and it owes its topic or content, to a distinct contemporaneous intuitional awareness of a presence. This helps to underline the primacy of the intuition, and the essentially dependent or second-order character of perceiving-that. In sum: despite the intimacy of its connection with the perception, perceiving-that turns out to be a distinct and dependent second-order phenomenon that is an event of a different type altogether, viz. a believing.

2. Distinguishing Intuition and Perceiving-That (2)

(a) Issues of substance

(1) The matter under discussion is of such central importance to a theory of perception, that I feel the need to pursue the question a little further. It seems to me that the purely cognitive Theory B of perceiving-that which I have been advancing can be strengthened by additional considerations. Here in Section 2(*a*) I address myself to that task, to further validating Theory B. Meanwhile, in the succeeding Section 2(*b*) I consider a problem raised by the fact that the typical objects of perception are complex in character.

It should be emphasized that *two* propositions of real substance are at issue in the discussion: (P1) That there exists *no* phenomenon that is a noticing—with propositional content—which is at the same time *not* a cognitive phenomenon like knowing/believing/suspecting, etc. And (P2) That 'aware' has *different senses* in 'he was aware of a whistle' and 'he was aware that a whistle was occurring.'

The arguments of the previous Section were expressly in support of P1. Now some may be willing to concede the truth of P1, and insist nonetheless that 'he was aware that a whistle was occurring' reports a perception: that is, they may insist that *two* distinct perceptions occur on such an occasion, one of which is a cognition and the other not. Then whether or not this latter claim has substance, depends in turn upon their response to P2. If they accept P2, the dispute is merely over words: it is over whether or not 'perception' is ambiguous, and whether one sense is 'believing that is causally sensitive to contemporaneous perception' (or some such). But if they reject P2, the dispute is substantive: it is over whether or not the unitary phenomenon of attentive-awareness takes direct *and* propositional objects. That is, in the way that is open to the unitary phenomenon of desire, which can take the two irreducible forms desire-to-do-act-Φ/desire-that-p-be-true (e.g. feel like shouting/desire that one's football team win). Yet having said that, we must immediately add that P1 is in effect a decisive proof of P2. Let me explain how this is so.

(2) The question is, as desire can take these two forms, can awareness take the forms: awareness-of-an-object/awareness-of-a-truth? I do not think it can. I think we are here talking of different phenomenal types along with different object-types. Now it is of great importance that no other psychological concepts come to our rescue if we wish to explicate the senses of 'desire to do act Φ'/'desire that p be true': we have in either case to make do with the irreducible concept of *desire*, and delineate the different kinds of its objects (and, incidentally, beat off misguided attempts to reduce one to the other).[1] An entirely different picture presents itself

---

[1] It is not possible to render 'I had an overwhelming impulse to shout' as (say) 'I overwhelmingly longed for it to be the case that I was shouting'. Plainly, these are reports of two quite different, and equally real phenomena, and simultaneously of two irreducibly diverse varieties of the unitary phenomenon, desire. Thus, each variety can be as intense as the other, each can lead to experiences of fulfilment (and pleasure) or frustration (and misery), each can be either rational or else merely inclinatory, and so on. The question we are considering is: is desire a satisfactory model for perceptual noticing? I am claiming that it is not.

when we consider the supposed two forms of intuitional awareness: direct-object awareness/propositional awareness. For here a quite distinct psychological concept comes at once to our aid in the explication of the *second* of the latter concepts—as soon as P1 has been conceded: to wit, that of belief. And it is clear that we are dealing with two irreducible psychological concepts here: a noticing, and a believing. The concept of noticing a whistle (say) simply cannot be explicated in terms of belief ('inclination to believe', etc.) or anything else, and of course neither can belief be explained in other terms. Now this is why 'aware' is ambiguous in 'he was aware of a whistle' and 'he was aware that a whistle was occurring'. It is ambiguous as 'wanted' is not in 'he wanted to call out with joy' and 'he wanted the roulette wheel to stop at the number 7'. Once the claim P1 is accepted, the fundamentals of the theory are in place. Namely: that perceptual or attentive events do not take propositional objects. They take public physical realities like material objects, events, colours, shapes—and relations, as object.

(b) The complex perception of complex objects

(1) This theory appears to be true, not merely of simple perceptual experiences of simple objects like whistles, but of the complex perception of complex objects. Thus, it holds of the structured seeing of a structured object: say, a recognitional seeing that is both *of* a tree and *as* a tree. Here, too, it is not possible to discover an attentive non-cognitive event with propositional object. And here, too, the naturally attendant belief both finds its content through the agency of, and owes its very existence to, the structured perception of a structured whole, namely to the recognition of a complex object.

And yet is there not a problem here? For how can one—not just *see* a tree, but *recognize* a tree—without seeing-that (say) something like tree shape is present? How can one visually identify such an item without seeing-that such truths obtain? The answer is, that one cannot: the full interpretational variety of seeing of a complex object cannot occur without the simultaneous occurrence of beliefs concerning the structure of that object. An extremely interesting and suggestive fact without a doubt, but in my view no reason for disputing the claim that perceiving-that is cognitive in character, and that perceptual or attentive events do not take propositional objects. We shall discover later on in this work, in the course of the discussion in Chapter 21 of the phenomenon of 'seeing in the round', that the mere experiencing of an object's visual appearance depends internally upon the utilization of cognitive attitudes concerning the spatial relations in which one stands to the perceived object. The moral to be drawn from these somewhat comparable cases is the same. It is that we should abandon forthwith those over-simple theories of visual experience which fail to appreciate the vitally important contribution of the intellect or understanding to the formation of perceptual experience. Perception may not be the same thing as discovery, but no more is it of the ilk of a blow between the eyes!

(2) However, a residual problem exists. For it looks perhaps as if perceiving-that might in these latter complex cases be *internal* to the phenomenon of perceiving-of, and this would amount to a disproof of the claim that perceiving-that is a dependent second-order phenomenon of perception. Thus, we have agreed that it is not possible to perceptually recognize a complex structured object without perceiving-that certain structural truths obtain. We might do so in the case of a bare simple object like a smell or taste, but with precious little else. For example, I cannot visually recognize a giraffe, I cannot record the presence of the distinctive giraffe-look, without seeing-that the bearer has a long neck *or* has spots *or* is tall, etc. True, I need not register any particular *one* of these, but I must register something more than 'sheer giraffe-ness'! Perceptual recognition of such complex structured objects cannot *itself* be structureless and ineffable, and cannot be *as of* structureless ineffables. Parts, and their interrelations, have to an extent to be noted, if the presence of an example of the object-look is to be noticed, and I must simultaneously record or be *aware-that* this is how the object is set up or constituted.

Then what may we deduce from the latter necessity? Does it show that perceiving-that is *part of* the perception of complex objects? But how could it be? A simple distinction makes the point. Thus, it is one thing to say: you cannot recognize (say) Rembrandt's 'The Night Watch' without noticing people, and as suitably related, say as standing together in a small group. It is another thing to say: you cannot recognize 'The Night Watch' without (say) noticing-that people are present therein, and that they are standing in a group. In my opinion, both claims are true, but, I suggest, only the first of these claims makes mention of *parts of the intuition*. Those parts surface to view when we give a *full description* of the perceptual experience: that is, fill in the full content of 'see as———', e.g. 'I seem to see a painting *as* The Night Watch and *as* of a group etc.' Then the perceptual discoveries (seeing-that———) in question are merely the inevitable necessary consequence of such a perceptual content. Thus, while it is true that such an intuition cannot occur without discoveries of this kind, so that they function as necessary intellectual conditions, those discoveries are no part of that intuition.

3. Distinguishing Perception and Thought (α): Three Differences

So much for the difference between *perceiving* and *perceiving-that*, which turns out to be the distinction between noticing-of something and belief-given-immediately-as-caused-by-a-now-noticing-of-that-something (or some such). I come at this point to the second main distinction to be drawn between perception and its closest experiential neighbours. This is the distinction between perception and thought: that is, between the perceptual experience and the thought experience. Then for the moment I put the phenomenon of perception to one side, and consider instead the nature of thought. I begin, in Section 3(a), with a few general observations concerning thought and the thought-experience. Once again we shall see that truth and the proposition loom large in the account.

324

(a) The thought-experience and truth

(1) Many events instantiate in time changes that can be timelessly specified, such as the change from being orange to being green, a change which we might find exemplified in an event like a traffic signal. And those events that are thought-events instantiate in particular minds at particular times thoughts that are either timelessly specifiable, like 'Sugar is sweet', or specifiable through a given sentence, like 'It is hot here.' Thus, we specify thought-events in such terms that different people might at different times 'have the same thought'.

Now it might seem that any old thought can rise to the surface of one's mind at any old time, but in fact it is not so. What thoughts can rise up into one's mind are mostly determined by one's system of beliefs. Most spontaneous thought-events are experiences whose entire content is a proposition that one believes to be true, they are events in which a seeming-truth surfaces into an individual consciousness. If the system of one's beliefs can be construed as a cognitive map of Reality, then the typical spontaneous thought-experience is a sort of visiting by the mind of a local sector of that map, an instantaneous trip to a point in one's internal representation of the World. One thinks 'the car lights are still on!', homing in as it were onto a point-fact. Now this is how it is with most thoughts, though not with all. Question-thoughts manifest no belief directly, and neither do the thoughts caused in under-standing the utterances of others. This is because the thought-event *as such* is an experience whose content is a thought-content. And so the constraints upon thought-experience must vary with the situation and state of mind of the subject. Thus, when awake and sane I cannot have 'I am Nero' rise up into my head; but I can if I am mad or dreaming, and can if I hear someone accuse me of being Nero, and can as part of a present complex thought.

(2) Now the thought which is the content of the thought-event is expressed by a sentence: 'This colour resembles that colour', 'Am I mad?', 'Sugar is sweet', 'I might not have been Nero', 'I am not Nero'. And so the thought-content can take the forms 'p', '~p', 'p?', '◊p', etc. Then the same holds of the thought-events themselves: say, 'As the clock struck one, I had the thought "I am not Nero".' And here we link a propositional form and content to a particular moment in time.

It is of great importance that thoughts are like beliefs in being conceived *under the aspect of truth*. Thus, if I have the thought 'possibly p' then I am thinking 'it is true that possibly p' or 'p is possibly true'; while if the thought 'not-p' enters my mind, I am thinking 'p is not true' or 'it is false that p is true'; and the thought 'p?' is thinking 'is p true?' No thoughts occur that are mere content, that are independent of truth-value. While a dog believes it is about to be fed without believing that *it is true* that it is about to be fed, I do not and I cannot. As all *self-conscious* beliefs are under the aspect of truth, so are all thoughts *of any kind*. Indeed, it is because animal belief cannot be under the aspect of truth, that animal thought is inexistent. This is because the capacity to negate, and hence to affirm in opposition to such negation, is essential to thought.

All important to the concept of a thought-event is the existence of a particular kind of *truth-gap* between it and Reality. Thus, the thought-event comes to its owner *as*: that which is capable of agreement or disagreement with Reality in the special mode of truth (a property it shares with beliefs in the self-conscious). It is above all this element that is missing in animal belief, which as a result constitutes an order of commitment-to or immersion-in Reality to which we cannot even aspire (and which has nothing to do with certainty). It is not just that the thought-event may or may not truth-agree with Reality, which after all is true of animal belief: it is that it is given to its owner *as*, what may or may not so agree. Indeed, this inner event is *experienced as* standing at such a remove from the World—almost like a sentence or a sense-datum! It is, in essence, in this regard, disengaged; or in a state of cognitive suspension, rather like a photograph or experimental 'mock up' of the real thing, even though typically it is experienced as in agreement with fact. But the truth-characteristic is absolutely indelible to the thought-experience. Now it follows from the above that a necessary condition of a mind's harbouring a thought-event is the capacity to distance itself in this special way from Reality, to interpose a kind of truth-screen between itself and the World. We gain much in having our minds wrenched away in this fashion from absolute or total immersion in the World: nothing less literally than an awareness of the World itself, the mental posture of those acquainted with Truth/Falsity (a 'Fall' comparable to the discovery of Good/Evil). On the other hand it is achieved at the cost of the coming into being of our awareness of this truth-gap, of the permanent possibility of agreement or disagreement of one's mind with the World. (What one might perhaps call 'Hamlet's problem'.) In any case a mind that can experience thoughts, is one acquainted with Negation and Falsity, along with Affirmation and Truth.

(b) Distinguishing thoughts and perceptions on the several counts: object/content/constitution

(1) So much for the moment for a few observations concerning the nature of the thought-experience. At this point I return to the specific problem before us. Namely, how do perceptions relate to thoughts? More exactly, in what ways are perceptual experiences to be distinguished from thought-experiences? Now a man who perceives what it is that he is perceiving in his environment *as* whatever it happens to be, puts to use an idea or thought-content in the constituting of that perceptual experience. What does this imply as to the occurrence of thought-experience at that moment in time? Well, to begin with it is clear that no thought-experience—such as 'That man must be Picasso!' (on seeing a figure disappearing into a doorway in Paris)—need *accompany* his perception. Then is it possible that a relation of *identity* holds between thought and perception? Might the perceptual experience and a thought-experience with one and the same content turn out to be identical? For example, suppose that one hears and recognizes a thump. Could this auditory experience *actually be* the having of a thought with the content 'I hear that thump'/'That thump is happening'?

326

There is simply no way in which it could be the same. To be sure, the perceptual experience is putatively *of* a distinct existent, but this object-directed character or representational content, a special variety or example of intentionality, plainly cannot on its own suffice to make of the perceptual experience a thought-experience. A series of considerations show this to be so. The first is, that the way in which the experience manages to be *of* what it is of, is of a wholly different order in either case. In the thought-experience it is achieved through the use of *concepts* in assembling a thought such that some object satisfies the individuating property given in the thought (e.g. 'that' [i.e. the one now engaging my attention] 'sound is now occurring'). Meanwhile in the case of the perception the relation noticing-of is established by very different means, even though concepts are here too pressed into service in constituting an interpretational content that is imposed upon a perceptual base. Those means are predominantly *causal* in character, for the attentive link is forged by the suitable engendering by its object, along regular mechanistic channels, of a suitable attentive event.

(2) Here we have one divergence between the perceptual-experience and the thought-experience. It is on the count: manner of discovering its *object*, which is to say the way (for example) a perception manages to be a perception of St Peter's and a thought a thought about St Peter's. I come now to a second reason for distinguishing perception from thought. This concerns the manner of acquisition of the thought-*content*. Thus, the thought with indexical perceptual content—'that thump is happening' (let us say)—must be a distinct existent from the perception of that thump, since it manages to refer to its object only through the *agency* of the already existing perception. Before the thought about the thump can so much as exist, the thump has to be a recorded object of consciousness: 'that thump is . . .' refers to what is *already* object for the attention. How else could the thought single out its subject? We could express the point by saying that the perception cannot be a thought with its own perceptually given object as referent. It cannot climb upon its own back!

(3) The third main difference between perceptual and thought experience is on the score of *constitution*. Unlike the thought-experience, perceptions exhibit a certain independence of concepts at their core. Even though it is true that 'intuitions without concepts are blind', intuitions cannot be constituted out of concepts alone. (As soon be made of words!) An infant who is crying with pain perceives that pain, and has no need of conceptual equipment to do so; and while this example is ridiculously slanted, the essentials of perception are nonetheless already in existence in so simple a case (viz. a distinct phenomenal existent is a direct material object for the attention). What this shows is, that in the typical more developed cases of perception concepts are somehow *impressed upon* the experience. They constitute a mutation in its character, but have no part in constituting the bearer of that interpretation. One needs no concepts to experience red, even though all of us will inevitably experience red *as* red. Perception does not *as such* need concepts, and

needs them only if it is to take the meaning-laden and cognitively valuable form it typically adopts. But the meaning is in all cases imposed. This is because intuition is acquaintance with its object, not merely in the *particular*, as in indexical thought, but in the *concrete*. The indexical thought 'That is a real backhand' (watching Donald Budge) is not to be confused with the perception which provides its concretely and indexically given content.

4. Distinguishing Perception and Thought-Experience (β): Negative Experience

(a) The agreement / disagreement of perceptions and thoughts with Reality

I come to the final fourth, and to my mind most significant, divergence between perception and thought: the mode of agreement/disagreement with Reality open to these two cognitively significant experiences. In my view, it is different in *kind*. After all, thoughts ('the kettle is still on!') are capable of truth and falsity, but we assign no truth-value to perceptions. 'A true hearing of a melody', 'a true tactile experience of something irregular' are, surely, senseless expressions. What a non-rational animal believes can be true, even though it cannot believe it to be true, but what beings of all and any type perceive cannot be true, let alone perceived as true. This is because we perceive objective phenomenal realities like material objects, or colours, or relations, none of which are capable of truth-values. To be real is not to be true, and to be perceived as real is not to be perceived as true. The nature of the error or disagreement with Reality open to perception, confirms this account. Thus, an illusion is the presence of an appearance, say a visual appearance or look, that corresponds to no matching reality; and an appearance, whether structured or not, is something other than a seeming truth. Illusions cannot be collapsed into delusions, not even when the illusion is relational in type (for example, an illusion of depth). In a word, the mode of agreement or disagreement with Reality is fundamentally dissimilar in the case of these two phenomena.

But the question at issue is of sufficient importance to warrant our embarking on a closer examination of the relevant perceptual data. And we ought in any case to take seriously the fact that some insightful philosophers, such as John Searle,[2] believe that all perceiving is perceiving-that, taking the content of the fully described perceptual experience to be *that* some state of affairs obtains. If this theory were correct, what one sees ('that p') would be true. Veridical perceptual experiences—which, after all, typically ground affirmative cognitive attitudes with propositional content that is true—would truth-agree with Reality.

Then let us for argument's sake suppose that perceptual-experience is like thought-experience in being *experienced as* something that agrees with Reality in the *truth-mode*. In short, let us assume the aforementioned 'truth-screen' exists in perception as well as in thought. What would this entail? The following, as it seems to

[2] *Intentionality*, 40. CUP, 1983.

me. We would oppose the perception of the true *as* true, to the perception of the false *as* false. And just as we know what it is to think 'not-p', so we should know what it is to perceive 'not-p': we should be able to have negative perceptual experiences, and do so even when the item to be negated is a simple object like a thump. But when do we encounter such a negative perceptual experience? If anywhere, surely when we hear a complete silence on an occasion when we were expecting precisely a thump. But exactly what goes on, on such occasions?

(b) The perception of absence

(1) At this point in the discussion I attempt to characterize the phenomenon, the perception of absence. However, to begin I want to make a few observations concerning the latter more particular phenomenon of silence, and the hearing of it.

Silence is non-specific, as 'noisyness' is not. Whereas 'noisyness' consists in the presence of sound, sound which of necessity is determinate, silence is not the absence of any one sound rather than any other: it is simply the absence of sound. Then being an absence, silence is nothing. Accordingly, hearing the silence cannot be the hearing of any sound, nor indeed of any thing, and is simply not a hearing. On the other hand it is something. Thus, it is something more than simply not hearing anything, for the permanently deaf do not hear anything and yet generally fail to hear any of the silences which may be surrounding them. Hearing the silence is logically equivalent to, and indeed is identical with, a sub-variety of hearing that it is silent. Accordingly, hearing silence and hearing that it is silent must relate altogether differently than do hearing a sound and hearing that a sound occurs, which are neither logically equivalent nor identical.

Then what *is* this experience of 'hearing that it is silent'? I have claimed it is not nothing, and in fact we are all familiar with the experience. I suggest the following as an analysis. Hearing the silence is a special case of coming-to-know of contemporary silence: namely, that in which one's knowledge arises immediately in an experience out of an absence of auditory experience which one knows to be a veridical perceptual reading. Therefore a cognitive attitude, with silence figuring in its content, is a necessary condition of hearing silence, as it cannot be in the hearing of sound (and animals must be unable to hear the silence). And to repeat: no hearing occurs when one hears the silence.[3]

(2) The hearing of silence is a special case of the perception of absence, which I now briefly discuss, using a simple phenomenon as a case in point. Thus, instead of the expected signature at the end of a letter you see blank white paper: you say, 'I saw that there was no name.' This reports an experience of absence, which is not to be confused with affective experiences like surprise which frequently attend it. The

[3] By contrast, seeing occurs when one sees the dark. A thing can look dark, as nothing can sound silent: 'the dark look' is a particular look, as 'the silent sound' is no sort of sound: the concept dark is of an appearance, the concept silence is of an absence. It follows, incidentally, that even though animals cannot hear the silence, they can nonetheless see the dark.

experience happened as you saw, and registered the presence of, a pure expanse of white. Then could this experience of absence be identical with the seeing of the white? Now the white, being no more the absence of a name than (say) of a drawing (or a rhinosceros!), cannot be identified with the absence of a name: after all, the white is something and the absence nothing. So how could the seeing of one *be* the seeing of the other? And yet the white can be visually experienced *under a negative aspect*, for example as *not being a name-bearer*—rather as an eskimo (say) might be experienced by a virulent Nazi as (before all else) 'non-Aryan'. Could such a negative mode of experiencing white *be* the experience of seeing name-absence? But seeing name-absence is a seeing-that something is missing, whereas the aforementioned negative experience is the seeing-of a presence *as* endowed with a negative property. In a word, seeing the absence neither is, nor is it a mode of, seeing the white.

Nevertheless the seeing of this particular absence was a definite experience, and it was occasioned by one's catching sight of the white (in the context of an expectation). You say: 'In seeing the white, I saw there was no signature', thereby timing the experience and internally linking it to the seeing of white. What can be the nature of this link? What sort of 'in seeing' is this? Well, it cannot be the well-known 'in virtue of' relation (familiar from visual perceptual theory), which concerns a single experience, for the experience of absence is neither identical with, nor is it an aspect of seeing white. I submit that these experiences are two, distinct, and causally related. That is, the experience of absence is *consequent upon* the seeing of white in the context of an expectation of seeing a name: it is consequent upon a comprehending seeing of white as a pure expanse of white. In short, a directly experienced causal relation links the two experiences. Thus, the visual experience causes the experience of absence, which is in addition directly given as arising out of the visual experience. The experience of seeing the absence of X is the experience of coming-to-know-of-the-absence-of-X-(directly given as arising out of a present visual experience of what shows no X). This cognitive experience is such that we experience the visual object *as* a presence endowed with a negative property. For example, we see the pure expanse of white *as* an unsigned-upon white expanse, as (so to say) bereft in a certain regard.

In sum, my supposition is that while the object is undoubtedly experienced as privative in a certain respect, it is thus experienced only because of one's presently occurrent *negative belief*. And that the negative belief in the first place arises out of one's seeing what is *there* (in the causally relevant context of an expectation of what will be there). It is *because* one sees the white as white, together with the intervention of a novel belief about what is present and missing, that one experiences the white expanse as privative in a certain respect. There is no intuition of absence.[4] So much for the general category: the perception of absence.

---

[4] *Pace* J.-P. Sartre, *Being and Nothingness*, 10, Methuen, 1957.

(c) The inexistence of negative perceptions

(1) At this point I would like to spell out the general significance of the foregoing discussion in 4(b) (above). I wish to show how it bears upon the enterprise of distinguishing perception and thought.

We know that thoughts, being conceived under the aspect of truth, can as readily take negative as positive propositional objects. If in thinking 'p' we are thinking 'p is true', this is because we can have the thought 'it is false that p', for in thinking 'p' we are consciously *ruling out* the falsity of 'p'. Thus, the very content of thought-experience depends internally on one's capacity to think the negation of the thought. I cannot think 'it is red', unless I can think 'it is not red': I need to be able to think, not merely contraries like 'it is green' or 'it is purple', I need in addition to be able to think the *contradictory*. In sum, thoughts are internally dependent on the capacity of the thinker to think the negation of the thought, which is to say that they are internally dependent on the existence of the afore-mentioned truth-screen (being in agreement or disagreement with Reality in the truth-mode).

Then if perceptions were a sub-variety of thoughts; and/or if they were conceived under the aspect of truth; and/or were in truth-agreement/disagreement with Reality—the same would be true of them. There would need to be an exact perceptual analogue of our capacity to think thoughts with negative propositional content. Such negative-object contrast-cases would be an everyday empirical reality, realized pretty much continually in everyday existence, as common in our perceptual experience as are thoughts like 'I did not turn off the car lights!' in our inner life. It was these considerations which led me just now into a search for perceptions with negative content. And it had at once to be admitted that, on the face of it, such phenomena abound ('I see there's no signature at the end of this letter', 'I see you've lost a front tooth', 'I see you've changed the furniture around in some way'). But only on the face of it, in my opinion. I decided to turn my attention onto the more general phenomenon that we describe as 'the perception of absence', for that seems to be the general type of those experiences that fall under 'perceive that not-p'. The aim of the inquiry being, to discover whether such experiences are to be classed as sub-varieties of perception.

Accordingly, I arrived at analyses both of 'the perception of silence' and 'the perception of absence': roughly, as experienced cognitions which were internally bonded-to and overtly fathered-by contemporaneous perceptual phenomena. Then the significance of such an account of these negative experiences is that set out immediately above. For the question I am concerned to answer is, whether the phenomena we describe as 'the perception of silence' and 'the perception of absence' provide the requisite negative contrast-cases to make the hearing of sounds and the seeing of objects *either* sub-varieties of thoughts *or* at the very least phenomena which agree or disagree with Reality in the truth-mode. As a result of the above analyses, the answer we must give is: no.

(2) It helps to set these findings in context to recall John Searle's general characterization of visual experience. According to Searle, all seeing is a case of seeing-that———,[5] it is an experience whose content is a whole proposition. As Searle expresses it, it is not just that a yellow station wagon is situated in my visual field, and that I see it *as* a yellow station wagon lying in a certain direction. The properly full description of the visual experience, the completed description of the intentionally directed phenomenon of seeing, is according to Searle typified by the utterance: 'I see that there is a yellow station wagon lying in a certain direction from me.' Now this is precisely the kind of account which the theory of perception that I am proposing rejects. My claim is, that while there is indeed such an experience as the above, it is in the first place a purely cognitive experience, and secondly is to be sharply distinguished from the intimately bonded contemporaneous perceptual experience. The theory I am advancing is, that noticing or perceiving is of *things* rather than truths or facts or states of affairs. Perception is as such of objects, events, qualities, and relations. It is of phenomenal realities.

It is of phenomenal realities, and thus invariably of what one might call 'positivities'. But if Searle's analysis was valid, negative perceptions ought to be possible. If what we see is that a certain state of affairs obtains, we ought equally to be capable of seeing that some other state of affairs does not obtain. Now this consideration sets the recent discussion in which we have distinguished thought-experiences from perceptions on the count of their relations to negation, into a wider context that manages to encompass the earlier discussion of seeing-that———, i.e. of 'perceptual discovery experiences' (at the beginning of this chapter). Since thought-experiences and seeing-that experiences are each propositional attitudes, they can each take negative objects, whereas an important consequence of the non-propositional account of perceptual experiences that we have given is that there can be no negative perceptions. There are no negative perceptions, any more than there are negative actions: that is, real actions that are the not-doing of some action. A word now about these last, since the parallels between perception and action on this count are multiple and illuminating. Those parallels extend to the explanation of the property in question.

(d) The inexistence of negative actions

A kind of act-machinery is operative in certain negative situations, which in my view easily misleads us, in effect causing us to hypostatize act-absence. Thus, there can be no doubt that there are such things as freely chosen decisions, and therefore freely formed intentions *not to perform* certain actions, and in addition freely chosen *abstentions from action* which are the expressions of those intentions. For example, I decide not to answer the telephone, and continue sitting and reading; and while I *need not* over that interval be expressing that intention (for I just might have forgotten it), I almost certainly will be—as is shown by my affirming with authority just why it was that telephone-answering did not occur. Now the expression of this

---

[5] *Intentionality*, 40, CUP, 1983.

special variety of intention neither transforms the phenomenon of sitting into an activity, nor ensures that the activity of reading falls under an additional activity-description 'not answering the telephone', nor engenders a special form of doing, nor indeed engenders *anything*. No event falls under 'not answering the telephone'. The chosen abstention from action simply does not 'take place'. It is merely a truth that one does not answer the phone, a truth for which one bears full responsibility. Such an active mode of responsibility for the non-occurrence of action must be sharply distinguished from the genuine act of producing no-change where change is the norm, e.g. balancing motionless on a tightrope. The latter is a real doing, while the former is no more than responsibility for a truth or fact, and it is obscurantism to collapse the performing of an act which consists in the producing of no-change where change is the norm, into the performing of an act which consists in *not* performing an act! The doing of nothing, is simply no doing. A 'negative action' is a contradiction: a nothing that is something!

Then as all actions are real events, and are directed to the production of real events in time, so also in the case of perception. All perceivings are of phenomenal somethings: objects, movements, shapes, holes,[6] colours, pains, relations—many of which have determinate appearances—and corresponding illusions in which appearance and object come apart. But what is the 'look' of no-name? What is the 'sound' of silence?

(e) Review

To review. The 'perception of silence' cannot provide the requisite negative that would make the perception of sound akin to thought. This is because the perception of silence is not a variety of perception. It is merely a rather special sub-variety of perceiving-that. Whereas there is *both* hearing-of a whistle and hearing-that a whistle sounds, there is *only* hearing-that it is silent. There is no such thing as the hearing-of silence: there is merely an absence of hearing-of anything, occurring in a self-conscious setting which is such that a cognitive experience occurs whose content refers to the prevailing silence. However, as we earlier noted, comparable claims cannot be made in the case of darkness, since both the seeing-of dark *and* the seeing-that darkness reigns are realities. In effect, this is because the absence of light

[6] The perception of holes is a true perceiving—but then a hole is not an absence. Even if a hole was an empty portion of space, the portion of space is not the absence of matter from that space; and in any case seeing a hole is neither seeing the *absence of matter* in a space, nor *seeing-that* matter is absent from a space. But anyhow a hole is neither a positive thing nor a negative thing, for it is a spatial quality of its owner. More, it is relative to a description, rather in the manner of shadows, so that it is not even an absolute spatial quality like sphericity. Thus, what is shadow relative to one patch of brightness is a patch of brightness relative to a darker shadow. Somewhat similarly the shape of an object with a hole can be described without recourse to the concept of a hole, indeed without recourse to the concept of negation. For example, one could as well say 'point p is at the bottom of a hole' or 'point p is surrounded by continuous cliffs'. In a word, there is no irreducible concept of negation at work here. This account of the perception of holes is confirmed by the fact that, exactly as bumps have determinate appearances, so too have holes, being phenomenal realities (like shadows). Seeing a hole is a certain way of seeing part of an object's shape, as seeing a shadow is a certain way of seeing the brightness-value of part of an object's surface (a pessimistic way, one might say).

and the presence of dark are separate realities contingently linked.[7] Therefore even though seeing dark is seeing the look that signifies light-absence, seeing the dark look is not *in itself* the seeing of an absence, but is instead the seeing of a presence signifying an absence. By contrast, hearing silence is the experienced cognitive accompaniment of an absence of experience signifying a further absence: it is the accompaniment of a lack of hearing-experience that signifies an absence of shock waves in a medium. And it is itself no form of hearing.

All this is true of the more general perception of absence. There is no perceiving an absence that is not a cognition, a perceiving-that an absence obtains. Real perceiving is invariably of the concrete, and therefore of the fully determinate in all phenomenal respects—which can scarcely be affirmed of negative objects like silence (which lack phenomenal being). In sum, the perception of presences is not opposed to the perception of absences, but to either *not* perceiving at all or to perceiving *other* presences. What one rules out in affirming 'he heard a thump' is not 'he heard a no-thump'/'he heard that there was no thump'. Rather, one rules out 'he did not hear anything'/'the hearing in question was of a whistle (knock, etc.)'. There is no contrast to a situation in which a negative object is perceived. Perception is of 'positivity', all the way.

5. The Concrete Character of Perception

(1) Thus, perception is uniquely of things, a property that emphasizes its unlikeness to *thought*. But it has another related property which does the same—with a vengeance: a property it is natural to describe as the *concreteness* of perception. This is something more than having an object that is a particular here-and-now phenomenal reality. And it is not to be confused with having an indexically given object. Perception gets at things 'in the flesh'.

In effect this property has already been sketched out during the course of the foregoing discussion. The property in question has at least four constituent parts, each of which has been remarked in passing. Namely: the special character of (i) the objects of perception, (ii) the perceptual relation, (iii) the phenomenon of perception itself, and (iv) perceptual validation. The first element we have just noted: that its objects are particular present phenomenal realities. The second concerns the manner in which perception acquires such an item as object, and was remarked earlier. This is mechanistic-causal in character, and to be opposed to the method open to thought and belief, that of concepts. Thus, sheer physical mechanism establishes a concrete link in perception, a contact 'in the flesh', almost an actual bridge or chain. And while a match of experiential content and outer object under minimal headings, such as holds between seeming-to-see a round red patch and the setting sun, is a necessary condition of that contact, only a mechanistic-causal linkage can establish the actual connection.

---

[7] Had we been differently constituted, the absence of light might have looked red: that is, the pre-stimulus neurological *status quo* might have caused or corresponded to red sensation.

The third determinant of the concrete character of the intuitional contact concerns the nature of intuition itself, and was also remarked earlier. Thus, unlike thought and cognitive attitudes generally, the constitutional core of perception is a-conceptual in character. This is apparent in the fact that newly born infants are responsive to and so aware of and thus perceivers of light and sound and pain, quite irrespective of their singling them out *as* anything. Intuitions, which are like physical actions in being eminently susceptible of redescriptive interpretation, are like them also in being—at the centre of the onion-structure of conceptually-determined interpretations—something without need of concepts to be. We require no concepts to see red or hear sound. Neither does one to move an arm. Will and perception are wholly distinct from the understanding, however closely and harmoniously enmeshed these faculties may naturally be.

(2) Each of the above three properties emerged in the course of the comparison of intuition with thought. But the comparison brought out a fourth and even more important (and 'concreteist') property: the mode of agreement and disagreement with Reality that is open to perception. Contrast in this respect veridical perception—and/or successful action—with true belief/thought. Only belief/thought finds its object through concepts, agrees in the truth-mode, and is capable of irreducible negative objects. While thought can range over positive and negative objects, over hypotheticals and modalities and much else, perception and action are alike in being bound to particular positive concrete actualities. There are no negative acts ('not answering the phone'), and all negating acts (murder, smashing, etc.) are *ab initio* willings and creatings (pulling a trigger, moving a hammer, trying to do either). And so it is with perception. It is not just that no perceptions consist in not perceiving something: no perceptions are of negative objects. The peculiar achievements of thought in this regard are simply closed avenues to perception and action. The upshot is, that the perceptual experience acquires its content through the possibility of perceptions with *contrary* content alone. In this it contrasts with the propositional attitude as such.

(3) It is interesting how much is in common between perception and physical action. These two psychological 'originals', the input and output points where mind interacts with the environment, share many important properties. Then how is it that they stand in so different a relation to consciousness? It is true that the mental life of the conscious is an active one, and that consciousness cannot occur without will. Nevertheless, the bond between consciousness and perception seems to be even more intimate. Thus, we saw that perception is a first derivative from awareness: it is awareness taking a non–reflexive extensionally given phenomenal existent as object. Nothing like this holds of will. You can juggle with the concept of awareness as long as you please, but nothing like 'striving' will emerge out of it. The very word 'awareness', which can signify perception or consciousness, points the way to such a conclusion. The most natural image for the emergence of consciousness is of a light going on, and the primary significance of light for man is as that which reveals

335

and makes knowable through sight. It seems that consciousness is in an important sense closer to perception and so also to knowledge than to desire and will, even though the latter are at least as necessary to the realization of our nature, and are perhaps the functional goal of consciousness.

6. A Review of the Present and Previous Two Chapters

Here I call a halt to the discussion. That is, to the investigation of the general nature of perception, which has gone on during the course of this and the previous two chapters. At this point I shall make a few general comments on the foregoing, and briefly summarize some of the central claims.

(a) The definition of perception in terms of consciousness

The aim of this and the last two chapters has been, to give an account of the essential nature of perception in terms of the neglected phenomenon of attention, ultimately in terms of the most central of all psychological phenomena: consciousness. In this way I hope to defeat a particular theory of perception, according to which it is merely the occurrence of an idiosyncratic event which puts one in a position to know about the physical environment. The method of departicularization that I adopted was that of definition via universalities: a dismantling of the concept of perception into fundamental indefinable concepts a priori to any concept of mind. Namely: awareness, and phenomenal existent. Perception simply *is* awareness of a phenomenal existent, where 'aware' has the basic and indefinable sense that it has in 'we are aware of our own experiences'. It is true that for this to be realized the phenomenon in question must take an extensional non-reflexive object (though these concepts are in any case non-idiosyncratic). However, since perception is the only intentionally directed event which discovers its identity under the concept of awareness, the above formula stands unamended. Perception simply *is* awareness acquiring a phenomenal object, in the central experiential sense of 'aware'. Logically, it is the unique case in which the genus term 'awareness' works as a species term: here we have a measure of the universality of the phenomenon! The idiosyncratic and highly contingent character of hearing, smell, and taste (say), tend to mask or obscure this universality of character. Perception is one of the two fundamental functional possibilities of the attention: to harbour experiences, to take phenomenal existents as object.

In what way does this theory explain perception in terms of consciousness? It is significant that the word 'consciousness' has *two* central occurrences: 'thanks to the anaesthetic he lost consciousness' and 'at that precise instant the stream of consciousness stopped.' It is true that the word 'consciousness' is strictly ambiguous here, as between 'state of waking' and 'experience'. But *why* the ambiguity in the first place? It is because the stream of consciousness is the *prime phenomenal manifestation* of consciousness. What the anaesthetic removed was a state that necessarily and immediately reveals its presence in a continuous stream of consciousness. And therefore perception simply *is*, the prime phenomenal manifestation of consciousness managing to acquire a phenomenal existent as object such that object and phenomenal manifestation are given to the subject in the same irreducible sense. When animality awakes in this World, mere physical things are as close to its mind as are its own inner experiences. This is the central message of this entire discussion.

The organized centre of consciousness that we call 'The stream of consciousness', which persists into dreaming and lapses intermittently outside waking, is a system of limited extent. This finitude exerts a causal power in the genesis of perceptual and all other experiences, not unlike that exerted by the walls of a containing room. Thus, it joins the perceived physical object, its internal sensory representative, and generally also to a degree the will, in bringing the event of perception to birth. I hear a message on the radio as a result of a number of factors: because of air-waves, the auditory sensations they engender, my firm decision that the aforementioned 'mental walls' will embrace such an occupant—whatever ejection of present tenants that entails (e.g. the ranting voice coming from the corner)—and the mental space in question. We call these latter two phenomena 'the availability of the attention' and 'its being subject to the will'. Then it is vitally important that we take note of the fact that the 'mental space' of awareness is literally constituted out of, rather than distinct from, the experiences filling the stream of consciousness. Failure to do so leads to a mythology in which Experiential Consciousness is misconceived as a second centre of awareness, a sort of internal gaze trained upon and harbouring in its 'field of view' the immaterial experience-'objects' of the moment! Experiences bring their own awareness with them (rather as material objects bring their own space): they stand in no need of such an 'internal gaze'.

(b) Perception and propositions

This brings me to the content of the present chapter. For what kind of a thing is perceiving, *so* conceived? We have claimed that the essence of perception is that it is the noticing of phenomenal existents. But what order of 'phenomenal existents'? At first one might wish to say: things, and facts. For on the face of it, noticing takes two forms: noticing-of ('I glimpsed her ankle') and noticing-that ('I saw that the roulette wheel had stopped at the number 7'). But here appearances are deceptive. I addressed myself to the elucidation of the second of these phenomena. It emerged that it is a cognitive event, and typically also an experience, of acquiring a belief in a proposition that is closely linked to the perception: a belief which is both constituted in terms of and typically also immediately and overtly caused by the content of the contemporaneous noticing-of. Since noticing-of is irreducible, and not to be explicated in terms of the concept of belief ('inclination to believe', etc.), noticing-of and noticing-that prove to be *different kinds* of phenomena rather than different varieties of the one kind: to wit, a noticing and a believing. This is the nub of the matter. While desire ranges over irreducible direct-object ('to do') and propositional ('that it be so') forms, and imagination does the same (imaginatively seeming to see Banquo/dreaming that you are Napoleon), perception is exclusively directed to particular phenomenal realities—to *things*, broadly understood: objects, events, qualities, relations. The attention takes no propositional objects.

But confusion threatens here. Thus, the conceptualized internal object of perception typically is a structured object. Therefore not only does the perceived object have perceptible parts (e.g. a clearly visible group of soldiers in a painting), the perception of such an object has matching parts as well ('I seem to see a painting containing a group of soldiers'). This conceptual content can easily be confused with a proposition, and cause one to mistake perception and the closely bonded simultaneous event of cognition for a single event. It is easy to confuse an attentive event possessed of a structured internal object and matching cognitive power, with the cognitive event with matching structural content it so naturally engenders, and mentally manufacture thereby an impossible hybrid. We readily transfer the content of the purely cognitive event of perceiving-that into the purely attentive contemporaneous event engendering it. And so we come to believe that the attention, like desire and the imagination, takes both propositional and direct objects. We very naturally take the content 'that a whistle sounds' from out of the cognitive event with such content, and insert it into the perception, and in that way arrive at a mythical attentive event of type hearing with propositional content. And the language—the existence of the speech-form 'hear that p'—encourages this error. And yet that it is an error is evident when one reflects on the irreducibility of hearing to believing, and remembers that hearing that p entails believing that p.

In sum, perception is of phenomenal realities, of direct and not of propositional objects. It is an irreducible *sui generis* mental event, the noticing or awareness of phenomenal existents. And it is non-cognitive in character, despite the fact that it is functionally endowed with the causal power of engendering knowledge whose content matches its causally potent internal object.

The Imagination (1)

Ah, Love! could you and I with Fate conspire
To grasp this sorry Scheme of Things entire,
Would we not shatter it to bits—and then
Remould it nearer to the Heart's Desire!

OMAR KHAYYAM

But, hark, what music?

Pericles, Act V, Scene 1

In Chapter 10 I continued the project of delineating the distinctive character of perception by differentially distinguishing it from two close experiential neighbours,
the 'perceptual discovery experience' and the indexical thought with present phenomenal content. This was accomplished largely through spelling out the diverse
relations of these phenomena to truth and negation. The fact that perception is of
concrete phenomenal realities significantly constrains the type of its objects, proscribing much of the realm accessible to thought. Then it seems to me that one other
close experiential neighbour ought likewise to be differentially distinguished:
namely, perceptual imagining. This also is because of the nature of its objects, for in
this phenomenon we have one of the few experiences in which the mind directly
encounters precisely those concrete items which lie open to perception. Just as we
can see material objects and events and *qualia*, so we can visually imagine those same
items. Charting the diverse experiential relations in which a person might stand
to such concrete perceptible items—the perceptual, cognitive, thinking, and imaginative—helps differentially to reveal the distinctive character of each of those
phenomenal relations. In the present chapter my specific concern is with the imaginative relation. That is, it is with perceptual imagining. However, in order better
to understand this important sub-variety of imagining, I begin by addressing
myself to the topic of the imagination generally.

1. A Classification of 'Imaginative' Items

(1) What is the *imagination*? What is it to *imagine*? These perfectly natural questions already assume too much: the first question assumes there exists something

that is the Imagination, presumably a distinctive faculty; the second that there is some one thing that is the phenomenon of Imagining, doubtless instantiated in diverse phenomenal forms. These assumptions may be valid, but they need not be. We ought not to prejudge these questions. Until we look more closely at 'imaginative' phenomena, we cannot really know how matters actually stand.

I propose to adopt a procedure which does not commit me on these issues. I will first draw up a classification of 'imaginative' items, separate out those phenomena which are imaginings, inspect each variety to see if any properties are common and peculiar to its members, and then look to see whether any properties are common and peculiar to all such types and thus to imagining as such. If there are, those properties ought to be the basis of an answer to the two initial questions (which I now put to one side).

(2) The classification takes this form. I start with the broadest category of all: items which owe their existence to the imagination (a term which I employ without prejudice). They range across material objects (e.g. sculptures), abstract objects (like music or poetry), actions (e.g. miming), perceptual experiences (like looking suitably at a photograph, viz. as showing sights and not just marks on a piece of cardboard), together with imaginings proper (say, mental imagery or phantasizing). Then while some of these items are *exercises of* the imagination, some are merely its *effects*. Thus, a man who mimes being a bear puts his imagination to work, but his acts of shambling and hopping are mere effects of those imaginative processes. By contrast, hallucinations are exercises of the imagination. Roughly, those items that are products but not uses of the imagination are only inessentially such. Thus, a fictional novel *might have been* a factual reporting which owed nothing to the imagination. By contrast, those products of the imagination that are also imaginings are for the most part essentially so (e.g. mental imagery and day-dreaming). My concern in this chapter is with the latter kind of phenomena—with 'exercises of the imagination'—exclusively.

'Exercises of the imagination' fall into at least three groups. (α) Imaginings taking a propositional object: say, the imaginings occurring in the mind of a man inventing a story. The remaining two groups take non-propositional objects. Thus, the group (β) consists of imaginative perceptions: say, looking in the right way at a photograph. The third group (γ) consists of perceptual imaginings: say, visual hallucinations or mental imagery. I sum up these classificatory facts in Figure 11.1.

(3) I have singled out three differerent varieties of imaginative phenomena (viz. the three kinds of 'exercises of the imagination'). Thus: α (propositional imaginings), β (imaginative perceivings), and γ (perceptual imaginings). I will examine them in turn, in the hope of uncovering properties common and peculiar to the lot. I have two main goals. First, to discover whether anything *makes* an imagining an imagining, and thus whether there exist defining marks of being an imagining, and so an analysis of the concept. And secondly, to discover whether imaginative

340

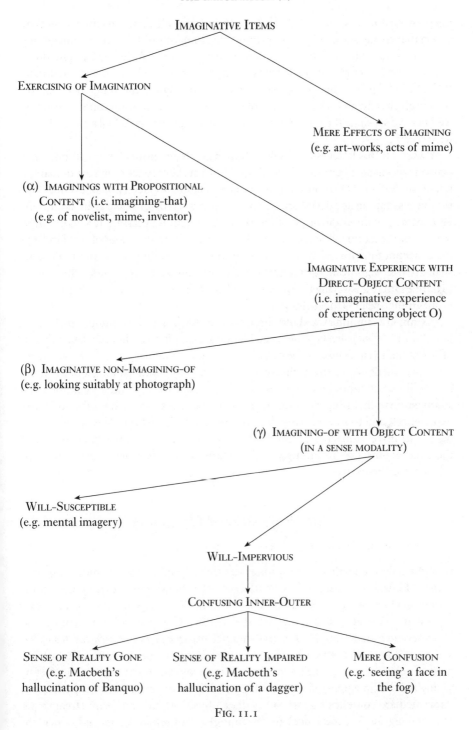

Fig. 11.1

phenomena are constitutively (or essentially, intrinsically, etc.) imaginative in type, and in that strong sense *sui generis* phenomena. Thinking of the fact that imaginings draw their raw material from our awarenesses of the World, one might doubt this last, for it seems as if imaginings might be constituted out of such materials. (Cf. Hume's 'pale copies of perceptions'.) Thinking on the other hand of the seemingly irreducible character of phenomena like mental imagery, one might well believe so, since the imaginative use of those raw materials looks on the face of it *sui generis*.

A word on this latter issue. Talk of 'intrinsic'/'constitutive' in the mind, while prima facie suspect because of the ubiquity of causal necessities in that domain, is not as such illicit. Thus, intentions are non-relationally determined even though they necessitate an act-desire origin, since nothing is redescribable as an 'intention'. By contrast, an intention origin with requisite content is necessary if a bodily striving is to be redescribable as (say) a searching or a flight. Distinctions of this kind give the concept of intrinsicality scope in the mind, however limited in extent. Then we shall discover significant differences between imaginings on this count which prove to be relevant to answering the questions asked at the beginning of the chapter: what is imagining? what is the imagination?

In sum, in examining the above three varieties (α, β, γ) of imagining, I am looking both for the *defining marks* of being an imagining, and for whether the determinants of being such as to exhibit those marks are *constitutive or relational*. Whatever properties are worth inspecting in this search for common ground amongst imaginings, they will one assumes be either relational or constitutive in kind. Then foremost amongst relational properties must surely be the causal properties of imaginative experiences, and most especially their origin properties. Meanwhile, when I speak of 'constitutive properties', I am thinking of such things as the characteristics of the internal object of imaginings, say its determinacy-properties. I turn now to the phenomena themselves.

2. (α) Propositional Imagining

(a) 'Propositional imaginings' versus 'direct-object imaginings'

It might at first seem that all imagining is a case of imagining that some proposition is true. Thus, it is natural to say of Macbeth that he imagined that he was seeing a dagger. However it is not strictly correct to do so, if only because Shakespeare represents Macbeth as in doubt on the matter. This particular imagining was an experience that (simply) *was* (no more than) *seemingly experiencing seeing-of-a-dagger*. Thus, that which is imagined here is an *experience*, rather than that a proposition concerning one's experience is true, and we might register this fact by saying that 'he imagines-of seeing a dagger'. His imagining takes an experience as its immediate content or as its 'immediate object'. It has the form: (Imagining-of) (Having an X-experience) or (Seeming) (X-experience); indeed, since the experience is of some object O, it has the form: (Seeming) (X-experience of object O). Meanwhile, there exist other imaginings which are not seeming X-experiences of objects, but are instead seeming cognitive relations to fact. Indeed, the two kinds frequently occur together in the one situation: Macbeth imagined *seeing Banquo* (i.e. he hallucinatorially saw) and in addition imagined *that it was true that* Banquo was present (i.e. he delusionally believed). I have tried to capture this difference by describing the latter delusion as a 'propositional imagining'. Whereas imagining-of a perception conjures up an experience whose perceptual status is in doubt, imagining-that something is true conjures up a seeming-fact whose factuality is in doubt. It is this latter mode of imagining that I am describing as 'propositional imagining'. Propositional imagining (α) is imagining that it is true that p. I now begin the general inquiry into imagining, by examining this propositional sub-variety.

(b) Active ('make-believe') propositional imagining

(1) Propositional imagining takes *two* main forms. First, a typically active experienced form in which a quasi-believing of quasi-fact occurs; second, an inactive non-experiential form in which a real believing of seeming-fact occurs. I shall briefly examine both varieties, in search of properties that are relevant to their status as imaginings.

Consider the active ('make believe') experienced form. The situation I shall discuss is that in which a man is narrating aloud to some children a story he is inventing on the spot. Clearly this man is imagining that certain states of affairs are realities: for example, he is imagining that a prince is journeying through a dark forest in a strange land. However, neither his acts of vocalizing, nor the speech-intentions to which they give expression, can be identified with the process of imagining. In between the originating intention of uttering a spontaneously invented story, and the vocal intentions and actions to which that intention gives rise, lies a processive continuity of internal imaginative experience. I say so because this man's mind is surely 'elsewhere' as he talks, being alongside the unreal events and situations which he threads into his narrative. Indeed, a characteristic physiognomy and demeanour tend to betray this fact: a faraway look in the eyes, a certain seriousness, a tone of voice, etc.

Why are we convinced that the above internal process is an *imagining*? Its very special origin must be one of the determining factors. That origin is a specific desire and intention, viz. to narrate the kind of narrative fact-narrators narrate—without narrating fact! This speaker intends to tell a story of 'unreals' in which the constraints imposed by Reality are severed, throwing memory, knowledge, and belief to the winds, turning instead to his own mind as final cause. And yet the words that emerge are not the chaos that infinite self-determination would entail. Evidently not *all* constraints have been abandoned in this enterprise, for the speaker assembles a structured intelligible verbal entity. Then the constraint determining this order lies in the fact that the process of speaking is *modelled upon* truth-telling, despite being generated by an intention which is expressly to narrate falsity. Such an origin automatically embeds the resulting words in a determinate verbal structure: falsity, after all, is structured, having determinate content. And, of course, it is not just *any old* falsity that concerns this speaker, say the falsity of something which he read in the paper that day: his interests are not so *negative*. Just as expressly, the intent is to narrate falsity which has the dual property of being liable to interest the children and of emerging in entirety from *the mind of the narrator* (and so, in a sense, from nothing).

(2) So why once again is it that we believe that the internal or 'private' experiences of this spontaneous fiction-narrator are imaginings? Consider the properties of those experiences, beginning with their causal properties (including those just noted above). The *origin* of that inner process is an intention directed to the production of what is at once modelled on 'a recording of reality' and yet paradoxically is of 'unreals' originating from the subject's own mind. Such unusual origins plainly have much to do with the narrative counting as 'a work of the imagination', and therefore also much to do with the creative mental processes being an imagining. By contrast, the *effect-characteristics* of the imagining, such as its cognitive ineffectuality, seem less relevant.

What of *constitutive characteristics*? One relevant constitutive trait is, that the internal objects of the process are experienced as falsities whose final source is his own mind: the imagining is directed *to* 'unreals' and *as* 'unreals' of *his* making, it is overtly concerned with 'unreals' emanating from his mind and not from Reality.

The conjunction of these origin and constitutive properties determines the imaginative character of this active variety of propositional imagining. And yet it is clear that neither property makes this active process of imagining-that into something which is wholly and absolutely *sui generis*. Thus, it cannot be an altogether *different type* of experience from that of a man who is narrating fact. For they are surely both forms of *thinking*. That is, the active self-conscious variety of imagining-that ought not to be *opposed* to thinking, being instead a sub-variety of the kind. A scientist who conjures up in his mind some experimental possibility, is both thinking *and* imagining that something is the case. So, likewise, here.

(c) Inactive (delusional) propositional imagining

The second and remaining variety of imagining-that is neither an experience, nor active in type. It is best exemplified in the phenomenon of dreaming, about which I now briefly speak.

Dreaming is a complex phenomenon which *is* (seemingly) (the conscious inner life of the wakeful). Typically dreaming has components: dream experiences ('dream seeing', 'dream agency', 'dream thoughts'), and conscious non-experience states ('dream believings'). For example, I dream (*seem to see* a tiger) *and also* dream (*that* a tiger is present), and the latter is distinct from the former. But why assume dream beliefs actually exist? The evidence for the reality of dream-belief is twofold: the character of the dream-report, and affect both within and without the dream. Thus, normally the dream-report of (say) one's 'perceptions' avails itself of the language of firm cognitive commitment to their content, and the attendant affect is typically consonant with this reading—such as fear in the dream at the presence of a tiger and relief upon awakening. Conscious but unexperienced cognitive commitment to the reality of what is seemingly perceived, is a typical constituent of dreams. Then this continuous inactive unexperienced cognitive phenomenon is an example of the second variety of imagining-that.

What attests to the imagining-status of these believings? Origins are a crucial factor in this case also. The origins of the dream, and therefore of its belief-elements, are the capacity to dream, the loss of consciousness and one's sense of Reality, and certain psycho-cerebral imponderables. Each is causally necessary. Now the loss of Reality-sense determines the non-rationality of dream-belief, and thereby at one stroke severs the binding constraint of Reality. This origin-property, in conjunction with the fact that dreams are modelled on waking experience of the World, determines the imaginative status of these beliefs.

(d) The non-cognitive character of propositional imaginings generally

One interesting property of imaginings-that generally—which I shall spell out in a moment below—plays a vitally important part in determining the imaginative status of both of the above forms of imagining-that. We come across this property when we consider the fact that, unlike the propositional imaginings of fiction-narrators, which are merely 'as if' beliefs, those of dreamers are real beliefs which posit their propositional object as true. The question naturally arises as to the *truth possibilities* and the *cognitive possibilities* of propositional imaginings. Let us consider these two issues in turn.

All imagination feeds upon Reality: real people, real types, even real events, are its raw material, and a novel like *War and Peace* is particularly instructive in this regard. Thus, if I report a dream and say 'I was in Paris', then both 'I' and 'Paris' successfully refer—which evidences a relatively robust relation with the World. Then suppose that I happened to be in Paris as I dreamed, would that make my dream-belief true? I think it would, as the following brings out. Suppose Banquo had not died from his wounds, and by some astonishing means coincidentally stood quite invisibly just where Macbeth hallucinated him, would Macbeth's belief that Banquo was at the table have been true? Surely, yes (whatever else it is). Similarly with dream-belief. Thus, propositional imaginings can be true. Propositional imaginings can be *real* beliefs, directed to *realities*, and *as* realities, which are *true*. And yet it is clear that their truth must be *accidental*. No propositional imagining can be a *knowing*. Here we have a universal relational determinant of their imagining status. It governs both (make-believe) quasi-believings and actual (delusional) believings. Propositional imagining is as such out of the cognitive circuit.

(e) A summary of the determinants of (α) propositional imagining

(1) *Origin-properties* are decisive in determining the imagining status of pro-positional imaginings. A necessary condition of a seeming-belief being an imagining-that is, that its origins so lie in the subject's mind that the constraint of Reality is avoided: no accredited mode of belief-formation operates, and knowledge must be unrealizable. However, since this is true also of irrational belief, we need a more differential statement of the origin-property of these particular imaginings. Then I suggest the following disjunctive origin-property as a logically necessary and sufficient condition (a condition ensuring that propositional imaginings cannot be knowledge, since in each case the mind is final cause).

> *Either* (i) the 'belief' has a will-origin which is directed to the generation of quasi-belief in 'unreals';
>
> *Or* (ii) an origin consisting in weakening-of-Reality-sense.

What of *constitutive properties*? The example of the spontaneous narrator of pure fiction raised hopes of discovering universal constitutive traits of pro-positional imaginings. After all, this imagining-that 'belief' is a mere quasi-belief (a 'suspension of disbelief' non-belief), which is directed to 'unreals', and as 'unreals'. However, none of this holds of the propositional imaginings of dreamers and madmen. These are real beliefs, directed often to real entities, *qua* in real situations, and are even occasionally true. The general conclusion must be that there are *no* universal constitutive determinants of being an imagining-that. And the overall conclusion must be that origins are the sole universal determinant in their case.

(2) The origins of propositional imaginings are such as to ensure that these imaginings cannot be knowings. They therefore guarantee that propositional imag-inings cannot instantiate the cognitive prototype upon which they are modelled. Therefore even though the constitutive traits exemplified by the internal object in self-conscious cases—being a mere quasi-belief that is directed to 'unreals' as 'unreals'—are not universal to the genus, the self-conscious case reveals a closely related and important truth which is concealed from view in unselfconscious cases. Namely, that the cognitive prototype for propositional imaginings is of necessity unrealized. Here we have a first significant hint as to the analysis of the concept of imagining.

3. (β) Imaginative Perception

(1) The remaining two categories of imaginative experience—dubbed by me β and γ—are directed to non-propositional 'direct objects'. These are experiences which take experiences of objects as their 'immediate object': they are the experiences of imagining-of (having [perceptual] experiences of events and people and things, etc.). And it is evident that they cannot be construed as directed to propositional

objects: for example, visual hallucinating is not imagining-*that* you see something. Then the variety (β) of imaginative experience we now discuss, is the odd man out among these direct-object imaginative experiences. It is the perplexing category of *imaginative non-imagining*. And by that I mean, those perceptual experiences in which the imagination openly assists in generating the internal object of the perceptual experience. Say, looking at a photograph of a landscape in the proper imaginative way (as opposed to looking at it as one might at a haphazard array of marks on a surface).

In what way does looking at a photograph utilize the imagination? Not, I think, in interpretationally pressing into use in the experience concepts whose content exceeds mere sense. After all, most visual experiences have a content well in excess of sheer colours and contours. Indeed, merely to see coloured photographic expanses sited in one's visual field *as* areas on a two-dimensional surface-plane that is tilted and set in three-dimensional space, is in that sense already interpretational. Where the imagination openly enters, is in the imposition of a special *second-order interpretation* upon the first. This second-order interpretation has certain interesting properties, which I will now spell out. One is, that it is not a distinct phenomenon in its own right, for it internally depends upon seeing the coloured expanses (as seeing those colours does not on it). It consists in seeing expanses of colour in such a way that, while remaining expanses of colour for one, they simultaneously in a special imaginative sense *bring a landscape into view*. For there are not *two* phenomena here: seeing coloured expanses on a piece of cardboard *and* seeing a landscape in a photograph. There is one complex phenomenon with two internal objects: namely, coloured expanses and landscape—the latter being second-order to the former. This complex phenomenon is therefore of the type, seeing, and not of the type, imagining. And that is why I describe it as *imaginative seeing* rather than as *visual imagining*.

(2) The next thing to say about the second-order interpretation is, that it is imposed on material whose visible elements stand in *projective relation* to the visible elements of the imagined object. And yet it is clear that such a projective relation cannot hold between *all* elements in the imaginative interpretation and elements in the visible interpretee: the one is not a simple replica of the other. After all, the coloured expanses on the photo surface do not *look like* a landscape, either in the round or from a point of view. If they did, the imagination would lack the necessary foothold for this kind of imagining. Thus, a perfect replica of a person at Madame Tussaud's does not give scope for an exercise of the imagination of this kind. A *difference* in appearance is a necessary condition of such imaginative work. Meanwhile the projective element guarantees a *similarity* in appearance. For it is important that the coloured expanses on the photographic surface share *some* appearance with (say) a landscape (from a point of view), such as a common contour and colour-distribution. Indeed, it is precisely this combination, of not-looking-like *and* having-some-looks-in-common, that provides the necessary foothold for the im-

agination in its special task of helping to constitute this special case of seeing. While it is open to the imagination to decline the option, the important thing is that the option or foothold exists. In a special imaginative sense a landscape is visible in these marks. It is visible to those who both know the look of landscapes and possess the art of imposing the second-order imaginative interpretation upon suitable patches located on surfaces. And yet in fact the landscape that 'appears' to one is invisible to one there and then as one inspects the image: *nothing* is there besides marks on a surface, i.e. a photograph!

Looking imaginatively at a photograph is like looking through a window onto a scene—with a difference. Something seems to open out behind the surface, a space of three dimensions appears to come into view, so that it resembles looking through an aperture into an illuminated box or stage-model—with a difference. The difference is such that it is precisely *not* visually the same, and the viewer sees it both *as* and *to be* so. If he did not, and if it was to him visually identical, there would be no scope precisely for the form of imagination we are purporting to characterize. This non-visual going-beyond in the very midst of vision itself, this flowering of a non-visual kind within a visual experience, is nonetheless a quasi-visual development or enhancement. Vision is its model, and the imagination its purveyor.

The fact that a discrepancy in appearance is a necessary condition of this exercise of the imagination, hints at something about imaginings generally. It suggests what is in effect a partial answer to one of the two central questions of this chapter, viz. what is an imagining? Namely: that imagining is *never* the same as what we imagine ('the real thing'), that it is always merely quasi- or modelled upon 'the real thing'. While the modes of being quasi- vary from imaginative type to imaginative type, the merely as-if character seems like a constant factor. Indeed, in direct-object cases the property of being merely as-if may be intrinsic. So, at any rate, I suspect. It is certainly true of the present case, bearing in mind the constitutive character of these phenomena. What is special about this particular variety of imagining is, that the raw materials on which the imagination works are located *within the very experience* that is in part its handiwork. This is a cause of puzzlement, and of properly philosophical interest.

(3) I return to the central issue. What accounts for the imaginative character of imaginative seeing? What determines it? Consider the causal and constitutive properties of the phenomenon, starting with the former.

Imaginative seeing, say of a photograph of a landscape, is caused by a non-landscape-look that encompasses part of a landscape-look, acting in conjunction with an internal factor, the capacity to imaginatively see. Such origins determine an effect-property, for the presence of the latter element in the origins ensures the epistemological functionlessness of the imaginative second-order interpretations. The 'leap' in object-content that occurs when a landscape comes imaginatively to view in an array of coloured patches, is not comparable to the 'leap' in object-content that constitutes a widening of perceptual consciousness—as when we suddenly see what we took to be a smudge of green paint on a window *as* the green of a distant meadow: it opens the door to imaginative, but scarcely to perceptual acquaintance. In a word, the normal causes of seeing are inoperative, and as a result the perceptual prototype for this form of imagining is certain not be instantiated in such cases. Then such *origin-properties*, together with the *effect-property* of failing to cause belief in the presence of its object (unlike the seeing of the above meadow), must play a part in determining the imaginativeness of these phenomena.

Do *constitutive* traits also determine imaginativeness in this case? I think so. It is not just that a landscape is not perceived. What is also relevant is that we encounter an avowed negative in the internal object of the imaginative experience. This quasi-perception of a landscape is not merely *not* a perception of a landscape: it is *avowedly* so: it is avowedly an 'unreal' perception of such an object. Such 'seeing' of a landscape is not merely relationally dissimilar from perceptual experience, it is *intrinsically* dissimilar, and the dissimilarity has entered the very content of the experience. The experience is *overtly* merely quasi-. It is like a form of conscious play at seeing a landscape. This is relevant to its imaginative character, and is a preliminary pointer to the general thesis mentioned above. Namely: that all imaginings are of necessity *merely quasi-* their cognitive or perceptual prototype. And it suggests that direct-object imaginings generally might be intrinsically so.

4. (γ) Perceptual Imagining (1): Causal Properties

I pass now to what, from the point of view of philosophy, is the most fruitful area for study: perceptual imagining. I opt for the visual variety, largely because the richness of the sense reappears in its imaginative reincarnation. In the present Section 4 I examine the causal properties of visual imaginings, while in the succeeding Section 5 I consider their constitutive properties.

There are at least three main kinds of visual imagining: mental imagery, visual hallucination, and 'dream seeing'. A word about each. *Mental imagery* comes in several varieties: the normal 'seeing in the mind's eye', the hypnagogic image (in which the image is frequently experienced in a direction and is endowed with superabundant detail), and the rather 'thin' and unconvincing case in which one might voluntarily imaginatively position an object at a point in visible space. The second main form of visual imagining is the *visual hallucination*, a phenomenon which can be conveniently grouped into those hallucinations experienced with belief (such as Macbeth's hallucination of Banquo), those which leave one in doubt (like Macbeth's hallucination of a dagger), and those one knows to be illusory (say, in the first stages of mescalin intoxication). A third variety of visual imagining is '*dream seeing*', which is distinguishable from the other two kinds (from hallucinations notably in its dispensing with an actual visual field) but about which I shall have little to say. I begin by attempting to delimit the most problematic of the above three kinds, the hallucination. I do so for two reasons: because its status as an imagining is put into doubt by the claims of some philosophers, and because I want to prepare the way for a theory I shall soon defend, viz. that perceptual imaginings are constitutively or intrinsically imaginings.

(a) Defining the hallucination

(1) Some philosophers describe psychotic 'seeing' *and* gross visual illusions as 'hallucinations'. It is a substantive issue whether they are right to do so. In my opinion they are not: I believe they confuse visual imagining and visual experience. An example helps to clarify what I mean. Suppose that scientists projected light-images of pink elephants onto my retina, so that I see pink elephants in mid-air (call them 'Reality Visions'). Then seeing the reality-vision is I suggest a *different experience* from an alcoholic 'seeing' of pink elephants: the former is a visual experience, the latter a visual imagining. That both are non-veridical 'seem-seeings' does not in itself automatically justify applying the concept of hallucination to both—else we should apply it to mental images. I submit that nothing could. No common nature is realized in these two phenomenal types. So, at any rate, I shall argue.

This substantive claim is best defended by defining 'hallucination'. Here are some of the necessary conditions of a visual hallucination:

H$_1$. Over area A of an actually existing visual field the subject seems to see some object O, i.e. a seeming visual experience E with direct object O occurs.

H$_2$. Experience E is indistinguishable to the subject from a visual experience of seeing O.

H$_3$. Experience E is not a seeing of O.

This still leaves it open that E might be of a visual illusion rather than a hallucination. For example, an *objective illusion*—as one could call them—such as a mirage, 'bent' stick, 'floater', or after-image—might have been actually seen. Accordingly, we now insert a clause to block the possibility that the explanation of E's not being a seeing of O lies in the ancestry of the visual field.

H$_4$. The non-veridicality of experience E is not due to the fact that area A lacks the regular physical causal ancestry requisite for the presence in the visual field of an O at A.

(After all, the real living and clearly visible Banquo might have stood exactly at the point at table and in Macbeth's visual field where Macbeth hallucinated him! This is one unusual way of managing not to see what is in your visual field! Here the visual field actually contains O, and thus area A must have the requisite ancestry for the presence of O in the visual field, and yet it harbours an hallucination of O precisely at the site of O!)

H$_1$–H$_4$ still leaves it open that E might be a *subjective illusion*—as one might describe (say) the Müller–Lyer phenomena. These last owe their existence to aberration, not in the ancestry of the visual field, but in the causal line between visual field and visual experience, and generally to psychological influences. It is *human mental nature* which lies at the root of the Müller–Lyer and moon-illusions, and one can easily imagine visually capable 'Martians' not experiencing them. By contrast, 'bent' sticks can be photographed, and should look bent to any 'Martian' who 'sees straight'! How are we to block the possibility that the putative hallucination of O is a merely subjective illusion? What distinguishes subjective illusions from hallucinations? It is a fine point, but one difference is that whereas hallucinations are not perceptions of *anything*, subjective illusions are *distorted perceptions*. In subjective illusions we *see* the item in question, only incorrectly. Accordingly, I add:

H_5. In experience E *nothing* is seen in seeming to see O.

(And although it is part of what I hope to demonstrate, I might have added:

H_6. Experience E is not a visual experience).

(2) I propose H_1–H_5 as necessary and sufficient conditions of visual hallucinations. Indeed, H_5 makes H_3 and H_4 otiose, and we are left with H_1 & H_2 & H_5 as a necessary and sufficient set: a visual hallucination is an apparent visual experience that is the seeing of *nothing*. However, people of a Naïve Realist persuasion may think that when I 'see' pink elephants that are generated by bizarre retinal phenomena then I also see *nothing*, may point out that this is not an imagining, and so reject the analysis. How to cope with this difficulty? While their characterization of these objective illusions strikes me as implausible in the extreme, a definition in terms of H_1–H_5 meets the objection. In any case, it is surely as obvious as anything can be that the 'retinal elephants' are real presences in the visual field.

And so the visual hallucination is an experience of seeming to see some O at a sector A of an actually existing visual field, that is to the subject indistinguishable from the visual experience of seeing O at A, and that is the seeing of *nothing*. Here we have an X which *no* physical device can remove—without first affecting the mind (in the imagination, negatively).

(b) The causal properties of visual imaginings in general

(1) So much for the delimitation of the hallucination, and for classifying it as an imagining. I turn now to the full spectrum of visual imaginings. What is it that makes all of these phenomena visual imaginings? Consider their *origin-properties*. One constant factor emerges.

Let us begin with the mental image. Now we know that mental images can be conjured into and out of existence at will, that they often arise and depart unbidden, and that the will lacks here the decisive and total control encountered in the willing of bodily movements. And so we may say that imagery at all times owes its existence to factors which are at any rate *susceptible* to the directives of the will. Their arrival is sometimes in our hands, and when it is not their persistence is something for which we bear a *limited measure* of willing responsibility. Will-susceptibility is a constant necessary factor in their occurrence.

The remaining two main varieties of visual imagination reveal an antithetical state of affairs. Thus, we are completely without choice as to whether we 'dream see' or hallucinate. And yet a different but equally constant causal factor appears in these cases (which we encountered earlier in certain propositional imaginings). Namely, a confusion of inner and outer reality that all but invariably proceeds from a disturbance of one's sense of reality. This factor is far from being a *sufficient condition* of the phenomenon in question, any more than is will-susceptibility in the case of mental imagery, since imponderables always play a part. Nevertheless, some measure of weakening of one's sense of reality functions as a *necessary condition* of the phenomenon. In every example of these two varieties of visual imagining the imagination substitutes its own objects for those of perception, and thus in the place of reality. This internal or mental cause I shall refer to as 'reality-weakening'.

Accordingly, the *origin-properties* of perceptual imaginings divide into: will-susceptibility (re imagining) *or* reality-weakening. Either one of these factors governs any case, or the other does, and never both. This divide is reflected in the *effect-properties* of perceptual imaginings. For precisely where will-susceptibility reigns, disbelief is a necessary concomitant, and precisely where reality-weakening reigns, belief tends to follow and to an extent that matches the extent of the weakening. And this in turn is reflected in a *constitutive property*. Namely: precisely where will-susceptibility reigns, the object is posited as unreal, and precisely where reality-weakening is a determinant, the object is posited as real to an extent that matches the extent of that weakening. In a word, where the object is avowedly merely imagined, disbelief occurs, and where the object is putatively real, belief to an extent which precisely matches the extent of that putative reality generally follows.

(2) One other universal necessary origin-property of all perceptual imaginings must be noted. It consists in the *absence* of the normal causal determinants of the perception being imagined (a property in line with the cognitive uselessness of propositional imaginings). That absence might take the concrete form of a breakdown somewhere in an actual perceptual causal transaction. For example, the breakdown in the perceptual causal pathway that is necessary if (say) an hallucination is to be occurring, might take place at a very late mentalistic ('processing') stage of an inner-to-outer seemingly perceptual transaction. Thus, it is in principle possible for a man whose visual field is *actually* and *completely* filled by the red of some wall, to be caused by that visually presented red to seem to see red from one end of his visual field to the other—hallucinatorially! If he was 'unhinged', and the red of the wall caused him (rather like Macbeth) to think of all the blood he had shed, which in a sort of ecstacy of intolerance his imagination proceeded to disgorge into his visual field. While the *actual presence* of red in his visual field is caused in normal

optico–ocular mechanistic manner, and while the latter visual presence causes the experience in question, it is in the *mode of production* whereby this visually presented red brings about the experience of seeming to see red that the required breakdown in the normal perceptual causal connection occurs. What we find here is not the usual immediate 1–1 causal transaction between sense-datum and attention that is obligatorily encountered in normal colour perception, but a mediate and *meaning-laden journey* which in this case passes through the conscience, indeed through the very soul, issuing in an imaginative rather than attentive event. This constitutes a breakdown in the working of the perceptual system.

(3) The summary situation concerning the *causal properties* of (γ) perceptual imaginings is as follows. The necessary origin-properties are:

A. Absence of the normal causes of perception, and
B. *either* will-susceptibility to imagining *or* reality-weakening;

   while the necessary effect-property is:

C. Belief follows on the heels of imagining to the extent that reality-weakening is a cause, and disbelief to the extent will-susceptibility is.

5. (γ) Perceptual Imagining (2): Constitutive Properties

Here in Section 5 I turn to an examination of the other main variety of property that we assume to be relevant to the imaginative status of perceptual imaginings, namely their constitutive properties.

(a) An either / or constitutive property of (γ) perceptual imaginings

Do any constitutive properties of (γ) (visual imaginings) determine their being imaginings? Might all visual imaginings be *de re* essentially imaginings? My own suspicion is, that this is how matters stand. In any case, we discover a lead on this issue from (α) *propositional imaginings* and (β) *imaginative perceptions.* Now both the active form of (α) (e.g. fiction creation), and (β) (imaginative perception), share the common property of positing both the putative cognitive-contact (knowledge, perception) and its object (fact, perceptible) as *unreal.* In other words, what one might call the 'cognitive prototypes' of these imaginings, as well as their imagined objects, are in these experiences given as mere 'play versions'. This raises hopes that we might have uncovered in this trait a constitutive characteristic universal to imaginings as such. However, the inactive variety of (α), namely delusional imagining-that, demonstrates that nothing akin to 'play' holds across the entire imagining genus. Nevertheless, a closely related *disjunctive property* proves after all to be common to (α) and (β) phenomena. Thus: to the extent the imagining is insightfully experienced as *imagining*, to that same extent both the putative cognitive-contact and its object are given as *unreal*, while to the extent the imagining is not so experienced, putative cognitive-contact and its object are given as *real.*

Turn now to the variety of imagination under examination, (γ) visual imaginings. Here we discover an exactly comparable situation. Thus, mental imagery is at once will-susceptible, and experienced as *imagining* and as the '*unreal seeing*' of an '*unreally presented object*'. This likewise raises hopes that one has uncovered a universal constitutive property of (γ) visual imaginings. However, once again the inactive varieties of the kind disprove the theory. 'Dream seeing' is mostly experienced as a real seeing of a real presence, and visual hallucinations are invariably experienced as visual experiences. In short, no property akin to 'play' is essential to visual imagining. And yet another related (disjunctive) property proves after all true of visual imaginings. Thus, to the extent a visual imagining is insightfully experienced as *imagining*, to that extent it is experienced as a mere *quasi-seeing* of an '*unreal presence*', while to the extent it is *not* so insightfully experienced as imagining, to that same extent it is experienced as a true seeing of a real presence. We just now encountered the identical disjunctive property in the other two main varieties of imagining (i.e. of 'exercises of the imagination'): namely, in both (α) ('propositional imagining') and (β) ('imaginative perception'). It is a universal property of imaginings.

(b) The intrinsic character of perceptual imaginings generally

The above property provides a lead concerning the intrinsic essence of perceptual imagining. In a situation of self-conscious insight visual imagining is revealed as a merely quasi-visual imaginative experience of 'unreals'. Then might this be a universal property of visual imaginings? Could it be that it is detected in the case of mental images *precisely because* insight there obtains? Might it be equally present in the other phenomena but obscured, precisely because insight is there absent? So I suspect. If it is true, visual imaginings will be constitutively imaginings. They must in themselves or intrinsically be incapable of being visual perceptions. They must as such be non-visual experiences

Are visual imaginings as such non-visual experiences? One prima-facie counter-example is the hallucination. Visual hallucinations are experienced as visual experiences, and this is a prima facie reason for believing them visual experiences. After all, experiences tend to be self-identifying. And yet this justification, which appeals to Cartesian translucency, is not absolute. While Cartesian translucency is a real phenomenon, it has limits. One such is the state of mind of the subject, peering into the supposedly crystal clear waters of his own mind. The mental eyesight of this observer can, I suggest, be misted over, not by obscuring mental *visibilia*, but by the fog of his own unreason. Hallucinators are mostly 'not themselves'. Why trust the introspective deliverances of a being in such a state? If dreamers can 'see' that 1 and 1 make 3, if in short they can misidentify events in their Understanding, why should not hallucinators fall into gross introspective error?

I shall argue that this is how matters stand with visual hallucinations. And I shall argue that the visual hallucination is a seem-seeing that is *not* visual experience.

Indeed, I will argue that this is true of visual imagining *as such*, which is a seem-seeing that is the seeing of nothing. The theory therefore is that the hallucination is the sub-variety of visual imaginings, directed to objects set in a real visual field, which is to the subject indistinguishable from visual experience. Meanwhile, the other varieties of visual imagining prove to be definable along comparable lines. Mental imagery is the sub-variety of visual imagining that is openly given as a *merely* quasi-seeing. And so on. These claims I hope now to justify.

(c) Visual imagining and the attention

(1) How to prove that visual imaginings as such are not visual experiences? I believe it is best accomplished through showing they are not *attentive* events. Now even the most unveridical visual experience is a form of attending: to wit, a noticing-of. Seeing a 'reality vision' of pink elephants that is caused by retinal interference is a visual attentive experience, even though nothing publicly visible is on view. I hope to show visual imaginings cannot be of this ilk, to show for example that Macbeth's seem-seeing of a dagger cannot be attentive in character. Now while some people believe all visual experiences are caused by a distinct psychological *visibilium*, namely a sense-datum, and many people do not, we can surely all agree that it is wildly unlikely that Macbeth's seem-seeing was caused by a distinct dagger-like psychological *visibilium*. It follows that proponents of sense-data could argue that hallucinations, indeed that visual imagining as such, must be non-attentive in character, through arguing that visual experience invariably entails a *three-term* situation, involving subject/seem-seeing/sense-datum, whereas visual imagining is a merely *two-term* situation, involving no more than a subject and a seem-seeing. In my opinion, this argument is valid and demonstrates the alleged dissimilarity of nature. However, it may not convince a Naïve Realist, so I turn instead to a different argument.

(2) The aim is to prove that visual imaginings are not visual experiences, and to do so by showing they are not attentive experiences. Then I think this can be achieved through appeal to the concept: *being an unrecorded part of what is present to attentive consciousness*. This well-formed concept is invariably applicable in perceptual situations. For example, it is applicable to (say) a particular face during a (brief, momentary) glimpsing of (say) 55 people who are noticed merely *qua* 'crowd of faces'. It is precisely the fact that the face was *present in the visual field* that was causally contributory to the noticing of the crowd. It was nothing less, nothing earlier in the causal transaction. It is not just that the light-image of that face on the retina causally contributed to the event. Rather, the light-image was thus causally contributory *precisely through* causing the presence of a face at a point in the visual field at the very instant a 'mere crowd' was noticed.

I know of no proper analogue in perceptual imagining. Consider what is perhaps the most plausible counter-example: an eidetic memory-image of a recent complex sight like a crowd, which as one studies it reveals image after image of each

355

individual face as it was at the time. Here one might be inclined to endorse the claim that objects can have been presented to imaginative conciousness and pass wholly unrecorded. And yet how could they? If 'recorded' means 'being part of the experience', the concept is simply contradictory. The following considerations bear out this claim.

(3) The distinction between being present to visual awareness, and being part of the content of a visual impression, which is applicable to visual experience generally, permits the concept of being present-to but missed-by to apply without strain in visual situations. This is because we have agreed tests for the presence of a colour-value at a point in the visual field when no colour at that point is recorded in the visual impression. Those tests depend on a vitally important property of vision: the existence of physical sufficient conditions for a colour-value at any point in a visual field. Such tests can be satisfied when the content of the visual impression includes no reference to colour at that point. In such situations the colour will have been part of the visible totality that was present-to and recorded-by consciousness (say, one daffodil in 'a host of golden daffodils'), will have gone wholly unrecorded by the perceiver, and will nonetheless have been causally contributory to the noticing of that visible totality.

No analogue of this concept applies to eidetic memory-images of complex sights. No comparable physical tests exist for the presence of colour-values at given points of memory-images, or for that matter in hallucinations or dream-images or perceptual imaginings generally. In effect, we are here drawing out the consequences of the *negative causal condition* of perceptual imaginings: namely, the absence of the causes of perceptual experience. How, in the absence of such causes, could we demonstrate the presence of a wholly unrecorded item in an imagining? In sum, concerning *all* perceptual imaginings we may say: truth-conditions do not exist for the application of the concept: present-to imaginative consciousness but absent from the content of the imagining experience.

The essential dissimilarity of imaginative and attentive experience is in any case something which is more or less openly apparent. Thus, the immediate material object of perceptual experience has a myriad of immediately perceptible parts which pass unremarked. A relevant case in point is, the teeming visual field of the present instant. All non-atomic perceptual experiences, which is to say experiences whose objects are of greater complexity than (say) a point in a visual field, are of necessity given as 'of an object with unremarked parts'. Indeed, the experience of *missing-much* is constitutive of visual experience in particular, and perceptual experience generally. This is not true of perceptual imagining. Therefore perceptual experience and perceptual imagining differ constitutively.

So much for perceptual imagining generally. And so much, for the moment, for this first part of the discussion, which has been undertaken with two aims in view. First, that of discovering whether there exist defining marks of being an imagining or 'exercise of the imagination', and if so what they are. Second, discovering whether the determinants of being such as to exhibit those marks are relational in kind, or constitutive, or both, or something altogether else. At this juncture I offer a summary of the foregoing inquiry, before moving on in the next Chapter 12 to an investigation of the logical properties of the concept of imagining, and thereafter in Chapter 13 to interpreting the overall findings in terms of my long-term topic: the distinguishing of perceptual imagining from perceiving.

6. Summary

(a) Unacceptable dichotomies

(1) I began by asking: What is the imagination? What is imagining? and immediately halted in my tracks, because it seemed to me that these questions assume too much. In particular, they assume there is some one thing, the imagination, and some one phenomenon that is its exercising, imagining. We simply do not know if this is how things are. Might not 'the imagination' do no more than name the capacity to engender items which on completely independent grounds we know to be imaginings? Alternatively, might it not be that items rate as imaginings solely through being the products of some distinctive universal agency, 'the imagination'? These are the fundamental questions which we must try to answer.

Now it should be noted that the existence of the capacity to engender phenomena which rate as imaginings, is not here in question. What is uncertain is (a) whether there is a distinctive universal bearer of the capacity, and (b) how imaginings come to be imaginings: whether it is through the operation of some special imagination agency like the latter, or through their own intrinsic essential imagining character, or by some other means. These issues are best expressed through two simple questions: Which comes first in the order of things, imagining or the imagination? and: Are imaginings constitutively or relationally determined as imaginings? Then starting out from the valid enough assumption that imaginings are some kind of replication of cognitively significant phenomena, three separate options come to mind.

(2) Suppose that all imaginings have an intrinsic unanalysable imagining essence: in short, assume they 'replicate' in a necessary distinctive and unanalysable manner, the 'imaginative way'. Suppose also that several dissimilar mental items happen to be endowed inessentially with the capacity to generate these distinctive mental phenomena. Then it seems to me that this would be to employ something like the thought-event as a logical model for imagining, seeing that thoughts are intrinsically thoughts and have heterogeneous origins. Now if this was how things stood, we would say that imaginings come first in the order of things and the imagination second. Accordingly, the imagination would emerge here as a sort of *goose that lays the golden eggs*. Just as artists rate as artists only through the nature of their works (despite engendering them), and humans as thinkers only through having thoughts, so on this theory certain beings will be said to be blessed with

imagination solely on account of their imaginings. Now this theory assigns to the imagination a role resembling that played in fact by stimuli to imagining, such as hallucinogens. As we shall see in the next section, the flaws in this account are multiple.

Suppose on the other hand that there was some sort of a mental agency, which was intrinsically essentially and unanalysably 'the imagination'. And suppose also that it is endowed with the power to engender certain mental phenomena, all of which are deemed 'imaginings' entirely because of their origin at the hands of 'the imagination'. Here the relation resembles that between the will to engender some artefact and the instantiation of that object-type in matter, and imaginings are assigned a role like that which is in fact occupied by (say) artwork products of im-agining. Then on this account the imagination is conceived of as something akin to (say) the Royal Mint, and rather as two objects could be indistinguishable and one a £10 note and the other a counterfeit, so it would be with imaginings. Now if this was how matters stood, we would say that the imagination came first and imaginings second. And as we shall see, the flaws in this account are also multiple.

One other logical model is worth mentioning: namely, that in which the imagina-tion and imagining arise in existence together, essentially predestined for one another. On this account both are said to be endowed with intrinsic unanalysable essences, one of 'imagination' and one of 'imagining', each necessarily endowed with the causal property which binds them together. The (exact) mental model here is something like the bipole of *act-desire and striving*, while the (less exact) non-mental model might be something like *acorn and oak*. Then while it is correct to say that imagination and imagining arise in existence together, it is incorrect to suppose that it could take the above form. I shall not list the failings of this theory, since they also will become evident in what follows.

Now it was in part to resolve these problems, and in any case to arrive at the correct account of imagining and the imagination, that I decided to take a look at the actual facts of the imagination.

(b) The defining marks of imagining

(1) The following emerged during the discussion. We have been concerned with five main varieties of imagining: 1. properly self-conscious propositional imagining (exemplified by the spontaneous author-narrator), 2. unselfconscious propositional imagining (exemplified by dream-belief), 3. imaginative perception (as when we look suitably at photographs or cartoons), 4. properly self-conscious perceptual imagining (say, common or garden mental imagery), and 5. unselfconscious per-ceptual imagining (say, hallucinations).

The first goal in the discussion was to discover what makes imaginings imagin-ings, what common property if any ensures that they are imaginings, in other words what imagining *is*. A clue was found in a universally applicable disjunctive rule governing *how we experience* imaginings. Thus: to the extent that full self-consciousness obtains, to that same extent imaginings are given as imaginings directed to 'unreals', and as merely 'quasi' their cognitive prototype; while to the extent self-awareness is absent, to that same extent imaginings are experienced, not as imaginings, but as what is being imagined, namely as the cognitive prototype, given as directed to 'reals'. Then not only is self-conscious imagining insightfully revelatory of the status of self-conscious imagining, it has proved to be revelatory of the nature of imagining itself. Imaginings turn out to be of necessity directed to mere 'unreals', and to be merely 'quasi' their prototype.

(2) The relevant facts emerged in the discussion. Thus, we saw in the case both of propositional and direct-object imaginings generally, that causes alone ensured they could not realize their prototypes. All imaginings arise from the subject's mind in such a way that the constraint of Reality is necessarily inoperative, whether through substituting one's will for Reality or through confusing 'subjective Reality' with Reality itself. The fact that the mind acts here, not as a representative of Reality but in direct opposition, guarantees that imaginings must be cognitively void. By contrast, while a mind reasoning on empirical matters is a causal force in the engendering of its own cognitive attitudes, the rationality of the process ensures that mind and Reality act here in consort. It is precisely not so in imagining. Here the mind operates genetically in such a way that the mental products are guaranteed not to realize their cognitive prototype, and Reality is simply short-circuited out of the causal transaction. Meanwhile, it also emerged in the discussion that constitutive considerations as well, the fact that absolutely all imaginative experiences are different experiences from the prototype experience, doubly guaranteed the identical conclusion. In these several ways failure to realize the prototype emerged as a universally necessary feature of imaginings.

And so the summary situation, so far as the analysis of the concept of imagining is concerned, is this. Imagining is '*quasi*' some cognitive prototype which represents Reality as endowed with a certain character, it *is not* that prototype and is thus *merely* 'quasi', indeed it is *of necessity* merely 'quasi', and it is as such directed to '*unreals*'. These are all necessary conditions of being an imagining. These properties together constitute a complex property which holds of anything that is an imagining. They are what I have been calling 'defining marks' of imagining, and constitute a provisional analysis of that concept, the final form of which must wait upon the logical analysis of the concept which occurs in the next Chapter 12.

(c) Constitutive or causal?

(1) But if this is what imagining *is*, the question remains: *by what means* do imaginings come to instantiate this complex property? Is it through origins? Or is it instead through constitution? Or is it in some other way? It was this question—along with the search for defining marks—which led me to examine the constitutive and relational properties of imaginings right across the board. Several highly relevant generalities emerged. (1) All imaginative experiences are constitutively imaginings.

359

(2) All direct-object imaginings are constitutively imaginings. (3) Propositional imaginings have an identity cast in terms other than imagining, whether it be under the concepts of belief or thinking. (4) No constitutive imagining-property holds of all imaginings.

The above generalities, ranging across all five sub-varieties of imagining, revealed in the first place that being an imagining cannot be a psychological unanalysable, in the way that belief and desire and much else in the mind are precisely just that. And they opened the door for analysis of the concept, of the kind just offered in provisional form above: namely, that imagining is of necessity *merely* 'quasi' some cognitive prototype.

(2) But they also reveal that imagining cannot be a purely constitutive characteristic. Then how does this fact bear upon the vexed question: is it through origin or constitution that imaginings come to *not* exemplify the prototype phenomenon (and satisfy the definition of imagining)? The resolution of this problem alerts us to an important property of imaginings.

And in fact a difficulty exists here, a problem which tempts one to split the concept of imagining. Thus, perceptual imaginings generally are not merely causally guaranteed not to be their prototype, they are in addition constitutively incapable of being the prototype, since they are at once both essentially imaginative and essentially different experiences from the prototype experience. By contrast, in the case of non-experiential propositional imaginings, for example the enduring persecutory or grandiloquent delusions of madmen, origins alone determine their imaginative status. Such a division in rationales threatens to split imaginings as a class into two camps, and appears to be inconsistent with the univocality thesis that imagining is the same across the varieties α—γ (a thesis which is expressible definitionally). Ought we to have resort to a theory of ambiguity? Might the concept of imagining have several senses? I have no doubt that we should resist the suggestion: the definition of imagining fits all varieties of imagining equally exactly.

To resolve this problem, it helps to remember the facts. We saw that a disjunctive causal rule applies to absolutely all imaginings, namely that the cause of imagining is: *either* the operation of will-susceptibility re imagining *or* a weakening of one's sense of Reality. This *origin-clause* alone ensures that imaginings cannot exemplify their prototypes (which are causally determinable types, to wit perception and knowledge). Meanwhile we know that imaginative experiences generally (images, hallucinations, 'make believe', etc.) are *constitutively* incapable of being their prototype. Then are (say) visual imaginings not-seeings because of origin or constitution? Plainly, because of both. Both constitution *and* origin guarantee a failure to exemplify the prototype in the case of perceptual imaginings generally. And since they are each sufficient conditions of that failure, they cannot be joint determinants. Then why choose one determinant at the expense of the other? The completely general conclusion which this points to is, that imaginings are imaginings neither through having a required constitution, nor through origins, and not even through a combination of these factors. They do so rather through satisfying the definition. That is, through instantiating the following character: being of necessity merely 'quasi' some cognitive phenomenon. The dichotomy: quality or relation? must be rejected. And that it must, provides us with an important lead as to the nature of imagining. Thus, the property of being an imagining is neither a relational nor constitutive property, even though relational and/or constitutive properties determine its existence. What matters is that a certain necessity is binding, namely that imaginings cannot exemplify their cognitive prototype. While there may be more to imagining than that, the above states a necessary condition. And it points us towards the possibility that what is so distinctive about the imagination is to be found in the *concept* rather than in the *phenomenon*.

(d) Provisional conclusions concerning Imagining and the Imagination

Bearing in mind these latter considerations, what can we now say by way of answer to the original questions posed at the beginning of this chapter? What is imagining? What is the imagination?

Imagining is quasi- a cognitive item (perception/knowledge) which represents Reality as endowed with a certain character, it is quasi 'the real thing', and necessarily never instantiates that prototype. Then in the light of this property, together with the fact that imagining is neither a relational nor constitutive characteristic, what can be said about the imagination itself? A full answer to this question must wait upon the completion of the analysis of imagining. However, we at least know that the doctrine of an essential common imagination agency is unacceptable, along with the theory of a common intrinsic imagining essence, and that the imagination must be the power to generate phenomena answering to the above definition of imagining. Then the fact that imagining is neither a relational nor constitutive property suggests that neither imagining nor the imagination can be definable in terms of one another. It suggests, without proving, that imagining and the imagination arise in existence together, on an equal footing. However, a more decisive answer to this question must wait upon our acquiring a better understanding of the logical properties of the concept of imagining.

12

The Imagination (2)

1. Completing the Analysis of the Concept of Imagining

At this point the discussion of the imagination changes direction, and I move on to its latter stage. I have managed so far to assemble a set of necessary conditions of imagining. And since that analysis applies equally to propositional and direct-object imaginings, as well as to both experiential and non-experiential imaginings, I find myself in a position to resist ambiguity theories and retain the univocality thesis. Meanwhile I reject the dichotomy: constitutive or causal? While recognizing that imaginings have to be constitutively so, or relationally and causally so, or both at the same time, since they can scarcely 'just' be imaginings, the concept proves not to be constitutive in type (unlike 'water' and 'pain'), nor relational in type (unlike 'radio' or 'irritable'). It is a different sort of concept altogether—a fact of some significance, as I hope to show.

But there is more to do. To begin, an important question remains regarding the analysis of imagining. Thus, it is unclear whether the aforementioned necessary properties constitute a sufficient set. And a further related question is, whether the concept of 'quasi' is unitary and self-explanatory. Finally and most important, I need to spell out the distinctive *logical properties* of the concept of imagining—since there is reason to think they are of a special type. I begin by addressing myself to the first question.

(a) Analytically constituting the concept of imagining

(1) It has emerged that imaginings are necessarily merely 'quasi' some cognitive prototype which represents Reality as endowed with a certain character. And yet there must be 'quasi's and 'quasi's among experiences with cognitive content. After all, while the non-imaginative 'quasi' of visual seem-seeing identifies the type of the experience with its seeing prototype, and allows for the possibility of its being a real seeing, the 'quasi' or 'seem' of imaginative experience permits neither. This fact shows quite clearly that the elucidation of the imagination can be further advanced only if we manage to arrive at an analytical account of the imaginative 'quasi'. Then in my opinion this is best accomplished through attempting piecemeal to constitute imagining out of its original or basic raw materials. The nature of the special 'as if'

should emerge in the course of the procedure. Accordingly, I embark at this point upon the process of analytically constituting an imagining. It takes the following form.

(2) We begin with a cognitively significant phenomenon of type knowledge (for propositional imagining) or perception (for direct-object). That is, with mental phenomena which represent Reality as endowed with a certain character. Then the imagining phenomenon is (at the very least) a *function* of that mental item, insofar as its essential description makes reference to that item. But of course it is that and more. Thus, intentions are necessarily directed to acts, and are therefore in that sense functions of another mental phenomenon, while some desires can be functions of cognitives like perception, for example the desire of a blind man to see. However, whereas desires can also be functions of non-mental phenomena, as (say) when they are directed to the weather (that it may improve), imaginings are necessarily functions uniquely of mental phenomena. More, they are of necessity functions *uniquely and only* of the fundamental mental cognitives—*knowledge and perception.* Here we have a first distinctive property of imaginings.

The example of desire alerts us to a second property. Namely, that whereas desires and intentions are *sui generis* 'first-order' psychological phenomena, imagining is 'second-order' in type. Thus, imagining necessarily 'feeds off' or is a 'shadow of' other psychological phenomena, which in turn stand in no such need of it. This property of being second-order can be formally explicated, as I hope now to show. Then the property in question begins to emerge when we ask: to what is imagining directed, what is its intentional object? Interestingly, it turns out that imagining is directed, not to the psychological phenomenon one imagines, but to the object of the psychological phenomenon. Whereas a desire to see some object O is intentionally directed to the seeing of O, the imagining of seeing O is by contrast directed merely to O. Thus, the indifference to existence when (say) I visualize Cicero, governs the reality of Cicero rather than of my seeing him (which is expressly negated in this experience!), and the same holds of referential opacity. In short, imagining and its prototype cognitive phenomenon are intentionally directed to the same object. And this is as true of propositional as direct-object imagining: a 'make believe' quasi-belief is intentionally directed to the very same propositional object as its cognitive model.

And so the intentional object of imagination must be distinguished from the (so-called) 'immediate object' of imagination, which is to say from the cognitive prototype or *that which is being imagined*—for example, in the case (say) of visual imagining from the visual perceiving of an object. To record this distinction between intentional object content and 'immediate object' content of imagining, I shall say that whereas the perceived physical item O is the intentional object of the imagining, the perceiving of that object is its 'filler'. In sum, the event of imagining is 'filled' by a perceptual experience which is posited as being intentionally directed to the very same object as the imagining itself. Each of these two psychological types has its sights trained upon the identical item. And the same is true of propositional imagining and its cognitive model. This strange state of affairs is part of what is being claimed of imagining when we say of it that it is 'second-order' in character.

(3) We can express the difference between 'intentional object' and 'filler' in different terms. Indeed, doing so leads to a discovery about imagining itself. And it helps thereby to uncover a property of perceptual imagining-of which is relevant to the overall project of the present discussion of the imagination in Chapters 11–13: namely, the precise delineation of perceptual imagining (ultimately, the exact differential characterization of perception).

Whereas the event of seeing finds its identity under 'see', imagining a seeing acquires its identity not under 'imagining', but under 'visual imagining'. This is because there is *no such thing* as merely imagining an object. And this is in turn a direct consequence of the fact that imagining is 'quasi' its 'filler' psychological phenomenon. There absolutely *has to be* some mental mode of relating to that object which imagining can 'shadow', take as prototype, be merely 'quasi', if it is to exist— something as true of those imaginings-that which find their identity under 'belief' as it is of perceptual imaginings-of.

This wholly general rule has interesting implications in the case of perceptual imaginings-of. Thus, being intrinsically essentially merely an imagining, imagining-of is of necessity *nothing but* a second-order being. Hence it needs a prototype, as opposed to an object, if it to so much as *be*. It is like an actor amongst its psychological peers, indeed one who is essentially pure Thespian! Such a measure of dependence of one psychological phenomenon upon another is without precedent in the mind. What is unique in the present case is, that the very type under which identity is acquired derives from another mental type. Accordingly, if I stands here for imagining, if O is some physical object, and ϕ is the mental type of the 'filler' phenomenon, then while we can perfectly well characterize the imagining as (say) $I[\phi(O)]$, it is more perspicuously to be expressed as $(\phi I)(O)$. The latter formula is structurally perspicuous, as the former is structurally misleading. For to repeat, there is simply no such thing as merely imagining an object. This fact should we borne in mind in the discussion in the next Chapter 13, where we will be concerned to delineate the various modes in which the mind can relate to physical objects. In particular, the perceptual mode.

(b) The elements of resemblance and confusion

(1) While we are coming nearer to a formal definition of the imaginative 'as if', and so to a more complete analytical characterization of imagining, two more elements in imagining need to find representation in this account. Although they do not add to the above analysis, they enlarge our understanding of the phenomenon. The first of these element is naturally described as 'resemblance'. Correlative with it goes a second property that one might describe as a tendency towards 'confusion'. Each

typify the special imaginative 'as if' that has application to both direct-object and propositional imagining, and each are derivatives of the nature revealed in the aformentioned analysis of the concept of imagining.

By 'resemblance' I mean that imaginings are not merely second-order to prototypes which they 'shadow', but that they imitate and are like them. You might say they are replicas of the prototype—only in another realm. When Hume described 'ideas' as 'pale copies', he was evidently thinking of such. Two features, already remarked, have much to do with 'resemblance'. The first is, that imagining and the 'filler' phenomenon are directed to identical objects. Absolutely every item that is object of one occurs as object of the other, whether it be material object, colour, contour, spatial properties—or proposition. The second feature is, that the only mode of acquaintance with that content open to imagining is that provided by the 'filler'. There are not *two* distinct ways of relating to an identical object-content, the perceptual way and the imaginative way: there is one way, and a 'shadow' of that way. This contributes to the special brand of 'likeness' holding between prototype and imagining-of.

(2) Closely connected with 'resemblance' is the second property, the tendency to confuse imagining with its prototype 'filler'. Thus, it is a substantive question why imaginings occurring when one's sense of reality is weakened, tend to be experienced as their 'filler' rather than as an imagining. (Somewhat like the Magritte painting of a painting which is resting upon an easel in a rural scene, whose content exactly matches a strip of the pictured scene: representation of a representation seemingly disappearing into mere representation!) Clearly, the identity of object-content, as well as of the first-order mode of experiential acquaintance that happens to be involved, have something to do with this property: in a word, the aforementioned 'resemblance' between imagining and imagined.

But it cannot be the whole explanation. Something else about imagining must determine this tendency to *not* experience a distinction which most assuredly continues to apply as one's reality-sense weakens. For we should remember that the property under consideration is not that whereby two experiences tend to merge, it is the tendency for imagining seemingly (but illusorily) to merge into its 'filler'. Then it is clear that the state of mind in which the *illusion of fusion* occurs must be such that the phenomenon of imagining cannot be experienced as *itself*, and, doubtless on account of the identity of mode and content, finds itself experienced instead as its 'filler'. It is rather as if, looking at the Magritte painting, one failed to experience the imaged image as anything more than simple (first-order) image: the sophistication of mind needed to grasp the wit and sense of the painting being unavailable. (Something which might happen with a young child already acquainted with pictures, who can by now 'read' representations, but not as yet *representations of representations*.) Analogously, the state of mind of the non-conscious or improperly conscious imagining subject must block the recognition of a mental representation of a mental representation for the meta-entity it is. The interiority necessary for mentally drawing back in the required way must be wanting. What is achievable in such a mental setting is merely first-order in type. This property is a direct derivative of the second-order status of imagining.

(3) At this point I conclude the analytical characterization of imagining. Here below is a brief overall summary of what has emerged in the discussion so far. It includes what has just now emerged concerning the special 'quasi' of the imagination.

What are imaginings? We answer this question by briefly recapitulating the process of constituting imagining out of its raw materials. We set out from a cognitive phenomenon, x, a perceiving or a knowing which represents Reality as endowed with a certain character. Then imagining x is a function only and uniquely of its prototype—a property which it shares with the seem-see of visual experience. And it resembles the latter also in the fact that its intentional objects are identically those of its prototype. However, these two 'seemings' with cognitive content sharply divide in a vital other respect. Whereas the seem-see of visual experience is 'aspirational' in allowing for the possibility of its coinciding with its own visual prototype, the 'seeming' of imagination stands at a polar remove on this count. Necessarily it *is not* its prototype, and necessarily it is not its prototype under *any description*. These few properties make of imagining a second-order ('meta') type. For under what heading can imaginings discover their identity? It can never merely be under 'imagine', since it is always an 'as if perceive/know', and it can never be under the heading of its prototype. Thus, it is cast in the role of 'shadow' 'actor' 'ghost'. Imagining is a 'seem' fated never to be what it 'seems'.

2. Imagining and the Imagination

(1) At this point I return for a final word on the two questions asked at several points in the discussion: what is the Imagination? how do Imagining and the Imagination relate? What follows is a brief summary which takes into account the recent observations concerning the analysis of the concept of imagining.

Is imaginativeness determined by constitution or by origin? The importance of this question lies in the implications of the two opposed answers as to the nature of the imagination itself. Suppose we ask: which comes first in the order of things, imagining or the imagination? The theory that constitution alone determines being an imagining, implies that what makes something the imagination is its causing *sui generis* items, and assumes that the imagination is to be defined in terms of imagining. The opposed theory opts for the reverse order of priorities, construes the imagination as a *sui generis* internal agency, implying that what makes a phenomenon an imagining is its arising from that source, and would put imaginings on all fours with 'works of the imagination'. The first theory confers a *sui generis* imagining-essence upon imaginings, and defines the imagination in terms of that essence, the second theory confers a *sui generis* imagination-essence upon the imagination, and makes the property of being an imagining an inessential property of its bearer.

Neither theory squares with the facts. The first theory is inconsistent with the fact that some propositional imaginings are imaginings because of origin, and have no imagining essence. The second theory is inconsistent with the fact that all direct-object imaginings are in essence perceptual-imaginings. Then instead of splitting the concepts of imagining and the imagination, instead of having recourse to a theory of ambiguity, we opt rather for the following account.

(2) The concept of imagining is not a first-order concept which applies essentially to whatever instantiates it. It is a second-order concept which applies, sometimes essentially and on other occasions inessentially, to its multiple instances. Accordingly, imagining must be a second-order concept which is not *as such* either essentialist or inessentialist in type. So much for imaginings.

What of their source, viz. the power to imagine? The imagination itself proves to have a character which is in accord with the above finding. The imagination is not a power to produce a first-order essence, nor a power to produce a second-order essence. It is a power to produce phenomena which fall under a second-order concept which has neither an essentialist or inessentialist role to play in the mind. It follows that the imagination must be capable of operating in widely dissimilar situations. Thus, it is undoubtedly at work when, largely because a state of consciousness obtains which is at once non-rational *and* capable of supporting cognitive attitudes manifesting contemporaneous time-awareness, a non-rational cognitive attitude occurs. It is at work here equally as much as when, with express intent, we summon up into our minds essentially imaginative phenomena like mental imagery. And yet both origin and its phenomenal effect are markedly dissimilar in these two cases. Accordingly, we may in general say: the imagination is the capacity to have arise in our minds phenomena which, whether because of constitution, or origin, or both, are of necessity merely as if a cognitive prototype which represents Reality as endowed with a particular character. This tells us nothing about the universal character of the items which manage to satisfy these two characterizations, whether we are thinking of imaginings or their imagination source—for in either case there is none. To suppose there might be such common characters, is to labour under a fundamental misapprehension as to the logical type of the phenomena involved. An excessive preoccupation with essences leads to the dichotomies, in which misunderstanding of this logical situation is manifest.

3. The Implications of the Special Logical Properties

(a) The 'corelessness' of imagining

(1) I would like finally to spell out the implications of the special logical properties of the concept of imagining. These properties have by now been delineated, but I want at this point to indicate something of their significance.

In characterizing the 'as if' of the imagination—as opposed (say) to that of visual experience—it emerged that it was *exhaustive* in character. Thus, when we come to analyse 'imagining', we find that what is distinctive about the 'as if' is that imagining is *no more than* 'as if': there is not a distinctive type of 'as if', there is rather the distinctiveness of being *merely* 'as if'. Now this property has to be expressed in terms of the concept, rather than its bearers. For while direct-object imaginings are no more than necessarily 'as if' the prototype, and propositional imaginings are something more (viz. thinkings/believings), nonetheless the concept which applies to them both affirms the property of being merely 'as if'. To be an imagining is not to possess the property of being a *something or other* that is of necessity merely 'as if' some prototype. Neither is it to possess that of being something that is *nothing but* 'as if' its prototype. Rather, it is to be of necessity merely 'as if'—whether or not there is more to it than that. This is what is meant by saying that the concept of imagining is neither a constitutive nor relational type of concept, and herein resides the impropriety of the dichotomous question, 'Which comes first in the order of things: imagining or the imagination?' The property of being exhaustively and merely 'as if' can coexist either with the property of being no more than that (say, an hallucination), or with that of being something else (say, a believing). In either case the 'as if' lies at the end of the conceptual line: there is nothing more to say about it. As we have already observed: the property in question has to be expressed in terms of the concept.

(2) Thanks to this property of exhaustiveness, the concept of imagining emerges as interestingly dissimilar from those of its familiar psychological peers: belief, will, desire, etc. To bring out this special character, it is illuminating to compare it with those phenomena, and discover the specific unlikenesses. Thus, suppose we compare imagining with a mental 'original' like belief. Now a mental phenomenon like belief is notable for at least two logical properties: it is indefinable, and it is intrinsically itself. Then the phenomenon of imagining differs on both counts. Consider the question of analysis. The sheer fact that we can successfully embark upon analysis of imagining disposes of the comparison, and the belief comparison must be rejected forthwith.

But 'success'-concepts like knowledge and perception and action are like imagining in being susceptible of analysis. Might (say) knowledge be a valid model for imagining? Surely not. If it were, there should exist a *sui generis* 'original' imagining-type core at the centre of imagining—and we would be back with the model of belief. For this roughly is the situation in the case of concepts like knowledge. Belief is the essence of knowledge, it 'aspires' to the condition of knowledge, and constitutes a core phenomenon which can find itself redescribed as knowledge. Nothing relates in this way to imagining. Thus, nothing 'aspires' to be imagining, finds itself redescribed as imagining, and there is simply no imagining essence. In short, while the analysability of imagining is accepted, it cannot be an analysability in terms of an unanalysable *sui generis* 'original' core-concept. For one thing, in the case of direct-object imaginings, which are intrinsically what they are, the core vanishes. It vanishes because these phenomena are in essence nothing but (or pure) 'shadows' of 'originals'. They are not pure distinctive types of 'shadow'—whereupon a core could be found in that distinctiveness, they are merely and nothing but 'shadow'. This is what I mean when I say that in direct-object imagining the core vanishes.

Then in precisely those other cases where a core concept does exist, namely propositional imaginings, one that finds itself redescribed as imagining, in short where one might suppose the model of knowledge applicable, the model breaks down on a different count. Namely, the core concept has nothing as such to do with imagining—being of the 'original' kinds of believing or thinking.

(b) The radical analysability of imagining

(1) So we shall have to accept analysability, but refuse the comparison with 'success'-terms like knowledge, since we reject the notion of a (say) belief-analogue lying at the centre of the concept of imagining. Then in dispensing with a core concept, we come upon one of the most interesting peculiarities of this concept. Notice how it comes about. We saw earlier that perceptual imagining finds its identity, not under 'imagining' but under 'perceptual imagining', whereas propositional imagining finds identity under 'believing' or 'thinking'. Common to both is that they do not discover an identity under 'imagining'. There is no imagining essence (which confirms the previous claim that 'imagining' is neither a constitutive nor relational concept).

What this means is, that 'imagining' is not merely analysable, it is *radically analysable*, almost analysable away. It is important that this concept is analysable almost into nothing: not into a distinctive variety of 'as if', but into pure 'as if'. This concept is 'as if' to the core: its core is pure 'as if'. It is (so to say) pure and sheer actor amongst its psychological peer concepts. A case in point, continuing the analogy. The greatest actor of our era, the one true genius, Laurence Olivier, at times conveyed the painful impression (at least in interviews) of lacking an identity, of 'acting' whatever he did: whether it was 'seriousness' in an interview, or 'everydayness' in everyday situations, and so forth. And then came resplendently into his own as Richard III, Henry V, Heathcliff, Shylock, The Entertainer, Coriolanus— where density of nature flowed in to fill the cavity in his soul. It was the price he paid for his greatness. In any case, it seems to me that the concept of imagining is of this kind, pure actor so to say, quintessentially and nothing but 'as if'. At the very end of the road it is still so—even if the bearer is not.

(2) In this sense imagining has no 'mystery', being *transparent* to the core. Conversely, however, had it been in possession of an impenetrable core, an essence or identity of its own, it would be shot through with contingency and idiosyncratic particularity. If it had been logically akin to belief, it would be a highly contingent and so to say wholly unanticipatable presence in the mind. The facts are precisely the reverse. The sheer property of corelessness, taken in conjunction with the fact that its prototype-content is one of a certain representation of Reality, make of this

concept one that is a priori-derivable from one's consciousness of Reality. Precisely the fact of lacking autonomy ('mystery') makes of it something unidiosyncratic and universal, and presumably a priori derivable from the very nature of the Mind as representer of Reality. It is because it is transparent, coreless, because there is no distinctive mode of being 'as if'—because 'as if' shrinks without remainder, that the radical definability of 'imagining' proves to be a unique example of definability in the mind: a definability *all the way*! To continue for a moment with the analogy of actor: it is as if he reverses the charge of emptiness of nature, and appears in the universal role of exemplar of the artist.

13

Imagination and Perception

The foregoing discussion of Imagining and the Imagination was undertaken in order to enable me to arrive at a precise analytical characterization of perceptual imagining. And that was carried out in order to help differentially distinguish perceptual imagining from perception. The ultimate goal is an enhanced analytical characterization of the phenomenon of perception.

1. The Special Character of Perceptual Imagining

It emerged that direct-object or perceptual imagining has a somewhat special character. I begin this chapter with a brief résumé of its properties. The special properties of direct-object or perceptual imagining proved to be as follows. Since all direct-object perceptual imaginings, I-of-x, are intrinsically essentially imaginings, and since imaginings necessarily never are their prototype, imaginings-of are *nothing but* imaginings. This has interesting consequences. It implies that the very type under which I-of acquires identity is not 'I', but 'φI' (where φ is the phenomenal type exemplified by the prototype x). Thus, imagining seeing an object O is a visual imagining that is intentionally directed to O, and is not an imagining that is intentionally directed to the seeing of O (by contrast with a blind man's desire to see O). As noted earlier, while we can perfectly well characterize direct-object imagining as (say) $I[\phi(O)]$, it is more perspicuously to be expressed as $(\phi I)(O)$. The latter formula is structurally perspicuous, as the former is structurally misleading.

This confers an unusual character upon direct-object imagining. It carries the implication that φI-of-O cannot be a bona fide first-order psychological phenomenon, not just in being essentially linked to φ and so dependent on another phenomenon, but in that the type 'I' cannot confer identity, whereas 'φI' (which utilizes the concept of the first-order φ) does precisely that. Such a measure of dependence of one psychological phenomenon upon another is without precedent in the mind. For example, we discover no comparable dependence even in those few psychological phenomena, such as the act-intention, which are essentially linked to other psychological types. What is unique in the present case is, that the very type under which identity is acquired derives from another mental type. Accordingly, 'act-

371

intention' cannot be comparable structurally with 'visual-imagining': 'intention' being the heading under which act-intentions gain their identity, 'imagining' failing to guarantee identity for visual-imaginings.

2. Negation and the Imagination

(a) Negation

At this point I return to the topic of perception. As we have just observed, the overall aim in writing the previous two chapters has been to pave the way for a more differential characterization of perception. Now in Chapter 10 I distinguished perception from thought through setting down their diverse relations to propositions and negation. Then the project of conceptually delineating perception will be significantly advanced if we can in an analogous manner distinguish perception from its close experiential neighbour, imagining-of. For there are at least *four* fundamental modes in which the mind makes contemporaneous experiential contact with a physical object: in perception-of, in imagining-of, in a thought-of the object (the latter probably only in a thought-about), and in knowing-of (in the discovery-experience). Of these four modes perception is undoubtedly the primal phenomenon. Thus, perceptual imagining is built upon the foundation of perception; the sophisticated character of thought ensures that developmentally it must have appeared later in the order of things than the other phenomena; and the discovery-experience owes both its existence and its content to the perception. In any case my immediate project in this present chapter is the distinguishing of imagining-of from perceiving-of and thought-of a phenomenal object (assuming there is such a thing as the latter). (The discovery-experience being sufficiently examined in Chapter 10.)

The feature that I select to effect such a differential characterization is once more negation. I intend to set down properties of imagining relating to negation. But first a word concerning negation and thought. A necessary and sufficient condition of the capacity for thought is, acquaintance with the concept of *truth*, and so also with *negation*. Now while humans are aware of these latter, non-rational beings are acquainted with neither. For this reason the content of merely animal belief has to be expressed though *contraries*: 'he thinks he is going for a walk' is opposed to (say) 'he thinks a kick is coming', rather than to 'he thinks he is *not* going for a walk', a fact borne out by our incapacity behaviourally to distinguish 'he thinks he is not going for a walk' and 'he has ceased experiencing a desire for a walk'. By contrast, a human who thinks he is going for a walk, thinks it is true he is going for a walk and false that he is not: the *contradictory* is implicitly negated in his belief. This difference between unthinking and thinking conscious animals implies that only the latter can entertain propositions under negative headings. In the thought one contemplates the propositional object *as* something which might disagree with Reality, for one encounters it under the aspect of truth. I do not mean that thought-events typically occur in the absence of cognitive commitment: rather, that a negative possibility is implicitly negated in all thought-events. In this special sense the thought may be described as non-commital in character.

(b) Negation and propositional imagining

(1) I turn now to imagining. We shall see that simply the fact that all imaginings are *merely quasi* a cognitive phenomena and all imagining experiences are essentially and constitutively imaginative, carries the implication that negation of the cognitive prototype belongs by right to imaginative experience as such. Whether or not this is overtly realized, turns upon the self-awareness of the imagining subject: rational wakeful subjects will do so, non-rational subjects will not.

Let us first examine *propositional imaginings*, beginning with the fully self-conscious sub-variety. Then it comes as no surprise to discover that the implicit negative informing all thought should be duplicated in the self-conscious propositional imaginings of wakeful rational beings. This is because in these subjects the capacity to propositionally imagine is indistinguishable from the sheer capacity to think. After all, it is essential to thinking that one be able to conjure up counterfactual possibilities of the kind exemplified by (say) philosophical or scientific 'thought-experiments', and these are at the same time exercises of the imagination. And yet something *more than* the implicit negation endemic to thought finds instantiation in the imaginative sub-variety of thinking. There exists in addition what one might call 'the negation of imagination'. Thus, the propositional imagining-that of wakeful rational beings has the special property of positing its object as a '*mere unreal*': the whole procedure being akin to 'play': a quite particular mode of negation as a result informing the experience. Negation overtly characterizes one's relation to the cognitive prototype in these insightful imaginative experiences.

(2) What happens to this special imaginative negation in the imaginings-that of rational beings in non-rational states, and in general in all the multifarious non-rational brands of imagining-that? It is invariably lost, in uninsight. Thus, the event of imagining in all these cases *is not* its prototype, and *that it is not* is simply lost to view. This is so even though the dream-beliefs of humans, being beliefs in the true and thus in the not-false, exhibit *thought's* mode of acquaintance with negation. What they lack is what is insightfully given to a wakeful human subject inventing a story, namely the 'play'-like 'suspension of disbelief', the overt consciousness of the non-cognitive, or at any rate non-knowing, character of the mental processes filling consciousness. In short, the property of being 'merely quasi'—the special negation of imagination—is obscured from view. In the light of these facts it seems to me that a valuable model for madness might be that of the actor who mistakes the play (*sic!*) for Reality: 'Othello' actually strangling 'Desdemona'! This image of uninsightful imagining emphasizes the fact that imagining is a phenomenon of such a kind that, when given in insight under its true colours, it is experienced as

pretence, play, or at any rate as merely 'quasi' a cognitive prototype it fails to be, and thus as falling expressly under a *negative*.

(c) Negation and direct-object imagining

(1) All properly self-conscious *propositional imaginings* veridically record the specific negation of imagination, since prototype and object are overtly given as 'unreals'. Now the negative of imagination applies equally to direct-object imaginings. Then consider the form that it takes in fully self-aware direct-object imagining-of: that is, in *mental imagery* (visualizing). Here, too, the negation in question stems from the fact that the imagining is, and is veridically given as no more than, quasi its prototype. Indeed, mental imagery embodies *two* overt applications of negation. First, the image is overtly given as not a visual experience, second the object of imagining is experienced as not now appearing to visual consciousness. (And these are different.) While one might just manage to visualize what one knows lies buried here and now somewhere deep in one's visual field, one could scarcely visualize what one now *veridically visually perceives*: at the same moment visually recognize object O *and* visually imagine the identical O! In short, self-conscious perceptual-imagining must be experienced as at once *not* a visual experience, and as *not* receiving its object in visual consciousness. An overt double negative will insightfully be registered.

Whereas this experience is insightful, all other direct-object imaginings are uninsightfully, indeed are erroneously experienced. Thus, Macbeth's hallucination of a dagger, despite his judicious doubts as to its character, was both uninsightfully and erroneously experienced as a seeing. And the same is true of the 'seeings' of dreamers. For we may in general say of the improperly self-conscious human being, caught up in his mind's creations, so to say enmeshed in his own 'play', that he fails to utilize the inherent capacity for negation which insight would have availed itself of. Meanwhile the non-rational animal, no matter what its state, simply lacks the capacity to invoke the negation which by rights belongs to all imaginative experience as such. And yet it is surely true that some animals undergo imaginative experience: say, dream and hallucinate. They simply fail to record the negative property which we necessarily imply when we bring those experiences under their proper descriptions. Interestingly, animals never initiate imaginative experience, precisely because doing so would necessitate acquaintance with that negation.

Let me briefly sum up what has so far emerged on the question of negation and imagining. All imaginings are 'as if', and necessarily 'are not', their cognitive prototype, being of the type of a mere 'shadow'. And the property of being an imagining is constitutively essential, first to all self-conscious imagining, and secondly to absolutely all imaginative experience. It follows that the property of 'falling short' of the prototype, must be veridically and insightfully experienced in all properly self-conscious imagining experiences. Thus, the character of 'not being seeing' is constitutively essential to visualizing, as is 'not being a real knowing' to the suitable inventing/listening/viewing of works of the imagination. In brief, negation overtly enters all self-conscious imaginative experience. Then while the negative will be lost to view in absolutely all unselfconscious subjects, it remains perenially applicable notwithstanding.

(2) One other feature relating imagining with negation is of considerable relevance to my enterprise. I claimed in Chapter 10 that perception no more takes negative objects than does the will: the *cognitive experience* of perceiving-that absence obtains (e.g. the cupboard is bare) paralleling the *intentional abstension* from action (e.g. ignoring the clamorous telephone). Thus, 'hearing silence' is not a perception, but a cognitive experience intimately linked to a contemporaneous self-aware absence of a perception. This property of perception is exactly duplicated in direct-object perceptual imaginings-of. Whereas there is such a thing as visualizing darkness, or propositionally imagining-that silence reigns, there is no such thing as the auditory-imaginative 'hearing'-of silence. In a word, perceptual imaginings-of no more take negative objects than do perceivings. While one can visualize a cupboard that is bare of food, one cannot visualize the absence of food of that cupboard. Why should it be *food*—rather than (say) *butterflies* or *a large hat*—that the image of wood and spaces (and etc.) is presenting absent? Only an imagining-that can take such an object as an emptiness of X.

3. Distinguishing Perception, Imagining, and Thought of an Object

(a) Distinguishing imagining-of an object from perception-of an object

The facts which came to light in the latter part of the previous chapter, in characterizing the special 'quasi' of the imagination, enable me at this point to further my long-term project of differentially delineating the perceptual mode of acquaintance with objects. Then let us first of all recall a few of the facts which we discovered about imagining. And then let us compare the situation which obtains in perception.

The following emerged. Neither a mental visual image of an object, nor a visual hallucination of an object, are imaginative consciousnesses of *seeing an object*: they are instead visual-imaginative consciousnesses of an *object*. This is because the identity of imagining-of is given, not under 'imagining of', but under 'ϕ-imagining-of' (where ϕ is a perceptual mode). There is no such thing as 'just imagining' an object: the imagination must be 'filled' before it can have identity, and the 'filler' of direct-object imagining-of has to be perceptual in type. And it has to be perceptual for the reason that it is a mere 'shadow' of the primary first-order direct encounter of consciousness with physical objects, namely perception. The 'play'-like character of imagining ensures that its autonomy is to this degree qualified, for it is by nature a 'borrower', an 'as if that is not——'.

How does this logical situation compare with that of perception? Must not perception likewise adopt a *mode* of perceptual relation to its object? After all, there is no such thing as 'just perceiving' a chair (any more than there is 'just moving' a chair). Must we not see it, or touch it, and so forth (just as we have to shove or drag or knock it)? Well, while these claims are undoubtedly true, the perceptual and imaginative situations are nonetheless fundamentally unlike. First, perception *can* take modeless form, say noticing a sensation, which is a sheer noticing of its object. For whereas one perhaps *sees* a chair and might instead have *felt* it, one *just* notices a sensation, since no alternative noticings exist in the case of sensations. Second, seeing the chair is in any case (just, sheer) noticing (and thus, perceiving) the visual sensations (regularly) caused by it. And so the perceptual event must *in essence* be a sheer noticing of a distinctive object, rather than a distinctive noticing of an object. And therefore third, it is not even a distinctive noticing of a distinctively (say) visual object: the reason being, that all that is distinctive to a visual noticing derives from the distinctive character of its immediate object, and nowise comes from the noticing itself. A visual noticing is not an auditory noticing, but the origin of the difference lies completely in the object. What we call a 'visual noticing' is merely a noticing of a distinctively visual object like colour, it is not a visual noticing of such a visible. There is simply no such animal! To what would it be opposed?

Since imagining-of is in essence a 'mock'-of something else, it can never be a pure imaginative consciousness of an object: it has to adopt a specific perceptual mode. By contrast, perception is precisely a sheer unmodified consciousness of its object. Yet it is easy to be misled by the variegation of perception's objects, and suppose the situations analogous. But in fact even though the perceptual noticing-of takes the different forms that we single out under 'see' 'hear' 'smell', the noticing-of taking place on these various occasions is one and the same phenomenon. In each case a distinctively different object—colour, sound, smell—comes as direct extensional object to awareness. No more: it does not come in any *way*, it simply *comes*. But the first derivative from this primal acquaintance with things, namely perceptual imagining, while imitating such a bare modeless acquaintance with a highly distinctive object, cannot but imitate as well the property of taking a distinctive object. The result is, that while the prototype is modeless, the copy is necessarily cast in the specific form of a sense.

(b) Distinguishing imagining-of an object from thought-of an object

Whereas perception is a sheer unmodified consciousness of its object, the imaginative consciousness of an object necessarily adopts a specific perceptual mode. How does thought compare on this count with these two experiential ways of relating to a phenomenal object? Is there such a thing as a sheer thought-of an object? As a mental image of St Peter's can swim into one's head, quite independently of other experience, can an ungarnished thought-of an object do the same? 'I suddenly thought of Z!' What does this exclamation convey? Does there exist *something else* besides a mental image of Z, and a thought which is a thought about Z ('What an amazing person Z is!', etc.)? I know of nothing to add to these two possibilities. While we discover in the latter case a thought-that which is a thought-about Z, in which Z is 'before one's mind' so to say in a 'propositional package', I can no more indicate anything that is a sheer thought-of Z, than I can in the case of an imagining-of Z. As Z comes to the imagination only through a perceptual modality, so it probably comes to thought only via a proposition. I shall tentatively assume that this is how matters stand.

But in any case the difference between the thinking and imagining relation to objects can be brought out independently of our stance on this issue. Thus, we can say of the imagining of (say) sounds that it is only because perception of sound exists that there can be imagining of sounds, since for the mind to pass directly imaginatively onto a sound *is* for one to imagine hearing-of that sound. By contrast, even if there existed such a thing as a non-propositional thought-of a sound, it would have no need of being a thought-of a *hearing* of that sound, and would presumably strike through to its object in one direct blow. In sum, thought probably encounters objects only in modeless propositional form, but even if it could encounter them *qua* direct-object, it would still do so modelessly. This establishes a fundamental structural difference between the relation of thought and imagination to the kinds of objects that are accessible to perception.

4. The Fundamental Experiential Relations to Perceptible Objects

(1) This terminates the enterprise of differentially distinguishing three fundamental experiential relations in which a person might stand to a perceptible object: perceptual, imaginative, thinking. This has been accomplished through appeal to the following characteristics: the autonomy of the phenomenon, its relation to direct and propositional objects, and its relation to negative objects. A summary word now on each phenomenon, beginning with perception.

(2) Perception takes direct objects ('a sound'), and discovers its identity autonomously under 'perceive———' ('perceive a sound'), but takes no negative direct-objects ('perceive a silence'). Perception takes no propositional objects ('that it rained last night'), and *a fortiori* takes no negative propositional objects ('that it did not rain last night').

The imagination takes direct objects ('imagine-of an object O'), though these events take the form of and discover their identity under 'imagine-of perceiving O' and never under 'imagine-of O' (there being no such thing), but the imagination takes no negative direct-objects ('imagine-of hearing silence', 'imagine-of an absence of auditory experience'). It goes without saying that the imagination takes propositional objects ('that I am now having auditory experience'), since this power overlaps with the sheer capacity to think. And it equally goes without saying that the imagination takes negative propositional objects ('that it is not now noisy', 'that it is absolutely silent', 'that I am not now having any auditory experience').

Thought probably takes no direct objects ('a mere thought of St Peter's Cathedral'), and *a fortiori* probably takes no negative direct objects ('a mere thought of silence'). However, if thought could manage to take direct objects, these events would autonomously discover their identity under 'thought-of x' and not under 'thought-of perceiving x', and thought would in addition take negative objects ('a mere thought of the emptiness of the cupboard'). Finally, it goes without saying that thought takes propositional objects ('that it is now noisy'), and it equally goes without saying that thought takes negative propositional objects ('that it is not now noisy').

(3) The discussion in this chapter has helped to bring into focus just what is involved when perceptual acquaintance with phenomenal objects is established. In distinguishing perception from imagination, and from its close relative thought, we have travelled further along the road to differentially delineating the precise nature of the attentive (i.e. perceptual) contact with phenomenal existents. When the attention takes a direct object, the event in question has certain essential properties that clearly mark it off from these neighbouring phenomena.

Indeed, it could with justice be said that we have been differentially distinguishing the *four* fundamental experiential relations in which a person might stand to a perceptible object: perceptual, thinking, imaginative—and cognitive. For to the above three phenomena we could well have added a fourth, namely the event which formed the subject-matter of Chapter 10, the (so-called) 'perceptual discovery-experience' ('seeing-that——'). The result is an enriched differential account of perception, exemplified in the following everyday situation. I am waiting at a traffic signal. Suddenly I catch sight of the green light. At that same instant I discover by seeing that the light is green. A thought passes through my head to the effect that 'that green is brighter than the usual green', and as it does an image of just such a green light swings into place in my mind. Then while these four simple phenomena, each endowed with a perceptual content, are all of them humdrum familiarities, they are nonetheless elemental constituents of a typical human stream of consciousness. And they are not to be confused with one another. My special concern in the latter part of the discussion has been with the primal event which, from a general point of view, is probably the originating father of the other three: the perception. And that is to say, with one of the two primary roles open to experiential consciousness.

14

Active Attending
or
A Theory of Mental Action

Much of our waking lives are passed, amongst other things, in looking at the objects and phenomena which surround us. Indeed, for the most part we are simply incapable of *not* looking at such items. This is a purely contingent genetically determined trait of humans, attesting no doubt to the power and scope of the sense of sight. Then it is of some significance that the process of looking is an *active* phenomenon. The world does not come upon us epistemologically like a clap of thunder, and we most of the time go more than half-way to meet it, actively directing our attention onto whatever outer phenomena happen to interest us. This state of affairs possesses two main assets so far as we are concerned. It helps us to determine the general content of our immediately future perceptions, say when one sees a car veering across the path of one's own car. Equally importantly, it enables us to synthesize perceptions across time, as when we see the path of a ball across a tennis court, or actively string together words on a page and make of them something intelligible. Stripped of the properties imported by the will, perception would tend to deliver to consciousness a mass of cognitive data which would be of little sense and less use. In short, epistemologically and perceptually we steer our own path through the world for much of the time, and for good reason.

And so it is of some significance that our perceptions occur in the setting of an active perceptual process, rather as the many separate frames out of which a 'movie' is constituted are located in an intelligible continuity of connected images. Then it is for reasons of this kind—and in the context of a general examination of the Attention and Perception—that the phenomenon of active attending calls for scrutiny. Just what is going on when this process is taking place? How do will and awareness relate? In particular, how does looking relate to seeing, or listening to hearing?

But there is another reason for investigating active attending. It is that the concept itself is *highly problematic.* We shall see later on in the present chapter that a puzzle exists over the very possibility of active attending, what I call the 'Antitheticality Puzzle', a puzzle located within the attention itself, arising out of the starkly antithetical characters of action and perception, resoluble only through dialectical means. This problem only comes to light when we pursue the analysis of the phenomenon of active attending to its later stages.

While the subject matter of the present chapter is the nature of active attending generally, it is in effect the analysis of listening and looking. For the most part I concentrate the discussion upon listening, because it is the simpler of the two phenomena yet such as to preserve the essentials of the problem. The question I hope to answer is: what is the structural analysis of active attending? Since we are concerned here with internal or mental actions, this problem leads me at first into an examination of mental actions generally. We shall discover that active attending realizes an entirely new sub-variety of the kind, not merely from the point of view of content, but from the more fundamental stance of structure.

1. Mental Actions

(a) Three distinct mental-act schemas

What are examples of mental action? The following: ratiocinating, phantasizing, trying to remember a name, talking silently to oneself, and surely also the phenomena that interest me here: listening and looking. Which mental phenomena are not mental actions? More precisely, which mental *experiential* phenomena are not actions? Examples are: seeing, dreaming, feeling emotion, experiencing pain. Then inspecting the above list of mental actions, it seems that they divide into active attendings and thinkings (provided the concept of thinking is sufficiently elastic to accommodate the active varieties of imagining). In any case listening, which is a mode of active attending, is a mental action. And that is to say—as I hope to show—an instance of a type that ranges over *structurally disparate* phenomena. It is my contention that mental actions, unlike physical or bodily actions, are not structurally all of one piece. This will become evident when we investigate the question: do mental acts consist in the—mediate or immediate—producing of some desired mental event? Various answers prove to be in order, depending on the type of the act, and these several answers have diverse structural implications. Mental actions prove to be structurally heterogeneous. This will emerge in the ensuing discussion.

My claim is that at least three different structures—call them (S1), (S2), (S3)—are exemplified by mental actions. I shall consider these three kinds in order, beginning with a somewhat surprising variety (S1) of mental action. Thus, there exist active mental phenomena which at first glance look to be the immediate producing of a desired internal event, but which on inspection prove to be the active producing of *nothing*: sheer doings, as one might say. The best example of this type that I can think of is the puzzling phenomenon of talking silently to oneself, which does not, I shall argue, consist in the active producing of imaginative phenomena in one's mind, nor indeed of any mental phenomena whatever. I will examine this case in the next Section (*b*), but I would like first to distinguish it structurally from two other varieties of mental action. The chosen exemplars of those other two varieties are, (S2) the phenomenon of voluntary recollection, and (S3) the case under discussion: listening or active attending. It is my contention that these three types, (S1), (S2), (S3), instantiate structurally dissimilar situations. More exactly, the claim is that the several whole-events that are necessary conditions of the occurrence of the act in question, instantiate three different structures. This more complicated formulation permits the structure under consideration either to include the *act itself* as one of its event-parts, or else to be the structure obtaining *within* the act. The value of this approach lies in the structural dissimilarities which it enables us to delimit, as a means to classifying mental actions.

(b) Structure (S1): talking to oneself

I begin this inquiry with a few words on the kind (S1) exemplified by talking silently to oneself. This phenomenon might take various forms: for example, in a permanently deaf person it could consist in signalling motionlessly to oneself. Since the expression 'silent talking' is as much a contradiction as 'motionless running', 'silent talking' must be a misdescription of a silent mental seeming-talking. This perfectly real internal activity is seemingly the public bodily activity of vocalizing. Then the question I wish to ask is, whether this activity consists in actively producing some desired mental phenomenon. For example, does it consist in doing internally what causes an imaginative 'hearing', or maybe an imagined 'sound', or perhaps an imagined perturbation of the larynx, or else a seeming act of vocalizing?

Well, it can scarcely be the producing by active internal means of a seeming-vocalizing, since a seeming-vocalizing is what precisely it *is*. When we speak of 'seeming', we here mean: a mental reproduction of some actuality; and that is what seeming-vocalizing is. And neither can it be the producing of a quasi-hearing, since the occurrence of hearing is strictly speaking irrelevant to the occurrence of vocalizing. A man can speak without hearing a word of what he has said: the experience of speaking does not entail the experience of hearing. And the same holds within. Why should we need to internally 'hear' if we are internally to 'speak'?

What remain as serious possibilities are that this internal activity consists in producing imagined sounds, or imagined laryngeal changes. Might silent speech be the active generating of such? But can a mental act be a seeming bodily act of producing a bodily movement ϕ, only if it is itself not merely an *attempted*, but a *successful* producing of an imagined ϕ? Must a man silently talking to himself really be trying to produce an imagined perturbation in the vocal apparatus? And must he be *succeeding*, what is more? Or must he instead really be trying to produce, and succeeding again, an imagined voice? But what explains his instantaneous success? For we can talk to ourselves with fluent speed, whereas as often as not mental images disobey our commands. And why in any case should success be of any account to him? Why should it matter to the silent speaker that seeming sounds *actually* issue forth in his own mind? They will not enlighten him as to the content of his inner willings. And is not the entire point of the exercise to bring a string of words before the mind? But that is accomplished from the beginning! Must he not be immediately aware of the verbal content of his intentions and his ongoing mental strivings? Does he need to 'hear' 'sounds' before he knows what he is doing? It is because of considerations of this kind that I believe of this case that it is the active producing of nothing. It is, so to say, will through and through. Here we have one structural situation (S1) in the case of mental actions.

(c) Structure (S2): recollecting

I turn now to the structural variety (S2) exemplified by voluntary recollection. The chosen example is, trying to remember a name. Unquestionably this phenomenon rates as an action if successful: an act of the type, jogging the memory. Then what are the constituents of such an act? In particular, is the event of name-appearance part of the act?

It is noteworthy in cases of this kind that just as typically one's endeavours are unsuccessful as successful. And it is significant also that the event of name-appearance which signals success, frequently occurs some few moments after the endeavour itself. What conclusions may we draw from these observations? The following, to begin with. First, that trying to remember has causal power. Second, that the power must be expressible in loose probabilistic terms which vary from occasion to occasion. Third, that normally one does not know why on any particular occasion one's endeavour was successful when it was. These conclusions may be summed up in the following generality: that successful tryings to recollect cause recollection through implementing hidden means which have a power that is expressible in loose probabilistic terms. In short, a highly fallible but nonetheless efficacious mental mechanism or *way of producing* must automatically be activated by the will to remember.

Does the existence of this mechanistic link between willing and name-appearance suffice to unite these two events under the event-head, 'jogging the memory'? I very much doubt it. I doubt it because one has managed successfully to 'jog' one's memory, even when the event of name-appearance occurs some few seconds after one stops one's mental exertions—and has one not done all that one is ever going to do when one ceases trying to remember? Evidently such acts do not encompass the event of name-appearance. But they are *as typical* as instantaneously successful cases. And are we to suppose these two varieties of acts structurally dissimilar? And does it not in any case seem likely that on all occasions of success, trying to remember causes and is thus distinct from the event of recollection? Then since in general successful tryings *are* the succeeded-in act, it would follow that the act itself will also be distinct from the recollection.

When these arguments are taken in conjunction with the consideration that the mechanism involved is fallible and unreliable, we have a strong case for the view that the act of jogging the memory begins and ends with the event of trying to remember, and does not include the distinct event of name-appearance or recollection which it causes. The structure of the act-situation encountered with (S2)-type actions like recollection, seems to be closely reminiscent of that realized in 'instrumental act'-situations in physical nature—with one important difference: that a mechanism is activated in the case of this sub-variety of mental act.

2. Comparing Listening and Bodily Action

(a) Setting up bodily action as a reference-point

(1) So far we have laid out two structural schemas—that of (S1) and (S2)—possible for mental actions, prior to examining the structural situation in the cases that are our prime concern, viz. active attendings. Then it is clear from what emerged concerning the above two structures that the most familiar example of the genus action, namely bodily action, cannot be taken as a structural model for either case. Both act-kinds so far mentioned—soliloquy, recollection—embody differently structured acts/act-situations from that encountered in bodily action, as we now see.

Thus, whatever one's precise views concerning the constituents of bodily action, it is certain that the bodily act encompasses the bodily movement as a whole-event part. Doubtless this is intimately linked with the presence in bodily action of two elements which were noteworthy absences in the (S2) case ('recollection') just discussed. Namely: the extreme reliability of the bodily motor-system, and the near-instantaneousness of its operation. These two factors must help to unite the events of willing, of mechanism-activation, and bodily movement, under the one event-heading of bodily action. Now these few comments serve to explicate the structural difference between bodily action and active recollection. Meanwhile, it is evident that both of these cases differ structurally in an identical respect from the (S1) type of act exemplified by silent soliloquy, since in this latter case there is no analogue either of name-appearance or willed bodily movement.

The question we must now ask is: which, if any, of the above three varieties of action, is a satisfactory model for the structural analysis of cases of the type of listening? Is listening to be compared to talking silently to oneself? Or to jogging the memory? Or to common or garden examples of bodily moving? I shall argue for the view that it is comparable to none of them, and that it realizes a novel active structural situation (S3) in its own right. We have here a fourth possible structure for actions.

(2) Nevertheless it seems to me that the discussion of active attending is best conducted by reference to the last of the three model cases, viz. bodily action. This most familiar and central example of the kind provides a reference-point when we come to consider the basic elements encountered in act-situations generally. And it has a second asset. Thus, bodily action is the most clear-cut or unambiguous example of the type action, the reason being that the distinction between active and inactive events is in the case of the body more decisive than in the mind, which by

contrast is populated with phenomena which have, and in continually varying degrees, something of a life of their own. The 'will status' (as one might say) of some mental occurrences is a 'grey area'. The 'would not'/'could not' distinction, so vitally important for the concept of responsibility, is notoriously difficult to apply in some cases.

Then I think we ought not to assume that bodily action must be a correct model for *any* mental phenomenon. As noted already, the mental *status quo* is so markedly dissimilar from the bodily that it would be intellectually foolhardy to do so. I say this, even though bodily action is surely the central, indeed almost the defining case of the type action. Yet that it cannot actually *be* the unique defining paradigm is evident from the preceding discussion, which brought to our notice fundamental structural differences between several varieties of action. While there exist necessary and sufficient conditions for action as such, and while all actions have one and the same essence (viz. striving), what has just emerged is that action has no *structural essence*, and *a fortiori* not that exemplified in bodily action. Nonetheless, this central example of the type provides a valuable reference-point. It contains clearly present elements which it is natural to look for in other examples of the kind, action. We shall bear them in mind as we embark now upon the structural analysis of cases of the type of active attending.

(b) Discovering the elements, the willing and the willed, within listening

(1) The elements of bodily action that I single out are the following: the willed bodily movement φ, the activation of the motor-mechanism M, and the phenomenon of willing (or trying or striving or attempting). Can we discover analogues of these three elements in attending or listening?

I begin this discussion by looking for an analogue of the willed bodily movement φ in active attentive situations. This bodily phenomenon φ has the following relevant properties. Thus, it is a continuity, that is in itself not an act, which owes its existence to the will, and that can in principle occur without will. Is there an analogue in listening? Can we discover there a phenomenon with these properties? A few simple entailments assist us at this point. Thus, listening to sound S entails hearing S, which in turn entails the here-and-now audibility-to-one of S, *and* neither entailment is reversible: the clock can be ticking away unnoticed, the slam of the door heard but not listened-to. Then these logical relations are more or less duplicated in bodily action, with arm-raising the analogue of listening, arm-rise that of hearing, and limb-freedom some kind of analogue of audibility-to-one-now. But the point that matters here is that hearing is an analogue of limb movement. And yet, it may be objected, limb movement is continuous, but can the hearing that is co-present with listening also be continuous? I can see no reason why it should not be. To be sure it may seem odd to say that continuous hearing is going on as one actively listens, but there can be no doubt that one hears at each instant in which one listens, and that those instants form a continuity.

(2) Thus far the comparison with bodily action holds. A continuity of hearing occurs which, give or take a certain leeway, would not have occurred were it not for one's engaging in listening. Later I shall have more to say about the 'leeway', but let us make the plausible assumption that *such* a hearing with *such* content would almost certainly not have occurred had one not listened. Turn now to the second element of bodily action: the essentially active element of willing or striving or attempting. This surely also is present: act-desire and act-intention find immediate expression in listening, the intensity of the desire matching the urgency of the enterprise, and in general when one listens one tries to listen. All listening is, and I think essentially is, something we engage in and 'do', in the special 'will' (and not just 'cause') sense of 'do'. All listenings are attempts or strivings or willings—however certain one may be of success. Just as 'believe' has the core sense 'hold to be true', which is consistent with unshakeable certainty, so I submit 'try' has the core sense 'attempt', which is consistent with the inconceivability of failure. Thus, despite a few misgivings on its exact productive function, the element of will encountered in bodily action is encountered in active attending also. In short, the comparison between the two cases is more or less sustained so far.

(c) The absence of mechanism in listening

(1) I come to the third element of bodily action: activation of a motor-mechanism, indeed of a motor-mechanism that for the most part works with a sort of flawless ease. We noted the presence of a mechanistic element, though highly flawed and expressible in no more than probabilistic terms, in recollecting, and its absence, for want of any putative mechanistically-effected product, in soliloquy. What is the situation in the case of listening or active attending generally?

At this point I will change the example. Since listening, or looking, or active attending generally, is the phenomenon under discussion, considerations of simplicity lead me to substitute the directing of one's attention onto a sensation. The example I propose is a naturally recessive sensation, say a sensation of contact. We shall suppose that the project is that of directing one's attention onto a medium-intensity sensation of contact, sited on the heel of one's left foot, for the span of a few seconds. And so one turns one's attention onto this psychological object, and of course succeeds, and instantaneously. Might a mental mechanism link these two events? Might a mechanism link the event of turning the attention onto or towards, and the event of noticing or making attentive contact with this object? If so, it must be a mechanism that works with the flawless ease and certainty of bodily mechanisms. Had it been the case that a mechanism linked talking to oneself with some inner 'sound', we would have had to say the same of it, since one embarks on inner speech with the same certainty and instantaneous success as outer. Then in either case one would have had grounds for suspecting that the situation had been misrepresented, for the simple reason that the mind's mechanisms seem invariably to be *flawed* (perhaps because the mental *status quo* is as mobile as flowing water). So to repeat: might a mechanism link directing one's attention onto, and noticing, a particular sensation?

(2) Does not the very idea seem suspect from the start? Where is the gap to be mechanistically bridged? It is worth remembering what in general the factor of mechanism accomplishes for a theoretical account. Thus, it bridges an explanatory hiatus, and does so through interposing a linked sequence of pellucid explanations as a means of explaining what otherwise stands unexplained. Then how can this concept find application when one turns one's attention onto a sensation? For is it not *explanation enough* of one's awareness of the sensation that one voluntarily turned the attention in its direction? What explanatory gap is there to bridge? What bridges that are an improvement on what already we have? Are we not in danger of regress in asking for more?

Let me express the matter slightly differently. A mechanism is a regular mediating device, a way of producing, a 'how', whose presence is attested by three factors. The first is the existence of a regular connection between input phenomenon and output product, the second is the occasional breakdown of regularity, the third is the existence of an explanatory hiatus that must be bridged. Is not this precisely the situation encountered in such a paradigmatic example of mechanism as that of the bodily will? Thus, regularity there obtains; and failure exceptionally occurs; and interposing between act of the will and bodily output lies nothing less than the whole mysterious divide of mind and body (as Hume observed in a cogent passage in the *Enquiries* (1748), sect. vii, pt. 1).

Of these three elements, I discover only the first in the example of attending. We have remarked already on the absence of explanatory hiatus. What about failure? When do we try to attend to a bodily sensation and fail? Here we should note a simple ambiguity in 'fail'. In the central sense of this term we conceive of failure as an unsuccessful attempt, but we should not overlook the existence of a subsidiary sense which merely means an omission to do (in a situation where doing is to be expected). In the first sense I failed to start the car one snowy morning, in the second I failed to keep a rather important appointment last week. Can one try and fail, in both these senses, in the simple case of trying to attend to a sensation? I do not think so: I do not think it is possible in the first sense. The only cases of trying and failing I can discover are of the second kind, viz. changes or abandonment of project, whether through fascination at the hands of some other object, or boredom, or sheer forgetfulness. Each of these causal influences might lead, not to unsuccessfulness of the project, but to its termination. It is true that we sometimes mean by 'trying to listen', trying to keep my mind on the task of trying to listen, trying for example to fight off the deflecting power of alternative attractions, and here of course one can fail—but they are not in question here.

I emphasize four simple points at this juncture. (1) The substitution of sensation for sound is irrelevant to the question at issue. Thus, the bodily auditory mechanism, which in regular fashion generates the here-and-now audibility-to-one of (say) a ticking upon receipt of stimuli from sound-waves, *precedes* the operation of the supposed mechanism under discussion, and it is the latter which I reject (for there is no mechanistic 'how' whereby an attempt to listen to a ticking clock succeeds). (2) I have restricted the discussion to simple cases like single sounds and sensations. The operative policy is: first things first. (3) By 'try' I mean, not 'try to get myself to try' (e.g. take a stiff whisky) or 'try to keep myself trying' (e.g. think of the money), not (for example) 'try to stand over myself and prevent myself from trying instead to listen in to that juicy piece of gossip over there'—but (purely and simply) 'try' (which cannot be better described). Whereas the former tryings are all of them second-order phenomena, the latter trying is first-order. (4) The issue is not, '*What does one do* to succeed in the enterprise?', but '*What mechanism* makes the enterprise successful?' My suggestion is: *no mechanism* makes a genuine trying to attend to a sensation, a genuine case of attending to that sensation. Regress is the nemesis lying in wait for those who keep insisting that we 'go on'.

It is for reasons of this kind that I believe we are dealing here, not with a flawless mechanism, but with no mechanism at all. This constitutes a breakdown of the model of bodily action, since mechanism-activation is of its essence; and a breakdown of the model of voluntary recollection, for the same reason; which we must set beside breakdown again of the model provided by soliloquy, in this case on the count of the inexistence of an analogue of hearing. We have here a demonstration of the earlier claim, that active attending instantiates a novel fourth act-structure. An act-structure, I should add, of which we are as yet wholly ignorant.

3. The Structure of Active Attending

(a) The Identity Theory

(1) The investigation of the structure of attending must be pursued beyond this point. We have just seen that the comparison with bodily action holds both in respect of the element of willing, together with that of the willed event, but breaks down on the count of mechanism. This simplifies the picture. We are concerned with nothing more than the relations between active attending, awareness, and the will to attend—with only a few structural situations possible. The problem of structure boils down to that.

However, the very factor which led to the deletion of the element of mechanism, raises a new difficulty: to wit, the spectre of necessary causation, from cause to effect, between distinct existents! Namely, between the attempt to direct the attention onto, and the event of awareness-of. To be sure the mind, almost like phenomena at quantum level in physical theory, has the habit of savaging principles which seem sacrosant; nonetheless one understandably quails a little before endorsing the reality of this state of affairs. And yet if failure, if only in the simple case under consideration, is in the primary sense of 'failure' downright inconceivable here, it is difficult to see how to avoid it. But now a desperate expedient comes to mind. Thus, it has frequently turned out, when necessary causation seemed on the face of it a reality, that we were in fact merely juggling with necessarily linked descriptions of the one and same phenomenal item. Could that be how matters stand in the present case?

What are the two elements supposedly linked by the improbable necessary bond? They are: the attempt to direct attention onto a sensation, and the event of awareness of the sensation. And yet why believe these phenomena are *two and distinct*? Why not endorse the simple view that they are one and the same event travelling under different descriptions? This view I shall dub the 'Identity Theory'. It is in effect a theory of act-structure, and its examination advances the overall project of uncovering the true structure of active attending.

Let me spell out what the Identity Theory involves. Now one might at first think, when (say) listening occurs, that three events are taking place: trying to listen, listening, and hearing; maybe distinct from one another, maybe overlapping in places, but ennumerable as three. The Identity Theory disagrees: where some may see three such events, and some perhaps no more than two, it sees but one: a solitary event travelling under three descriptions. What is said to justify the multiplicity of characters available to this one phenomenon is the complex character of its immediate origins. When a hearing occurs which is the immediate effect of certain act-progenitors that are expressly dedicated to its occurrence, which is to say phenomena like act-desire and intention with hearing as their projected content, the resultant hearing qualifies for the additional descriptions, 'trying to hear' and 'listening'. Thus, listening is on this account the *active occurrence* of hearing, not in the relatively uninteresting sense in which arm-raising involves or realizes the active occurrence of arm-rise, but in the strict and simple sense of identity. *This hearing,* on this occasion, *is* this listening. That is the claim. Accordingly, the activeness of this example of hearing/listening must on this account be a derivative and inessential property: this phenomenon will be essentially a hearing, inessentially a listening, and inessentially active. This is what the Identity Theory implies.

(2) This theory has distinct theoretical assets, over and above the virtue of eschewing necessary causation, from cause to effect, between distinct existents. Thus, it identifies the successful attempt and the deed, and this is in accord with a general principle which, for reasons which I shall not rehearse here, strikes me as extremely sound. And the offending element of mechanism is, on this theory, banished from the scene. And a precedent exists for the very simple act-structure envisaged by the theory: namely, the strangely simple structure exemplified by the aforementioned phenomenon of silent speech or soliloquy. In addition, the theory has the merit of keeping listening and hearing together—which is surely a virtue: thus, it does not postulate them as two and distinct, and in the strongest possible sense listening on this account involves hearing. Finally, it has the virtue of vindicating the intuition that listening is active through and through, for on this theory no alien inactive element is introduced into listening, which is to say a supposedly inactive hearing-part. And, of course, the theory has economy and simplicity.

(3) Nevertheless, these advantages do not constitute a demonstration. And in fact there exists a more or less decisive disproof of the Identity Theory. A first indication of its falsity is given merely by the oddity of some of the things that would hold were the theory correct. There should be such a thing as rational hearing; we should be able to be 'engaged in' or 'occupied in' hearing; and we would have our own reasons for hearing, which would exhaustively constitute its cause. An even more significant argument against the theory lies in the fact that *all* listenings are active, while some hearings *at the very least* are inactive. This latter fact constitutes convincing reason for believing that hearing must as such be inactive. This is because the mind is full of phenomena whose will-status is fixed by their kind: belief, emotion, desire, intention, and for that matter trying or willing itself. It seems like a completely general rule that, while some inactive phenomena can actively be engineered with varying degrees of immediacy, no phenomenon that is sometimes inactive *ever* occurs as active—and vice versa. When is a willing inactive? When is a believing a doing? Accordingly the fact that *some* hearings are indubitably inactive is reason for believing that hearing *as such* and therefore the hearings *contemporaneous with listenings* are also inactive.

Finally, we encounter an even stronger argument against the Identity Theory when we come to consider the question of origins. It goes without saying that listening is an activity, and so also goes without saying that it has its immediate source in phenomena like act-desire and intention. Then there is no room amongst these immediate progenitor-phenomena for the sensation that is the immediate object of attending, or for the sound that is the object of listening. Thus, if I choose to attend to a sensation, that sensation is a cause of my attending only insofar as it appears as incentive in the intention and desire generating the attending. It cannot function as immediate cause in the way that is open to act-desire, snap-decision, and suchlike appointed act-sources. But the Causal Theory of Perception requires that any event of perception have its source, at least in part, in the perceived object. If it did not, how would perception be a *way of knowing* about the World? Then when the object of perception is an immediate object like sensation, the causation has to be at once immediate and unrationalized. And the perception that occurs when we actively or voluntarily attend to a sensation, can be no exception to this rule. While the will is implicated in its origin, so too of necessity is the sensation, acting directly and without the mediating assistance of desire, intention, decision, and the like. This after all is the rationale underlying the impropriety of the aforementioned speech-form: 'my reason for hearing'. In sum, if listening *were* active hearing, the sound must be an immediate unrationalized cause of listening. But it cannot be. How could listening ever be rational if it were?

Accordingly, I reject the Identity Theory. And in fact I do not see how one could not reject it. If the theory were true, a particular example of perception would have to be identical with a particular trying, striving, act of the will! But can *any* perceiving ever *be* a striving to do? Surely perception, of its nature and therefore universally, is a responding-to or suffering-of at the hands of its object, howsoever much this may be intentionally engineered by the being who suffers such self-engineered experience.

(b) The structural analysis of attending

(1) The situation is as follows. I am attempting to provide a structural analysis of listening, or more generally of the activity of voluntarily attending. I began by comparing it to what I take to be the best understood instance of the act-genus: namely, bodily action. I uncovered in listening two precise structural analogues of the latter: first the act of the will, second the event that the will is bent upon immediately producing, in this case the continued awareness-of or hearing-of the entity that is actively attended-to or listened-to. Meanwhile it emerged that a third and vitally important element of bodily action, the mechanism whereby willing achieves its goal, is nowhere to be found in active attending.

Then in the light of the breakdown of this basic model, and the abandonment of the Identity Theory, what structural theories of active attention remain as viable options? Three theories suggest themselves—call them (A), (B), and (C)—which I now represent diagramatically (L standing for listening, S(L) for striving-to-listen, H for hearing). I discuss these theories in the order given by the diagrams in Figure 14.1.

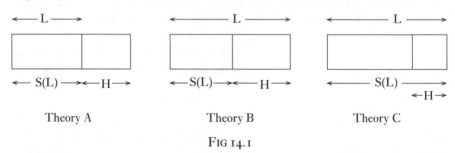

Theory A   Theory B   Theory C

FIG 14.1

(2) To begin with, a possible image or model for listening. Namely, that of reaching out a hand and touching something. Thus, noticing is in certain ways like the mind being touched by a psychic thing. Then why should we not *actively* produce such an event? Why should we not conceive of active attending as akin to the active extending of a mental hand in order to generate the inactive event of psychic contact? Alas, persuasive as this picture may be, it must be rejected forthwith. If it were true, that which is active when we attend would lead to and fall outside the confines of the goal event: attentive-contact. This is the first (A) of the above three structural theories (A)(B)(C), and is plainly wrong. What in effect it claims is that listening *causes* the hearing which listening entails. But it is absurd to suppose that listening and hearing are two and distinct. They cannot as we have just seen be identical, but equally as certainly they cannot be held apart. There can be no doubt that listening *involves*, but is not actually to be identified with, the hearing that is guaranteed by its occurrence.

Only two theories appear to be viable at this point. Let us remember that the structural raw materials consist of just three items: listening, trying to listen, and hearing. No more; and in particular no mechanism, no concealed sector, no subterranean unexperienced part. Finally, we have the following constraints upon theory-formation: the falsity of the Identity Theory, and the non-distinctness of listening and hearing. All that remains is to decide between Theory (B) that makes trying to listen part of listening, and Theory (C) which identifies listening and trying to listen. (That is, if the above three theoretical accounts exhaust the possibilities—which they certainly seem to do.)

I will be brief here. The one theoretical asset of Theory (B) is the fact that according to this theory the exercise of the will is explanatory of hearing. By and large this is true; though with qualification, as we shall shortly see. For the most part, had one not *listened* one would not have experienced *such* a hearing as in fact occurred. Now this is the doctrine that involves grasping the nettle of necessary-or-near causation from cause to effect between distinct existents, since according to it the act of the will is distinct from and cause-in-part of hearing; and this relation must, at least in the simple cases under consideration, verge upon necessity. No doubt this characteristic does not automatically disqualify the theory, but it is certainly a disincentive. In any case other considerations render it unacceptable. First it runs counter to the general principle that the successful attempt *is* the succeeded-in deed, which for a variety of reasons—notably, being demonstrably true of absolutely all instrumental acts—recommends itself. Second it embeds one act as non-distinct part of another, despite the fact that the supposed 'two' deeds have token-identical act-producer origins. And so on.

(3) The remaining third Theory (C) is the doctrine that identifies the phenomenon of listening with the attempt to listen, and locates the event of hearing as an inactive non-identical part of that listening. Let me now briefly run over a few of the theoretical virtues of this account.

It eschews mechanism and necessary causation between distinct existents. It identifies act and successful attempt. It disidentifies listening and hearing, yet at the same time holds them together. Thus, it does not suppose listening to be distinct from, and a necessary cause of, the event of hearing: instead it recognizes that listening *involves* hearing. Again it does not construe listening as a mere amalgam of an active first half and an inactive resultant second half, offering a sort of oil-and-water account from the point of view of the will: it does not do so, since on this theory listening itself *is* an action, and that is that. To be sure listening is said to include the inactive element of hearing, but that no more splits the act into act and non-act than does the presence of arm-rise in arm-raising. In a perfectly good sense, both acts are acts through and through to the end, despite encompassing elements which are not in themselves active. Hearing goes on in its own right in listening, literally overflowed by the will. What, by contrast, must be avoided in any acceptable account of this phenomenon, is the supposition that the event of willing produces a

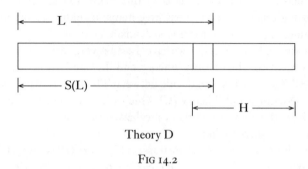

Theory D

FIG 14.2

distinct inactive hearing—which would as a result 'come at one' rather like the recoil of a gun. But on the present account hearing no more 'comes at one' than does the event of arm-rise in arm-raising. So much for the virtues of Theory (C). I accept it—qualifiedly. We shall see that it stands in need of qualification: namely, the emendation that we replace 'hearing is part of listening' by the rather *outré*-sounding 'the part of hearing that occurs because of will, is part of listening'. Let us call this final theory Theory (D) (see Figure 14.2). (But, as we shall see, the time for pictures is past.)

Because this emendation is a consequence of the special explanatory situation obtaining within listening, a proper explanation of that final emendation must be postponed until Section 5. In the meantime I deflect the discussion towards the explanatory issue.

4. Justifying the Existence of Active Perception

(a) The problem of the double causation of listening

Let me at this point review the account of listening which Theory (D) provides. The situation is something like this. A sound exists, or perhaps a sensation, of which already we are aware, and for some reason we choose to actively attend to it. And so a will-to-listen takes place, that proves to *be* a successful listening, in relation to which the sound is at once immediate material object *and* immediate unrationalized part-cause of the hearing-sector of this same listening—a sector which is identical with that part of the hearing that owes its existence to the will-to-listen. This rather complex state of affairs is what is said by Theory (D) to be realized when we engage in listening.

One element in this Theory (D)—indeed, for that matter, in Theory (C) as well—is worthy of special note. Namely: the necessity of immediate unrationalized causation of the hearing-sector of listening at the hands of a distinct external sound-object. Just how does this element fit into the theory? I ask, because I detect a difficulty. Thus, the sound-object is assumed to have nothing to do with the immediate genesis of the willing, but much to do with the immediate genesis of the hearing it encompasses. But surely if the sound helps cause part of listening, it must help to cause listening itself? What is the way out of this difficulty? It is to differentiate causal roles. The sound is not immediately responsible for the occurrence of the event that is a listening, but has much to do with its acquiring the status of listening. Rather as biceps-contraction has nothing to do with the occurrence of the event that is arm-raising, but much to do with its being an arm-raising, so here. The immediate progenitors of action, which include act-desire and act-intention and belief, cannot include sound or sensation—and that is that. It is a universal rule, applicable alike to listening and arm-raising. Rationality in action depends on this property.

(b) The problem of the double causation of hearing

(1) This response may answer the problem of double-causation of *listening,* namely the problem of the simultaneous causation from within (by act-desire) and without (by sound) of listening. But does it constitute an effective response to a closely related second intuition: namely, that the self-originating character of active perceiving may be inconsistent with the elsewhere-originated character of the perception involved in that activity, in the present case of the *hearing* involved in listening? Is there not a serious difficulty here?

And so the problem posed by Theory (D), a problem which by implication questions the very possibility of (say) listening and in effect requires it to justify its existence, relates not so much to listening as to hearing. The real problem posed by Theory (D) lies in the account which it seems by implication to give of the genesis of the hearing involved in listening. For it looks as if it *shares this out* between will and sound-object. Yet how can a veridical perception owe its existence, in howsoever slight a degree, to an immediate will-source? Is it not like supposing that rational belief might arise in part out of desire? How can a belief be rational and derive in even the least degree immediately from desire? Must not its rationality be qualified precisely to that degree?

Here we have a serious problem concerning the hearing that occurs in listening, indeed more generally over the awareness occurring in active attending, and in consequence a difficulty concerning the very viability of the concept of active attending. Because it stems from the antithetical character of will and perception, I shall dub it the 'antitheticality puzzle'. Then since active attending actually exists, since Reality so to say presents us with a *fait accompli,* the natural supposition is that the resolution of this puzzle should proceed *pari passu* with a fuller account of the facts. In short, with a better characterization of Theory (D). We shall see that this consists in a fuller account of the *explanatory situation* prevailing in active attending.

(2) Before I can begin to meet the above difficulty, I must make a few general comments concerning the structural analysis of listening implicit in this Theory (D) of listening. The first thing to say is that, at least from the point of view of the other three act-models—(S1)(Soliloquy), (S2)(Recollection), and Bodily Action—listening proves on this theory to have a *decidedly odd* structure. The Theory (D) that we have endorsed might at first look like a vindication of the bodily act model, minus the element of mechanism. Thus, in both cases the successful act of the will encompasses, so to say as its crown or culmination, the event that was the aim of the whole enterprise: namely, the hearing-sector that would not have occurred were it not for the exercise of the will. However, on closer inspection it can be seen that in actual fact the structural situation realized in listening does not duplicate that of basic bodily action, with or without mechanism.

Thus, a condition of listening is, not merely as in physical action that the desired goal-event owe its existence to will, but that this very same sector of itself be simultaneously caused by an external event! Nothing like this exists in physical action. And the very oddity of its make-up forbids our construing listening as instrumental action of any type, say as a mental contacting of its immediate object. For a necessary condition of listening is, not as in instrumentality that it *cause* a distinct external event, but a somewhat mystifying inversion of that requirement, according to which a sector of itself must in part be *caused by* an external! Indeed, the comparison with instrumentality is doubly askew. For an instrumental act *is what it is* irrespective of causing the manipulated event: thus, it might be a turning of a key or a moving of a limb; but listening in the absence of part-causation at the hands of the sound proves to be nothing more than a failed striving to listen. And that is why I say it has an odd structure. It actually *completes itself* through external assistance. To be sure, physical action stands in need of causal cooperation from the environment if it is to come to birth, for it is a necessary condition of limb-moving that limb-movement be possible—but surely not in the same way. In a word, listening, and indeed active attending generally, realizes an unusual and novel act-structure (S3), to be set alongside the three other exemplars: active recollection (S2), silent speech (S1), and physical action. All are, I suggest, 'originals'.

(3) I return to the problem raised by the intuition that the hearing sector of listening is a genuinely problematic phenomenon, and that as a result the very phenomenon of active attending must itself be problematic. Indeed, the problem is double. It is double because it involves a double paradox, one concerning action and the other concerning perception. Thus: how can there so much as *exist* an act-structure in which the actively engineered goal-event (of and within the act) owes its existence in part to an external event? And: how can we immediately and willingly produce in ourselves that which of its very nature (as a reliable recorder of outer reality) must be determined from *without*?

How are we to meet these difficulties? As I have already observed, it is the very special character of the explanatory situation prevailing in active attending which lies at the root of these problems. Now we know that in physical action willing leads causally to the desired bodily movement through the regular working of motor-mechanism. Given certain familiar standing conditions, willing is at once a tight sufficient condition-of and explanation-of willed bodily movement. Then how does listening compare on this count? What are the causal powers of the will to listen? What explanatory situation prevails in active attending generally? We shall see on investigation that it is nothing like so exact or clear-cut a situation as that realized in the physical case, and that it is entirely without precedent amongst acts of all kind. And so it is plain we shall not have completed the specification of this third (S3) type of mental act-schema, until we have filled in this explanatory part of Theory (D). Accordingly, the explanatory situation in listening comes to the fore, partly to fill this gap in our account of listening, partly to resolve the aforementioned puzzle—which is in effect to explain the possibility of such an unusual act-schema as that of active attending—the nub of which (here) lies in the explanation of the hearing involved in listening. Then note before I begin, that the process of delineating the explanatory situation, and *pari passu* of resolving the 'antitheticality puzzle', continues to the end of this chapter.

(c) The function of listening

(1) So at this point I raise a simple but fundamental question which until now I have ignored. *Why* do we listen? What is the *purpose* of listening? More exactly: is the function of listening to generate *hearing*? And a subsidiary query: does trying to listen *causally explain* hearing?

To explain why we listen, must be to discover the content of the impelling desire and intention expressed in the exercise of the will. In listening we aim to take control of our hearings, to remove them from the disordered wilderness of chance and site them in a structured network of our purposes, exercising a measure of choice as to their content. Then is the aim of listening the production of hearing? I think the answer is: yes, and no. An interesting counterfactual reveals something of the complexities in this issue. Namely, would we have heard the sound we listened to, had we not listened to it? Strangely enough, in many cases the answer is that we would! And yet, despite the force of this consideration, the content of the impelling act-desire cannot but be to produce hearing! Only it is not just any old hearing that we seek, it is a select hearing that is endowed with certain desired properties: some of those properties being external properties, some others internal and pertaining to content. Thus, one might listen simply in order to hear; but sometimes it will be, not just to hear, but to hear *for certain*; and sometimes it will be, not so much to hear, but to hear *well* or *continuously* or *for all of five seconds*. These are external properties. But one can in addition pursue internal properties of content: for example, a differential perception of timbre, or of pitch, or volume, or the full propositional content of some statement. And so on.

(2) Given these several kinds of properties of the internal object of trying to listen, we now rephrase the earlier explanatory question, taking due account of their existence. Does trying to produce a hearing that is (say) guaranteed, and continuous, and a good example of the type; that is of timbre, or pitch, or whatever it be—does a trying with such differential content cause a hearing blessed with just such properties? What, in other words, does listening *actually accomplish*? This should tell us what is its causal role or *natural function*.

Once again a counterfactual sheds light on the situation. Let us assume that there exists a soft monotone sound S which endures for n seconds; and suppose you bring to bear such a listening project upon it; and at the end that you have heard S, continuously, well, and so forth. Can you assert that, in the absence of such action, such a hearing would not have occurred? One can say nothing so simple. The answer must be given both differentially and in probabilistic terms. Thus, you can say that in the absence of such a listening project it is *very unlikely* that you would have experienced a hearing endowed with the full battery of desired properties. And you can say that it is *unlikely* that you would have experienced a hearing that was (say) both a case of hearing well and continuously. And you can say finally that it is *quite possible* that you would have heard the sound itself. Then these facts have causal repercussions of corresponding character. Thus, what you cannot do is to assert *categorically*: 'trying to listen, with such and such an internal object, aided and abetted by the sound itself, was causally responsible for a hearing endowed with such and such properties.' But you are entitled to make a series of probabilistic causal claims. Thus, you are entitled to say: 'very probably, trying to listen, taken in conjuction with the sound-object, was causally responsible for the fact that a hearing occurred that was endowed with the full battery of desired properties.' And you are entitled to say: 'probably, trying to listen was causally responsible for the fact that a hearing occurred that was both continuous and a good example of the kind.' And finally: 'possibly, trying to listen caused the very event of hearing itself.'

Thus, willing is in general a probabilistic causal explanation of the hearing that occurs in listening, an explanation whose probability-value must rise with the expansion and development of the content of the hearing involved. But it is never entirely certain, never categorical, always probabilistic: a fact which is doubtless a reflection of sorts of the natural turbulence of the mind, of the fact that there is no stationary *status quo* which is disturbed more or less by will alone—by contrast with our limbs. So what is the answer to the original question, viz. what does listening accomplish? There exists a much closer match between what is actually heard and what one sought to hear, than between what is heard and what listening accomplishes. What listening accomplishes consists in, what is heard less what would have been heard had the listening not occurred: an answer that must be cast irreducibly in probabilistic terms. So much for the causal role of listening.

(3) It should be emphasized that the above property constitutes a decisive break, on the count of explanatory character, with the basic physical model of action. We

have already noted a significant dissimilarity between listening and this physical paradigm, consisting in the absence of any listening-mechanism; and an even more radical dissimilarity, namely the fact that listening stands causally in need of assistance from without if it is to complete itself. But the gross unlikeness of the rationale linking will and success in these two cases, takes us far afield from the original physical model. It serves to emphasize the truth of the earlier claim that we are in the presence of a fourth wholly 'original' schema for action.

(d) The special causal properties of the will to listen

(1) So much for the causal accomplishments of the will in active attending, and for the justification of the claim (in Theory (D)) that (say) the hearing sector of listening consists in something less than the hearing co-present with that listening. I undertook this task with two aims in mind. First, in order to provide a more complete characterization, and indeed justification of Theory (D). Second, to put us in a better position to meet a difficulty which had arisen over the genesis of the awareness involved in active attending, and ultimately therefore over the phenomenon of active attending itself. Now earlier we noted that the resolution of the (simple) problem of the double causation of *listening* lay in the differentiation of the modes of causation open to listening and to the hearing involved therein. Then it seems to me that analogously the resolution of the (complex) problem of the double causation of that *hearing* lies in differentiating the modes of causation of hearing, open on the one hand to striving-to-listen, on the other hand to the heard object itself. Let us at this point begin upon this task.

(2) We just saw that the former brand of causation must be expressed probabilistically. And yet there can be no doubt that the will-to-listen has genuine causal power, and that it truly explains certain events. Not categorically, not on its own, and not through the use of mechanism, but probabilistically and with assistance from the distinct external auditory object. Then how does it do so? Perhaps the first thing to note by way of reply is that the causal power of the will-to-listen is a function of its *internal object*. Thus, given a fixed external auditory object, one might bring to bear upon it various intentional listening-strivings—each with different causal power—and result.

This power is in the nature of an *attractive power*, and its presence is determined by choice. Freely selecting whichever feature interests us, say the timbre of the sound, we overtly *open the door* to timbre's causal influence upon the attention. And we actively do so. We actively make the attention *open to influence* at the hands of timbre. We do what deflects any occurrent hearing in this direction, thereby ensuring that the attention tends to light upon timbre. In this regard, the act is not unlike an instrumental act—though strangely in reverse. Thus, we actually *enlist* the timbre of the sound as an external cause of timbre-hearing, through specially 'grooming' any possible hearing for timbre-affectedness. This trying, that the attention be thus influenced, is the continuous inner creation of a causally

397

influential internal mould; and as the desired effect of this continuous mental work occurs, which is to say a hearing of the desired kind, an act-edifice is completed, namely listening to the heard feature of the sound.

What are we to say of an act which unites free choice with external determination in producing its object? How can such a thing be possible? I think we should say something along the following lines. That the very nature of the enterprise is the setting-up of an attractive force that draws chosen responses upon itself; that the creation of that force is almost in the nature of suction, the creation of a vacuum apt specifically to be filled by whatever item the mind of the listener so desires. Then that the completion of this process should occur from without, does not imply that it is either some kind of chance or lucky accident, since the force that took the form of striving or listening-for had as its object just such an occurrence. Thus, the external influence or sound, though in itself external to the listening and indeed to the mind as such, is not an unchosen external influence: its power was conferred upon it from within: it was a chosen external influence. In this sense the external sound, while no part of the listening process, is part of a natural causal system. Perhaps this constitutes explanation enough. Perhaps this resolves the puzzle.

5. The Rationale of Theory (D)

(1) And yet it seems to me that the final Theory (D) still stands in need of elucidation. For example, in what precise fashion do listening and hearing overlap? How can that overlap take a merely probabilistic form? I am therefore of the view that the explanatory situation has not been fully characterized, and in consequence that the 'antitheticality puzzle' must still have life to it. Then I think it will help me to put forward a final differential statement of that theory, if at this juncture I examine the closely linked concepts of *structure* and of *part* that are appealed to in the Theory (D). These special concepts are central to its character.

All of the Theories (A–D) are *structural* theories. Now in general we may say that characterizing the structure of any item consists in charting the relations that constitute the item out of its parts. Just what those parts are, depends on the principle of partitioning being employed. And this can take multiple forms. Thus, it could be any one out of a number of purely spatial divides, or it might instead be purely temporal in type, or it could divide the item into self-subsistent individuals—and numerous other possibilities exist. Accordingly, some parts of an item will be autonomous individuals, such as the battery part of a car-object; while some contingently will not, such as the first half of a skid-event; and some parts could not conceivably be individuals, like the moral part of the mind. And so on. Roughly, partitioning an item consists in itemizing 'what goes to make it up'. As noted above, the 'what' is protean.

Theories (A–D) are structural theories, not merely of *mental actions*, but of the *whole situation* needed if a mental act of a certain kind is to occur. For example, the

Soliloquy proved on investigation to have *no* event-parts and therefore *no* event-structure—and this constitutes one structural possibility. Meanwhile the structure of event-parts in Recollecting, is the structure of an act-situation encompassing the act itself, and mechanism-activation, and the distinct event of remembering. However, we recognize that other principles of partitioning would yield different structures of different parts in either of these two cases. This option becomes increasingly relevant when explanatory considerations highlight the shortcomings of the penultimate Theory (C). Thus, the analysis of listening into *event-parts* turns out to be an inadequate instrument for understanding the relation holding between listening and the whole-event hearing that is contemporaneous with listening. We must avail ourselves of parts of a different kind—as will emerge below. This confirms the above supposition that Theory (D) still stands in need of further elucidation.

(2) At this point I need to delineate several related concepts: some of them actualities, some merely ideal. These concepts will be of use in characterizing the explanatory situation which obtains in listening.

(A) The set of all the audible qualities of a sound: $\{q_s\}$.
(B) Maximal listening: a maximally intense listening to all of $\{q_s\}$: $L_{max.}$
(C) Maximal hearing: a maximally intense hearing of all of $\{q_s\}$: H_{max}.
(D) Actualized listening: a distributed-intense listening to part of $\{q_s\}$: L_{act}. (That is, the ordinary or actual variety of listening.)
(E) Actualized hearing: a distributed-intense hearing of part of $\{q_s\}$: H_{act}. (That is, the ordinary or actual variety of hearing.)

Meanwhile, actual and ideal explanatory situations are as follows:

(X) L_{max} occurs, & H_{max} occurs, & (L_{max} completely explains H_{max}).
(Y) L_{act} occurs, & H_{act} occurs, & (L_{act} completely explains H_{act}).
(Z) L_{act} occurs, & H_{act} occurs, & (L_{act} partially explains H_{act}).

A few comments on these concepts and supposed explanatory situations. The ideal listening (B) and hearing (C) are doubtless unrealizable, and so too *a fortiori* is the explanatory ideal (X). The explanatory conjecture that I find interesting is (Y). This claims that ordinary actual examples of listening *completely* explain the co-present ordinary enough examples of hearing. Then is this particular explanatory ideal (Y) in principle realizable? Now the causal and explanatory power of a will-to-listen is a function both of the range of its internal object, and the intensity of the will-to-listen. For of what else? Accordingly, a valid guiding principle must surely be: the more a listening approaches L_{max}, the more it tends both to engender *and* to explain an H_{max}. Then how could an L_{act} ever *maximally* explain an H_{act}? If a particular listening is (say) merely to the qualities a and b (let us call it L_{ab}), and if it is very far from intense in character, how could it ever *maximally* explain a contemporaneous hearing H_{abcd}? And it could not. This demonstrates the unrealizability of

(Y)—and the validity of (Z); which, anyhow, was evident from the earlier discussion concerning the *accomplishments* of listening. In a word, not all of any hearing that is contemporaneous with listening to that heard, owes its existence to that listening.

(3) It was this fact which pushed us beyond Theory (C) to Theory (D). Now we have just referred to 'all of' a hearing, and thus implicitly to parts. But what *principle of partitioning* is involved? We must settle upon a determinate kind of part if we are to capture the above insight and offer a clear statement of Theory (D). Then the partitioning of the hearing must be such as to help us answer 'What goes to make up an H_{act}?' And it cannot be temporal in character since it applies in each instant. It must surely be a divide along these lines. In this particular framework we will assemble (say) an H_{abcd} out of the parts H_a, H_b, H_c, H_d, where 'a' 'b' etc. designate qualities of the sound-object (e.g. timbre, pitch, etc.), without our supposing that we are referring to actual or potential individual existents. For example, we may descriptively assemble an H_{act} that is an H_{abcd} out of (say): H_a (very well) & H_b (hardly at all) & H_c (marginally) & H_d (well). It is clear that this is the variety of part that we need if we are to state Theory (D), and do justice to the explanatory situation which came to light earlier. However, we need in addition to discover the principle governing *act-constitution* that is to be applied to listening L.

One prime consideration helps us in this task. For it becomes clearer what that principle must be, when we address ourselves to the following question. If a sound is listened-to and one of its qualities (call it q) is heard or noticed; and if that noticing is due in only some slight degree to the occurrence of the will-to-listen, so that the audible quality q would almost certainly have come to our attention had we *not* engaged in listening; then what can be the justification for assimilating the hearing of the quality q inside the boundaries of the phenomenon of listening? It is because I can think of none, that the following principle recommends itself to me. Namely: to the extent that the part of the hearing (viz. H_q) under consideration owes its existence to the will-to-listen, to that same extent that H_q part of hearing is part of the listening.

It is clear that this principle governs the H-constitution of L. And it enables us to determine the extent of the overlap of L and H. Then as we have already discovered, that extent can only be *probabilistically expressed*! This is because the explanatory justification for citing such an extent is probabilistic in character. And so—in this final differential statement of Theory (D)—we shall find that we have to make somewhat unusual claims of the following kind: that it is m% likely that part H_a is part of listening, and n% likely that part H_b is part of listening, etc. And we shall have to accept that that is the end of the matter! And we will in addition have to acknowledge that listening-hood is never anything more than probabilistically realized. *Absolute listening* proves to be a myth!

It is a strange state of affairs, to be sure. And yet to my way of thinking it is not all that alarming. Thus, it does not imply that listening has only probabilistically-given boundaries, since the concept of will rather than of listening binds this phenomenon in one piece. Neither does it carry such an implication in the case of the hearing contemporaneous with listening, for the concept of hearing likewise unifies this particular event. On the other hand it undoubtedly implies that what listening is said to encompass in the way of hearing, has only a certain likelihood of being located within the hearing, and that in consequence the instantiation of listening-hood is only probable (however high the measure of probability may be). Many a 'listening' is a case of 'not properly listening', as few arm-raisings are malformations or 'under-realizations' of the type. As we have already observed, it is all very strange. But then why not? This unusual structural state of affairs is after all being realized in a unique sector of the World, viz. the Mind. Why should it take its cue from elsewhere?

Before I conclude this discussion, I must try to complete the resolution of the difficulty that I called the 'Antitheticality Puzzle'. This was left in a state of suspension at the end of Section 4(*d*).

6. The Resolution of the Antitheticality Puzzle

(1) It is significant that the Antitheticality Problem presents itself in the form of a puzzle. A puzzle has the form: certain unexceptionable premises p and q appear to drive one irresistibly towards a contradiction; and finds expression in a question of the form: *How can it be* that p & q? The presence of contradiction suggests the possibility of dialectical resolution: the replacement of false antitheses through the emergence of a novel, more developed, and enlarged concept of the elements involved. Something like this seems to be at work in the present situation. Now the Antitheticality Puzzle is not: How can it be that the hearing involved in listening owes its existence to the will?, seeing that we continually stage-manage our own perceivings through such active bodily means as head-swivelling, eyelid-opening, sniffing, etc. The puzzle follows upon the expulsion of mechanism from listening. It is expressed in the question: How can the veridical hearing that is involved in listening derive in even the least degree *immediately* from the will? The difficulty being, that willing in and of itself is entirely without cognitive significance, while perception is of necessity a kind of window opening out onto Reality. How can a Reality-recorder be absolutely-immediately responsive to the instructions of the will?

Underlying this puzzlement is a particular conception of the genesis of the hearing involved in listening. Thus, the abandonment of mechanism and the rejection of the Identity Theory, taken in conjunction with the truth of the claim that the will-to-listen explains the occurrence of the hearing involved in listening, demonstrated that the will-to-listen immediately causally explains the hearing that completes listening. But the Causal Theory of Perception requires that the sound—and in my view its internal sensation-representation—also cause the hearing. Thus, the hearing occurring in listening must have *two* simultaneous causes, one operating from within and the other from without. Indeed, if the theory of the auditory sensation is correct, that hearing must have two simultaneous *immediate psychological causes.* More, two simultaneous causes which are *distinct existents.* And so it looks as if this hearing is fathered into existence by two distinct causal agencies, acting in consort simultaneously and from opposite directions. Such a structure of causes seems to be the only operative possibility in the case of the hearing involved in listening. Accordingly, the only variety of causal power open to the will-to-listen appears to be of the type, Contributory-Condition.

The Antitheticality Puzzle shows that there is something wrong with the above account of the genesis of the hearing involved in listening. It is true that one might try simply to sidestep the puzzle: for example, by abandoning the theoretical position we adopted on the issue of mechanism, that is by reintroducing mechanism into the act of listening. But the arguments against such a move are, I think, too strong: notably, the argument from regress (of explanations). I can see nothing wrong with Theory (D), nor with the idea that the hearing involved in listening is at once caused by sound/auditory-sensation *and also* simultaneously and immediately causally explained by the will-to-listen. What I believe is at fault is the assumption that the causation involved is of the type of *multiple determination*: that it consists in the operation of distinct causal agencies. More specifically, the fault lies in the natural enough supposition that the unquestionably distinct existents will and sound are *distinct causal agencies* in the generation of the hearing that is involved in listening. But precisely how this can be so, remains to be established.

A preliminary indication is given by the singular fact that no matter *how much* the will-to-listen is causally explanatory of the hearing contemporaneous with listening, there is never any danger that it will become the *sole* explanation, nor even that it will *monopolize* the explanation—to the exclusion of the sound! The object of a perception must in an absolute and non-quantitative sense be a causal agency in *any* perceiving—quite irrespective of the causal efficacy of the will. Plainly, these two causal agencies cannot act in the manner of 'joint contributors', for if they did one could outstrip the other in the extent of its 'contribution': a fact which strongly suggests that, even though these phenomena are distinct existents, they cannot in this transaction be distinct causal agencies. Now such a theoretical position as this last pushes one towards the *instrumentalist* reinstatement of mechanism in listening, according to which the will-to-listen activates a device which ensures that the sound act causally upon the attention; for this account accords with the non-distinctness of the causal roles of will and sound. However, I do not follow that course. And yet it has at this point to be acknowledged that the resolution of the problem has something in common with instrumentalism—without being instrumentalism. Rather, it lies at a dialectical remove from it.

(2) To resume. Let H stand for hearing, s for the sound, S(L) for strive-to-listen; and let us assume that we are attempting to discover which, among the experienced events at the time of listening, is the final or last determining cause of the hearing involved in listening. Then the question originally posed was: is $H \longleftarrow s$ or

S(L)—→H or S(L)—→H←—s the correct account of the causal situation? Bearing in mind the strict cognitive significance of perception, one cannot but feel that H←—s must be correct. And I think it must. Nevertheless, we earlier saw that precisely to the extent to which H is absorbed into L, to that same extent the immediate causal claim S(L) —→H must also be true. Therefore a certain interpretation of S(L) —→ H←—s must be correct, only it cannot be the interpretation according to which S(L) and s are 'joint contributors', which we might depict as

$$S(L) \searrow$$
$$s \longrightarrow H.$$

And neither is it the instrumentalist interpretation, in which a suppressed or hidden mechanism M appears in the above: viz. S(L)—→M—→(H←—s). The correct interpretation is in my opinion the theory—a theory bearing a certain resemblance to instrumentalist theory—which we characterized earlier as lying at a dialectical remove from instrumentalism.

The raw materials for that theory, and for a different conception—for a sort of dialectical advance in our understanding—of the causation in question were noted already in Section 4(*d*), when we drew attention to the specific type of the causal power of the will-to-listen: namely, *attractive*. This is the idea that the causal role open to the will-to-listen is akin to the creation of a kind of vacuum in the attention, which is apt to be filled uniquely by a particular sound. Now the creation of a vacuum is the doing of some deed x, that generates a vacuum y, which we suppose to be specifically apt for the generation of a unique filler-event z. Then it is clear from the preceding discussion that this valuable model, despite its undoubted virtues, must be flawed in some fundamental respect. If it was correct as it stood, the instrumentalist account would be vindicated and mechanism reinstated within the act of listening.

The correct theory, as I see the matter, differs from the above precisely on this score. Thus, this theory does not analyse 'strive-to-listen' as 'willingly generate some y that is specifically apt for generating hearing'. Rather, according to this account the phenomenon striving-to-listen-to-sound-s simply *is* a doing that is specifically apt for generating s's causing hearing-of-s—and it is nothing more. That is, it is an active event which is directed towards a sound-object, that is specifically endowed with the following causal power: to cause its sound-object to cause hearing of that sound. Now such a causal power as this last might well be possessed by any number of ordinary enough phenomena. For example, a sustained training which repeatedly stressed the importance of hearing some specific sound, makes it more likely that one notice that sound when it occurs, more likely therefore that the sound cause hearing of itself, and for these reasons such a training must be credited with the aforementioned causal power. Then what is special about the phenomenon will-to-listen is that the means it employs are *non-existent* and the power it possesses is *essential*.

(3) The will-to-listen S(L) is an active event directed towards hearing H, with the power to cause the causing of H by the sound s: a characterization that is at once

essentialist and exhaustive. S(L) is thus an active power to confer a power—with which it is non-identical and which it takes unto itself; for S(L) comes by the power to cause hearing by conferring that power upon the sound. It is therefore a strange situation: S(L)'s causing a causing neither instantiates an instrumental causal structure, nor collapses into S(L)'s causing H, and yet S(L) and s share a token power to cause H. Let me now elucidate these latter three somewhat perplexing claims in order.

First, even though S(L) causes a causing, it does not do so instrumentally. 'Cause a causing' must not be understood in this sense. There are not *two* causings: S(L)'s producing some y, which produces s→H; nor S(L)'s producing s, which in turn produces H. There is *just* S(L) producing s—→H. Yet how does S(L) do this? What is its way? S(L)'s very being is its 'way': for S(L) *is* a way of getting s to cause H: it is pure 'way'. That is, S(L) *is* the subject doing what—a 'what' that is never to be unpacked—causes s to cause H. And that is *all* that it is. So much for instrumentalist readings of 'cause a causing'.

I turn now secondly to the reading that collapses 'cause a causing' into 'cause'; that is, renders S(L)'s double-headed object as the causing of H. This likewise is a misconstrual. The truth of the matter is that S(L)'s causing of s's causing of H entails, but does not collapse into S(L)'s causing of H. If it did, s would drop out, and we would be left with the unacceptable S(L)→H. But in fact S(L) can cause H only if s causes H as a result of S(L); and this demonstrates that s has an indispensable irreducible causal role in this transaction.

The third thing to say is that even though the causal powers of S(L) and s are non-identical, they are also non-distinct. S(L) and s are the one causal agency in this particular H-producing; for S(L)'s producing of H *is* the producing of H by an s that derives its power from S(L). Thus, the token power to cause H is shared by S(L) and s. But it is not 'shared out' between them. This power is shared, not through division, but in common possession: they both possess the one token power—in entirety. It is the same relation as the 'in virtue of' relation of Perception Theory. Just as the appearance of the north side of Mt Blanc is shared with Mt Blanc (from the north) without being shared out between them, being instead in common to these two non-identicals; so here.

In short, will and sound are distinct existents with non-identical causal powers, which are simultaneously token-identical causal agencies in the generation of hearing: not in the mode of 'jointly contributory' agencies, nor that of instrumentally-linked agencies, but in a novel mode which bears a similarity to instrumentality. This novel mode, whereby distinct simultaneous existents can, non-instrumentally and non-distributively, share the one token causal-power, is the novel mode of causation pointed towards dialectically by the seeming contradiction visible in the original puzzle.

The correct picture is: not H←—s; not S(L)—→H; not S(L)↘

not   S(L) —→s—→H;   not   S(L)—→M—→(H←—s);   s—→H;

but S(L) —→ (H←— s).

7. Conclusion

(1) My topic has been a phenomenon in which are intimately fused two fundamental yet antithetical elements of animal mental life, action and perception: namely, the process of *active attending*. The phenomenon in question proves on consideration to be highly problematic, as we have just now seen in the 'antitheticality puzzle'. That problematicity has an evident source. In action we change the World, in perception the World changes us. Such a polarity in nature underlies a natural intuition that it might be unintelligible to suppose we could immediately perceive our own willings or immediately will our own perceivings. While the mediate instrumental versions of these phenomena are plainly realities, difficulties arise when in these situations immediate mental causation replaces mediate causation. At that point these two elemental antithetical mental phenomena look as if they might be too close for their own good.

And in fact they are too close in one case. For there is reason for endorsing the first intuition, which proscribes the immediate perception of one's own willings. Despite the profound cooperativeness of action and perception in animal life generally, these phenomena are such as to disallow the epistemological gap necessary if the putative immediate perception is to have functional space. Because action has its origin in phenomena like cognition and desire, which virtually already closes that gap, the immediate perception of willing lacks a functional cognitive rationale and thus a foothold in existence. That is, it is because action comes into being already firmly contained within a cognitive setting, that action cannot be a psychologically immediate object for the attention. What this conclusion boils down to in plain fact is, that if I try to move a limb and completely fail, then I know that an event of trying or willing occurred, not through the occurrence of an immediate perceiving or noticing-of that psychological event: I simply and immediately know it occurred.

(2) What of the other intuition proscribing the immediate willing of perception? That is, of a relation which some might suppose to be realized in the course of a phenomenon like (say) listening. The natural initial presumption was that the symmetry would hold, that 'wishful hearing' would parallel 'wishful thinking', and prove to be an equally tainted concept. Strangely enough, matters have turned out differently, and the original intuition stands discredited. The analysis of listening and looking which we reached during the course of the present chapter has endorsed the contentious 'immediate willing of perception'.

What went wrong with the intuition? The trouble stemmed from the concept, *the immediate willing of* ——. This perfectly legitimate concept conjures up in our minds the model of the bodily will, leading to the assumption that 'the willing of ——' must designate a phenomenon of *pure invention*. However, if this was how matters in fact stood, we would have something of an antinomy on our hands, and the active modes of attending would simply have to be outlawed out of existence. In effect, we would be able to determine the character of a sector of Reality at will!

405

It is vital to understanding the failure of the second intuition, to grasp that the structure of these active modes (listening, looking, etc.) is different from that of the bodily will and is in any case *decidedly odd*. Thus, we earlier saw that listening completes itself only with outside assistance, that it becomes something more than a merely failed striving only through the causation of its hearing-component at the hands of its distinct external sound-object. And we subsequently discovered that this causing is precisely to be identified with the causation of that hearing-component by the listening which encompasses it. So the 'willing of hearing' must depend for its success and indeed existence upon the causal action of a distinct 'public' reality. Such a 'willing of hearing' is anything but 'pure inventing'. In short, I suggest that the intuition foundered through one's bringing the central or proto-typical purely inventive conception of *the willing of*——(viz. bodily will) to bear upon a phenomenon which could not sustain it. It is an understandable mistake, since the phenomenon incarnates an unusual structure, but it is a mistake nonetheless.

(3) The failure of the intuition can be viewed in another light. Thus, we saw that the completion of the event of listening from outside is non-instrumental in type, seeing that instrumental acts acquire their status as an act of that type by causing events lying at a remove from their boundaries, whereas listening in a strange rever-sal of structure acquires its status as listening by inverting the direction of instru-mental causation. Nevertheless, something *reminiscent* of instrumentality is realized in listening, for the will here *uses* its distinct sound-object to cause what it seeks to cause if it is to be what it seeks to be.

Now we have already remarked that the instrumental mode of 'doing' one's own perceivings (as when one opens one's eyelids to see) presents no particular problem for the understanding. Then I suggest that the cases in which we manage immedi-ately to will our own perceivings, namely listening and looking, are not merely reminiscent of instrumentality, but lie at a *dialectical remove* from instrumentality. It seems to me that the only way in which antinomy can be avoided and causal imme-diacy preserved in active hearing, is by the appearance in Nature of a phenomenon which in the one stroke goes *outside of itself* causally without surrendering its own immediacy of operation—and that the will-to-listen dialectically accomplishes this seeming impossibility. The original intuition was born of the incapacity to imagine such a manner of coming into existence for the hearing component of listening.

Part III

Seeing

Introduction to Part III

1. Experience and Perception

(1) In Part I of this work I proposed an analytical theory of consciousness in which I dismantled this phenomenon into its constituent elements. Those parts were as follows. The presence of an unbroken 'stream of experience'; an accessibility of the attention to perceptual contact with outer phenomena; and what I called 'The Apparatus of Rationality', consisting in the closely bonded circle of phenomena and powers which make up the occurrent rational condition of self-consciously conscious beings (rationality, self-knowledge, etc.). This tripartite analysis brings into prominence the importance of the epistemological function of consciousness. Thus, the typical relation between the above three parts is, that when the 'stream of experience' encompasses phenomena in which the attention makes perceptual contact with the environment, the apparatus of rationality is brought to bear upon the data of sense leading to knowledge which tends often enough to find expression in intentional action upon the perceived environment.

This fact suggests, not merely that perceptually founded empirical epistemology is an essential function of consciousness, but that it is one that is charged with a wide significance. And there is an independent reason for thinking so. The content which enables the representational intentional powers necessary for mentality as such, could not exist without perception of a kind that occurs only when one is conscious. In sum, we have every reason to believe the relation between consciousness and perception to be intimately close, and that when perception occurs in consciousness it is a predestined occurrence. It is at once the expression of a necessary function, and the event in which consciousness comes face to face with the World it putatively represents, and thus the event through the agency of which is effected the process of internalization essential to the very existence of mentality and consciousness.

(2) It was with this in mind that I came in Part II to investigate, not whether perceptual function is essential to consciousness, but precisely how it relates to consciousness when it occurs. Interestingly, we find that when perception occurs in consciousness, it does not spring up on its own: perception invariably appears amidst a colony of other experiences. In short, perception appears as an occupant of the 'stream of consciousness' that we know to be analytically entailed by

consciousness. This contextual property of perception led me to embark upon several related enterprises. The first was that of characterizing the 'stream of consciousness' in which perception appears, a phenomenon which is to be identified with the whatever-it-be that objects come in perception as objects-to, viz. the Attention. It proved on investigation to be a mental space of experience, logically necessitated by consciousness, constituted out of experiences rather as a mosaic is constituted out of its parts. In short, it is not in the nature of a *frame* of awareness, something which can precede and outlive its occupants, and it leads to serious confusion to espouse such a conception of the Attention. But it is a system, for it exhibits properties which justify its being characterized as a system in the sense our beliefs form a system (one's 'cognitive map of the World'), or the visual sensations of the moment constitute a system (the visual field). Systematicity is apparent in the common kind of its occupants, their principle of individuation, the distinctive type of the relations holding between them, as well as in certain other properties of the system: notably, its relatively fixed extent.

It is in this mental space that perception finds its place. Accordingly, I investigated the nature of perception and the relation it bears to this setting. Reasons emerged for thinking perception a very special example of the type constituting that setting. This is because its specific kind is derivable from the type of the covering genus, viz. experience. Then it was along these lines that I came to propose a completely general theory of perception. More, a general theory in which the analysis is cast in universal terms, concepts of which one is apprised a priori: namely, the concept of experience, and that of taking an extensional object. And so we arrive at a theory of perception, in which we intimately link this phenomenon with what is in turn analytically entailed by and barely to be distinguished from consciousness itself. As one might express it: (sheer) awareness, leading to (directed) awareness, leading to (extensional) awareness. We discover through the above two theories, one of the attention and the other of perception, just how naturally perception arises within the stream of consciousness. They show the concept of perception to be already logically prefigured, insofar as it was derivable by a purely formal operation upon the concept of what was the 'stuff' of the stream of consciousness, viz. the experience. Conjoining this property with that of expressing an essential function of consciousness, it justifies the characterization of perception as a predestined occurrence in consciousness.

(3) Thus, the system variously dubbed 'The Stream of Consciousness', 'The Attention', 'Experience', 'Awareness', turns out to be capable of encompassing one quite special and peculiarly universal phenomenon: the experience-of——, extensionally understood. In this phenomenon the system of experiences brings to awareness, not as a constituting occupant of itself but as object, concretely given particular structured phenomenal realities. In order to demonstrate how this was so I embarked upon a third enterprise, to be added to the first of delineating the nature of the attention and the second of arriving at a general theory of perception.

Namely, to augment the latter with a general theory of the *objects of perception*: that is, continue the enterprise of providing a general theory of perception by advancing one of its objects. The theory I proposed was to the effect that those objects were as described above: individual structured phenomenal realities—*things* (broadly understood). In particular, they are to be sharply distinguished from the propositional objects of the cognitive experiences which almost invariably accompany them and which it is the essential function of perception to generate. My claim was that these two closely bonded experiences are causally and indexically related, in that the perceptual experience both causes and provides the cognitive experience with its indexically given topic or object. This more exact characterization of perception, in which sheer attentive contact with particular phenomenal realities is distinguished from the experience of discovery which typically accompanies it, led naturally to a further enterprise in which I continued the project of more precisely delineating the nature of perception. Thus, it sheds light on that nature to differentially distinguish perception from certain other cognitively significant experiences which share with perception the property of being directed to the phenomenal objects in the environment. More exactly, from those examples of thought and imaginative experience in which, in whatever way lies open to these phenomena, one relates mentally to the objects amidst which we lead our lives.

The net result of these several enterprises is that perception emerges as rather less interior and less intellectual in nature than its more highly developed experiential brethren: to be precise, than imagination and thought and even than discovery. Despite the fact that perception generally incorporates the closely integrated application of the Understanding, it is itself a blunt and unthinking contact of 'Experiential Consciousness' with mere *things*. And this restrictedness of scope is scarcely surprising, bearing in mind its developmental antiquity, for we have every reason to believe perception antedated the emergence of thought and imagination by hundreds of millions of years. This history leaves its mark on the phenomenon. That peculiar imprint I attempted to bring to light in the later part of Part II in the discussion in which I continued the process of differentially distinguishing perception from those generally more developed interior phenomena which were capable of taking propositional objects, hypothetical objects, negative objects, and the full gamut of articulable object that becomes accessible with the onset of complexity and ultimately of rationality and self-consciousness itself.

2. Visual Perception, the Attention, and the Understanding

(1) Then if this is the general nature of perception, what of particular perceptions? What happens when a particular example of this phenomenon occurs? The most notable case is *visual perception*. In this highly structured phenomenon experience takes an extensional and visually presented object as it moves beyond the stream of consciousness out onto the environment. And when I speak of 'visually presented' I mean, presented through the mediation of the secondary quality

colour/brightness and ultimately through the visual sensation which is its source. The vast powers of sight that we know so well are inessential to the sense, but the latter property is of the essence. Sight might have taken a form no less simple than smell or taste, and the spatial content which is of such great importance to us formed no part of its content, which would in those circumstances have been confined to colour/bright analogues of smell and taste. In fact however it is not so, and it is sight as we know it that I investigate. That is, a sense in which spatial content is of overriding significance.

One thing which becomes apparent as we study this sense is its scope. That is, the range of the objects that lie open to the attention when it makes use of the visual channel, which is to say when awareness encounters items in the environment through the mediation of visual sensations which are embedded in the highly structured psycho-physical causal context realized in humans. In the case of visual perception the attention makes its most extensive and ambitious journeys, and the understanding undertakes its maximum labours. The result is that both attention and understanding reap their greatest rewards. Material objects and physical space come to awareness in this sense, and through the interpretational work of the understanding they identify themselves to the mind for what they are in the one and same event. That is, the place-filler of our typical veridical 'see as——' experiences is of great scope. Indeed, it would be no exaggeration to say that typically in visual experience we set eyes upon physical space itself, as we see a sector of outer reality stretching on and on into the distance. In this regard all the other senses seem impoverished. Moreover, in sight alone amongst the senses we encounter *perception at a distance*. Here, uniquely, awareness takes as its extensional object concrete realities set for the most part at a distance in space from ourselves, in fact in some cases set at a remove to be measured in light-years! The directional character of sight must be a necessary, though insufficient condition of this property of visual perception.

This stretching of the attention into a third spatial dimension more or less without end is accomplished through the agency of a sort of 'accordion effect', closely akin to that whereby the multiple causally related event-objects of instrumental action accrue to the one event of willing. Thus, the line of awareness in one and the same event takes in a whole sequence of items as it journeys outwards from the stream of consciousness and late in the day makes a qualitative leap into a third spatial dimension. What explains the unique achievements of the attention (and understanding) in sight is the high differentiation of the visual field and the uniformly regular causal projective relations in which it stands to the environment. Ultimately, and via the processes of evolutionary development, it goes back to the omnipresence in the environment of rectilinearly propagated electro-magnetic radiation steadily emitted by the sun and reflected by objects. Then the end-point of this notable line of awareness is the physical object set in three-dimensional physical space. And here in these items we encounter a concealed complexity, which is of such a nature as to call extensively upon the understanding and by implication also involves the whole containing spatio-temporal framework of physical reality. This meeting of the attention and physical objects in more or less unlimited three-dimensional physical space and time confers upon sight—wholly contingently but actually—a universal significance. This is because sight realizes to the full that concrete transaction between consciousness and physical reality that I have described as logically prefigured and predestined.

(2) As we approach this phenomenon at close quarters, certain questions strike me as being of especial importance. The first concerns the essential nature of visual perception. I have already referred to the essence of visual perception in supposing the taking of objects endowed with colour/bright secondary quality to be a definitional attribute of the sense of sight. But the property which interests me to begin with is the most primal of all, its experiential status. This has been under assault of late, when the ill-digested discoveries of Cognitive Science lead some philosophers to question the very authenticity of the concept of experience, and some to actually disengage visual perception and experience. It is the latter of these two doctrines that concerns me here. I am convinced that such a theoretical step would be tantamount to throwing the baby out with the bath water, and endeavour in the discussion of 'blindsight' to show how this is the case.

The next issue which impresses itself upon me is the exact character of the early stages in the life of the visual experience, so to say its 'infant waters'. It seems to me that an important distinction must be drawn between what in the very first place is presented to awareness in the case of sight, and what is accepted by awareness as the first visual object. The former of these two realities I have seen fit to describe by the time-honoured expression 'The Given', the second I shall contend is none other than the 'Sense-Datum'—opposition to which appears at times to verge upon the ideological. In order to cope with the problems which in my opinion cause many to reject sense-datum theory I address the question of the visibility of light. This is an important issue in its own right, surely of great relevance to the formation of a satisfactory theory of visual perception generally. However, in the present context it has a special interest. One reason lies in the fact that it enables one to synthesize the phenomenon of directional perception with that of depth perception, my contention being that the purely directional seeing of light is one and the same event as the seeing of material objects (which unites in the one experience directional perception and depth perception). However, the main relevance of this discussion is that it enables me to illustrate in detail some of the properties of the visual attention, in particular the manner in which the 'accordion effect' or 'Transitivity of the Attention' is realized in visual perception, misunderstanding of which lies in all probability at the root of the rejection of sense-datum theory.

The work of the understanding is of great importance in this experience. In visual perception the labours of the understanding are directed to the formation of the internal object of the visual experience. Thus the achievements of the attention in sight are to be distinguished from those of the understanding, and to an extent they can occur independently of one another. But only to an extent, else the cognitive function of sight could not be exercised. For it is important in general that the internal object of the experience match the objects which the attention has managed to contact. This fact leads me into a discussion of the formation of that internal object. The theory which I propose has two branches. The first concerns the work of the attention in the instant, as in the instant it internally develops in such a way as generally to match the outer objects encountered by the attention. The second addresses itself to the task facing the attention when the physical object under scrutiny is the material object 'in the round'. Here the synthetic and interpretational work facing the understanding, which utilizes the above achievements in the instant, takes the form of a process extending across time, and is of such a nature as of necessity to make due allowance for the relevance of the spatio-temporal situation of the visual observer. Two notable truths emerge out of this. First, the supposed subjectivity of appearances proves in a certain sense to be mythical, since the appearance 'in the round' can be constituted only by reference to physical space. Second, the divorce of attention and understanding proves likewise unreal, since in this case the two work essentially in unison.

(3) The final topic upon which I shall make brief comment before I begin the discussion has already been noted above. Namely, the rich and complex character of the end-point in the 'journey outwards' of the attention in visual perception. I mean, the material object set down in a realistically-perceived universal physical space. I aim in the discussion to lay bare the raw material which has to be synthesized by the attention, aided of necessity by the understanding, in constituting what by implication is nothing less than physical reality as presented to consciousness at that moment. This confers a special significance upon sight in the context of this work. It has been one of my main claims throughout this book that consciousness 'keeps a date' with the World in the phenomenon of perception. Now this is scarcely apparent in the case of simple relatively uninterpreted senses like those of smell or taste. And even in the case of the sense of touch what is disclosed to awareness is circumscribed by the fact that it is given in body-relative space, albeit a body-relative sector of physical space. But it is openly on view in the complex phenomenon of sight as we know it.

15

'Blindsight' and the Essence of Seeing

The purpose of the ensuing discussion is to defend the doctrine that perceptions are essentially experiences. This theoretical position is what one would naturally assume if the conclusions of the previous Part II are correct. The theory there advanced characterized perception as an event in which a phenomenal item comes as object to the attention or awareness. And can awareness be so engaged in the absence of experience? Indeed, what else is 'experience' but precisely events of such a kind? All this strikes me as relatively obvious. However, phenomena like 'blindsight' (so-called) are thought by some to cast doubt on these near truisms. I shall argue in this chapter that those truistic propositions are part of the very foundation of the concept of perception, and that their abandonment would be tantamount to jettisoning an indispensable part of what one might call our 'conceptual heritage'. With this in view I propose to take a closer look at the phenomenon in question.

1. Introduction

(1) There are are at least two phenomena one might consider in this context, 'blindsight' and 'subliminal seeing'. However, I will confine the discussion to the former phenomenon. But first, a preliminary word about each. In 'blindsight' subjects with damage to the visual cortex claim that they see nothing, yet upon being asked to guess whether (say) a light is before them make guesses which are (say) 80 per cent accurate. In 'subliminal seeing' visually normal subjects are confronted (say) with a light for so many milliseconds, and once again their experience is apparently of nothing yet their guesses are (say) 80 per cent correct.

Common to both cases is that the visual apparatus is affected by light, not quite as it normally is but similarly, that there occurs as a result a cognitively significant phenomenon whose content tends to match that present in normal visual situations, and that the subject claims to have had no visual experience. These cases seem as if they might show that the real nature of seeing cannot be what we naturally take it to be: an *experience*. They raise two important and closely related questions. First, do such phenomena demonstrate that seeing is not necessarily an experience, that seeing might occur without visual experience? Second, do they demonstrate the need thereby for a general theory of seeing which is cast in purely physical cerebral terms? Might empirical investigation in this way lift the lid upon what seems quintessentially experiential in character, and demonstrate a pre-eminence of cerebrality over experientiality? If this can happen to visual experience, it looks as if it might happen to absolutely any other experience. Accordingly, we seem faced with the possibility that the true theory of the mind might be one in which experience plays no part!

All depends upon whether in blindsight visual experience is absent, and seeing present. The following considerations seem to show so. The evidence favouring the thesis that no visual experience occurs is that a subject in a rational state of mind firmly avows that none is occurring. The evidence in favour of the thesis that the subject truly sees is a little more complicated. Two facts suggest it might be so: first that the visual pathway is activated for most of the way, second that a cognitively significant phenomenon results—of type latent or potential knowledge—whose content approximates to that normally purveyed exclusively by sight. This latter fact cries out for explanation. And what else could the explanation be but seeing? Thus, we seem driven to the view that seeing is going on in the absence of visual experience. And thus to the falsity of the claim that seeing is necessarily an experience.

(2) Something in us resists this conclusion. One way of trying to avoid it is by claiming that the issue is merely one of words, to affirm that the unwelcome conclusion can be avoided once we grasp that 'see' is ambiguous. The supposition is that there really are *two* phenomena, See$_1$ and See$_2$: an experiential seeing, and a closely related but distinct cerebral phenomenon which enables cognition or latent cognition; and whereas 'See$_1$ $\longrightarrow$ an experience occurs' is true, 'See$_2$ $\longrightarrow$ an experience occurs' is false. Just as experiential heat is one thing, and of the nature of a mind-dependent sensible quality, and physical heat is another, and mind-independent in character; just as it is misguided to fret over whether or not they are identical, when in fact they are not even in the same line of business, so roughly in the case of seeing. As there is Heat$_1$ and Heat$_2$, and a simply ambiguous word 'Heat', so there is See$_1$ and See$_2$, and the word 'See' proves to be ambiguous. However, this facile account of the matter is not likely to appeal to many. The significant common territory between experiential seeing and blindsight cannot be ignored, and it is this which impels one to say, 'What else but seeing could explain the blindseer's cognitive powers?' There seems to be no way in which we can avoid the force of this appeal.

The failure of this verbalistic attempt to sidestep the problem leaves the question as to the reality of non-experiential seeing wide open. And it opens the door to the second main question. Namely, whether blindsight has shown that we stand in need of a new and comprehensive theory of seeing, a theory cast in non-experiential cerebral terms, capable of explaining both experiential seeing and blindsight. If the issue is not one over words, and if it is true that the one phenomenon seeing really does occur in both situations, whatever it is that guarantees seeing must obtain on both occasions, presumably some cerebral reality. But which? Well, what is the natural function of sight? *Why* do animals see? Surely to acquire information concerning the environment as it relates to the animal's body there and then that will be of use in intentional action that promotes life. This fact suggests a theory concerning the nature of seeing. Namely, that seeing is the X causally sandwiched between the very last point of physical input within the visual system—a point in the visual pathway which must be situated well beyond the optic nerves—and the cognitively significant phenomenon that is directed to the initiating object-cause. Since it is inessential that X take experiential form, and since seeing nonetheless occurs on both occasions, X must be expressed in purely physical cerebral terms. Thus, seeing proves to be physical in character before all else. Prior to the discovery of blindsight a physicalist might have advanced a theory of seeing which was cast simultaneously in cerebral *and* experiential terms. However, blindsight seems to have shown that we can now drop the concept of experience from the account. So much for the supposed theoretical importance of the phenomenon of blindsight.

2. Criticism of the Argument

(a) Preliminary reasons for doubting the theory

(1) Several considerations ought to make us hesitate before accepting this theory. The first concerns the relatively *low-key* power of blindsight. Thus, blindsight is restricted to 80 per cent correct guesses, mostly unspontaneously elicited, concerning a few phenomena like lights and their orientation from us. Why not 100 per cent firm conviction, indeed actual knowledge, let us say that a circle is just a little on the oval side or that two shades of green are a trifle dissimilar? It is true that in marginal extra-foveal seeing the visual content and even the attendant certainty can sometimes fall short of the norm in ways that are comparable to blindsight, and blindsight might be construed as an analogue of those cases—but then proper or fully foveal seeing also exists with highly determinate content. Why do we not come across its blindsight equivalent? Why do we not encounter seeing without experience that is nonetheless endowed with high discriminatory power? Indeed, are we even prepared in principle for such a possibility? We are prepared for the possibility of a situation in which someone knows all that vision tells us, knowledge which owes its existence to full activation of the visual pathway, who insists at the same time that he has no visual experience. But are we prepared to classify this as a case of 'blindsight'? Why the uncertainty? Why cannot blindsight shake off this limitation?

(2) The second reason why we should hesitate before accepting that blindsight is sight without visual experience is, that there is evidence that blindsight might be a '*borderline*' *case* of seeing. It seems to me to be an obligatory principle when we are dealing with phenomena which evolved into being, that borderline examples are conceptual and empirical realities. While there may be no such thing as borderline

417

examples of categories like number, there absolutely have to be borderline examples of such ontological categories as Life and Mind, as there must of such particular psychological phenomena as action, knowledge, and seeing. Thus, we *know* that borderline self-consciousness was to be found somewhere on Earth between 10^7 BC and 30,000 BC; and we *know* too that borderline examples of life and mentality must have occurred somewhere between (say) 5×10^9 BC and 5×10^8 BC Seeing cannot fail to have made its appearance in this creeping form.

So much for demonstrating the reality of the type, borderline seeing. Now we have no reason for supposing that blindsight occurred as a stage of development. But we do know that seeing takes time to develop into being in the brain, as the optic message travels down the visual pathway. While it cannot yet be a reality as that message is arriving at the optic chiasma, it is surely in existence by the time the message has reached certain extra-striate regions of the visual cortex, and presumably this does not occur discontinuously. Then what I would suggest is, that we now try to assemble the kind of data that would constitute evidence of cases of borderlineness along this particular avenue into being. Let us put together the various possible such evidences, and see how blindsight stands in relation to them.

There ought to be no great problem in doing so. For we can in general readily enough put together data that would be indicative of marginal visual classifications of various kinds. For example, in the case of peripheral vision: say, being right 60 per cent of the time that some dark and smallish object sited 80° right of visual-field centre is now on view against a white wall. So why should we not do the same for a marginality that derives from an imperfect realization of the cerebral phenomena requisite for seeing? Then why not when that imperfection is pathological? Must not such a state of affairs exist? There are various modes in which seeing can shade into non-being: through brevity in its object, or smallness in its object, or indeterminacy in its object, through an evolutionary primitiveness of physical realization, through an insufficient utilization of the visual pathway—and surely also through pathologically falling short of the cerebral requirements of true seeing. I suggest that blindsight might be an example of the latter. If not blindsight, then *what*? What *would* count as an example of a borderline seeing whose marginality derives from pathologically falling short of the cerebral processes requisite for seeing? While I do not advance this as a demonstration of blindsight's marginality, I think it shows it is a serious possibility.

(3) The third reason for hesitating over accepting the theory is the fact that normally, usually, and far and away so, seeing is an experience. It is not just that in 99.99 . . . per cent of cases seeing is *co-present with*, or that it *involves* an experience. In 99.99 . . . per cent of cases seeing *is* an experience: the relation is one of strict identity. The Causal Theory of Perception teaches us that a suitable visual experience with the correct causal ancestry, is a *logically sufficient* condition of the experience being a seeing. Then what we are being asked to believe is that in (say) 0.001 . . . per cent of cases the very same phenomenon takes non-experience form! (And constitutes a revelation of nature in so doing!) Yet *when else* does such a

mutation happen in the mind? When do experiences slip out of their normal experience guise and reappear as non-experiences? It is at best a rare occurrence. When do we encounter mental images that are not experiences? Or visual hallucinations? Or dreams? While it is true there is an experience of acquiring a belief, and belief is usually no experience, the experience in question is the awareness of belief-onset rather than the belief itself. Perhaps the most plausible counter-example is desire, which as readily takes experience as non-experience form. For example, I can experience a desire to punch someone's nose, or harbour such a desire without experiencing it. Yet once again we do not seem to be dealing with the same phenomenon. Thus, the experience-desire might last a minute, the non-experience a year; and if during that year I own up to harbouring a desire to do such a deed, and presumably at that moment make epistemological contact with that desire, it seems to me that I need not at that instant experience the inflaming mental fuel that I felt over that minute. Evidently, they are not the same thing.

In sum, I can think of no phenomenon that is a convincing counter-example to what looks like an inflexible rule in the mind. Namely: once an experience, always an experience. Experientiality looks as if it might well be an essential property of experiences, whether we are thinking of individuals or types. The indications are that seeing—like mental imagery and the hallucination—simply is an ex-perience-type. This, too, gives us reason to hesitate before endorsing the contentious interpretation of blindsight as inexperienced seeing.

(b) Setting out the contentious argument for the claim that 'seeing is not necessarily an experience'

(1) So much for justifiable scepticism concerning the significance of blindsight. Now I am at present concerned with the claim that blindsight demonstrates that *seeing is not necessarily an experience*. The phenomenon of blindsight is taken by some to demonstrate this questionable claim, partly on the grounds of the strength of the subject's conviction that he does not see, partly because of the relative accu-racy of blindsight guesses. Then I intend at this point to set out in a little more detail the argument which such a line of reasoning expresses. The argument falls into two halves.

The first half of the argument seeks to prove that *blindsight does not involve a visual experience*. The argument in favour of this claim is, that it is rendered certain through the obtaining of the following factors:

   (i) the honest insistence of the subject that he does not see,
   (ii) the near certainty that the pathology in the visual pathway leaves his rationality unimpaired.

(2) The second half of the argument seeks to prove that *blindsight involves seeing*. The argument proceeds in stages. Thus:

(i) in blindsight a cognitively significant phenomenon (say, latent knowledge) occurs,

(ii) whose content approximates to that normally purveyed by sight alone;

(iii) the cognitively significant phenomenon is caused by activation of the visual system,

(iv) the cognitively significant phenomenon demands explanation,

(v) the only possible explanation is that seeing occurs.

In sum: the first stage of this argument is taken to demonstrate that no visual experience occurs in blindsight, the second that seeing does nonetheless occur in blindsight. The two together are taken to prove: $\sim[\Box\,(x)\{\text{seeing } x \longrightarrow (Ey)(\text{experi-}$ ence $y \ \& \ x = y)\}]$.

(3) In the immediately succeeding discussion I will examine what I take to be the three main strands in this argument. Each of these claims seems vulnerable to objection. Thus, I shall be considering the following three assertions:

A_1. The firmness of the conviction that one does not see, demonstrates that visual experience does not occur in blindsight.

A_2. The content of the cognitive phenomenon is uniquely or truly visual.

A_3. Given that the cause of the cognitively significant phenomenon is activation of the visual system, and that its content approximates to that normally purveyed uniquely by sight, only seeing could explain the cognitive phenomenon.

(c) Examining the first main claim in the contentious argument: (A_1) that visual experience does not occur in blindsight

(1) In this present Section (c) I confine the discussion to A_1, the supposed demonstration that visual experience does not occur in blindsight, and then move on in Sections (d) and (e) to examine the remaining two claims (A_2 and A_3). Now it must be emphasized that during the course of the argument as a whole, as well as in the discussion of the present claim A_1, the truth-value of *more than one* debatable proposition is at stake. Namely, each of the following (possibly inconsistent) quasiprinciples is in question:

α. No visual experience occurs in blindsight.

β. Seeing is necessarily an experience.

γ. Experiences are necessarily veridically accessible to their owners.

δ. Borderline cases of seeing are empirical realities.

These several propositions are, it seems to me, 'in the ring' together during the debate. Thus, if claim α is made, it is surely done so through appeal to γ and in disregard of δ. And yet how certain is γ? As it stands, it is false: after all, dreamers do not know that their experiences are imaginings. True, this is merely a *misclassification*, and it might be argued that a subject cannot be ignorant of the *sheer existence* of an experience. However, this also must be false: a subject might look back in time and realize that he had felt a pang of jealousy when he had thought he experienced nothing on seeing his rival talking to his girl friend. Nevertheless, there can be no doubt that there is a natural presumption of self-knowledge in the case of normal wakeful experience. Then the question we have to consider is whether this natural presumption can legitimately be invoked in blindsight situations.

(2) Depending upon one's attitude to the above four debatable 'principles', α–δ, any of the following three conflicting deductions might be endorsed:

(i) Borderline experiences need not be known of—→blindsight might be a borderline visual experience.
(ii) Experiences need not be known of—→blindsight might be a visual experience.
(iii) Experiences are normally known of and blindsight is not a borderline seeing —→ no visual experience occurs in blindsight.

Then the deduction (iii) is (roughly) a statement of the argument A_1: that is, of the first of the three main strands (A_1, A_2, A_3) in the central argument pro the occurrence of non-experiential seeing in blindsight. It implicitly involves a rejection of the two alternative deductions (i) and (ii). Then in so doing it exhibits preferences amongst the 'principles' α–δ. Thus, it in effect plays off the certainty of γ against an appeal to δ. And yet is it right to do so? Perhaps not. Thus, how do we know that we are not dealing with a measure of borderlineness that is such that valid enough 'insight' yields a null reading? This is the first challenge to be made to A_1. The second challenge, which is along the same lines, takes off from the fact that A_1 is affirmed in the course of an argument dedicated to the disproof of the intuitively compelling β. Namely: is the likelihood of an exemplification of γ greater in these circumstances than the likelihood of β? More, is it greater than the likelihood of β, in a context in which δ has to be taken into account? I do not think it is. We have noted that 99.99 . . . per cent of cases of seeing *are* seeing-experiences: after all, we have to grub around in our search for putative exceptions to β, combing through much pathological data before emerging with a debatable and at best flawed example like blindsight, whereas error relating to one's present experience is common enough in everyday life.

The general conclusion forced upon us from the above considerations is, that while it is certain that blindsight does not involve full-blooded visual experience, it remains uncertain whether *no* visual experience, or a phenomenon *midway between* visual experience and its sheer absence, or a *highly marginal* visual experience, is taking place. When one recalls the kind of phenomena that occur in (say) peripheral vision, and when we remember that the data prima facie supporting the thesis that seeing occurs in blindsight consists in 80 per cent correct unspontaneous guesses which are short on determinacy of content, this non-committal account of the situation seems not unreasonable. The categorical conclusion that no visual experience occurs, lacks justification.

(d) Examining the second main claim in the contentious argument: (A₂) that the content of the cognitive phenomenon in blindsight is 'truly visual'

I turn now to claim A_2, the claim that the content of the cognitively significant phenomenon occurring in blindsight is that typical of sight (or 'truly visual').

Before I consider this question, a word in passing on 'truly visual content'. In fact, there is no such thing. What we should rather speak of is 'normal visual content'. Visual content might in principle take *any* value, simply because sight might in principle adopt *multiple* forms. All we need for a sense of sight is the occurrence of visual sensations which stand in regular relation to outer stimuli, and this might very well take a form no less primitive than smell or taste. Thus, when we speak of 'truly visual content', we are thinking mostly of the typical spatial and colour/brightness content of human seeing.

Then what in the present context we should in fact say is, not that the content of the cognitively significant phenomenon occurring in blindsight is 'truly visual', nor even that it is 'normal visual content', but that the content *falls within the province of* normal visual content. I say so because it seems to me to do a major disservice to the facts to claim that the content of blindsight is 'normal visual content'. In doing so, we brush sand over the important respects in which it falls short of that of normal seeing. The following normally present elements are missing:

(i) Temporal finesse: for example, seeing a light go on and off once every second, or seeing that a light is oscillating between two points p′ and p″ (say 5° apart) once every second.
(ii) Type perception: say, seeing a nearby human as and to be a human being.
(iii) Depth perception of much scope.
(iv) And thus also perception of the size and position of most nearby objects.
(v) Perception of the shape of movement, and possibly also of movement itself.
Etc, etc.

We have already noted how the content of peripheral vision falls short of that of properly foveal vision in partially comparable ways. For example, colour and shape differentiation, depth and object-type, are generally absent. I am nonetheless struck by the fact that even the most marginal examples of peripheral seeing tend to conserve the element of temporal finesse, and as a result conserve in addition a sensitivity to *movement*. It is life-preserving for a whole range of animal species that they can be aware, within a mere split second, of a sudden movement occurring—at whatever distance seems not to matter—in the outermost sector of their visual field. This instantaneous responsiveness, such that visually perceptible phenomena keep strict time with the *very tempo* of the inner domain (where 10^{-4} seconds is undetectable and 10^{-1} seconds is differentiable) is one of the great assets of sight, and doubtless reflects the fact that in sight the mediating phenomenon travels with a speed that might as well be infinite. In sight the mind passes onto an object in the very instant in which the object stands before it, and as a result sight equips animality to cope practically with flying missiles, striking snakes, escaping rabbits, sudden

BLINDSIGHT AND THE ESSENCE OF SEEING

chasms—even as the animal-subject moves speedily through its environment. We would do wrong to play down the fact that the phenomenal objects of visual experience 'pace' the inner world: it is a feature of the utmost importance. Then it is surely a noteworthy fact that peripheral vision realizes, and so far as I know blindsight does not, this sensitivity to the refined experiential 'now'. To me it suggests the likelihood that blindsight lies somewhere the far side of peripheral vision, along the road which passes through the no man's land of the borderline into the region in which sight is simply non-existent.

(e) Examining the third main claim in the contentious argument: (A₃) that only the presence of seeing could explain the 'truly visual content'

The final claim A_3 is the most important element in the argument. It runs: *what else but seeing could explain a cognitive phenomenon whose content is more or less unique to sight, which is caused by activation of the visual system?*

Then in a sense the above question answers itself: activation of the visual system! However, the question must surely assume that if activation is to be explanatory of the cognitive phenomenon it will *have to be* (or to 'realize') seeing. But upon what is this 'have to be' based? Plainly, the appeal must in some sense be to *intelligibility*. Yet how can that be? There is nothing unintelligible in the supposition that a (merely) cerebral event should causes cognition of some kind or another; and in the case of blindsight a causal sequence leading from physical objects to light to retina, and thence along the visual pathway, shows pellucidly enough how the information involved manages to enter the mind. What is the reason for supposing that to appeal to cerebrality without appealing also to sight, is to stray into nonsense?

Then could it be that the unintelligibility in question derives from the fact that, to envisage blindsight along the lines we have followed and not deduce the occurrence of seeing, is to contravene the definition of 'see'? Might not such cognitive accomplishments necessitate sight? But seeing cannot be defined in terms of knowledge. There is no tighter link between sight and knowledge than the fact that sight *puts one in a position to know* its content (a position one need never realize). Thus, seeing necessitates neither knowledge nor belief, and even though seeing tends to breed belief which tends to be knowledge, nothing remotely approaches necessity here. It is true that we attribute seeing to other beings largely on the basis of their possessing a visual system and knowing certain here-and-now facts about their environs, and while this is scarcely a matter of necessity it undoubtedly constitutes a powerful constraint. Could this be the source of the supposed unintelligibility in failing to attribute seeing in blindsight? But this could verge upon unintelligibility only if in blindsight the cognitive accomplishment and its cerebral basis decisively matched the norm. But they do not. They are the kind of phenomena one might expect either in the most marginal of seeings, or else in truly borderline cases located between seeing and its absence. Accordingly, I can find no substance to the claim that it is unintelligible to seek to explain the cognitive achievements of blindsight through appeal to visual-system-activation without simultaneously invoking sight. So much for '*What else* but seeing could explain the cognitive achievements of blindsight?' So much for the claim A_3. And so much for the moment for the argument purporting to demonstrate that blindsight is seeing in the absence of visual experience.

3. Theoretical Deductions from the Phenomenon of Blindsight

(a) A theory of seeing ('anti-experientialism')

(1) The discussion in the foregoing Section 2 was directed against a certain interpretation of the phenomenon of blindsight: namely, as an example of seeing in the absence of visual experience. My claim is, not that this interpretation is palpably false, but that it has in no way been demonstrated and that it is an *improbable reading* of the situation. Far more likely is, that blindsight is either a borderline seeing (and borderline visual experience) or else a merely cognitive close precursor of these latter. The central point of the above discussion was, that no case has been made for the contentious claim that seeing need not be an experience. To me it seems as likely that seeing is essentially an experience as it is that (say) mental images or awarenesses of pain or hallucinations are essentially experiences. Are not awarenesses *essentially* experiences? Or is that a tautology? It is indeed a tautology—and true!

Resistance to the idea that seeing might be essentially experiential, stems from the assumption that the identification of seeing is like the identification of physical natural kinds, an epistemological encounter with something whose natural depth is not on view. Since first-person incorrigibility is a myth, since some form of physicalism may be true, *how could* a phenomenon exist which *of its very nature* wore its heart upon its sleeve? And yet is not this last precisely true of (say) the colour yellow? How could one conceivably burrow beneath the surface of yellow and discover its hidden essence? How could we in such a manner *finally fix the sense* of 'yellow'? How could we come in this way to know *just what it was* we had been talking of all along? What would be a 'twin earth' yellow? It would be yellow—notwithstanding! After all, not everything in the physical domain has a natural depth which is revelatory of the nature of its bearer: for example, simple artefacts like knives and chairs, simple pre-scientific items like lakes and mountains. Such objects have *no* hidden nature! Why *must* the nature of pain or yellow be hidden from immediate awareness? What is the principle supporting this edict? Could it reside in the fact that the sensations in question are 'embodied'? But the works of Titian are comparably 'embodied'—in paint; and does that mean they are not open to immediate awareness?

(2) Despite these personal convictions, I intend in the ensuing discussion to set aside the case I have made in support of the claim that blindsight does not prove that seeing is not essentially experiential. The reason is, that I am interested in following up the *theoretical implications* of the contentious interpretation of blindsight as non-

experiential seeing. In short, I shall play devil's advocate: I will assume the truth of the contentious claim, and see where it leads. Accordingly, we set out from the assumption that blindsight teaches us that seeing can occur in the absence of visual experience. Now *something* must make the seeing of blindsight a case of seeing. That something must one assumes be present both in experiential seeing *and* in the non-experiential seeing of blindsight—else what would be the interest of blindsight? And it cannot consist in the presence of a suitably caused visual experience. Then what can it be? Well, it is worth remembering how we managed to *identify* seeing in blindsight. It was via the presence of the right or regular outer (optical) input, the right inner (ocular) input, the more or less adequate activation of the visual system, and the more or less adequate psychological cognitive output—a form of potential or latent knowledge. If blindseeing is seeing, whatever makes it seeing must be set out in this list.

These facts suggest a theory as to the nature of seeing. Namely: that seeing *is* suitable activation of the visual system that is possessed of the right causal properties, viz. being caused by the right inputs *and* cause of a latent knowledge of the public physical situation that caused the outer input. Any cerebral phenomenon that is endowed with these several properties must rate as a seeing.

(b) The type of the nature of seeing supposedly discovered through blindsight

(1) Such a phenomenon as the above must be present, both in the vastly familiar or (so-called) 'folk' experiential examples of seeing, and in more out of the way non-experiential cases of seeing like blindsight and subliminal seeing. This common ground between 'folk' and scientifically discovered instances of seeing must be what seeing *really is*. Here we have a comprehensive theory of the nature of seeing, covering both familiar and unfamiliar territory, a theory in which the concept of visual experience finds no place. Let us call this theory of seeing: 'anti-experientialism'.

The question arises as to the correct interpretation of the above theoretical statement. This is because the theory as stated might be variously understood. In particular, is it a theory as to the real essence of seeing? or is it rather a functionalist-type statement of nominal essence? or has it some other interpretation? Now I think we may assume that all parties are agreed, in accordance with the Causal Theory of Perception, that input causal properties of the right kind are necessary conditions of seeing. What is however debatable is the necessity or not of certain constitutive-cerebral properties *and* of the cognitive-type output causal properties. Then what might we expect an anti-experientialist to say on this issue of the nature of seeing? In principle anti-experientialists might opt for any one of the following four interpretations of their theory as to the nature (N) of seeing:

N₁ Suitable causal input, and the occurrence of suitable constitutive visual-system phenomena, are necessary and sufficient for seeing—in any life system.

N_2 Suitable causal input, the occurrence of suitable constitutive visual-system phenomena, and suitable cognitive-type causal output, are necessary and sufficient for seeing—in any life system.

N_3 Suitable causal input, and suitable cognitive-type causal output, are necessary and sufficient for seeing—in any life system.

N_4 Seeing has neither nominal nor real essence. Typically it is caused by the optical causes of sight in humans, and is itself typically cause of cognitive phenomena with matching and distinctive content.

(2) Initially the case favouring an N_1-interpretation or an N_2-interpretation of anti-experientialism looks strong. Thus, the anti-experientialist theory claims to range across experiential and non-experiential varieties of seeing, and to be capable of identifying the phenomenon in novel forms. One is reminded of identifying carbon in its various allotropes: as diamond, graphite, or charcoal—stuffs with diverse superficial qualities, but with the same deep constitution and the same fundamental causal properties. Then if this comparison were accurate, we ought to be credited with the discovery of the *real essence* of seeing, and we should endorse either theory N_1 or N_2.

However, theories of blindsight which invoke deep or hidden natures—whether physical or mental in type, real essences as I should call them, face a number of serious difficulties. For example, unlike the situation encountered with carbon, the properties taken to demonstrate that seeing occurs in blindsight, namely the possession of *such* causal properties by some requisite sector of a visual tract, are at least in part a priori knowable in advance, and that alone disqualifies the claim that we have uncovered a real essence. This counts against both the N_1 and N_2 theories. More specifically: one reason for rejecting N_2 at least is, that the argument supporting this theory takes the cognitive powers conferred on blindseers to be of absolutely decisive importance, which is surely inconsistent with a real essence analysis. But there is in any case another and completely conclusive consideration that militates against both real essence theories, N_1 and N_2: namely, the already noted familiar fact that suitable visual experience with suitable regular causal ancestry constitutes a *logically sufficient* condition of seeing.[1] How could such a rule be squared with a doctrine of real essences?

But yet another problem exists for real essence theories of blindsight. It concerns what the real essence (let us call it xyz) is to *guarantee*. Thus, H_2O guarantees being water, but what is realized by xyz independently of its ancestry? An event? But of what type? The (so-called) 'folk' seeing we all know is an event and experience, which is such that in the absence of the required ancestry the event falls under 'seem see——'. But what occurs in a blindseer whose blindseeing has the *wrong* ancestry, arising let us say because of eccentric events in the optic nerve? What is the *type* of

---

[1] There is nothing circular about this claim. The psycho-physical nomic requirements of perceptual contact enable us to distinguish genuine from merely apparent examples of such contact. In short, we know what to look for to identify cases of 'the right ancestry'. This suffices to dispose of the charge of circularity.

the event—here falling short of being a seeing—realized on this occasion by the constitutive property xyz? It must be whatever normally gives rise to the latent cognitions of blindsight. And what is that? It cannot be a seem-seeing: there can be no visual 'seemings' in one devoid of visual experience. Nor can it be any kind of experience-type. Yet if xyz is a real essence, it ought to realize *something* both real and mental. It therefore looks as if we shall have to *invent* a new psychological type: to wit, whatever non-experiential mental event becomes a blindsight seeing when endowed with the right ancestry! Etc., etc. These rather desperate conceptual manœuvres strike me as decidedly unconvincing.

The final difficulty facing theories positing a real essence for seeing is of a rather different kind. It would seem to follow, if such theories were true, that unless animals in other life systems had similarly constituted sensory brain-centres, they could not *conceivably* be seeing—quite irrespective of whether all input–output properties, including all behavioural responses in similar environs, were the same as those of visually endowed animals on Earth. Now I readily grant that it might be difficult to *know* that these animals had a sense of sight. But what perplexes me is how one could *know* they could not *conceivably* have a sense of sight! I can see no way around this difficulty. It surely disqualifies Theory N_1 and N_2 as possible interpretations of anti-experientialism.

And so the theory that seeing *is* suitable activation of the visual system that has the right input–output causal properties, cannot really be likened to the theory that carbon *is* a suitable configuration of protons (etc.) that is endowed with the right causal properties. Whereas constitution alone gives the a posteriori-disclosed essence in the theory of carbon, anti-experientialists seem to assume that causal properties are part of an a priori-given essence. It therefore looks as if they must be endorsing either Theory N_3 or N_4 as to the nature of seeing. That is, eschewing 'depth' accounts of seeing altogether.

(3) Theory N_3 dispenses with real essences, and affirms the overwhelming importance of causality, for it is a functionalist-type statement of a supposed nominal essence of seeing. Such a theory could perfectly well endorse a supplementary thesis to the effect that it is the cerebral constitution of seeing that determines its possession of the all-important causal properties. In fact it could readily agree that a regularity across an entire species might obtain governing constitution. But the theory can still at the same time consistently maintain that what makes the cerebral phenomenon a *seeing* is its possessing the right input–output causal properties.

The final theoretical possibility, Theory N_4, hardly seems to be a theory at all. Indeed, it is doubtful whether the recipe for seeing which it offers is equal to the task of designating *anything*! And yet I suspect that something of this kind lies at the back of the mind of many anti-experientialists: seeing is taken to be that bodily X whose presence a familiar mix of constitutional and causal considerations typically indicate. To my mind the danger facing such a theoretical position is, that in dispensing altogether with essences and demoting visual experience from its usual pre-eminence, they will have succeeded in dissolving seeing out of existence! They run the risk of denying it a nature of any kind!

(4) In short, it seems from these considerations that anti-experientialists must opt either for N_1, N_2, or N_3. And, in the light of the recent discussion concerning real essences, it seems that they have little choice but to settle for N_3 among those three alternatives. Just as the essence of pain cannot be wholly given by its input–output causal properties *and* wholly given by c-fibre constitution; and just as the essence of pain cannot be the conjunction of c-fibre activation *and* input–output causal properties; so those who eschew experientiality as a necessary property of seeing must get off the fence and opt *either* for a physical-constitutive *or* for a causal-functionalist theory of seeing. Then judging by the weight accorded the cognitive accomplishments and causal ancestry of blindsight, and the insuperable difficulties facing both physical-constitutive theories and real essence theory generally, my surmise is that they are obliged to opt for a causal and thus functionalist theory— which is a priori known in advance. At once the scientific setting of blindsight proves to be so much hocus-pocus, at least in the hands of many science-bemused philosophers. (They might as well have carried out a much despised 'thought-experiment'!)

(c) The physical constitution of seeing

(1) Before I can assemble a final statement of the type of nature that is implicitly posited by anti-experientialists for seeing, I must first answer two related, though separate questions. The first question is: what is the physical constitution of seeing? This question I shall consider completely in its own right, independently of these contentious issues.

Clarification is gained through asking a second simpler question: what is the physical constitution of a bodily sensation? Two theories of constitution seem plausible, both resting on the reasonable assumption that some kind of psycho-physical law governs the occurrence of sensation. The first theory T_1 states that a bodily sensation S which is sited feelingly at limb point l_s in the body, is constituted of the entire tract of neurological phenomena stretching from that point of causal input l_s to and including those at the relevant brain centres b_s. The second theory T_2 confines S's physical constitution to the latter cerebral phenomena at b_s, which is to say to phenomena necessary and sufficient for S to be feelingly at l_s. Now both theories T_1 and T_2 could agree that the cerebral phenomena at b_s are necessary and sufficient for S to be at l_s, but differ as to whether the neurological phenomena at l_s join them as a non-necessary 'outpost'-part of S.

Both of these theories can marshal reasonable arguments. Thus, T_1 can point to the fact that nomicity links the input at l_s with events at b_s *and* the occurrence of S; that the function of that input is to lead to such events at b_s that a sensation S is felt at l_s; and argue that no principle exists whereby we may divide up the neurological syndrome into S and non-S sectors. However, the case in favour of theory T2 is decidedly stronger. For example, if T1 were true, it would not be correct to say that events at l_s caused S, and we would have to say that S had already begun by the time of those events at l_s. Both assertions are highly counter-intuitive. Accordingly, I opt for T2. (Note that this is a theory concerning the constitution of a *sensation*, and must be sharply distinguished from any theory as to the constitution of the *perception* of that sensation.)

(2) The above conclusions have a direct application to precisely analogous issues concerning seeing. Thus, it is evident from the above that a theory which identified visual perception with the entire input into the visual system, beginning with retinal events and concluding with events in the visual cortex, is open to the same objections as the theory identifying bodily sensation with the full range of phenomena stretching from bodily extremity to brain: for example, we should be unable to say that seeing was caused by stimulus to the optic nerves. The first and tentative theory which we must therefore adopt concerning the physical constitution of seeing is, that the phenomenon of seeing is made up out of events located beyond the optic chiasm and situated for the most part in or around the visual cortex. This completely independent but plausible conclusion can then be added to the previous interpretation of the 'anti-experientialist' account of seeing. The result is a more complex statement of the natural theoretical consequences of anti-experientialism. Namely: seeing is constituted out of the above cerebral events, and is an event whose essence is wholly given in the causal functional terms already elaborated.

(d) A final statement of the theoretical implications of anti-experientialism

Before we can finalize the statement of the natural theoretical consequences of anti-experientialism, we need one last ingredient. This is because of a feature one easily overlooks. The anti-experientialist theory of seeing as a physical X in the visual cortex which is causally sandwiched between ocular input and cognitive output, suffers as it stands from a major (though readily correctible) flaw. Namely, it fails to note that in seeing we are concerned with *two* phenomena and not one, the causal properties of which are far from being identical. Those two phenomena are: the *presence* of a visual field ('being visible to one there and then'), and the *perception* of a content of that visual field ('being perceived/noticed/seen by one as——'). The causal properties of the first phenomenon are: being caused by optical and ocular input, and tending to cause seeing when suitably abetted by such factors as the right attentive-posture. The causal properties of the second phenomenon are: being caused (amongst other things) by the first phenomenon, and tending to produce whatever cognitive phenomena seeing tends to produce.

It is vital that we draw this distinction if we are to finalize the statement of the theoretical implications of the anti-experientialist reading of blindsight. Just as we distinguished the literal physical cerebral site of a bodily sensation from that of its perception, so we must first of all affirm that the site of the phenomenon, visibility-to-one, which is to say the sheer existence of a visual field, must lie somewhere beyond the optic chiasm and encompass events in the visual cortex. And we should then in the second place note that the site of the distinct event of seeing must lie at some point even farther down what I suppose one might continue to call 'the visual pathway' (despite the breakdown of nomicity at this point). When we conjoin this differential statement of site and constitution to the causal functionalist analysis of essence, we arrive at the final statement of the natural theoretical consequences of anti-experientialism.

4. Criticism of Anti-Experientialism and the Novel Theory of Seeing

(a) A statement of anti-experientialism and the novel theory of seeing

What theory of seeing is open to anti-experientialists? What according to them makes a seeing a seeing? A real essence? Causal properties? Let us recall what emerged in the recent discussion.

We saw there that real essence interpretations of anti-experientialism face numerous difficulties. The fact that we identify blindsight as seeing through a priori-given tests: the fact that it is surely at least intelligible to wonder whether seeing might occur in very differently constituted beings in different life-systems; the fact that there seems to be no agreed phenomenal type that the real essence in and of itself guarantees; and above all the fact that the existence of a suitable visual experience with suitable causal ancestry constitutes logically sufficient conditions for such an experience being a seeing.

The theory of seeing which these and other considerations seems to force upon anti-experientialists is, that the necessary and sufficient conditions of seeing are, that there exists a phenomenon sited somewhere along the visual pathway which has the required optical-ocular input and the required cognitive output. Seeing simply *is* the cerebral bearer of these latter causal properties. Then two features of this theory strike me as highly questionable: the absence of visual experience from the essence, and the supposition that the cognitive effects of seeing are part of that essence. Since the former is the main question at issue, I shall concentrate my attentions upon the latter topic.

(b) The causal properties of seeing (1): the visual field

Many psychological phenomena have closely allied causal properties, some of which are essential to those phenomena, some of which are not. Thus, while the causal properties of the antecedents of action are essential traits, those of sensations are not. Even the tight link between itches and the urge to scratch can scarcely be necessary. There is simply no contradiction in supposing there to be a species in whom itches have no more mental effect than do mild tingles in humans. And yet there can be no doubt that the presence of sustained scratching in an animal is good evidence of itching, and it seems a near certainty that itches evolved with the function of generating such behaviour. We must therefore accustom ourselves to the idea that psychological phenomena can have causal properties which are at once profoundly typical, highly functional, and yet inessential.

What is the causal situation in the case of seeing? The first vitally important fact to emphasize—a fact just noted—is that *two* closely related visual phenomena must be brought under scrutiny in this regard: visibility to a subject (i.e. the existence of a visual field), and the noticing of the visual field (under a certain organizational and interpretational aspect). For example: a room fills a visual field for 0.5 seconds, and the subject notices 'a room of modern furniture'. These are *two* phenomena, and they have diverse causal properties, as we shall now show. In the present section I discuss the causal properties of the *visual field*, and in the next those of its *perception*.

The causal properties of a visual field are, that it necessitates a physical non-psychological cause which obeys psycho-physical law (which typically we discover in retinal optical stimuli), and that it tends to generate visual noticing of itself. How essential is the latter trait? Well, how necessary is it that a sensation of contact generates, or tends to generate, noticing of itself? I can discover nothing approaching necessity here. And so it is in the case of the visual field. It is perfectly conceivable that some blind-from-birth animals have unchanging visual fields which no more capture their attention during their entire lifetime than did the sensation of contact on your left heel during the last five minutes. There can be no possibility here of a necessary power which we might build into a causal analysis of the phenomenon: possession of a visual field.

So much for the tendency of visual fields to generate noticing of themselves. What of the additional causal property of tending to generate interpretational and organizational determinations in these noticings? No regularity is possible here either. Thus, the one and same visual field might generate any number of such characteristics, depending on the contents and properties of the containing mind. Here also we must abandon all hope of discovering causal traits which might be introduced into a causal analysis of the phenomenon, *having a visual field*. In a word, such analyses are bound to fail in the case of this phenomenon.

(c) The causal properties of seeing (2): noticing

(1) What of the causal properties of the *noticing* of the visual field? Here we come to a quite different and important question. For it is this event that normally gets brought under the concept of seeing. This is what seeing *is*.

Consider first the *origin-properties* of the event. These origin-properties necessarily include stimulus at the hands of a visual field. However, this cannot be the only source of that noticing. Since the noticing is endowed with organizational and interpretational determinations, other causal factors must be at work besides the visual field. And they will vary from case to case, depending on the mental furniture present in the perceiving mind. In short, there can be no regular origin which might constitute the input-half of a causal analysis of the noticing event. All sorts of psychological phenomena play a part in its genesis. While causation at the hands of a suitably originated visual field is necessary, they are only part of the ancestry.

(2) Matters are more complicated in the case of the *effects* of visual noticing or seeing. At first one might be inclined to suppose that seeing necessarily generates knowledge of its object—but this must be wrong: one can see items one knows nothing of. Then might it be that it necessarily generates belief in its seeming-object? But humans believe what they seem to see only if they have reason to trust their sense of sight. Thus, if they know the sense is completely unreliable, all the experience might produce is a mere *feeling as if* matters are as they appear in the visual field. As an example, there is simply no tendency to believe in the existence of the 'moons' one seems to see when one presses an eyeball. And the reason for this is that one knows that an index finger, rather than a moon or a light, engendered the visual experience in the wrong or a–perceptual way. And they need not even believe in the existence of the seeming object under its least ambitious description, say as 'a moon-like psychological object', since many who disbelieve in the existence of sense-data will deny the separate existence of any such object.

Then might it be that seeing has a near universal albeit conditional power: that of causing belief in its internal object all else being equal (which is to say, provided other causal agencies do not interfere)? Well, it seems likely that seeing has some such property, give or take a certain leeway in the case of the perception of after-images and suchlike. More specifically, it seems that *visual experience* has a property roughly along these lines, a property that helps to characterize that experience, bearing in mind that the experience is one of apparent concrete confrontation with objects in space. But I can discover no reason for supposing this property *necessary*. What is the difficulty in supposing there to be an experience of seeming to see a landscape that occurs without any tendency to believe in the presence of the land-scape? Why should it not happen? True it is unnatural, true it probably will not happen, but why should it not? Doubtless if it does not actually ever happen it must be because Nature has reason for proscribing it, bearing in mind that the natural function of seeing is to generate knowledge that facilitates intentional manipulative physical action that is endowed with natural advantages. But this is scarcely the same as necessity. And what at the moment I am seeking are the supposed necessary effects or powers of seeing. And I can discover nothing of the kind.

A final comment on this issue of necessary power. Suitable causal input, in conjunction with suitable visual experience, constitute logically sufficient conditions of seeing—come what may. Then amongst the 'come what may' one could locate the causal powers of the visual experience. So how can there be a place for causally necessary powers in this vastly familiar experiential situation? So how in general can there be such a rule?

(3) It is because of the above considerations that I reject any theory which analyses seeing in input–output causal terms. Such theories have no chance of being valid, irrespective of whether we take 'see' in the normal and accepted sense of *notice what is a content of the visual field*, or in the abnormal sense of *being present in a visual field*. Then if in the light of this discussion the causal analysis of seeing has to be set to one side, and if the same is true of real essence theories of the phenomenon, what intelligible reading remains for the novel and anti-experientialist theory of seeing supposedly flowing from the lessons of blindsight? Indeed, if this is how matters stand, how can 'see' even manage to retain a sense?

(d) Anti-experientialism and the being of seeing

(1) A serious difficulty seems to have arisen at this point for anti-experientialists. Namely, how if $\sim[\Box(x)\{\text{seeing } x \longrightarrow (Ey)(\text{experience } y \ \& \ x = y)\}]$ can seeing have a nature of its own? How can seeing so much as have being?

This difficulty comes to the fore when we review what recently emerged concerning the issue: What kind of a nature can anti-experientialists take seeing to have? Bearing in mind the many serious problems which have emerged for real essentialist depth-theoretical interpretations of anti-experientialism, they can scarcely suppose it to have a real essence. Nor can it be that seeing might have a causally specified nominal essence, since seeing has no rigorously linked powers, and in particular no rigorously linked cognitive power, through which we might thus define it. But if, as anti-experientialists claim, seeing can occur without visual experience; if seeing has no real essence which might anchor it in reality; if its powers generally and its cognitive powers in particular prove to be merely functionally important but inessential properties of the phenomenon; then why on an anti-experientialist understanding of the facts should we believe that the word 'see' has managed to corner in its sights *any* sector of the real? Why think such a 'seeing' is *anything* at all?

(2) Let me now ask a closely related question. What rules are there whereby seeing might exist in very differently constituted beings in whom it happens to have *different cognitive effects* than it does in us Earthlings? Here it seems to me we have another problem facing anti-experientialists. Experientialists have a ready and simple answer to this question, an answer mentioning neither real essence, nor causal powers, nor cognitive causal powers of any kind. The rule they would quote in reply takes this form: a logically sufficient condition of seeing occurring in such beings is the presence of a visual experience which is endowed with the required origin-properties linking it to the visually perceived material object. While they or we may in fact be unable to detect such an experience in these 'Martians', indeed while such experience may even be impossible in those beings, they can nonetheless confidently affirm that *if* it were to occur with the right origin-conditions, then seeing will have occurred.

When we turn to anti-experientialists we meet a different situation. It seems that, even though they *in no way* deny the existence of visual experience, they can give no answer to this question. Either they will disallow a priori the very possibility of seeing in differently constituted beings in whom seeing does not generate the usual cognitive attitudes—and in doing so contravene the above inflexible and wholly valid a priori rule—for their theoretical position does not as such proscribe visual experience with the requisite ancestry in these beings. Or else they should bring forward the conditions which on their account of seeing permit the above rule to be valid in their case. It is up to anti-experientialists to show how on such occasions these beings might manage to satisfy the *supposed universal requirements* of seeing which blindsight prompted them to uncover—tests which are said to transcend those utilizing the concept of visual experience. Since they can be expressed neither in experiential, nor in real essence, nor in causal terms, I do not see how anti-experientialists can meet this challenge.

(e) The primacy of experience

(1) One principle has stood firm throughout this discussion, and it raises difficulties for anti-experientialists. Namely, that we are apprised already of logic-ally sufficient conditions of seeing which are cast in terms of visual experience and its origin-properties. What are anti-experientialists to make of this fact? How do they account for it? Indeed, two questions urgently impress themselves. Why are there *logically sufficient* conditions for seeing which are cast in terms of visual experience? And why on those occasions is the visual experience *identical* with the seeing?

Once again experientialists have a ready answer to these embarrassing questions. In response they can assert that seeing simply *is* visual experience that suitably derives from the visually perceived item. This analysis of the concept of seeing at a stroke brings rhyme and reason into what, from the point of view of anti-experientialists, must appear strange. Thus, the tight link to visual experience cannot be explained by the supposition that scientists have no choice but to set sail on their Columbus-like voyage into the cerebral unknown from a familiar port (here, visual experience). After all, no necessary port existed for scientists in the many situations in physical nature in which their original access to a phenomenon proved to be ambiguous in significance: the scientists concerned just threw away their epistemological ladders in the end. If seeing simply *were* a bringer of distinct-ive knowledge, or simply *were* a cerebral constitution which in Earthlings typically was a bringer of such distinctive knowledge, then it is difficult to comprehend how visual experience could play so central a place in seeing. And let us not forget: we are talking of 99.99 . . . per cent of the actual examples of seeing. It is not as if blindsight related to experiential seeing as does (say) diamond to graphite: the very most that anti-experientialists can hope for is that blindsight seeing prove to be an eccentric or damaged outcast of the tribe!

(2) Once we accept that seeing *is* visual experience with the right causal ancestry, much falls into place:

1. We understand how seeing can be a bringer of knowledge, without being necessarily such: it is the non-accidental or causally significant match between its content and its *ancestry*, rather than any *essential power*, that is the actual basis of the latent knowledge that is essential to perception generally.
2. The fact that seeing naturally generates belief in non-rational Earthlings, is merely Nature putting that match to contingent practical use.
3. We meet the requirement of being when we affirm that visual experience is the essence of seeing, accepting that $\Box(x)\{$seeing x $\longrightarrow$ (Ey)(experience y & x = y)$\}$.
4. It becomes readily comprehensible that logically sufficient conditions for seeing exist which are cast in terms of visual experience.
5. And readily comprehensible how on those occasions the visual experience and seeing are one and the same thing.
6. We do not find ourselves supposing that the same item can sometimes be an experience, and sometimes be a non-experience.
7. We meet the abstract need for a phenomenon that is 'borderline' to seeing, whose frontier character derives from a pathological falling short of the cerebral requirements of seeing.

That more or less concludes my criticism of anti-experientialism. However, before I leave the topic I would like to separate out for special consideration one other interesting, and altogether different, flaw in that theoretical position. (And a corresponding asset in 'experientialism'.)

5. The Function of the Experientiality of Visual Experience

(1) Plainly seeing has a function, a function which is cognitive in character. To affirm the necessity of its origin causal properties, and deny the necessity of its effect causal properties—as I have done—is perfectly consistent with recognizing both the existence and functional role of these latter. Nevertheless it would be an error to suppose that the concept of seeing is a functional concept. Rather, it is endowed with an intrinsic essence, and has a functional part to play in the mind. Then in claiming of seeing that it can occur without visual experience, anti-experientialists evidently believe that the function of seeing can be discharged without discharge of the function of one of its most familiar traits. I am thinking of the property of being an *experience*.

For does not experiencehood have a function in the mind? It seems to me likely that it has a vitally important function. Just what that function is, is not something into which I can much enter at this point, and I must content myself with a few general comments. To get a rough idea of the function of experience as such, one need merely imagine a mind devoid of experience at some moment in its existence, say during sleep, and note what else it lacks as a result. Considerations of this kind bring to our attention two particularly significant properties of experience, both relating to *time*. Namely: a concrete awareness of the present moment, and an occurrent short-term memory of the recent experienced past. These two accompaniments of experience enable a subject to differentiate each instant from its immediate neighbours, and plot a future which relates him to a sector of the empirical world as it has just been. Then let us here settle for these few functional properties of experience itself, and consider to what extent they are realized in visual experience.

The specific issue I am now raising is: what is the function of the *experiencehood* of visual experience? One power it confers is, that of enabling a subject to be aware of his environment under as refined a temporal framework as human experience can manage: say, using a grid of 0.1 second duration. This capacity enables much. Thus, the subject manages to see phenomena like the motion of a nearby missile, or of a nearby snake, and other like items with survival interest. Such sights breed knowledge with comparable temporal determinations, and lead in turn to intentional physical actions endowed with the same refined temporal properties. Meanwhile visually experiencing subjects carry with them occurrent short-term memory of the recently perceived environment, and this inevitably helps to condition intentions and intentional actions which take due account of its character. And so on. Here we have a rough picture of some of the elements of animal life which owe their existence, not merely to the occurrence of seeing, but to the fact that the seeing is an *experience*.

(2) How much of this is realized in blindsight? Well, it may perhaps be that a blindseer experiences a vague 'feeling as if . . .' with a propositional content at the time of his supposed seeings. However, since many of his latent quasi-cognitions are uncovered only through promptings and guesses, one cannot be far wide of the mark in supposing that a sizeable proportion of the above powers will be unavailable to him.

What follows from this conclusion? Two comments come to mind. The first is, that it is surprising that those (viz. anti-experientialists) who are naturally drawn to a functionalist analysis of seeing, should lay no emphasis on the functional accomplishments of experiencehood. Ought they not to be impressed by the large-scale cognitive shortfall of blindsight? Should it not cause hesitation in adopting a non-experiential analysis of seeing? Why stress the cognitive assets of blindsight and ignore its cognitive shortcomings? I think this tendency may stem from a reluctance to credit experiencehood with any functional role whatsoever, due perhaps to a prejudice based on the supposition that experience escapes the reach of science. In any case, the utility of experience is an incontrovertible fact. Experience *evolved* into being, and doubtless did so for good utilitarian reasons.

The second comment is this. Due recognition of the fact that blindsight does not discharge the function of the experiencehood of visual experience, permits us to ask the central question under debate in a different form: one cast in terms of function. Namely, whether we are *functionally justified* in interpreting the phenomena of blindsight as anti-experientialists see fit. Thus, we understand that blindseeing discharges some of the function of sight. Yet clearly it does not discharge all. Then does it discharge sufficient to make it reasonable to infer that seeing occurs in the absence of visual experience? Here we have a question that is couched in non-analytic exclusively functional terms. Then I have to say that the case in favour of such an interpretation strikes me as relatively weak: a merely latent, or unconscious, less than cognitive attitude, that is right 80 per cent of the time, concerning normally visible data, which confers certain powers on its owner which may but very well may not condition his conduct. Such is the data supporting the above reading. By contrast the negative case, assembled out of all those elements of normal seeing that are absent from blindsight, looks formidable: instantaneous experienced conviction, cognitive attitudes which are right 99 per cent of the time, high-speed awarenesses, a continuously mutating record of the immediate environmental past, and above all the vitally important element of leading to responsive intentional physical action relating the subject to his immediate past, present, and future. Think of the extent to which these features are realized even in impoverished examples of seeing like the perception of movement in the outermost edges of the visual field. These considerations strengthen the case against anti-experientialism.

6. Conclusion

(1) What has emerged from this discussion of blindsight? The most important point relates to *essence* and *being*. Starting out from the Causal Theory of Perception, together with due recognition that a suitable and suitably originated visual experience constitutes a logically sufficient condition for that experience being a seeing of the originating stimulus, we confirmed the natural presumption that the essence of seeing is visual experience. Experientiality guarantees, not identity as *seeing* to seeing, but identity *for* seeing: it is that property without which seeing would lack being. While seeing has an origin-type necessary causal condition, it also has a non-causal and constitutive other necessary condition. Then whereas the former property is no more than relational in type, the latter is intrinsic—and herein resides the being of seeing.

The requirement of being, that the expression 'see' has sense, cannot be met unless certain standards are observed. Faced with the demise of family-resemblance and 'cluster' theory; finding real essence theory inapplicable in this case, and functional or causal input–output theory the same; something is needed to guarantee that we designate *anything* by 'see'. Then merely to gesture towards the ocular causal nexus and affirm of seeing that it is 'what typically is lodged causally between ocular input and the cognitive marks of seeing', is inadequate. It is not merely the fact that two, rather than one, psychological phenomena find themselves thus causally 'sandwiched'. Because seeing need not have had the cognitive-output property it has, the individuative recipe cannot be sufficiently exact. And it cannot be exact because of the several possibilities that are left open—as the following shows.

(2) Function appears in the mind in more roles than one. For example, some psychological items have a near unitary a priori-given essential function: say, the antecedents of action such as intention and act-desire. Thus, while these phenomena need cause nothing, they cannot but have the power they have, and the more or less unitary power they have more or less exhausts their nature. By contrast, certain other phenomena have a priori-given essential causal powers which, in being multiple, go no way towards explicating the concept. An example is belief, which has the power to rationally cause other beliefs, or non-rationally to cause beliefs, or to cause desire, emotion, or action, and so on. Meanwhile some other phenomena have overwhelmingly typical, immediately mentally accessible, but at the same time non-necessary functions. Thus the itch has the function of generating scratching (which typically removes an irritant), and perception that of generating knowledge of the presence of the perceived object, and while both powers are the very rationale of the item's existence, neither are necessary. Finally, some psychological phenomena have purely contingent a posteriori-disclosed powers: for example, the power and function of dreams to (say) preserve sleep. In sum: intention, belief, perception, and dream, each exemplify markedly different functional situations.

Then when seeing is singled out as 'that which is causally "sandwiched" between ocular input and typical cognitive output', each of the following functional states of affairs remain open possiblities which have yet to be closed off if the given specification is to be determinate. Namely, the cognitive output is either:

   (i) unitary, essential, a priori-given, or
  (ii) unitary, inessential, universal, and immediately accessible, or
 (iii) unitary, inessential, universal, and a posteriori-given.

Which of these three possibilities should be endorsed in the case of seeing? In my opinion seeing exemplifies type (ii). This is because its origin and intrinsic character wholly determine its existence as seeing, and the cognitive powers of seeing are inessential: seeing is merely *raw material* for cognition rather than a source of knowledge *as such*. Meanwhile, those who believe that merely to indicate the causal nexus between input and output suffices to delimit the phenomenon of seeing, must either suppose that seeing falls into category (i), or else simply fail to differentiate between the several functional options. Until we know which of those possibilities is intended, we do not I suggest have even a putative sense for 'see'. This vagueness is compounded by the fact that *two* psychological phenomena fill the 'sandwich'.

16

Seeing the Light

O, she doth teach the torches to burn bright!
Romeo and Juliet, Act 1, Scene v

Perception begins in experience. It occurs when the attention takes a phenomenal reality as its distinct and extensional object. Now in the case of the visual perception of extra-psychological physical objects the attention is unable to reach its goal at one fell stroke, it cannot do so without the attentive mediation of epistemologically more proximate visible phenomena. Then by what means does one discover the existence of those mediators? One guide we must do without if we are to identify the most proximate objects of the attention: the work of the understanding in the fashioning of the visual experience. This is because it is one thing for something to come to the attention, and another for it to be recognized or conceptualized in the content of the experience, and there is no reason why in veridical visual experience all that one notices should be identified. How, then, are we to discover the identity of those early mediators? We cannot turn to the understanding, which is to say to the content of the experience, nor to the attention in the form of finer discriminations of the objects of experience. It seems to me that we must avail ourselves instead of tools of an altogether different and non-observational kind: namely, those of argument. Indeed, of argument of a purely philosophical order. This is my *modus operandi* in the discussion which now follows. Through such means I hope to uncover one of the most important proximate objects of the attention in visual perception, one that is imperfectly individuated in the content of the visual experience, viz. light. In doing so we shall encounter facts about perception which have a direct bearing both upon the present optical case and upon the vexed question of the existence of 'sense-data'.

1. Introduction

In 'A Defence of Common Sense'[1] G. E. Moore attempted to persuade his reader of the existence of 'sense-data' by telling him to look at his hand and 'pick out something . . . it is . . . natural . . . to take . . . is identical with . . . parts of its surface

---

[1] 'A Defence of Common Sense', in *Contemporary British Philosophy*, ed. J. H. Muirhead, New York, Macmillan, 1925.

'. . . but . . . (on a little reflection) . . . it is doubtful whether it can be identical.'
The inadequacy of such directions is one of the main disincentives to believing in
'sense-data'. If these elusive items really were inhabitants of the visual field, there
ought one assumes to be such a thing as their visual individuation. But what is it?
When we follow the above directives and inspect the visual field we seem to
encounter nothing but material objects and the like. Where are the 'sense-data'?
Now it is of some interest that we encounter an identical difficulty when we try to
pick out the light which (as I believe) fills our visual fields. This suggests that if we
can resolve the latter difficulty and meet the demand for visual individuation in the
case of light, we will have resolved the former difficulty—and smoothed the way for
'sense-data'. In any case, the seeing of light is my topic. More generally, the perception of mediators in the perception of objects.

The difficulty in picking out the light is admitted. Yet surely we *sometimes* see and
identify examples of light. For example, a torchlight shining across a dark and dusty
room. This is something that has a shape and position, that can be viewed from
angles and exhibits foreshortening, that can be individuated and singled out in
opposition to particular objects like the furniture. So is this not a paradigmatic
example of the seeing of light? In fact, it is an a-typical instance of the seeing of
light. Indeed, it is because one naturally selects such phenomena as paradigmatic
that one begins to doubt that the light that makes sight possible is itself on view. One
knows that there are beams emanating from all the things we see—but where are
they? I think it is fair to say that those beams, criss-crossing the room inches from
our very eyes, are for the most part completely invisible. More, we see *nothing* and a
fortiori no light between our eyes and the objects that we see; and, looking then side-
ways at the space between the object and the place where our eyes had just been, we
see nothing again. And there seems to be no such thing as the individuation within
the visual field, and in opposition to the visible material objects, of the light beams
that are coming to our eyes from those objects. Nor do we see any such beams as
shaped and positioned and foreshortened (etc.).

In a word, if we see light all the time then it must be markedly unlike the seeing of
objects—or of a torchlight across a dusty room. For the truth is that the seeing of
this torchlight is thanks to the seeing of objects rather than the reverse, that it is the
seeing of an object-collective of the nature of a crowd, viz. a cylindrical collection
of dust particles. Indeed, for the most part the beam itself is invisible, and those
shining specks are like so many Man Friday's footsteps—evidence of the unseen!
Then because these cases of the seeing of light are in many ways on a par with the
seeing of material objects, we may falsely assume that all cases are, and go looking
for something of the nature of a Light Object. Thus, we may go looking for something of the ilk of rainbow or hologram, misunderstood in the process as a something that is *there* (say, a mile off) and a something *thus-shaped* (say, a bow), and,
inevitably, come away disappointed. No such luminous ghosts get between us and
the things we see: as remarked above, all is empty between eye and object. Accordingly, the absence of these Light Things from the field of view, the presence of

nothing in three-dimensional space that is visible but material objects (disturbed intermittently by events), may lead to the conviction that light itself is altogether banished from the picture, lurking instead beneath the visible as an essential causal foundation, a sort of invisible plinth. Thus, we may arrive at the theory that while the light is playing an indispensable causal role, it itself is no more on view than are the causally necessary phenomena occurring in our visual apparatus. This account manages to demote light to a position not unlike that of X-rays!

My own view on this matter is closely analogous to what I think about perceptual (and above all, visual) sensations. Namely: once you allow the existence of a single case, you must be prepared for a complete 'take over' by the item in question. As after-images demonstrate the reality of visual sensations, and thereby open the floodgates—so that every point of every visual field is necessarily visual-sensation-inhabited, so if we ever see light at any point in the visual field, we must always see light at every non-black point of every veridical visual field. Now either we never, or sometimes, or always see light. Then who will say we *never* see light? Catching sight of torchlight, of car headlights, the sun, moonlight, a distant window in the forest at night, all rule out this possibility. And it will be allowed that in general we only see the lighted or the luminous. This makes it seem likely that we always see light. It remains to actually demonstrate that we always see light. Indeed, in a certain sense *only* light. Contingently.

2. Why We Must See Light Whenever We See Physical Objects

(a) A first proof: from the cognitive properties of visual experience

Some sensations are only loosely linked with environmental phenomena, and are as a result unsuitable as a medium for perception. The tingle is such a sensation. Others, like the sensation of heat, regularly correlate with specific environmental phenomena, and this suffices for a sense-perceptual capacity to exist. All that we require for such a capacity is that the sensation be a regular effect of a given outer phenomenon. We do not even require that the regularity be two-way, for it is conceivable that sugar and saccharine work on our taste buds in the generation of the sensation of sweetness through different traits. Nor have we any need as such for a specialized sense-organ like eye or ear, bearing in mind that taste and touch are as much senses as sight and hearing. In a word, the requirements for perceptual power are relatively simple, and a sufficient condition is regular sensory responsiveness to the environment.

Whenever a sensation possesses this property, it is a potential source of information. While it is true that the sensation need not have had the property, for it is a contingent truth that (say) visual and auditory experience have regular environmental cause, if a sensation does in fact have a regular outer cause then it both guarantees the existence of a sense and the necessary epistemological utility of the sense. Accordingly, it must be prima-facie evidence that we are in the presence of a perceptual power, when the occurrence of a given sensation in specifiable condi-tions is compelling evidence for the presence of some spatially and qualitatively determinate environmental item. Then it must surely be relevant to the question of the perceptibility of light, that the occurrence of non-black visual sensation, in anyone whose visual system is healthy and not otherwise stimulated, is compelling evidence for the occurrence of light here and now at the eyes. The human visual sensory system is a splendid apparatus for detecting the presence of a specific range of electromagnetic radiation at a selected site, viz. the range of radiation that we call 'light', located at the eyes.

Thus, given the occurrence of visual sensation in the required circumstances, a man could with justification say: 'I know there is light here and now on my retina.' Then why not also: 'I know because light is in my visual field'? After all, we can cor-relate presence, intensity, and colour of visual sensation in the visual field, with presence, intensity, and colour of light on his retina. I conclude that we can know we are seeing light simply from the occurrence of visual sensation in suitable circum-stances. And all this can be known *before* we know whether and what material objects are seen. Precisely this 'beforeness' is the fact that light is the perceptible mediator for the seeing of material objects, and not vice versa.

(b) A second proof: from the nature of shadow

Here is another proof. Suppose that, even though the shutters of a room are drawn, a bright strip of sunlight appears on the carpet. Presumably, if we ever see light we see it when we catch sight of that vivid patch. Meanwhile the rest of the room is in shadow. But shadow is not *darkness*. More, shadow is only *relative*, shadow is not an absolute. What is shadow for light can in turn be light for shadow. For shadows can harbour darker shadows, whereupon the lighter part of the shadow has every right to be described as a patch of light, and would be so described by one suddenly emerging from darkness and catching sight of this limited sector of the scene. Accordingly, this person will have seen a patch of light. Why cannot a patch of light be dim? It is not the joke it sounds. Then what holds of the above shadow holds in turn of those darker constituent shadows—and so on until we encounter a shadow that cannot contain darker shadows. That is, a strip of pure darkness. Herewith, light vanishes from view. Then everywhere else light was visible, light of varying intensities, which is to say of differing degrees of brightness, ranging from the unutterably dim to the blindingly brilliant, for the visibility of light *is* the visibility of brightness—of any degree. I conclude: wherever in a veridical visual field it is not absolutely dark it to a degree shows light. Now this is not just a way of characteriz-ing the internal character of the visual field: it is a precise and literal characteriza-tion of its contents. It says: any non-black point of a veridical visual field is inhabited at that point by light. That is, our visual fields are all but filled with light—indeed are filled with light irrespective of whether material objects also appear. This is what I had in mind in claiming earlier that in a certain sense we see only light. Light epistemologically precedes the objects it brings to view. It is a visible mediator between us and those objects.

The nub of the above argument is to be found at its very beginning. Namely, in the claim that seeing a bright strip of sunlight on a shadowy carpet is a case of seeing light. This proposition is then assisted by the unexceptionable claim that light and our experience of it is subject to quantification. In effect, the nub of the argument lies in the supposition that we *sometimes* see light. It was for this reason that I remarked earlier that once one allows the existence of a single case, one must be prepared for a complete 'take over' by the item in question. And yet is it not preposterous to suggest we *never* see light? What is it that violet radiation *has* that ultra-violet radiation *lacks*—if not visibility? For why the 'ultra'? What is the blue 'what' that we see when we see the blue sky above, if not the light raining down upon us? Do we not see light when we see rainbows? stars? conflagrations?

(c) A third proof: from the analogy with sound

Here is a third even more decisive argument. Seeing might have taken a more primitive form than it in fact does. For example, it might have been such that, even though our visual fields lit up *only* with the impact of light upon the retina, mapping relations onto individual object-sources were the exception rather than the rule and mapping relations onto the contours of object-sources simply did not exist. If light were more scattered in its approach to the eye than it is, this might well have been the position. Nevertheless, that light would be an objective reality that our visual experience reliably detected. Thus, a solitary torch in the dark that sent light to the retina would still cause brightening of a determinate region of the visual field, and the more of and the more intensely it did so the closer that light-source—even though we would in daylight no more manage to see *all* the objects that cause lightening of the visual field, than we hear all the constituent cars in hearing the roar of the traffic. In a word, seeing might have been much more like hearing than it in fact is.

The question then arises: what if anything would we *perceive* under these circumstances? That is, what would we perceive with the *sense of sight*? What possible reason can there be for *not* saying that we would perceive the light coming from objects? If we smell their smells, and hear their calls, why cannot we see their luminous effluvia? All that makes for perception in the olfactory and auditory cases obtains to a nicety in this. Very well then, we shall assume that we do see light in this situation. Meanwhile, we must assume that the inexistence of mapping relations renders it at least doubtful whether we also perceive their object sources. As I do not perceive the bird that sings in the morning even though I perceive his song, so it seems unlikely that I would in the above circumstances see the object sources of the light that I see.

Let us now suppose that for some abstruse physical reason the scattering of light were suddenly to cease. Let us suppose that beautiful mapping relations were all of a sudden to become the rule rather than the exception. In short, let us upgrade the above imagined seeing from the aforementioned more primitive form to what we in fact now know. Can such luxuries render the recently visible light *invisible*? I have heard of many causes of invisibility, ranging from screens and masks to fogs and darkness itself, but never of such an excellence in a sense! Can the coming to view of what lies *beyond* the visible render the near-at-hand visible invisible? It can stretch the attention, it can stretch it to goals we did not even dream of, and in that sense open up new worlds to view, it can thereby stretch our concerns into wholly new territories—but can it *blot out* or *obscure* or *hide*? Then if the light is indeed visible, it must *fill* the visual field. But if it fills the visual field, it must be possible to *see* it. When? Evidently, it is seen the whole time.

This argument trades upon the similar perceptual role played in sight and hearing by mediating wave phenomena: by light waves, and by shock waves in a medium respectively. These phenomena differ greatly in velocity, they differ in their reflective powers, and differ also in the way they approach through space to the specialized sense organ, but the relation in which they stand to the minds of men is in each case very similar. For example, they are each *causally sufficient conditions* of perceptual phenomena, and they are each such that relatively tight laws connect the intensity and *qualia* of those phenomena with the intensity and wavelength of the impacting phenomena. Thus, light of (say) λ_1 ångström units wavelength impacting upon a healthy visual apparatus is a causally sufficient condition of (say) a yellow visual field, and intensities of light and *qualia* likewise correlate with one another, exactly as vibrations of 256/sec in air (etc.) are normally sufficient conditions of the audibility of the sound middle C. The major difference between the two wave phenomena is, that light relates spatio-temporally to its sources vastly more precisely and regularly than happens in the case of sound waves. No more. Why should such an excellence render imperceivable in one case what is perceivable in the other?

3. The Characteristics of Seeing Light

(a) The non-representational character of sound-perception

(1) Let us suppose that in a dimly lit room a spherical frosted orange lamp glows in a corner, lit by a very low wattage globe. It is as if none of the light spills beyond the surface. And yet I see the light. That is, I see not merely 'a light' in the uninteresting sense of 'a lamp', I also see the *light* emitted in this strangely self-contained manner by the luminous sphere. Then *where* is the light that I see? One is inclined to say: it is within and on the surface of the lamp (rather as if it were the fluid in one of those fluorescent tubes popular once in physics labs). That would cohere with the idea that the light is self-contained; and it is undoubtedly true that the sphere, its colour, and even its luminosity, are seen at a distance in three-dimensional physical space. Nevertheless, it seems to me that to affirm the same of the light that I see would be to fall into the error of postulating light-things or light-stuff: roughly,

hypostatized holograms. In effect, it would be to remain still within the province of the perception of objects in three-dimensional space. What is needed is a radical break from this paradigm. We must recognize the existence of a more primaeval mode of visual perception, which fails to measure up to the requirements of this sophisticated structure, lying buried within the usual variety. Namely, a seeing which takes light as its object: a purely directional seeing.

(2) A salutary comparison is with the other great mediator sense: hearing. Where is the sound of the piano that I hear? Note that we hardly ever ask such a question of sound; not because it lacks a sense, but because our practical interests primarily centre upon the character and locality of a sound's source. Yet one might ask it. For example: 'Where is that beautiful voice sounding now?'—'In the drawing-rooms of the very wealthy'. Or: 'Where was the sound of the Krakatoa explosion an hour later?'—'In Australia, India, Japan'. That one and same sound—assuming a single individuatable roar occurred—might simultaneously have reached all those places (while all was silent at Krakatoa); exactly as the first note emitted by Heifetz's violin at some concert, and heard by a thousand listeners, will have reached the farthest recesses of the auditorium $1/5$ of a second after coming into being; which implies that 'it' inhabited all those places by that time and had left the violin for good.

So where is the sound of the piano that I hear? To cope with this question we must draw an obvious distinction: between the locality of a sound's origin, and the region occupied at any instant by the sound. We would do well to liken a sound to a single ripple spreading out across the face of a glassy pond (irrespective of whether sound and air waves are one or two); and just as we distinguish 'Where does the ripple originate from?' (which cites one place) from 'Where is the ripple now?' (which names a disc-like region), so too with sound. This utterly obvious distinction tends to find itself obscured by the fact that our auditory experience of space is an experience of (largely, directional) location of source. That is, one both hears a sound and *that* it comes from that direction/there/him (etc.). This makes it seem as if we hear a sound that is *at* the place of its source, and hear in addition *that it is at* that place, rather as we both see a patch of colour that is *at* the place of origin of the light that we see in seeing the patch, and see too that it is at that place. In short, there is a tendency to fail to grasp that the auditory perception of space is largely directional in character, and to model it upon the visual perception of physical objects, which are visibly set both in *directions* out from us and in addition at *depths* away from us in three dimensional space. In imputing to the auditory mode more than it can achieve, we misunderstand its true nature and tend as a result to overlook its actual accomplishments.

Thus, hearing the sound to be coming from p very readily seems to be a case of hearing that the sound is *at p*—prior to reaching us. Then, according as we read that 'prior' as temporal or spatial, we will give a different (mis)interpretation of auditory spatial experience. If we take it temporally, we will construe 'I hear that the sound is coming from the corner' on the model of 'I see that the arrows are coming from the corner'; whereupon hearing that it is coming from the corner will be thought to involve (a) hearing the sound, (b) when it is at the corner, and (c) when it is on its way to us, and (d) when it arrives, and so (e) hearing its motion; just as seeing that the arrows are coming from the corner involves (a) seeing the arrows, (b) when at the corner, (c) when on their way, (d) when arrived, and (e) seeing their motion. As one perceives the arrow at a distance through experiencing it where one is, so it might be thought one perceives the sound at a distance through experiencing it where one is. But in fact when I hear a sound it has already reached me, unlike the arrow that I see at the corner; and *a fortiori* I do not hear it when it is at all of the intervening places between the corner and me, unlike the arrow which I see at all those intervening places; and so I do not perceive the motion of the sound, unlike that of the arrow. Finally, I hear the sound through hearing nothing else, whereas I perceive the arrow through perceiving the light which it reflects.

Here we have one way of (mis)interpreting our spatial experience of sound. It incorporates an illusion of temporal differentiation in the object of that experience. A second equally natural (mis)interpretation incorporates an illusion of spatial differentiation in the object. Thus, instead of modelling 'I hear that the sound comes from the corner' upon 'I see that the arrows come from the corner', we may instead model it on 'I see that the highway comes from the north.' Thus, we may suppose that hearing a continuous sound to be coming from the corner is like looking down a pole stretching from eye to corner, thereby replacing the illusion of temporal diversity by one of spatial diversity. But the model is equally defective. For I simultaneously see nearer and remoter sections of the pole, but do not simultaneously hear all of the (temporally spaced and spatially spaced) parts of the sound (which is at once a creature of space and time); and I see the straight line of the pole at any instant, but cannot hear the path traversed by the sound; and see the whole pole through seeing light simultaneous with it, but immediately hear the sound.

(3) Thus, hearing the sound to be coming from point p is not a case of hearing it to be *at p*. This is because the sound that I hear is *where I am* when I hear it. Yet this latter fact is liable to elude us because, while we have the auditory experience of hearing that a sound *comes from p*, we do not have any experience that it is here where it now sounds. (Rather, we work that one out.) And this is so for a very interesting reason: namely, that we absolutely never immediately perceive sounds to be *at* any place. (Inference from auditory data being another thing.) *A fortiori* we never perceive their motion, even though they most assuredly do move, and we never perceive their spatial extent, even though they range at any moment over a region of space. *A fortiori* once more, when we perceive that they come from some direction or even place, this perception is not constituted out of perceiving that they are at some one or variety of places—whether we have in mind a temporal or spatial modality of change: it being neither the perception of change of place through time, or change of place through space. Indeed, it is simply not constitutable out of any other supposedly more ultimate perception. This directional experience, which is caused by

the discrepant time of arrival of air waves at eardrums, is in itself an absolute irreducible.

In sum, while the sound originates at a distance and we can hear that it is coming from a direction and even place, and while there is no auditory experience of hearing that the sound is where we are, the sound that we hear is nonetheless where we are. Meanwhile the sound has two sorts of temporal dimension: the temporal extent of the sound, as well as the 'longevity' of what has that temporal extent; so that while the roar of Krakatoa may have lasted one minute, that minute-long sound may have lived on for several hours. Therefore sounds have both a spatial and temporal *history*, as movements do not, rather as a hurricane has as it waxes and wanes as it moves across the ocean. It follows that the sound that we hear may be where we are and no longer where it originated from, and in any case the part of the sound that we hear must be where we are and cannot be where it came from.

And so there can be no sound-representative account of sound perception, as there has to be a light-representative account in the case of the visual perception of material objects. Whereas I see material objects at a distance through seeing light that is where I am, I do not hear sound that is taking place on a platform through hearing sound that is where I am. This is because of two features of the situation. First, the sound that one hears is no longer sited at the platform, being located instead where we are; and secondly, we do not in any case perceive either that the sound is or was at that platorm or anywhere else. Rather, in hearing sound that is situated where I am, I hear sound that came from and sounds to have come from the same direction as a platform. I perceive its direction, and more or less nothing else of a spatial variety.

(b) *The non-representational character of light perception*

What holds of sound holds also of light. Here, too, there can be no light-represent-ative account of light perception. Thus, I do not see light that is at a far-off window at night through seeing light that has reached me, for the light that is at that window has not yet been seen by me. Yet looking at a dull luminous orange lamp in a corner, it can easily seem that the light that I see is there where the lamp is. After all, the glowing lamp may be visually indistinguishable from an orange-painted sphere, and the orange of that sphere is there where the sphere is. As I see the orange of the sphere through seeing orange light where I am, so it can seem that I see orange light that is there where the glowing sphere visibly is through seeing orange light that is here where I am. But the truth of the matter is that I see orange light that visibly emanates from the glowing sphere, not through seeing light of any kind—orange or otherwise—here or at the sphere: I simply and immediately see orange light that emanated from the sphere. And through it I see the orange of the sphere that is sited where the sphere is sited. Even though the orange of the light is a distinct instance of orange from that of the sphere, seeing the one is seeing the other. (Such is seeing.)

The speed of light, fabulous beside the snail's crawl of sound, may seem to put all this in doubt. Then it clears the head to consider an astronomical example. We shall suppose a vast stellar orange body, with the angular dimensions in our sky of the moon, situated a light year away. Assume this object to be almost always unilluminated and invisible to us. Then let us suppose that for one second an intense beam of white light falls upon its surface at 9 p.m. on 1 January 1999 (GMT) The orange light reflected in that second reaches our eyes at 9 p.m. on 1 January 2000. For a second we see 'orange light', 'an orange light in the sky', 'a heavenly object', 'an orange surface', 'the orange colour of a heavenly object'—not all that different in appearance from the orange sphere glowing in the corner of the room, or the normally illuminated orange-painted object in the other corner. Where is the heavenly object? A light-year away. Where is the orange surface? Ditto. Where is the orange colour of that surface? Ditto. Where is the orange light in the sky? Ditto (for this is the sense in which we say, 'I saw a light' [i.e. something bright] 'moving slowly down the mountain side'). Where is the orange light? Where our eyes are. The temptation to postulate a light-representative theory of light perception—such that we set eyes upon light that is light-years away through setting eyes on light that is here—comes to the fore in the tension between the last two questions and answers.

I conclude: that when I look at the orange lamp glowing dimly in the corner of the room, and the properly illuminated orange-painted sphere in the other corner, then (A) I see the two spheres, as and at where they are, (B) I see their colour as and at where it is, (C) I see their surfaces, as and at where they are, and all of this is both identical with and due to the fact that (D) I see in either case orange light that is where *I am*. This constitutes a light-representative theory of the visual perception of objects. We shall see that the theory is contingent a posteriori.

(c) Directional seeing

(1) The light that we see, in seeing objects at a remove in space, is not merely located where we are: to be precise, it is located upon our *retinas*. It is not situated on the surface of the eye, nor a little in front of the eye, nor a mile or light-year in front of it, for the radiation at these points has yet to encounter the visual system—and be seen. And whether or not we also see the effects within the brain of light, those effects can nowise be identified with the light that is their source: after all, such effects might be chemical rather than energic. Then just as the sound that we hear is where our ears are situated, so too is the light that we see upon our retinas. Perception at a distance, which is something that light effects for material objects, fails to obtain in the case of each of these immediate mediators. The light and sound that we perceive are invariably close at hand. More exactly, they tend to be sited on or just within our perimeters.

But what kind of an experience could it possibly be to set eyes upon light that is situated at the back of one's eyes? The answer to this question is simple: it is no different from any other visual experience. And the reason for this is equally simple: it is because it is one and the same experience as those familiar experiences. However, that they are the same experience is concealed by the interpretational content of most visual experience. For just as we see material objects at a distance in and through seeing light that is on our retina, so in reverse fashion we see light that is situated on our retinas *in the mode of* seeing material objects at a distance.

Yet having said this—and it has all the look of sidestepping a highly problematic issue—we can go some way towards meeting the spirit of the question. We do so by answering a different question: what would it be like to see light on the retina *not* in the mode of seeming to see objects at a distance? What would it be like to see it in the mode of *seeing light*? Then in answer to this question, we need merely to conjure up the situation that would have obtained had the sense of sight resembled hearing in the ways earlier adumbrated, which is to say had it not been fortunate enough to link to the environment with the spatial precision it in fact exhibits.

It would be an experience not all that dissimilar from the one we encounter when we close our eyes in daylight. We would experience a continuous visual field, populated by coloured patches, given in particular directions out from the head, containing visible spatial structures of the kind of circles and lines. No more. What would be absent would be experiences of depth, of spatial structures like hemisphericity, indeed of material objects generally, and the near flawless typing of contents ('car', 'tree', 'chair', etc.). Then if such visual experience were to be generated veridically by light, and in a manner sufficiently resembling our present experience of sound, we would I suggest be seeing the light that is located on our retinas—without seeing its material object sources. And we would presumably see that light *as* light. This reply seems to meet the *spirit* of the above question. It shows what it would be to *avowedly* visually individuate the item which the theory claims we unawares visually individuate and experience all the time. It demonstrates that the concept is not empty.

(2) And yet even though in this imagined situation we experience the light on the retina as *light*, we do not experience it as *on the retina*. And in fact there can be no 'meeting the spirit' of perplexity over locale. For it must be emphasized that, just as we do not hear the sound which is situated at our ears *as* or *to be* at our ears, since our experience of sound is purely directional experience, so likewise in the case of the experiencing of light. We do not see the light that is on our retinas *as* on our retinas, let alone see it *to be* there. To believe so would be to misconstrue the present theory as involving the rather wild supposition that we see our own retinas in seeing material objects. Seeing the light on our own retinas is not to be likened to seeing a patch of light upon a carpet. While the latter necessitates the differentiation of a surface within a space of three dimensions, the former does not. This is because it is purely directional in character. Light is given in directions, but not in depths, out from the body. The third dimension of light is simply invisible.

It remains but to observe that the visual perception of material objects in three-dimensional space *unites* the property of directionality with that of differentiation in depth. This permits us, not to identify the material objects of sight with its light objects, but to allocate (say) the orange of an orange patch lying in a certain direction to two *quite different varieties of object*. On the one hand to (say) the surface of the orange sphere situated at a distance and lying in a particular direction, on the other hand to the orange light reaching us from precisely the same direction. This is what I had in mind in claiming that a more primaeval mode of perception lies buried within the sophisticated seeing of familiar experience. The *merely directional* seeing of immediately proximate light is going on at the very same time as we are seeing the surrounding environment in terms of a framework which is at once three-dimensional *and* directional. Then despite being one and the same phenomenon, the primaeval element can be dredged up into view by the means adopted above: namely, through the reconstruction in thought of a relatively primitive mode for seeing. Such a procedure constitutes, as one might say, an imaginative or conceptual form of 'filtration'.

4. The Transitivity of Attention

(a) Reliability

The light that comes from the orange sphere travels down a cylindrical path and is itself orange, and it is no accident that a transverse section of cylinder and sphere is in each case a circle. Here we are dependent upon the laws of optics, which ensure that the light that reaches our eyes is as fitting a representative of the orangeness and sphericity of the sphere as is (say) a coloured photograph of that object. Visual appearance, which bears witness to but a slender few of the properties of its possessor, is wholly dependent upon the properties of light. Standing where we are at a point in space, the light that comes to us from the object represents the colour and contour of that object. Thus, in seeing the colour and contour of the light and thereby also of the object, and in that way experiencing the visual appearance of that object, we are dependent upon a reliability that is situated, not just within our perceptual apparatus, but externally to our bodies in the environment. We make use of this feature of the perceptual situation when we construct artefacts which, in preserving the aforementioned reliability, are justly described as 'extensions of the senses'. Mirrors, windows, periscopes, camera obscuras, televisions, microscopes—as well as mirages and glassy stretches of water, all exemplify this reliability in the transportation of light; and even though in some cases it is insufficient to ensure an actual seeing of the item (e.g. television), it is sufficient in some others (e.g. microscope, window, mirage); and it is a reminder that a causal theory of perception should take due note of 'deviant' and 'non-deviant' physical causal chains both within and without the perceiver.

This hardly holds of touch and taste, and only to a degree of smell, but it is necessary in the case of a sense that presents its objects for perception through the mediation of wave-phenomena that are themselves perceived. One has only to think of distorting mirrors in funfairs, of the viewing of garments under mercury vapour lamps, to see that the perception of shape and colour, and hence of the object itself as a single determinate entity endowed with these properties, is grossly dependent upon the lawlike character of the natural devices linking the optical phenomena taking place where we the viewers are, with the optical phenomena happening at the place at which the visible item is situated.

(b) Two principles

Then it is this continuous non-accidental preservation of an image across space, reminiscent in ways of the causally bonded continuity of memory, that helps to make possible a phenomenon that is of absolutely central importance to Perception Theory. I refer to the 'Transitivity of Attention' (as I shall call it): the principle that, when certain reliability-conditions are satisfied, noticing or attending to X *is* noticing or attending to Y—even though X and Y are two and distinct. It is a reminder of the fact that it is the essential function, and hence an essential causal property, of the attention that it make possible a knowing of its object, and since sense-perceivings are merely modes of noticing, an essential function of sense-perception also. Sense-perception is one might say a form of contact with its object, but the contact is epistemological rather than literally spatial: a basis for knowledge rather than some (occult) variety of mental touching (which is the flawed model for this strange phenomenon that one might have at the back of one's mind).

Hence it is that a sequence of regular links, in preserving the basis for knowing down the line, preserve the epistemological contact and with it the contact with the attention. Thus, when the orange light from outer space comes to my attention on 1 January 2000, under whatever conceptual heading, so too does an object, its surface, and their colour—as they were on 1 January 1999. It does not matter whether I think an after-image has appeared, or a shower of light from outer space, a planet, or anything else. The fact is that this single episode in my consciousness *is* the coming to my attention of light that is here, and of planet, surface, and their colour that were there a light-year away in space. The reliability of the mediating phenomenon, obeying such laws as the rectilinear propagation of light, helps to make possible this multiplication of the objects given to view, and hence multiplication of the objects given to the attention. This is how the Transitivity of Attention comes to be a reality in the case of sight.

Then it casts no aspersions on the Transitivity of Attention to say that an even more fundamental and closely analogous principle makes it possible. I refer to the 'Transitivity of Presences' (as I shall call it), which encapsulates the facts of *representation*. Thus, presence in the visual field of a round orange sensation *is* presence in the visual field of a cylindrical beam of orange light, which *is* in turn presence therein of an orange sphere. Suitable causal links between these distinct items, in preserving the ground for knowing, preserve the epistemological contact that *is* being given for visual consciousness, i.e. being on view there and then to a particular consciousness. It remains merely for the attention to avail itself of the fecund epistemological situation prevailing at that instant in the mind. It has merely to make any one of these three listed items its object, to make the other two simultaneously its object. The foundation for knowledge, not to be confused with the knowledge itself, is there and then established.

(c) Transitivity and Moore's instructions

Then it is the Transitivity of Attention that renders invalid Moore's instructions for picking out the sense-datum. And in precisely the same way it renders invalid comparable instructions for picking out the light that causes the sense-datum (i.e. sensation). The only picking out that is possible is the variety that forms the subject-matter of this chapter, viz. a picking out by conceptual rather than attentional tweezers, aided and abetted by argumentation.

An example helps to make the point. Looking upwards into the sky I can, I believe, truthfully say to myself: 'The moon has just now come to my attention, and so also has some light, and this is one and the same event differently conceptualized.' Here in a thought I separate out two objects given to my attention at the very same visual site. But I cannot accomplish this differentiation by using my *gaze* as separator—as when I manage to distinguish the rim of the moon from a slight halo enveloping it; nor by using my *attention*—as when I notice a faint hint of violet in an otherwise pearly moon. The aforementioned identity between the noticing of moon and light logically precludes the possibility of *such* discriminations. But the *mind*, equipped with concepts and arguments, is I suggest equal to the task. Rather like peeling a transfer off a page, it detaches (translucent) light-here-and-now from (opaque) object-there-and-then—without splitting gaze or attention. And the same holds of the visual sensation, a further mediator of an entirely different type. Thus, the attention reaches through the sensation to the light, and in turn reaches down the light to the object; but not in the first place as it reaches through coloured glasses, nor in the second place as it rakes an avenue of trees to a house at the end of a drive. In an entirely different way our sight reaches beyond the here and now, and we see through and down the line in a special representative mode that is not to be modelled upon these channels.

5. Sound and Transitivity

It remains to explain how it is that the visual medium can accomplish what the auditory cannot, both in the way of representation and of perception. And, in any case, to provide an intelligible account of certain fundamental differences between the role of the mediating phenomenon in seeing and hearing.

Some might put it all down to this: that sounds of objects are *emitted* by objects, whereas sights are not. This 'explanation', while registering some kind of a difference between these perceivings, seems to me to take shelter in ordinary language— and obscurity. It is true that we speak in this way, and doubtless do so for reasons of some sort, but it is up to us to uncover those reasons rather than merely invoke the linguistic practice. And what in any cases are those 'sights', which exist without being emitted? Optical images of visible objects? But it can be of little interest that most of the light reaching our eyes is *reflected* light: objects would be pretty much as visible as they are were they all like the example of the dimly lit orange lamp; and there might after all have been some sort of auditory 'sun'. Nor can we accept the suggestion that the mediator phenomenon is perceptible in one case (sound), but not in the other (light). However, what is surely true, and of the first importance so far as these senses are concerned, is that the Transitivity of Attention, which holds of sight, is inapplicable in the case of hearing. The following example helps to illustrate this truth.

Let us suppose that a faint rustling sound comes to my ears, which I may or may not correctly interpret. Then in neither case is the rustle's coming to my attention identical with its maker's doing so. Thus, even if the sound is correctly interpreted and heard *as* 'rustle of X', so that X is in this special sense present to my mind, it is with the aid of thought or concept (which are conjured up by *my [individual] mind*) that this contact is accomplished. Now this is not an 'intuitional' or attentive contact with X. Rather, it is a 'thought contact' (personally effected, as one might say). Then this example beautifully points up the distinctive features of the attentive 'intuitional' relation. For here the attention goes onto a sound only to stop there, irrespective of whether the mind travels a stage further; whereas in the case of sight, as when I glimpse an orange object in the night sky, the attention goes onto the light and passes beyond to its object source, quite irrespective of whether the mind knows that it does (for one can be ignorant of the leaps of one's attention as one cannot of one's thoughts or beliefs).

What accounts for this difference between the two senses? I think it derives from two features of the perceptual situation. It is to begin with a consequence of the fact that visual sensations form a continuous two-dimensional array, which is to say that they constitute a true sense-field; whereas simultaneous auditory sensations, which are incapable of sustaining relations of contiguity, and of quantitative specification by the use of two variables in the manner of coordinate geometry, do not. It just seems to be a 'brute' fact that visual sensations alone of the two have this property—though it doubtless owes its existence to the superabundance of optical data in the environment; for it seems certain that, in one of those astonishing coincidental non-coincidences, sense and sensation evolved to put to use the vast cognitive potential of those light rays. And yet on its own this sensory difference between the two senses is insufficient to account for the fact that the Transitivity of Attention carries through to material objects uniquely in the case of seeing. One needs in addition to invoke the special optical and ocular features of the case. Namely, that the laws of reflection and rectilinear propagation govern the transmission of the mediating light, together with the fact that psycho-physical law links such optical stimuli with the aforementioned differentiable elements of the field of sensations which those optical regularities helped engender.

453

Then the conjunction of these inner and outer facts makes possible a sharp optical and sensuous representation, set down in continuous optical and sensuous systems respectively, providing thereby sufficient data for identification and positioning. Thus it comes about that the visual field miraculously presents to view a spatially ordered world of already labelled objects, rather like the trees and bushes one encounters in a botanical garden: wherever the gaze ranges it lands upon 'moon', 'man', 'table', 'grass' (and the occasional 'unidentified flying object'), duly positioned like so many exhibits; and this I believe constitutes the magnificence of the sense. Contrast the sense of touch, which conveys in each instant little more than anonymous nudges. And sound, which just as characteristically conveys 'a sort of rumble' as 'the sound of footsteps', and in any case never manages to bring those footsteps to the attention. It is simply that the dearth and diffuseness of sounds, taken in conjunction with the properties of auditory sensations (which doubtless also evolved coincidentally non-coincidentally to utilize the flimsier data), fails to meet the lawlike requirements which would permit the attention to travel onwards to its source.

6. A Defence of Transitivity

(1) Then in the case of sight it is precisely the continuation of the attention, according to the Transitivity Principle, beyond the mediator phenomenon as far as the object itself, that makes it impossible to pick out the light *in opposition to* its object source, i.e. to follow 'Moorean'-type instructions with regard to the mediator phenomenon. But now a difficulty appears. For now it looks as if an attention that takes as its object a transitively linked sequence of items should be unable to focus selectively upon any single object (which, incidentally, would divest it of epistemological utility). Clearly, this is false: one has only to open one's eyes for material objects to come unambiguously to our attention. Then how can the Transitivities of Attention and Presence accommodate such selective power on the part of the attention? How is it, if noticing a hand in one's visual field *is* noticing the light from it, that we can obey instructions to 'look at the hand' in a way that we cannot to 'look at the light coming from the hand'? Ought we not to conclude that it is simply a myth that the light comes to the attention, and deduce in consequence that the Transitivity of Attention must likewise be a myth? To try to answer this question, I shall now describe a possible though highly unnatural history of the sense of sight in an individual.

(2) Consider the case of a man who has been blind from birth, in whom optic nerves and visual centre are nonetheless intact. Then we could repeatedly stimulate this man's optic nerves in such a way as to generate red and blue visual sensations, and teach him to name those sensations under the correct terminology, so that he could eventually identify red and blue visual sensations. Next, assuming him to be already acquainted with the meaning of 'round' and 'square', we could doubtless also after a time induce the capacity to identify occurrences of visual sensations

which he and we would naturally dub 'a red circle', 'a blue square' (etc.). Then note that up until this point in the story, the subject's visual attention has ranged no farther than the psychological domain, and he may be presumed to know that this is so.

Now let us suppose this man's blindness (unknown to him) to have been completely cured, and suppose him to inhabit a very special environment which is such that he sees light without (it may be) seeing material objects as well: for example, sees the blue sky, sees bright light through closed eyes, sees dazzling headlights near at hand, and suchlike. Then whether or not he actually also saw minute dust particles on the first occasion (and why should he?), or blood in his eyelids on the second, or light-globes on the third, it seems certain that in each situation he saw light. Finally, let us suppose that these visible phenomena are visually indistinguishable to him from the visual sensations he has already encountered.

Then whenever this subject thinks his attention has been caught by (say) a blue sensation, it will I suggest have been caught by blue light. For would he not retrospectively say, concerning the very first visual experience after cure, that that was the first time he saw phenomena in his environment, and that the first thing he saw was blue light? Would we not say, not merely that blue light inhabited his visual field, but that it caught his attention? Would we not say this even though his attention had 'aimed' only at his sensations—for could he not later *remember* that light? But more, would we not also say that he noticed the *blue sensation* that was equally present in his visual field? For if a blue sensation is visibly present in his visual field, and if he singles out precisely that blue sector of his visual field under 'blue sensation', how could we say that his attention had not landed upon that sensation? If we did assert such a thing, it would have to be on the supposed grounds that his attention was also caught by a blue light. But this is to misconceive the attention as a kind of groping hand (and there certainly is no such thing as a 'Transitivity of Grasping'!)

It seems that this man's attention might be caught by sensation alone (prior to cure), or by light and sensation simultaneously (post-cure), quite irrespective of his believings and knowings on the matter. It seems that an item's coming to the attention is independent of one's knowing either the object's specific type, or even its broad category of being. Then all that we need to complete the description of this case is to suppose that, again unbeknown to the subject, red spheres and blue cubes (etc.) which present an identical appearance to all he has hitherto seen, should now make their appearance in his visual field. In that case I think we would be entitled to say that when a blue circle enters his visual field and catches his attention, then he has in that one instant noticed sensation, light, and physical object. And that concludes the 'thought-experiment'.

(3) This thought-experiment was designed to save the Transitivities, which seemed threatened by the fact that the visual attention appeared to focus uniquely on a material-object object. Then the thought-experiment defends Transitivity in the following way. It shows that whether one's attention is directed onto light, or

material object, or both at the same time, is determined by other factors *as well as* by the character of the visual field, and that it is independent of the beliefs and knowledge, and to a degree also the experiences of the viewer. Therefore that the back of one's hand should seem to come to one's attention, but not the light from it, when one studies it in the manner suggested by Moore, proves nothing as it stands. To think it does is to be deluded into believing that the attention discovers its objects as thoughts do. I suggest that we are here victims of the relative *unambiguousness* of this and most visual fields, which pre-reflectively have a clear material object interpretation. I would point out in the first place that such unambiguousness is *belief-relative*, and I would secondly suppose that in taking our cue solely from our own experience, we are in effect confusing attention with *thought*.

The thought-experiment undoes these influences by choosing a simple visual field that is ambiguously capable of multiple multi-level interpretations. Then by shuffling the attendant cognitive attitudes and extra-visual optical facts, while keeping the visual field unchanged, it clearly shows that one and the same visual field is consistent with the attention's finding a variety of different objects at a variety of ontological levels under a variety of *true and false* headings. Even as I am inclined to say, 'I cannot imagine what it would be to pick out the light from this hand', I must recognize the theoretical possibility that I have in fact already picked out light rather than my hand. It is the pressure exerted upon my mind by my *beliefs* that cuts me off from entertaining this real possibility, rather than some supposed immediate experience of one's attention finding a material object rather than a light object. And the same can be said of the possibility that, in picking out my hand, I have in addition simultaneously picked out the light coming from my hand. Here, too, experience and preferred description are not the only guides. And that fact suffices to steer the Transitivity of Attention clear of the present difficulty.

(4) But the situation described in the thought-experiment, because of its extreme simplicity, helps to defend the Transitivities in a second quite different way. It counters their counter-intuitiveness. For despite its high explanatory power, the thesis of Transitivity is I think at first blush somewhat implausible. Several factors conspire to make it seem that only one item can be given to sight and attention at any one point in the visual field. I am thinking of the following. The tendency to misconceive the attention either as a form of literal mental contact or else as a mode of thought; as well as the sheer impossibility of using either one's gaze or attention as a resolving instrument for singling out the several mediators in visual perception; and above all a puzzle not unlike that posed by the Christian mystery of the Blessed Trinity.

Thus, we wonder how three that are distinct and of different status can yet be one, we wonder how this *one thing* in our visual field can somehow *be* three distinct things, we feel we are succumbing to 'metaphysical triple-vision' no less! And, of course, such a 'puzzle' can have no resolution. Then the thought-experiment helps in this way. When avowed total ignorance of the prevailing physical situation

456

obtains, and the visual field is (say) no more than a blue circle set upon black, we recognize that we might at that very moment be attending to sensation, to light, to object—perhaps to all three at once, perhaps to two, perhaps only to one. Then what is of great interest is that one does not, or at any rate should not if one thinks, say, even as one stares at the blue circle: 'I do not know what is the status of this item that is lodged in the middle of my visual field.' This would be to treat the blue circle like a mysterious package: open it, and it might prove to be internal and psychological, or external and energic, or external and planetry, or somehow miraculously all three at once! We do not *first* single out a particular individual and *then* puzzle over its status: rather, we wonder what is making its appearance in this sector of the visual field, which leaves it open whether one alone or alternatively several distinct items and levels of being might simultaneously be appearing in sight and to the attention at that one place. The peculiarities of visual presence, the distinctive character of the attention, find due recognition in this thought.

7. Rules for Seeing-as

(a) The phenomenon of 'Selectivity'

The difficulty facing Transitivity was that even if noticing the hand *is* noticing the light (as Transitivity affirms), the event will inevitably be experienced as 'noticing the hand' and not as 'noticing the light'. However, this proved to be less of a problem than one might have thought. What emerged in discussion was that the visual attention finds its objects with the aid of extra-psychological factors, and that the character of the attentive experience cannot legislate as to what those objects are. This leaves it open that the Transitive identities hold, unscathed by the selective deliverances of the attention.

Nevertheless, such selectivity on the part of the attentive experience remains mysterious. The phenomenon of Selectivity shows clearly in the recently elaborated thought-experiment. This erstwhile blind man at one point in his history noticed a blue sensation as 'blue sensation'; and was at the same time noticing (unawares) blue light as 'blue sensation'; and when apprised of the prevailing facts of the case would doubtless then have seen the very same blue light as 'blue light'; and so on. And in fact all sorts of permutations of internal object are veridical possibilities here, despite the continuing presence of one and same visual field. But what it seems is not open to this man is, to notice the one blue patch in his visual field as *both* 'blue sensation' and 'blue light'—even though the appearing of a blue patch in his visual field *is* the appearing at that point of both sensation and light, and even though he may know so. There is nothing to prevent his bringing the one event in his attention under both descriptions (which he will do if philosophically 'wised up'), but the event itself cannot come to his consciousness under two such disparate headings. His mind has no choice but to opt for uniquely one, at the expense of the other.

How does the property of Selectivity relate to the phenomenon of Transitivity? Illumination on this question is gained when we remember that attentive experiences have both 'internal objects' and 'external (or "material") objects'. For it is clear that the puzzling phenomenon of Selectivity governs only the former. Thus, the situation with regard to Selectivity is clear enough in the case of external objects. Sheer presence in a visual field is a pre-attentive phenomenon, and it is clear that there can be no such thing as Selectivity regarding which objects it can hold, since that is determined by causal regularities extending beyond the mind. Then since the external object of the attention *is* the content of the visual field at the attended point, it is scarcely surprising that Selectivity should not obtain in the case of the external objects of the attention either. However, when the objects of the attention are internal, we are dealing with an altogether different situation. Factors of a wholly different kind are at work here. Then which factors are they? In effect, what we are now concerning ourselves with are the rules governing the formation of the internal object of the visual attention. That is, the determination of the value of 'x' in the attentive sense of 'see — as x'.

Then it is plain that, whereas the attention finds its material objects with the aid of such extra-psychological factors as physical causal chains, the determinants of its internal object must be psychological items like the character of the visual field and one's attendant beliefs. Three principles govern this causal transaction: 'The Principle of Helplessness', 'The Principle of Selectivity', 'The Principle of Maximization' (as I shall call them).

(b) 'Helplessness' and 'Selectivity'

Concerning 'Helplessness', it is worth remembering that action is grounded on possibility. Thus, one can move an arm only if arm-movement is physically possible. Likewise, (active) looking is grounded on (helpless) seeing, and I can only look at what I can see. Therefore what we can actively visually-attentively single out must depend in the first place upon how things visually appear to us: the voluntariness of the looking process should not be thought to circumvent the constraints upon how things look to us. Then it is here that the 'Helplessness' in question makes its appearance. While certain examples of 'seeing-as' are subject to the will, the variety that is my present concern is not. This is the familiar sense in which I see a cat as a cat. I can no more in this sense *choose* to see a cat as an infant panther than I can believe it to be an infant panther: in either case I run my head up against hard fact. Therefore when the light from my hand enters the visual field and comes to my attention, and always assuming the truth of Transitivity, there can be no such thing as 'picking out my hand and then *at will* picking out the light'. Since I am incapable in the familiar sense of seeing the colour of my hand *as* of the light, I am necessarily incapable also of *choosing* to see it so. Here we have one source of the difficulty posed by Moore's active instructions.

The second source of the difficulty has already been noted, and it is what I called

458

'The Principle of Selectivity'. Roughly, this principle affirms that irrespective of whether a succession of distinct items come to the attention at some point in the visual field, that attentive experience must be given to its owner as directed uniquely to one item. And yet why should this be so? Why cannot I seem to see light *and* sphere at the very same point in my visual field? Well, it seems that there is a fence the mind cannot sit on, and at the behest of a form of commitment that is conceptual rather than moral. Many a psychological experience has two *external* objects, but how could it have two *internal* objects? Would it not have to split itself first? But might it not have a single conjunctive internal object, as when I visualize my two hands? But visualizing my left hand *is not* visualizing my right hand, just as desiring fish *is not* desiring chips—even if one refuses to eat them apart. If someone were to suggest that we might see the blue patch in the visual field as of light *and* as of a sphere, they are not providing us with a conjunctive internal object, they are offering experience two internal objects and inviting it to split itself! In any case this principle lives in a continual state of tension with the Transitivities. It generates the illusion that only one object can be given to the visual attention at any one point, arising out of our proneness to lose or embed the (multiple) external objects in the (unique) internal object of experience. Thus, it generates the need for philosophical inquiry to recover the truths underlying everyday experience, forgotten like the insights of childhood.

(c) 'Maximization'

The third 'Principle of Maximization' states that not only does the visual experience not posit multiple items at specific points in the visual field, it conceptualizes them epistemologically as ambitiously as possible. Suppose a blue sphere to have entered someone's field of view. Transitivity ensures that the blue patch in his visual field is at once sphere *and* light *and* sensation (in the 'is' of presence rather than of representation or identity). Selectivity requires that the attention settle for only one of these three possible headings. Then what I am calling 'Maximization' claims that if the subject believes his visual field to be inhabited by all three items, his experience must be 'see sphere' and cannot be 'see light' or 'see sensation'. If I hear what I take to be a very faint 'ringing in the ears', and discover that I am in fact hearing a faint real ringing, not only is my *experience* now not 'hearing ringing *and* "ringing"' (in accordance with 'Selectivity'), it has to be 'hearing ringing' and *not* 'hearing "ringing"'. Seated in a concert hall, I simply cannot have the solipsistic experience of being 'alone with my auditory sensations'—whatever my philosophical theories of perception. What accounts for this phenomenon? Not the holism that knits belief and attention, for why the epistemologically most successful belief? Bearing in mind that all noticing is perception, and that the function of perception is to prepare the way for knowledge, it may perhaps be that it is of the very nature of the attention that the experience in no degree neglect this function.

But is this principle true? Cannot I knowingly see a hologram of an apple as an *apple* (notwithstanding)? But what kind of 'seeing-as' is this? The question is: is there logical space between a sense of 'see as' that affirms, would-say-it-was-from-looking-if-I-could-trust-looking, (which seems to be operative in the case of the hologram), and a sense in which we (so to say) merely 'paste' our beliefs over the objects we see (as in 'I see him as famous' or 'I see him as the man who broke the bank at Monte Carlo')? I think there is, and it is far from recherché. I am talking of the bluntest reports of what we see, according to which I see the contents of Madame Tussaud's (including by error the odd attendant) as 'waxen', holograms as 'unreal', and Mr Jones as 'Mr Jones'. Hearing a doorbell, and irrespective of my knowledge of the reality of auditory sensations, I have no choice but to describe my experience as 'hearing a bell' and to exclude 'hearing an auditory sensation'. I would need to be mad to say and to be meaning the latter. Sanity and common knowledge of the language impersonally ensure it shall be so.

Thus, 'Maximization' brings it about that seeing has the following experiential character. The light that catches my visual attention is here and now, whereas the coloured surface and object that also catch my visual attention were there and then (perhaps a light-year off, perhaps a year ago); yet given my cognitive presuppositions, I cannot but see the shade of orange (say) that is in my visual field as of *object* and *surface*, even though the engaging of the attention by object and surface is through the coming to the attention of the *light*. A deflection of time and place occurs that is the reverse of the order of dependence. Cognitively I am attuned to what lies beyond me; and this is as it should be, since the function of visual perception is to lead us, attentively and cognitively, outside of our sensations and their immediate causes to the environment at large. Thus, considered solely from the point of view of content, the attention lands uniquely at a distance, even though the means by which this is accomplished recede conceptually from view, creating a sort of field area for philosophical reclamation. Thus, 'Maximization' likewise ensures the failure of Moore's instructions.

(d) Moore's instructions in the light of these rules

The following are the conclusions we must draw. That if I know it is a real sound that I can hear, and if in addition Transitivity is a fact and I am attending to both sound and sensation, then sanity and common knowledge of the language ensures that I describe this process as one of 'listening to the sound', while only philosophy will help me to bring it under the equally valid 'listening to the sensation'. Therefore when someone says: when I see my hand and know it is my hand, I simply cannot engage in attending to its light; what rather he should say is the following. When I see my hand and know it is my hand, sanity and common knowledge of the language ensures that I and my mind will conceptualize this experience as 'noticing my hand'; but common knowledge of the language does not ensure that I do not also, so to say off my own bat and personally, conceptualize this phenomenon as one of 'attending to the light'. Rather, the language is silent on this issue, and it is only at the prompting of philosophy that we discover that the activity had all along been in addition one of attending to the light. And a visually indistinguishable example of attending to the hand could, in different cognitive circumstances, and now at the prompting of sanity and the language, have been correctly conceptualized as 'seeing the light'. For example, if the sense of sight had in someone's case a special two-stage history, in which it mutated from taking only immediate physical objects like light to taking mediated material objects as well. Such a being, ignorant of this development, might well find himself correctly conceptualizing the seeing of his own hand as 'seeing light'.

Small wonder then that most people will not know what to do if one says, as they look at their hand, 'attend now to the light that is coming from your hand'. For all that this order could legitimately mean is: 'continue doing what you are now doing.' Then sanity and common knowledge of the language ensures that they must do what they are doing as 'looking at the hand', and ensures also that 'the learned' (philosophers) will join 'the vulgar' (humanity) in doing precisely the same; but only philosophy brings it about that some of these philosophers—when like G. E. Moore they engage in 'a little reflection'—will *also* do it as 'attending to the light' (in a non-visual mode of 'seeing-as'). Shift the cognitive presuppositions however, and the suppressed characterization of the attending will now at the prompting of the language come to the fore.

8. Mediators and Contingency

(1) *Perception* ('intuition') requires (stipulatively) that either the perceived item or its 'material base' cause an awareness-type (or attentive) event in the perceiver via a causally reliable path. Meanwhile, *sense-perception* requires in addition that the reliable causation of that awareness-event involve causal mediation by a sensation which at the same time acts as attentive mediator. Accordingly, awareness of pain rates as perception, and so does proprioceptive awareness of limbs, but neither count as examples of sense-perception. The former satisfying neither requirement, the latter failing to meet the attentive requirement—since sensation-representationalism breaks down in the case of proprioception. By contrast, awareness of heat and smell on this definition count as examples of sense-perception.

Some sense-perceptions are less immediate than others, for example smell than contact, and occur anyway at a spatial remove from their object. In such cases phenomenal mediation occurs—of varying kinds. Thus, we may smell a particular object (e.g. a giant cheese), and do so through smelling the smell of mediating particles; yet this diffusion of particles, while a phenomenon in its own right, is not a mediating phenomenon in quite the sense sound is, for what we perceive in perceiving the mediator is in this case identical with what we perceive insofar as we can be said to perceive the mediated, viz. the smell of its stuff. By contrast, in the central cases of phenomenal mediation—those of light and sound—we perceive a mediator that is altogether different from the mediated object, for light and sound are distinct and diverse from their material object sources. And yet here too a notable difference exists. For the Transitivity of Attention applies in the case of light, and does not with sound. Then while it is an impossibility that it should with auditory sensation in its present state, and evidently possible it should in the case of visual sensation, it is a posteriori that the latter possibility is realized. Sight might have taken a more primitive form. For example, had our visual fields registered the presence and colour of light, but been unresponsive to its spatial layout. In that case Transitivity of Attention and Presence would not have held of the sense.

(2) At this point a second difference between sight and hearing comes to the fore, which is on the face of it even more important than that of Transitivity—and yet I suggest it be taken with a grain of salt. Namely, while it is contingent that light mediates the visual perception of objects, it is probably necessary that sound mediates the auditory perception of objects.

Let me begin by substantiating the claim concerning sight. Now we individuate the four sensuous senses, not all that surprisingly, through appeal to the type of the sensation that is at once causal and attentive mediator. Therefore whenever visual sensation plays such a role in a perception, we can know that the sense involved is sight. This account allows there to be primitive forms of sight which fail to realize the rich potential of the visual sensation (a potential suggested by the refined spatial structuring to which the sensation lends itself). Thus, sight might have been much nearer to smell than it in fact is. For example, most visual fields might have been black most of the time, only to light up with vivid magenta flashes when coffee particles were on the wind, or pink spots if cheese particles were in the offing, or gold streaks when roses wafted tiny fragments of themselves our way, etc. In these circumstances we would see material stuffs, rather as we now smell them, and see individual objects in the thoroughly second-rate way we now smell them. In that case we would have an example of seeing, first without light as a mediator, second with a mediator in the sense smell has a mediator.

Meanwhile, this account of a sense also permits there to be examples of seeing, first without light as a mediator, but secondly with a different mediator that mediates precisely as does light. Thus, provided visual sensations regularly match the physical surrounds as they now do, and an intervening phenomenon plays a causal role similar to that of light, we will have realized a case of seeing that is indistinguishable from present seeing, with a mediator playing the same role as light. And it is irrelevant whether the match is produced by light or some other phenomenon. Theoretically we might see objects by seeing electrons. Indeed, we might even manage to see without mediator phenomena either of the kind found with sight or smell: for example, if the causal agency were magnetic action at a distance. I conclude: that it is a merely contingent matter of fact that the Transitivities holds of seeing; contingent that we see objects through seeing light; and contingent that we see objects through seeing some intervening mediator phenomenon.

Then if it is contingent that we see objects by seeing light, how can it be necessary that we hear objects by hearing sound? Well, it just may not be. But in any case this has nothing to do with the senses concerned, and merely reflects the mode of individuation of the mediator phenomenon in vogue at the time, which in turn probably reflects the state of development of the physical sciences of the mediator. The issue boils down to the familiar question: is sound identical with waves in a medium? And this in turn is ultimately a stipulative linguistic issue. Whether sound is wave motion turns upon whether it has extra-psychological physical causal powers, e.g. cracks glass. It is natural but absurd to be puzzled over this. One puzzles as to whether there is a sort of non-physical publicly perceptible sensory *thing* (the sound), that quasi-magically (and very like a spirit) splits the glass. Likewise, we may think it obvious that a smell cannot tarnish the silver. After all, what does the silver know about the smell? Probably our concept of smell is such that a smell cannot tarnish silver. Yet if we decide that smell is causally powerless in the physical realm, it is easy to overinterpret this fact, as if it demonstrated the existence of a public non-physical mental domain which our senses somehow enable us to contact. In fact, all that it shows is that 'sensible' (i.e. secondary) qualities are consciousness-relative grade II-objectivities, mere projections of the *qualia* of sensations onto the environment. And all that really matters is the reality of purely physical mediation, and the reality of the perceptual sensation. The rest is historical accident and stipulation.

Now *if* a 'sensible' phenomenon has well-known physical effects along with its sensory effects—as holds of light in its well-known gymnastics across lakes and through windows, and heat in its power to melt and cook—*then* probably men will have the concept of a deep physical X that has both these sensory and merely physical effects. This is true of heat. It is true of light. But probably it is not true of sound. Yet philosophically it is of no moment either way. The only issue of philosophical interest is, that we can in absolutely all of these cases constitute a bona fide concept of 'the property of φ-ing as the φ sensation reveals', e.g. of 'smelling as the coffee smell sensation reveals' or 'feeling as the heat sensation reveals'. The concept of taste is already of this kind, for necessarily if something tastes sweet it has a sweet taste; but the concept of heat is not, for something can be cold but feel hot (e.g. some new plastic at −60 °C). Yet side by side with the concept of heat is the concept, feeling as the hot usually feels, which is just as good a property as smell. Berkeley addressed himself to this latter real property—and was wrong to do so; but no harm done, provided he knew so—which he did not. And the physical 'impotence' of feeling-hot, like that of smell, is not a substantive lack, but a mere conceptual trifle.

It may be that our term 'sound' vacillates between a use where it refers to a hidden physical item, and a use where it refers to an analogue of smell. It may even have changed with the progress of Physics. Nothing much hinges on it, provided we grasp these facts. Then this is what I mean when I say that, while it is a contingency that sight is mediated by light and very probably a necessity that hearing is mediated by sound, this should be taken with a grain of salt. Even if hearing were mediated by electrons rather than shock waves, 'The Messiah' would remain a sound-concept. An analogue of sound can be constructed for light, 'lightt', just as feeling-hot, 'hottness', sits side by side with hotness. This grade II-objectivity moves with the speed of light, rather as rumours travel fast. And just as we feel the hotness and hottness of the sun, so we see its light and lightt—in one and the same event.

Now it is no coincidence that sound and light are at the meeting of the ways, both for the Transitivities of Attention and Presence and the a posteriority/a priority of the mediator. It is no coincidence that precisely at the point at which Transitivity comes into its own, the mediator should be a posteriori-given. For what ensures Transitivity, which is above all the ubiquity of simple law in the transmission of spatial facts, likewise ensures that the profound physical facts of the case, the inhuman and grade I-objectivities of Physics, will sooner or later have semantic priority over the human-relative 'sensible' phenomena.

17

Sense-Data (1)
or
The Ways of the Attention

The problem which led to the discussion of the previous chapter was that of identifying the early objects given to the attention in visual perception. That is, those visible phenomena which in coming to the attention enable epistemologically more remote objects to do so. These phenomena are not overtly conceptualized by the understanding in the visual experience, so that we cannot turn to the content of that experience to identify those early objects, and are instead compelled to have recourse to philosophical argument. The example of light is particularly helpful in this regard for several reasons. One is, that it is difficult for anyone to actually deny that we see light, and yet the way in which this fact is conceptualized in our normal visual experience is of such a nature as to make the thesis of Chapter 16 both substantive, contentious, and a means of demonstrating in the concrete that the content of the experience is no certain guide to the identity of its objects. The mere fact that the light that we see all over the visual field is situated upon the retina, even though given merely directionally to the experiencing subject, shows how poor a guide is visual content, and indeed common sense of a kind, to the identity of the objects given to the attention. However, the main reason for studying the perception of light is that it brings clearly to our notice the phenomenon I called 'The Transitivity of the Attention', misunderstanding of which is in my view the main obstacle to understanding the attentive situation that obtains in the case of visual perception, and in particular to grasping the fact that visual sense-data engage the attention before anything else.

1. Introduction

(1) One extremely common theory of visual perception affirms the existence of one and only one experienced psychological phenomenon at the time of visual perception: namely, the visual perception itself. Nothing more, and in particular nothing that matches the traditional specifications of the sense-datum. Sometimes this theory is embellished with a diagnostic account of the thought-processes of those who believe in sense-data. They are sometimes said to confuse the real

immediacy of the visual experience with that of some supposed immediately given psychological object, either in believing that visual experiences are themselves seen, or else in hypostatizing the internal object of the experience, taking it to be a distinct and immediate psychological object of an awareness. The claim is that when people speak of 'sense-data', they are in all probability referring to the 'objects' of such mythical encounters!

Thus, sense-data theorists are supposed either to think that we see *our own seeings*, or else that we see a distinct psychological something which is the *content* of our seeings. An example will illustrate the second of these two confusions. Suppose that one sees a red apple *as* a red apple. Then those who believe in sense-data are supposed to think that this event of seeing consists in or analyses into an awareness-event, together with a distinct psychological object that is at once red, hemispherical, of apple-type! Some such, and in any case a theory that leads inevitably to regress. After all, the content of the awareness of this strange meaningful mental object will doubtless in turn suffer hypostatization. And so on—endlessly!

Well, it seems to me that not too many believers in sense-data have consciously or unconsciously embraced these crass accounts of visual perception. Berkeley thought that the 'proper and immediate' objects of sight were 'lights and colours', and G. E. Moore illustrated the kind of thing he had in mind in talking of 'sense-data' by referring us to an after-image,[1] and neither doctrine suffers at all obviously from the aforesaid thought-ailments. In any case a theory of sense-data can be defended which comes close to the traditional theory and which eschews the undoubted errors of these caricature theoretical positions. It takes the following form. We shall assume that we are giving an account of a normal enough example of seeing: more exactly, of monocular seeing (for simplicity). Then in the first place the visual experience or perception is understood to be an event in the attention: more precisely, an event of noticing. Secondly, the object of noticing is something that is sited in the visual field. The third and most contentious part of the theory is sense-data-ist in character. It claims that the immediate object of the above attentive event is a visual sensation: more specifically, the colour and two-dimensional properties of a two-dimensional array of visual sensations. Meanwhile the visual sensation itself is taken to be a psychological individual of type sensation, which is located in the visual field, and endowed with colour-brightness and an extent that is characterizable through the use of two variables (such as right/left and up/down). The theory concludes with the contentious and representationalist claim that the seeing of this sensuous phenomenon is *identical with* the seeing of whatever public physical perceptible it manages to make visible. Thus, the one perceptual or attentive event is said to fall under double descriptions: one involving reference to the sensuous object, the other to the physical object.

A word at this point about the descriptive headings under which the objects of seeing are given to the perceiving subject. The theory in question does not suggest

---

[1] *The Philosophy of G. E. Moore*, ed. P. Schilpp, 629–32, North-Western University Press, 1942.

that the attention is directed onto the colour of the sensation *qua* (or *as*) of a visual sensation. Despite falling under the above two descriptions, the perception is said to be experienced under only one head. Thus, the attention is said normally to go onto the colour of the sensation *qua* colour of the public perceptible item, and the claim is that generally this will not be in error, for normally the colour of the one *shows* the colour of the other. Now this account is representationalist in that it is *in* (or *through*) experiencing the colour and contour of the immediately perceived sensation that we experience the identical colour and contour of the distinct and mediately perceived public perceptible. The claim is that the immediate material object of the visual experience is the visual sensation—a senseless psychological primitive with colour and expanse—and it is nothing else. It is not the public physical object, for it is the sensation; not the experience, for no experience can be its own immediate material object; and it is not the content of the experience, for the content is not distinct from the experience and is not an individual. It is a senseless psychological primitive that is endowed with only *some* of the experienced properties of the public physical perceptible, namely its colour and two-dimensional layout. This theory is very different from, and should be clearly distinguished from, the above improbable doctrines.

And yet how can scaling down the immediate psychological object of sight from one that is meaning-laden and three-dimensional to one that is senseless and two-dimensional, bring sense-datum theory any nearer to answering the charge that it involves an hypostatization of the internal object of the perceptual experience? Is not the difference between the two putative objects little more than a matter of degree? Well, the answer to the above charge is that it rests on a misunderstanding. The sense-datum theory propounded above practises no form of hypostatization. Neither does it depend on the assumption that intentionally directed experiences with (say) colour content necessitate *as such* the existence of distinct mental colour objects—witness hallucinations of colour where none exist. And neither does it (fantastically!) assume that intentionally directed experiences *analyse into* an awareness-event conjoined with a distinct immediate psychological object. All of these conjectures are mistaken. Rather, the theory supposes that any truly visual experience with colour content invariably (and probably necessarily) takes a direct immediately given distinct psychological colour object, exactly as any experience with the intrinsic character of a pain-awareness invariably (and probably necessarily) takes a direct immediately given distinct pain object. So much for misunderstandings.

At this point I think I should declare the evident enough fact that I myself endorse the above theory. Such a limited representationalism is, in my view, forced upon us by the 'sense' in 'sense-perception'. In any case, whether or not it is true it is evident that it is free of the gross failings mentioned at the beginning.

(2) Why should one accept this theory? Before I bring forward reasons in its favour, let me note that the very content of the theory depends decisively on the

sense of 'visual sensation'. What do we mean in using this expression? In my opinion examples of the type under consideration abound in everyday visual experience, and could be readily singled out there. However, it is better to explain the expression uncontentiously. Then I will do so by indicating as an instance a simple and familiar psychological item: to wit, a visual after-image. Here we have an unexceptionable defining example of the type under discussion, an example with somewhat special origin-properties but with nature intact. Then what is it to believe that visual sensations so defined are an essential element in the normal visual perceptual situation? What is it to believe in sense-datum theory? The following is a very simple explanation of the doctrine. Suppose that one turns one's face upwards to the heavens and opens one's eyes, which are suddenly inundated with the blue of the sky. To believe in the existence and omnipresence in normal seeing of visual sensations is to believe that at that very moment *something blue came into existence*: something blue, psychological, and one's own. It is the existence of such a something that is the fundamental point at issue.

One final comment before I begin the discussion. It is interesting that people feel great confidence in their intuitions on this matter, in the nearly complete absence of an inspection of the central phenomena—the *two* central phenomena—involved: to wit, the *sensation*, and above all that unique and extremely important psychological phenomenon, the *attention*. I have subtitled this chapter 'The Ways of the Attention', not as a quirk, but because the conclusions I reach, and most especially the *defences* of those conclusions against attack, travel hand in hand with a piecemeal charting of the very interesting peculiarities of the intuitional attention. Only through understanding just what this phenomenon is, and just what it accomplishes (its 'ways'), can one truly find oneself in a position to entertain views on the questions: Are there such entities as visual sensations? Is sense-datum theory true?

2. A Prima-Facie Case for Sense-Data

(a) A preliminary reason in favour of the sensation theory

First, a preliminary consideration favouring the theory that visual sensations both exist and play the role suggested. It is based upon the reliable causal action of the body in determining the character of the visual field. This last is of the nature of a principle, a principle which bears decisively upon the present discussion.

Let us assume that a condition of visual normality obtains in some human subject, and let us in addition assume that the retinal area under consideration is sufficiently central to permit full perceptual colour differentiation. Then given these background conditions, (a quotum of) light of colour c_1 at point p_1 on the retina is in such a conscious being a causally sufficient condition of colour c_1 being present at some corresponding point p_1' in the visual field. Now let us make one more innocuous assumption. Let us assume that the c_1-light at point p_1 effects the appearance of c_1 in the visual field through locally generating some chemical α.

Why not? It must do it some way. Accordingly, α at p_i must in the assumed standing conditions be a causally sufficient condition of colour c_i being at point p_i' in the visual field. This truth will hold of a normal visual system irrespective of whether the chemical α is induced by light from the environment, or by some other means. Thus, it holds even if α is directly introduced by scientifically accomplished chemical intervention. Then to repeat: the presence of the chemical α at p_i is a causally sufficient condition of colour c_i in the visual field—given the above few assumptions.

This simple proposition is of some moment. It is in my view already weighty argument in favour of the view that when in normal vision c_i-light impinges at p_i on the retina, it causes a visual sensation of colour c_i at p_i' in the visual field. A series of considerations point to this conclusion. First, the instance of colour c_i at p_i' in the visual field when the cause is the scientifically effected introduction of chemical α, is immediately perceptually accessible uniquely to the consciousness of the subject, and this fact strongly suggests that such an occurrence of colour must be a psychological phenomenon. Second, this phenomenon will surely be present whenever light of colour c_i impinges at p_i on the retina, since α is present on both occasions. Third, a sort of local psycho-physical law seems to be exemplified by the latter psychological phenomenon and its (c_i-light at p_i) cause. Fourth, it is a law which holds irrespective of the presence or absence of sophisticated or developed mental items of the kind of concepts, intellect, rationality; indeed, the only relevant psychological condition is the absence of a state of general unconsciousness. Fifth, there furthermore exists a regular determination of intensity: intensity of c_i-light at p_i determining the brightness of c_i at the visual field point p_i'. Sixth, and perhaps most important of all, no reference is made to the *attention* or *awareness of the subject* in the conditions governing the law. In sum, there is reason to think that when in normal vision we see a public perceptible colour c_i, then a colour c_i that is a psychological phenomenon, that is capable of intensity, and that exists independently of intellectual and attentive events, is quasi-nomically determined by bodily events.

All of the above five features are exemplified in the relation holding between the bodily causal conditions of pain, itch, tickle, and these paradigm instances of the type, bodily sensation. Thus, a kick in the shins regularly causes pain of roughly corresponding intensity in the shins. And it does so irrespective of one's state of mind (barring sheer unconsciousness), and of the contents of one's concept-system, and of whether one is awaiting pain or absorbed in a book or overwhelmingly involved in some searingly intense experience. Then in view of the striking similarity between bodily sensations, and the occurrence of colour c_i at p_i' in the visual field that is at once psychological in nature *and* guaranteed either by the incidence of c_i-light or by chemical α at point p_i on the retina, the burning question seems to be: how can one *avoid* postulating visual sensations in seeing? And perhaps equally urgent: what is it about the visual situation that makes for *resistance* to the sensation theory?

469

(b) Diagnostics and an alternative theory

(1) Consider the latter question. There can be little doubt that the answer is to be found in the character of the closely related phenomenon of visual attentive consciousness. Several factors are at work here. Perhaps the first thing to say is, that nothing seems more immediate in experience than the objects of visual perception, and this fact alone makes the sensation appear otiose and even downright intrusive. The supposition must be, that if the sensation existed then it would have to make its appearance as one visible standing *in the way of* or before another. Now this is, I think, true, but it does not follow that it appears as an *obscuring* agency. Precisely the opposite is the case. It *makes visible* what would otherwise lack an appearance at that point in the visual field. But, anyhow, the mediation of the sensation is a mediation of mere colour-brightness and its contour: it is not that of a visible object set at a distance from us in three-dimensional space; and there is no reason why such merely directional mediation should disturb the experience of immediacy. The example of light, which exactly analogously mediates the perception of objects, beautifully illustrates this fact.[2]

Here we have one possible cause of resistance to sensation theory. But it may be that the main reason the phenomenon of visual attentive consciousness engenders scepticism concerning the existence of visual sensations is, that visual consciousness is almost always directed to public *visibilia* lying beyond the psychological given, so that we never seem to encounter the supposed mental go-between on its own. It is rather as if one were to doubt the existence of some supposed paint stuff out of which pictures are said to be created, on the not unreasonable grounds that one has absolutely never encountered the stuff outside the context of a picture. Why believe in its separate existence? Well, protagonists of visual sensations can I think meet this challenge: they can effect the required separation. Thus, they could in response bring forward the unusual but perfectly possible example of visual sensations of determinate colour and intensity which some scientist manages systematically to induce in certain congenitally blind people through stimulation of their optic nerves. Those blind subjects may well experience those novel colour patches merely as novel sensations blessed with *quales*. Then here we would be encountering visual sensations in the absence of any representational interpretation. Alternatively, sense-data theorists could proffer an example like a completely unnoticed after-image. And here we would be encountering visual sensations in the absence of an impression of any kind. Nevertheless, these cases may not produce conviction: they may well be dismissed as 'rudimentary', 'degenerative', 'pre-perceptual', 'already interpretational', etc. We shall return to them later.

(2) So much for diagnostics. What about the other question? How might one get by without postulating visual sensations? Well, many people seem not to have felt the strength of the case in their favour, despite the impressive array of con-

---

[2] See Chapter 16.

siderations marshalled earlier. One who has, and hopes nonetheless to avoid drawing the conclusions I am inclined to draw, is Christopher Peacocke in his book *Sense and Content*.[3] Peacocke aims at conserving the bulk of the characteristic properties of visual sensations while dispensing with visual sensations as individuals. Roughly, in his ontology the sensation is consumed in entirety by the visual experience; though not 'without trace', for he endows the latter with a distinctive few 'sensational' content-properties ('red', 'bright', etc.) which possess special characteristics. I shall say little here about Peacocke's views, except to say that I believe he has done us the service of drawing to our attention the existence of this interesting sub-class of the properties of visual experiences. Then as I should express it, these properties of the experience are those contentual elements that are simply and immediately caused by the visual sensation (in a sense that should become apparent below). But let me now explain the concept of a sensational property without recourse to debatable issues.

Stipulatively, I shall take the 'sensational properties' of a visual experience to be those elements of its experiential content that would still have been present in visual experience, even if visual experience had never managed to go beyond its immediate sensuous objects onto outer physical objects. (Something which would have been the case had visual experience during the course of evolution never made the grade as a sense, never succeeded in 'hooking onto' the environment, for want of the right causal connections.) Then it is important to note that absolutely all of the elements of such a primitive and purely sensuous content would have *survived* a revolutionary evolutionary developmental leap in perception's objects from 'inner' to 'outer' (or as I would prefer to express it: from 'inner' to 'inner and outer'). For example, 'red' would have survived, and so too would the two-variable characterization of its contour. While we in fact visit the former upon public physical objects in projective manner, and the latter upon them non-projectively, neither of these two *visibilia* would have vanished from view at such a developmental watershed: they were seen beforehand, and they continued to be seen afterwards. In short, 'sensational properties' prove to be realities and the concept is vindicated. So let us not confuse the plausible doctrine of sensationalism ('sense-datum' theory) with an implausible rejection of the thesis that the visual experience is endowed with this special sub-class of properties.

3. The Argument

(a) Demonstrating the reality of the visual sensation

(1) The vital question now facing us is: does acknowledgement of the existence of such properties of the *visual experience* as have been dubbed 'sensational', render unnecessary the postulation of a separate psychological entity which is the original source and bearer of such properties? In my view it does not. I say so, for the

---

[3] *Sense and Content*, Oxford, Clarendon Press, 1983.

following reason. There exist truth-conditions for the state of affairs in which a particular point in the visual field has a determinate colour-brightness value, while no public perceptible is at that point *and* the contemporaneous visual experience lacks any such sensational property. What makes this state of affairs possible is something very simple. It is that *the* determinant of the colour-brightness value of every differentiable point of the visual field is completely physical non-psychologi-cal. If a man is conscious, and his visual apparatus normal, and light impacts over the full extent of the retina, then the colour-brightness value of the entire visual field is rigorously fixed. This determination is at once causal and (in a certain sense) necessary. While it is contingent that a particular light-value causes a particular colour-brightness value, it is necessary that the latter is at every point in the visual field wholly determined by bodily non-psychological phenomena. The mind has nothing to do with it. The cognitive utility of vision depends on this property.

Turn now to the visual attentive experience. It is inconceivable that it should be wholly determined by such factors. Clearly, the content and character of our glimpsings and watchings must in part be determined by mental items like one's concept-system, one's experiential history, one's cognitive and attentive posture, and the like. I can scarcely have the experience of seeming to catch sight of a blue wren if I have never heard of wrens; and it must be relevant to the fact that I had such an experience that I was watching expectantly for just such a wren's appear-ance at just such a point in the brambles; and so on. This holds, not just of physical representational contents like wrens, but of mere sensuous contents like a particu-lar instance of blue, where attentive-posture at least must play a causal part. And so a gap appears between the *causal determinants* of the visual experience and the causal determinants of the visual field. This divergence makes its presence felt when we come to compare the *content* of the visual field and the content of the visual experience. So let us now make that comparison.

(2) How do we determine the content of the visual experience? How do we dis-cover just what it was that I seemed to see? The means are multiple, convergent, and to a degree inexact. Thus, it is attested by the description I would give; or by the painting I would execute if with lightning speed and limitless expertise I embarked on the enterprise of representing it immediately after the experience; or the common territory of all the three-dimensional replicas of content that I would accept as nearly veridical to my experience. Some such—and with an irremediable element of uncertainty. Then the point to be emphasized now is that the painting will have gaps, and the common model will have gaps, and the narrative will be lit-tered with gaps and indeterminacies ('a few chairs', 'some large shape', 'a bright patch', 'something', '——'). So much for the content of the visual experience. Then a strikingly different situation meets us when we consider the content of the visual field. For the only indeterminacies that occur in the characterization of the visual field are, first the indeterminacies stemming from the fact that the visual field is not infinitely fine-grained, second the indeterminacies that inevitably gather as

we move out from the centre towards the peripheries. No more. And in particular, nothing answering to the indeterminacies in the narrative characterizing the attentive experience. For example, nothing will answer to the lack of specificity of 'a few chairs'. If chairs are in the visual field, then necessarily some one number is their number. And nothing will correspond to the gaps in the painting or model. And so on. In a word, while much that is in the visual field will find its way into the content of the visual experience, much will not. At some point there is and must be a tuning out in the visual experience. (For it is a *limited container*.)

(3) What is the significance of this discrepancy between the contents of the visual field and those of the visual experience? What account are we to offer of the fact that, at a point in the representational painting where there is a gap, and a gap in narrative and model, there is in the corresponding region of the visual field a small but clearly differentiable yellow circle? A natural if complacent response is to say that it just shows that something yellow and round was in the visual field at that point and that it went unnoticed. Certainly it shows as much. But I think it shows more.

Let us remember that in a visually normal human subject yellow light at point p_1 on the retina is a causally sufficient condition of yellow at a corresponding point p'_1 in the visual field. Then what if the small yellow circle in the visual field owes its existence, not to some publicly visible yellow item lying before one in the field of view, not to yellow light impinging on the retina, and not even to some technically induced chemical phenomenon α in the retina that is exactly the same as that which is normally generated by the incidence of yellow light; what if it arises because of some sudden accidental or pathological event deep within the visual system? In that case the yellow in the visual field cannot be the publicly visible yellow of some publicly visible item. And yet this yellow is real enough. It is not imagined. After all it can be carefully scrutinized, it has a determinate shade, a repeatable cause, and so on, even though we are supposing on this particular occasion that it escaped notice.

The question then arises: *what* is yellow? It is pointless trying to discover some publicly visible item whose publicly visible yellowness is on view in the visual field: neither a visible surface, nor a spot of yellow light, nor the pathological event deep within the visual system, nor anything else of a publicly visible nature meet the requirements. Now this instance of yellow is of necessity reserved uniquely for the consciousness of its owner, who can as we have remarked carefully scrutinize and experience it as we cannot. Evidently, this occurrence of yellow is a psychological phenomenon. Of what type? Well, it is not the contemporaneous visual attentive experience that is yellow. And since *ex hypothesi* yellow is no part of the content of such an experience, it is not even the non-autonomous internal object of the visual experience. It is not an imagining that is yellow, and no part of the internal object-content of an imagining. Meanwhile, it exhibits the following traits: it has and must have a regular bodily non-psychological cause, it has a phenomenological character,

473

it has intensity, it has extensity, it lacks all sense or meaning, it owes nothing to its owner's concept-system or mind generally, it is capable of being noticed or vaguely noticed or missed altogether by the attention. Now all of these traits are shared by pains and tingles and itches and suchlike phenomena, and by nothing else. Plainly, this phenomenon is of the type: sensation. It is the familiar sensation that we bring under the description, 'sensation of yellow'. What other type is there to fit to such a phenomenon?

Here we have a proof of the fact that a psychological phenomenon, that is a sensation of yellow, can exist in a visual field and pass wholly unnoticed. And so the existence of that special sub-class of properties of visual experiences that are called 'sensational properties', fails to obviate the need to posit visual sensations. In short, visual sensation theory withstands the seeming threat posed by these properties. And it seems highly probable that the visual sensation must be the original source and bearer of 'sensational' properties.

(b) Representationalism

This conclusion takes us almost all the way to a representationalist theory of visual perception. The final step takes the following form.

Let us at this point adjust the above example a little. In the light of the above argument, I would like at this point to return to the earlier prima-facie reasons advanced in favour of the existence of sense-data. Thus, let us now assume that the small unnoticed yellow circle in the visual field owes its existence, not to some publicly visible yellow item lying before one in the field of view, not to yellow light impinging on the retina, and not to an accidental or pathological event deep within the visual system. Let us instead suppose it derives from a technically induced chemical phenomenon in the retina, one that happens to be exactly the same as that which is normally generated by the incidence of yellow light: in a word, the aforementioned chemical α. Then for the identical reasons as were just now advanced, this instance of yellowness must be predicated of a sensation of yellow. That is, it must be predicated of the very same bearer as was singled out through the example of ocular accident or pathology: a psychological individual of the type sensation.

Now the above instance of yellowness was present when the yellowness of nothing that is visible to mankind was present at that yellow point in the visual field. However, when the yellowness of something that *is* yellow to mankind is visible at that very same (x, y) point in the visual field, the physical item in question must be reflecting light which *ex hypothesi* when landing on the retina generates such chemical phenomena as were responsible for the above sensation of yellow. But those chemical phenomena are causally sufficient conditions of the sensation of yellow in a visually normal human. I conclude: when a publicly visible item which is yellow to mankind enters the visual field of a visually normal human, it causes the sensation of yellow precisely at the point which it itself occupies. But there is only one instantiation of yellow at that visual point, so that the one yellowness at that point must be at once *of* sensation *and* physical object. This is a representative theory of material object perception.

4. Counter-Arguments

This argument, like any argument, can be endlessly resisted. But it can be intelligently and interestingly resisted in no more than a limited few ways. I propose at this point to briefly outline the only counter-arguments I can take seriously, and answer them as best I can. Because of the centrality of the question to perceptual theory generally, and the strength of people's convictions on the matter, I devote a fair measure of space to meeting those counter-arguments. However, as I remarked at the outset of this chapter, this procedure travels hand in hand with a piecemeal charting of the very interesting peculiarities of the intuitional or perceptual attention. And that is the only way we have of arriving at a properly considered judgement concerning the existence or not of sense-data.

I shall make one proviso. I propose to discuss the above argument up until the penultimate Section 3(*b*): that is, to defend the argument for the existence of visual sensations when the internal psycho-physical situation is identical to that in normal cases of colour perception, since that in my opinion is the nub of the matter. Accordingly, the instance of yellow under discussion must from now on be understood to be, the small yellow circle generated in the visual field by a technically induced chemical event of the type normally generated by the incidence of a circle of yellow light at that point of the retina. And the assumption is that such a small yellow circle goes completely unnoticed on some occasion. Then the first four of the counter-arguments which now follow dispute the claim that on such occasions *the point in the visual field is yellow*. And the reason they do is, that such instances of yellow seem to demand a psychological bearer of the type of sensation, and to be internally indistinguishable from normal cases of colour perception. The remaining four arguments dispute that *anything psychological is the bearer of yellowness at that point*. The counter-arguments are these.

(a) The point in question is not yellow, for the reason that 'yellow' is predicable of something only when that instance of yellowness is in principle visually accessible to mankind.

(b) The point in question is not yellow, for the reason that it is simply not in the visual field.

(c) The point in quesion is not yellow, for the reason that the character of the visual field is wholly revealed in or by the character of the visual experience—as the hallucination demonstrates.

(d) The point in question is not yellow, for the reason that its colour-brightness value is indeterminate.

475

Four more counter-arguments exist. They are directed, not against the supposed yellowness of the point in the visual field, but against the deduction that something psychological is the bearer of that property.

(e) The point in question is yellow, and *something* is yellow, only it is not something *psychological*: yellowness is predicable of certain elements in the causal chain leading from point p, on the retina to the visual centre.

(f) The point in question is yellow, but it does not follow that *anything* is yellow, for the reason that the yellowness enters the visual experience *qua* constitutive-contributor-to-the-internal-object-of-the-experience.

(g) The point in question is yellow, but it does not follow that *anything* is yellow, for the reason that yellow is part of the content of the visual experience; and what makes this possible is, that the content of visual experience is wider than that of visual noticing and encompasses the entire content of the visual field in all its detail.

(h) The point in question is yellow, but it does not follow that *anything* is yellow, for the reason that the utterance merely affirms a conditional binding upon the contents of visual experience.

We shall consider these arguments in order.

(a) *The point in question is not yellow, for the reason that 'yellow' is predicable of something only when that instance of yellowness is in principle visually accessible to mankind.*

If this is how matters stand, the seeming colour of after-images must be accounted some kind of illusion or error. But is not a 'yellow after-image' really yellow? After all, it *looks* yellow. Some will demur at this however, affirming that only the publicly visible can look *any* way. I find this principled pronouncement dubious in the extreme; but it will in any case be allowed that the yellow after-image looks yellow *to its owner*, and that he is unlikely to be in error on this issue. So surely it *is* yellow for him. True, it does not look yellow to others, but why must what is yellow for him look yellow to others? After all, our familiar colour attributions are relative to human viewers, so what is untoward about making a colour attribution that is relative to one viewer? Indeed, I suggest that the yellow after-image is a special instance of yellowness in that *necessarily* it looks yellow to someone, viz. its owner. Why should not 'yellow' name precisely the look that is necessarily on show to the owner of a 'yellow after-image'? In that case, the yellow after-image will be necessarily yellow. And it will be neither here nor there to its yellowness that it does not look yellow to others.

I think that is how matters stand. But it does not really matter if I am wrong. It does not at all matter if some other property, 'yellow'', has to be affirmed of the point in question. It will still be a reality, and truly predicable of a psychological reality. And the properties of that psychological reality are such that it must be an example of the type, sensation. Does it not still have a particular phenomenological character, yellow-ness notwithstanding? Is it not capable of intensity and extensity? Is it not senseless in that it is generated completely independently of the intellect? Must not its cause be regular physical non-psychological stimuli to the visual system? Cannot it be noticed or vaguely noticed or missed altogether? Etc. Etc.

(b) *The point in question is not yellow, for the reason that it is simply not in the visual field.*

The suggestion is, that just as those publicly visible points that are sited opposite the blind spot are not even in the visual field, so too are those points corresponding to gaps in the representing painting (or narrative, or model)—irrespective of whether we are talking of publicly visible object-points situated at a distance in space from the subject, or merely of angularly mapped points in the visual field (e.g. 10° left from centre and 20° up). If there is a gap in the painting 10° left 20° up, then neither public visibles lying 10° left 20° up nor mere colour-brightness values can be sited there in the visual field—for the visual field is not even black at that point: it is non-existent! Accordingly, hiatuses must spring up like mushrooms all over the visual field as the attention wanders! I find this suggestion wildly implausible. In effect, this theory at one stroke rejects the doctrine that the contents of the visual field are of necessity wholly determined by bodily non-psychological factors. Instead it supposes that if the light impinging on the retina of a visually normal human were to remain absolutely unchanged over an interval of time, then the contents of the visual field will nonetheless constantly mutate as the focus of the attention shifts and wanders. Not the focus of the *gaze* be it noted, but merely that of *attention* or interest. Thus, the attention joins the visual apparatus as a mental-causal force in the setting up of the visual field! More, it helps to cause that which stands forth as its own object!

This argument makes confident use of the concept, presence in the visual field. (As do I.) But just what does it mean to say of a point that it is 'in the visual field'? What is it that the things behind my head *are not* that everything of middle size in front of my head *are*? Feebly, one says: visible now to me. But what does 'visible' mean here? Will be noticed *if*—? If what? Suppose we say: if noticed. Then the claim collapses into tautology. Suppose we say: if attention is drawn to it. But often it will be noticed whether or not attention is drawn to it, yet what happened seemed to be made possible precisely by its presence in the visual field; while occasionally it will not be noticed despite all attempts to bring it to the attention (e.g. in negative hallucination). Suppose we say: can be noticed. But I can notice what I turn my head to inspect. Suppose we say: needs no condition if noticing is to occur. But noticing must have a cause. Suppose we say: all necessary physical non-psychological conditions of noticing are met. Here we come closer to the concept to be analysed. Yet is it not still a little *negative*? The 'in' of 'in the visual field' seems intuitively to correspond to something *concrete*.

All of these obscurities are conjured away at a trice by the theory of the visual sensation. According to it, presence in the visual field *is* the concrete presence of suitable visual sensations with suitable causal properties. More exactly, all physical non-psychological conditions must be met for the truth of 'noticing those sensations *can be* noticing the occupants of the visual field.' However, it is not my purpose at this juncture to defend this analysis, but to assess the claim that where there is a gap in the painting (narrative, model) *nothing* is in the visual field. Then it tells against this claim that the two most plausible analyses of 'in the visual field' are inconsistent with it. Thus, the theory of the visual sensation detaches the concepts, 'presence in the visual field' and 'presence in the content of the visual experience', while the theory that presence in the visual field *is* the state of affairs where all physical non-psychological conditions of noticing are met, allows that the latter state of affairs can obtain even as the attention fails to take up the option.

To this argument from plausibility, I now add a verificationist argument. Let us address ourselves to a more modest question than the issue of analysis: namely, whether from the point of view of verification a distinction exists between present-in-the-visual-field-but-wholly-unnoticed and absent-from-the-visual-field. Then I think it clear that one does. The tests for the former include the demonstration of here and now noticeability ('visible to one'), the tests for which rest on the presumption of a repeatedly instantiated physical state of affairs which is kept constant as potential mental-causal influences ('attend 10° left 20° up', etc.) are introduced into the situation. Meanwhile the test for absence from the visual field *is* the test for unnoticeability ('not visible to one'), and this simply repeats the above test-situation only to look for a contradictory result. In a word, verificationist considerations support the claim that these concepts are different.

But it is in any case obvious that these concepts are distinct. Indeed, the very concept of the visual field derives its validity and utility from this distinction. In effect, to assert that the yellow circle is not even in the visual field, is to abandon the concept of the visual field. If presence in the visual field simply *is* presence in the content of the attentive-experience, we might as well dispense with all talk of visual fields. Presence in the visual field collapses into, being a seen part of a seen expanse. I suggest that this is a deformation of the concept, which is in fact such that we readily make utterances like: 'Let us introduce the object into his visual field, and see if he notices it.' Meanwhile an additional part of the justification for speaking of a 'field', lies in the phenomenon of sensuous continuity, and this has by implication been extirpated. And in any case the visual field is 'presented to view' rather than 'taken (or had) in viewing'. And so on.

(c) *The point in question is not yellow, for the reason that the character of the visual field is wholly revealed in or by the character of the visual experience—as the hallucination demonstrates.*

This argument is at one with the previous argument in rejecting the principle: the colour-brightness value of each point in the visual field, veridical or not, is wholly determined by bodily non-psychological causes. It very interestingly adduces the hallucination as disproof. Thus, Macbeth hallucinated Banquo, let us say in a red cloak, let us say in front of a visible blue wall. Then the argument begins with the claim that the colour at that point in his visual field was red, and, no point being able to be red and blue, not blue. After all, did not something red appear in his visual field? Is not that precisely the way of hallucinations? But the causes of the hallucination were knowledge of a murder, overwhelming guilt, general mental unhingedness. It follows that the colour at that point in the visual field owes its existence to psychological factors like knowledge, guilt, insanity. Therefore the principle is false.

Note that I am using the word 'hallucination', not in the unfortunate sense loosed some few years ago into the philosophical literature by writers like David Lewis[4] and others, but in the traditional sense whereby the insane and the overheated and the drug-laden are its natural habitat. If a light-image of pink elephants were to be projected onto my retina, then in my terminology the resulting visible elephants would not rate as hallucinations. This is not stipulation, for this phenomenon is different from the above: my pink elephants are sensations which are real autonomous existents, but the pink elephants of a sufferer from *delirium tremens* are merely the internal objects of visual imaginings, and the traditional term 'hallucination' is justly reserved for a sub-variety of perceptual imagining. In short, the above items are altogether different in type, and fall under different categorial concepts. In any case, the present argument depends upon our understanding 'hallucination' in the traditional sense.

Then the reply to the argument is, that the point in Macbeth's visual field would have been blue and not red. People constantly underestimate the extremity of much hallucinatory experience, which is capable of such oddities precisely because it is a direct manifestation of a loosening of one's grip upon reality. Then part of the lost reality here is, the colour of that sector of the visual field. That we should site a red imaginary object at a blue point in a visual field, is no more problematic than that we should eidetically imagine a dark road against a white wall. What is problematic is that we should lose epistemological contact with the wall in so doing. Then the truth of the matter is, that Macbeth did not have a visual experience with red content, let alone a visual experience with red content and distinct red material object: he had a visual-*imaginative* experience with red content and an unremarked blue object at that point in his visual field. This special visual-imaginative experience was of such a kind as to 'stymie' *any* visual experience—whether with blue or red content—of that same point, but not through some red something *obscuring* any something else from view. Mental forces like unassimilable guilt made it impossible for him to visually experience what was there, through causing him to substitute at that point the deliverances of his visual imagination.

(d) *The point in question is not yellow, for the reason that its colour-brightness value is indeterminate.*

It is allowed that something can be in the visual field but wholly missed by the attention. It is allowed that when the something is a public perceptible like a red

---

[4] 'Veridical Hallucination and Prosthetic Vision', *Australasian Journal of Philosophy*, vol. 58, 1980.

balloon, that which is in the visual field will be of determinate colour. And it is allowed that determinate colours can be in the visual field and noticed. What is not allowed, whether we are talking of public perceptibles like red balloons or merely psychological phenomena like after-images, is that a *determinate colour* can be in the visual field and *wholly unremarked* by the attention. Note that we are not talking specifically of the peripheries. A small yellow light could appear in the middle of the visual field, and because one's attention is riveted on the peripheries go wholly unnoticed, and the suggestion will be that at that moment yellow is not in the visual field at that point. At that particular point the visual field is said to be, not empty, but indeterminately bright and indeterminately coloured. I shall make two comments on this claim.

The first is, that even if it were true that the visual field was not yellow at that point, the desired counter-argumentative conclusion does not follow. To be indeterminately coloured and bright is to be just that, and since this can be true even as the painting (or the narrative, or model) harbours blanks at that point, a wedge is driven between the content of the attentive experience and the content of the visual field. Then since this discrepancy can exist when no public visible is appearing at that point in the visual field; and since such an example of colour-brightness is of necessity attentively available uniquely to the consciousness of its owner, and must in consequence be rated a psychological phenomenon; and since not even the indeterminacy said to characterize this sector of the visual field appears in the content of the visual experience; it follows that some other psychological phenomenon must be invoked as its bearer. What else but the sensation? And why in any case should not a visual sensation be less than fully determinate in colour-brightness value? That, after all, is precisely true of the visual sensations encountered at the edge of the visual field.

My second comment is, that the only explanation in the offing for the alleged indeterminacy of the brightness-value of the unnoticed point is, that the point in question is completely unnoticed whereas it is necessity that every point in a visual field be of *some* more or less determinate measure of brightness. But in what way do these facts add up to an explanation? What is the rationale? Are we to assume that the fact that the content of the attentive experience omits all reference to that sector of the visual field, somehow *causes* indeterminacy in colour-brightness value at that point? But how could it? And in any case this is to postulate the experience and the indeterminacy as *distinct existents*, and that thesis leads almost inevitably to the postulation of the sensation as the bearer of the indeterminate colour-brightness.

Finally, no reason has been advanced for jettisoning the view that the visual field must remain unchanged if the light impinging upon the retina remains unchanged—even as the attention wanders. We have been give no reason for abandoning the view that physical non-psychological factors are of necessity the sole determinants of the contents of the visual field. (After all, visual fields typically reflect the contents of the non-mental physical environment, being by nature cognitive indicators somewhat akin to mirrors.) No reason has been advanced in support of the thesis that the internal object or content of the visual experience provides the ultimate criterion for determining the character of the visual field.

(e) *The point in question is yellow, and* something *is yellow, only it is not something* psychological: *yellowness is predicable of certain elements in the causal chain leading from point p_1 on the retina to the visual centre.*

(1) This first of the counter-arguments which accept the yellowness of the point in the visual field, strikes me as wild and yet interesting. The claim is, that the yellowness in the visual field is truly predicable of something publicly visible, and thus need not be predicated of some psychological bearer. The argument proceeds as follows.

We see 'floaters', and we see light that is at the retina, *directionally* (at the very least). That is, we see their directional and two-dimensional properties, irrespective of whether we also see their three-dimensional properties. Then could it be that we directionally see the regular effects *within the visual system* of retinal events? If it is true that we can directionally see a circle of yellow light situated on our retina, might we not directionally also see a sequence of causally linked representatives of that circularity within the visual system? If so, when the yellow circle is induced by chemical α, and even though we at that moment see neither light nor any outer reflector-source of light, we would still see the yellowness (for us) of causally linked physical neural phenomena that normally are representatives of light at p_1. Then note that the validity of this objection turns upon that of the claim that we normally see such neural occurrences when we see physical objects in the environment.

A comparison helps to explain this last suggestion. The one act of raising an arm falls under many act-descriptions. It falls under the '*basic*' act-description of 'raising an arm', and also under *instrumental* act-descriptions like 'lifting a cup', 'moving an arm-shadow', etc. (under only some of which is it intentional). But in addition this same act falls also at the same time under certain other non-instrumental non basic '*constitutive*' act descriptions (as one might call them): for example, 'producing muscle contraction', 'producing neurological change', etc. And I say of these descriptions that they are of *actions* for the following reasons. It is because being an act is not description-relative; and because one can intentionally obey orders to non-instrumentally effect these same bodily phenenomena simply by moving one's arm (provided one knows the relevant bodily facts); and finally it is because one does *the very same thing* when one moves one's arm ignorant of those facts. These considerations are sufficient to demonstrate the existence of 'constitutive' acts.

(2) Might such acts be a suitable model for sight? Might the one attentive event fall under 'see the sun', 'see the light at the retina'—*and also* under analogues of the above 'constitutive' descriptions of actions? Suppose the sun looks round and yellow, and the patch of light on the retina is round and yellow, and that there exist a regular sequence of causally related event-segments C_1, C_2, etc. down the optic nerves. Might it be that these event-segments are directionally seen when one sees

481

the sun? And might they also be yellow for us? And round? And are these supposed instances of these properties also directionally seen?

Now if circularity is seen in both sun and light, circularity must in principle be *recoverable* at each causally linked stage in the visual system: that data must in some form be preserved all the way, since the perception is veridical. This might seem like a reason for saying the event-segments C_1 (etc.) must be directionally seen on such occasions. And yet must those segments be themselves *circular* if the circularity of sun and light are seen? I can think of no reason why they should be. All we require is regularity, with circularity as its steadily recoverable content down the sequence C_1 C_2 etc., and this need not take the form of *spatial projection*. The equation $x^2 + y^2 = a^2$ in some mode or another suffices. But can an item be directionally present in a visual field if *no* spatial projections relate it with visual representations in the visual field? I do not think so. The following is why.

I can imagine a far-off balloon in the sky visible as a mere point, set in a visual field in which spatial relations have been systematically distorted through systematic reorganization of ocular-neural paths. Here neither shape nor even direction of object are visible, even though the object itself is. Now the very existence of such a possibility might seem decisively to detach visibility from spatiality as such. However in reality the facts do not bear this interpretation. Thus, the visibility of the balloon was made actual only because of spatially determinate correlations holding between points in the visual field and points in the visible scene, rather like the correlations exemplified by mirrors and prisms. Then how could presence in a visual field be realized if *no* spatial projections relate the item in question and the visual field? We can hardly perceive the object and dispense with the perceptibility of the space which individuates it! While sight might have taken a more primitive a-spatial form, we should remember that, in the case of the visibility of an object in visible three-dimensional space, such as the aforesaid balloon, we are obliged to discover a principle whereby we can identify a point in the two-dimensionally ordered visual field as that in which the visible item appears or shows itself. How could this be accomplished in an *a-spatial* perception of item and setting?

These considerations show that, whereas we really do 'constitutively' 'do' the events in the motor-system, we do not 'constitutively' see the events in the visual-system. The situations are disanalogous: 'doing' muscular events helps 'do' limb events, but were we to set eyes upon C_1, it would actually obscure or *stand in the visible way*—as light does not and as 'floaters' do. What we are concerned with here is the fundamental distinction between a *perceptible mediator* and a *perceptual mechanism*; and whereas we *actively* generate the elements of motor-mechanisms, we do not *perceive* the elements of perceptual mechanisms. In a word, these considerations demonstrate that we do not see the regular neural effects of chemical α, and that the yellowness at p' cannot be predicated of them.

(3) It is because light travels in straight lines that we see, not just light but light-sources as well, and it is because visual sensations spatially correlate with each that

we see both. Then these perceptions reveal the perceived item *and* its spatial properties, as the perception of sound or smell need not. The requirements of visual
individuation are such that one cannot have the one without the other. Now the
mediation between retinal light and visual field is not in fact spatial-projective all the
way, and has neither need nor even possibility of being so. Therefore even if it had
been the case that the very first event-stages C_1 (etc.) were normally directionally
seen, yellowness could still be sited in the visual field at p′ while C_1 (etc.) had been
rendered invisible through scientific intervention (by introducing some chemical β,
say)—and we would be back once more where we began—namely, at a situation in
which the yellowness at p′ is predicable of no non-psychological object! Thus, the
supposition that 'constitutive' seeing might conceivably have been a reality for the
very first part of the visual pathway, can in no way succeed in making the original
bearer of yellow a public visible.

5. The Argument from Parts

The next counter-argument is sufficiently important to deserve a section to itself.
And it has the virtue of helping to delineate some of the distinctive features of the
visual experience. It therefore also assists in the delineation of the distinctive
characteristics, the special ways of functioning, of the visual attention.

(f) *The point in question is yellow, but it does not follow that* anything *is yellow, for
the reason that the yellowness enters the visual experience* qua *constitutive-contributor-
to-the-internal-object-of-the-experience.*

(1) The suggestion is, that every point in a continuous visual field can have a
determinate colour-brightness value, even though some points may not be registered in the visual experience under a fully determinate heading or indeed under
any heading at all, without our needing to postulate a separate bearer for those
colour-brightness values. What is supposed to make this possible is that the colour-
concepts continue to find application in the characterization of the internal object
of the attentive experience—only in a very special way: namely, *qua* constitutive-
contributor-to-the-internal-object of that experience. Thus, the yellow patch does
not at the time of the visual experience lead an existence outside the scope of that
experience, even if it happens to be completely unnoticed. Whether or not that particular instance of yellow is individually registered, it is nonetheless collectively
registered (like a fish in a netted shoal) under a heading of the form 'contributor to
item X' (e.g. as 'one of a host of golden daffodils').

This counter-argument stands in need of elucidation and elaboration, so I shall
set it out once more in stages, beginning with what seems to me to be a genuine
insight.

(2) Our immediate concern is: the noticing of collectives. An appeal to a democratic principle has just been made, upon the following lines. If a collective (of 3, or
of 1003) is noticed; and if no unit is more (or less) noticed than any other; then the

noticeability of the collective must be due in part to each unit. Each unit must make a definite and equal contribution both to the noticeability of the noticed and thereby also to the single event of noticing. Therefore the relation of the attention to a completely unnoticed occupant of the visual field cannot be compared to its relation to something lying outside the visual field. To speak of a completely unnoticed occupant of a visual field as if it were a *lost thing*, lying out of sight and mind like a coin at the bottom of a well, is to introduce into the visual world an alien element drawn from the world of material things, with its distinctive modes of loss. Such an item is not *out of sight* in the visual field, precisely because it is *in* the visual field. Here we come across the real reason why gaps in the experience-representative painting (or narrative, or model) cannot be construed as indicating holes in the visual field. Whereas a gap in a visual field makes no contribution to what is seen, any particular visual atom part of the visual field makes its self-sacrificial democratic offering to the recorded *visibilia* of the moment.

All of this strikes me as unexceptionable. Indeed, it seems to me a truth of some significance. I think it puts its finger on an important difference between visual impressions and mental images (where both constituent atom and democratic principle are inexistent). Crudely, one might say we have here the explanation of the congested or overinhabited impression made upon one by the visual field—in contrast to the underpopulated expanses of the mental image. It is not just that the visual field is fully occupied, 'all seats sold out': it is that every single point in the entire visual field stands in a functional and engaged relation with the attention. I do not mean in the familiar relation that we bring under the heading 'noticed', but in another special and causally efficacious relation. Thus, the unnoticed points of the visual field do not in being unnoticed recede from view into invisibility, leaving the visual field to the recorded *visibilia*. On the contrary, these visible items play their constitutive part in making visible such *visibilia*. While they are in competition with them for our attention, as is absolutely everything in the visual field, they are not in competition for existence. Rather, the small is in general ready to assist in the constitution of the large—which simultaneously they help bring to our notice. Then let us *completely stipulatively* and without prejudice characterize the relation holding between the attention and a constituent of a noticed totality, as a 'part-noticing'. Accordingly, the constituents of a very small and noticed collective (e.g. of 3) will be both 'noticed and part-noticed', while the constituents of a very large collective (e.g. of 1003) will be at once 'completely unnoticed and part-noticed'.

(3) What follows from these considerations? Consider the small yellow circle that occurred in the visual field at a point corresponding to a complete blank in the painting (etc.). This unnoticed patch has not slipped out of sight in the visual field. Instead it is part-noticed by the attention, since it as least helps to constitute the entire visual field, which is something that certainly came to our notice or attention. Therefore it has not separated itself off completely from the attention. *A fortiori* it has not separated itself off completely from the attention only to stand as a result in

484

need of some psychological bearer other than the attention. Yet it stands in need of a psychological bearer. What? Not the attention as the *subject of qualification*, for the attention cannot play such a role: thus, this noticing-event is not itself yellow, nor is it yellow at point p_1' of the visual field (whatever that state of affairs might be). And not the attention as the *bearer of a content* either, for this small yellow circle finds no place in the content of the attentive experience. Then what can the psychological bearer of yellow be?

It is at this late stage in the discussion that the counter-argument under consideration is advanced. The claim is, that 'yellow' finds its application, not in qualifying some psychological bearer something, nor in characterizing the internal object of the attention, but in characterizing a part-object of the attention. It is through playing such a role that yellowness can eschew the role of constituent-of-content, and at the same time permit justice to be done to the fact that yellowness is instantiated in the visual field. In this way we sail between the Scylla of indeterminacy and the Charybdis of sheer absence, even as we wield Ockham's razor and manage to give an acceptable account of the complexities of visual perception in which we postulate no more than one experienced psychological phenomenon at the time of seeing: the visual experience. So far the argument.

(4) Before I discuss this argument, let us remember that we are considering an instance of yellow in the visual field that owes its existence to an artificially induced chemical phenomenon in the retina, of the type that is normally engendered by yellow light at that point. Now the above argument appeals to the fact that the visual attention has part-objects. It claims that, while point p_1' in the visual field is indeed yellow, this is to say *no more than* that the part-object of the attentive event at p_1' is yellow—and claims that this fact obviates any need to predicate yellow as a quality of some distinct psychological individual. But precisely what are we *saying* in claiming that the part-object of the attention at p_1' is yellow? It seems clear that we are saying *no more than* that the event of noticing some inclusive totality $\Sigma x_{1\,\text{to}\,N}$ owes its very existence to (many) such facts as (say) that the concept yellow is instantiated at point p_1' (including that very point). Thus, we put this colour concept to use when we characterize the visual field at point p_1', and it is because we *in general* find ourselves in a position to apply such concepts across the visual field that there comes to exist an intentional object $\Sigma x_{1\,\text{to}\,N}$ for the attention. An internal relation holds between the existence of a noticing event with a collective content and the collective applicability across the visual field of concepts like (say) yellow. Such a state of affairs is of the very essence of visual and indeed of perceptual experience generally. It typifies the entire breed.

However, just as blood cannot be wrung from a stone, so no amount of stipulation can dress the above relation up as one of being object for the attention. Thus, each person in a crowd of 1003, while contributing to its noticing through helping to at once cause it and compose its object, is not thereby noticed. But if some particular part-object of the attention is no sort of object for the attention, no mention of it under *any* description appears in the most exhaustive possible description of the attentive experience. It simply falls outside both the qualitative character *and* the intentional content of the experience. And it is in my opinion a serious error, based upon a confusion of internal and material object, to suppose that a visual experience is psychologically *underdescribed* until mention is made of each of its part-objects.

All this is true of the present instance of yellow. This visual experience with yellow part-object is not itself thereby yellow, whether to its owner or *qua* cerebral event; and the fullest possible psychological description of the visual experience will begin by classifying the type of the experience, will predicate relational or qualitative predicates like 'unexpected' or 'momentary', and it will be *completed* upon our providing the fullest possible description of its internal object. Then absolutely nowhere in this descriptive enterprise will we have discovered a use for the concept of yellow. But if the point p_1' in the visual field is a beautifully clear example of the colour yellow, and the phenomenon itself is psychological in status, the concept of yellow must be put to use in characterizing *some* psychological something or other. Surely, the visual sensation, descriptively. I conclude that the counter-argument fails.

(5) But I concede the reality of the phenomenon, being a *noticeable and unnoticed part of the noticed*. Precisely here the concept of the sensation is indispensable: it readily accounts for the facts. Thus, sensations have the property of being immediately accessible to the attention, of being able to elude the attention unless overwhelmingly intense or affectively charged, of tending to capture the attention the more intense and the more extensive, of merging into totalities. For example, we can immediately attend to the most unobtrusive sensation of contact, and just as easily fail to notice it, and the intenser and more widespread a sensation the more we tend to notice it, and as one sensation. Such features lead inevitably to the part-object phenomenon noted above. For a sensation can lie open to consciousness, not noticed but helping to constitute an extensive sensation-complex which *is* noticed. Thus, a hundred simultaneous light sharp contacts on the back of the hand generate a sensation-complex ('prickles') which would not be noticed were it not for the unnoticed contribution of the likes of any one of the hundred small sensations of contact. Then a *causal function* must be allotted to each single sensation together with a *constitutive function*. They are not *objects of awareness*, but *part-causes* of an awareness of *that of which they are unnoticed parts*. They are part-causes of awarenesses of the objects they go to constitute.

This is precisely the situation encountered with the visual field. The experience of overpopulation produced in us by the teeming detail of the visual field, owes its existence to the fact that each single point, noticed or partially noticed or completely unnoticed, is at once part-cause and part-of-the-material-object of the visual experience. However, being part of that object and cause is not the same thing as being part of the representational content of the experience which represents that object. The existence of such a psychological gap is essential to the very manner of being of the sense-perceptual experience. On the one side of the gap the experience, on the other side the sense-datum. These two remarkably (and perhaps even ontologically) dissimilar phenomena are (so to say) face to face with one another, and a strange (but incomplete) transference of content occurs across the gap. Such a special variety of epistemological communication constitutes a sort of Jacob's ladder within the mind!

6. The Argument from the Experience/Noticing Distinction

Like its predecessor, this argument warrants a section to itself. It is like it also in pro-viding a means whereby we may further delineate the distinctive characteristics of the visual experience. And therefore also the special ways of functioning of the visual attention.

(g) *The point in question is yellow, but it does not follow that anything is yellow, for the reason that yellow is part of the content of the visual experience; and what makes this possible is, that the content of visual experience is wider than that of visual noticing and encompasses the entire content of the visual field in all its detail.*

(1) *Expounding this objection.* The concept now under scrutiny is the visual ex-perience; indeed, the experience itself. The suggestion is, that the *visual experience* has a wider content than that of *visual noticing.* Now experiences are phenomenal episodes: hearing someone laugh, feeling a surge of pride, having a mental image swim into one's head, trying to recall a name. They are events. But so too are noti-cings: noticing an unusual smell, a slight twinge in a molar, a friend on the other side of the road. Accordingly, if visual experiences and the co-present visual noticing have non-identical content, and the latter is narrower than the former, then *either* these phenomena are two simultaneous distinct events *or* noticing is an event-constituent of the experience-event *or* noticing simply *is* the experience—under a more restrictive head. No other possibilities exist.

The first possibility can be immediately discounted: visual noticing must of necessity at the very least contribute to the visual experience. The second possibil-ity is equally unacceptable. Thus, when do we ever encounter the visual noticing-event in the absence of the supposedly complex experience-event? It seems clear that these 'two' events are logically equivalent events. Then how could the visual noticing that is said to be *part of* the visual experience be itself an *autonomous* event? How could it have an *event-identity* of its own? So how could it be an *event*-part of the non-distinct autonomous experience-event? There seems no way of distin-guishing these events as *events.* Accordingly, we are left with the third theory. This theory identifies the visual experience-event and the visual noticing-event, yet somehow supposes the content of the experience to be *broader*—perhaps as a paint-ing *qua* representation can have properties ('pink-cheeked at p') which it does not have *qua* painting ('pink at point p'). And yet how can the internal content of a mental event be description-relative?

(2) _Criticism_. Let me briefly resume what has emerged so far. The only alternative to identifying _both_ the experience and the noticing _and_ their content, seems to be to identify the events and dis-identify their content. Personally, I cannot understand how this could be accomplished. However, let us take a closer look at the theory. In particular, I would like both to assess it and understand how one might come to endorse such a doctrine.

According to this objection (g) the content of the visual experience under discussion is said to include the yellow circle at p_1. Presumably, this experience must be expressible as '_seeing the yellow circle_ at p_1'. Yet what kind of seeing can this be? It will be allowed that there is a familiar usage in which it would be correct in this present situation to say: 'I did not see the yellow circle' (under _any_ description). We are therefore being asked to suppose that there exists a sub-variety of experiential seeing of coloured patches which is non-identical with (i) noticing the patch, or (ii) noticing some totality (for example, some garden) of which that coloured patch is a noticeable part. Then is this strange non-noticing mode of seeing a _form of awareness_ of the seen item? How can it be a _perceptual experience_ and not be? And so we are being asked to endorse the existence of a visual consciousness or awareness of a momentary yellow circle, that is not under any heading a noticing of it. More, an awareness-of that circle that can be completely divorced from knowledge of it, since whatever visual content is visually known-of must necessarily be visually noticed-of. Once again I confess my incapacity to make head or tail of such an 'awareness'.

What might lead one to endorse so strange a theory? Perhaps the rationale goes something like this. We saw earlier that the teeming detail of the visual field was causally active, and we have no choice but to include the yellow circle in question among these many active mini-agencies. Then how—one asks oneself—can a circle be _causally contributory_ to a visual consciousness without itself being an _object_ of visual consciousness? Must it not precisely be through being an object for consciousness that visibles can manage thus to be causally contributory? Therefore the yellow circle must somehow come through to visual consciousness even though it fails to come through to the visual attention. Now I myself can feel the persuasive power of these utterances, and yet as they stand they plainly do not constitute a valid argument. To be part of an object of awareness is not _as such_ to be an object of awareness, for although some parts are indeed objects of awareness, it is clear that some others are not—the attentive event being less fine-grained in content than its immediate material object. And so the argument is variously flawed. It underestimates the indivisible unity of the visual experience, blurs the distinction between internal and immediate material object, and practises what might be called a _reductionism upwards_. Thus, it reduces 'noticeable but unnoticed element of the noticed' to a kind of unnoticing noticing! It seems to assume there is in some other usage an entailment from 'noticeable element of the noticed' to 'noticed': that is, that in this strange usage 'noticeable but unnoticed part of the noticed' is simply contradictory. I can discover no reason for endorsing this doctrine. Why accept so unperspicuous an account of the perception of collectives? And we have in any case been over some of this terrain already in 5(e)(above). Etc.

(3) *Awareness of bodily sensations*. At this point I turn away briefly from visual perception to the less puzzling phenomenon of bodily sensation, in search of clarification. We shall see that we encounter here a similar (and equally illicit) inclination to postulate unnoticing experiencings (of perceptibles). We shall see also that the perception of bodily sensation-collectives instantiates an identical causal-attentive structural situation to that postulated by sensationalists in seeing. I begin the discussion with an examination of the two closely related concepts: awareness of bodily sensations, and experience of bodily sensations.

We distinguish *faint* awareness of *intense* sensation from *intense* awareness of *faint* sensation. The governing principle is, that degree of awareness of a sensation is distinct from the degree of the sensation. Therefore the degree of attention directed onto a sensation need have nothing causally or logically to do with the intensity of the sensation. A faint or marginal awareness of an intense sensation is thus a genuine possibility: a sensation need not diminish in intensity as a result of the poverty of attention coming its way. Then why not the occasional *total* unawareness of some sensation? Or are we to believe that, as a medium-intensity sensation passes from faint almost subliminal awareness into total unawareness, it automatically topples off the ledge into non-existence? I can see no justification for this view. And we have a powerful counter-consideration in the fact that this theory would entail the existence of a sophisticated *mental (partial-) cause* of mere bodily sensations like toothache—namely, attention-*distribution*! After all, it is a near truism that attention-distribution cannot be a part-cause of bodily sensations like toothache. I conclude: a sensation can exist completely unnoticed or unawares. Why not? It will scarcely split the mind into schizoid halves to accommodate this measure of disunity. In fact it seems to be happening all the time in the case of sensations of contact and pressure. The wearing of clothes would be a distracting nightmare otherwise: an unending 'hair shirt' situation!

Now we say of a bodily sensation that we 'feel the sensation'. This can be understood in two senses. That the sensation is a *feeling*, or that this feel-type sensation is *experienced*. (And these are not the same.) What is 'experiencing a sensation'? Far and away the most natural view is, that it is having the sensation come to the attention, that it is noticing-of it. However, another possible theory—one in line with the present objection (g)—might be that experiencing a sensation is a rather strange and complex phenomenon: namely, the noticing-of the sensation *conjoined with* a second phenomenon which is dubbed 'feeling the sensation'. But does anything answer to this latter expression? Why believe in a 'feeling experience' that is additional to attentive experience? One possible reply is: that we should believe in it because the sensation is *no mere thing*, is a *feeling*, and therefore must *merely through being real* be felt and experienced. And that in turn seems to imply that the sensation will be felt otherwise than through the mere vagaries of the attention.

Consider this latter account of sensation-experience. How does the phenomenon of noticing-of relate to this supposedly co-present 'feeling-of'? Well, the rationale advanced seems to imply that the 'feeling-of' ought to remain perfectly steady even if the noticing-of experience were to dwindle away towards zero. I say so, because the theory deduces the existence of such feeling-of from no more than the *feeling-status* of its object. But just what *is* this steady element of the experience of a sensation that persists unabated and unaffected as attentive consciousness of the sensation dwindles towards (and even arrives at!) zero? Can one seriously believe in an *experiencing* of bodily sensation that is wholly independent of the degree and distribution of the attention? And can one even make sense of a variety of experience that is in principle (as this should be) wholly detachable from *knowledge* of its own existence? In short, the aforementioned complex 'experiencing' seems to be sheer moonshine.

In a word, experiencing-of a sensation must be the awareness-of or noticing-of or consciousness-of that sensation. These are all one and the same thing. Then this phenomenon has *degrees*, and can *fade away towards zero*, and actually *vanish*, even as the sensation persists unaltered. Thus, the existence of another mode of 'feeling a sensation' besides 'the noticing-of a sensation' and 'the having of a sensation', is surely a myth. Only one interior phenomenon occurs, an attentive phenomenon, and only one psychological object phenomenon occurs, the sensation given to the attention. And I can think of no term or description which is capable of singling out the conjectured non-attentive mode of experiencing a sensation. Nor can I think of any reason for postulating its existence.

(4) *Perceiving sensation-collectives*. We are at present considering bodily sensations. We saw that they can exist wholly unnoticed. We also saw that noticing-of or awareness-of these phenomena is synonymous with experiencing-of them, and that nothing answers to a 'feeling of a bodily sensation' that is neither the sensation itself nor the noticing of it. Accordingly, a sensation must be able to exist *wholly unexperienced*. Let us carry this result with us as we turn now to consider the perception of bodily sensation-collectives. (Here we return to an example already employed a little earlier.)

We shall suppose that at time t_1 a thousand point-places all over one's body are given a short sharp non-painful contact. At t_1 you for a moment feel 'prickles all over'. Consider sensation 728 situated on the left side of the left knee. This is as real as any other sensation and as the sensation-totality itself, and can be attentively singled out each time we repeat the overall stimulus, and for these reasons must be deemed to have existed at the original time t_1. Now the discussion in (3) (above) demonstrated that sensation 728 *might be* at once real and unexperienced. So let us assume that this possibility is actualized at the time t_1. Meanwhile we have assumed that the sensation-collective is perceived merely as 'prickles all over', and that the content of this experience included no reference to 728 (under *any* description). Then we can see from these few observations how the content of a veridical perception of a sensation-collective generally will be less rich than that of the collective itself. Bodily sensations can contribute both to causing the perception-of, and at the same time to constituting its object, without themselves being objects of that perception.

Those wedded to the doctrine that sensations cannot be completely recessive within experience, must argue against the total experiential recessiveness of sensation 728. For example, they may say: 'Sensation 728 was real at the time t_1 at which one felt "prickles", so it must at t_1 have been *felt and therefore experienced*; for if no one of the thousand is experienced all of the thousand are not experienced, but since the thousand was in fact experienced each of the thousand must have been experienced.' This argument assumes that, whereas 'an unnoticed but noticeable part of the noticed' is intelligible, 'an unexperienced but experiencable part of the experienced' is not. But the argument equivocates over the sense of 'the thousand was experienced'. In effect it denies the *sui generis* and special character of the experience of collectives: it assumes that it consists in the mere summation of experiences of all of the constituents. Rather as one cannot whitewash a thousand fences without whitewashing each of the thousand, so in the case of experiencing a thousand! But this misrepresents the distinctive character of this very interesting phenomenon. It supposes a definite experiencing-of for every single sensation. But what can that experience be? I can think of nothing measuring up to the given specifications.

(5) *The visual case*. I return to visual perception. In the light of the above discussion of bodily sensations, why in the visual situation should we be surprised that a perceptible part of a perceived collective might pass unperceived and unexperienced? After all, that precisely is the possibility realized when the perceptible is part of a complex bodily sensation-collective. Indeed, what we have witnessed in the case of this sensation-collective is something of general import. It is the *very ways of the attention*.

A word here about those 'ways'. They are in marked contrast with those of imagination and thought. Perceptual attention, 'intuition' so-called, is a unique mental phenomenon in which the mind enters into contact 'in the raw' with phenomena lying beyond itself, without reproductively internalizing the fine grain and disorder of the contacted realm. At exactly this point in the perceptual causal chain—a chain leading from outer physical object to an internal event of awareness—a load of potential data is jettisoned. And it is no accident that a significant disparity is thereby established between the content of the 'raw' intuited object and that of the immediately adjacent contacting intuition. Since perception is the unique site at which mind concretely engages with non-mind, acting as a one-way messenger between two profoundly dissimilar realms, it must have the special Janus-like property of operating simultaneously in highly dissimilar ways on two distinct fronts.

On the one side it engages with a physically presented non-mental sector of the

491

teeming world, on the other side with the holistically bonded phenomena of the mind—and most especially with the phenomenon of knowledge (which it is the express function of perception to engender). Then just as the mind cannot be clogged with useless knowledge projectively matching the minutiae on immediate view, so likewise the engendering perceptual experience cannot be overloaded with mere visual bric-a-brac. Why should it be? What would be the function of this excess material? Then why not jettison it at once? Only a confusion between *the experience-of* and *the experience-ed* could lead us to insert this excess baggage into the content of the perceptual experience. Here the vital distinction between a causally engaged immediate material object (such as a sensation-collective that is noticed), and a resulting internal experiential object, comes into its own. And here we have the source of the puzzling gap between the visual field and visual experience that determines the disputes arising in this area.

The beauty of the example of the perception of bodily sensation-collectives is this. We actually *set out from* an example of the very type under dispute—to wit, sensation, and proceed to demonstrate that gaps may be expected and do indeed exist between the sensation-object and the content of the perceptual experience of such a collective. This in turn demonstrates that no valid principle exists to the effect that perceptual consciousnesses and their sensation-collective object cannot co-exist and have non-identical content. Thus, we saw how such a disparity is a reality in the case of bodily sensation-collectives. Then all that holds of the perception of the latter, holds of the perception of colour patch collectives. If it is possible for a single bodily sensation to exist wholly unexperienced, if it is possible for a single sensation (such as 728) amidst an experienced collective to exist wholly unexperienced, if significant gaps can in this way appear between the content of sensation arrays which are experienced and the internal content of the experience of those arrays— then why not in the case of a complex visual field containing a small patch of yellow? And that suffices to distinguish visual object from consciousness of that object. This present chapter is in effect the construction of a device whereby we may prise apart two closely intertwined psychological items: the visual field, and our awareness of it. The independent psychological reality of the visual field *is* the existence of visual sensations or visual sense-data.

7. The Argument from Conditionals

Like its two predecessors, this argument warrants a section to itself. And at the risk of seeming mechanically to repeat myself, I will add that it is like them also in providing a means whereby we may further delineate the distinctive characteristics of visual experience, and thereby also the special ways of working of the visual attention.

(h) *The point in question is yellow, but it does not follow that anything is yellow, for the reason that the utterance merely affirms a conditional binding upon the content of visual experience.*

The suggestion is, that 'point P in the visual field is yellow' *means*: if the attention has P as internal object, then it also has yellow. The rationale of this analysis is, that the verification of yellow at P is, attending to point P and experiencing yellow. To postulate behind such experience a distinct yellow psychological object is, it is claimed, to introduce a redundant *thing* into the world of sight. Why try to break out of the circle of experience? It is not necessary, and it is therefore theoretically unjustifiable.

The chief failing of this paean to experience is, its neglect of the causal presence of the physical. Such an approach is actually valid in the case of mental imagery, where experience is all that we have to go on, but it is wholly misguided with a phenomenon like the visual field which is, from one end to the other, necessarily causally engaged with the physical visual apparatus (unsurprisingly, in view of the informational value of the visual field). It is because a link of this kind does not exist in the case of mental imagery, that experience is here the only court of appeal. Let me try now to justify this rejection of the present counter-argument (h). This begins with an examination of bodily sensations. These less contentious phenomena should help once again to shed some light upon their more problematic perceptual brethren.

A. SENSATIONS AS INDIVIDUALS

Attentive phenomena

Much of what this counter-argument asserts could equally well be affirmed of bodily sensations. It is important therefore at this point to understand why we countenance bodily sensation individuals. Why believe that pains are individual somethings? Why do we think that, in attending to a toothache, one psychological individual takes another as object? Why are we not introducing a redundant psychological *thing* here? How do we manage in this case to break out of the circle of experience to the sensation individuals beyond?

Why believe sensations are individuals? Certainly, the language suggests so: we speak of 'it' being intense concerning pain, of 'that tickle', and so forth. But a much more substantive reason resides in the fact that we stand seemingly in an *attentive relation* to sensations. Even if no pain individuals exist, even if pain is merely the internal object of an awareness-event, the latter is nonetheless a *putative-attending* to pain. Now other modes of mentally relating in an experience to individuals occur besides intuitional attention. For example, a thought-of (as when I think about someone), or an imagining-of (as when a mental image of a friend comes into my mind), or affective relating-to (as when remorse over someone afflicts me). All of these are thought-mediated, in that my capacity to think of the individual is somehow tapped in the phenomenon. By contrast, the 'intuitional' attention relates us concretely 'in the flesh' to its object. And that it is to be contrasted with thought-mediated relations is evident, when we remember that perceptual relations are validated through appeal to causal considerations which for the most part lie outside the mind.

The phenomenon we describe as 'noticing a pain' is of this type. A pain can be noticed irrespective of concepts, beliefs, rationality, for noticing a pain simply *is* experiencing it, and newly born infant and dumb beast are as adept as anyone at experiencing pain. Now successful and unsuccessful putative-attendings are common enough phenomena, and we have accredited paths through which to distinguish one from the other. When the required link exists, perception occurs. And when it does, a basis for knowledge is realized. The intuitional attention is a path to knowledge—by contrast with the *thought*—or the will. Indeed, it is the 'royal road' to knowledge of the world lying outside our own minds. Whenever in our experience we encounter putative-attendings, there exist accredited paths to which we may appeal through which the attentive link can be established, and therewith a basis for knowledge identified. Such reliable paths exist in all varieties of sense-perception. They exist even in the immediate proprioceptive perception of our own body and its postures.

Then it is evidence that we are dealing with an accredited way of knowing that the event in consciousness we describe as 'noticing a pain' is of the type, putative-attending. From the mere fact of being, not a thought-mediated relation, but a putative attentive relation to something in the flesh, it is reasonable to conclude we are in the presence of a way of knowing, and hence with a phenomenon which in suitable circumstances rates as a perception. But the putative object of perception in noticing sensation is the sensation itself. And so there should exist circumstances in which an attentive relation to a sensation is established. Surely, when normal waking consciousness inheres in the putative-perceiver—no more! In that case the sensation must exist as a real something which is distinct from the attentive awareness of it. Thus, it must be an individual.

Note that there are putative-attendings and 'putative-attendings': for example, the seeming to see of genuinely visual experience and that of dream-seeing. It is evident that we are dealing here with two highly dissimilar phenomena: a truly attentive, and a merely imaginative that is an imagining-of just such an attentive experience. Then when I assume in the above discussion that the phenomenon we describe as 'noticing a pain' is not thought-mediated, by implication I classify it with the first of these. To my mind, this requires no justification. For to repeat, what we call 'noticing a pain' *is* what we call 'experiencing it', and whatever else the latter happens to be it is not thought-dependent in character. It is on the basis of such an assumption that the argument proceeds.

The explanatory situation

(1) The argument for scepticism concerning sensation individuals is, that the only mode of access to sensations is through consciousness of them, and just as no psychological something lies behind an image-consciousness, so nothing lies behind a sensation-consciousness. Such a theory must analyse *all experiential situations*

involving sensations purely in terms of our consciousnesses of them. For example: familiar phenomena like noticing a sensation, failing to notice it, noticing it imperfectly, and so forth. Consider one of these states of affairs, unnoticed pain at P. The theory under consideration will analyse this as: (i) the bodily causally sufficient conditions obtain for the truth of the proposition, the attention is on P—→the attention is a pain-consciousness, and (ii) there is at the present moment no consciousness-of-pain-at-P. Or consider the state of affairs, imperfect noticing of pain at P. Here the proposed analysis is: (i) the bodily causally sufficient conditions obtain for the truth of, the attention is on P—→the attention is a pain-consciousness, and (ii) there is at present a consciousness-of-some-sensation-or-other-at-P. And so on.

Why do we not accept such analyses? No doubt because they patently dissolve away the sensation as a reality (for it simply vanishes from the analysis). No doubt also for the reasons recently advanced above. But a further reason comes to light when we examine the *explanatory situation*. More exactly, when we look for an explanation of the *known experiential properties* of pain. Now for the most part these properties are causal in character. Then it is natural to assume that several of them must have been of vital import in man's sometime original framing of the concept of pain, and reasonable therefore to believe that the phenomenon thus singled out must have been *explanatorially justified* by their existence. In a word, an explanatorial case must exist for hypothesizing the separate existence of bodily sensations generally, and of pain in particular.

Amongst the causal and experiential properties of pain we note the following: (a) being caused by c-fibre stimulation. And, in addition to this scientifically disclosed property, those familiar experiential causal properties of pain which are accessible to almost any self-conscious being who has experienced pain. Thus: (b) usually causing noticing-of-pain events, (c) if faint in intensity and one's attention is riveted elsewhere causing no such events, (d) if a little less faint and one's attention is riveted elsewhere tending to cause noticing-some-sensation-or-other events; etc. Now these causal properties are not stray unintelligible phenomena. They do not perplex or surprise us. The reason is that they are readily explicable in terms of *two fundamental principles*: (A) Pains are obtrusive to the attention, sensations of contact are recessive, etc.; and (B) The more the attention is free, the more sensations and their determinations tend to be noticed.

(2) Here we have some of the more basic causal experiential properties of pain. Then how does the conditional or non-individualist theory of sensations cope with the phenomena (a)–(d)? Can it manage to explain these familiar properties of the sensation? Because sensation individuals are not countenanced by this theory, the properties (a)–(d) must now be expressed (very roughly) as: (a') c-fibre stimulation (C_f) causes the truth of a conditional linking noticing-bodily-part and noticing-pain events, (b') stimulus C_f causes noticing-of-pain events when the attention is free, (c') if the bodily conditions obtaining are C_{f*}, which regularly cause noticing-of-

faint-pain events when the attention is free, then if the attention is riveted elsewhere no such events occur, (d′) if the bodily conditions obtaining are C_{f**}, which regularly tend to cause noticing-of-rather-less-faint-pain events when the attention is free, then if the attention is riveted elsewhere noticing-some-sensation-or-other events tend to occur; etc.

These somewhat tortured claims are how some of the more basic experiential properties of pain, namely (a)–(d) (above), are to be expressed if the conditional analysis of sensation is accepted. Then can that conditional analysis *explain* these few basic experiential facts? Can it bring order into them? For example, how is such a non-individual analysis to explain *property* (d′) (which analyses the phenomenon of marginal awareness)? It is not to be accomplished by appeal to the Principles A and B, nor can it be effected by offering mental-causal explanations which appeal to the mental-causal properties of psychological individuals (for the sensation-individual is not countenanced). Rather, we must first of all assume a standing state in which the attention is directed elsewhere than the body part; and then introduce the bodily condition C_{f**}, which with the aid of certain novel principles governing the occurrence of noticing-of-pain-events, supposedly explain the noticing-some-sensation-or-other event. These novel principles are (something like): (A′) Bodily stimulus C_f causes noticing-of-pain if the attention is free; whereas the distinct bodily stimulus C_g, which has the property of causing noticing-of-sensations-of-contact-at-the-body-part-contacted if the attention is directed onto that body part, tends to cause no such phenomenon if the attention is free, etc.; (B′) The more the attention is free, the more a value and a more determinate value will be given to the sensation-place in the resulting event of type noticing-an-x-sensation when bodily conditions obtain such that if the attention goes onto the body part it will be a noticing-of-a-sensation event!

(3) Thus, it looks at first as if a fantastic but nonetheless real explanatory rationale might be available for the causal experiential properties of the sensation content of attentive-consciousnesses, when sensation individuals are not countenanced and are conditionally analysed. However, the explanations are more complicated, and more ultimately *obscure* than those familiar explanations which introduce into the causal picture a sensation individual blessed with a few regular mental-causal powers, and a psychological attentive setting with the same.

An example will help to bring out this obscurity. Thus, the substitute principle (B′) claims that diminution of attention to a body-part reduces determinations in the internal object of a sensation-consciousness directed onto that part. But *why* should it be so? It cannot be explained through appeal to the general characteristics of the attention: namely, having fewer determinations in the internal object of a directed consciousness when diminished attention is directed to its material object. The reason being, the theory does not countenance a material object for a sensation-consciousness. And so it proves to be a sheer rock-bottom opaque fact of nature.

But, it may be replied, do not believers in sensation individuals likewise ground their explanations on rock-bottom fact? *Why*, the more the attention is free, should sensations and their determinations be better noticed? Is not that also a sheer opaque fact of nature? But the more the attention is free, the more *anything* and its determinations are noticed. But is not that likewise a sheer opaque fact of nature? Could it not be the other way around? Might it not in general be that the more one attended to something the more one noticed something else? Might it not be that if you wanted to hear conversation X properly that is going on at this table, you would be well advised to listen with rapt attention to conversation Y going on at the next table? But how could you be listening to conversation Y if you are hearing conversation X so well? Presumably, you don't hear much of conversation Y!

This Alice in Wonderland chaos gives way to rule and reason when we assume that the mental-causal properties of mental items are windows into their very being; that is, drop this talk of 'sheer rock-bottom fact'. The attention simply has to be something like a light which reveals more of what it lights upon, and it is to properties of this kind that the mental-causal explanation in terms of sensation individuals appeals. But conditionalists are in no position to make a comparable claim on behalf of conditional propositions, since it is only when the sensation is object for an awareness that any attentive conditional propositions with sensation-content acquire a semblance of necessity. For what must be emphasized is, that in jettisoning sensations as individuals one loses the right to appeal to the general characteristics of the attention in explanation.

(4) Let me sum up. We set out from the assumption that the theory of sensation individuals explains the familiar causal facts which first prompted our ancestors to frame the concept of sensation. Then our immediate concern has been with the following question. If we do not countenance sensations as individuals, can we likewise explain these basic known properties of sensations?

At first blush it looked as if a real even if less cogent explanatory system was available. However, on closer inspection it seems not to be so. This is because the explanatory principles to which we appeal are both restricted in scope and not susceptible of broader explanation in terms of the general properties of the attention (and are in that sense *ad hoc*). In supposing a special sub-category of putative-attendings which even in principle could take no material object, we automatically deprive ourselves of the right to appeal to the general characteristics of the attention. In effect, we are paying the penalty for failing to draw the conclusions imposed by the broad spectrum of facts; that is, for failing to opt for the propositions which, in the light of the known facts about the attention in general, explain the known facts about the sensation in particular. I mean, that bodily sensations are psychological individuals, with distinctive mental-causal properties; and that the same is true of attentive events; and that these two phenomena causally interact in ways which are pellucidly explicable in mental-causal terms.

B. NON–BODILY SENSATION INDIVIDUALS

(1) The immediate aim of the foregoing has been, not to persuade us that bodily sensations are individuals, which to my mind has never been in doubt, but to bring to light the reasons which persuade us that it is so. That is, the reasons why we believe there exist not merely episodes in consciousness with a sensation object-content, but distinct psychological phenomena of which those episodes are intuitional consciousnesses or *perceptions*. And the aim of the whole exercise has been, to discover whether in the case of supposed examples of *non-bodily sensa-tions*—say phenomena like after-images—reason exists why the arguments based on the absolute primacy of experience, which proved ineffectual in the case of bodily sensations, should in their case be effectual. In short, is there a case along those lines for proscribing the countenancing of non-bodily sensation individuals?

Consider the phenomenon of 'ringing in the ears' ('tinnitus'). What we want at this point to discover is: do there exist psychological individuals of type sensation called 'ringings in the ears'? Or is the position rather that there only exist individual episodes of attentive-type consciousness whose internal object is a 'ringing'? My suggestion is that there exist both, and that the former are the distinct and immediate material object and cause of the latter. In a word, the familiar situation encountered with pains, tickles, sensations of contact.

(2) What reason can there be for declining to postulate these 'ringings' as sensa-tions, and as individuals? Let us consider these two questions in order, beginning with the question of *sensation-status*.

The only consideration that springs to mind which might seem to count against their possessing sensation-status is, that 'ringings' are not (quite) experienced in the body. And yet how is that relevant? The claim is not that 'ringings' are *feelings*, and in any case there can be no justification for collapsing 'sensation' into 'feeling'. Then all the reasons militating in favour of classifying pains (and tickles, etc.) as sensa-tions, point to the same conclusion in the case of 'ringings'. Thus, it shares with pain the property of having a standard bodily cause: namely, whatever it is that future medical science will expunge from the body when the condition is cured. It shares with it the property of in no way calling upon the concept-system of its owner in coming into existence. And of being capable of intensity, a quality that is standardly caused by the degree of its bodily cause. And it shares with it above all a similar relation to the attention. Can there be any doubt that 'ringings' are noticed? Or that they frequently escape the attention? Or that the attention registers fewer of its determinations the more the attention is unavailable? And so on. So much for sensation status.

(3) Now let us consider the question of the *individual status* of these 'ringings'. If we are prepared to postulate pain-individuals and tickle-individuals, the case for postulating 'ringing'-individuals looks impressively strong. For there can now be no objection in principle to the supposition that an attentive event might take as its dis-tinct material object another mental phenomenon, provided the latter is a senseless

498

or intentionally undirected primitive item of the type of mere sensation. It is true the attention cannot accomplish this feat in the case of thoughts, or images, or visual experiences, or indeed in the case of experiences generally, and this might make it seem that it is in principle impossible throughout the mind. And in fact it very nearly is. But sensations are the exception that prove the rule. There is no reason why the attention should not take as its material object a primitive senseless individual of this kind: witness, pains and tickles and sensations of contact, etc. A relation of intuition can be established in their case, a contact 'in the flesh', which would be impossible if the putative object was of the type of an intentionally directed consciousness-of—.

So there can be no objection to the suggestion that the attention might take as its immediate material object another psychological item of the type of a pain or for that matter a 'ringing'. Then the reasons why we countenance bodily sensation individuals apply with equal force in the case of 'ringings'. For example, what we call 'noticing a ringing' is at the very least a putative-attending, being no more thought-mediated than is experiencing pain (in contradistinction to desiring, fleeing, hating, imagining, etc.). I will not repeat the argument earlier advanced why the fact that this 'noticing' is a true putative-attending, constitutes reason for supposing that circumstances exist in which the 'ringing' is a perceived individual, and that those circumstances are normal waking consciousness. Meanwhile, explanatorial considerations point the same way. Far and away the best explanation of the attentive phenomena of this case is given when we postulate 'ringings' as individuals endowed with a given set of mental-causal powers, and attendings as the same. For example, facts like the increasing indeterminacy of the object of noticings when the attention is increasingly unavailable, which are best and most universally explained in mental-causal terms of the type already elaborated. Once again, I will not repeat those reasons: they apply without qualification.

C. CONCLUSION

The argument from the primacy of experience against bodily sensation individuals failed, first of all because our experience of bodily sensations is an attentive consciousness, second because explanatorial considerations demonstrate the individuality of those sensations. For exactly the same reasons a similar argument against 'ringing' or after-image individuals fails, their individuality being established on the same dual grounds, viz. that they are object for an attentive-type consciousness, and that the hypothesis of individuality best explains the known facts of attentive experience. Accordingly, non-bodily sensation individuals must likewise be countenanced. A categorical non-conditional analysis must be given of 'there is a yellow after-image at point P in the visual field' (and *a fortiori* of 'there is an unnoticed yellow after-image at P'). Therefore 'point P in the visual field is yellow' cannot *mean*: yellow is part of the content of any attentive-consciousness of P. And so the counter-argument (h) must fail. This discussion has had the virtue of bringing to

the surface two additional related arguments for the existence of non-bodily sensation individuals; and, since the step from the latter theory to a representative theory
is a small one, for a representative theory of visual perception.

8. A Summary Statement

(1) The several counter-arguments (a)–(h) help to point up certain significant
properties of the attention, of the visual field, and of their interrelation. These are
set out summarily below.

The following emerged about the *attention*. The intuitional attentive relation is
concrete, 'in the flesh', an experiencing-*of* its actually existing material object,
rather than a thought-mediated relation to that object. In contrast with the thought,
imagination, will, affect, even belief, attending is as such a way of knowing, being a
legitimized bridge to empirical actuality. And the intuitional attention has in addition the following important properties. First, it is distinct from its existent object,
and whatever is its object might have existed unnoticed, for no object necessarily
causes its own noticing. Second, the more it is available and the more directed to its
object, the more both the object and its determinations are noticed. Third, it can
take distinct psychological phenomena as material objects, provided they are not (so
to say) pure experienced intentionality—which is tantamount to saying provided
they are not consciousnesses-of or experiences (but are instead constituted of mere
'psychic stuff'). Fourth, some sensation types are attentively obtrusive (e.g. pain
and itch), others attentively recessive (e.g. sensations of contact and warmth).

And the following emerged about the *visual field*. We distinguish imagining
something to be sited in the visual field (e.g. Banquo's red cloak or an eidetically
imaged road) from its actually being there, since only real existents manage to enter
the visual field, irrespective of whether those existents are psychological in status
(like sensations) or not (like physical objects). Then for something X to be at a point
in the visual field, which is to say *visible* at that point, a categorical rather than
conditional requirement must be met. Namely: visual sensations must exist, and
all physical conditions satisfied for the truth of 'noticing these sensations *can be*
noticing X' (where 'X' ranges over sensations, light, objects, and their shapes).
Next, whether or not it is veridical in character, any (monocular) visual field must
have a single, continuous, two-dimensional, point-by-point, colour-brightness
description, which may be limited in differentiability and determinacy in various
places such as the peripheries, and will in any case be limited in extent by hiatuses
and boundary. Finally, the character of that description is of necessity wholly determined by bodily non-psychological causal factors.

Following upon this account of attention and visual field, certain facts emerged
concerning their *interrelation*. It is not just that the attention has no part in determining the visual field. It is not even in the nature of a *mirror* of the visual field, for
the content of a veridical noticing of the visual field never coincides with the
content of the visual field. For example, indeterminacy at some points can and

indeed must obtain in the content of a veridical noticing of the visual field, quite irrespective of indeterminacy at corresponding points in the visual field. And gaps in attentive-content need not correspond to hiatuses in the visual field, bearing in mind that the concept of absence from the visual field is not that of absence from the content of a veridical noticing of the visual field. And so on. Yet having said all this, it is time to call a halt to the process of *prising apart* attention and visual field. Thus, the total content of the visual field is of necessity the cause and object of any veridical noticing of the visual field. Accordingly, no point in the visual field can be so small, so dull, so undistinguished, as not to be part of the cause and part of the material object of such a noticing. Any such visual noticing necessitates its playing such a role. Mere presence in the visual field ensures as much. Inessential as it is in the particular, it is essential in the general.

(2) These insights into the nature of the main *dramatis personae* of the visual perceptual situation formed the basis of the central theses of this chapter. Two contentious claims were made. First, that there exist non-bodily sensation individuals; second, that their perception mediates, in a certain determinate way, the perception of publicly perceptible items in the case of sight, and probably also of hearing, smell, and taste. The sense of touch presents a very different picture. It is not just that the sensations involved in tactile perception are bodily sensations. More to the point, they mostly do not play the role of mediator for the attention in the perception of objects. I have therefore chosen to concentrate the discussion on the case of visual perception, partly because the theory applies to sight, partly because of the importance of the sense.

The centre-piece of the argument has already been noted. Namely, that the colour-brightness value of every point in the visual field is of necessity determined in entirety by bodily non-psychological causes. In particular, the attention has nothing to do with it. A visual field could in a congenitally blind person just lie there—like a hidden pool in a corner of the mind: multi-coloured, unchanging, unremarked, perhaps never to come to the attention, forever dormant. This highly unnatural state of affairs is a real possibility, and that it is opens up an all-important space between consciousness and the visual field, even though the visual field of its nature lies open to consciousness. Then the autonomous individuality of each point, determined in entirety by the body in veridical and non-veridical cases alike, and therefore psychological in status before all else in all cases, requires in all cases a psychological type as bearer, viz. visual sensation. Herewith the case is stated for the existence and omnipresence of the visual sensation in visual perception and visual experience generally. This is the first truth of visual perception.

18

Sense-Data (2):
Additional Arguments

Disbelief in sense-data is so firmly entrenched in many minds, that I find myself obliged to marshal a series of additional arguments in their favour. They are further to the main argument in the previous Chapter 17.

1. Perceptual Sensations and General Principles

(a) The existence of visual sensations

(1) The theory of sense-data that I defend posits the existence of visual sensations, and claims that they causally and attentively mediate the visual perception of material objects (etc.) and light.

The first strand of the several arguments supporting this theory consists in a demonstration of the sheer existence, and some of the general properties, of visual sensations. The most unproblematic example of the kind is the after-image, which I now briefly discuss. Then note before I do, that it is merely one example of visual sensation. A variety of stimuli to optic nerves (etc.) can lead to 'lights' (etc.) in the visual field which are equally unproblematic examples of visual sensation. I select the after-image merely on account of its familiarity. An analogous example from another sense is that of tinnitus or 'ringings' in the ear, which have a different kind of ancestry from after-images. Here, too, we encounter a perceptual sensation stripped of its usual environmental causes.

Look at a bright window in a darkened room for (say) twenty seconds, and then close your eyes. One seems to see *something* bright and rectangular, fading rapidly. This 'something' is surely distinct from one's awareness (experiencing, noticing, seeing) of it, just as (say) a sensation of contact is unquestionably distinct from one's noticing of it. Thus, the awareness need not fade or in any way diminish as the after-image is fading, indeed it may even wax; and if one chooses to attend more to one part of the image than another, one will notice and discover more of that part's properties than another part's; and physical causal conditions confirm the fact that this fading item has an existence distinct from one's awareness of it. Then note that this fading image is a real individual, and precisely is not the hypostatization of the internal object of the awareness-experience. The fading after-image is at once the distinct immediate material object, and the immediate cause, of that awareness, standing to it in the same relation as the sensation of contact stands to an awareness of it. If we are prepared to countenance bodily sensations in our ontology, it is difficult to see how we can fail to acknowledge the existence of after-image individuals.

(2) Despite these considerations it is possible that someone might hold that the 'something bright and rectangular and fading fast' is merely the internal object of an intentionally directed visual experience, illusorily appearing to be the external object of an awareness event. Now if this were the position, no noticing of anything can have occurred on such an occasion. After all, noticings cannot occur without something being there to be noticed. Then let us consider just what it is that noticings imply in the case of bodily sensations generally. I am thinking of facts like these: that had one chosen to attend harder one would have noticed and learned more of the sensation, that what one discovered depended in part upon what one was seeking, that noticing was one's way of knowing about it, etc. In short, evidence which confirms the obvious truth that the awareness is one thing, and its sensation object a distinct and autonomous other. When we say that we notice a sensation, the above array of properties are generally understood to obtain. Then there can be no doubt that they are all of them realized also in the case of our experience of visual and auditory sensations. For example, in order to discover the exact character of the 'lights' or 'ringings' in the course of medical tests, one would surely attend closely to those items, come in that way to notice certain properties, and so make discoveries about them which might otherwise not have occurred. We would not be prepared to affirm a lesser claim than that of noticing in such cases, any more than we would with bodily sensations—and for the identical reasons.

In these important respects there seems to be no significant difference between awareness of bodily sensations like tingles and itches, and awarenesses of after-images and 'ringings'. And in fact I can discover no more reason for supposing that after-images and the 'ringings' of tinnitus are mere reified internal objects, than I can in the case of bodily sensations. But the case against refusing to countenance bodily sensations is impressively strong, as we saw in the discussion in Section 7 of the previous Chapter 17. In short, unless one simply fails to countenance sensations generally, I cannot see how one can resist the proposition that after-images are the distinct and immediate material objects and immediate cause of events which are of the type, noticing.

(3) Here is an additional argument in support of the thesis that there exist perceptual sensation individuals which are not bodily sensations—an explanatorial argument. I choose to discuss here the auditory sense, because I believe that the rich interpretational content of visual experience stands in the way of grasp of some of the main elements of sense-perception. However, all that I assert

in the following argument carries over into the experience of visual sensations generally.

Let us suppose that in some human subject a temperature over 100 °F was a sufficient condition of a temporary tinnitus. More exactly, we shall assume the following obtains when 100^+ °F occurs.

A. The subject sometimes finds himself having an experience he would naturally describe as 'noticing a faint ringing'.
B. Whenever he listens for such a 'sound', he invariably hears it.

Then it seems to me obligatory that we interpret these facts as evidencing the continuous presence of a 'ringing' which is distinct from the intermittent awareness-experiences of which it is material object and cause. This is how we interpret exactly comparable facts in the case of bodily sensuous experience: say, awareness-experiences of tingles in the fingertips (which are likewise caused by 100^+ °F). Given such facts we would all agree a tingle is going on continuously. Then why not here also in the case of a 'ringing'? Indeed, how could one possibly *not* postulate continuous 'ringing' individuals in this case? In particular, what account could one then give of the causal situation? Well, let us suppose a disbeliever in 'ringing' individuals were to advance the following theoretical interpretation of the facts (viz. A, and B) of this case.

α. Temperature over 100 °F is causing no experienceable psychological phenomenon between the intermittent experience-episodes.
β. It causes intermittent unchosen experiences naturally describable as 'noticing a faint ringing'.
γ. And causes it to be the case that whenever the subject engages in an activity he would naturally describe as 'listening for a ringing', he has an experience he would naturally describe as 'hearing a ringing'.

Now those believing in 'ringing'-individuals would explain the mental events mentioned in A and B in the familiar mental-causal attentive terms we employ with bodily sensations. Thus, they would say:

a (concerning A). The persistent 'ringing' caught his attention, perhaps because his attention was relatively free. (As we would say of tingles etc.)
b (concerning B). The experience occurred because, when some audible s is present, listening for s normally causes hearing s. (As we would analogously say of tingles etc.)

These a/b explanations, which turn upon the mental-causal properties of the attention, are not available to the 'anti-sensationalist'. In neither case can he invoke mental-causal dynamics involving the attention, since he denies the existence of the main sensory causal protagonist. He might conceivably say that it is on account of *some* mental-causal reason or another that events like A frequently occur, but it is grossly unclear what that reason might be. Meanwhile, the event B must seem to him even stranger from the explanatorial point of view. Thus, because of the hypothesized regularity we are all of us obliged to accept that 'listening-for' causes 'hearing a ringing' (something for which 'sensationalists' have a simple mental-causal explanation). However, that causal transaction cannot on the anti-sensationalist account be understood to be one that is *mentally mediated*: given 100^{+}°F, 'listening-for' must be said to *just* cause 'seeming hearing a ringing'—no more! But is not this explanatorially unsatisfactory? And how is this theory intelligibly to *relate* the episodes A and B: that is, the fact that 'ringings' both *seem* to catch the attention and *seem* to lend themselves to discovery and scrutiny? The only answer available on the theory is bluntly to quote the 100^{+}°F temperature as common ground—and that is all an anti-sensationalist can say! He can appeal to nothing in the way of a *mental rationale* to bridge these A and B episodes. Explanatorily, it all seems to be a mess; one which is neatly resolved by positing a sensation individual, endowed with the mental-causal and attentive properties of sensations generally.

(4) All of the causal and attentive properties noted above in the case of after-images and 'ringings' (etc.) hold equally of bodily sensations. Then on top of these particular properties of after-images (etc.) we encounter a series of additional properties all likewise exemplified by bodily sensations. Thus, after-images have regular purely bodily causes, they are capable of intensity, and of extensity of a sort, they are experienced as inhabiting body-relative physical space, being seen as lying in a direction out from one's body, they are possible but not necessary immediate objects of noticing, they are thing-like and in themselves senseless, etc. In short, after-images must be deemed a species of sensation, and distinct from one's awareness of them.

In sum, there looks to be no way of avoiding the conclusion that the coloured patches which we see in after-image experience, and the 'ringings' heard by tinnitus sufferers, are a species of sensation and distinct from the awareness of them. That is, that the type 'sensation' ranges farther afield than bodily sensations, and encompasses a variety that could be described as 'non-bodily perceptual sensations': sensation individuals which are individuated in body-relative physical space, like their bodily sensation brethren, and which are to be encountered in the various senses of sight, hearing, etc. And I labour the point that there exist such sensations, in part because the sheer existence of perceptual and especially visual sensations seems to me to be the nub of the arguments supporting the existence of sense-data, in part because of the importance of sense-datum theory to any account of the nature of perception, but also because of the fact that many philosophers appear to be almost ideologically opposed to sense-datum theory.

(b) A preliminary principle

(1) The next proposition of importance is, that some after-images are for a few

moments visually indistinguishable from—that is, look the same as—present the same visual appearance as—certain publicly visible physical non-psychological items. A faint smudge of green paint on a wall, and a green after-image, can present one and the same visual appearance to consciousness. The experiencing of one is indistinguishable from, indeed is internally or in itself the same as, the other. Then as a consequence of this fact, the following Principle X may be affirmed.

Principle X: For any visual field which is veridically filled with physical non-psychological items from one end to the other, there in principle exists an after-image from which visually it is indistinguishable.

At first blush Principle X seems implausible. However, this is only because most of the after-images we encounter are 'thin', short-lived, fading, etc. The differences are merely those of degree. Imagine looking long and hard at a stark and simple and vivid scene, peopled by sharp-edged objects which are either very bright or else darkish, let us say for five minutes on end with one's head and eyes rigidly fixed—and then closing one's eyes. Apart from colour reversal, for a moment the scene might well seem to stand forth before one! For to repeat, it is merely a matter of degree. So let us now embellish Principle X with a further detail, bearing in mind that the genesis of after-images obeys psychophysical law, as does the genesis of visual fields generally (a causal property which is the foundation condition of the epistemological utility of visual fields).

Principle X′: For any visual field which is truly or veridically filled with physical non-psychological items from one end to the other, there in principle exists a complex bodily stimulus, ΣS_B, which would cause an after-image of such a kind that it would be visually indistinguishable to a normally conscious subject.

2. Arguments

(a) Argument 1

(1) Let us suppose that the visual system of humans generally slowly mutated over many years in the following way. Thus, it became such that the light from objects facing one induced, not the stimulus $\Sigma S_B'$ they now normally induce, but the above ΣS_B. Accordingly, while complementary colours would then fill the visual fields of humans, they would nonetheless regularly do so in exactly the same sectors of the visual field as before. Now would not this be an exercise of the visual sense? After all, the full cognitive powers of the sense would be preserved under these circumstances.

It may be objected that 'it would no more be a case of seeing than is seeing on the TV'. But in the case of TV images, spatial and temporal relations to the imaged objects are grossly irregular. And do we not really see objects in (say) mirrors and periscopes, where spatial and temporal relations are properly regular, even though the spatial relations are distorted—regularly? Does not the attention manage to pass onto the object, whether it be in a mirror or periscope or in the above imaginary situation? It may be replied that 'it really only passes onto an *effect* of them'. But why should it not pass onto *both*, as it does in normal visual situations, where the attention takes both light and material objects? It seems to me that this latter protest labours under the idea that the attention must be some kind of psychic thing, a sort of mental wand or hypostatized gaze which touches its object! But in actual fact attentive contact is of a wholly different order. It is a cognitive link, that is embodied in regular connections, which is such as to lead naturally to knowledge.

(2) It may finally be conceded that seeing occurs under such circumstances. But it may now be said that 'there must be two sorts of seeing, direct and indirect'. But here, too, I cannot see what work 'indirect' does in this claim, bearing in mind that the seeing of objects is mediated by the seeing of light, and yet in a decent enough sense rates as 'direct'.

Now what does this Argument 1 actually prove? As it stands it does not demonstrate that sense-data at the present time mediate human visual perception. But it shows that in principle seeing might have taken that form, and that it might conceivably do so in the future. It therefore furthermore shows that there can be no significant conceptual error in the hypothesis of sense-data. And it shows also that opponents of sense-datum theory can at best make the claim that the theory is false as an empirical matter of fact. In short, it demonstrates that even if sense-datum theory were false, it would not be a philosophical error. It would merely be one of contingent empirical fact.

(b) Argument 2

(1) We shall assume we are dealing with normally conscious sane humans. Then if they were to have an experience which is exactly the same as that which is induced in the attention by agonizing toothache, this would constitute overwhelmingly strong evidence that at that moment these subjects harbour pain. This truth holds right across the board of bodily sensations. It leads me to state the following second principle.

Principle Y: In the case of bodily sensations generally, the presence of an awareness-experience which is the same as that induced by an intense example of any given sensation, taking place in conditions of conscious normality etc., constitutes overwhelmingly strong evidence for the presence of a distinct sensation cause and object of matching kind.

(2) Turn now to the auditory sense. As we have already seen, the phenomenon of tinnitus clearly demonstrates the reality of auditory sensations. For here we have something which can pass unnoticed, or noticed, or merely vaguely noticed; that is capable of various intensities; that may be experienced as lying in a direction out from one's body; that has a merely bodily cause; and so on. Then this phenomenon tends to cause in its owner, for some but not for all of the time, an experience consisting in awareness of the 'ringing'. Just as low sounds can be going on in one's presence without one noticing them, so in the case of the 'ringings' of tinnitus.

Now suppose that an actual sound is heard by someone, and that the sound is a ringing which experientially is absolutely indistinguishable from the steady 'ringing' heard by tinnitus sufferers. Then the sheer presence of such an experience seems to me to constitute powerful evidence for the existence of a matching sensation cause. After all, bodily sensations cause an experience of an attentive kind with an exactly matching content. Is it not natural to suppose that when an auditory experience occurs which is identical to what tinnitus causes, it will likewise have a matching sensation cause? The causal deduction proceeds in both directions in the case of bodily sensations generally, so why not here with this perceptual sensation? This suggests the following principle, which merely generalizes Principle Y. While it is less obviously true than Principle Y (which strikes me as incontestable), it is difficult to see how it could be false. Indeed, the only reason it is less apparent, in all probability lies in the fact that, thanks to the Transitivity of the Attention, sensations are heavily interpreted in the case of auditory and most especially visual perception. This results in the sensations being singled out under a physical terminology, and this acts as a sort of conceptual mask which hides the sensation from view.

Principle Z: In the case of sensations generally, the presence of an attentive awareness-experience which is exactly the same as that induced by an intense example of any given sensation, taking place in suitable conditions of conscious normality etc., constitutes overwhelmingly strong evidence for the presence of a distinct sensation of matching kind.

(3) Now if Principle Z is true, and is conjoined with Principle X', we arrive at an argument for a thesis which is stronger than that demonstrated by Argument 1. Namely, not just that visual perception might have been and might conceivably in future be mediated by sense-data, and that at worst sense-datum theory is merely contingently empirically false. We arrive at an argument for the stronger claim that visual perception must here and now be so mediated. If a non-veridical visual field of visual sensations looks exactly the same as a veridical visual field inhabited by material objects, then the latter visual field must also be populated by the same visual sensations as filled the visual field of after-images.

It seems to me that the onus lies with opponents of sense-datum theory to justify their implicit assumption that material objects are capable of causing visual experiences without the assistance of visual sensations. That is, the onus is on them to justify the supposition that physical objects can cause what visual sensations incontestably cause, without needing to call upon the assistance of visual sensations. We incontestably know that after-images cause genuinely visual experiences without the assistance of material objects, just as we know that an identical state of affairs holds with bodily sensations like pain and itch. Why should we assume that the situation is any different when the cause of the visual experience happens to be a material object that is seen?

(c) Argument 3

(1) The following argument trades upon the breakdown of intentionality, more precisely upon the breakdown of the intentional indifference to existence, that is encountered in the case of sensations generally.

Now we know that a man when awake and having a visual experience, let us say of a patch of red before him, can know that something red is in front of him. He will do so if he knows he can trust his sight, and that the viewing conditions are as they should be. But let us supposes he knows neither. Then he still at least knows that he 'seems to see red', that he has 'an experience as of red before him'. But it seems to me that he is in addition in a position to know something else on top of this: namely, that *something red* lies before him. And it seems to me that such knowledge is more or less irrefutable. This is because it exemplifies an immediacy precisely of the kind that is encountered when we more or less irrefutably know that we are aware of a pain or itch or tickle. That is, a mentalistic immediacy. Then if this is true, it will follow that there must in this situation be something red, that is of a psychological nature, that is the distinct and material object of an awareness-experience, of a noticing. In short, a visual sensation. And this deduction holds equally in veridical and non-veridical cases of perceptual experience. Thus, the sense-datum must be immediately perceived in veridical experiences of public physical occurrences of red.

(2) To help clarify the main issues raised by this argument, indeed to help demonstrate precisely how it constitutes an argument at all, consider a properly visual but wholly non-veridical situation. Return to the example, used in Chapter 11, in which (say) one's optic nerves are so stimulated, let us say by chemicals or electrodes, that elephant-looking entities appear in the visual field ('retinal elephants') which proceed to caper before one's eyes. In short, we are supposing that simple psycho-physical regularities linking visual system and visual field are here tapped—completely bypassing the higher centres!—as a means of altering the visual field. Then I would like very strongly to emphasize that the proper characterization of the situation is, not just that one seems to see real physical objects lying in one's visual field, but that real psychological objects have *actually* entered one's visual field. Whereas Macbeth's 'dagger' was not a real psychological entity that entered his visual field, even though Macbeth really seemed to see a real dagger set in his visual field, a 'retinal elephant' or an after-image is a real psychological entity that truly does enter the visual field: after all, a 'retinal elephant' or a very vivid sustained after-image will momentarily *blot out* whatever lies in their part of the visual field, whereas by contrast the objects of the imagination never do.

This distinction between the objects of visual 'seemings' is of the utmost importance. The 'retinal elephants' are of an altogether different ilk from the objects of imagining. They are no less real than are after-images or itches—or even 'floaters'. Thus, one can notice them, and do so either well or marginally, actively attend to them, fail to see them when they are present and then suddenly catch sight of them, learn more about them by studying them, state physical causally sufficient conditions for their existence, and so on. Such properties ensure that the 'elephants' are not to be construed as the mere reification of the internal object of an experience, any more than are after-images—or pains, itches, tickles, etc.

These 'elephants' provide us with a salutary lesson regarding visual fields generally. They teach us that a wholly non-veridical visual experience, that is in no way different from the normal visual experience of material objects, can involve the direct confrontation of the attention with *something psychological*. And that it can do so when a heavy physical object interpretational overlay is built into the experience. In this way they bring out the radical unlikeness of visual experience as such to imagining, the fact that it as such involves a direct confrontation with an extensional object which is necessarily present. The error committed by many opponents of sense-data lies in the assumption that situations of visual illusion are on all fours with that of the visual hallucination, which is to say with a situation in which *absolutely nothing* is presented to view (being an exercise merely of the visual imagination). And this is surely false. The essential distinction between visual experience and visual imaginative experience goes by the board otherwise. The seeing of 'retinal elephants' and Macbeth's 'seeing' of a dagger are essentially dissimilar phenomena: the first phenomenon really is a seeing—though not of elephants!, the second is no more than an imagining-of seeing (i.e. it is a 'seem to see' in the imaginative sense of the expression).

(3) Ultimately, the flaw in the thinking of many opponents of sense-datum theory lies in their inability to realize that intentional inexistence fails to hold in the case of sensations in general and sense-perception in particular. It consists in the failure to grasp the concreteness of the perceptual contact, something which is a reality only because of psycho-physical causal regularities. And it all goes back to the fact that perception is a phenomenon which at its *core* is pre-conceptual in character. A newly-born infant wincing at the light sees light—whatever else! It is upon such a core that the work of the understanding is imposed. Over-intellectualization and over-interiorization of the animal mental condition seem to me amongst the main dangers for perception theory. The positing of pure intentionality in the case of sense-perception is to my mind in the nature of a retreat backwards into the realm of interiority. It is, so to say, a flinching from a raw contact with Reality.

I suggest that it is simply inconceivable that one have a real visual experience and *nothing* be on view. And I suggest also that it is inconceivable that one have a real visual field and *nothing* be experientially present in the mind but a seeming awareness with such an internal content. Let us suppose that my visual field is filled with the colour red, and that this has been caused by scientific intervention deep in the visual pathway, so that the phenomenon is both properly visual and physically non-veridical. Then I suggest that something red *has* to be present on such an occasion. And if in these circumstances I then undergo literally the experience which I would normally describe as 'noticing red before me', then I suggest also that something red *has* to have been noticed. Now here once again we may be accused of reifying the internal object of the visual experience of seeming to see red. And yet is this accusation in the least convincing? Is it credible to suppose that *nothing*—not even *black*—lies before one when one *really* does have a visual field—which is *wholly* non-veridical? And *nothing* noticed when one apparently notices it? Indeed, what would it be like to have such an experience? That is, have a visual experience directed to a real (though non-veridical) visual field filled with (say) red, and absolutely *nothing* be either given to the attention or noticed? I simply cannot imagine it, any more than I know what it would be to have a visual experience which *overtly* was of nothing!

And yet is it not possible that I seem to myself to have a visual experience of red, and *nothing* be showing to me? It is indeed, because it is possible that I am hallucinating. Although vivid hallucinations are a rarity in most people, they cannot automatically be ruled out.

(4) There are two comments I want to make upon this valid enough observation. The first is to say that, from the fact that I seem to myself to be having a *visual experience*, it does not follow I am. Thus, if I am *visually hallucinating* it will seem to me that I am having a visual experience, but this would be an error of immediate identification (comparable to that occurring when a 'dream seeing' is experienced at the time as a visual experience), and is usually a clear index of some causative mental disturbance. *A fortiori* such a situation cannot qualify as a case of a visual experience with *nothing* given to awareness. However, this analysis of the situation may be disputed, so I pass on to the second more obvious rejoinder.

Namely, that the same possibility may equally be raised in the case of bodily sensations, without in any way qualifying the truth of the claim that we know with mentalistic immediacy of the existence of itches and pains and tickles, even though hallucinations of sensations occur. And just as I cannot imagine what it would be to have the very experience one has when one is aware of searing toothache without *pain* being present (despite the possibility of hallucination), so I cannot imagine what it would be to have the visual experience I have when I see a vivid red wall without *something red* being present to view. I know what it would be to go searching for an El Dorado that does not exist, indeed I could imagine engaging in such a search and thinking 'but it may all be mythical', but I do not know how to do this when experiencing pain or redness: that is, attend hard to these apparent entities and have the thought 'but it may all be mythical' 'nothing may be there at all'! In short, I can think of no analogue of the search for El Dorado in the case of redness or pain. The visual experience, indeed the sensuous experience generally, simply fails to exhibit the indifference to existence encountered almost universally in the mind. The visual experience that is caused in us when we see the red of something guarantees the presence of something distinct and red given to one's attention. The possibility of serious hallucination in no way weakens the point.

(5) Return now to Argument 3. It follows from the above that when we have visual experience, one is in a position to know with mentalistic immediacy that something sensuous lies before one—to the extent that one knows one is not hallucinating. But the overwhelming majority of the human race for almost all of their waking lives do know they are not hallucinating, and know in a very strong sense. It follows that they are in a position to know that something real and sensuous is being given to their attention. Accordingly, it follows that such a something is being presented to their awareness: in short, a sense-datum.

(d) Argument 4

(1) The present argument might be described as one that is based upon the contingency of the developmental history of the sensuous senses. Then for the moment I confine myself once again to the less complex, and far less heavily interpreted sense of hearing, since the lessening of the interpretational factor enables us to filter out certain fundamentals of perception. Then the following state of affairs seems intelligible. It is conceivable that at some point in evolution auditory experience existed, and that almost all its causes were of an internal bodily sort, pretty much like what obtains at present with tingles and itches. Thus we are hypothesizing next to no outer connections of a regular sort, and even then only at the hands of sudden events like (say) blows. Those causes might have ranged over (say) dryness of the skin, sudden blows, highish temperature, even stress.

If this were the case, the situation would not be dissimilar to that at present existing in the case of tinnitus. Such things as 'ringings' would be experienced, sometimes in some sense in the ear, sometimes merely directionally, and the odd example merely as 'there' where one is—as happens in fact in the case of certain diffused humming sounds. Now if this was the situation, we would be undergoing auditory experiences in the absence of publicly audible sounds. And we would not as yet have acquired a sense of hearing. Two sorts of phenomena would be taking place: on the one hand 'hummings' and 'ringings' and 'tinkles', and on the other hand the noticing or awareness or experiencing of those mental objects. And that would be all: in short, a situation not very different from what occurs at present with (say) itches and tingles. It is true that we would in fact perceive those sensuous objects (as we do itches and tingles). However, since we would not perceive anything extra-psychological in having such experiences, these capacities would not qualify as the possession of a sense.

(2) Then over many thousands of years we shall suppose that the environment slowly alters. For the first time sound or shock waves occur in the atmosphere and water etc. *Pari passu* with these changes evolutionary selection singles out those creatures who, already the site of 'ringings' etc., gradually come to acquire causal powers similar to what we now possess. By that time a proper sense of hearing will have evolved into being.

Let me justify the claim that powers like our own could be imposed on such a base, by filling in details. Thus in this new situation we assume that the cerebrally profound phenomena which caused auditory sensations like 'ringings' continue to be activated, only now it will not be by (say) dryness of the skin, but by novel cerebrally superficial events which are regularly caused by whatever bells do to media. And we assume that a similar situation prevails in the case of all the other auditory sensations. Then in that case the old sensations will still be caused, since whatever was the previous profound cause of 'ringing' will still be operative. The old deep regularities continue, except that they are now joined by new cerebrally more superficial as well as by external or extra-bodily environmental regularities. These novel regularities do not cancel the old deep regularities out: they merely enrich them. And so directional experience of sensation will correlate with direction of the origin of the shock waves, type of sensation correlate with type of cause generously conceived (thuds, thumps, knocks, scratchings, etc.), and so on. Here we have a potential source of knowledge, and unquestionably a sense of hearing no different from our own.

(3) So in this imagined situation we hear a ringing sound in the air, through and in hearing a 'ringing' sensation. And this is a sense-datum analysis of a variety of auditory perception that differs from our own merely in its history. Then all that we say here concerning auditory sensations could equally have been said of visual sensations. Of course additional complexities are ushered in with sight, such as the perception of depth and of material objects, together with the individuation of the objects of sight. However, these are no more than complications, and in no way affect the basic situation or the argument.

What must be emphasized about those senses which depend upon the use of secondary qualities is, that they were not absolutely or a priori fated to develop into senses. The existence of auditory and visual and smell and taste experience does not entail that they have regular extra-psychological environmental causes. We might have heard 'ringings' which rate as sensations, seen patches of red which rate as visual sensations, and experienced smells and tastes which are olfactory and gustatory sensations, and the regular links to the environment simply be non-existent. That shows that it is sheer contingency that the character of the experience take place in the context of a sense. The present Argument 4 trades upon this property, by imagining a different possible history for these senses.

In effect, we have been constituting these several senses from the direction, inside to outside, rather than from both points of view at once. In actual fact it seems likely that these sensuous experiences evolved into being simultaneous with the evolutionary development of the cerebral sensitivities and regularities which determined that they arose in the context of a sense. But it need not have been that way. Imagining a different order of development brings into the open the autonomous inner life of perceptual experiences, the fact that they were not of their nature or essentially fated to lead the attention out onto the environment, nor fated to take such ambitious internal objects as to refer to the environment. However, they are essentially and not merely putatively directed onto extensional sensuous objects. Then it is the conjunction of these two properties of sensuous perceptual experience that guarantees the existence of sense-data. This is what the present argument reveals and demonstrates. This is its substance.

(e) Argument 5

Assume the occurrence of a veridical monocular visual experience Ve_v of the physical environment.

(i) The owner of Ve_v has a visual field Vf with an exhaustive description D_v in terms of right/left up/down angular coordinates and colour-bright values of diminishing finesse as the angles increase: a minimal 'pointillist' description.

(ii) There exists a complex of visual sensations S with identical D_v-description.

(iii) There exist regular causally sufficient cerebral conditions C_s for S.

(iv) When the subject notices S, let us say with roughly the same distribution of attention as in the above veridical case, he has a visual experience Ve_s more or less the same as Ve_v.

(v) When Ve_v occurred physical cerebral conditions C_v caused there to seem to be a visual field of character Vf.

(vi) C_v is a regular causally sufficient condition of the latter state of affairs, since this property is a condition of epistemological veridicality.

(vii) But if C_v had happened to have a merely intra-cerebral cause, C_v', rather than a precipitating first cause in light and physical object light-sources and light-reflectors, then a non-veridical visual experience Ve_v' would have occurred which would be the same experience as Ve_v and Ve_s.

(viii) Thus, C_s causes S which causes Ve_s, and C_v' causes Ve_v', and neither of these two indistinguishable visual experiences is a perception of the environment.

(ix) The psychological situation on the occasion of Ve_v' is the same as that on the veridical occasion when Ve_v occurred.

(x) There are no grounds for distinguishing the psychological situations that obtained on the occasions of Ve_s and Ve_v': in each case causally sufficient purely cerebral conditions are responsible for the same visual experience.

(xi) The existence of visual sensation individuals—e.g. after-images/phosphene (etc.) individuals—is no less certain than the existence of bodily sensation individuals.

(xii) Since the psychological situations on the three occasions are identical, and sensation S was the cause of Ve_s, it follows that when the veridical Ve_v occurred sensation S must have been present and cause of that visual experience.

19

Secondary Qualities

If sense-data exist, which is to say perceptual sensations that attentively mediate the perception of phenomena in the environment, their qualities must be perceived in a way that is not *in competition* with the latter. That property is guaranteed by the Transitivity of the Attention. It enables qualities of the sensation to have an identical value to those of objects situated at a later point down the line of the attention. Now in the case of monocular seeing what we attribute to the sense-datum is a complex of colour-bright qualities set in a two-dimensional ordering system, such that the parts of the sensation complex are given as both standing in ordered spatial relations to one another and in ordered directions out from the body in body-relative physical space. These few properties manage to accomplish much, leading the attention out onto the World at large. For example, through the circularity of a red sensation one becomes aware of the round profile from a given direction of the setting sun, and through the redness of the sensation one becomes aware of the redness of the latter. However, whereas profiles exist purely objectively and independently of consciousness, redness surely does not. This asymmetry raises problems concerning the status of the property one attributes to an object when one describes it as (say) red. It is this question which I want now to investigate. More exactly, the character of the property of which we become aware in being aware at one and the same instant of the redness of sensation, of light, and of the setting sun. In short, the nature of secondary qualities.

What is a secondary quality? It is a quality that necessarily is perceived by only one sense, and through only one genus of sensation. Indeed, a catalogue of the secondary qualities rigorously matches one of perceptual sensations: taste and smell corresponding to sensations of taste and smell, sound to auditory sensation, and colour to visual sensations. Being an appearance-quality, namely a quality whose character is wholly determined by our experience of it, the secondary quality is almost always relative: relative in the first place to which beings it appears to, and generally relative also to the conditions under which it does so. Thus, to say of some publicly perceptible item that it has secondary quality S, must be to say: 'it is S *to* perceivers P *in* conditions C.' Here we have one firm principle. This is the general form of all of our familiar secondary quality attributions. Whenever we encounter a statement to the effect that some material object or physical stuff or light (etc.) possesses a particular secondary quality, we must understand there to be an appended 'to——, in——' clause, inscribed as it were in invisible ink. To state that an apple (say) is *absolutely* red, in the way in which its shape is absolutely spherical, is simply without sense.

A second equally important principle follows from the fact that secondary qualities are appearance-qualities that are perceived through the occurrence of a unique sensation. Namely, to say that an item has secondary quality S, is to say that it senses S-ly, e.g. to have a sweet taste is to taste sweet, to be red is to look red, and so on. This principle functions as a vital test. Through it we may decisively exclude heat from the class of secondary qualities, for it is conceivable that some novel plastic both feels warm at −20 °C and as warm as water and much else at 60 °C, and therefore as items of differing measures of hotness. These facts entail that feel cannot be the sole determinant of hotness. Therefore heat is not a secondary quality. But side by side with the wholly objective property of heat, goes the usually co-present and absolutely distinct secondary quality of feeling hot. This little remarked second shadow quality is every bit as *bona fide* a quality as having a pineapple taste or smelling as coffee smells. Accordingly, the novel plastic at −20 °C must be at once colder than and feel as warm as water at 60 °C. This shows we are dealing with two distinct properties.

The central concept is that of sensing in a distinctive qualitative way: of tasting sweet, of looking red, of feeling warm, and suchlike. The problem of understanding secondary qualities is largely the problem of arriving at a correct analysis of (say) 'looks red'. Now if 'looks red' were like 'feels electrified' there would be no great problem. Thus, we determine the presence of the objective phenomenon of electrification through appeal to ammeters and electroscopes and suchlike instruments, whereupon having the property of feeling electrified would be having the disposition to cause the feeling which mildly electrified objects cause in most humans. This seems like a valuable model to put to work with secondary qualities. But in fact the model cannot as it stands be applied. An apparent circularity appears with secondary qualities, threatening the concept with vacuity. If the ultimate test of being red is looking red, if there is in this sense no gap between appearance and reality, how can 'red' and therefore 'looks red' have content? It seems as if we are saying something empty like: 'to be red is to look as things which look red look'; which is no doubt true, but fails to tell us just *how* those things in fact look! How can we inject a content into this specification if there are no objective tests for the presence of redness?

The threatening circle appears to be broken when we uncover the phenomenon: the sensation of red. This 'subjective-objective' seems like the anchor that we need. For surely we could begin by naming that sensation, and proceed to define the secondary quality in terms of it. While this is not the usual order of development, there can be no doubt that it might in principle have been. Why should not visual experience in general have developmentally preceded visual perception of the environment? Humans might first of all have had and named the experience of red without perceiving any public physical items thereby, and only much later managed to perceive physical objects through this experience. This latter state of affairs would become a reality when the human body evolved in such a way as to regularly generate the experience of red in its owner in response to determinate environmental stimuli. Accordingly, the problem of secondary qualities looks at this moment to be pretty trivial. It seems that having the secondary quality of redness simply *is* being such as to cause in most humans that sensation which we at present bring under the description 'the sensation of red': a sensation we could ostensively single out by asking people to stare long and hard at a bright green light, and then look at a white wall and pick out the patch that fades from view. In other words, a dispositionist analysis of 'looks red' seems unavoidable.

1. Materialist, Power, and Dispositionist Theories

(1) However, the above analysis does not satisfy me. One reason lies in the fact that secondary qualities seem to be predicable of their own distinctive sensation. If this claim is true, it is inconsistent with a dispositionist analysis, since sensations lack the power to cause more of their own kind in us. Nonetheless, the claim is undoubtedly contentious in character, and stands in need of argumentative support. I try to provide that support in the discussion which follows. But first I would like to consider secondary qualities from a more general standpoint, to briefly investigate several theories as to their nature, and lead up in that way to the dispositionist theory that is my main interest.

To facilitate matters, I will sometimes make use of a hypothetical and very simple example of a secondary quality: an example that is similar in many respects to the aforementioned 'warm feel' secondary quality. Namely, the so-called 'pain patches' mentioned by Wittgenstein in *Philosophical Investigations*.[1] The advantages are, first the simplicity of the phenomenon, second the fact that whereas some people might doubt the existence of the sensation of red, few will question the existence of pain. Then let us call the secondary quality in question 'painyness', which we will take to be a sub-variety of feel, relating to feeling hot pretty much as tasting sweet relates to tasting sour. Roughly, the details of the imagined situation are these. Let us assume that a certain Mr L has merely to lay the tip of his right index finger upon certain determinate stuffs: silver, beryllium, etc.; whereupon a stinging pain instantaneously occurs on his skin at the point of contact and ceases the moment contact is broken. Call whatever it is in silver (etc.) that explains their effect on Mr L, 'x_1'. Finally, call whatever it is in Mr L which explains their effect upon him, 'y'.

Here we have all that is needed for a secondary quality to exist. It exactly parallels what obtains in the case of the 'warm feel' secondary quality. Namely, the regular causing in repeatable physical conditions—which roughly include stimulus of the bodily surface by some regular item in the environment—of a particular sensation. We do not require that this be true of the vast majority of humans. It could even

---

[1] *Philosophical Investigations*, 312, Blackwell, Oxford, 1953.

hold uniquely of a single man. Indeed, it might only last for five minutes. Then for five minutes silver, beryllium, etc., were painy for Mr L. And all that happened when those stuffs became painy was, not that they altered in the *least degree*, but that Mr L's body acquired state y. That event falls under the description, 'the becoming painy (for Mr L) of all the stuffs in the Universe of the type of silver, beryllium, etc., whether past, present, or future.' For in general we may say: when secondary qualities arose in the Universe, all the relevant phenomena occurred in animals. Eyes and ears appeared, not to gather in the sights and sounds waiting like fruit to be harvested, but to engender experiences of sights and sounds that could function as clues to the presence of nearby physical items relevant to the furthering of life. What was waiting to be harvested was the immense cognitive potential of omnipresent and well-ordered (light, sound) wave phenomena intervening between the animal and items in its surrounding environment. This absolute objectivity preceded and is not to be confused with the mind-dependent realm of appearances. The emergence into the World of 'the look of things', back to the Big Bang and forward to the Heat Death of the Universe, *was* the development at some time of the visual apparatus.

(2) Before I come to the main topic in the next Section 2, which is the question whether secondary qualities are predicable of their own distinctive sensation, I shall make use of the simple model of painyness to assess several theories of the secondary quality. I begin with a theory favoured by some Materialists.

What is the relation between the painyness of silver and the x_1 in silver that is its 'material basis'? Let us call the 'material basis' of the painyness of beryllium 'x_2'—without prejudice. Then there is no binding reason to assume x_1 must be identical with x_2. Even though the 'material basis' of most secondary qualities is uniformly the same across nature, there is no necessity for it to be so. Why must the sweetness of sugar be determined by the selfsame factor as makes for the sweetness of saccharine? Why should not the *size* of sugar's molecules and the *mass* of saccharine's molecules be the causally relevant properties that activate the taste buds in the same sweet way? So let us suppose that $x_1 \neq x_2$. Then could the painyness of silver *be* x_1 and the painyness of beryllium *be* x_2? Only if 'painyness' names different qualities on each occasion. But how could it? Is not the quality of yellowness that we attribute to sulphur the *very quality* that we admire in sunflowers—whatever else? Accordingly, painyness cannot be x_1, or x_2, or etc.; nor can it be an open-ended disjunct x_1 v x_2 v . . .—seeing that painyness is a determinate quality and more or less anything might in principle find its way into this disjunct. And painyness can scarcely be identified with the physical painyness-determining feature y that is found in Mr L, bearing in mind that painyness is predicated of stuffs like silver but not of Mr L; and anyway some other factor z might be the factor in Mr M which determines the appearance of painyness for him. These considerations seem to dispose of a simple materialist analysis of secondary qualities. I turn now to another possible analysis.

(3) Might the property of painyness be the *power* to produce pain (in the right way) in animals? Let me at this point make a comparison. Consider the case of an 'uncomfortable' chair. This chair has a causal power. However, so too have its human users. For while we attribute the uncomfortableness to the chair, we no more implicate the chair and exonerate its users than the reverse: the causal explanation of uncomfortableness distributes responsibility all round. Chairs could as easily speak of the 'touchyneness' of humans (to certain chairs) as humans of the 'uncomfortableness' of certain chairs (to humans). Then so it is with silver and Mr L. We attribute painyness to silver, from the standpoint of Mr L—but the powers are independent of standpoint. Is the power of silver to cause pain in Mr L's right index fingertip, different from the power of Mr L to have pain caused by silver in his right index fingertip? It is in part because I see no difference between them, it is because I do not wish to speak of two mutually entailing yet distinct realities here, that I see no reason to identify painyness with that power; for the power seems no more in silver than in Mr L, and yet the painyness is predicated of silver and not of Mr L.

Then is the painyness of silver (for Mr L for those five minutes) the *disposition* on the part of silver to (suitably) cause pain in Mr L's right index fingertip? Bearing in mind that all that may be needed for painyness to inhere is such a causal relation, and therefore the existence of such a disposition, it is a natural thing to say. And yet dispositionist analyses seem alien to the very nature of secondary qualities. For example, the nature of redness seems discordant with such an idea, especially when we remember that the presence of a disposition is ultimately determined by a conditional proposition. For redness is an appearance-property, part of the look of a thing, something that has reality only consciousness, a distinctive *quale* ('brave and warm like the sound of a trumpet'), that wears its entire heart on its sleeve in giving itself up to intuition, that has no hidden reverse side, that is infinitely superficial, that reveals its 'all' in a simple sensation, that is known only through direct concrete acquaintance. How could *that* be the kind of item that was most perspicuously 'unpacked' in an 'if . . . then . . .' proposition? Surely *that* is best explained confrontationally!

Well, I shall not labour the point. I will regard the case against the dispositionist analysis as unproved. Indeed, I shall do the same for materialist and the causal-power analyses. The time has come to grapple with the question from a different angle.

2. Can We Predicate Secondary Qualities of Their Own Distinctive Sensation?

Let us return to where we began. What account are we to offer of redness? This is equivalent to asking: what is the analysis of 'looks red'? The immediate difficulty that we encountered was an apparent circularity: if being red is looking red, how can 'red' have content in 'looks red' and how therefore can 'looks red' have content? The circle appeared to be broken when we came across the *sensation of red*. For it seems as if naming could begin here, just as it did with pain in the case of painyness, whereupon the concept of red might be constituted out of that of such a sensation. Two analyses of redness, cast in these terms, naturally suggest themselves: an *intuitionist*, and a *dispositionist* account. Does 'looks red' mean (a) has that look that comes to immediate acquaintance when a sensation of red is noticed, or (b) produces the distinctive sensation that the things we call 'red' produce in us?

The nub of the matter is, are pains painy? Does the sensation of warmth feel warm? Is the sensation of red actually red? In other words, do sensations have an appearance? If they do, both the causal and dispositionist analyses of secondary qualities can be rejected, seeing that sensations have no propensity to cause more of their own kind in us. The example I shall consider is colour. And I will address myself to the general issue, by considering the specific question: are those entities we all call 'red after-images' really red? Why might one suppose they are not? Either because they do not cause sensations of red in us whereas all agreed red things do, or else because they are 'private'. Why might one suppose they are? One compelling consideration is, that a man could discover what it is for something to look red merely by making the acquaintance of a red after-image; indeed, might learn the meaning of 'red', and so come to know what redness itself is, through confronting the sensation. Is not this a case of knowledge by acquaintance? Does he not precisely encounter redness itself?

A dispositionist could reply in two ways to the latter suggestion. He could first of all say, that in making the acquaintance of the sensation of red, in coming to know what 'sensation of red' designates, we come to know what is the very *cornerstone* of the use of 'red', around which the remainder of that use is readily constructable along the general well-known lines governing the use of taste and smell (etc.) words. So it is scarcely surprising, he could say, that this is all one need know to know what a red appearance is.

The second rejoinder that a dispositionist might make is even more interesting. He could say: the only conceptual space available for 'the after-image is red' is already occupied, and the truth-conditions are different from those appealed to by the intuitionist. Namely: (t_1) the red after-image is identical with a cerebral phenomenon, and (t_2) that cerebral phenomenon looks red to normal sighted human viewers in white light (etc.). Now the dispositionist is here implicitly reminding us that when ordinarily we say of something that it is red, we imply that it presents a red appearance to normal sighted human viewers in normal viewing conditions. Who can deny it? Then why should the after-image be an exception? If Physicalism is true, it is difficult to see why this physical phenomenon should fall outside the scope of the rules governing the attribution of colour. If Physicalism is true then t_1 & t_2 must be the truth-conditions for 'the after-image is red'. Accordingly, the answer to the question: 'Is the red after-image really red?', now seems as if it must be: 'Nobody as yet knows, but the probable answer is that it is not.' This if Physicalism is true; while if Physicalism is false, there will be no truth-conditions for an after-image being red. Either way, the inference, 'The after-image is correctly described as "a red after-image" and therefore it is red', emerges as invalid.

3. Viewing Conditions

(1) It is beginning to look as if those who say red after-images are red, are confused over what it is to have a colour. And there seems to be no valid principle to the effect that after-images necessarily have the colour we name in correctly describing them, for it seems that for anything to have a colour X it must cause sensations of X in visually normal humans in normal viewing conditions. But now just what *are* these 'normal viewing conditions'? They are the generally prevailing and presupposed conditions that lie in the background of ordinary speech concerning visibles. Yet those conditions are in no way absolute. For one thing, they vary with the type of item under view. Thus, red light looks red and is red, but it is irrelevant whether or not it is viewed in conditions of white light. Red light looks red in the dark. But the spatial point of view of the perceiver is relevant. Consider a situation in which a slender beam of red light is crossing a vacuum transversely to the gaze. Despite the fact that this light is invisible to us who are staring at the tract of space wherein it resides, it is visible to someone situated in line with it. But is it then *visible*? It is—to people who stand in line. Then is it not merely *partially* visible? It is not; for partial visibility requires, as in the case of a man in the dark who extends an arm into the light, that part be visible and part invisible. The red light crossing the vacuum is no more partially visible than any material object, which after all requires that we face towards it to see it (etc.). Implicit in 'the table is visible' is, not only 'to humans' and 'in white light', but also 'facing' and 'at a reasonable distance from' and even 'at a velocity of less than (say) 1000 m.p.h.' (etc.). (Doppler red-shift holding for colour viewers travelling at appreciable fractions of the velocity of light.) What the example of red light underscores is, that *all we ever mean* by 'visible' is 'visible to——, in——'. It reminds us that *all* claims concerning visibility and colour, are relative to observers and generally also to viewing conditions.

The next thing to note is the utterly democratic nature of these last. For those observers, and those conditions, under which an item can (say) be truly visible or (say) truly look red, can include *more or less anything*. In this respect, there is nothing absolute or even special about humans and light. An item could be visible in electron beams and invisible in light; visible to ichthyosauruses and invisible to humans; visible even in electrons uniquely to the human individual that would have resulted from the fusion of a particular male and female seed; etc. If sulphur looks blue down a microscope and yellow in normal viewing conditions, the blue has as much right to the sulphur as the yellow. If the earth looks blue from the moon and yellow from a nebula receding at 7/8 of the velocity of light, the yellow has as much right to the earth as the blue. And so on. There simply is no limit to the conditions we might quote. Therefore a colour predicate might stick even if the attendant conditions do not include 'to human', 'in daylight', 'facing', 'nearby', 'slow', etc. For no conditions have priority. No conditions are absolute. None are 'true'. The above familiar conditions are merely the norm for us, and hence the conditions most useful to assume in public human communication.

This is the sole interest of these particular conditions. However, from a different point of view the conditions implicit in attributions of sensible qualities have another significance, different from either the exigencies of communication or the overt acknowledgement of relativity. For they are in addition conditions in the *statement of a law*. Thus, many laws hold only under certain conditions, e.g. Boyle's Law. Then sense-perception links physical properties of environmental items with sense-experience via laws which likewise require conditions. The important thing being, that a sensory experience be caused by a physical item in repeatable circumstances, such that a law cast in terms of some physical concept and the sensory concept be instantiated. When that happens, sense-perception of the physical item occurs, the attention makes concrete contact with the item, and a foundation for knowledge is established; and at the same time the secondary quality of the sensation which made possible such attentive contact finds itself objectified in the environment, automatically qualifying the 'public' perceptible it helped bring to awareness.

Then it does not matter what the conditions are under which this attentive contact and sensory objectification are established. All we need is the regularity, and it is accomplished—no matter what the participants. Thus, electrons may happen to be blue, for only five minutes, uniquely for some Mr N. Then this instance of blueness is no less real than the greenness of grass or the redness of blood. It is simply unshareable and of no immediate use to others. A man might even have a new sense, with a whole new genus of sensation, the content of which might even in principle be incommunicable to his fellow men until they experienced the sensation.

(2) Let us now return to the suggestion that for the red after-image to be red, the after-image would need to be a cerebral phenomenon that presents a red appearance to normal human viewers in white light (etc.). This is supposed to be an application of a principle to the effect that, for anything to be red, it must present a red appearance to visually normal humans in white light. The above discussion now makes us want to drastically qualify this principle. Taken in one way it unites the blemish of the pathetic fallacy with that of tautologousness, affirming that 'what looks red to *us* in white light, looks red to *us* in white light'. While taken as a statement of perceptual standpoint, it has no absolute need of holding for everyday material objects. The normal viewing conditions might have been electron beams. Indeed, the very notion of normality along with that of numbers can be dropped, seeing that it is imaginable that no more than one eccentric human could manage to see in the presence of electrons (etc.). We can shake off this tyranny of populace, species,

numbers, or whatever it be; for all that matters is nomicity and its conditions. Instead we shall say: for anything to be red—to observer O—in conditions C, it must present a red appearance—to O—in C. A tautology, to be sure; but worthy of reiteration.

4. Do We See the After-Image?

Given this principle, what are we to say of the red after-image? Circularly, that if it is to be red—to mankind—in normal viewing conditions of white light (etc.), then it must look red—to mankind—in white light (etc.); and doubtless for this to be realized, some version of Physicalism must be true. However, no one who claimed that red after-images are red would take himself to be affirming such a proposition. What, then, would he actually mean? Well, we have seen that 'normal viewing conditions' are one thing for material objects and another for light. Then why should they not be a different thing again when the item under view is an after-image? And why should not the red after-image be red in those special viewing conditions—whatever they may prove to be? Again, we know that blood presents one colour to humans and another colour to some other animals. Then why should not the red after-image be red for its owner under the above special viewing conditions? This may be his claim. This may be what he means in saying it is red.

Some will wish to resist this suggestion, along the following lines. They may claim that, if anything has a colour, it must be *visible*. And therefore if the after-image is to be red, it likewise has to be visible. But how else could such an internal psychological phenomenon be visible, unless it be through the visibility of a brain phenomenon with which it is identical? Therefore the only possible redness for 'red after-images' would be the redness of certain cerebral phenomena in white light (etc.). Now this argument appeals to the concept of visibility. But what *is* visibility? And why should visibility be reserved uniquely for what is in principle open to the gaze of the (or some) public (or other)? To this it might be replied: to be visible *is* to be visually perceivable; and it is for precisely this reason that we refer to the normal viewing conditions of white light (etc.).

But now it seems to me that we are in danger of being bemused by 'perceivability' in place of 'visibility'. And again we ask: just what *is* 'perceivability'? Perceivability, I suggest, is being such that some conscious being or other might in principle—not *know* of it—(but) be *aware of* or be *conscious of* it 'in the flesh' and in such a way that knowledge could flow naturally from this episode in consciousness. Then why is not an after-image perceivable? For all that the above definition affirms is that the perceivable is *intuitable*, i.e. is capable of being noticed-*of*. Is not this true of the after-image? But, it might be replied, the definition also asserts that we naturally *come to know* of the perceivable through noticing-of it. But do we come to know of the after-image through noticing-of it? Indeed, does one in general usually or even ever come to know of a sensation through noticing-of it? When would we speak of a *way of knowing* in relation to one's own present toothache? (Quite apart from Wittgenstein's 'it can't be said of me . . . that I *know* I am in pain.')[2] Well, there can be no doubt that we very often come to know of sensations through noticing them. Even though other ways of knowing are possible, as when one discovers one last night had toothache through learning that one groaned (etc.) in one's sleep, noticing-of a sensation is both the *usual* and in the present tense *the* way of knowing of the existence of a sensation in oneself. It is true that one cannot set out to discover through the active method of attending whether (say) one has toothache. But this in no way alters the fact that one knows one has toothache, notices one's toothache (since mostly one cannot help noticing pain), and would not know one had toothache had one not noticed it. Knowing of pain is one thing, noticing it another, and generally the latter causes the former. An example drives the message home. Thus, for five ghastly seconds a man's car goes into a protracted skid, during which time he failed to notice the momentary twinge that sprang up in his tennis elbow, and is as a result forever ignorant of this sensuous episode. Clearly, it was the riveting of his attention beyond the confines of his own body that caused this ignorance. Conversely, the capture of his attention by the sensation would have caused knowledge of its existence.

Therefore the after-image is *perceivable*. And, being an entity uniquely visual, it is *visually* perceivable. And while we do not use our eyes to perceive it, its very existence depends on the visual apparatus of retina, optic nerve, visual centre. So must it not be *seen*? Well, it may be said, perhaps it is visually perceivable, but it is not visually *sense*-perceivable, for we do not become aware of it in and through becoming aware of a causally intervening sensation. This interesting claim is undoubtedly true. But what interesting proposition follows from it? Some may say: it follows that we do not *see* the after-image, for the reason that seeing is a mode of sense-perception. But this pronouncement seems to me to be sheer stipulation. What is its justification? I can think of two kinds of justification for stipulations of this kind: considerations of usage, and considerations of nature. Neither support the present stipulation. Thus, it will be agreed that we at least *say* that we 'see the after-image on the wall'. Then do we withdraw a claim to 'see a red mark on the wall', when we discover it is a mere after-image? For what it is worth, we do not. We may say 'there was nothing on the wall'; but we do not say 'I was aware of nothing', and neither do we say 'I did not actually *see* the after-image'. (By contrast with: 'I only imagined, or thought I saw, a shadow' (uttered jitterily).) So I find no support in usage for the thesis that the visual perception of the after-image is not a seeing of it.

What about considerations of nature? Here, too, we find no support for the stipulation—precisely because of the unlikeness of the latter 'nervy' visual imagining and the visual perception of an after-image. The event in the attention when we notice a red after-image on a wall, is of the *very same type* as the event in the attention when we notice on a wall a similar looking red stain that rapidly fades. By con-

---

[2] *Philosophical Investigations*, 246, Blackwell, Oxford, 1953.

trast, an imaginative event of seeing a mental image is a wholly different kind of phenomenon from the seeing of the after-image or stain; and with this in mind we say that seeing the mental image and seeing the after-image are not different species of a *single seeing genus*. But seeing the after-image and seeing the stain *are* different species of a single generic type: visual noticing. But if an event x is a visual noticing of some real existent y that is present in the visual field, then in an unproblematic sense x is a seeing of y. For seeing *is* noticing what is sited in one's visual field. Therefore both the immediate noticing of the after-image and the sense-mediated noticing of the red stain are different varieties of seeing, viz. immediate and mediate. Therefore we see the after-image.

5. The Conditions for Viewing the After-Image

(1) It seems that the relativity to conditions and viewer, of colour and indeed of sheer visibility, opens up the possibility that the red after-image is seen and is red. The suggestion therefore is, that the red after-image looks red to its owner. But *under what conditions?* When he notices it? Or (to rule out brain viewings) when he notices it *immediately?* Here we must tread carefully. When we say that roses look red to humans, we affirm a proposition whose truth-conditions make no reference to the attention. All we require if roses are to look red to humans is, that they cause sensations of red in humans in normal viewing conditions. No more. While they need not actually ever cause such sensations, it is necessary that they should when the viewing conditions are realized—but that is all that is needed: noticing is unnecessary. Thus, the truth-conditions are to be cast in terms of visual sensations but not in terms of the noticing of them.

But a difficulty now presents itself. For if the colour of the visual sensation normally caused in man by roses is actually noticed, then that noticing experience will be a seeming to see red. It follows that if roses normally look red to humans, roses must in normal viewing conditions cause in humans sensations such that if their *quale* is noticed, then that noticing experience must be a seeming-to-see-red experience. So here we have necessary and sufficient conditions of looking red which are cast in terms of both the sensation *and* the attention. Then why should we prefer the former simpler set which are expressed merely in terms of the sensation? Is it just a question of simplicity?

Simplicity is no more than a clue to the real reason. That reason is, that just as effects cannot determine their cause, and just as knowledge cannot determine its objects, so the attention cannot conjure up or create its own distinct material objects. Colour determination *precedes* the noticing of it. What happens in the attention is a consequence therefrom, and this is the reason why the conditions are to be expressed in terms of the sensation. But there is another reason why the truth-conditions for (say) roses looking red to humans must be cast in terms of the sensation of red rather than the noticing of that sensation. This is, that while we can state necessary and sufficient causal conditions for the occurrence of a sensation of red, we cannot do the same for the noticing of it. This implies that we cannot propose a tight or nomic rule of the following form: if roses look red to humans in white light (etc.), then in white light roses must cause in humans a seeming-to-see-red noticing experience. The reason being, that no 'etc.' is equal to the task. At best we can assemble a proposition the probability of whose truth asymptotically approaches 1 as we pile on a welter of psychological conditions, e.g. sanity prevailing, attention free, etc. But the colour of things is given via a simple categorical law which omits all reference to the psychological state of viewers: it is nothing so complicated, nothing so mental (as one might say). Therefore the truth-conditions must be cast entirely in terms of the sensation.

(2) Then what are we saying when we say that *the red sensation looks red to its owner*? It now seems clear that we do not mean: when noticed. Surely we mean just what we say: that the red sensation presents a red appearance to its owner. But is this utterance properly elucidatory? For what about the fact that the after-image might be blue to its owner peering at his own brain in a mirror in purple light? Here the after-image will present a blue appearance to its owner! So how are we to differentially distinguish the specific claim that we wish to make?

Ought we by way of explication say that the after-image looks red to its owner *in the mind*? But what does 'in the mind' mean? Does it mean anything more than that the sensation is a psychological phenomenon? If not, it should be pointed out that the sensation does not cease being a psychological phenomenon when viewed in purple light in a mirror by its owner. Then perhaps we ought to construe 'in the mind' as importing the special observational conditions that there prevail. Might this enable us to make the required differential claim? But what are those special conditions? In the case of sensations there exists at least one important mental epistemological peculiarity: namely, that sensations can be the immediate cause and immediate material object of a noticing-of experience. So why should we not, instead of speaking of 'in the mind', say by way of explication: the after-image looks red to introspection? But this supposes that introspection is a different procedure from looking. But it is not. A person who is looking at a red after-image on a wall *qua* red stain, is introspecting every bit as much as one whose attention is self-consciously turned inwards onto a toothache. Then should we say: the red sensation looks red when it is *immediately noticed*? But we have just seen that the truth-conditions governing the attribution of colour appearance must be cast entirely in terms of the visual sensation. So how are we to explain the utterance in question? What do we mean when we assert that 'a red after-image looks red to its owner'? How are we to differentially explicate this claim? How are we to cope with the problem of conditions?

(3) What is the way out of this impasse? It is to drop all reference to conditions in the case of the sensation of red, when we affirm that 'red sensations look red to their owner'. Not because no one can get their head into the head of another and

introspect their sensations; that is, not because the sensation is necessarily *for* its owner alone: the reason being, that it is not. From the point of view of appearance, absolutely anything is *for* anyone: the reverse side of the moon had a colour *for* dinosaurs; and so on. And neither is it because of the near infallibility of introspection in relation to sensations. Thus, it is not because only the owner can see it in this special immediate way, and he is almost immune from error. This still makes it relative-to, and conditional, albeit in an Observer's Heaven where observations lead a charmed life. We must drop any reference to conditions in this case for a quite different reason. Namely, because colour-determination *stops* at the sensation, not at the observing or noticing of it.

As the chain of reasons must come to an end, as instrumental actions must go back to basic acts, so here with colour appearance. The sensation of red *in and of itself* is red: 'red' *names* the X that this sensation has, that is *immediately on view* to its owner. For this is where it all begins, this is the fount from which the whole language of colour flows, for it is at this point that 'red' gets its sense in an ostensive naming. Then this fact permits us to say that a red after-image necessarily and therefore conditionlessly looks red to its owner. And this in turn is perfectly consistent with saying that in purple light it contingently looks blue to its owner (peering at his brain in a mirror). But it is the unconditional redness of the sensation of red, or blueness of the sensation of blue, that is the ultimate foundation of these colour attributions.

(4) Earlier we noted that all familiar agreed colour-attributions imply the truth of a law. If roses look red to humans then roses in white light (etc.) must cause sensations of red in visually normal humans. And another law holds in the case of light that looks red to humans. And so on. Then where is the governing law when we say of red after-images that they too look red to their owner? Now the laws invoked when we attribute a colour either to (say) a material stuff or a mediating wave phenomenon like light, relate that physical existent and a sensation: for example, blood and a sensation of red. Then clearly nothing like this can hold of the sensation of red: it stands in no nomic relation to more of its own kind. Accordingly, whoever claims that 'those after-images that we normally call "red" necessarily and conditionlessly look red to their owners', must dispense with the usual nomic link between the perceived and its internal sensuous representation. Thus, if there exist grounds for claiming that the red after-image looks red to its owner, they must be something other than the familiar nomic grounds which enable us to say of a pillar box that it looks red to a perceiver.

What is the *role* of law when we attribute colour to material objects? It is something like this. The applicability of such law is a necessary condition of an object's colour appearing in the visual field, precisely because it functions as a basis for knowledge of the cause of the colour sensation, and so to say retrodictively for the attention's managing to make contact with an item in the physical extra-psychological domain. The role of law is to permit the attention to range farther afield than the sensation and to land upon both mediating light and even remoter causative object. Then no comparable problem exists when our concern is merely with the sensation. All we need here is a free and searching attention, whereupon the sensation immediately and more or less infallibly is revealed to it—and cognition is available. It is in this way that one who claimed that red after-images look red to their owners, might shrug off the absence of the usual psycho-physical law linking object and sensation.

Indeed, we have seen he can go further in his eschewal of law and conditions in this case. For he could in addition claim of sensations of red that they of all things *cannot fail* to look red. The question is closely analogous to the question that is so often addressed to volitionists, with a view to embarrassing them: namely, are volitions themselves voluntary? To which I think volitionists should reply: they are the *only thing* that is voluntary! And for a very simple reason: that to be voluntary *is* to be a volition! Somewhat similarly our protagonist might say: not only are red visual sensations red, they are the only item in any possible world that is red *in itself*. Just as we do not deny the voluntariness and reality of instrumental actions, despite the fact that volitions are all that is voluntary, so we do not deny the redness and reality of the projected or public physical red, despite the fact that the red sensation is the only thing that is or that can be non-projectively red or red in itself.

6. The Look of the Red After-Image

(a) One absolute amongst countless relativities

Then is it in fact true that red after-images look red to their owners? Let us suppose that a subject sees two red circles on a wall, and judges them identical in appearance—whereupon one fades. This was the after-image. The question is: was he right? Or consider the following assertion: after-images on walls are sometimes mistaken by their owners for stains, because for a moment they look the same to them. Is this statement true? Plainly, both of the above claims are true. It is beyond dispute that a red after-image looks red to its owner. That is, has a red appearance for him; and conditionlessly so. Whereas blood has a red appearance for mankind in white light (etc.), red after-images have a red appearance for *any* owner in *any* conditions. Even if a red after-image is cerebral in nature, and, seen in purple light in a mirror that happens to be trained upon his own brain, turns out to look blue to its owner, the red after-image continues to look red to its owner—as those very conditions prevail; for 'in purple light' means 'when illuminated by purple light', and 'in a mirror' means 'the light reaching the eye is reflected from a mirror', and neither situational factor threatens the necessity that a red after-image looks red to its owner. Indeed, even if a red after-image is experienced as blue by a subject in a psychotic state, the after-image continues to present a red appearance to a consciousness that simply fails to receive what is offered it. Then if red after-images look red to *someone*, they have as much right to be described as red as do items like blood which look red to a whole species. But *necessarily* red after-images look red to someone. Therefore necessarily they are red.

If Physicalism is true, red after-images must have a myriad of contingent properties, such as being sited *here* in the brain, and having *these* neurological constituents, etc. However, one property they *must* have, viz. being/looking red (to their owner, conditionlessly). This absolute is the source of all relative attributions of redness, since we explain the relative redness of things in terms of the absolute redness of the sensation of red, but cannot explain the necessary redness of the sensation in terms of anything. It is *because* blood causes in humans in white light (etc.) sensations which are necessarily and conditionlessly red to their owner, that blood is red to humans in white light (etc.); but it is because of nothing that those sensations look red to their owner. Far from being a dubious instance of redness, the sensation of red is the only thing in the Universe that is necessarily red to one standpoint. It is sheer contingency that anything else is red. That is, whereas anything else that is red to one lot of observers might have been non-red to these and all and sundry observers, it is necessity that the sensation of red is red to its owner (whatever else it is to its owner). This necessity is the absolute which permits the countless relativities we have had occasion to chart.

(b) A difficulty posed by the existence of object-directed and reflexive uses of 'sensation of——'

One additional difficulty stands in the way of our accepting that the red after-image looks red. It arises out of the fact that, in some uses of 'feeling of——' or 'sensation of——', the word 'of' leads outwards beyond the bearer to a distinct object, whereas in some other uses it involutes reflexively back onto the bearer. As an example of the first, 'feeling of smoothness' or 'feeling of furriness', as an example of the second, 'feeling of discomfort' or 'feeling of weariness'. The sensible quality of painyness helps to highlight the difficulty this duality creates. Thus, if red after-images are red, pains must themselves be painy. Something in us protests at this. After all, one cannot tactilely perceive pains, and surely one can predicate painyness only of that of which one can have tactile perceptual experience. Indeed, thinking of 'feels bumpy' or 'feels smooth' or 'feels furry', there is a tendency to assume that for anything to feel any way, it is necessary for us to engage in a process that is at once active and tactile. But this is not possible in the case of pain. So how can pains be painy? This is the difficulty.

Doubtless all this is true of the 'feeling of bumpiness'—but bumpiness is a primary quality. However, our concern is secondary qualities; that is, qualities transmitted through the timeless character of a sensation. This immediately ensures that we can dispense with the factor of time, and therefore also of activeness in the sensing of the sensible quality. Likewise, tactile perceivability is equally dispensable in the case of sensible quality 'feels'. For example, we can perceive the sensible quality warmth of a stationary fluid wholly in the absence of anything one could call tactile experience. So when I say that pains feel painy I must not be supposed to imply that I think I have lain a kind of mental hand upon a mythical pain surface, let alone have actively stroked that supposed surface. When we are talking of mere sensations, and their corresponding simple sensible qualities, the above provisos fall by the wayside. Red things look red to us, red after-images are red for us, irrespective of whether we engage in looking activity, or indeed of whether we even notice them. The character of the sensation is the sole determinant. In short, it is a case of 'sensation of——' in which 'of' involutes reflexively, not one in which 'of' leads outwards to a distinct object. And so it is with the other sensible qualities. Since the taste or smell or feel of things is likewise wholly determined by the *quale* of a sensation, pains passively feel as painy things passively feel and must be accounted painy; and the feeling of warmth in the hands passively feels as warm-feeling things passively feel; and the sensation of red presents to view the self-same look or appearance as do red things, and must in consequence be said to be red for its owner. Thus, the sensation of red survives this difficulty: it possesses the red look notwithstanding.

(c) 'Red' names a determinate look: a look that comes from the sensation of red

(1) 'Red' names a specific look, a determinate visual appearance, that all manner of things can have. But we can intuit this look in something iff we immediately intuit the red look of the one and only thing that necessarily has that look, viz. the sensation of red. For we may in general say, that acquaintance with the 'sensible' sensation is a logically necessary condition of acquaintance with any instance of the corresponding sensible quality. More, it is a logically necessary and sufficient condition of acquaintance with the quality itself. As noted earlier, we could introduce a permanently deaf man to the whole world of sound, including the full range of the art of music, merely by inducing the right auditory sensations. Likewise a permanently blind man might have decided preferences amongst colours and even paintings, and all in the absence of the usual situation in which sensations are caused by the item whose appearance one is concerned to assess. In what sense has this man yet to make the acquaintance of colour? In what sense have appearances been withheld from him? True, he has never actually set eyes on the Mona Lisa, but he knows all that is really important about it, for he has made the acquaintance of that which Leonardo laboured to create, viz. a particular appearance. (Painting being an art of creating durable static appearances through two-dimensional physical means.) For what kind of appearances must they be that can of necessity come forward to consciousness only when appended to a public visible? Is not the character of an appearance determined precisely by what comes through to *consciousness*, wholly irrespective of how?

Thus, 'red' names the red look, a look predicable necessarily of but one item, viz. the sensation of red; and contingently, and derivatively, of much else. It is for reasons of this kind that I would wish to say, that a world in which sensations of red occurred but no public physical existents were red, was a world in which redness was instantiated. But a world in which red mental images occurred but no sensations or public physical existents were red, would be a world without redness (always supposing such a world possible). Red after-images are red; red mental images, which is to say mental images of red, are not. Red after-images have an appearance; mental images of red have not, being mere imaginings of appearances. For redness is the intentional object of a mental image of red; so that the function of 'of' in 'mental image of red' is to lead beyond to what is putatively independent of the image, as it is in 'mental image of Paris' and 'mental image of water'. But the function of 'of' in 'sensation of red' is not to lead beyond to anything; for the role of 'red' here is precisely to characterize the sensation itself, exactly as happens with 'feeling of warmth' or 'feeling of discomfort' or 'feeling of pain', which reflexively turn back descriptively on themselves in the final term.

(2) Something in us resists this account, inclining us to reject the reflexive reading of 'sensation of red'. Thus, we are inclined to say that the sensation of red only fulfils its destiny when it lands projectively upon some physical existent like a balloon, rather as if redness belonged by nature to the physical world at large as bodily sensations belong by nature to the body. But this comparison is completely misguided. For one thing, bodily sensations are necessarily putatively set in body parts, whereas in no sense is (say) the after-image that we experience with closed eyes necessarily putatively set in a physical recipient. Nothing putatively comes to consciousness in the after-image. The only reason one might be inclined to propound such a theory about the sensation of red is, that the sensation is usually successfully projected onto the environment, and it is not projected onto a body part. But these facts lend no support to the theory that the sensation of red is essentially putatively projected onto the environment. Humans as a species might have had visual sensations without those sensations ever functioning as sense-perceptual mediators. Who would talk of a projective destiny then? All one could be thinking of in saying such a thing would be the fact that those sensations have an untapped potential; but then the same is true of pain—witness 'painyness'! Has pain, likewise, a 'destiny'?

(3) Since 'red' names a particular look, to be red is to have that look. No more. In particular, it is not to be such as to cause in viewers sensations of red, for red after-images are red but cause no sensations of red in us. Nevertheless, whereas all that the sensation of red need do to be red is be itself, for a material object to be endowed (projectively) with the red look, it must be such as to cause sensations of red in viewers (be they humans, cats, or fleas) in determinate conditions (be they electrons, at $7/8$ the velocity of light, or whatever). Accordingly, I do not wish to *play off* the state of affairs in which (say) a rose has the red look, and that in which it is such as to cause sensations of red in viewers in the required conditions. Since these two descriptions are logically equivalent, they refer to the same state of affairs. Then one state of affairs is a sensation's having the red look, and a quite different state of

affairs is a rose's having the red look. So are we attributing one thing to the rose and another to the sensation in predicating redness of each? We are not. To see this, let us suppose that the attention lands upon the sensation of red. Then if that sensation has the right causal ancestry, this same event *is* the red of the rose coming to the attention. So a *single look* has here been intuited, in intuiting both sensation and rose, and in consequence we predicate this one look of both the sensation and the rose. Even though different truth-conditions exist for these intuitional contacts, they are the one event with the one internal object. In a word, different kinds of truth-conditions exist for predicating the self-same red look of inner psychological and outer physical object. But in each case we are doing no more than predicate *that look* of something. This is common territory.

(d) Redness necessarily owes its being to the sensation of red

(1) Redness is a visual appearance or look. And looks are what any looking must see, what any viewer must immediately encounter, so to say looking back at us the viewer. (Like the monkey at the keyhole.) Then necessarily all red looks appear to minds only in the appearing of the sensation of red; and while redness is a property of many things, it is a necessary property uniquely of the sensation of red. Then how does the redness of a sensation of red relate to the sensation? If Physicalism is true the sensation of red must have many unknown physical traits which are inessential to its being the sensation of red, in which case being red cannot exhaust the being of the sensation of red; while if Physicalism is false, the sensation is a phenomenon with at least two characters, viz. being a sensation and being red. Either way the sensation of red cannot *be* its own redness—though they may *seem* identical, since redness is the only quality of the sensation of red that we notice, for even the brightness and intensity and distribution of the sensation are predicable of its colour.

(2) Then it is important that we do not misconstrue the fact that the 'is' in 'the sensation of red is red' is one of predication rather than identity. For example, it would be a misconstrual to suppose that redness might have *pre-existed* or been *independent* of the sensation of red, as the formal property of circularity pre-existed and did not need instantiation to be real. Necessarily, this is false of redness. If there had been no such thing as a sensation of red, there would be no such thing as redness. The example that clears the head is 'painyness'. It is evident that painyness could not pre-exist pain, even though if Physicalism is true there is a vast amount more to a pain than its (necessary) painyness (to its owner). It is obvious that 'painy' has meaning only because there is such a thing as pain. The same is true of red and the sensation of red.

But why does 'red' have meaning only if the sensation of red exists? Whatever the explanation, it must cohere with the fact that 'red' stands, not for the sensation of red, but for one of its (perhaps many) qualities. Now the latter fact implies that even though all statements of the truth-conditions for the inherence of red in anything must be cast in terms of the sensation of red, these statements cannot define 'red'. The reason is, they do not say what 'red' designates, for they fail to specify *which* of the (perhaps many) properties of the sensation is the property that ensures the inherence of redness in something. In fact, that property is the *look* of the sensation of red. And this is that property of the sensation of red that is immediate object of the attention when the sensation is immediately noticed. Then this latter definite description fixes *which* property of the sensation is the redness-determining element in any statement of the truth-conditions for the inherence of redness in things that is cast in terms of the sensation. For this property alone is relevant among all the (perhaps many) qualities of the sensation. Two more of its traits further identify the property in question. First, the sensation of red looks red in all worlds in which it occurs; second, only the sensation of red looks red in all worlds in which it occurs. So looking red is a property such that uniquely the sensation of red has it in all worlds in which it occurs. Then if we return to the question: why does 'red' have meaning only if the sensation of red exists? the answer must be, that 'red' names what is an essential property uniquely of the sensation of red, and derivatively of all else it qualifies.

We noted that all statements imputing redness are logically equivalent to statements cast in terms of the sensation of red. When this is conjoined with the fact that uniquely the sensation of red has the property of being red in all worlds in which it occurs, we deduce that all worlds without this sensation are worlds without redness, and worlds without redness worlds without the sensation. Therefore redness cannot have pre-existed the sensation of red. Redness arises in any world in which it does arise only through the sensation of red.

(e) The causal power of secondary qualities

A word on the causal properties of secondary qualities. Since secondary qualities of material stuffs and light are relative to consciousness, we cannot attribute causal power to these examples of secondary qualities. Thus, we cannot make a claim to the effect that (say) the smell of hydrogen sulphide tarnished the silver: the statement is simply unintelligible. Nor can we even say that the smell of coffee caused us to smell coffee-smell: rather, it is the non-identical 'material basis' of the coffee's smell which produced this experience. However, we cannot then go on to say, as I was once wont to say, that secondary qualities *as such* lack causal power, nor even that secondary qualities as such lack *physical* causal power. The reason being, that the secondary quality of the corresponding sensation causes an event in the attention: for example, the redness of a visual sensation of red causes an event of seeming-to-see-red. And if Physicalism is true, and the event in the attention is of physical status, the secondary quality of the corresponding sensation must have caused a physical event of a psychological sort. It is true that the rationale of the latter causal transac-

533

tion has to be expressed in psychological rather than physical terms. Nonetheless, this instance of a secondary quality will have a causal power, which if Physicalism is true is also a physical causal power, that is built into its very nature.

7. The Attention and the Secondary Quality

(a) The sensation as mental object

(1) The foregoing discussion has been an attempt to demonstrate an intuitionist, as against dispositionist, analysis of secondary qualities, largely through assembling arguments favouring the attribution of secondary qualities to sensations as well as to public perceptibles. The case strikes me as very strong. And yet it is hard to shake off the feeling that the dispositionist analysis also cannot be far from the truth. After all, a disposition to generate sensations in given conditions is a necessary and sufficient condition of the inhering of a secondary quality in a public perceptible. This fact alone makes the analysis seem plausible. One feels that the difference between the two theories may be no more than a matter of words. Why throw out so attractive a theory on account of a single recalcitrant case? In my opinion this line of thinking should be firmly resisted. Despite these persuasive considerations, dispositionism proves on further examination to be far from the truth.

(2) I believe the prime interest of secondary qualities, perhaps the main reason we ever coined a terminology for these phenomena, lies in a property which dispositionism simply fails to come to terms with. What is of central significance, outweighing the above causal considerations, is that the *quale* one experiences in the case of secondary qualities is immediately given to awareness in the mode of *material object for the attention*. For it is not just that red objects regularly cause experiences with red-content, that they have such a disposition. What equally matters for the existence of secondary qualities is that this experience is of the type *perception*. This vital property prepares the necessary ground for the situation in which the *quales* of certain sensations prove to be projectable perceptually onto the environment, whereupon the secondary qualities of physical objects are born. While it is an insufficient condition of such projectability, it is a vital and necessary one. And it is realized uniquely in sensations.

For we are in the presence here of the *only* psychological item which can be an immediate material object of noticing. Neither the bodily will, nor affect, nor indeed anything else in the mind, can appear in this role. *A fortiori*, since the sensation is endowed with a *quale*, we are in the presence of the one phenomenology ('what it is like') that can be object for the attention. In a word, with the one phenomenology that can be *immediately perceived*. We ought to be struck by this property. It is absolutely unique to the sensation. All other phenomenologies, whether of mental imagery or dream-experience or joy or amusement or anxiety or shock, come to consciousness solely as the *internal object* of the experience: they never come as well as its distinct and perceptible object: they never appear in the mind in this double mode. While the phenomenology of these items manages to invade our consciousness, it does not simultaneously stand outside-of or confrontationally-to it within the mind, simultaneously objectified in some bearer psychological object. This the secondary quality precisely does. It is at once both objectified, in a sensation (and maybe environmental object as well), and also internalized in the perceptual experience of these latter. It appears within the mind as internal *and* external object of one and the same attentive experience. This dual property is unique to the secondary quality.

From this unique property, compounded with the psycho-physical nomic situation governing its objectification, flows the special potentiality and utility of the secondary quality. Namely: to take its place as material object for the attention in an experience in which it simultaneously qualifies a whole string of causally interrelated items: sensation, light, surface, side, object. These multiple instantiations of the secondary quality take their place in a single attentive line which moves in a direction leading from the mind out onto the environment.

And so the secondary qualities of items in our physical surrounds are realities, not just because we regularly undergo determinate experiences in given physical situations, but above all because of what we manage through these experiences to be aware of or *notice* in the environment. Through its presence in the sensation we become concretely conscious of mere things lying beyond the mind. The phenomenon of the secondary quality enables us to trace out the objects of the attention in the visual perceptual situation: to map the phenomenon of attentive projection ('Transitivity of the Attention'). But these momentous achievements are in the first place made possible through the immediate perceptibility of this phenomenology. Then it is above all those *attentive accomplishments* which confer significance on the phenomenon of the secondary quality—not the fact that we regularly undergo sensuous experience at the hands of the environment. The disposition needs to be supplemented by the property of attentive projectability. And this fact disqualifies dispositionism.

(3) To see this, let us compare the property, possessed by sudden loud noises, of causing shock: of being a 'shocker', as one might say. This is the disposition to produce certain experiences in given subjects in specifiable circumstances. Plainly it is inadequate as a model for the secondary quality. Thus, we do not *perceive* 'shockingness' through the experience of shock, whereas we *perceive* the red (say, of a setting sun) through the experience of red (say, seeming to see a red circle). What accounts for this difference? Well, it cannot be relevant to the difference that these environmental items possess the *disposition* to generate determinate experiences in given subjects. And in neither case do we *perceive* the experience in question: for I no more perceptually feel the shock than I see my seeming to see red. What truly accounts for the different attentive properties of the two experiences is, that whereas the attention is *occupied by* both experiences, only in the case of visual ex-

perience does the experience arise through having the phenomenology of some psychological something *come to the attention* as its distinct or material immediate object. Seeming to see red *is* noticing or perceiving the redness of some psychological bearer, feeling shock never *is* noticing the 'shockingness' of anything.

(4) The unique possibility of intuitional contact with the sensation is consistent with the fact that the sensation is an undirected senseless psychological product of merely bodily events. Here, too, it is almost unique amongst mental phenomena. It occurs solely at the instigation of superficial physical stimuli, in accord with psycho-physical law, and such an origin helps to ensure that the sensation is no more than a sort of *psychic thing*, a mental something devoid of intrinsic sense or meaning. Then it is in all probability this quasi-material merely sensuous character that permits consciousness to make intuitional contact with this phenomenology. I have concentrated the discussion upon the perception of the sensation for two main reasons. Because of the fact that it brings out the fundamental weakness of the seemingly plausible dispositionist analysis. But above all because it simultaneously reminds us of the unique property of the sensation phenomenology that is the very cornerstone of the phenomenon of secondary qualities. Namely, the capacity to be immediate material object for the attention. It is this which, when in conjunction with certain causal regularities, makes possible the state of affairs whereby a phenomenology is projectable onto the environment in such a mode as to constitute an attentive awareness of the physical recipients of the projection. As we have already observed: it is in this way that the secondary qualities of physical objects are born.

(b) 'Projecting' a 'private quale' onto the environment

(1) There is no reason why a concept like 'red' should not have come into existence in the first place as the name of the *quale* of a sensation, and only secondly been projected beyond onto the environment. Indeed, had the course of evolution been different, this might very well have been the actual history of the concept: the two usages *temporally* staggered. Why should not 'red' have gained its sense in this fashion? For why should not 'red' be the name of what comes immediately to awareness when a 'red after-image' is seen? Why should it not thus name what is an intrinsically essential quality uniquely of that sensation (and derivatively of all else that is red)? Or is this an illicit 'private ostensive definition'? But what is illictly 'private' about it? Self-conscious beings, armed with a public conceptual system and the public concept of 'sensation', coin a subsidiary concept to single out what comes to attention when one attends to a publicly and readily specifiable instance of the type 'sensation'. For the concept of this property begins its life here, exactly as happens in the case of the concept of any other *quale* of any other sensation. But the difference in this particular case is, that the concept then finds itself put to special and derivative uses, thanks to certain special contextual properties.

Now when this look is appended onto a material object, we do not of course suppose that the object *is* a sensation. Rather, a conceptual operation ('projection') occurs that is based upon the fact that the sensation, in a given psycho-physical situation, *is* the presence for attentive awareness of an object in the environment: merely to notice it, *is* to notice a physical bearer. There are two determinants of this state of affairs: the noticeability of the sensation, and the nomic psycho-physical relation in which the sensation stands to the environment. It is upon this dual basis that 'projection' occurs. The argument explicating its sense goes as follows.

(2) A material object can come to visual attention only if one of its qualities does—for no physical item can be 'just' seen. However, the only way one of its qualities can come to visual attention is if a quality which is at once simultaneously of the sensation and the object does the same. For how else? But the object *can* come to the attention through the red of the sensation. Therefore the red of the sensation must *in some sense* be predicable also of the object. Now since the object is not a sensation, that sense cannot be intrinsic, and must rather be relativistic: to perceiver, to time, and situation. Accordingly, if we assert 'The object is red' (meaning for him, here and now, in these circumstances), then what we are saying is: noticing the red of the sensation would here and now be noticing the object. Then here we have what goes into the 'projective' adaption of what ('red') starts its life non-projectively and intrinsically essentially of a *quale*. This is what it is to attribute so subjective a thing as a 'look' onto a mere chunk of matter. The colour of a physical object is the colour of the sensation that, in the appropriate nomic conditions, *would be* the presence of the object *for* attentive awareness. It is a subjective guise which it might wear as it enters the subjective domain: it is, so to say, its entrance ticket into another realm.

537

20

The 'Perceptual Given' and 'Perceptual Mediators'
or
The Formation of the Visual Experience

In Chapter 16 I argued for the thesis that the visual perception of light mediates the perception of physical objects at a distance in space, given in the visual experience in appropriate three-dimensional spatial terms. It does so in a way which closely resembles the mediation of sense-data that was examined later in Chapters 17 and 18. In both of these situations the mediating phenomenon is merely directionally perceived in body-relative physical space. However, these early objects in our visual perceptual transactions with the environment are not in general conceptualized by the understanding in the visual experience. By contrast, the objects given as lying at a determinate distance in three-dimensional space are thus conceptually demarcated for awareness and so also for cognitive use. This difference generates problems concerning the detection and/or individuation of the early merely directionally perceived phenomena. The method of resolution of these problems proved to be neither that of inspecting the content of the visual experience, nor one of finer attentive or perceptual discrimination of the objects of perception, but the wholly different method of argument of a purely philosophical kind. Now so far in the examination of visual perception I have confined myself to considering these questions concerning the type of the early objects given to the attention. Nevertheless, certain other related problems exist which are as yet completely unresolved. In particular, it seems to me that we need a better understanding of the *formative history* of the visual experience of the moment. After all, visual experiences do not arise out of sense-data through the means of a simple transfer of content, but spring instantaneously into existence with a content that is for the most part highly differentiated and markedly interpretational in character. How does this come about? It is above all to this question that the discussion is now addressed.

1. The Epistemological Gap

Consciousness is situated at an *epistemological remove* from almost everything in the phenomenal world—bar a few mental items (such as one's own experiences). Almost nothing in the phenomenal world is immediately accessible to us epistemologically. Hence it comes about that if we are to know anything about anything in physical nature, we will often have to make do with merely hypothetical and uncertain data. This holds just as much of concepts as anything else. Far from knowing essences first and then discovering their instantiation in the world, we hypothetically label items in the world long before we know just what it is we have named, indeed long before we know whether we have succeeded in naming anything. Think of our first namings of metals and disease entities.

Even prior to these encounters with natural kinds, even more fundamental and beset with the same uncertainty, is our encounter with the data on which these surmises and concepts are based. I mean, with objects and events in the environment. This is accomplished perceptually. Here, too, and for the same reason, we meet with the same epistemological gap. And it could not be otherwise. When we visually perceive an object it gives us little to go on with, an appearance and that is all, and certainly nothing one could call absolutely immediate acquaintance. This holds quite irrespective of whether Direct Realism or Representationalism is true. In sense-perception the mind simply cannot strike through to its goal in one immediate and infallible blow (as, here and there, it does intra-psychically). As we have just noted, not even our concepts do that. Accordingly, if some outer object is to be identified, it can be known only through the agency of epistemologically more immediate items which link us with the object and which can themselves be more readily identified. In short, we need the intervention of phenomena *near at hand*.

In the case of visual perception those intervening 'bridge'-items take more than one form and play more than one role. My concern in this chapter is with *two* such items. Namely, with what has been called the *perceptual given*, and with what I shall call the *perceptual mediators*. More exactly, since these are philosopher's terms of art, I am concerned to at once stipulate senses for those terms and single out two important realities that are to be sited within the aforementioned epistemological gap between the mind and the environment.

The rough ideas behind these terms is this. By 'perceptual mediator' I mean a perceptual go-between or agent: an epistemologically nearer perceptible item that is non-identical with the perceived object, which stands in proxy-wise for it, enabling us to make perceptual contact with what is in some perceptual situation epistemologically remoter. A familiar example is, the visible near side of a visible material object.

When we turn to the concept of perceptual 'given', matters are a little less clear. The concept that I have in mind differs from that of 'mediator', and yet the two concepts are closely related. Whereas mediators are second-best substitutes which are proxy for the real thing, what the concept of the given seems to be aiming at is some kind of perceptual *beginning-point*, something of the kind of perceptual *raw material* (or some such). I shall not try to be more precise at this point, since it is possible that several such items exist. However that may be, it is my intention in this chapter to try to fashion credible and veridical concepts of *two* essential auxiliary elements in the perceptual situation, and having done so to spell out the nature of their relation. The natural order for discussion seems to be, from the more to the less primitive: that is, to begin with 'the given', and pass from there to the 'mediators'.

2. The 'Perceptual Given'

(a) Explaining the concept

(1) What is the 'perceptual given'? It is up to us to stipulate a sense for this philosopher's expression—though it is a substantive issue whether anything exists which it is natural to describe in this way. Then I think that when philosophers have talked of a 'perceptual given', they have often had in mind a mental raw material, which is at once the initiating stimulus of a perception *and* that which simultaneously is perceived in terms of an organizational/interpretational framework which is imposed upon it in that very perception. More exactly:

- (i) something produced in the mind by the senses alone,
- (ii) whose parts are perceptible,
- (iii) which is susceptible of various organizings/interpretings; and
- (iv) which finds determinate organizing/interpreting
- (v) in the content of the perceptual experience
- (vi) it is 'triggering' into being,
- (vii) which simultaneously is directed onto it
- (viii) in such terms.

This statement embodies a theory of the *origins of perceptual experience*. The theory of the perceptual given is a causal theory, and the given is itself a causal posit. Paradoxically expressed, the idea is of a sort of 'sub-perceptible', underlying and causing a perceptual experience which is directed onto it, utilizing a certain framework in so doing. The suggestion is, that some mental item X is produced by the senses—an X which engenders a perceptual experience that is directed onto itself—and that properties of order and sense in the perceptual experience arise through the mind's perceptually discovering these characteristics in the originating X. The expression 'perceptual given' is coined to single out this hypothesized X. Thus, it stands for a supposed relatively unorganized and wholly senseless raw material which is said to be at once causal 'trigger'-agency *and* the subject-matter of mental organizing and interpretation within a perceptual experience which is directed onto it in those terms. Here we have a natural sense for 'perceptual given'.

(2) Does anything in reality answer to this specification? It seems to me enormously likely that, in the case of hearing, an array of sound is given to auditory consciousness in just such a fashion. For it seems certain that the mind orders and interprets *audible data* in various ways. Thus, (adapting the old joke) the barmaid, instead of hearing 'tickle your arse with a feather', might easily have heard instead 'particularly nasty weather'. Was there not something audible here upon which her mind got to work in constituting her auditory experience? In short, I think the idea of a 'perceptual given', taken in the stipulated sense stated above, is unproblemat-

ically applicable to hearing. And I think it can readily be generalized to cover most other examples of perception.

But not everyone will agree, seeing in this example nothing more than the familiar ambiguity in meaning and structure which we encounter in some perceptions. In particular, they may find therein no evidence of a *mental raw material* which is the subject of a mental 'processing'. Then let me now assemble the argument in favour of the existence of such an item. Before I do so however, I should like to offer a brief preliminary sketch of that argument.

What convinces me of the existence of the 'given' is that there is reason for thinking that when sense-perceptual experience occurs, a *two-stage* but synchronous causal transaction takes place: the first stage consisting in the creation purely by the senses of a psychological phenomenon of sensuous kind, the second consisting in the engendering by the latter phenomenon of a mental process which subjects that senuous item to organizing/interpreting within the very bosom of a perceptual experience that is directed onto it. Thus, first of all a psycho-physical transaction (not unlike that which occurs when (say) c-fibre stimulation causes pain), and then a resulting psycho-psycho transaction (not unlike that which occurs when (say) pain causes pain-awareness): in short, body-to-mind causation first, leading secondly to mental causation. Here we have an empirical theory of the origins of perceptual experience. Then if this aetiological account is correct, if the perceptual experience has a causal ancestry with this structure and those participants, we will need a name for the psychological product of the first transaction. The name proposed is, 'The Perceptual Given'. This is the justification for availing myself of this antiquated expression. Its use is necessitated by the peculiar *bifurcated type* of the causal ancestry of the perceptual experience. The 'given' is the hypothesized middle term in a hypothesized causal triple.

(b) The example of pain as a preliminary model

By way of justification of these claims, let us begin by examining in a little more detail the above example of pain, which I propose to use as a model. We shall assume that in a particular being (Mr N) c-fibre stimulation of intensity i at bodily point p is a regular sufficient condition of pain of intensity I (roughly) at point p. Certain standing conditions are required if this is to hold: say, neurological normality in some determinate regard, the absence of a state of unconsciousness, etc. And let us note in passing that these conditions do not include the distribution-situation in the attention, and require only that attention be available.

Now let us suppose that on one occasion Mr N is anxiously awaiting the arrival of just such a pain at point p, on another occasion listening to riveting news on the radio—when c-fibre stimulation of intensity i at p strikes. On each occasion a pain of intensity I (roughly) occurs. Yet Mr N's experience of the pain will surely differ on these two occasions. After all, a faint awareness of an intense pain is not the same as an intense awareness of a faint pain, so why should an intense awareness of a pain of intensity I be the same as a diminished awareness of a pain of the same intensity I?

And so we have no choice but to offer one explanation of the occurrence of the *pain*: namely, c-fibre stimulation of intensity i at point p in a conscious Mr N. Meanwhile we must offer a quite different explanation of Mr N's *experience-of* that pain: namely, the conjunction of a pain of intensity I and a certain situation in the attention. Accordingly, we offer the following two-stage explanation of the occurrence of Mr N's *experience*: c-fibre stimulation—in a psycho-physical transaction; and the conjunction of pain and an attentive preparedness/or lack-of-preparedness—in a psycho-psycho transaction. In a word, first a psycho-physical causing and then a mental causing. Note that we can offer this account, and separate out the pain as a distinct existent and causal agency, even though the two causal transactions occur in the *one instant* of a single experience. Even though we cannot *attentively* or *experientially* single out the pain independently of its effect upon us, we can nonetheless single it out and distinguish it from its effect—thanks to causal considerations. This is a matter of considerable importance, and should be borne in mind when we come to consider a similar situation in the case of sight.

(c) Body-to-mind causation in visual perception

The example of pain provides in my opinion an accurate model for most examples of perception—it is *itself*, incidentally, a case of perception—and justifies us in speaking of a 'perceptual given' in the sense stipulated in the case of pain. But let us turn now to the all-important sense of sight, and for simplicity's sake let us confine the discussion to monocular vision (binocular vision introducing complexities which are irrelevant to the existence of a 'given'). Then we discover here a psycho-physical law governing the origins of the visual field, closely analogous to that operative with pain. We shall see that this is the thin edge of a wedge leading to the legitimate postulation of a 'visual given'.

Before I do, I must stress a point of some significance. Namely, that even though the model of pain appeals to the existence of a directly experienced mental object, and despite the similarities in the causal ancestry of pain experience and visual experience, the theory of a visual 'given' is not in any obvious way dependent on sense-datum theory. The example quoted earlier in which a given audible phenomenon was variously ordered and interpreted, on the face of it makes out a case for an auditory 'given' without appeal to sense-datum theory. The nub of the matter is, that there is reason to believe that mental causation at the hands of the visual field plays a part in the genesis of the visual experience, and even though a sense-datum interpretation of this theoretical position is natural, it is not the only possible reading. Then I turn at this point to spelling out the precise nature of the first of those two causal 'tiers' in the case of sight. That is, the psycho-physical law governing the origin of the visual field.

The law takes the following form.[1] In a wakeful visually normal human, yellow light (let us say) of intensity i (say) at a point p_r on the retina, is a physically sufficient condition of yellow of brightness b (roughly) at some corresponding point p_v in the visual field. This regularity can be generalized across both retina and visual field: continuous yellow light across the full extent of the retina is a causally sufficient condition of yellow across every point in the visual field. And the generalization may be extended to all colours, and govern the colour-brightness properties of all visual fields. It does not matter how the light got to the retina: whether it reached point p_r from the surface of a nearby buttercup, or whether it was introduced by scientists, or whether it simply sprang up spontaneously within the eye, in each case the visual field at p_v will exemplify the same colour as the light at p_r. The phenomenon of 'colour constancy' in no way qualifies the following fact: that if the retina of a visually normal conscious human is flooded with yellow light, then so too will the visual field be filled with yellow. And neither do the vicissitudes of the attention: *holes*, after all do not appear in the visual field as the attention wanders, any more than do *dimmings* or *fadings*! Does the visual field grow dim when you hear electrifying news? Does it so much as alter an iota? Immobilize a man's head and eyes, fix the character of the light impinging on his retina, and keep this physical situation constant for a minute; then provided the subject does not lose consciousness, the character of the visual field will stay unchanged over that time. And it will do so quite irrespective of the direction of his attention, indeed of his mental state generally. He could go mad and his mind fill his visual field with demons, with purple demons if you wish, and it remain yellow! The property of being a reliable 'port of knowledge' concerning the environment, ensures this independence of the mind.

(d) Mental causation in the genesis of the visual experience

How close does that bring us to demonstrating the existence of a 'perceptual given' in the stipulated sense? It more or less takes us all the way. Does not the visual field have a purely physical origin at the hands of the senses alone? Must not this psychological item be a fixture, provided there is a fixed stimulus to the senses? And must it not be susceptible of multiple organizings and interpretations in leading to the perceptual experience? For will not the one visual field, of some given colour-bright character, find itself variously 'processed' by various minds which find themselves in various attentive and cognitive states? And does not the character of the visual field play a significant causal part in the genesis of the final experience? In short, is not the causal ancestry of the visual experience *bifurcated* in the required way?

What is at issue is the occurrence here of a specific example of *mental causation*. Now for the reasons just given, body-to-mind causing clearly occurs. But why posit

[1] Making due allowance throughout this discussion for the dramatic lessening, both in determinations and finesse of discriminability, as we move towards the peripheries.

mental causation as well? Why not a single body-to-mind causing of meaningful ordered visual experience? Certain considerations indicate the presence of mental causation, which is to say not just causation *by* mental phenomena, but causation that is exclusively *intra-psychic*. To begin, Mill's methods alert us to the existence of a working causal power on the part of the attention: thus, the one and same retinal input with varying attentive postures (expectation, distraction), leads to diverse visual experiences. Now precisely what was it that caused those attentive responses? Perhaps on one occasion the presence of a bright light before one. But not just bright light before one *in space*. And not just bright line *on the retina*. To affect the attention the light must actually *enter the visual field*. Then whatever analysis one might wish to give of this state of affairs, it was *this* which caused noticing in a mind poised (let us say) for just such a visitor. And this causation must be distinct from the body-to-mind causation. After all, these two causings have different 'logics': the body-to-mind explanatory schema is that of simple nomic regularity, whereas by contrast the attentive explanation mentions intelligibly related mental events and properties exclusively, and is unable to appeal to strict regularities by way of eluci-dation (being irremediably susceptible to a measure of causal influence at the hands of the rest of the mind). And we cannot telescope those two rationales into a single rationale, nor into one another. Then the presence of mental causation suffices to demonstrate the reality of the visual 'given'. The 'given' precisely is that mental cause. It is the initiating mental cause in the mental causation of the visual experience.

3. Justifying the Atomistic Characterization of the Visual Given

(a) The problem of minima

In short, the visual given is a reality. But an important question remains unsettled: namely, the content of that given. In particular, since the given is assumed to be the subject of organization and interpretation, a problem exists as to the measure of structure and meaning attributable to it in its own right. After all, that it suffers organizing and interpreting does not entail that it is itself a senseless chaos! Then could it perhaps be that it is simply a two-dimensionally organized atomistic array of colour-brightness values? Many philosophers have felt so. And yet the truth-value of this claim is far from obvious. And, in any case, *what* 'atoms' are we speaking of? And are we really talking of discrete distinct atomistic sensory entities?

It is greatly to the credit of Hume, Berkeley, and others, that they recognized that the visual field was not infinitely divisible. Sensation is in this regard absolutely unlike material stuff. Humans cannot see germs, not because those germs might perhaps be dullish in colour, not because they may be transparent, and not because something else could be obscuring them, but simply because of their *size*! Germs do not subtend so much as $1''$ of arc in the visual field, and the human eye cannot resolve anything less than $10''$ (at the very least). To note this important fact, which is a kind of *quantization* phenomenon, those empiricist philosophers spoke of '*minima visibilia*', and we shall here assume that they postulated, not the existence of discrete sensation individuals, but the existence of an inevitable and determinate coarse-grainedness in perception. No more.

Consider what this implies about the character of a visual field. Let us make the preliminary assumption that humans cannot see anything below (roughly) $10''$ of arc. If this figure gave the lower limit for the entire visual field, we would need to specify the colour-brightness values of something of the order of $(180 \times 60 \times 6) \times (100 \times 60 \times 6)$ points, in a grid of $180° \times 100°$, if we were to completely specify the colour-brightness character of a visual field. That is, we should need to give about 2.3×10^9 values (2.3×10^{10} being ten times otiose, 2.3×10^8 being ten times under-described)! No doubt the real figure is vastly less. So let us now—and simply for argument's sake—assume that something like a million differentiable points exist in the average human visual field: meaning merely that a million colour-brightness values, drawn on a two-dimensional (x,y) grid, are necessary if we are to fully characterize the colour-bright character of some monocular visual field. That is, of the psychological whatever-it-be that a fixed pattern of light on the retina completely determines in a waking visually normal human.

And so the colour-brightness character of the visual field will be wholly *describable* by one million two-dimensionally ordered colour-brightness values, and wholly *explicable* by one million distinct psycho-physical transactions. This reality has this internal character, and this causal ancestry. And that internal character, when suitably abetted by the attentive and cognitive situation prevailing then in the mind, causally assists in determining the character of whatever visual experience takes place whose objects are set in just this visual field.

(b) The structural character of the raw material of perception

(1) May we from these few facts conclude that a *visual given* exists that is to be described by one million two-dimensionally ordered colour-brightness values? Can we conclude that what we are 'given' in visual perception is of the nature of an ordered array of *sensory points* or *minima*?

Naturally enough the answer to this question depends upon the sense of 'given'. Then the stipulated sense is that the given is the bodily produced psychological factor (X) which interacts with the mind in generating the perceptual experience. And we saw that in visual perception, the visual field meets that causal specification. However, as it stands such an answer fails to specify the precise content of the given, which is to say the causally operative properties of the visual field. Then how are we to meet that need and finalize the specification? Well, we know that the visual given must be the visual analogue of the array of sound which gets heard one way by one person, another way by another, a different way by a third, and so on. It seems therefore that for any fixed visual field, the given must be *so* characterizable as to transcend specific orderings, and to be common to all actual or empirically possible orderings. To doubt this last would be to doubt the causal role of attention-posture and of the mind generally in the genesis of perceptual experience.

Does it follow from the above that (say) the mononocular visual given consists in (say) one million two-dimensionally ordered colour-bright values? Is the common or transcendent character of the pure contribution of sight towards the genesis of the visual experience, one cast uniquely in terms of mere colour-brightness points (of an order of finesse matching the *minima*) extending in ordered fashion over an unbroken continuity of given angular span? While this theory somehow seems natural, it is not immediately obvious whether or not it is true.

(2) Causal considerations enable us to resolve the uncertainty. Thus, the given is the hypothesized psychological product of the senses which interacts with the mind in generating the perceptual experience, and in the case of sight the visual field proves to be that agency. But it is not *just* the visual field: it is the visual field *under a certain description*. For what we have singled out as 'given' are the *causally efficacious* features of the visual field in this causal interaction. Now any visual field can be described in many spatial ways. For example, we might describe it through tracing linear structures, somewhat as one might draw a scene using an array of continuous lines. And many other descriptive systems might be employed. Then amongst these multiple specifications of a visual field occurs one which registers *no* structures. Namely, the 'pointillist' or merely atomistic listing of point *minima* in a two-dimensional framework. A mere list—assembled in any order—in which we specify a sequence of x, y position-values and corresponding colour-bright values.

The theory which I shall defend singles out the latter specification. The theory is, that the visual given is susceptible *only* of this description. In short, I suggest that the visual given has but one description: the absolutely *bare minimum* description. And that is to say that whereas a visual field may contain yellow straight lines and blue circles and patterns of all shapes and forms, the visual given realized by that visual field contains points of many colours set in all sorts of positions in space, but no lines, no patterns, no structures of any kind. Although the lines and patterns (etc.) are really there in the visual field, and even though the visual field is given to one, the lines (etc.) form no part of the given!

(c) The argument for atomism

(1) The argument sets out with a few preliminary observations. Let us begin by repeating what it is that requires demonstration. It is a claim of the following type: that whereas lines and circles and triangles are in the visual field, they are no part of the visual given. Instead they are said to *follow from* what is given: that is, from the minimal description of the visual field given in terms of spatially positioned *minima visibilia*. Now if these particular shapes are a deductible consequence of that basic description, so too must be a multitude of other spatial structures. If straight lines

are deductible, so are pentagons and octagons and forty-one-gons and one-thousand-and-one-gons, etc. Some of these shapes are simple and familiar, some are outré and complex, some are outrageously outré and complex; but in the sense in which *any one* of these shapes is present, so too are *all* of the multitudinous others.

Then it is an interesting fact that *only a few* of this vast array appear in the content of our visual experiences (generally being either simple or familiar shapes, and probably also certain shapes which evolution selected us to individuate). Equally interesting, we have no way of telling which it will be that is independent of the character of the containing mind. No betting odds of any kind exist on this matter. Nothing about those structures gives any hint as to which will come to awareness. Looking is useless. If we say that simple shapes are 'more noticeable', this is merely to say that they are more noticeable to minds that notice simple shapes. If we say that yellow lines 'stick out', this is merely to say that they 'stick out' for those for whom yellow lines 'stick out'. Considered merely in themselves all spatial structures and colours have as much probability or improbability of appearing in the content of the visual experience. As remarked above, there are no 'betting odds'!

Now it must be emphasized that I am not denying that some of those shapes and colours *cause* visual experiences with themselves as content. What rather is being claimed is, that whether or not they do is determined by the *character of the mind* into which they are inserted. By that—and by nothing else. The causal power of a line to cause noticing of itself *is* the susceptibility of the harbouring mind to be affected by stimuli of this kind. More, the latter susceptibility *confers* the former power. It is *because* the mind has this susceptibility that the line has this power. In many another mind the line might have no power whatsoever. Lines are not of the nature of forces. Lines have no power *in themselves*.

(2) We shall now see that this conclusion is, in effect, the argumentative justification for which we are looking. Let 'VF' stand for visual field, and 'VE' for visual experience. Then the causal equation [{(VF containing lines) & (Mind in such and such a state)} —→(VE of lines)], is undoubtedly true in some cases. But the above discussion has shown that this causal equation is not as explanatory as it looks. Thus, it is not to be likened to: [{(Rubber stamp with raised lines) & (empty white page which registers stamps)} —→(image of lines)]. This last is truly explanatory. It puts to use the familiar model of the parallelogram of forces, each added force having an absolute measure of its own. Then to endorse this model for perception would be to endorse the idea of the Attention as a *tabula rasa* for the visual field to write upon. That is, it is to conceive of the Attention as a simple reflector of impressed impulse, as if there really were such a thing as 'Mental Physics'! This is profoundly misconceived. It misunderstands both the nature of the attention, and the type of its causal properties, neglecting the contribution made by the attention itself and the mind generally to the attention's interaction

with the visual field. Above all, it fails to grasp that the efficacy of the 'impressed force' derives entirely from the 'simple reflector'.

Accordingly, while we cannot but accept [{(VF containing lines) & (Mind in such and such a state)—→(VE of lines)] on some occasions, we would do well to replace it by the following causal equation: [{(VF with minimal description such that large continuous yellow lines are deductible) & (Mind in such and such a state, including susceptibility to lines)}—→(VE of lines)]. The latter is not merely perspicuous as the former is not—remembering that nothing in a visual field's contents gives *any* hint of their causal power: the latter actually *explains* the former. If the former appears to be perspicuous, this is because we are under the sway of the *tabula rasa* model. And the model is inapplicable. The causal power of lines in the visual field is at once relative to, and wholly determined by, the minds in which they appear.

We are therefore entitled to single out the visual field under its minimal specificatory description, as the psychological stimulus which is brought to bear upon the mind in the genesis of the visual experience. This is the second of the two justifications for positing a given of this kind which we have been seeking, and it too is a causal justification. On the above causal grounds we say that the two-tiered causal origins of the visual experience, begin with a psycho-physical causing of the visual field under its *bare specificatory atomistic description*; and that it is completed by a psycho–psycho or mental-causing by this visual field impacting upon the remainder of the mind, leading thereby to a visual experience wherein order and interpretation are manifest. This is the causal argument for the view that the visual given is, the visual field described in atomistic *minima visibilia* terms. For to repeat: the theory of the perceptual given is a theory as to the causal ancestry of perceptual attentive events. It is a causal theory.

(3) The existence of a visual given of the above kind, is forced upon us by nothing more than a few simple considerations.

(a) The character of the visual field is wholly determined by bodily non-psychological factors.
(b) The senses have finite powers of discrimination.
(c) The existence and character of the visual field is a causal agency in the genesis of the perceptual experience.
(d) The order and meaning in the content of visual experience is wholly determined by the susceptibility of the perceiving mind.

No more. And yet it can sound alarming to postulate a visual given in such 'pointillist' terms as we have employed: the constituting 'points' mere constructs, the unstructured array essentially unperceivable, the whole thing seems to reek of empiricist mythology! Good sense tends to be restored when it is pointed out that the theory is merely a two-tier theory of the causal ancestry of visual experience, taken in conjunction with a due recognition of the fact that the synthetic and inter-

548

pretational properties of perceptual experience stem in the final analysis from the experiencing mind alone. In effect, the positing of a visual given is an affirmation of the role of the mind in the constituting of visual experience.

4. The 'Perceptual Mediators'

(a) Explaining the concept of 'perceptual mediator'

(1) I turn now to a quite different, though closely related concept, that of 'perceptual mediator'. This is the concept of a perceptual go-between or proxy. It is of that, the perception of which is the means or form taken by the perception of some x. Thus, it is a y such that we perceive x *by* or *in* or *through* or *in virtue of* perceiving that y. For example, we see Mt Blanc by seeing its south side, we see the setting sun thanks to seeing a sliver of red between some leaves, we see a perfectly clear block of glass in virtue of seeing a fine coat of blue powder on its surface. What are the characteristics of the 'in virtue of' relation? For the most part I shall concentrate on the sense of sight.

How do we come by the concept of mediator? I think in the following way. Whereas we 'just' see after-images, we never 'just' see material objects. There is no such phenomenon. We always see these particular x's *by* or *in virtue of* seeing some y which is non-identical with x. In the case of material objects and the sense of sight, if we are to make perceptual contact we are obliged to discover something epistemologically nearer us than the object, indeed ultimately something *so* near that the chain of dependencies reaches its last link, and set eyes upon that. Generally in perception there is more than one mediator, but there invariably is in the visual perception of material objects. Here the mediators are at once multiple and intermediating. And they can vary both in *kind* and in the *structural situations* they realize. For example, I see Mt Blanc through seeing its south side, its south side through seeing its south surface, its south surface through seeing a patch of snow thereon, and so on. But I might instead have seen the mountain through seeing its profile against the stars at night, simply short-circuiting side and surface out of the transaction. Thus, in sight the mediators are not merely multiple and intermediating, they also instantiate multiple structural possibilities.

What can we say in *general terms* about the relation between a perceived item x and its perceptual mediator y? The first thing is, that x and y must be non-identical. Thus, y can be a side or profile, and so non-distinct from x; or y might instead be light or a sense-datum or a fine coating of snow, and thus both distinct and non-identical; but in either case the y is non-identical with the x it brings to awareness. The second thing is, that the mediators or y's must have a first term y_f such that we perceive that y_f through perceiving *nothing*: a y_f that we 'just' perceive. The third characteristic is, that the perceived object x and its mediators y must stand in regular and probably causal relation: Mt Blanc does not cause its south side, but material objects are for the most part stable causally-bonded wholes with sides and surfaces. In sum: mediators often form a sequence of regularly bonded non-identical items, and, apart from the first mediator y_f and the last mediated x, anything playing the role of mediator in one direction will simultaneously be a mediatee in the opposite direction. At any rate, this is the situation in the case of sight.

We should distinguish *quality* from *part* from *entity* mediation. All these items can act as mediators, though in the case of sight *two qualities* have a special role to play amongst mediators: the secondary quality of the sense, and the two-dimensional shape it assumes. Thus, each y-term in any particular sequence of visual mediators has to present the very same colour-brightness and profile value to consciousness. Whether it is simultaneously of this or that entity or part is a separate matter altogether—and in the case of sight we know that various mediatory situations are possible—but the one and same colour and profile must be visible all the way down the line of mediators. A typical situation might be something like the following: the entity a triangular coat of white snow might mediate the perception of a white mountain, and so on through other triangular white parts or entities until we reach a triangular white sense-datum, where both entity and colour-profile mediation come to an end.

(2) Now even though the relation between the *mediator y* and the *mediated x* is one of non-identity and regular concomitance, the relation between the *perceiving of x* and the *perceiving of y* is neither. It is that of *identity*. Seeing x and seeing y are one and the same event. Thus, seeing material object x falls under multiple descriptions, according as the variable y takes different values, which relate to one another rather like the contents of a Russian doll. A whole string of 'in virtue of' relations stands revealed as we list the nested sequence of descriptions of the single attentive event: a sequence of epistemological priorities coming clearly into view in those various mediating y's, which edges nearer and nearer to the epistemological beginning-point where redescription and epistemological dependence come to an end, and we 'just' perceive some y.

(b) How the attention manages to go beyond the secondary quality of the sense in the case of sight

(1) Mediation by secondary qualities is a necessity in the case of those senses that are *built upon* secondary qualities, viz. sight, hearing, smell, and taste. A notable feature of all of these senses is, that they need not have made the grade as senses. Experience might have been stranded with a mere secondary quality *quale*—and nothing else. In fact however in the case of each of these senses we perceive an outer reality in virtue of perceiving a secondary quality. Then whereas in the case of smell we do no more than perceive a material stuff through perceiving its smell, in visual perception we encounter a *whole sequence* of mediators, including the colour-brightness of sense-datum and of light and material stuff and side, leading 'out' as far as (and culminating in) the material object itself. This sequential phenomenon I

have dubbed 'The Transitivity of Attention',[2] to record the fact that a single event in the attention takes a string of non-identical objects, each succeeding object making possible a successor in the one extended line. It is pretty much the same phenomenon as the so-called 'Accordion Effect' in instrumental-action theory. Just as we cannot immediately will the opening of a door, so we cannot immediately see a door, and just as we manage nonetheless intentionally to open doors thanks to the intended mediation of a push, so we succeed in seeing doors thanks to the visible mediation of sides and stuff and light.

(2) The question arises as to the origins of the very special situation prevailing with sight. How does it come about that the visual perception of material objects is possible through the agency of a complex sequence of mediators? Alternatively: how can the visual attention manage to reach out in space through colour and light to material objects situated at a distance? It is not so in the case of (say) hearing. How comes it that the gaze can string so many entities down a single line?

A comparison with another phenomenon assists us here. Once again the situation can with profit be likened to that of physical instrumental action. Just as the will there interacts with what lies at a *remove in space*, so the attention in the visual perception of material objects interacts with what likewise stands at a distance. This gulf in space attests to an important feature of both situations: namely, in either case the mind relates *extra-systemically* but regularly and thus meaningfully with something lying outside the system. As the door we open is no part of our motor system, so the door that we see is no part of our ocular system. And yet in either case it is *almost as if* we managed to bridge this systemic gap (somewhat as in the case of physical skills it is *almost as if* we had managed to extend our inborn motor-powers). But in each of these cases it is an illusion: the door does not join the motor system, any more than it does the visual system (and the skilled agent does not in his skill instantiate the relatively tight psycho-physical law of motor-power, for skills are to be expressed instead via psycho-physical statistical law).

These considerations help us to understand how the visual attention manages to extend its range as far as it does. For remember what is the function of perception. Thus, even though perception is not a *mode* of knowing, it is as such a *way* of knowing. Every perception must have the capacity to generate knowledge. Then since the perceptual experience and the perceived object are parts of no encompassing system, the basis of this latent knowledge has to be provided by the novel data encountered in perceptual experiences, taken in conjunction with the standing conditions. The absence of encompassing systemic conditions ensures that it cannot be *presumed* to obtain: no pre-ordained harmony existing between visual experience and surrounding environment: nothing like the relation between (say) kidney-function and liver-function. And so in the case of those senses which grew out of our experience of sensible qualities, the required foundation for the latent knowledge of perceptible items has to be realized in regular outer connections.

Then in the special case of sight the latent knowledge manages to extend out as far as the material object, and this is made possible by the general stability of material objects and the law-governed transmission of optical images by light. Such regularities 'underpin' the simultaneous journey out from the mind of the twin phenomena, *latent knowledge* and *noticeability*.

In sight those regular connections are realized between items lying down a line in physical space which we call 'the line of sight'. The various mediators relate evidentially to one another: a patch of white in the visual field of a visually normal perceiver being evidence of white in a direction, a white surface evidence of a side, a side of an object. It must be along these regular evidential lines that the attention moves outwards beyond its immediate colour objects. The end-point in this line is an item with a complex spatial nature, which is capable of throwing off the trappings of the particular direction in which it was encountered. Namely, a self-subsistent material object. This is the final attentive object in seeing.

5. The Relation between the Given and the First Mediator

(a) Can we see the given?

The given is the middle term in a hypothesized three-term causal transaction which begins with physical input into the ocular system and terminates in the visual ex-perience. It is the more primitive and initiating partner ('the stimulus'), in a mental-causal transaction with an attentive-standpoint and cognition (etc.), the fruit of which is a phenomenon of seeing in which its own parts occur as object-parts. If this empirical hypothesis is correct, and such a middle term exists, the stipulation is suc-cessful and we have an agreed sense for 'Visual Given'. The question arises: do we *see* such a given? Now *ex hypothesi* all of its parts are visible, and this might seem to entail that the given is itself seen. However, bearing in mind that the concept of the given is that of a pre-organizational item, and seeing entails a preferential descrip-tion and presumably therefore also organization, the very idea of 'seeing the given' looks to verge upon contradiction. In any case it seems to me that the most natural sense to attach to the question we are asking is, whether visual experiences can exist in which *no* organizing/interpreting of perceptible parts occurs. Then even though this extreme requirement must surely be unrealizable, it is illuminating to spell out just why it is so.

We are looking for a visual experience whose internal object is to be described by the bare specificatory piecemeal description of the monocular visual field in terms of two-dimensionally ordered *minima*: a mere litany expressible in no preferential order. And it must be an experience such that synthesizing descriptions like 'many of——' can have no application in its content, for a feature of collective experience is that it is achieved at the expense of its constituents. Just as we tend in normal vision to single out objects at the expense of their surrounds, rather like a focused photograph in which the background is a blur, so we notice a host of golden daf-fodils at the expense of the individual daffodils, and a sort of attentive blur appears *within* the crowd of daffodils. In short, attentive preference occurs. But in the conjectured seeing of the given, preferences of all kind give way to absolute egalitarianism. And so on.

In sum, we are looking for a visual experience that is devoid of all synthesis and meaning, and therefore of both figure-on-ground and collectivization structures as well as physical interpretations, whose proper description is an ordered litany of point-values expressible in any old order. Plainly, such experience is not even in principle possible. But I specify the full extremity of the requirements, in order to justify the claim that the visual given is not visible. Such a conclusion is of great relevance when we come to give an account of the *very first stages* of the formation of the visual experience—an important question considered in the final part of this chapter, Sections 6 and 7.

(b) The first mediator

(1) I turn now to the delineation of a close relative of the visual given. Before I can do so, I must clarify several minor matters.

It is worth noting how perceptual mediation reveals its existence to mankind gen-erally. It does so in two ways. On the one hand through the several descriptions of the one visual experience *automatically available* to any competent speaker apprised of the empirical facts of the case. Thus, suppose a man sees a blue wall in front of him *as* 'a blue wall'. Then while I can intentionally characterize his experience as 'seeming to see a blue wall', I can also describe his experience extensionally as 'seeing a blue expanse', 'seeing the paint situated on a wall', 'seeing the surface of a wall', 'seeing the side of a wall', 'seeing a wall', and so on. Any competent speaker aware of the relevant empirical facts can variously describe this one experience in terms of multiple objects which are all given extensionally to the perceiver's atten-tion. Meanwhile it is evident that, since the paint is nearer the viewer than the wall and sight is a directional sense, the blue of the wall must derive from that of the paint rather than vice versa. Then these factors together determine the common knowledge of mediators. That is, it is the above interchangeability of objects, taken in conjunction with the order of epistemological priorities, which reveals the pres-ence of perceptual mediation to any competent speaker.

But there is one other way through which we might come to know of perceptual mediation: namely, through *philosophical inquiry*. A man might come to believe, as a result of philosophical considerations, that sense-data exist and mediate the per-ception of material objects. In short, while some mediators are overtly given to us all, others are matters for philosophical debate. Then as a general though not invari-able rule that debate will concern epistemologically proximate items like sense-data and light.

The operative principle is, that when an item is mediated through a sequence of items, the mediators must be seen and therefore as a matter of course *attentively* individuated by the subject. But they need not be *cognitively*, nor therefore also descriptively, individuated by him. Those familiar mediators openly accessible to competent speakers doubtless as a general rule are cognitively individuated, but the same need not be true of mediators whose very existence is disclosed only through philosophical inquiry. Thus, while some mediators can be visible and unproblematically accessible, others can be at once visible and seen and yet cognitively hidden.

(2) These considerations are relevant when we attempt to discover which mediators lie epistemologically closest to a perceiver. Since mediators cannot be infinite in number, and a chain of epistemological dependence relates these items, there must always be something which is the epistemologically nearest mediator. This item I shall call 'The First Mediator'. From what we have seen, its identity must be a matter for dispute. No doubt colour-brightness and contour figure in its description in the case of sight, but it is a matter for philosophical debate which *entity* is the first bearer of that colour-brightness and contour.

What can we say about the character of the first mediator? In particular, what do we know about its *descriptive content*? Well, a perceptual mediator is a perceptible item which is epistemologically closer than the perceptibles it mediates. Indeed, each mediator is both explained by and revelatory of those epistemologically more distant mediatees: for example, we see white light because it is reflected off the mountain side it reveals. It follows that the veridical mental or internal representation of each mediator (e.g. of a covering of white snow) must involve *one interpretation less* than the representation of its neighbouring mediatee (e.g. of an object-side). And it follows also that the representation of the first mediator cannot involve interpretation of any kind. On the other hand experience of the first mediator must already embody *synthesis*, since all visual experiences have preferred descriptions. Here we have a significant constraint upon the descriptive content of the first mediator.

The first mediator will therefore be an item which is seen via the seeing of nothing else, whose description is non-interpretational yet such as to incorporate syntheses of the kind of structuring and collectivization, and such also as to answer the philosophical entity-disputes. Accordingly, if (say) sense-data exist, the first mediator in a particular seeing might be something of the ilk of (say) a round red patch which is a sense-datum. Now it is natural to say of each mediator that it 'goes beyond' its predecessors in the line of mediators. Then at the very beginning of this line stands a mediator which 'goes beyond' nothing else. This is 'the first mediator'. Since it goes beyond nothing, it must be immediately accessible. Since it is immediately accessible, it must in some sense simply be *given* to us. Here we have a *second* perfectly natural sense for 'The Perceptual Given'. Namely, the first mediator in any line of mediators.[3]

---

[3] But I emphasize that throughout this chapter I employ the expression in the original sense.

(c) Does the given help to constitute the first mediator?

How are these fundamental items related? This question is of some interest, for it is directly relevant to a phenomenon which I hope soon to characterize: namely, what one might call 'the birth of the visual experience'. That is, the process whereby the fully fledged visual experience somehow arises out of and at the prompting of the visual given.

How does the given relate to the first mediator? It is clear that these two important and 'early' variables in the perceptual situation play very different roles in that situation. One difference in their causal properties is, that we can see the first mediator but not the given. Now the concept of *seeing the given* is not that of seeing some kind of primitive psychological entity, it is that of a certain kind of seeing, viz. a seeing of the contents of the visual field without organization and interpretation. Since the attention is not a *tabula rasa* for the visual field to write upon, this is impossible. Then how do the given and the first mediator relate? Well, we know that the *minima* which are 'given' occur in the same visual site as the several visual mediators—amongst which sits the first mediator. Ought we to conclude that elements of the given constitute the first mediator? It seems a natural conclusion. But we must first take a closer look at the facts. At first blush it looks as if two theoretical accounts might be possible, depending on one's theoretical commitments.

Consider an element of the given: say, a blue point in the visual field. This point is part of the given, being part of the psychological stimulus to visual experience. But is it a distinct psychological existent? Only if sense-data exist. Now if sense-data exist, they are the first perceptible object of the attention, and thus the first mediator. Therefore this blue sense-datum point must go to constitute the first mediator, and so also must the given as such. Suppose on the other hand that sense-data do not exist, and that the blue point is the point-appearance of light/of side/of object (say)—all showing in the one visual site. Then whichever of these happens to be the first mediator, the point-parts of the given will still help constitute the first mediator. Thus, the general conclusion holds, independently of the existence of sense-data. That is, the parts of the given go to constitute the first mediator.

Accordingly, the first mediator must come to awareness when *the mind is such that* the given has a particular causal power. Namely: to cause a *noticing*, whose material object is constituted out of *elements of itself*, which is the *interpretation* of nothing, and which exhibits *structural/organizational* properties (like 'round', 'scattered right and left', etc.). This formulation spells out some of the important links between these two 'early' fundamentals of the visual perceptual situation.

(d) A note on the concept of the visual field

I have assumed throughout this discussion that there exists something called 'the visual field', which is psychological in status, and inserted by the ocular system into the mind as 'psychological stimulus to visual experience production' (which is its *natural function*). Some may think this an unwarranted reification of a mere property of visual experience, and tantamount to endorsement of sense-datum theory. Well, it may be that implicitly it is so, since the facts of the matter cannot but 'hang together', and sense-datum theory seems true. However, the theory of the visual given is no more than a theory to the effect that both psycho-physical causation *and* mental causation occur, and in sequential manner, in the genesis of visual experience. Then it seems to me that this theoretical position can be affirmed in its own right without overt appeal to sense-datum theory, and irrespective of whether we conceive of the visual field in reified terms as a distinct autonomous psychological existent.

Nonetheless, I shall now advance a few considerations which put the existence of a visual field so conceived beyond doubt. A first decisive consideration is the following. Namely, that there *must* exist as a real empirical possibility a visual field of determinate character in which *nothing* of a publicly visible nature is on view. And such an empirical possibility is not difficult to realize. It is a significant fact that, provided a human subject has a workable visual system and is conscious, he *must* have a visual field: maybe no more than a black visual field—though at least that, and anyhow a black visual field is not a black nothing. It is a notable fact that we know of no way of erasing the visual field in a conscious human who can see. Thus, a complete absence of outer and inner physical stimuli to the visual system of a conscious being, inevitably results in a steady unchanging black or dark-grey. Under these extreme conditions the visual field continues to exist, continues to have an angular amplitude and colour-value, indeed a colour-value which might have been (say) yellow had we been differently constituted.

Then *what is it*, under those extreme conditions of *null stimulus*, that shows as (say) grey in this visual field? What is the *bearer* of grey? It is no good claiming the visual field is not grey, that all is illusory. Nor that, while the visual field is grey, *nothing* shows as grey. Cannot we attend and dis-attend variously to this physically determined unchanging phenomenon? This grey expanse stubbornly retains its existence and colour and intensity, independently of one's state of mind in general and attention in particular. Then the Causal Theory of Perception forbids that the bearer be a public physical perceptible. And since the colour is immediately near-infallibly perceived by its owner alone, whatever is grey in this null-stimulus situation must surely be psychological in status. Call that grey something Z_ψ. Then Z_ψ must be a sufficient condition of a grey visual field. And, since one can know irrefutably one's visual field is grey, Z_ψ must be a necessary condition also. Therefore 'The visual field is grey' must at the least affirm the existence of the grey psychological something Z_ψ which shows as grey in the null-stimulus situation.

(e) A preliminary sketch of the formation of the visual experience

There can be little doubt that Z_ψ is the first mediator in any visual perception. It is organizationally constituted out of the given as immediate object for the attention by the mind's imposing a structural order upon the already spatially ordered given. Then this *structural order* transfers automatically onto the remaining mediators and mediatees in that perception. That is, onto those items as they come to awareness in the attentive event.

Now the phenomenon of *perceptual interpretation* is something quite other than the above automatic transfer of structural properties onto the sequence of mediators/mediatees. It takes place when the mind constitutes, at whatever instigation, the *several internal objects* of the one and same perceptual experience ('seeming to see white *stuff*', 'seeming to see a white *surface*', etc.). And it has no binding need of mirroring the actual string of mediators/mediatees, even though it will typically mirror some at least. Thus, I might see a blue patch/surface/roof/etc. merely (and erroneously) *as* a blue patch of sky. And in any case the *very first interpretation* in the visual experience invariably represents a point located some distance down the line of sight: it never mirrors the first, nor for that matter the second mediator in that line. The reason is, these last are not directly given to self-consciousness. (Hence the need for philosophy at this point.) For example, no experiential interpretation corresponds to seeing that causally vital mediator, the light which is situated at our retinas. Perceptual experiential interpretation is the result of the mind's bringing to bear upon the already structured mediators which are given to the attention under minimal pre-interpretational headings, certain mental facts which permit the experiencing mind to go beyond that data. It takes place wholly independent of one's philosophical convictions, and goes on automatically and invisibly somewhere within the mind. This thought conducts us into the remaining theme of this chapter.

6. The Formation of the Interpretational Objects of Visual Experience

(a) The minimum visual experience

The question I want now to consider is: how does it come about of any particular visual experience that it has the *internal objects* it has? Is there a general form to the explanation of their existence? Can a general account be given of the constituting of the visual experience? I shall approach this important question through a subsidiary issue.

What is the *minimum possible* content of monocular experience? Now when visual experience occurs, attentive confrontation with a visual field occurs. Then in a good sense the visual field is a two-dimensional entity (arising out of the directional character of sight). While it may perhaps be described as 'two dimensions in three dimensions' in the case of binocular vision—which is akin to confronting a surface convoluting in three-dimensional space, a surface is nonetheless a two-dimensional creature. Thus, two variables suffice to *single out* any point in a binocular visual field (a third dimension telling us no more than where in depth the already individuated point lies). But anyhow the z-dimension is *inessential* to visual experience and the xy-dimension essential: there *need be* no visibility in the depth-dimension: depth can be invisible as breadth not. Thus depth can be no part of the minimum content of visual experience.

Accordingly, the following seems to encapsulate the bare necessities of visual experience. An attentive confrontation with a two-dimensional visual field of some colour-bright character, whose parts are experienced as lying in various directions out from the body,[4] in which a measure of two-dimensional spatiality is recorded. Depth need not be experienced, nor interpretational 'going beyond' to physical phenomenal types. We approximate to such a minimum when we shut our eyes in broad daylight and visually attend. We notice a visual field that is a unified sensuous continuity, spread out in a continuity of body-relative directions facing out from the body. It may be that we also see the occasional circle or line or pattern, but as a general rule we remark little else. Noteworthy absentees are depth and objects of any kind. While one can whittle away here and there at this reduced content, one cannot I think delete much. It seems reasonable to assume we are here close to the minimum.

(b) The first work of the attentive-system

Whenever we visually experience, a content *at least* matching this minimum must have been constituted by the attention out of the visual given. The insertion into the mind of the two-dimensionally ordered psychological stimulus to vision, namely the visual given, will have helped engender a visual experience with at least such an internal object. While visual givens sometimes exist in the absence of visual experience, if visual experience does occur then the given must have acted in causal consort with parts of the mind, and inevitably with the distribution of the attention, in generating an attentive event whose content at least matches this minimum. Colour-bright continuity will be present, a measure of two-dimensional organization, and body-relative directions out from the body.

The suspicion arises, that the construction of such a minimum internal object might be the *first work* of the attentive-system in the constituting of visual experiences generally. And yet this is no more than a suspicion. Could it not instead be the case that while the above measure of organizational 'synthesis' of the given *must* be accomplished in any visual experience, it is accomplished *alongside* other inessential interpretational 'syntheses', and so cannot be the *first work* of the attention? Might not several *distinct* internal objects come into being simultaneously, constituting a whole whose parts relate merely additively to one another? In my view not, and I shall soon offer reasons why the internal structure of the visual experience cannot be of this kind.

[4] For in general we individuate sensations, whether bodily or merely perceptual in type, in terms of body-relative public physical space.

(c) The causal theory of internal-object formation

When I speak of the 'first work' of the attention, I am thinking of *causal-explanatorial* rather than temporal priority. The theory of experience-formation I propose is, that the attention in the first place assembles an internal object consisting of a two-dimensionally organized array of colour-bright shapes, and that this attentive accomplishment *helps explain* the acquisition by the very same experience of additional internal objects of a more ambitious interpretational character. Thus, the theory is that the least ambitious internal object functions as a *part-cause* of the additional interpretational and environment-sensitive internal objects, which gather in the instant around it like the formative layers of a pearl. If short, the relation between the several internal objects of the visual experience must be anything but merely additive. This is the theory which I shall defend.

This development is something quite other than what might be called 'the journey outwards of the attention'. That is, the state of affairs whereby the one event of visual noticing acquires a whole string of non-identical *material objects*, viz. the mediators. This last is non-occurrent in character. Because certain causal relations are realized, certain entities come to be objects of a single attentive event—but nothing need *happen* for this to be so. My present concern is with something altogether different: the acquisition by a single visual experience of a series of *internal objects* (which typically match most of the mediators). This is truly phenomenal, since an experience here suffers transformation in its intrinsic character. While time does not separate the appearance of each internal object, my contention is that causality does. It is an occurrent and not merely relational matter.

The question is: why should we believe that constituting a mere two-dimensionally organized internal object from the given, explanatorily precedes the acquisition of (say) three-dimensional material object internal objects? Well, there can be no guarantee that such an enrichment of content will in fact occur. Nor guarantee that any such enrichment of content will match any actual material objects of vision, viz. any mediators. No argument exists to the effect that if the attention acquire (say) N external objects, it will have a correspondingly enriched content of N such internal objects. Nor vice versa. The visual experience might be rudimentary in the extreme, remaining at the minimal content of mere 2D-organized shapes, even as the attention ranges far and wide. And vice versa. My question is: when enrichment of content does occur, what explains it? In answer, I have proposed a specific causal theory, one which sets out from the minimal visual experience.

(d) Indirect explanation

(1) Once again: why should we believe that the mind constitutes out of the visual given a merely two-dimensionally ordered internal object, and that this *explanatorily precedes* the acquisiton of more ambitious internal visual objects?

Why should not the unambitious and the ambitious internal objects come into being *independently?*

One obvious reason why not is that internal objects *constrain* one another, and in the direction required by the causal theory. Thus, I cannot seem to see a red cube in seeming to see a blue circle. This fact at least disposes of any theory of *sheer independence*—and raises the question as to why such constraints exist. Then for the most part the answer is one cast in projective-geometrical terms. The directional character of sight requires that 3D-figures project a given 2D-profile onto a plane at right angles to the line of sight. This implies that only *some* ambitious objects are possible for any given unambitious internal object, and lends some kind of preliminary support to the causal theory. However, it is one thing to dispose of the theory of independence, and another to establish that the requisite dependence is causal from beginning to end. That is, demonstrate the contentious causal theory under consideration.

That task I undertake in Section 7. In the remainder of this present Section 6 I shall fill in the details of that theory. The part of the theory which stands most in need of elucidation, concerns the character of the putative causal relation holding between the internal objects of the visual experience.

(2) The case for believing in the existence of the causal relation, begins its life with the observation that the public items named as less ambitious internal object constitute *evidence* for those named under more ambitious headings. I seem to see a treelike profile and I seem to see a tree, and the presence of a tree-profile in public physical space is evidence for the presence of a tree lying in a certain direction. Then while this might suggest that I seem to see a tree *because* I seem to see a tree-profile, it cannot prove it. Thus, it is possible that my mind, aware that trees embody natural syndromes, simply defers to this regularity in throwing up internal objects which evidence one another. In short, being evidence-for cannot be enough to demonstrate causality. More is needed. In particular, the causal theory seems implicitly to assume the truth of the following problematic claim. Namely, that the fact that the unambitiously named object constitutes *evidence* for the ambitiously named object, actually *plays a part* in the arise of the ambitious object.

(3) I must now say something about the kind of part open to such evidential facts. In my view it can only be *indirect.* The evidentiality in question could be functionally effective in the generation of the internal objects of the visual experience at best only *epiphenomenally* (so to say). Were the visual experience a rational phenomenon, being evidence-for could act *directly* in the genesis of the ambitious object. However, the visual experience is never rational. In this regard it is to be contrasted with the phenomenon to which I have likened it in so many ways: namely, intentional instrumental action. Thus, the one act which falls under a string of intentional headings, generally does so because it is a rational event and because of the agent's understanding of the situation. The fact that a kick to a door constitutes *evidence* for the impending occurrence of a door-opening, plays a *direct role* in

ensuring that the act of kicking was intentional under both 'kicking the door' and 'opening the door'. It is *because* the agent understands that the two events are related as evidence-for and evidenced-by, that an act can come into being which has two such intentional internal objects.

We must not look for anything of this kind for the internal objects of visual experience. While visual experience across time exhibits an intelligibility of kinds, visual experience of the moment is a sheer given to its owner. By contrast actions are often rational, their origins are in general immediately accessible to their agents, and humans are for the most part responsible for their own actions. Perception lies at a polar remove on each count. The famous illusion in which the moon looks larger at the horizon than in the zenith, succinctly makes the point. One might brilliantly fathom the explanation of this illusion—as the illusion stubbornly persists! Its existence is entirely independent of one's knowledge of the reasons for its existence. And in any case those reasons cannot be rational causes—and not because the illusion is some kind of aberrative breakdown of a mental system: it is because no perceptual experience of the moment can be rationally determined. Indeed, there cannot even in principle be such a thing as an immediately given mental cause of the internal objects of the visual experience. One is not accountable for one's visual impressions.

So the relation of evidence-for cannot—in the manner exemplified by intentional action—play a direct part in the arise of the ambitious internal objects within perceptual experience. Just why one ambitious object rather than another comes to be, is a matter upon which immediate (Cartesian) authority is wholly inexistent. The perceptual impression arises with the same bluntness and opacity as the moon illusion. We can at best entertain surmises as to why the visual experience appears in one form rather than in another. Then how can the fact that the unambitiously named object (e.g. tree-profile) is *evidence for* the ambitiously named object (e.g. tree), manage to *play a part* in the development of the more ambitious internal objects of the visual experience? How can the obtaining of external evidential relations between outer mediators constitute reason for hypothesizing a mirror-like causal relation between the several internal objects of the visual experience? What sort of an 'indirect' 'epiphenomenal' role is it that might exist for those external evidential relations?

(e) The model of belief-formation in the non-rational

To see what it might be, it is advisable that we turn to the phenomenon of belief-formation. My suggestion is that a significant likeness exists between the formation of belief in non-rational creatures and the formation of perceptual impressions in rational and non-rational beings alike. Then how is it that animals acquire beliefs? And how does it happen that some of those believings rate as knowings?

Natural selection has much to do with it. We may express the matter thus: that

Nature selected for existence those beings whose mode of belief-formation, in the first place mimics *Nature's regular ways*, and secondly actually exemplifies a kind of internalization of the *specific natural regularity* governing the distinctive subject-matter of the belief. The property which I have in mind travels under the familiar title 'the power of association', but it is I think with more illumination viewed in the above terms. Let me be specific. Regularly experiencing a conjunction between certain items α and β, typically so affects animals that experiencing an example of α tends to generate expectation of β. That is, experiencing the regularity so affects, in this special cognitive regard, just those beings that were selected to have just such a mode of belief-formation. And it is plain *why* they were thus selected: their beliefs tend towards the *true*—bearing in mind Nature's regular ways and their responsiveness to natural regularity—and truth-believers tend to out-survive falsehood-believers. All this is made possible by the fact that animal beliefs concern matters in which simple overt perceptible regularities are the norm. Had it been the case that the perceptible phenomena in the environment manifested only covert or highly complex regularities, animality could not have evolved.

These surface regularities helped select beings whose beliefs were addressed to the effect-phenomenon, viz. β. Given their experience of α, and such a personal and evolutionary history, they expected β—which tended to obtain. Thus, animals prove to be *instruments of prediction* of a kind, and just as valid instruments tend to indicate truth, so animal beliefs tend likewise non-coincidentally towards truth. It is *as if* the perception of α generated mental processes which were an internalization of the objective rationale linking α and β, but of course it is not so. It is often enough so in the case of *rational* animals, who may well understand *why* β occurred. Otherwise, however, not. Explanations do not appear amongst the contents of non-rational animal mental life, and the mental or cerebral processes linking α-perception and β-expectation have nothing to do with comprehension or inference. Rather, they may with illumination be compared (say) to the electrical phenomena linking the contents of a petrol tank and the readings on a fuel gauge.

Now when the environment is in certain fundamental ways the same as that which selected these animals, when β-expectation derives suitably from α-perception, and when β in fact occurs, then the belief generally rates as knowledge. A dog knows he is going for a walk when he see his master approach holding a lead and making the familiar signal noises. On such occasions the veridical belief is *well-formed*, since this belief is suitably caused by the dog's present and past experience. Meanwhile belief or expectation is well-formed in the *rational* when with proper comprehension they come to expect what generally happens. And so we may with justice subsume both examples of knowing under the head: well-derived instances of non-accidental belief in the true. Thus, these rational and non-rational examples of belief-formation satisfy a rule which comprehends both the simple–naturalistic and the more developed rational cases.

(f) Visual experience

The naturalistic mode of belief-formation in non-rational beings provides a model for the formation of visual experience in rational and non-rational perceivers alike. Here, too, we are dealing with a naturally selected mode of origin. Now we have seen that Nature selected beings whose beliefs tend towards the true, and within this group selected in turn those special beings whose mode of belief-formation had the flexibility and scope imported by rational comprehension. We saw also that such 'luxury developments' as this latter rational mutation must necessarily be barred to visual experience, since the perceptual experience of the moment simply comes upon us with the unaccountability of the moon illusion. In sum, whatever causation is responsible for perceptual experience, it must be non-rational non-inferential in type. While the multiple internal objects constrain one another, and those constraints accord with rational principles, reason cannot generate ambitious internal objects out of the less ambitious. Nature simply sees to it that one object arises from the other suchwise that the constraints are operative. And the selective process which led to beings with such interpretational internal objects as content, must have been such that in suitable environments those beings saw what they seemed to see.

Before I move on in Section 7 to arguing for the causal theory, a note on the causal transitions that are our topic. It is interesting that we have no general name for 'veridical seeings'. That is, seeings in which the match of content between seeming to see X, and the seen X, is non-coincidental and the exercise of a *power*. The reason is, that veridical seeing is generally the exercise of a *non-visual* power, viz. the power to put to use contextual knowledge in reading the significance of visual appearances. Strictly speaking it is not the task of *sight* to distinguish bearers of identical appearances. Then I emphasize that the causation of internal objects which here concerns me is one that corresponds to an *achievement of sight*. Thus, the transition from the internal visual object 'round red sphere a foot in diameter' to (say) 'balloon' will mostly not be an instance of the kind of transition that is my topic. Rather, that from 'round red expanse' to 'red sphere' better exemplifies the development of visual internal objects under examination. Appearances lie at the end of this particular line.

7. Demonstrating the Causal Theory of Internal-Object Formation

(a) Résumé, and statement of the problem

(1) The case for the Causal Theory begins with the observation that the nearer mediators relate evidentially to the remoter. Thus, treelike profile in physical space evidences tree in a certain direction, yellow patch evidences the sun, etc. The intuition is that the corresponding internal objects of the visual experience (treelike profile, tree, etc.) somehow *recapitulate* this relation through the less ambitious internal object causing the more ambitious: that one so to say *earns one's way out-*

wards from the unambitious internal object (e.g. white patch) to the ambitious (e.g. mountain) by causal steps (e.g. to snow, to surface, to side) which are in some way *legitimized*. The problem facing causal theorists is, to discover a bridge leading from the evidential relation holding between the public physical mediators to the intuition concerning internal objects. This is the same project as that of discovering the legitimization in question.

It is clear that the evidential relation holding between the mediators on its own proves nothing. If the intuition of an internal recapitulation is to be vindicated, the outer evidential relation must actually *play a part* of a legitimizing kind in determining the internal objects. And any such part has to be *indirect* in character, since the visual experience and its internal objects are non–rationally determined, indeed are of necessity non–insightfully determined. Then the model of belief-formation in the non-rational demonstrated how evidentiality can play just such a decisive but indirect part in the determination of non-rational phenomena. One could call such non-rational determination by evidentiality 'quasi-rationality'.

(2) The time has come to justify the application of this naturalistic model, and in effect to demonstrate the Causal Theory. Let me be specific. I need to show that the evidential relation holding between the mediators explains the existence of the visual internal objects, and does so by determining a *causal relation* between those internal objects. That is, the outer material objects $O_1, O_2, O_3, \ldots$ relate evidentially, and I have to show that this fact explains the existence of the corresponding internal objects $IO_1, IO_2, IO_3, \ldots$, and does so by determining that IO_1 causes IO_2, which causes IO_3, which causes . . . . Then as we just now noted above, this cannot be accomplished *rationally*. It could if (*per impossibile*) we could use the outer evidential relations as rational justification in selecting the internal objects of the visual impression (as actually holds of intentional instrumental action). My suggestion is that the outer evidential relation does in fact determine the internal situation; only indirectly, non-rationally, naturalistically, and in an evolutionary-determined manner that exhibits quasi-rationality of the type encountered in belief-formation in the non-rational. Thus, I hope to demonstrate that the objective evidential relation *non-rationally but quasi-rationally* determines that IO_1 cause IO_2, etc.

(b) Two competing theories of internal-object aetiology

All important in demonstrating the theory are two simple facts. First, that perception is a potential source of *knowledge*. Second, that the visual experience relates *non-systemically* with its objects. We encountered these two fundamental facts earlier in discussing the need for mediators in visual perception. Those same considerations find a place here in examining the formation of the visual experience.

Consider the first of these 'principles'. We know that perception is non-accidentally linked to cognition. Where there is perception, there is latent knowledge. Perception is like money in the bank: it licenses payments, and does so irrespective of whether one knows one has credit. If one perceives something, one is *in a position* to know of that item, whether or not one does know. And the general rule is that one does. Perception has the function in animal life of generating knowledge of the physical here-and-now. Now perception can discharge that function only if the *internal objects* of the perceptual experience tend in general to match the outer objects. The following considerations show why. Non-rational animals automatically believe what they seem to see, naturally believing in the existence of what occurs as the internal object of their visual experiences; and rational animals non-automatically, but unthinkingly and for good reasons, do precisely the same. Then these believings in the internal object tend to be *knowings* of the outer seen object. Accordingly, there must in general be a match between the several internal objects of the visual experience and the outer mediating material objects.

This match cries out for explanation. *Why* does some IO_R (i.e. 'rich' or complex internal object IO_R) correspond in general to O_R (i.e. some 'rich' outer material [and mediated] object O_R)? Now there can be no doubt that *evidence* of the presence of the outer 'rich' O_R must somewhere be *entering the visual system* of the perceiver. How else could latent knowledge and the regular correspondence between the two obtain? Plainly, that evidence enters the system in the form of the retinal image (call it $MO_{Retinal}$). This phenomenon must either itself be, or must at the least somehow imply, evidence of the presence of the outer mediated material object O_R. More, $MO_{Retinal}$ must lead to IO_R in such a fashion that the evidence of IO_R contained in $MO_{Retinal}$ non-accidentally determines IO_R. The question we must settle is: how does it do so?

Two possible causal structures need to be considered: call those two possibilities, Theory A and Theory B (see Figure 20.1).

Theory A asserts:

Theory B asserts:

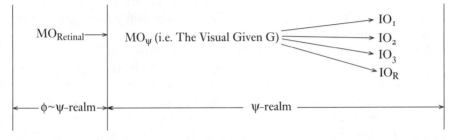

FIG. 20.1

I hope to demonstrate in the ensuing discussion the correctness of Theory A, and the incorrectness of Theory B.

(c) 'Learning from experience' and 'seeing from experience'

(1) It is at this point that the *second guiding principle* comes to our assistance (and does so through putting to use the naturalistic belief-formation model for the formation of visual experience). The above 'principle' reminds us that the physical objects of vision relate extra-systemically with the working of the visual system, yet manage to relate in the special regular way necessary for visibility. As intentional instrumental action allows the will to enlarge its scope and range beyond the body, through utilizing regular relations which connect it suitably with what lies outside the motor system, so mediated perception permits the attention to reach beyond the immediate sensuous objects of experience to items which lie outside the visual system. In either case a regular systemic connection manages to unite with a regular a-systemic bond lying beyond itself, and extend thereby the scope of the mind.

The a-systemacity is of the utmost importance. Consider for a moment the implications of Theory B. Theory B posits a causation of IO_R at the hands of MO_ψ (the Visual Given), a causation which is unmediated by IO_1, IO_2, IO_3, and posits the same kind of unmediated causation of IO_1, IO_2, and IO_3. Now remember that our aim is to explain the *natural correspondence* between the internal IO_R and the outer object O_R, which we know to be causally mediated by the phenomenon $MO_{Retinal}/MO_\psi$. Then the implication of Theory B is that this correspondence is 'just a fact', that the internal object IO_R 'just' corresponds with the outer object O_R. Thus, it assumes a natural correspondence of a *quite different order* from the above between a perceived outer object O_R and the mind. In effect, it assumes a systemic connection. That is, a relation such as we might discover were we to learn (say) that bodily organ α functionally needs and transforms the highly specific organic compound Q, *and* that some other bodily organ β functionally and wholly independently manufactures precisely Q! Only if the outer object O_R related *systemically* with the visual system could O_R and IO_R 'just' correspond. How otherwise could the visual system be in harmony with the evidential bonds linking the external items O_1, O_2, O_3, and O_R? What does it know of the ways of working of the environment? Unless of course it were, in a virtual or 'so to say' manner, to know them all in advance—which is tantamount to systemically binding the visual system to the outer visual objects!

The appeal to the naturalistic model of belief-formation in the non-rational, implicitly recognizes the a-systematicity of the connection. It comprehends that just as it is of the essence that animals 'learn from experience', so likewise it is of the essence that they 'see from experience'. That is, their visual experiences must be sensitive to and shaped in part by their visual experiential history. The regularity put to work in perception and action lies in a certain respect midway between the merely haphazard irregular and the systemically bonded. Animality must as such be sensitive both to the uniformities *and* the vagaries of experience. Animals must respond not merely to familiar regularities in experience, but to *novel* regularities: indeed, to novel and unexpected regularities which replace or *overturn* old ones. This in no way conflicts with the need and even necessity for an innately-endowed determinant in perceptual experience: 'we see from experience' is perfectly consistent with 'we see by inheritance'. If 'x' stands for the percentage of the determination of cognitively significant processes by experience in the animal, then the true situation is always expressed by $0 < x < 100$: x being nearer to 0 in the insect—where innate 'programming' factors count for so much; while x will be nearer to 100 in more-developed animals—whose flexible openness to the lessons of experience is so enhanced. Innate factors will *always* be operative in the determination of animal visual experience, but never suchwise as to shake off the susceptibility to experiential factors.

(2) The upshot is, that the transition from MO_ψ to IO_R cannot be presumed upon in advance. The ultimately unanticipatable nature of the publicly perceptible world, its actual ways of working, must find representation in that transition. Therefore experience must be engaged in one way or another. That way is naturalistic and non-rational. The approved model points the way. Nature selected those beings whose visual experiences were determined by regularities in experience in such a manner as to constitute an 'internalization' of the outer regularities—exactly as happened in the case of non-rational belief-formation. In this way the essential *ambiguity* of perceptual experience finds due recognition. Thus, the transition from the mediator treelike profile to tree object is *as such* capable of being overturned by experience, and Nature selected beings whose visual internal objects would in the face of such unexpected experience mutate correspondingly in a way which 'tracked' reality. That is, beings who—faced with sustained experience of a novel regularity and the overthrow of the old—would come eventually in the one experience to at once both seem-to-see-profile-P (hitherto of trees) *and* seem-to-see-X (where X is something other than a tree), directly and as a result of that sustained (though novel) experience. In short, beings who 'see from experience'.

Ambiguity, and the essential responsiveness to experience, requires—not merely mental causation (which holds after all between MO_ψ and IO_R)—but a mental causation which manages to *interpose between MO_ψ and IO_R* the causal mediation of IO_1 and IO_2 and IO_3. Only thus can the responsiveness to the contingent regular evidential links binding the outer objects O_1, O_2, O_3, and O_R, reliably determine a general matching correspondence between the internal object IO_R and the outer mediated material object O_R. Just as we never 'just' see material objects, but see them only through seeing non-identicals which relate regularly with them, so we never 'just' harbour internal objects such as IO_R which naturally match the outer object O_R. As we earlier remarked—and it is a direct consequence of the essential openness to experience of animality on cognitive matters—we must 'earn our way' outwards if we are to harbour internal objects which naturally so match up with the physical environment. It must be both mediated (by internal objects like IO_1, etc.) and legitimized (by our having been selected as natural 'instruments' reliably responsive to the contingent regularities in the environment). In this way the (earlier noted) constraints exerted upon one another by the internal objects, whereby (say) I cannot seem to see a red cube in seeming to see a blue circle, become readily understandable. We merely build upon the first in a causal manner which is determined by our 'instrumental' properties.

(d) The parallel between physical action and visual experience

Thus, the least ambitious internal object of the visual experience functions as *part-cause* of the additional interpretational and environment-sensitive internal objects, which gather in the instant around that germinal core like the formative layers of a pearl. For the visual experience is at once constituted out, and at the same time completes, an instantaneous causal sequence which is internal to its own being. In short, the experience incorporates within itself an instantaneous history—if that is not a contradiction in terms.

There is a striking parallel to be drawn between this developmentalist sequence, and a comparable phenomenon encountered in the formation of bodily action. Here, too, there is what one might describe as a germinal core. I am referring to the event of willing, which begins with the activation of the motor-mechanism, and spreads out causally and developmentally as far as the limb-movement that is 'willed'. These developments are inessential burgeonings in an event whose essence is already realized—as willing (for striving is the essence of bodily actions). Thus, it is not that the event of willing *causes* the activation of the motor-mechanism. Neither is it the case that the event of willing is to be identified with the *first event* in that activation. Rather, the event of willing begins (and is already a willing) with the beginning of the developmental sequence, being initiated by phenomena like desire and intention, and is complete (as a limb-moving) only by the time of the willed limb-movement. This is because the willing, and activation of the entire sequence, are one and the same phenomenon.[5] Then all of this is incorporated into the single act of moving a limb, just as a visual experience incorporates into itself the sequential formation of internal objects.

Despite these significant similiarities, the unlikenesses between these situations should also be noted. In particular, whereas the internal sequence of the motor-mechanism exemplifies a nomic regularity, the internal visual experiential sequence does not. The latter, but not the former, can be affected by repeated experience. Hence it comes about that we 'see by experience' (as well as 'by inheritance'). By contrast, one might say that we move our limbs solely 'by inheritance' (i.e. through inherited constitution).

---

[5] See B. O'Shaughnessy, *The Will*, Vol. 2: 212–14, 286 (ix), CUP, 1980.

(e) The origin of the visual experience

The origin of the visual experience is represented diagramatically in Fig. 20.2: the arrows indicating either 'causings' (as happens between the internal objects, and between *some* of the mediators) or else 'causal bondings' (as happens between such mediators as sides and surfaces).

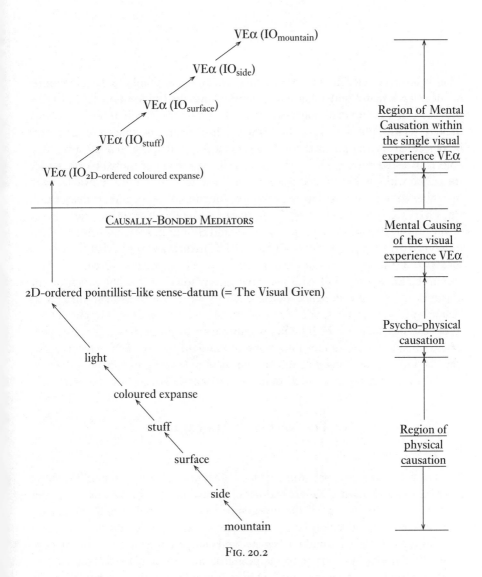

$VE\alpha$ ($IO_{mountain}$)

$VE\alpha$ (IO_{side})

$VE\alpha$ ($IO_{surface}$)

$VE\alpha$ (IO_{stuff})

$VE\alpha$ ($IO_{2D\text{-ordered coloured expanse}}$)

CAUSALLY-BONDED MEDIATORS

2D-ordered pointillist-like sense-datum (= The Visual Given)

light

coloured expanse

stuff

surface

side

mountain

Region of Mental
Causation within
the single visual
experience $VE\alpha$

Mental Causing
of the visual
experience $VE\alpha$

Psycho-physical
causation

Region of
physical
causation

FIG. 20.2

569

21

Appearances

The visual experience in the instant comes into existence thanks to the joint efforts of the attention and understanding, prompted into operation in the first place by the emergence in/for consciousness of visual sensations given merely directionally in body-relative physical space. In this way consciousness becomes aware, not just of objects at a distance in three-dimensional physical space, but of structured objects in a structural mode. In short, typically we recognize those objects: we see them, and with justification, as what they are; and tend to acquire knowledge with matching content. In this way the cognitive function of perception is discharged. But what exactly *is it* that we see? We do not see the temperature or electrical charge of the object. By contrast, we see its colour and lay-out in space. Wherein lies the difference between properties of this kind? The natural answer is, that these latter form part of the *appearance* of the object: it *looks* red, round, but scarcely anything else in the same sense. Indeed, this seems strictly to be all that one gets from the object in the visual experience, nothing but its look. Not its temperature, or its valency if it is an element, or a limitless array of other properties. Merely its look, its appearance, behind which lie an unending array of properties of diverse kinds. These considerations lead me into an inquiry into the nature of the whatever it be that the object does thus give to consciousness in visual perceptual experience. What is this badge of sorts which 'doubles', and look-alikes generally, share?

1. The Nature of Appearances

(a) Introduction

What is an appearance? Some will say that there is no such thing, counselling us not to be bemused by what is a mere manner of speaking. Whether or not this is how matters stand, the concept of the appearance seems nonetheless to be completely indispensable to us, given the kind of lives humans lead. How could we make use of the sense of sight if we could not register and compare the look or appearance of things? In any case, it is certain that appearances matter vastly to us. Think of 'the face that launched a thousand ships'. Here we are talking of the peculiar efficacy in human life of a mere visual appearance. It was the *look* of Helen's face, rather than its chemical or electrical or pheronomic properties, that caused such a furore.

570

Again, the arts of painting, sculpture, and architecture, are more or less exclusively concerned with visual appearances, while the film, drama, and even opera, address themselves in part to our capacity to respond to visual appearances. Importance may not be everything, but it strongly suggests we are dealing with something more than a myth.

The next thing to be said about appearances is, that the concept gives every sign of being at once bona fide and rule-governed. For example, we would all I think agree that, short of radical change in the human species as a whole, appearances necessarily *supervene* upon the physical properties of the bearer, so that if the look of a painting changes in any respect whatsoever, something absolutely must have happened to the paint. In addition we have the precise and valuable concept of the visual facsimile or 'double', which is the concept of one who is visually indistinguishable from another, and therefore of one who *shares a visual appearance* with another: a fact which shows that appearances must be such a kind of thing as to be transcendent of their bearers.

This latter observation provides a clue to the nature of the appearance. It reminds us that one and the same visual appearance can find instantiation in distinct individuals, which in turn suggests that a visual appearance might be a complex universal, compounded presumably out of colour, brightness, and spatial appearance. Accordingly, the claim that there are no such things as visual appearances, which some people may be inclined to make, could perhaps be better recast into the following unexceptionable assertion. It is not that the word 'appearance' is devoid of sense. And neither is it that those who make use of the concept of the appearance are the bemused victims of a mere manner of speaking. It is rather that the complex universal that is a visual appearance does not find instantiation in an object through designating some further individual which stands in close and special relation to the bearer of the appearance. In other words, not only is a visual appearance not something of the ilk of an ineffable covering skin or shell (or whatever it be), it is not any sort of inner psychological analogue of them either, for instance a construct out of visual sensations. The reason being, that it is not an individual.

(b) The uniqueness of visual appearances

(1) It is interesting how we drift all the time from talking of appearances to talking of *visual appearances*. Why? Is it because of a simple prejudice in favour of the visual? I think it is for a better reason than that. I think it is because the only appearances material objects have are visual appearances. This is not to say that the only sensory qualities they have are visual, nor that they alone have appearances. It is to deny to smell and taste and sound, and the properties disclosed to touch, the property of being part of the appearance of their material object owner or source.

What is the rationale of this exclusion? Better, why is there such a thing as the visual appearance of a material object? Two properties, both possessed by sight, are I think responsible. The first is, that when in sight the attention lands upon a colour it lands thereby *in addition* upon its material object bearer; the second is, that it lands upon the material object *in and through* (or 'in virtue of') landing upon its colour or brightness value. In other words, the visual attention manages to pick out material objects, and does so through picking out the secondary qualities of the sense.

Sight differs in the first respect from smell, taste, and hearing, and differs in the second respect from touch. Thus, when I notice the smell of an object I do not thereby notice the object that is its source; and this is because, thanks to the inexistence of anything one could call a 'smell field', and *a fortiori* the absence of mapping relations from object onto such a field, attentive individuation of smell sources is not possible. While the attention encounters the appearance-clothing (as one might say) in the case of the three sensuous senses, it does not encounter a material object owner to suit. It is precisely the other way around with the non-sensuous sense of touch. While the attention does in touch manage to land upon individual material objects, it does not do so in and through (or 'in virtue of') landing upon any tactile analogue of colour or brightness: for example, through our noticing its furry feel or its coolness. This lack of sensuous mediation in the case of touch is doubtless internally linked with the fact that tactilely we individuate objects across time through spatial phenomena rather than instantaneously via phenomena of sense. Various philosophers have noted this immediacy. Berkeley in *A New Theory of Vision* when he claimed that the 'proper and immediate object of touch' is the material object itself, which is to say that no secondary quality is or could be to touch what colour or brightness are to sight; Wittgenstein also, it may be, when in his 1946–7 lectures he described the idea of 'tactile sense-data' as a mere 'stunt' (though we will shortly give reason why the concepts of appearance and of sense-datum must be sharply distinguished). In a word, in touch the attention encounters the potential owner of the appearance-clothes (as one might say) but no sense-clothes to match. Only in sight do these properties come together, only here is the dual requirement satisfied. And this is why I claim that material objects have but one appearance: a visual appearance. It may be that coffee-stuff has an olfactory appearance, and this turns upon whether the attention passes automatically from smell to bearer, and it is in any case certain that light and movement share with material objects the property of having a visual appearance. Yet neither fact affects the important truth, that the only appearance that material objects possess is their look.

(2) This is a contingent proposition. First of all, it is a contingent proposition that objects have an appearance at all. Indeed, it is sheer contingency that anything physical has any appearance whatsoever. Thus, material objects would have had no appearance if sight had either not existed, or had taken a more primitive form in which mapping relations from visual field onto object-space were non-existent. And object appearances would in general be non-existent if sense-perception was confined to touch (something which would constitute a mighty privation for animal kind, but scarcely a metaphysical disaster for man or the World). The second thing to note is, that material objects might have had several distinct appearances. For

example, if other senses had existed which shared with sight the property of enabling us differentially to individuate material objects in a sense-field. In that case the good-(look)ing might simultaneously be bad-(something-else)ing; for even though mapping relations would hold between the two senses, and a formal similarity exist therefore between sight and the novel sense, that resemblance need not suffice to overcome the possibly deleterious effect of a wholly dissimilar sense-content: that is, of dissimilar mediating secondary qualities. (Think of the effect of garish make-up.)

Then because sight is a contingent attribute of animality, while touch, taken as it seems we must take it in a broad enough sense to encompass the sheer capacity to encounter and locate obstacles through awareness of our own limbs, verges upon necessity, we may make the following summary claim. Parodoxically, it is because there need not have been such a thing as sight that there can be such a thing as the visual appearance of a physical object, while it is because there had to be such a thing as touch that there can be no such thing as a tactile appearance. This is because appearances depend upon secondary qualities, and therefore upon senses which are gross contingencies.

Finally, we must note that appearances are relative to observer and point of view. Objects look different from inside and outside, different to the colour-blind and to animals with different colour vision, and they show more or less of their appearance according as we glimpse more or less of the object. For the most part when in normal conversation we speak of an object's appearance, we are concerned with the appearance of the object to normal-sighted humans from outside and nearby, which is to say from the standpoint from which we visually individuate it from its fellow *visibilia*. That is, from the point of view whereby we can determine the shape and the colour (to us) of its exterior. I follow this practice in the discussion.

(c) The nature of the appearance

(1) And so an appearance exists when an item can in the first place come perceptually to the attention, and in the second place do so in and through the coming to the attention of its secondary qualities, which is to say in and through the coming to attention of a perceptual sensation. When a veridical double transaction of this sort takes place, that experience is the experiencing of the appearance of the item, and the character of that appearance is determined by the internal object of the experience. More exactly: in the first place, by that element of the internal object that records the secondary quality attributed to the object; and secondly, when the formal properties of the secondary quality are the means whereby the attention individuates its object, by those formal properties also. This enables us to say what an appearance *is*. It is the character with which an item is endowed for the attention, when the item is veridically individuated by the attention through its secondary qualities. This account accords with the supposition that the appearance is a complex universal.

This theory affirms that, when an item comes to the attention though its secondary qualities and is individuated for the attention through their formal layout, the formal properties join the secondary quality in constituting the appearance. This is not applicable to red light as such, which merely looks red, nor to red material stuff as such, which does the same, but holds of material objects. Thus, I characterize the *look* of a balloon, not merely by saying that it *looks red*, but also by saying that it *looks spherical*. The latter formal look joins the former sensuous look of which it is form and without which it cannot exist, in constituting the look or visual appearance of the balloon. While an appearance necessitates that the attention individuates its bearer through its sensuous qualities, it is clear that in the case of material objects it cannot do so through those sensuous qualities alone, but must in addition put to use the formal characteristics of the sensuous property. It is because space is the framework within which we individuate material objects that 'looks spherical' enters the characterization of the visual appearance, and it is because colour-brightness is the sensuous quality through which we experience the object that 'looks red and bright' completes it. In short, it is no accident that the visual appearance is exhausted by the colour-brightness look and the spatial look. Suppose one asks: why should there be two and not twenty-two appearance variables? The answer is, I suggest, simple: colour-brightness comes from the sensuousness of the sense, spatial look from the sense's capacity to projectively map the individuating spatial properties of the object.

Then out of these flimsy two properties, behind which lie a dense and perhaps limitless array of other properties about which they are silent, we assemble the appearance. This functions like a badge or marker through the aid of which we gain epistemological access to those other multitudinous and ultimately more significant properties. For however important appearances in their own right may be—and our interest in beauty and art and general surface glitter show how much—such matters pale in significance besides life and reality (with which we must engage). It is as a guide to such ultimates that appearances find their appointed place in the scheme of things. The natural function of the look is to generate knowledge of its bearer.

(2) Appearances are thus something more than a myth. And yet they are not individuals, unlike material objects or light or sensations. Each of the latter are objects of perception, and are *seen*. Then do we *see* the look of material objects? We see their colour, which is part of their appearance, and we see (say) their sphericity, which is no part of their appearance, even though there is a sphericity look which we at least *experience* when we see their sphericity. But do we *see* that sphericity look? This is tantamount to asking: is the sphericity look something that is there in space, an item which is visible and set some distance away from us? Well, all that seems to be *present* before us in space is, first the colour of the object, second the sphericity of the object, and all that happens when we experience its appearance is that we experience the colour *as* spherically laid out in space. Then whereas we see the object through the mediation of seeing its colour, we do not see it through the mediation of

seeing its sphericity. The seeing of sphericity lacks the epistemological ambiguity that is so central to sensuous mediation, indeed to mediation generally, and it is perhaps this property which ensures that there can be no autonomous sphericity *visibilium*, and determines the immediacy of sphericity perception. Thus, the sphericity look must be disanalogous to the colour look, and the governing concepts dissimilar.

Then it may be stipulation concerning the use of 'appearance' when I say that the internal object of the attentive experience of the colour and shape of an object gives us the content of its appearance. But it is certainly not stipulation when I claim that experiencing the sphericity look *is* noticing the sphericity of the bearer, and *is not* the noticing of *something* that is the sphericity look. These are issues of substance. Accordingly, it is I believe muddled to think: what a strange thing an appearance must be, compounded as it is out of a noticeable quality, a colour, and a merely experienceable non-quality, a sphericity-look! For whereas the look of an after-image is one of its qualities, the look of a red balloon is not I think a quality of the balloon.

These facts are puzzling. But the puzzle probably arises through the assumption that the appearance of a material object must be either an individual, or else a complex quality which is open to the perceptual attention. Neither view is acceptable. The truth is, that there exist complex appearance-concepts, which find instantiation in individuals, and that the suitable or individuative visual experiencing of that individual *is* the experiencing of its visual appearance. And yet it does not seem that we actually set eyes upon an object's visual appearance. The visual experiencing of the look of a material object is not the seeing of that look. Rather, the suitable seeing of the object is the experiencing of its look. Just how this can be so, will emerge when we come to discuss appearances in the round.

(d) Appearance versus sense-datum

(1) Two things follow from the above conclusion. First, regarding sense-data; second, regarding consciousness.

Thus, we do not see the visual appearance of material objects. Rather, we experience their visual appearance when we perceive the bearer to be endowed with precisely those visible qualities which visually individuate it for us. Roughly, the appearance is 'how' or with-what-character the bearer veridically comes through sensation to attentive consciousness. What does this tell us about the relation between appearance and sense-datum? In particular, might the appearance be identical with the sense-datum? I think the suggestion can be rejected forthwith. The reason is, if the sense-datum exists it must be an individual, and on one reading of 'sense-datum' an individual that is seen. Whether the sense-datum is taken to be nothing more problematic than the visual impression, or nothing less problematic than the visual sensation, it remains in either case an individual: on the first reading an individual of type episode of consciousness, which is of course not seen; on the second reading an individual of type sensation, which is I believe seen and in any case certainly noticed. Meanwhile, the appearance of the material object is the character with which it is endowed for the attention when the object is veridically individuated by the attention through its secondary qualities. On either reading of 'sense-datum', the appearance is not a sense-datum.

(2) The second thing to be noticed on the present account of the appearance of objects is, its close tie with attentive consciousness. If appearances are mediated by secondary qualities, appearances must from the start be relative to the minds that experience them, since the secondary qualities of physical objects are relative to the beings for whom they exist. We have already remarked on this fact, and noted in addition that appearances must be from points of view in space. But we shall discover also that appearances are relative, not merely to particular minds and places in space, but to perceptual episodes of the type of awareness-of or consciousness-of, and in a stronger sense than applies with secondary qualities. Exactly in what way this is so, will emerge immediately below as well as in the ensuing discussion.

I think this strong relativity to consciousness is responsible for some of the more interesting properties of appearances. Thus, our interest in the appearance, why we have the concept at all, stems from the fact that epistemologically it is sandwiched between sensation and knowledge. Not being aesthetes to the core, we recognize that the natural function of appearances, and hence also of perceptual sensations, is to generate knowledge of the bearer of the appearance. Then in the case of material objects in space this function can be satisfactorily discharged only if the *understanding* has a causal role to play in the genesis of the experience of the appearance. This is how it comes about that the appearance must be defined in terms of particular consciousnesses-of which are causally sensitive to *cognitive factors* as well as to sheer sensation. Insofar as we hypostatize the appearance, construing it as an individual of the type of sense-datum, we neglect the vital role played by the intellect in the constituting of material object appearances. While sensuous individuals come directly to consciousness without enlisting the labours of the intellect, the intellect is an essential element in the experiencing of the appearance of a spatially complex item like a material object. The full force of this truth only becomes properly apparent when we consider in detail what kind of a thing a material object appearance is.

2. Looks in the Round

(a) Introducing the concept

(1) The following has emerged about the appearance of a material object. In the first place, it is not an individual. Therefore it is neither the object itself, nor any sort of mediator entity through which we make epistemological contact with the object. In particular, it is no kind of psychological entity of the type of sense-datum or complex sensation-construct. Again, it is not a quality of the object, nor even a descriptive conception of the object. Then what is it? It enters experience when the attention encounters the material object through the mediation of the *quale* of

sensation. The experience is not *just* of the object, and neither is it *just* of the sensation-*quale*, but is an experience of the object in a certain sensuous presentation. It is an experience of the object 'thus' sensuously presented. Then that the object can come through to consciousness via such a mode of presentation is at once a contingent property of that object *and* consciousness-dependent in a strong sense. The appearance is essentially tied to episodes in consciousness, to episodes *of* consciousness; and it is this feature which enables concepts and sectors of the intellect to play their part in the phenomenon of sensuous presentation. Rather than being a descriptive conception of the object, the appearance is a way or guise in which we encounter the object 'in the flesh' or intuitively, which is to say *attentively*. The appearance is no representer-entity, but may perhaps be characterized as a representer-*way*: as it were the object simultaneously filtered through sense and mind.

Let us at this point consider the appearance of a material object in a little more detail. What goes to make it up? Not just secondary qualities, but spatial appearances also, indeed three-dimensional spatial appearances. For there can be no doubt that the dimension of depth contributes to the look of things. Is there not a 'convex look'? And surely also there is a distinctive appearance that we experience whenever we see a sphere, 'the sphericity look'—think of a full moon as it is rising. Then is there such a thing as 'the cubical look'? In the sense in which there is '*the* sphericity look' there is not, for cubes looks different from different angles but spheres do not. Then if no views reveal '*the* cubical look', do some reveal '*a* cubical look'? Because only some looks can be presented by cubes, while others such as 'the sphericity look' can never be, we could quite naturally stipulate of any of the looks the cube does present that it is 'a cubical look'. But it would be a misleading stipulation. For it suggests that if a look rates as 'a cubical look', then it cannot also rate as 'a pyramidal look' or any of a limitless array of other looks. And this is false. Absolutely any three-dimensional look that is a view or aspect can be presented by any of an infinity of different shapes. Every three-dimensional view is limitlessly ambiguous. While every such look is necessarily not a look of an infinity of figures, for the sphericity look is necessarily never presented by any cube or pyramid etc., it also necessarily is a look presented by an infinity of other figures.

Therefore the cube must be typical of the species as the sphere is not. And we have just now noted that what we see in a single view of any shape is something *infinitely ambiguous*. Clearly, we make a mighty leap beyond the visual datum in recognizing cube or sphere or any shape whatsoever in a single view. Then how to close the epistemological gap? How do our minds make this transition? If we had no other resources but sight, the only method would be by resort to the visual data given to other points of view in three-dimensional space. Well, we have other resources, and in any case we do in fact identify shapes on the spot. And yet I think we may in general say that when we identify shapes through a single look, the presumption is that the object will present the required array of looks to other points of view. Indeed, this presumption, far from being 'unthinking', functions as a cornerstone in the visual determination of shape. In a word, a relation of profound dependence holds between the visual discoveries of the instant and visual appearances in the round.

(2) These simple facts about the visual appearances of material objects, and generally the primacy of appearances in the round, tend to be recessive and neglected. When we think of appearances our minds fly at once to what meets the gaze in the instant: we talk of views, of elliptical pennies, of perspective, and suchlike. Why this obsession with the single view? Is it that human constructs like photographs and paintings and signs generally lead us away from the realities of visual experience? After all, these images likewise show their 'all' to a single look. Whether or not this is a factor I cannot say. But that it can scarcely be the whole truth, seems likely when we press the question: why in the first place do we respond to two-dimensional representations? And the answer to this question must surely be, that the monocular visual 'given' is two-dimensional in character, which in turn probably derives from the fact that the sense of sight is a *directional* sense (the attention travelling down 'the line of sight' to its object). In any case, we most of the time identify objects and therefore presumably also shapes as well by no more than a single look.

It seems to me then that it is the nature of sight itself, rather than the influences of civilization, that is largely responsible for our tendency to underestimate the extent to which sight is three-dimensional in outlook. Indeed, it is difficult to see how sight could have its colossal informational virtues, ranging as it does across light–years of space, and not be directional in character. It may be that indirectly we are paying for the assets of the sense in our tendency to underestimate the full extent of its three-dimensional commitments. This present discussion may be seen as an attempt to redress something of the wrong that we tend to do to this sense, arising out of its peculiar fusion of two-dimensionality with three-dimensionality. For it is I suggest above all the fact that we see depth only directionally, that leads to a neglect of the equally vital truth that the visual data of the single view rests firmly upon a foundation of 'seeing in the round', or, as one might better express it, 'seeing in the spherical'.

These facts are of more than philosophical interest. They have been remarked far and wide, and most especially in the arts, probably for the reason that an entire world-outlook can find symbolic expression in our methods of representation. Cubism for example has to its credit that it reminds us of the artificiality of a mode of representation that is concerned to reveal no more than a single aspect of its object. After all, we most of the time see material objects *as* such as to present to other points of view aspects of which we ourselves are apprised. Then Cubism, or more precisely the later paintings of Picasso in which this doctrine receives its ultimate justification, works a few such aspects into a visible synthesis which represents something wider than the visual experience of the moment. It goes beyond the visual experience of the moment, but not beyond the momentary experience of the one who sees; that is, beyond the *visual* brand of seeing-as, but not beyond that *extra-visual* variety in which we see the pillow as soft and the pool as inviting. All painting in this sense goes beyond the visual experience of the moment, so that a whole extra-visual world of experience can with luck show in a representation of a single aspect. What is novel about Cubism is that the added dimension that goes beyond the visual experience of the moment, is itself visual in character. I do not mean to suggest that it is *merely* visual, for in hands as great as Picasso's Cubism was a device for liberating into the art of painting forces which had lain dormant under a great tradition, but at the very least visual.

(b) The relation between aspect-looks and looks in the round

(1) We have already noted that, in the sense in which there is such a thing as '*the* sphericity look', nothing counts as '*the* cubical look'. And yet it is certain that 'cubes look one way and spheres another'. Therefore there must in another sense be something that is the cubical look. Hitherto, in speaking of '*the* sphericity look', we have been speaking of the look we experience in the instant, which is a particular aspect-appearance. Then of what do we speak when in a legitimate sense we talk of 'the cubical look'? Evidently, of the look in the round. That is, of something of the same general type as whatever it is that two visually indistinguishable material objects must share. In short, a whole-object appearance in contradistinction to an aspect-appearance. For the look in the round is no artificially concocted creation, no fashionable analogue of theatre in the round or even Cubism. It precisely is the look of a material object. In other words, *the* pre-eminent appearance amongst all appearances.

Then what is it, this look of a material object? At first blush it hardly fits our definition of a visual appearance as 'the internal object of the veridical visual consciousness of its bearer'. For we see objects from angles, but the look in the round is never released to particular standpoints. And yet it does manage to reveal itself as we look at the object from diverse standpoints, and we can at least say which visual phenomena reveal which looks in the round. Accordingly, I will begin this inquiry into the look of an object, by addressing myself to a subsidiary question concerning the visual data which reveal that look. Namely: what are the *visual implications* of (say) looking cubical? To attribute a cubical appearance is, at least by implication, to attribute a near-infinity, not of possible looks from possible positions, but actual looks from actual positions. For example, straight out from any face the cube looks exactly as does a square face of a rectangular parallelepiped from the same angle. And so on *ad infinitum*. Whatever it is to have a cubical appearance, it must be such that the bearer presents an infinite set of determinate three-dimensional aspect-looks to an infinity of points of view. Whatever the having of a single visual appearance of the type possessed by material objects actually is, necessarily it is such that the bearer is the possessor of such an infinitely complex property.

These are the visual implications, in some sense the *very content*, of having a particular appearance in the round. Indeed, a logical equivalance links attributions of the two kinds of looks: for example, 'X looks spherical' is logically equivalent to 'X presents a sphericity look to all places and angles from which its shape can be seen.' So the connection between the two kinds of look must be very close. In fact, one wonders whether looks in the round may not actually be *reducible* to aspect-looks. Whether or not this is so, a puzzle has arisen both over the character of the look in the round and its relation to the aspect-looks through which it is revealed.

(2) One lead to understanding the look in the round is, our undoubted capacity to specify examples of the kind. One imagines that the rules by which we do so ought to put on display the rules by which a whole set of aspect-looks come together to realize some single determinate look in the round.

How do we manage to specify looks in the round? We have merely to append the operator, 'the look of', to the name of an object, 'a rose', and the task is accomplished. However, this valid enough answer already helps itself to the concept of look in the round. What we rather want is a specification which is independent of any bearer, we want a specification which assembles a determinate look so to say from scratch. The most natural answer to this is something absurdly complex. Theoretically, we achieve this goal by listing an infinite set of triples, consisting of direction out from every point on the object's surface, distance out from that point, and attendant three-dimensional aspect-look; and the set must encompass *all* directions and *all* distances from which it is visible (for objects look not merely of different size, but different anyway from different distances). Now this answer gives us what we have asked for, since it suffices to specify a particular look in the round, but it suffers from certain defects—quite apart from the factor of infinitude (which is simply an idealization). One disadvantage is, that we all of us know the look of thousands of objects, but neither think of those appearances in such terms, nor come to learn of them in such terms, nor specify them to others in such terms.

(c) Specifying looks in the round: practical paths

(1) It is worth remembering what we would do to either learn or else acquaint someone else with the look of some material object. Perhaps this will reveal a 'structure', binding together many aspect-looks, which is of such a nature as to realize a single object-look. Mostly, if the object is large we would go for a walk or flight around the object, while if it is small we might perhaps revolve it within our field of view on a disparate series of axes. It will be admitted that for every path followed an infinitude of possible other paths remains neglected. And yet a few such circumambulations or rotations will often suffice to give a person a fair idea of the look of an object. However, we should note that it is one thing to *specify* a look, another to fully display its *content*. Even if after a certain stage it is from the point of view of specification otiose to mention other aspect-looks from other places, from the point of view of content such itemizing can never be otiose. For the visual appearance is expressed, not by an infinite set which suffices to ensure that it is the visual appearance that it is, but by an infinite set which encompasses all possible views of the bearer.

We very often 'structure' our knowledge of appearances in terms of paths followed by observers, to which are appended a corresponding ordered series of aspect-appearances. Such schemas are at once more limited and more local than a total itemizing of positions and views, and they are often direct relics of our own epistemological history in relation to the object. Thus, our knowledge of the look of a tract of landscape is mostly organized along such lines. For example, my knowledge of the look of Hampstead Heath is in the first place limited and partial, since I have little idea what to expect visually from helicopter height let alone wormwards, and is secondly specified largely in terms of particular paths through which I have come to know this land.

So here we have one familiar organizing principle whereby spatial paths can be used to structure our visual knowledge. But it must be recognized that other schemas are possible. For example, we would employ a different schema if we were astronaut-sculptors bent upon discovering the look of an illuminated object in dark outer space, with no fixed stars to guide us in our journeyings. Here we would rely above all on regular repeatable sets of aspect-looks, coming up regularly as we intentionally flew by (say) gyro-compass in chosen directions around the object. Then what is especially interesting about this schema is, that the whole investigatory procedure and the knowledge it leads to, leans openly and explicitly upon the law-abiding character of physical nature. It reminds us of the great truth that, if we are to come to know something as seemingly subjective and consciousness-dependent as the mere look or appearance of material objects, we must depend absolutely upon physical natural law, whether it be in relation to the bearers or the discovers of those object-appearances, and we must in addition depend upon our knowledge of the physical situational facts of the case. And the intellect or understanding must lie at the heart of the entire process.

In each of the above two cases we 'structure' the knowledge in terms of paths traced out by a subject in his role as an observer. Often, but not necessarily, those paths will have been actively and intentionally followed by an observer who perhaps walked or flew, or who maybe turned the item around with his hand; indeed, sometimes the structuring path will have taken account of the speed at which the observer moved around the observed. As we have already noted, knowledge schemas of this kind are usually relics of our epistemological and often active history in relation to the object. Such schemas have this importance, that they guarantee the observer a reliable way of getting from any aspect at one point to another at another, and in the absence of a comprehensive mental map of the region, so that in effect the schema constitutes a sort of epistemological short-cut. But the schema has this additional importance, that it puts on display an ordering principle whereby out of a knowledge of aspect-looks we arrive at a knowledge of a look in the round.

In cases of this sort a limited, associatively bonded, and regional type of knowledge is acquired; and the units of the structure are (say) that look L_1 at point P_1 follows look L_0 at P_0 and is followed by L_2 at P_2, and suchlike. What is missing is knowledge, both spatial and visual, of relations that are independent of particular associative links: for example, whether a more distant prospect would show the constituent elements of L_1 and L_{10} as near or far from one another, or the constituents of L_0, L_5, and L_8 as lying in a straight line. And so on. Visually this object has been mapped by no more than a few associative threads, and the resultant knowledge is both limited and regional (Fig. 21.1).

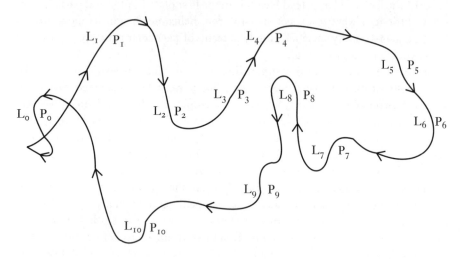

FIG. 21.1

(2) Then common and interesting as such cases are, it is clear they cannot be a satisfactory model for understanding the look of material objects. It may be that our early acquaintance with the look of things took some such form, so that the infant first learned to know a (regional) mere segment of the look of (say) the table and drinking mug via a ritualized sequence of acts on his part. But if this is how things once were, and often still are in the early stages of our visual acquaintance with things, in the case of most objects these practical paths into the space and appearance of things have vanished without trace, are transcended by something universal and ahistorical, and the epistemological ladder has simply been thrown away. The smaller and more familiar the object under consideration, the more this is likely to be the situation. Since I am confident I could recognize a teapot from almost any position, my knowledge of its appearance must have transcended any such ordering principle. All I need know about the teapot is my relation in space to it, and I will know what look to expect, and conversely all I need do is see it from any angle, and I will know that this look is a look that teapots present.

(d) Looks in the round and space

So the practical-path model, through which we hoped to understand how a set of aspect-looks come together to realize a single look in the round, positing association as the synthesizing agent, proves inadequate. The model is too primitive. A simple object like a teapot refutes it, and returns us to the account in terms of an infinite set.

Yet earlier this analysis struck us as unsatisfactory. At this point another theory suggests itself. Thus, we know that cubes cannot present the sphericity look, and spheres cannot present any look the cube presents. It seems there must be entailment relations between looks and the spatial qualities of the bearers of those looks. Then may we legitimately conclude that aspect-looks are merely a priori-determinable projections of the visible parts of an object, and looks in the round no more than the figure thus projected? Has it not become increasingly difficult to keep apart knowledge of looks and knowledge of spatial traits? May we not dispense with these infinite lists and replace them by a single succinct formula or shape? The answer is that we may not. And the reason is that the sense of sight, and visual appearances generally, are mere contingent presences in the world; indeed, even in a world with sight, visibility remains a contingent property both of the physical objects that have it and the parts of the object that are visible. In a word, looks in general and looks in particular need not have existed. By contrast, those geometrical projections are sense-independent necessities, just as it is a necessity that a sphere projects onto a plane as a circle.

And yet it must be acknowledged that the link between the a priori-determinable projection and the aspect-appearance is close. Corresponding to each projection is a look which could not be other than it is if sight is a sense in which, as we earlier claimed, linear projective mapping relations exist from material objects into the visual field. So we could succinctly specify a recipe for the look in the round when we are dealing with easily defined shapes like the cube: we simply say that it is 'the look of a cube', and add that this is such that the cube presents the look corresponding to each a priori-determinable projection. But having said this it must be emphasized that not all shapes are expressible by simple formulae; second, that each new detail of a shape relates additively and contingently to its fellows; and third, we simply repeat that looks are contingent properties of their bearers. In a word, specification of appearances must in general adopt the piecemeal form we have used until now.

At this point I must record that all this talk of an infinity of distinct appearances is an idealization, designed for 'perfect viewers', always supposing the concept of perfect eyesight is viable. However, it plainly is not. The infinite divisibility of matter may or may not be a viable concept, the infinite divisibility of sensation is surely not, if only because of the essential bond between sensation and awareness. As the hoary but perspicacious empiricist doctrine of the *minimum visibilium* reminds us, the senses are not limitlessly fine-grained, in fact or in principle. When I say that an infinity of appearances shows us the appearance of a material object, I am illicitly extrapolating from an infinity of distinct geometrical projections to a supposed infinity of distinct corresponding looks. No matter. While plenty of supposed looks must merge, plenty of real looks remain.

(e) Experiencing the appearance

(1) The puzzling question we are considering is: what kind of a thing is a look in the round? And how does it relate to the aspect-looks through which it is revealed? We concentrated on the second question, in the belief that answering it will answer the first question. However, the fact that the look in the round is rigorously specified by an infinite set of triples, did not bring us any nearer understanding the nature of the look, nor its relation to those triples. The reason being that object-appearances are an important part of our lives, but these infinite sets are not; and, anyway, our knowledge of looks in the round is an ordered knowledge, whereas there is no mention of any ordering principle in the infinite set. It was precisely this lack of structure in the infinite set that drove us to turn to certain ordered phenomena in human life. Thus, we asked the question: how do we learn, and how do we communicate to others, particular appearances in the round? Here in some cases we discovered an order, that of associative threads which were the relics of our own practical history; but while this account fitted certain examples of limited regional knowledge, it was too primitive a model to apply to those vastly familiar and numerous cases in which we have simply thrown away all epistemological ladders.

At this juncture I think we should ask ourselves a question concerning *procedure*. Why, in discussing what can be rigorously specified by a randomly arranged infinite set, do we take our cue from human knowledge of that item and the supposedly orderly character of the object of such knowledge? Why should the orderliness of the latter be of any relevance to the character of the former? Well, if the look in the round were a *thing*, a very complicated thing to be sure, it is difficult to see how the one could be of any relevance to the other. But the look of the object is not a thing, being no kind of individual; and, if aspect-looks are any guide, is probably determinable as the internal object of a veridical individuating attentive-consciousness of the bearer of the look. Therefore consciousness and its objects must be our guide, only in such a way that it leads directly outwards onto the bearer of the look.

The difficulty is to steer a path between a subjectivism that is only concerned with inner entities, and an objectivism that refuses to recognize the essentially mind-dependent character of appearances. We must grasp that the look does not get between one and the bearer, and yet has reality only for consciousness. Without falling backwards into ourselves and hypostatizing the look as an internal entity, nor forwards into an objectivism that makes of the look a mind-irrelative quality of the bearer like its shape, we must allot to it a status such that this consciousness-relative non-individual something is given in visual attentive experience through its secondary qualities first of all and thereby also through its formal or spatial properties.

(2) Accordingly, the character of the experience of the look in the round becomes now of central importance. Then when and how do we experience the look in the round? Necessarily, it is not accomplished in an instant, nor from a particular point of view. Necessarily, we experience the look in the round only if the object is

seen, over a period of time, across a tract of space, from all visually differentiable angles. But is that enough? Suppose I see every possible view, but have no idea whether I am north, south, east, or west; whether a foot away now, or a mile away then; and so on. Have I seen the object? I have, repeatedly. Indeed, I have seen all there is to see of it. But do I know what it looks like? I do not. In fact, I have not the slightest idea. And even if this procedure is repeated many, many times; and most especially if the order is different each time; I will come nowhere near to learning it. And this seems true, even if I can clearly call to mind every single one of those disjointed views.

Suppose now that I were to be told *where it is* that I am situated each time I see a specific view. But suppose in addition that those places are a mere random selection of positions scattered in three-dimensional space; and suppose further that the aspects presented to view seem as unrelated as (say) a hippopotamus head and a car wheel! Then once again I have seen all there is to see of the object. Yet once again I have no idea what the object looks like. And even if the process is repeated many times, and most especially if the order is different each time, I will come no nearer to learning it. Indeed, it seems to me that I have not learned it even if I can call to mind every one of these many disjointed views together with the position in space from which it is seen. After all, I have no idea of the object's shape. I do not know whether from afar the object looks like a porcupine or the interior of a television set. I have not the faintest idea what it looks like. How can I be said to have discovered its look in the round?

The next question to ask is: have I managed nonetheless to make the visual acquaintance of the object's appearance? The trouble with this suggestion is, that such a putative experience of the look in the round leaves no memory of itself: all I can remember is a multiplicity of looks. But if I have experienced the object's appearance, indeed done so repeatedly, how come I have not learned what it is? And yet how else may one learn the look of a thing but by repeated experience of it? Plainly something more than these aspect-experiences and knowings is needed, something facilitating the kind of *synthesis* those experiences are susceptible of. Then it seems to me that what in addition is required is that certain specific relations are perceived; and not just some relations, we need to perceive the *right* or synthesizing relations. For example, if I am to make the acquaintance over time of an object's visual appearance, I would need to perceive such relations as that *this* look greets me as I turn the corner of what is showing at the edge of *that* look. It is not that a material object is an inherently meaningful progression across space as an audible sentence is across time. It seems nonetheless to be true that making the acquaintance of an object's visual appearance must be an ordered and intelligibly bonded procedure. Above all, it ought to be such that repetition tends to generate knowledge of its individual character. Above all therefore, it ought to be such that repetition tends to generate knowledge of the bearer's colour and spatial character. But for this to happen, synthetic processes in the understanding must intelligibly connect the contents of those experiences. This is why order is essential.

(f) The appearance itself

So what is the look in the round? What is the look of a material object? We at least
know the following about it: that it is necessarily experienceable uniquely through
sight; necessarily not experienceable from a single direction; necessarily experienceable only across time, rather as a melody is necessarily experienceable only
across time; necessarily experienceable only across space, whether it be viewer or
object that mutates in position; necessarily experienceable only through an ordered
comprehending viewing procedure which ensures that the spatial relations between
elements of views are also perceived; such that repetition of the experience leads
naturally to knowledge of the look; and thereby also of the colour and spatial qualities of the bearer of the look; and so on. It is not the sum total of the aspect-looks
through which it reveals itself, else making the acquaintance of a haphazard array of
aspect-looks would be making its acquaintance. It is not the view cast in the mind of
God, for it is no kind of view at all. *A fortiori* it is not a view given in an instant to
some impossible awful encompassing gaze of many eyes which closes around the
object from all directions simultaneously, rather as a hand does around a pebble. It
is not this last, precisely because such an encompassing gaze is an impossibility, for
whenever we glimpse or in an instant gain a view of something it must in principle
be possible to set something else behind it as background—thanks to the directionality of sight—but this imploding vision buries its object in a pocket of its own, set
against nothing.

Then what is it? It seems to me that the aforementioned definition of the appearance applies here, despite the added complexity introduced by time and a third
spatial dimension. I see no reason, in the case of appearances in the round, to
dispute the claim that 'the appearance of a material object is the character with
which that object is endowed for the attention, when the bearer of the appearance
comes to the attention through and as endowed with the secondary and thereby also
the formal or spatial qualities which individuate it for that sense.' An object coming
to attention in a single view satisfies this formula, for we experience its aspect-look
in seeing that side of the object to be endowed with the colour, contour, and depth
properties which visually individuate it. Equally, the same formula holds for the
more complex phenomenon of appearance in the round. Thus, we experience that
appearance when the object so comes to the attention, across space and across time,
that we perceive it to be endowed with the three-dimensional colour and spatial
qualities which visually single it out from its fellow perceptibles in the world given
to sight. We can succinctly describe that very complicated visual character by saying
of the object something like 'it looks red and cubical', and a whole world of experience is condensed in that utterance, a condensation that could not have occurred
without the intervention of the understanding.

Yet it is difficult not to feel one is being denied something in these answers. One
keeps searching for some kind of apparitional *thing*, set somehow in three dimensions and from no one direction, that one immediately encounters in experiencing

the look in the round. But such a quest is fundamentally misguided. We must shake off the idea that the look in the round is either an entity or a visible that might in the instant be given to intuition, however bizarre in type. (Regress would inevitably follow as we in turn proceeded to intuit that visible!) At the same time we should understand that the visual appearance has to be experienceable. And we must recognize that time, and also public physical space, are essential to the revelation of the appearance in the round: time for the necessary unfolding to the attention of the complex visual data; space for the due relating and therefore also comprehending of the data that thus unfolds to view. It follows that this datum of sense cannot be assimilated to the immediate private givens of consciousness. Here we are in the public world of physical space and time *from the very beginning*. We do not 'work our way' from inside to outside like prisoners escaping from some fortress, but are (so to say) 'liberated' from the start. Naturally, one ought not overestimate this fact, supposing it to dissolve in a trice epistemological problems which have troubled many philosophers. Nonetheless, it is of some moment that the acquisition of visual awareness is the natural function of the sense of sight, that it is accomplished all the time by animals of many types, and that in all probability we begin our visual life doing so.

3. A Summary Statement

The visual appearance of the object is not the object itself. Indeed, it is not an individual; *a fortiori* not an internal or mental individual such as a construct of visual sensations—in two or three quasi-spatial dimensions; and no kind of shell, spatial or qualitative or sensational, that somehow in the visual field fits the object like a skin. It is not a quality, and *a fortiori* not the qualities of colour and shape revealed to sight. It is not the sum total of the aspect-appearances through which it reveals itself. In fact, it is not even seen.

And yet it is not nothing. For it is experienceable, through sight, across time, across space, via an ordered and comprehending viewing of aspects, which is such as to culminate in a veridical seeming to have seen the colour and spatial qualities of the bearer. Acquaintance with the appearance *mediates* embarking upon the looking procedure and the resultant knowledge of the colour and shape of the bearer; yet not as an intervening event-effect of looking—like a flash of insight. (A dawning, rather.) To experience the appearance ('seeing what the object looks like') *is* so to visually experience the object across space and time that seeming to see—and, normally, knowledge-of—its colour and shape transparently ensue. One so assembles the aspect-looks in one's mind that awareness of colour and shape emerge at the end; for experiencing the appearance *is* seeing the colour and shape. And that is all that it is.

Then it must be repeatedly stressed that this experience crucially depends on events in the understanding—if only because of the natural tendency to hypostatize the appearance. For we have seen that the activity of looking to discover the visible properties of material objects cannot lead to that complex perceptual experience without parallel mutating knowledge of one's changing spatio-temporal relations with the object. Then that cognitive factor helps to cause the perceptual experience—intelligibly. Indeed, what is going on as one makes the visual acquaintance across space and time of material objects, is nothing less than the constituting across space and time, out of visible parts, of a complex being endowed with multiform properties, mostly of structural import: a being with an interior, rear, sides, and stability. Then as noted above, positing the appearance as a visible, whether it be of the type of individual or complex quality, leads inevitably to regress. This follows from the fact that the understanding plays an essential part in the experience of the look in the round. No mental *thing*—no material object for the attention—is equal to the task of providing what the understanding alone can provide. The meaning that knits the aspects together across space and time has no equivalent in *visibilia*. Meaning cannot be hypostatized. The reduction of what the mind encounters in the appearance in the round to visibles, has no prospect of success.

4. Visibility

(a) Necessary conditions of seeing

So much for the nature of the appearance, and our experience of it. The question remains: how do we put this phenomenon to use in the visual perception of the physical environment?

Seeing necessitates the interaction of a *visual appearance* and the *capacity to see*. These factors are interdependent, for as we have noted the appearance is not an irrelative ingredient of the extra-psychological physical world, so to say an ethereal skin somehow fitting its bearer. Rather, any particular appearance is a consciousness-relative instantiation of an appearance-concept. Visual appearances, which can be shared by individuals and types, are complex universals. Thus, I specify the visual appearance A_1 by conjoining brightness, blueness, and sphericity-look; and this A_1 look is possessed by anything that is a bright blue sphere. Yet even though A_1 is a mere 'look', and therefore of necessity *for* consciousness, it is nonetheless an irrelative and unconditioned appearance-universal. It is true that when I say of some object that 'it has A_1', I usually speech-pragmatically imply: to humans in daylight. But were I to be talking to animal psychologists who were forever studying ichthyosauruses in red light, I might instead imply: to ichthyosauruses in red light. To repeat: A_1 *as such* has nothing to do with humans or daylight or even light, being a complex universal, and it finds instantiation in the physical world relative to observers and viewing conditions.

Then to see an item is to become visually acquainted with the several *visibilia* (as I shall call them) that constitute its visual appearance, e.g. its colour, brightness-value, 3D-shape. In a decent case of seeing these will all be on view, together with relational properties like direction, depth, 3D-movement, etc. But objects can be seen when almost none of these properties are visible, e.g. a flock of birds appearing as a speck in the sky. All that we see here is (a) expanse > O, (b) ± brightness, and (c) directional location at some distance. In short, we merely see 'something of some width, of ± brightness, "there"' some way off (pointing). Then apart from depth, I do not think we can shorten this short-list any further, for remove any other item and you remove them all. Therefore ± brightness & expanse > O & 'there (perhaps some way off)', constitutes the ultimate minimum in the way of *visibilia*. After that—invisibility! (The fate of the wind—because neither bright nor dark, of the germ—because too small to have visual expanse, of the future—because nowhere.) All particular appearances, $A_1 A_2 A_3 \ldots$, approximate towards this degenerate case as they are denuded of *visibilia*.

Now when an object is seen it must *look to be* as its visual appearance *shows* it to be. The object cannot at once be seen *and* retreat incognito as a mystery behind its *visibilia*, for in seeing objects through seeing *visibilia* we see them *as* so endowed. And however few *visibilia* may appear, we cannot see something without setting eyes upon some of its *visibilia*. Accordingly, if an object is visible it must at least *look to be*: bright or dark or in between, and somewhere, and of some expanse. I mention this fact because, as we shall discover in a moment, it can function in certain cases as a sort of simple litmus-test of visibility.

(b) Guide lines for distinguishing the visible from the invisible

(1) That which is invisible may at the same time be eminently detectable by visual means. Thus, while orange light is visible, ultraviolet light is not, and this property of ultraviolet light is perfectly consistent with the fact that when it strikes some chemical substance, the latter invariably emits orange light. Even though we can *visually tell* that ultraviolet light impinges at some point, the radiation itself (which can scarcely be an orange ultraviolet!) remains invisible. Likewise the wind that scatters the autumn leaves. And the solitary α-particle causing a white track of tiny water droplets in a Wilson Cloud Chamber. And the heat that makes an iron bar glow in the dark. And the itch that is causing the dog to scratch. And the snap decision to vote 'Yes' that caused Smith's arm to suddenly rise. In a word, there is much that is invisible that can yet be visually detected in a trice. The concept of seeing easily accommodates such strains. Thus, we distinguish seeing-*of* from seeing-*that*; and seeing-*x-occur*-in-y from seeing-*that-x*-when-x; and etc. So when I see the dog scratch, I see the *dog* and see *that* he itches and see him *as* itching *when* he itches— but I do not see the *itch*; and will only if Physicalism is true and the right brain event discoverable. Now it is not in some strained sense of 'see' that this is true: it is so in *the*, public perceptual, commonest, and certainly central sense of the term. It is simply and bluntly true that orange light and blushes are visible, and that ultraviolet light and feelings of embarrassment are not.

Then what distinguishes the actually visible from the merely visually detectable? What rules govern the attribution of visibility? How is it for example that we can see a nebula in seeing an image in a telescope but cannot see the wind in seeing the swirling autumn leaves? Why is it that we can see a skin diver who is covered from head to foot but not an α-particle as it 'visibly' crosses a Wilson Cloud Chamber? Well, seeing is already from the start mediated by light and sensation, and in certain cases that mediation is extensible. These cases are of *two* kinds, exemplified by the nebula on the one hand and the diver on the other. Namely: those cases wherein an existent appearance is *transported,* and those wherein an appearance is *borrowed.*

The first cases occur when, thanks to the reliable transportation through space of existent *visibilia,* an appearance that physical circumstances have rendered inaccessible is reconstituted once again at a new site. It is in this way that we permit seeing to be via periscopes, mirrors, telescopes, and microscopes. Thus, in all these cases it is as if the viewer mutated spatially on a kind of 'magic carpet': rose, turned, went and grew, went and shrank; at the end of which one re-creates the normal viewing situation wherein one makes the visual acquaintance of the visual appearance of the in any case visible item. For these 'extensions of the senses' *recover* rather than confer appearances.

But the second class of cases are those in which a mediator *shares* its appearance with an item, and here an appearance is actually conferred upon what might otherwise be without an appearance of any kind. In these cases we validly transfer the *visibilia* of the mediator onto the mediated, thanks to the reliable preservation in the mediator of *visibilium*-type properties that causally derive in the first place from the mediated. As an example, properties like shape and position, which must obtain in but need not be visible in the mediated prior to mediation. Take the case of a perfectly clear invisible block of glass that is rendered visible through being covered by a coat of fine blue dust. Here the blue of the dust transfers onto the glass because the dust and glass surface spatially coincide and the glass surface causes dust-adherance. In short, regularities linking *visibilium*-type properties rather than actual *visibilia,* first in the mediator and then in the mediated, play the central part in licensing the transfer of *visibilia* from mediator onto mediated. Once these requirements are met, the visual appearance of the mediator *is* that of the mediated.

And so we must not say, 'the invisible glass is made visible through utilizing an appearance that does not belong to it', but 'the invisible glass is made visible through acquiring an appearance that belongs to something else'. In short, the dust's appearance *becomes* simultaneously the glass's appearance, for nothing can 'falsely' be made visible. The appearance is shared—without being divided.

(2) Then under these conditions the glass actually *looks to be* blue and round and 'there' (where rightly or wrongly it shows). As we have already remarked, when an object is visible it looks to be as its appearance shows it to be. This is a fundamental truth of visual perception. Indeed, it is a principle of kinds. That principle can help us to delimit the visible from the invisible, merely through appeal to our unstructured knowledge of whether or not an object looks to be a certain way, without requiring of us that we explicitly invoke the rules governing the divide.

Thus, the nebula that shows as a point of light in the sky actually looks to be bright, of some expanse, 'there' some fairish way off. And the diver looks black ('a dark figure') and human-shaped ('like a man') and to be entering the water ('there'). By contrast, the α-particle neither looks white, nor thread-shaped, nor of some expanse; and is in many ways like a distant tank crossing a desert, throwing up vast clouds of sand as it goes, which visibly signal the object's presence but wholly conceal it from view: plainly a 'seeing-*that*' in the absence of a 'seeing-*of*'. (If it were a seeing-of, *what words would be left* if we were actually to glimpse the tank itself amidst the swirling sand?) Then it is *because* the α-particle neither looks white nor thread-shaped, that we class this vastly smaller than an invisible virus item as invisible. And so it is with the other examples of invisibility. The autumn wind that swirls the golden leaves does not itself look golden or serpentine-shaped. The ultra-violet light does not look orange. The heat in the iron bar does not look red. And the tank neither looks sandy coloured nor a hundred metres high!

22

Perceptually Constituting the Material Object

The function of perception in general, and above all of visual perception, is the acquisition of knowledge of the physical contents of local space in the near present. This requires acquaintance not merely with the look or appearance of material objects, but with sufficiently complex perceptions as will enable one differentially and more or less definitively to identify those objects as physical objects and of some specific kind or another. It is with this ensemble of experiences, and the processes in the Understanding to which they are subjected, that I am now concerned.

1. The Inessentiality of Perceptibility

(1) In this chapter I aim to set out what is implicit in the self-conscious or human perception of physical objects. This differs in certain fundamental respects from the perceivings of unselfconscious beings, for it incorporates a use of concepts, and an awareness of object-structures, of a kind not found amongst such creatures. Thus, when humans visually recognize an object, an almost limitless array of perceptual properties and procedures are by implication condensed into an instant. My aim is to bring something of this to light. But before I do, it will set those findings in perspective if we take stock of a few general properties of the relation between objects and perception.

From the point of view of the perceptible objects, perceptibility is of absolutely no account: it is 'consciousnesses' who need perception, not the objects themselves. Perceptibility is a wholly contingent attribute of whatever possesses it (apart from sensations). And it is invariably a relativistic property (apart again from sensations). What is perceptible to this sort of being in these circumstances, is imperceptible to the same kind of being under different circumstances, and to another variety of being under either circumstance. In sum, when we are dealing with non-psychological phenomena, there can be no a priori guarantee of perceivability to anyone, and anything that is perceptible is so relative both to perceiver and conditions.

(2) This fundamental gulf between object and perceivability is compounded by the fact that almost nothing comes to the perceptual attention simply or of its own accord. Apart from proprioception and the perception of sensations, perception is never 'just' perceiving. That is, the perception of objects is through the perception

of certain mediating X's which are non-identical with the object, and the same is true of the X's themselves. With the single exception of proprioception, mediation is needed for the entire gamut of publicly perceptible items in physical space (proprioception evading the rule through being an intra-systemic phenomenon). Epistemologically almost everything in physical nature lies at a remove. Mediation is a near-universal necessity, and is exemplified in the perception of material objects, light, movement, colour, sound, and much else.

And so the perceivability of physical non-psychological items is a contingent property of the bearer, is relative to perceivers and conditions, and apart from the special case of body-awareness, is made possible by the perceptibility of items linked to but non-identical with that perceptible (the slide to regress being halted by the sensation). I see a tree against the night sky thanks to catching sight of a silhouette, but the tree might have been invisible to me or any other being, in more or less any imaginable circumstances, and the silhouette might have been some trick of the light, etc. These few facts set the phenomenon of perception in a realistic framework, militate against overestimating its significance from the point of view of cosmic ontology, and should be borne in mind in the ensuing discussion. In particular, when we speak of 'perceptually constituting the object', this must be understood to be free of all idealistic connotations.

2. The Visual Perception of Material Objects

(a) The unique achievements of sight

(1) My aim is to bring to light the complex presumptions of a perceptual kind underlying the typical human perception of material objects (especially the seeing of them). This is tantamount to the following reverse project. Namely, setting out first the full perceptual (and particularly visual) evidence for the presence of a material object, and then providing an intelligible account of the mental process by which a self-conscious mind undergoing such experiences would in the end seem to itself to have perceived a material object, a process some might call 'constituting the object out of perceptual experience'. When one visually recognizes (say) a tree one unreflectively assumes it presents a multiplicity of appearances to a multiplicity of distances and angles, and it is simultaneously true of most humans that upon experiencing those sights in those situations they would in the end seem to themselves to have seen a tree. Such fundamental assumptions 'underpin' the normal visual experience of the moment.

(2) To help bring the full visual implications of visual perception into the open, we must first understand *precisely which items* we perceive when we see a material object. Then as a way of separating out the several objects given visually to the attention, it is clarifying to consider the objects of perceptual experience in the case of those senses (of which sight is the prime example) which are attentively mediated by sensation. In short, let us list the various objects which come to the attention in

the case of sight, hearing, smell, and taste, and in the natural order in which they do. I suggest that in each case the perceptual transaction begins in the following way: that we first immediately perceive the secondary quality (and perhaps also layout) of the sensation through which we demarcate the sense in question. This *sensation* is the first perceptual object in a sequence of objects which that sensation brings to the attention.

Then in the case of the two most developed of these senses, sight and hearing, we in addition *directionally* perceive physical wave-phenomena, namely light and sound, which are nomically linked to their physical source, which is generally situated at a distance at a point in three-dimensional space. That is, we perceive the directional properties, relative to our bodies, of these wave-phenomena, together with their secondary qualities, which they acquire from and share with the sensation. Indeed, in the case of sight we also perceive the *two-dimensional shape* of the sector of the wave-phenomenon that is sited at the sense organ (say, the roundness of a light beam), though not in the case of hearing (for we never hear roars to be round or bellows square), where we merely perceive two-dimensional distribution of the type of 'scattered' or 'concentrated'. Then since the depth-properties of the wave-phenomena are not perceived, and since the perceived sector is located at the sense-organ (retina, eardrum) (though imperceptibly so), we naturally describe the perception of light and sound as 'merely directional' and 'merely two-dimensional'. In short, in the case of these physical wave-phenomena we perceive a select few depthless two-dimensional spatial properties, together with the secondary quality definitive of the sense.

(3) Now the above set of perceptual accomplishments might have been all we achieved through the use of the four sensuous senses: sight, hearing, smell, and taste. Through their use we might have perceived no more than lights, sounds, smells, and tastes: these phenomena might have been the end of each perceptual line. This would have been the case if there had been a dearth of causal relations of individuative import between the 'outer' perceptible wave phenomena and their 'outer' physical sources. Had that been how matters stood, our sole perceptual acquaintance with physical and specifically material objects, given differentially in three-dimensional physical space, would have been through the 'body senses', proprioception and touch. However, it proves not to be so. For in the case of sight uniquely the attentive perceptual line extends a *stage further*, taking a qualitative leap into three-dimensional space. Thanks first to the fact that two-dimensional structures are visible, both in the case of light and visual sense-data, and thanks secondly to the linear projective properties of light, material objects are visible through the visibility of the secondary qualities *and* the directional *and* the two-dimensionally individuative properties of both visual sense-data *and* of light. All of these traits take the identical value in the case of all three objects, all are equally visible at the same time, and all are perceived simultaneously in the one attentive event.

594

And so in the case of the material object uniquely amongst these latter few visible objects, *depth* is visible: here directional and lateral perception is enriched by a *third dimension*. It is not so with the light or sensation objects given to sight, but it is of the material objects. While depth and the three-dimensional properties of objects need not as a matter of necessity be visible in any particular visual experience of material objects, they must in principle be visible if the objects are to be visually perceptible. Then this enlargement of the scope of sight into a whole new spatial dimension brings with it an entirely new range of objects: pre-eminently material objects, but much else as well. Thus, matter generally in all its formations of gas, liquid, object-collectives, along with events involving these items as bearer, whether movement (of a cloud, say) or colour change (within a lake, say), come into view. The whole material realm and the three-dimensional space containing it become visible. The order and differentiation in the visual field, bearing witness to the abundance in the environment of linear EM-waves originating in the sun, make possible this qualitative leap in the objects accessible to the attention. Perception *at a distance* enters existence for the first and only time with sight. Physical objects, situated miles and even light-years away, come concretely to awareness at this point. (An almost inevitable concomitant of this colossal enlargement of perceptual power is directionality: how otherwise would one perceive (say) the nebula M31 in Andromeda?)

(4) Note what this extensibility of the attention in the case of sight implies. Whereas (say) sound-sources do not come to the attention when their sound does, light-sources do at the same time and in the same event as the light they transmit. And they do, whether or not one knows so. However, perception would be functionless in the absence of knowledge of its objects. This fact conditions the character of the visual experience, which so enlists the aid of the understanding that its internal objects typically match the additional achievements of sight. Thus, at any moment typically one sees what one sees *as* (at the very least) 'something—in such and such a direction—of such and such two-dimensional shape—and near-side three-dimensional shape—at such and such a distance'.

(b) The perceptual implications of positing the perceptibility of a material object

We, being thinking creatures, add considerably to the above content. Our minds naturally position 'out there' at a distance and direction in space all sorts of items: light-sources, colours, movements, material formations, but centrally and pre-eminently *material objects*. Then what *beliefs* does this latter classification presuppose in the mind of a perceiver? What properties would one automatically suppose that material object to possess? Well, there is no necessity that one posit, say, the rule of the Laws of Chemistry, etc. However, certain other traits must be presumed by any perceiver to obtain in the item, simply through its being a material object: for example, shape and solidity. Now of these essentials some at least are visible. So which properties are at once necessary, assumed by us to be present, and accessible to sight? Answering this question should help to uncover the *visual presumptions* implicit in the visual recognition of material objects.

Here it helps to remember mediation. Which items act as mediators in the case of the visual perception of material objects? Now speaking quite generally it is a sheer contingency of anything physical, and *a fortiori* of any of a material object's perceptible properties, that it is perceptible. For example, it is a contingency that its heat rather than (say) its valency is perceptible. Nevertheless, some select few properties are in a way conditionally necessarily perceptible. Thus, no property of a material object can be seen unless its *object-bearer* is also seen: we cannot perceive (say) the colour of a material object without perceiving its object-bearer at a remove in space. But we have just seen that we cannot accomplish the latter unless the special properties which permit the visual attention (but not hearing) to range differentially into three-dimensional space are realized. This acts as a constraint when we look for the visual mediators in the case of the visual perception of material objects. Certain visible properties of structural import are obliged to play that role. Once we posit the visibility of material objects, we necessarily posit that of a select sub-class of its properties (and vice versa). One cannot have the former without bringing the visibility of certain spatial differentia in its wake (and vice versa).

In short, those spatio-temporal properties which enable us *attentively to individuate* material objects (etc.) in space, must be among the mediators that are visible when material objects are visible. If what we perceive is a material object at a distance, many suitably ordered such properties must also be visible. And so a whole set of visible spatially differential properties will be presupposed in the object when one sees it as a material object. Thus, the *visual presuppositions* and a sub-class of the *visual mediators* of visual object perception coincide. Now in general when we see an item as a material object, we mostly take it to be showing a side, to have sides it is not showing, an interior, a boundary surface, to be constituted of material stuff, in solid state, to present a different appearance from different distances and directions, and so on. And most of these properties are visually detectable. If they were not, how could we visually discover that what was in the visual field was, say, not a lingering mist but a material object? What humans need to know to be credited with visual experiences with such content, is of the inherence in some occupant of space of such properties.

It is thanks to such knowledge that human visual experiences can manage to have a *material object* as its intentional content. The subject of experience has to know what kind of visual data would tend to confirm that the item appearing as incarnating such a content does in fact possess those multiple necessary traits. One needs to know what it would be to undergo a set of visual experiences such that at the end one would naturally say: 'that, analytically speaking, seems to indicate the presence of a material object'. In the face of such data, and aided by suitable contextual beliefs, one's mind tends to assemble the properties given to sight, and come up automatically with the legitimized object of visual experience: (say) 'material object' ('chair', 'tree', 'man'). This procedure might be dubbed 'visually constituting the material object out of one's visual experiences of the object.' Of course one does not undergo such a sequence of experiences whenever one visually recognizes a material object, nor recapitulate somewhere within one's mind whatever synthesizing phenomena normally get brought to bear upon such raw material. Nevertheless, it is implicit. One needs to be able to reopen the question, and presumes upon the occurrence of such experiences and syntheses. All this lies in the background, acting as foundation for normal perceptual experiences of the moment, for the typical 'see as——' of humans.

(c) Constituting material objects out of visual experiences of visual mediators

(1) Let us be clear what is going on when we 'visually constitute a material object'. That is, understand what takes place in our minds when we undergo a sequence of visual experiences of visible mediators from numerous places and directions, such that at the end of the process we appear to ourselves to have just seen a single material object. It seems clear that something of a mental character is being assembled. What is less apparent is: exactly what.

The absolute contingency and relativity of perceptibility shows that it must all be a far cry from any idealist project of assembling a construct—say of the ilk of a 'logical construction'—which we take to be the material object itself. Indeed, in the absence of knowledge of a stable physical setting, and one's spatio-temporal and causal relations to it, those many visual experiences would be as useless as a scattered array of photographs lying around in disorder. Without a physical situation to contain them, and even assuming the veridicality of the visual experiences, no one visual construct would have any more validity than any other. The domain of experience rests fair and square upon the mindless realm of physical nature, and can have no epistemological significance apart from it. In short, there is no possibility that the myriad visual experiences, gathered from a multiplicity of distances and directions, might be used to constitute a mind-irrelative entity like a material object. And in fact this entire process of visual inspection has to be assumed to be occurring in a mind apprised of its changing position in space and time. Without that knowledge the whole procedure would be epistemologically valueless.

(2) And partly for the same reason there can be no possibility that the visual experiences might together constitute a mind-relative entity, construed as the visual appearance of the object. Thus, it is not as if the multiple sights encountered in those visual experiences were assembled by one's mind to make up some three-dimensional visual entity which somehow attaches to the outside of the material object. Visual appearances are not *things*, 'out there' at the place of their bearer, to be assembled and fitted to the bearer. It is of the utmost importance that we cannot *first* assemble a visual appearance and *then* discover that it is of a bearer. Such a supposition suffers from a 'cart before the horse' weakness: it fails to take account of the fact that the determination of the appearance of material objects depends internally on one's *already* positing a material object bearer for the appearance. In the absence

of such a 'tethering point', no unifying principle binds the many particular appearances. This internal dependence upon the object is evident in the fact that any intentional activity of discovering a material object appearance, must take a form in which we investigate actual or supposed material object individuals. How, otherwise, might one go about the task?

The temptation to hypostatize the visual appearance as a coloured something 'out there' in space where the object is, that is visible in a sector of three-dimensional space and evidence for the presence at that site of the *merely inessentially visible* object to which it belongs, to conceive of it almost as a sort of coloured three-dimensional shadow of the object, such a tendency can cause misunderstanding precisely concerning these matters. First, it naturally leads us to overlook the role of the intellect, specifically the understanding, in the process of 'visually constituting the material object out of one's experiences of the object': hypostatization or 'the flight to mental things' proving here to be (as so often) a 'flight from meanings'. But secondly, in splitting off the appearance from its bearer, it causes us to conceive of that material bearer as something *behind* its appearance and the merely secondary and indirect object of the attention and the perceptual project. Both are misrepresentations of the facts. The proper corrective is first to note how much in the way of cognitive commitment to a public physical world is present from the start as we embark upon these investigations. It is secondly to observe that the entire procedure is from its inception a 'whole object'-enterprise, being as firmly committed to the provisional presence of a single unifying physical object as one is categorically committed to the existence of a containing physical setting. But above all it is to recognize the vital role of a synthesizing intellectual agency in the perceptual process.

(3) In short, we neither literally assemble a material object, nor an entity 'the visual appearance' to append to it. And yet what in fact we do assemble might be mistaken for either, for it stands in close relation to both. That mental construct is in the first place the internal object of a protracted visual experience: more exactly, it is its *terminal value*. It follows that it must encapsulate a *grasp* of what we have just now been witnessing during the course of that temporally extended experience. This is because during the perceptual procedure, the understanding is steadily brought to bear upon each new fragment of visual data, which is interpreted in the light of the preceding data, whereupon the internal object of the experience mutates, culminating in the aforesaid final value. Now that value is at once of an appearance *and* of a material object. For these are not two entities. They are one entity and a purely relativistic property that is revelatory of certain (largely) non-relativistic properties of that entity (such as its shape). And so in the second place and primarily, our minds are engaged in constructing in the concrete a conception of a material object through the construction of a property which is a partial revelation of its character. Thus, the visible character of the material object is the terminal goal of the entire process.

It must be emphasized that the two processes, of uncovering a visual appearance and visually confirming that a single material object is being seen, advance *pari passu* to their goal. Rather like the building of Neurath's ship these processes proceed in tandem, neither in advance of the other, both incomplete as they go, each as liable as the other to collapse in disarray. It does not matter in either case whether the goal is entertained merely as an hypothesis: if it is hypothetical that a single material object is on view, so is it that a visual appearance is there to be apprehended. The very existence of an intentional enterprise of 'perceptually investigating a single material object', which depends on suitable cognitive assumptions, shows it is so.

(d) The limitations of sheer perceptual scrutiny

(1) Before I examine the differential concepts which we employ in characterizing the perceptual data encountered in a fully elaborated perceptual, and above all visual experience of a material object, a few preliminary clarifications.

I should first emphasize that the complex visual property of material objects of which I am speaking, is wider than what generally we refer to in talking of visual appearances. Visual appearances are relative, not merely in our own case to humans, but usually also from the vantage point from which we individuate one material object from its fellow objects, namely from the *outside.* However, we might instead be interested in the appearance from the inside—or any other point of view. Then my present concern is with something which 'comprehends' all these traits: roughly, with the suitably ordered sum of all the visual experiences one would expect if every readily accessible part of a material object were visible, taking due account of the situation of the viewer.

The second thing to say is, that we ought not to overestimate what sheer perceptual inspection can accomplish. In such inspection we are, so to say, mere tourists of the object, standing to it in a relation not unlike that of viewers to Chartres Cathedral, who walk around the outside and enter the precincts of that edifice, eyes agape as they go, discovering as much and as little as that permits. To begin, we know that perceptual experience without knowledge cannot even discover the appearance of an item. Yet even when we are acquainted with a visual appearance, its epistemological limitations are considerable. For one thing appearances are *essentially ambiguous.* But anyhow sheer appearance alone cannot tell us whether it is of a *single* object, since several objects might fuse at a point to constitute one mass but not one object. Finally, we should remember that material objects might in whole or part be *invisible.* Then in the ensuing discussion I simply assume we are dealing with one fully perceptible material object. Without that assumption we might for all we know be 'constituting', out of those multiple perceptions, merely the visible part of a continuous material mass which was several fused material objects.

(2) Here I resume. What is it that is going on when we carry out the multiple procedures and undergo the requisite visual experiences one should expect if we are engaged in visually confirming that we are in the presence of a fully visible material object?

Plainly, it depends on the *intention* driving the active procedure. As we proceed we assume we are inspecting a single example of a material object type, and that what we see is not the merely visible part of some larger object. Then the project is at least one of visually inspecting a material object. However, we have a *wider purpose*. It is not the idealist constituting of a material object. Nor the constituting of the material object out of its properties. Nor the constituting of an entity, 'the visual appearance'. And neither is it the constituting of an essential attribute of material objects. Indeed, it is not even a decisive proof that it is a material object. The intention determining the project consists in fact in a *hierarchical structure* of integrated intentions with the following contents. In the first place we are engaged in visually experiencing as much as we can of a given material object. And this process is in addition the construction of an extended visual experience with a suitably visually justified internal object. And this in turn involves our assembling, in an integrated and intelligible structure, a sizeable fraction of the visible implications of being a single fully visible material object. In this way we seek to effect in ourselves an extended experience of the visual appearance of that object. And thus also of the full spatial and colour properties of the bearer of the appearance.

3. Standpoint in Visual and Tactile Perception

(1) So far I have confined the discussion to the sense of sight. Yet even though sight is epistemologically in the ascendant almost all of the time in our perceptual relations with the environment, it is necessary to cast the net more widely in this inquiry. Since the topic is 'the constituting of the material object out of perceptual experiences', we must include tactile sense as well. This is because sight and touch are the senses through which we individuate material objects, for they alone directly acquaint us with their spatial properties. Accordingly, sight and touch provide the data which our minds integrate in the manner to be investigated in the ensuing discussion. Now a vitally important feature of those perceptions is that they depend on our *spatial situation*. Corresponding to this property is the fact that the data which they provide is *partial and aspectual*, being of sides and surfaces and parts and suchlike. Then how do sight and touch compare in this regard? Are both senses 'situational' in the same sense? While there is common territory, there are significant dissimilarities. The following is a brief account of the facts.

We look at and see a side of an object, from a distance, from a direction, and from a part of our own body. Then the differences in the case of touch are notable. Thus, even though we feel an object's sides, or its inside or outside, and while we can can approach a side from a direction, one cannot feel sides either from a direction or distance. Even though we sometimes speak of feeling a side from a position, we refer merely to the position of our body rather than to a perceptual standpoint. Accordingly, it is above all on the count of *directionality* and *distance* that we must contrast these two senses: while they are essential to sight, they are simply absent in touch. This shows in the following interesting fact. Whereas it is tautologous to say we feel the side that we approach and then feel, it is by no means tautologous to say we see the side facing the direction from which is directed the gaze directed onto it: a gap exists which is bridged by the directionally determinate 'line of sight'. And this has no analogue in touch. Now it is for reasons of this kind that little is asserted in saying we feel objects from a side. The vitally important property of directionality is missing.

Then in speaking of 'perceptual standpoint' I shall mean either that a perception is directional and from a position in space, as in the case of sight but not touch, or that in the perception we encounter a side of the object, as in the case of both senses. We should bear these dual possibilities in mind in the ensuing discussion. These properties help determine the content of perceptual experiences, its fragmentary character, and the need for integration of the sort I describe. They each reflect the *situatedness* of the perceiver.

(2) Different consequences flow from the 'situatedness' of these two senses. In particular, the relations to space as a whole, as a single unified totality, are unlike. Thus, sight sees its object set amongst other objects, and in the space of all objects, indeed as set in the world itself, which is simultaneously seen as visually organized around the visual subject. By contrast, in the case of touch we do not feel the object as set in the world, along with all other objects, but as situated (say) merely in the hand. This is because with touch all space that we perceive is relative to the body of the perceiver. Touch can have as its object one thing alone, and if two then two alone; thereby one experiences the object in remove from the world of objects, and isolated in the tactile domain of (say) a hand. And so the single all-encompassing public space that every perceiver inhabits is not perceptually apparent within one's grasp, as it is in one's field of view. We can point to the sky that we see with the words 'It goes on and on', but there is nothing analogous in the case of what we feel in our hand.

In sum, seeing in the instant is from a direction and distance and position in space. And even in the case of seeing in the round across time, seeing must still be from the outside, which is a totality of directions, and from a medley of distances. And so in both senses of the word sight is from a standpoint. Touch, on the other hand, is neither from a distance, nor direction, nor position in space. And yet because it is sides that we touch, we have a right to say of the tactile perception of objects that it too is from a standpoint.

4. Material Objects

(1) At this point I think we should examine the units out of which the 'perceptual constituting of the material object' is assembled. More exactly, the *structural concepts* which are put to use in these many experiences. Such conceptual elements help to constitute the content of the perceptions. Indeed, they are that out of which the concept of the object that is gathering in our minds is ultimately constituted. They are what we must now consider.

For the most part the conceptual scaffolding is either spatial or of spatial import, space being the prime individuating characteristic of material objects. It is of interest that a perceptual investigation of a material object culminates in a characterization, not in terms of (say) deep scientific or pre-scientific stuff-concepts, but with something assembled out of 'primary' and 'secondary' qualities (of which only the former are truly objective). That spatial structuring can be of several kinds. Thus, one way of dismantling the material object, of putting on display what of a perceptible character goes into its make-up, is through an analysis into spatially delimited perceptible *parts*. And yet not all that we perceive in investigating objects is of the type of part: for example, its *surface* is not. And its perceptible character must enter the catalogue of items revealed in a purely perceptual investigation of an object. In short, such concepts will also be put to use. The 'scaffolding' employed in perceptually assembling a material object out of the data revealed in an extended perceptual investigation of a material object, consists of such concepts as those of part, side, surface, outside, and so on. Accordingly, their delimitation becomes of central importance to the present enterprise.

(2) Before I undertake that task in the following Section 5, I will set out some of the main properties constitutive of the concept of a material object. Material objects are:

(i) Material.
(ii) Solid.
(iii) Materially continuous from any one point in the object to any other.

And they possess the following spatial properties:

(iv) A boundary surface.
(v) An outside.
(vi) As many sides as there are directions onto the object from outside.
(vii) Surfaces wherever there are sides, and vice versa.
(viii) An interior.
(ix) Possibly an interior boundary surface, and if so
(x) an inner side (or 'inside').

And material objects are composed of parts, in some at least of the following senses of that protean term. Namely:

(xi) Object-parts (e.g. of a watch).
(xii) Segment-parts (e.g. of a 'rainbow' cake).
(xiii) Insides (e.g. of animals).
(xiv) Spatially delimitable parts (e.g. the north half of Mt Blanc).
(xv) Qualitatively delimitable parts (e.g. the nickel part of a meteorite).

(3) We should always remember that matter exhibits a density of nature that is limitless. While matter is nothing if not primaeval, indeed one might say infinitely

undeveloped, it is unquestionably mysterious in its depth, and the eternal life of the subject Physics is a reminder of that depth. I mention these facts concerning its density of nature, to remind us that matter lies at the heart of objectivity and Reality. And so it really should not surprise us, when we come to explore the concepts of matter and of the materially constituted, that a labyrinth of linked concepts is exposed to view. This is reflected in the existence of a familiar and impressive conceptual structure: the conceptual apparatus which we avail ourselves of when we come to describe our perceptual experiences of material objects.

5. Material Objects and Perceptual Standpoint (1): Structural Concepts

At this point I address myself to the delimitation of the structural concepts put to use in the perception of material objects. More specifically, the Section which now follows is concerned in the first place to demarcate those concepts, constitutive of the material object, that are needed if we are to analyse the object in terms of the differentials, without and within, and whole and part. This is because my subsequent concern is with the object as it is given in perception to multiple *standpoints*, and with the *synthesis* of such perceptions, and because the above concepts are put to use in the content of those perceptions. And so my preliminary aim is to understand just what it is we predicate of an object when we attribute a property perceived from a standpoint. When we engage in the analytical perceptual exploration of material objects, we perceive at each moment data which is appended to these structural items. It is those items that are the subject of the ensuing inquiry. More exactly, it is the concepts of such items.

But how in the first place did we come by those concepts? It must have been internal to the formation of the very concept of a material object, and will have proceeded *pari passu* with that primal development in our conceptual system. Accordingly, what follows is a sort of mythic reconstructive gloss. Then I think it happened in something like the following way. When one sees an object from some position in space one perceives a variety of spatial and sensible qualities. Now these qualities must be predicable of the object—for of what else? However, as it stands such a characterization is an unsatisfactory rendering of the facts, for these attributions can qualify the object only *partially*: after all, we do not 'just' see material objects, but something falling short of that unreachable simplicity. How is one to make good this imperfection in our rendering of the facts? Suppose I see the red colour of a material object from some vantage point. Then the structural concepts which are our present concern come to our assistance, enabling us to do justice to the *particular* object of perception without compromising the *whole* object. The red, we say, is of a *side* of the object, and it is of the object *only in so far as* it is of that side: we literally acknowledge the multi-facedness of the material object, and recognize at the same time the necessity of mediation: we put on record a specific measure of complexity which this dense existent, the concept of which is gathering in our minds, is capable of incarnating. Meanwhile it is clear that the very same instance of red must equally be of the nearer *part* of the object. Then how do these two bearers, each of differential import, relate to one another? And how is it possible that each can be bearer of the one token quality? It is to answer such questions that I embark upon the following exploration of concepts.

(a) The material object

(1) *Parts and sides and surfaces*

(1) *Parts.* Here are some uses of the word 'part'. If the part of the meteorite that is nickel is merely 'some of the meteorite', it is a *quantity*. But if half of the block of ice-cream is pink, it is a bounded portion or *segment*. Let us call the thumb of a hand a *structural part*, and a readily separable part of a clock a *structural piece*.

Now consider parts along the organizing axis of inner/outer. We oppose the shell to what it contains, the skin to what it covers, the outer layers to the inner; and these are all material objects, distinct from though perhaps connected to others. Within the casing or main body of an object are objects which are *contents* if separate or *insides* if connected to the whole. But a *core* is one, central, and may but need not be an object. Again, the outside part of a cake may be cooked, unlike the inside part, and is a segment of kinds rather than an object (and this is the usual part-sense of the term 'outside').

The items in the second classification, whose principle or organization is differentially spatial, fall simultaneously under the headings of the less specific first classification, whose principle of differentiation lies in the degree of autonomy of the parts, in their likeness and unlikeness to material objects. Thus, a core may be a segment, or it could instead be a structural piece, the insides and generally the skin are structural parts, and the shell and casing structural pieces, and so on. Any hesitation is due to the rough and ready nature of these distinctions, which are drawn solely for present purposes.

(2) *Sides.* The word 'side' has several uses. It occurs in one way in 'the six sides of a dice', and in another in 'the south side of Mt Sainte Victoire', though in each case we are speaking of aspect-sides. In the first use there are a fixed number of sides, whose identity and number is unrelated to the orientation of the object, and which may be viewed from many directions. But in the second use of 'side', the sides are originally identified through orientation, and it is a convention whether the number of sides are (say) four, as is generally the case with mountains, or maybe instead twelve, and it is perhaps unsettled whether such a side may be viewed from different directions. The aspectual sense of 'side' seems to me the central or primary or primitive sense of the term, other uses of the term being adaptions of that sense.

Meanwhile it appears that the sides of objects cannot constitute a realm of being, that sides are not sorts of existents, unlike colours or shapes or even surfaces. For even though there are *descriptions* of sides, as there are of colours and shapes, there are not *kinds* of sides. Rather, while the outside is the standpoint that reveals the object as object, a side of an object is merely the *object* as it differentially reveals itself to one particular standpoint amongst others. This is the only way an object has at any instant of giving itself to sight, which cannot in the instant encompass it in the manner of a hand or mouth.

(3) *Surfaces.* Though one almost always sees a side of whatever object one sees, one need not see the surface of that side, which is a narrower concept of spatial character. What we attribute to a surface we generally attribute to that side of the object, but the reverse is not true. Surfaces are of sides and objects, but are different from either. While there are many concepts that are applicable to objects but not to sides, such as 'thin' and 'cubical' and 'accelerating', there are many that are. And there are far fewer in the case of surfaces. A side can be beautiful, shaded, frequently painted, renowned, ornamented, as well as red, smooth, hard, and hot. A surface can be smooth, spherical, plane, dusty, but we hesitate to apply many of the above predicates, and if we do they may be applied differently, as is generally the case with 'beautiful'.

Surfaces are predicable, not (say) of belts of radiation, but of enmattered entities, notably material objects, and of the two material differentia under examination, viz. sides and parts. Thus, we refer to individual surfaces through referring to (say) liquids and objects, to parts, to sides, and parts of sides. We speak of 'the surface of this object', which we can call rough or smooth in describing its texture, or spherical if spatially characterizing it. Then whereas a spherical rock is a sphere, a spherical surface is not, for it makes no sense to speak of the volume of a surface. 'Spherical' describes the rock through describing its shape, but if we speak of the surface of an object as spherical we do so not through describing its shape, but through describing that of the object. It is important that we understand the rules governing the use of (say) 'spherical surface', since failure to do so can lead one to conceive of surfaces as somehow separate from their object owner, to think of a surface as a kind of two-dimensional three-dimensional entity which for some reason one can never encounter on its own.

That concludes the preliminary delimitation of the three fundamental concepts—part, side, surface—put to use in analytical explorations of material objects. Then it seems to me that of these concepts that of the side is the most centrally relevant to the phenomenon of perception from a standpoint, which is I must emphasize my ultimate topic. I turn now to the consideration of the pre-eminent sub-variety of that type.

(II) *Outsides*

(1) In the primary aspectual sense, the outside of an object is not its surface. Neither is it the shell or skin, any more than it is the outer casing or the outside part of the object: in short, it is not a *part* of the object. If there is an inner side, it is the outer side which is opposed to the inner side as is the right side to the left, the front

to the back. But, unlike the inner side, it is a necessity. Even a sponge has a face with which to meet the world. No object, however tortuous its interior, can dispense with this necessity. Only the outside can constitute it as object. Thus, from the vantage of a hollow within it would be perceived as no more than a material continuum, since here there can be no picking out the object *qua* object. And yet one would still see the object, only now from a non-individuative standpoint. And still the interior of the object would lie the far side of the side that we see. For that is always true. There is always that which is essential to the object's being which lies outside the scope of perceptual awareness: it is a measure of their essential inwardness, of their 'mystery' as one might say. In sum, while there exists adapted uses of 'outside' to outside-part and surface, all that we say above holds of that central usage in which we are speaking of the outer *side*. This is the aspectual sense of 'outside'.

The purpose of the expressions 'inside' and 'outside' is in the first place to enable us to speak of the inside of the object. But it is not only that, it is in the second place to speak also of the outside—an achievement of a wholly different order. We discover that there is more to the object than that outside for which we have for the first time found not only words, but thoughts. It is, in short, a peaceful revolution in our relation to the object, an awakening. For the development of the system of structural concepts is at once an enterprise of analytical exploration and of synthesis, the synthesis of what in uniting those differential properties proves in the end to be nothing less than the concept of a material object. It is to introduce into the object of unreflective, of pre-rational experience, a new degree of logical complexity, beyond the inchoate preliminary or pre-rational standards for objects, and beyond those of surfaces: it is to allow it to be the synthesizing repository of contradictory predicates, almost like a miniature Absolute; and all of this is possible only because of the essential inwardness of the material object (in contrast to the surface, which 'wears its heart upon its sleeve'). It is to find oneself all but thinking such thoughts as that 'it is smooth but also——if only you knew and in a way . . . rough!' For if, *per impossibile*, one could imagine conversing with a being struggling towards the light of self-consciousness and the acquisition of the concept of material object, one might speak in this way of the material object which he has yet mentally to demarcate. Paradoxically, it involves a suspension in our attitude towards the object as object, since what is withheld from view is for the moment set on a footing with what is there and then visible outside, and the logical primacy of the latter is for the moment set aside.

In this primary sense of 'outside'—which I describe as 'primary' because it is an adaption of the central aspectual sense of 'side'—we will say of any property that can be of sides, that is apparent to standpoint, and that is of the object itself, that it must be of its outside (hence we speak also of the 'pre-eminence' of the outside of the object). Examples of such properties are the following: rough, hot, red. They are to be contrasted with properties like (say) heavy or accelerating: the former (token) properties, but not the latter, being shared by object and its outside. This is implicit in saying of the outside that it provides the standpoint from which the object is individuated.

(2) Here is a summary statement of the situation in the case of material object outsides/insides. While objects have sides as well as surfaces, they have a pre-eminent enclosing surface and a pre-eminent outer side. They have moreover an 'inside' that is either the inner quantity or segment (etc.)—*part*; or the inner side to the outer side, the side that may be (but need not be) within; or else that which is the far side of the surface, that which is within the object, its interior. These are all different senses of 'inside', and they each correspond to different 'outsides'. Thus, objects have an outside that is either the outer segment or quantity (etc.)—*part*; or the outer side to the inner side, the side that is without; or else the outer surface of the object. And so in speaking of the 'outside' we could be speaking either of a part of the object, or of its surface, or the object as it reveals itself to the stand-point that constitutes it as object. The latter use I have taken to be the 'primary' use of the term.

(b) The 'inner-outer' problem for secondary qualities

So much for the system of analytical concepts which we bring to bear upon the object when we put on display what of a piecemeal perceptual nature would be involved in a sustained perceptual encounter with a material object. These concepts enable us to give such differential aspectual reports as that 'The north face of the Eiger looks blue from here', or 'The inside of the hollow conductor feels smooth at this point', or 'The near side of the moon looks hemispherical from earth', or 'The outside of Notre Dame is grey'. From now on my topic is the integration that occurs when we pass from these fragmentary aspectual findings, which reflect the fact that the perceiver is situated in a sector of space, to perceptual experiences and judge-ments which to a degree or even totally shake off this characteristic. The integration in question assembles both the perceptual experiences as parts of a sustained experience of the object, and their contents as the properties of a single material object.

What follows is a brief sketch of what goes on in the course of the perceptual integration of secondary qualities: for example, of heat ('feel') and colour. (This is undertaken prior to discussing the integration of the more fundamental spatial properties in the ensuing Section 6.) One of the interesting features of secondary qualities is their independence of material form: these properties can belong to matter with or without shape or structure, and to both the surface and interior of material objects. Now while some attributions of these properties are related to per-ceptual standpoint, some others are not. Then the reason for now briefly examining the attribution of heat and colour to material objects, is a problem which is a conse-quence of this diversity. What one might describe as 'the inner–outer problem with material objects' is raised in a very clear form in the case of such properties. I mean the problem posed by the fact that perception from the outside of the object is the normal access to the perceptible character of material objects, and thus to a single materially continuous entity with an interior. This raises questions as to the implications, so far as that interior is concerned, of those attributions from the outside which are in depth.

(I) *Attributions in depth from a standpoint*

Heat is predicable of material objects. Then while this attribution is non-directional, it is nonetheless from the outside and thus the product of perception from a standpoint. This is reflected in the fact that such attributions are to material objects *and* their outsides. And yet there is an inclination to say that it is *material objects* alone, rather than their *outsides*, that are capable of sustaining heat, as if the concept of perceptual standpoint was inapplicable in this case. Then while this objection correctly assumes that heat needs material stuff as bearer, it seems to conceive of the outside as some kind of immaterial metaphysical shell. But this misunderstands the situation. After all, the outside contrasts with a possible inner side and an interior, but in no sense with the object itself or its material stuff. Then in general our primary concern in attributing 'feel' properties to material objects is with their outside, for such properties are detected through the sense of touch. Indeed, since this is the only way we have of perceiving secondary 'feel' properties, it can be in no way second best to alternatives. Accordingly, even if one were to break open the object in search of their ('real') heat, we would still never escape from the outside of objects as the bearer of that heat.

And yet how can the outside of an object be hot? For if all of its interior were cold, what would be left to be hot? But here it is illicitly assumed that to predicate heat of the outside is by implication to contrast it with the state of the interior. But this is to confuse the outside of an object with its outside surface. And in fact nothing in the concept of an outside being hot rules out the possibility of our discovering a fine layer that is hot—whereas by contrast we already know on logical grounds that (say) smoothness cannot be in depth (being a property reserved uniquely for surfaces). Then is there a regulative principle to the effect that some depth must be hot if the outside is hot? I think there is, and in practice it might amount to the claim that we have yet to encounter the other side of the layer that is hot—however fine that layer may be. 'Hot' is not like 'smooth', reserved only for surfaces, nor is it like (say) 'juicy', which implies some more or less reasonable depth in its bearer. As if the only alternatives lay between predicating heat of an immaterial shell, or else of part of the interior merely through indirect evidential indications accessible to us from the outside. If there is predication of heat, it is given in logical form: that is, it is regulative.

(II) *The integration of sides in depth*

So much for the *aspectual attributions* from a standpoint to the prime enmattered object-structure (viz. side) capable of bearing the secondary qualities in question.

Let us now consider the *integration* of such aspectual properties, and the way it leads to a characterization of the whole material object of which they are aspects.

If each of the many outer sides of an object with an outer and an inner side is warm, we might say that 'The whole outside is warm', and here the contrast will probably be with the inner side of the object. But if every side of an icy object was momentarily warm from the sun we might say 'The whole outside is warm', and here the contrast will probably be with the interior, and in the process the use of 'outside' switches from the above aspectual sense to the surface sense. Such specialized integrative attributions are to be distinguished from the most familiar syntheses. Thus, if each of the many sides of an object is warm we mostly simply say that 'every side is warm', and having said that our orientation and that of our speech naturally changes to the whole object, as opposed to the whole of its outside. We now simply say that 'the object is warm', and what led (analytically) as a bridge to that (whole-object) orientation falls into disuse.

It may be objected that all we are really doing is integrating parts of the outside into the whole outside, and then deciding to use 'the whole of the outside is warm' interchangeably with 'the object is warm'. According to this account of the predication of heat, which is resistant to the thesis that we synthesize from (mere) sides to (real whole) objects, when we say 'This side is warm' we might as well say that 'this part of the outside is warm'. However, if the transition from side to object were to take place in the manner suggested, we should in the case (say) of a hot sphere be able to substitute 'this half' for 'this side', replacing an integration of sides with one of parts. But if a hot sphere is divided in two the new exposed surfaces may be cold, whereupon the two halves would not be described as hot, and it might be argued that we should retract the original claim that 'the object is hot'. But this conclusion does not follow. And it shows that 'Both halves of the warm rock are warm' differs from 'Both halves of the juicy orange are juicy' and 'Both halves of the camera are heavy'. The transition from parts to whole in the case of heat is not that of quantity-parts to quantity-whole or structural-parts to structural-whole. It is an integration of a wholly different order, one that is specifically perceptual.

6. Material Objects and Perceptual Standpoint (2): The Synthesis of Visible Shape

I come now to the most important of perceptual syntheses: seeing the shape of material objects. Here we have a phenomenon as fundamental as any in perception. It at once provides the structure through which the visible properties of objects (colour, texture, etc.) are ordered in perceptual experience, and is at the same time the essential basis of the visual recognition of objects. Now the visual perception of object-shape is a complex phenomenon, constituted out of units which are themselves also made up out of parts. Then how do we assemble seeming to have seen the three-dimensional shape of a material object out of momentary visual experiences? The unit out of which the whole is constituted is the seeing of the three-dimensional spatial properties of the sides of objects. Then these experiences are in turn made up of simpler elements, whose nature needs to be understood. Meanwhile, with the increasing complexity of the spatial object, three additional significant variables make their appearance during the process of perceptual synthesis: mental activity, the spatial relations between observer and observed, and processes in the understanding. I begin by examining the simplest of shape perceptions, since they play a part in the constitution of the experience of the shape of sides.

(a) Two-dimensional seeing

(i) 2D/2D seeing

By 'two-dimensional seeing' ('2D-seeing') I mean seeing two-dimensional shapes like ellipses. And by '2D/2D seeing' I mean the sub-variety wherein we see no internal three-dimensional spatial property of its parts. Then this encompasses two sub-varieties in turn. First, cases in which the bearer of the shape inhabits a purely two-dimensional continuum: say, seeing the shape either of after-images with eyes closed, or of neonlit tubes in dense fog. Second, cases where the bearer is visibly set in three-dimensional space: say, seeing the shape of a constellation like the Southern Cross, which I see to be 'somewhere above me', even though the third dimension within the constellation is invisible (hence 'the floor of heaven' of the poets).

When I see an after-image, or constellation, or in dense fog see a round neonlit tube that is tilted from the vertical, I experience a specific two-dimensional appearance, say an elliptical look. Corresponding to every two-dimensional shape is a single two-dimensional look which is unique to it and transcendent of both colour and ontological type: for example, the round look is common to a round red after-image and a circle of silver stars. Let us call such a look '$L_{2D\ round}$'.

(ii) 2D/3D seeing

(1) By '2D/3D seeing' I mean seeing a two-dimensional shape that is at the same time the seeing of some of the internal three-dimensional spatial properties of the bearer of that shape. Examples are: seeing the rectangular shape of a carpet, or of a door, both set in an ordinary room. Then provided the obliquity is not excessive, these shapes are usually veridically seen in a single oblique look.

Such cases are puzzling. What happens when, from an angle of (say) 20° from the vertical, I see the roundness of a dinner plate? One is inclined on the one hand to say that one does not really see the roundness—on the grounds that we do not see $L_{2D\ round}$. But conversely one is also inclined to say that, while we do see roundess, this can be no more than seeing-that roundness is present—on the grounds that we see $L_{2D\ ellipse}$, which is merely visual evidence of roundness.

I reject both theories, and suggest that the facts are a little more complicated than either suggest.

The first argument correctly assumes that $L_{2D\,round}$ is not seen, for it is simply not on view; but mistakenly supposes that $L_{2D\,ellipse}$ is seen, and that in general to see any 2D-shape S necessitates seeing $L_{2D\,S}$. If it were true that I see $L_{2D\,ellipse}$ whenever I see a tilted circle, then on such occasions I ought to be able to draw the ellipse I saw— and often cannot with any confidence. But it is in any case certain that we sometimes see circularity that is at 20° or less, for we can tell merely by a single look that the shape is circular (as we cannot when the tilt is 80°). This shows there is no principle to the effect that the seeing of 2D-shape necessitates experiencing the ('2D/2D') 2D-look.

(2) The second theory, that while we see the roundness of the plate, this is merely seeing-that roundness obtains, is also false. It correctly accepts that we see roundness and do not see $L_{2D\,round}$, but mistakenly supposes we see $L_{2D\,ellipse}$. Doubtless this theory is sensitive to the fact that the circular object occupies an elliptical sector of the visual field, and that this fact is causally contributory to our seeing roundness. What more natural than to suppose it makes that contribution through causing the seeing of $L_{2D\,ellipse}$, which causes a seeing-that circularity obtains? But in fact $L_{2D\,ellipse}$ is visible only to those who cease to see the layout in three-dimensional space (perhaps because of dimmed spectacles). This seeing-of roundness defies reduction to any form of seeing-that: what we see here is a particular 2D/3D look that is uniquely one of roundness. It defies reduction to both 2D/2D-seeing and to seeing-that, and is *sui generis*. And it is a more complex synthesis than the 2D/2D variety.

In such a 20° case one sees-of roundness, which causes a distinct see-that roundness obtains. We neither see $L_{2D\,round}$—which is *not on view*, nor $L_{2D\,ellipse}$—which is *neither noticed nor properly visible*. But while seeing examples of a 2D-shape S does not in general entail seeing $L_{2D\,S}$, it does *as a completely general rule* entail seeing a look that uniquely is a look of S: namely, the look of S-at-tilt-t. Then when t has the value 0°, the unique look in question is $L_{2D\,S}$, as happens in the case of after-images and constellations. But in the present case t has a value somewhere between 0° and (say) 30°, and here the look L is that of circle-at-such-a-tilt. This enters the content of the visual experience, whose full description is not (just) 'see-of a circle' but 'see-of a circle-at-such-a-tilt'. The look of a circle at 0°, which is $L_{2D\,round}$, *is not* the look of a circle-at-tilt-t (where t ≠ 0°), which is $L_{2D/3D\,circle-at-tilt-t}$; and it is the latter we encounter in the present case of 2D/3D seeing. The principle that a unique look corresponds to the spatial content that is perceived, remains unscathed, as does the irreducibility of see-of to see-that.

(3) In sum, in 2D/3D-seeing the perceptual object is not just (say) round: it is round-at-t° (tilt into the third dimension). It is therefore a *more complex object* than that of 2D/2D-seeing. And while we do not encounter anything that is '*the* look of roundness', we nonetheless encounter a look that is *uniquely a look of roundness*, viz.

the look of roundness-at-t°. Nevertheless, seeing roundness at t° entails seeing *roundness* (which is in this sense detachable from the more complex object) *and* seeing the third-dimensional t°-tilt at which it is set (likewise detachable). In short, in such a 2D/3D case we encounter one of the *many looks* uniquely showing round-ness-presence, attesting to a gathering complexity in visual experience and visual object. Though roundness at t° looks different from roundness at z° (say), it nonetheless looks uniquely *round* at all those different angles. It is perhaps this fact which generates the puzzlement which is natural to this case.

But one other factor remains perplexing in the extreme, and causes me to embell-ish the above account. Namely, the ever present element of *degree*. I mean, the fact that between tilts of (say) 20° and 85° lies a continuous spectrum of diminishing extents of 2D/3D-seeing, and increasing extents of 2D/2D-seeing that are embed-ded in a seeing-that context. This shows that, whereas we can have *pure* examples of 2D/2D-seeing, we cannot of 2D/3D-seeing, and have to acknowledge an irre-ducible element of 2D/2D-seeing in all cases—despite the existence of veridical depth-perception. It is a corrective to an oversimple understanding of 2D/3D-seeing that probably uses 2D/2D-seeing as model, and reveals a qualitative unlike-ness between the two phenomena. Whereas in 2D/2D-seeing we encounter a mental *thing* as the original bearer of shape, namely the visual sensation, nothing mental is the *bearer* of experienced 2D/3D shape, for in this experience the ele-ments of interpretation and intellect have already made their appearance on the visual scene, and for that no mental thing suffices. And so it might be said of 2D/3D-seeing that variously well-formed or less well-formed examples of 2D/2D-seeing must be a constant subliminal presence: examples which will be increasingly well-formed as t° waxes in extent and 2D/3D-seeing fades from the scene. Nonetheless, 2D/3D-seeing remains an irreducible and *sui generis* phenom-enon.

This discussion has shown that 2D/3D-seeing cannot be constituted out of 2D/2D-seeing. The reason is, that a whole new variety of look is encountered in such seeing. A whole new order of experience comes into being in those cases in which the third dimension within the object is an irreducible element of the content of the experience.

(b) The fundamental unit: 3D-seeing of object-sides ('3D face-seeing')

2D/3D-seeing occurs, not just when one sees the shape of a window or a plate, but the shape of the rim of one of the faces of the Great Pyramid at Gizeh. However, something more happens when I see, not merely that *rim* in three dimensions of space, but the *general three-dimensional spatial properties* of the face. Whereas 2D/3D seeing is of ellipses and squares at tilts in space, this ('3D face-seeing') is of (say) 'the triangularity and concavity of a surface', also at a perceptible tilt. Then such a variety of seeing constitutes an even more complex synthesis than the preceding varieties. Thus, 2D/3D-seeing involves the seeing of the *object* of the decidedly less complex 2D/2D-seeing, which is deductively detachable from it: for seeing a circle at tilt 20° entails seeing a circle, which is precisely an example of that which is the sole possibility of 2D/2D-seeing. Similarly 3D face-seeing is a more complex synthesis than 2D/3D-seeing, since from it we can likewise deductively detach the seeing of the object of 2D/3D-seeing. Thus, seeing the planeness and triangularity and tilt at t° of one of the faces of the Great Pyramid, entails seeing a triangle at a tilt of t°—which is precisely what 2D/3D-seeing accomplishes.

Now this form of seeing can be generalized to encompass the wider primary aspectual sense of 'side'. Accordingly, its object is now permitted to range not just across faces like those of the pyramids, but over 'the south side of Mt Sainte Victoire', etc. For example, such seeing occurs when one sees the round profile and hemisphericity of our side of the moon. Then here in this perceptual experience we have the unit out of which is constituted the seeing of the shape in the round of material objects. However, that complex perceptual phenomenon involves an important factor which has so far been missing in the discussion: mental activity. This must now find its place in the analytical account.

(c) The synthesizing power of mental activity

(1) When our minds synthesize the visual experience of the three-dimensional shape of material objects out of these units, it is made possible through the mental activity of looking at ordered sequences of the sides of the object. Aspect gives way to aspect in visual experience, each somehow uniting with what has preceded it, culminating in the end in a single complex object of visual consciousness. The discussion which now follows examines what is the simplest example of a phenomenon of this kind: perceiving the shape of linear motion. But the aim is general. It is to understand how mental activity of the right kind can effect the unification of spatial data in our own minds. It is to discover the general form of such syntheses.

(2) I begin with the simple unit which is to be synthesized in the present case. Consider a familiar example of the sort of phenomenon I have in mind: seeing the (rapid, brief) path of a shooting star. This event is the inactive seeing of a shape which unfolds across time (to be contrasted with (say) seeing an apparently instantaneous streak of lightning). In this phenomenon we see the shape of a movement. It is almost as if one set eyes upon a *thing* bearing that shape. But in fact the shaped entity that we see is something that sheds into the past parts of its being as it progresses, and gathers from the future parts of its being in completing itself. What is astonishing is that a look possessed by an a-temporal entity like a plank of wood, should be possessed by one which relates so to time, and at each instant shows not a *whit* of that look! And yet these grossly dissimilar items share a 'look' in a unitary sense of the term.

So we are supposing that we see a star suddenly and rapidly trace out a straight line. Now this is a single visual experience with a single spatial object, bearing a look that can be worn by a plank. Then because this appearance is a *purely spatial* appearance, time-order is irrelevant to experiencing that look. If from t_1 to t_2 I see an object trace out a path t_1 ⌒⌣ t_2, I would experience the very same look when from t_1' to the later t_2' it reverses its tracks t_2' ⌒⌣ t_1': though the experiences are different, the spatial look we experience is the same. However, it is one thing for a structure to be instantiated in something, it is another for it to be visible and seen: if it is realized in an hour hand, it will be neither! Then the causal agencies determining this *double phenomenon* are A) Suitable velocity (unrealized in the movements of snails and nearby tracer bullets), B) Mental constitution (as Berkeley noted, the rate at which 'ideas' traverse the mind might have been different, we might have perceived across milliseconds, and seen very different events), C) Visual 'grasp' (one's capacity to synthesize parts into greater wholes), etc.

(3) Now let us consider an example of the synthesizing power of mental activity, with the above perceptibility of motion-slices as unit. What occurs here in the mind is the same in these regards as what goes on in perceiving the overall shape of material objects, but in the interests of simplicity I restrict the discussion to perceiving linear shape: (say) that traced out by a firefly wandering across a field at night. Then suitable mental activity is capable of synthesizing examples of the simple phenomenon examined above.

Thus, visibility-for-one of the shape can be created by the mental means of looking with a suitable relatively ambitious *internal object*. Instead of looking merely at 'a light crossing a field', one needs to be looking at 'the shape of the light's path'. Thereupon the willing that is such a looking acquires a new causal power, the domain of the visible-to-one enlarges in one respect, and ⌒⌣⌒⌣ may appear in visual consciousness, generating knowledge and recollection of itself. At the end of the procedure memory seems to contain a single sine wave spread out across space and time.

What is going on during the activity? At any instant the enterprise is at once a looking-for the next spatial change and looking-for the enlargement of the foregoing. Such striving with such an internal object has a causal power that is determined by that object. It determines the power to effect a seeing whose novel object-sectors unite in consciousness with that already seen, constituting thereby a spatially enlarged object. Thus, it tends—albeit with increasing difficulty—to engender a *continually enlarging* visual object. This mental activity is a continuous willing such that the attention tends to be *causally responsive* to wider and wider spatial spans of the path of the light. That willing *is* 'priming' the attention to be responsive to just such an item. This is how spatial synthesis across time is effected in one's mind.

(d) Mental synthesis

(1) The present discussion seeks to understand what happens when the mind synthesizes perception of overall object-shape out of aspect-experiences. However,

the term 'synthesis' as used in mental philosophy needs to be understood—and 'taken with a grain of salt'. Understood because different situations are so described, taken with 'salt' because talk of 'synthesis' can arouse false expectations. Now the use of the word 'synthesis' in Chemistry is reserved for situations in which more complex stuffs like ammonia are created out of simpler, by the application of a 'synthesizing process'. It is this physical paradigm that causes the need of the 'grain of salt'. We must understand that we can legitimately speak of 'synthesis' in the mind and elsewhere when the paradigm is wholly inapplicable.

As an example, intention origin can synthesize distinct act-events as parts of one act. Then while the unified acts are analogues of nitrogen and hydrogen, nothing is an analogue of the synthesizing process, for here there is no event of uniting. And this variety of 'mental synthesis' is only one of several. Indeed, for much of the time when we speak of 'mental synthesis' it is of what is from the start already accomplished. We encounter the 'synthesized' as a whole-event, and in many cases can discover no whole-event parts. Mostly the concept of synthesis is merely the conceptual other side of analysability. We need discover no separate 'synthesizing process', no autonomous 'raw materials', no analysability into parts which might have existed on their own or otherwise combined: merely analysability. In a word, both the chemical and the act syntheses are simply two familiar varieties of a kind that ranges far and wide.

Thus, where synthesis exists, so does divisibility; and vice versa. And where divisibility exists, a Principle of Partitioning exists together with one of Synthesis. That is, rules whereby given some item we may discover a set of parts; and vice versa. And such a pair of principles can take multiple forms, depending on the variety of part. Accordingly, 'synthesis' is always relative to such a principle-pair. The rules of synthesis consist of tests whereby a set of items may be deemed to constitute a single item. Such rules are implicit whenever we characterize something as a 'synthesis'. We ought to be able to specify the putative parts, as well as the criterial tests which ensure that they constitute the required whole.

(2) Then consider seeing the overall shape of the path of a light. Here the putative parts are the short-term seeings continuously occurring between (say) t_a and t_p. Then how do we tell if these last really are parts of the former? The necessary conditions are simple enough. There must exist a visual experience lasting from t_a to t_p whose object is the shape of the overall path; and at any instant t_k in that interval the visual experience must be enduring through to $t_{k+\epsilon}$ (where t_ϵ is the rough time-extent of such seeing); and the latter must be identical with the short-term seeing from t_k to $t_{k+\epsilon}$. We simply 'thought-slice' the seeing from t_a to t_p into seeings of t_ϵ-duration. The 'thought-joining' of such 'slices' is all we need to be able to speak of the synthesis of long-term seeing out of short-term. It is a simple reversal of such partitioning.

Nowhere do we discover mention of a causal criterion of unity. We make no appeal to the active mental cause which was operative in determining the existence of this synthesis, as a way of showing that synthesis exists. Indeed, we make no appeal to a synthesizing agency. It seems that the chemical synthesis involving a synthesizing event, and the act synthesis involving a synthesizing desire and intention cause, both give misleading prominence to causation. They misleadingly suggest that 'synthesis' obtains only when a distinct causal agency brings separate existents into a state of union. But in fact synthesis out of given parts is determinable merely through discovering the existence of an entity with such parts. Though mental activity plays such a causal part in the present case, it is not what we refer to in speaking of synthesis.

(e) The understanding and spatial self-reference in visual experience

(1) But if this is what synthesis is, and if synthesizing of object shape is effected through mental agency, it remains unclear how seeming to see a *shape* emerges out of that procedure. After all, we are not glueing together parts of a mental *thing*. Why should a sphere rather than an ellipsoid appear to have been seen? There can be no doubt that the intellect is closely involved. This emerges in the fact that the experience of shape is internally dependent upon belief. Thus, the paradoxical fact to be interpreted is that perceptual experience of the spatial properties of objects is internally sensitive to beliefs concerning one's spatial relations to the object.

An example bring this out. We shall suppose that from the vantage point of an unbelievably fast spacecraft we (a group of astronaut-sculptors) are viewing the shape of some luminous minuscule moon of a remote planet, and that the only way of knowing our speed and height is from instruments. At any moment we stand in various spatial relations to this moon: we are at a certain height above its surface, moving in a certain direction, at a given speed. Then let us assume we circumnavigate the moon, believing as we do so that we adhere to a norm of constancy of height and speed, and at the end of the procedure seem to have seen a certain shape. What role was played by self-referential spatial belief in the genesis of this experience of shape? Assume the moon was pear-shaped, and suppose also that during half of the flight the instruments went askew, falsely indicating constancy in the above values. Thus, as we neared the larger end of the moon the spacecraft imperceptibly slowed to half-speed and half-height: a state of affairs which persisted until we had rounded that end, whereupon the craft imperceptibly resumed the norm. We had thought the flight was so ⌒⌒⟩ at constant speed and height, whereas in fact it was ⌒⌒(½)speed. Then one is likely to seem to see not ⌒◯ , but ⌒◯⟩, and all the more so if the whole situation is repeated half a dozen times, and if the entire journey can be accomplished sufficiently rapidly for the mind to knit the many view-experiences into one extended complex spatial perception. If one's self-referential spatial beliefs ($\Sigma\ B_{sr}$) and the ordered set of the view-experiences $\{Ve\}$ are as in this example, it seems likely we will have a (non-veridical) visual experience of seeming to see ⌒◯ .

(2) Now there is no reason why we should not have *chosen* to halve speed and height for half the journey, nor any reason why such a viewing procedure should not result in a veridical perception of shape. Call the attendant self-referential spatial beliefs in this case ΣB_{s2}. Then the following emerges: had one held one set of beliefs (ΣB_{s2}) one would seem to have seen ⌒◡, while had one held another (ΣB_{s1}) one would seem to have seen ⊂◯—even though the ordered set of view-experiences $\{V_E\}$ was identical in either case. Therefore belief must in either case be one of the causes of the perceptual experience of shape. And this is the norm.

Let me explain why. Experiences of perceiving shape in the round are non-redescriptively, indeed are essentially, putative perceivings uniquely of three-dimensional shape. Now if such experience is to be a way of knowing, it requires supplementation by knowledge, first that one's visual system is intact, second of the spatial conditions of viewing. Therefore the need for such knowledge must in a general sense be recognized in the experience itself. The very institution of (such a mode of) visual shape-perception depends on our knowing (as a general rule) the attendant spatial conditions. In an environment in which they had become unknowable, the institution would fall into disuse and the phenomenon simply vanish from the scene. For one cannot accidentally perceive shape in the round, as one can circularity. If, in a context of veridical views, a rag-bag of false beliefs somehow engendered seeming to see shape S_R, and S_R truly is the shape of the seen object, this cannot be the seeing of S_R: the reason being, that its causal history is not of a kind that leads to a corresponding outer reality. Therefore knowledge of spatial conditions must be the norm in the visual perception of shape in the round.

(3) This suggests that when spatial conditions causally condition the overall spatial experience, they do so in a way that is intelligible to the subject. When perceiving shape in the round S_R, both the shape S_R *and* the attendant spatial viewing conditions (C_v) *explain* the ordered set of momentary view-experiences $\{V_E\}$. Then *that* they do, and *how* they do, is not hidden from the subject. Normally one knows both the spatial conditions, and that and how they enter into the explanation of one's seeming to have seen S_R. The projective geometry is, to a degree, understood. One's mind interprets the views, in the light of C_v, and comes up by the end with an *experience* of an object (viz. S_R) that explains $\{V_E\}$. We can see this in the following.

As the moon continues to grow in the window of the space craft, the subject believing he is travelling at the same speed and height, it *looks* to be enlarging. Though the set of looks $\{V_E\}$ is ambiguous, his experience across time constituted one reading of that ambiguity. The set of view-experiences $\{V_E\}$ leads to seeming-to-see-S_R, thanks to one's knowing conditions C_v, *through one's understanding* the spatial implications of $\{V_E\}$ in the light of C_v. Thus, given the views one experienced, and one's attendant beliefs, it comes as *no surprise* to the viewer that he seemed to see ⌒◡. Normally, having seen such an S_R, one knows why the views were as they were in the order that they came. The understanding is overtly implicated in the genesis of the experience. Normally one knows, in projective-geometric terms, and in the light of C_v, why it is one both saw such views and seemed to see S_R. After all, if the understanding had been wholly inert, then the set of views in conjunction with the beliefs simply would not have led to the experience of seeming-to-have-seen S_R. In short, we know that, and how, C_v was involved. We will mention our belief that C_v obtained qua part of the reasons for the fact that 'it looked larger'. That is, our beliefs in the spatial viewing conditions are internal causes of the visual experience of shape in the round.

(4) Now this is how it comes about that a sequence of visual experiences can synthesize to realize an experience of the three-dimensional shape of a material object. While we saw in the discussion of 'synthesis' that it is inessential to the existence of such a synthesis that it was made possible through the occurrence of mental activity, it remains nonetheless as likely that one would have had the unified experience of shape-in-the-round in its absence as it is that one would have understood a clearly audible conversation without in any way listening to it. Then all of the above is implicit when we catch sight of and recognize a familiar material object like a tree. We know that in so experiencing a shape in our visual field, we would expect in the appropriate circumstances to be confronted by a sequence of aspect-views of the kind examined above, which are such that in a context of knowledge of our mutating spatial situation a tree shape would have come to consciousness.

7. Conclusion

(1) We synthesize across time our *perceptual experiences* of colour and heat and texture, simultaneously with the more fundamental syntheses of shape, in particular the visual syntheses of contour and three-dimensional relief, which bring order and structure into all of these experiences, whether sensuous or structural in type. And we synthesize the *objects* of those perceptions as we do, which are characterized in physical concepts of the kind elaborated earlier. All of this occurs in the course of a unifying complex perceptual project in which we posit, before we even begin, the existence of a single material object, which is the extensional object of an ensuing sequence of perceptual experiences. In the end an object with a determinate perceptible character seems concretely to have come to awareness: a material thing with a three-dimensional shape, with colour properties that are internally linked to the latter and ordered thereby, and temperature and texture characteristics similarly connected to spatial layout.

Much is omitted when we engage in this enterprise. In particular, there are two main respects in which the above is only a beginning. For one thing, what we encounter in this way is nothing more than a flimsy array of superficial ('apparitional') traits, which might in principle be possessed by any number of individuals and types. If we are to resolve these ambiguities, inquiry into other characteristics is the only possible course of action. And this is further to the process described.

(2) But there is another dimension, more pertinent to the topic of this chapter, along which one might partly redress a specific shortfall. Namely, if the object of perceptual investigation is a material object, there can be no end to the processes set out in the preceding discussion. While it is true that sides do not have sides, nor *a fortiori* outsides outsides, any more than do surfaces have surfaces, parts have parts more or less without limit. And those parts lend themselves in turn to perceptual scrutiny of the kind adumbrated, whether they be object-parts or segment-parts. I have commented already on the density of being of a material object. The sheer property of materiality automatically determines a complexity of nature which lies open both to deep scientific analysis *and* a vastly complex conditional perceptual project of exploration along with it. It is the latter of which I speak.

We can in principle dismantle or dismember or dissect or simply arbitrarily divide a material object, in all cases arriving at an ordered set of material object parts, each of which exhibit the properties laid out in the preceding discussion. True, we do not engage in such procedures when we perceptually identify material objects. Nevertheless, we know that in principle we might, and that such perceptual properties are implicit. When we describe ourselves as 'perceptually constituting the material object', we simply have to draw the line at a certain arbitrary point, rather like a painter laying down his brush. But we know as we do that these implications are real and presumed, and might to an extent be realized. While perceptibility is a contingent and inessential and relativistic property of the object, it remains nonetheless one which has almost limitless ramifications.

Note (to page 551)

But to grasp how close it might come, note the following. The great batsman Donald Bradman signalled his arrival in England in 1930, 1934, 1938, with innings of 236, 205, 258; and, at the age of thirty nine in 1948 relented to the extent of notching up a mere 107. Each of these innings was played at Worcester, they were the first first-class innings in each tour, and he made four tours in all. And yet cricket is supposedly noteworthy for its marvellous 'uncertainty'! But this was the man who hit over 300 in a day in a Test Match against the truly great bowling of Larwood and Tate, and without taking any risks. And it was he of whom Constantine wrote, on witnessing his 254 in the Lord's Test Match in 1930: 'it was like an angel batting'. Indeed, it was Bradman who said of McCabe, who played three innings of genius in Test Matches, that he had the impression that he 'played beyond his means'. And it is entirely credible to suppose that he did, and that Bradman did not do this. After all, we are talking surely of the greatest sportsman who ever lived. Small wonder, then, that I should like for a moment to bask in the glow cast by that wonderful career. And to propose a toast, at this distance in space and time, to 'the Don'.

Part IV

Perception and the Body

Introduction to Part IV

1. The Achievements and Significance of Sight

(1) We saw earlier that consciousness involves a 'stream of experience' which typically encompasses use of an accessible attentive capacity in the form of perception. Now in the case of sight especially those perceptual experiences reach far beyond the stream of experience attentively, and because of the work of the understanding typically adopt a developed interpretational form in which the internal content of the experience matches the later objects of the attention. The end-product of these twin agencies is veridical 'see as——'experiences in which the mind encounters physical phenomenal realities lying at a remove in three-dimensional physical space, which are suitably conceptualized both for what they are, and for where and when they are in the broadest possible setting, viz. the World. Thanks to the rational apparatus accessible in consciousness this 'realistic perception' of the contents of physical space-time leads usually to knowledge, and often enough to informed active intervention in the environment which puts that knowledge to use, in all probability re-enacting in these deeds the very rationale which lay in the first place behind the evolutionary development of mind and consciousness.

My claim throughout this work has been that the perceptual and cognitive encounter between consciousness and physical reality is, from a general point of view, essential to the very existence of mind and thus also of consciousness. The reason lies in the fact that this interaction in the concrete is the avenue of the internalization of outer reality that is a necessary condition of the intentionality essential to mind. I suggested that the central importance of the phenomenon of perception for consciousness is reflected in the intimacy of their relation: in particular, in the fact that perceptual experience arises in consciousness in predestined fashion. In part this is because it is an essential function of consciousness; but it is a consequence also of the fact that, thanks to its universal and a priori-given character, the concept of perception constitutes a 'logical moment' in the concept of the core phenomenon analytically entailed by consciousness, viz. experience.

(2) The perceptual experience which most clearly illustrates the manner in which in perception consciousness concretely encounters physical reality—and *as it is* or in its ultimate ontological (i.e. physical) form—is visual perception. This is due to the fact that it alone of the senses manages to both reveal and instantaneously

to identify physical objects lying at a remove in three-dimensional physical space, indeed renders visible the containing space and indirectly also the temporal relations between them. This great epistemological power, which causes us to epistemologically more or less live through our eyes, owes its existence to the high differentiation and order in the visual field and the regular projective psychophysical causal relations linking the visual field with the environment. The attentive accomplishments of sight take the form of a 'journey outwards' from the stream of experience. It is a journey which leads the attention first of all immediately onto a merely directionally given sensory field which is set already in body-relative physical space, then onto merely directionally given optical phenomena likewise set in body-relative physical space (to be precise, on the retina), both of which are seen by the attention though not conceptualized by the understanding, and then along the same directional line makes a qualitative leap into three-dimensional space and distance, arriving finally at overtly given properly conceptualized visible qualities which mediate and bring to view physical phenomena and pre-eminently material objects.

Now whereas the understanding fails to conceptualize the sensory and optical objects of the visual experience, as a general rule it 'paces' the final or maximal achievements of the attention and conceptualizes those objects. Thus the final attentive accomplishments mostly are matched by the work and achievements of the understanding. Let me here briefly set out the several stages in this complex phenomenon. In the very first place the visual experience is immediately caused by a sense-datum, which appears as object for the attention, which in one and the same experience imposes *structural* properties upon a 'Given' of spatially ordered colour/bright point-values in singling out that object. Then this experience incorporates in the instant a developmental causal sequence, beginning with the minimal internal object of the visual experience and terminating in the maximal, and herein lies the *interpretational work in the instant* of the understanding. The end point in that developmental progression is a visual experience whose internal object tends to match the later objects given to the attention.

In this experience the understanding played no part in bringing objects to awareness. However, it does so elsewhere, and in a way that has implications for the experience of the moment. Thus, in the final analysis the visual experiences of the moment stands in a relation of mutual dependence with the experience of seeing 'in the round'. Now this latter phenomenon is in its own right an occurrence of some importance, for in it the attention encounters what is the primary or ultimate object of visual perception: the appearance of a material object (that which is shared by a man and his double). But it is also an instructive phenomenon. For here the understanding plays an essential causal role in bringing objects to the attention. This is because the perception of the instant finds itself embedded in a perceptual process extending across time, which is assisted by self-referential knowledge of the bodily position of the visual observer in relation to the object, all of which has to be grasped by the understanding as the process unfolds, leading finally to the attentive individuation of the physical object in three-dimensional space. Plainly this attentive individuation depends internally on a comprehending mind. Then it is of some interest that this process has no exact point of termination, and could in principle be pursued indefinitely. Thus the visual individuation of the physical object can be no more fully complete than is the painting when the painter lays down his brush. It is a phenomenon which in principle incorporates infinitude of a kind: in the first place insofar as objects are individuated through siting them in relation to other objects and the encompassing uncircumscribed space in which they are set; but also in a polar opposite direction, in that the analytical perceptual constituting of the physical object continues in principle without limit within the borders of the object: a microcosm reflecting a macrocosm—and not distinct from it. The open-endedness of the process of visual individuation carries such an implication.

2. The Body

(1) Then despite the magnitude of the achievements of sight, and quite apart from the extent to which we are reliant upon this magnificent sense, so far as the ultimates of animal mental life are concerned it is all sheer contingency. And in fact the entire procedure of perceptually constituting the physical object in space-time, which is generally accomplished by sight, depends in the final analysis on the body-related senses of proprioception and touch. This is because the latter senses are essential to the animal condition as we know it, while those senses that acquire their objects through the mediation of a secondary quality and thus via perceptual sensation, including it has to be said sight, are sheer contingent presences. And the relation of implicit dependence is asymmetrical. There is no reason why the two primordial body-senses should not constitute the entire perceptual powers of an animal, for the body-senses have no binding need of the deliverances of sight or the other senses, and their content is the all-important spatial properties through which we individuate the contents of space-time. In sum, these two senses act as a recessive foundation on which the others depend. It is an indirect dependence, but since Mentality strictly necessitates internalization of the World and the body-senses alone are essential to animality, one that is actual and ultimate.

Proprioception is put to use so long as we are conscious in enabling us to lead our lives as embodied entities in physical space, and most especially in providing the necessary epistemological foundation for the physical deeds central to animal life. One item of truly major importance for the functioning of this sense is the inherence in the mind of something it is natural to describe as a 'Body Image'. This is a problematic object of inquiry, largely because difficulties occur over its conceptualization. In part those difficulties derive from the fact that there exists an imaginative and far less elusive phenomenon which it is also natural to describe as a 'body image'. In the main however the problems appear when it comes to formulating the sense of the expression that is relevant to proprioception. In my opinion the very first thing to emphasize is that we are dealing here with something vastly more primitive than the aforementioned imaginative phenomenon, for this variety of 'body image' plays a vital role throughout the animal kingdom, seeing that animals are aware of their bodies in precisely the sense and way we are. Many people make the error of failing properly to differentiate the two phenomena, and as a result speak unguardedly of a 'body image' with nothing clearly in mind. At this point I shall merely note that the philosophical problems in this area consist for the most part in assembling a viable concept which fits the primitive reality that I claim to be a necessary condition of proprioception, and providing an account of its role in proprioceptive experience.

There is one other property of proprioception, and implicitly therefore also of the body image, which is of great epistemological importance, since it constitutes an essential part of the underpinning of all the sensuous senses. Thus, the principle of individuation of sensations is spatial, indeed body-relative spatial to be precise, so that what makes it possible for two qualitatively indistinguishable pains to exist simultaneously in (say) left and right thumbs is the fact that they are given to their owner at diverse locations in a bodily spatial framework. The existence of that framework is internally dependent upon proprioceptive experience and ultimately on the possession of a body image. Then the same principle of individuation applies when the sensations in question are what one might describe as 'perceptual sensations', the sub-variety mediating the perception of the environment: smell, taste, auditory, and most notably visual sensations. It is because one after-image is given as 'directly in front', and so pointable-to along that line in physical space, and another qualitatively indistinguishable other as 'a little to the left' along a different line in the same physical space, that we can simultaneously confront two such items. In the complete absence of body-sense, and the orientation it involves, and ultimately of a body image, it is difficult to conceive of an adequate system of differentiation of sensory phenomena. Remove direction and orientation—and what is left? In the light of these considerations the possession of a body image must on a number of counts be rated as part of the very foundation of absolutely every form of perception and thus ultimately of consciousness itself. As the point of input for time is the experience, so in the case of space it is the bodily spatial framework opening onto universal space. The body image underlies almost everything else in the animal mind.

(2) On this understanding of the situation proprioception, and the body image along with it, must be fundamental causally engaged elements of human and animal life generally. On the other hand the role of the sense of touch, at least from a functional point of view, is of lesser significance. True, the small-scale active manipulations that are an important part of our dealings with the environment probably make use of tactile experience: for example, in driving a car or opening a door; and this is of some consequence. But it pales in significance besides the essential contribution of proprioception to physical action and sensuous perception. Now here the yardstick of significance has been functional utility. However, we saw

above that from a different standpoint both senses have another and equal importance, since they are essentials of the animal condition, indeed are mutually supportive, completely self-subsistent, and sufficient on their own for an animal to lead
a life. On these counts they are to be placed on a level, and to be contrasted with all
the other highly contingent sensory powers. Together they play an indispensable
role in animal existence as a recessive but nonetheless essential foundation upon
which rests the achievements of the other senses, notably sight. While they are
not put to direct use in the main epistemological transactions of consciousness
with physical reality—apart from the aforementioned role of proprioception in the
individuation of perceptual sensations, they are nonetheless there as a constant
presence, something for the other senses to fall back upon, an essential foundation.
In sum, before I come now to look more closely at these two phenomena the main
conclusion I think we should draw from the foregoing considerations is, that
whether one perceptually constitutes the physical object by sight, or else more
laboriously and no doubt more with the aid of rational intellectual processes does so
by means of touch, awareness of one's body and the deliverances of touch together
constitute a self-sufficient foundation upon which the perceptual constituting of
physical reality ultimately depends. Thus, they must each in their different ways be
necessary conditions of the development of mind and consciousness.

23

Proprioception and the Body Image

1. Is Proprioception a True Perceiving?

(1) At first blush the phenomenon of proprioception[1] looks like a bona fide example of perception. And yet it is natural to entertain doubts on the matter. For one thing proprioception is attentively recessive in a high degree, it takes a back seat in consciousness almost all the time. Might it perhaps be that we are misdescribing as a perceiving or noticing what is in fact no more than an immediate knowledge of limb presence and posture, caused let us say by either cerebral events or postural sensations produced by limb posture? Why posit an intervening event of perception? May it not be functionally otiose? In addition, if perceiving is the same thing as noticing, and noticing invariably makes demands on the attention, surely bodily perception ought to obtrude in some distracting fashion in our daily practical dealings with the objects in the immediate environment. But this is not our experience. Catching a ball, we do not find our limbs attentively getting in the way. The body does not appear to consciousness as a rival object of awareness as we actively engage with our surroundings. Why not abandon the theory of a body-directed attending, and substitute in its place an account in which we postulate an immediate knowledge of limb presence and posture which is generated by psycho-cerebral phenomena regularly caused by such bodily states of affairs?

I am convinced that this would be a mistake. To help explain why, I will begin this examination of proprioception by considering an atypical example of the species. Namely, the case in which we involute some of our perceptual attention away from its usual visual and auditory objects, and actively turn it instead in an immediate mode onto some body part like an arm. This is an atypical example of proprioception, partly because of its purely inquisitive character, but above all because it draws its object out of its natural obscurity into the full light of awareness. Yet I doubt whether it differs much from the everyday recessive examples in other significant

---

[1] The term 'proprioception' might be used in various ways. I employ it to stand for the familiar immediate experiential awareness of our own limbs and body. It turns out on inspection that this consists in an attentively immediate intuitional awareness uniquely of these material objects: in short, a distinctive sub-variety of perception. It follows that proprioception is not 'a kind of information', if that means the holding of cognitive attitudes. And it is to be sharply distinguished from the attentively immediate awareness of bodily feelings like fatigue or warmth: the reason being, that these latter are mentalistically-immediate perceptions of psychological objects.

respects. In any case, it is surely an example of perception. Thus, it is an experience, of type attending, whose content is caused non-deviantly by its object, and it can form the basis of an inference to the existence of that object. Above all, it is no kind of cognitive attitude, nor tendency to entertain a cognitive attitude, even though, as befits perception, it causally sustains one. Thus, it is not a case of knowing, believing, suspecting, or any such, since one could in principle have this experience when one knows that the bodily facts are other than they seem in the experience. In short, we have here an attentive experience in which a small sector of physical reality appears one way, which is to be sharply distinguished from cognitive attitudes of all kinds, even though it naturally sustains such. In a word, a perceiving.

(2) Is it a new or sixth sense, to be added to the famous five? The concepts involved here are perhaps too vague to admit of an exact answer, and I will not pursue this issue. Instead, I will ask another more precise question, namely whether we have reason to distinguish proprioceptive perception generally, and not just the above self-conscious sub-variety of the kind, from the mode of perception closest to it in character: the sense of touch. It will I think on investigation emerge that these two types of perception differ in a number of respects, and that as a result neither can be subsumed under the heading of the other. In any case let us at this point make a few comparisons between these two body-related varieties of perceiving.

But first, what is to count as an exercise of the sense of touch? Whatever the answer to this question, it is clear the sense encompasses heterogeneous phenomena, ranging from instantaneous point contact with a material object to active tactile exploration in which, as it seems to me, one's own bodily movements play a mediating role of a causal and maybe also attentive type. Then common to all these cases is a property which bears directly upon the question under consideration. Namely, in every instance of tactile perception a proprioceptive awareness of one's body *stands between one* and awareness of the tactile object: it is only through being aware of one's body that one becomes aware of the objects given to touch. And so the sense of touch must depend upon proprioception, as not vice versa. Therefore whether or not proprioception is *absolutely* immediate, it must be immediate in ways not open to touch. This differentia between these phenomena, carries the implication that neither mode of perception can be a sub-variety of the other.

Here we have one major difference between proprioception and touch. A second major difference lies in the character of their perceptual objects. One glaringly obvious difference consists in the *scope* of the objects open to them: whereas touch ranges far and wide without restriction, proprioception is more or less of necessity confined to the body of the perceiver (non-trivially, surely). But another important difference lies in the *type* of the properties, and in particular the type of the *spatial* properties, open to these modes of perception. Through the sense of touch we discover surface properties (like roughness and smoothness), shape properties (like sphericity and cubicality), and in general a broad array of fully determinate spatial properties. Then it is surely of some import that not all of these are accessible to proprioceptive discovery. For example, roughness and smoothness are not. And determinacy of shape seems to be discernible only in rather unusual cases of proprioception: thus, I can see no reason why we should not across time proprioceptively discover complex shape properties of (say) one's hand movements, such as the property of moving along a rectangular path. But there are limits to what spatially can be disclosed to this sense. For example, there seems no real prospect of proprioceptively discovering, either instantaneously or across time, that (say) a particular limb is a cylinder or sphere or cone, or suchlike.

Whether or not the latter differences in the type of spatial object given to the two kinds of perception constitute a major difference between them, the mediacy/ immediacy difference undoubtedly does. This difference is fundamental, and if anything could prove that these two modes of perceiving are different senses rather than the two sub-varieties of one sense, it surely ought to. However, since the very same type of sensation is put to use in these perceivings, even though no secondary quality is essential to either, and since these two closely related properties are usually definitive of senses, it begins to look as if the concept of a perceptual sense is *vague* and as if we ought not to press the issue. Perhaps we should settle for the following more exact claim concerning these two varieties of perception. Namely: that while the sense of touch and proprioception are closely related and body-oriented senses, they are nonetheless dissimilar in a number of fundamental respects, and neither can be reduced to the other—and leave the matter at that. When we reflect that they each in different ways depend inextricably upon the existence of the other, this guarded conclusion seems all the more judicious.

2. Proprioception and Physical Instrumental Action

(a) A preliminary problem

(1) So much for the question whether proprioception, including the highly self-conscious variety of the species that I singled out earlier for discussion, is to count as an example of perception and as the exercise of a new or sixth sense. I want now to take a look at cases of proprioception that are far more typical than the latter sub-variety. After all, introspective proprioception (as we might call it) is the exception rather than the rule. Even self-concerned bodily acts, such as occur when a cat washes behind its neck, take place in situations in which the attention passes beyond the active limb and focuses on a distinct object (which in this case happens to be part of its own body). Thus, the mode of proprioception involved here cannot be what I am calling 'introspective proprioception'. What is special about 'introspective proprioception' is merely that the limb is the *focal point* of the attention at the time of proprioception. While this might look like a form of introspection, in that we involute the attention away from its outer mediated objects and turn it immediately onto something in oneself, it is so markedly dissimilar even from attending to a sensation

that I think it should be acknowledged that the title 'introspective proprioception' is a little misleading. Its value lies in the emphasis it places on the somewhat unnatural involution of the attention that occurs in such cases.

Then what is it that occurs in most animals most of the time in the way of body awareness? If it lacks this interioristic convoluted character, might it not be something different, indeed might it not simply be non-existent? I do not think so, and will address the issue below. In any case, I now intend to consider what are probably the most common examples of proprioception. I propose at this point to examine the part played by proprioception in *physical instrumental action*. More exactly, the variety of proprioceptive awareness that occurs when we are engaged in intentionally manipulating objects, such as a newspaper or a car or a tennis racquet. In short, when we are in the midst of the most familiar and typifying of deeds.

A difficulty appears at once. I have mentioned the problem already in Section 1, and address it again in the hope of resolving it. The problem arises out of the fact that at any instant we have only so much attention to go around and no more. If perception consists in the coming to attention of some item, and if proprioception is a variety of perception, proprioception must make demands on the attention. But if attention needs in part to be absorbed in proprioception of the acting limb, it rather looks as if when we engage in intentional manipulative action the phenomenon of proprioception ought to be a discordant and distracting item, competing for our attention with both the act itself and (say) visual perception. Yet this is not our experience. When we play a stroke in tennis we are not conscious of a conflict within the attention, we do not experience the limb as competing for attention with the ball (whose path occupies so much of our attention), nor with the playing of the stroke (which does the same). Ours is not the experience, say, of a novice juggler. What is the explanation of this state of affairs? Given the rather impoverished content of introspective proprioception, one might begin to question whether proprioception occurs at all in such cases. Might it not be that it simply drops out of the picture, and that the attention is wholly directed onto (say) the path of the ball and racquet, to the exclusion of the body? This conclusion initially recommended itself to us at the beginning of this discussion, and as we shall see some philosophers incline to this view.

(2) The first thing we should do, if we are to meet this point, is reaffirm a simple principle first formulated by Elizabeth Anscombe.[2] Namely: that acts can be intentional under *multiple descriptions*, some instrumental and some 'basic'. Thus, a particular act can be intentional under both 'unlocking a door' and 'turning a key', and we bring this out by saying things like 'I decided to unlock the door by turning the key'. Then in cases like this we might very well have added 'I decided to unlock the door by turning the key by swivelling the hand that grasped the key'. Here both ends and means are chosen and hence are intentional, and the means

---

[2] *Intention*, Blackwell, 1956.

in this example are chosen right down to the basic bodily means of swivelling a hand. The next thing to say is that swivelling is generally a *proprioceptively detectable* phenomenon: if someone swivels my left hand unexpectedly, I am usually immediately and proprioceptively aware of the existence and type of that movement. Finally, we should note that intentional acts are known to their owner under the headings under which they are intentional. The conclusion in such a case as the above is that the act will be known to its owner under the heading 'swivelling a hand'. Then since one can scarcely know one has swivelled a hand without knowing one's hand has swivelled, and since one must discover this last proprioceptively, we are forced to conclude that in a case of this kind—where an act is intentional under both instrumental and basic-act descriptions—*and* where the latter is a spatially determinate description like 'swivel'—one must have been proprioceptively aware of a determinate bodily movement and therefore also of body positions across time.

And so, despite the fact that the attention in such cases is probably focused ahead of the actively intervening limb, and despite the natural epistemological recessiveness of limb movements, when an instrumental act is intentional under a description that mentions spatially determinate bodily means, proprioceptive awareness of the bodily phenomenon is a necessary condition of the deed. If playing a sudden snap forehand volley is intentional not merely under 'hitting the ball to the corner' and 'playing a forehand volley' and 'swinging the racquet' but also under 'moving my right hand forward thuswise', then proprioception of arm position is a necessary condition of the deed. Even though one's attention is focused primarily on the path of the ball, and doubtless also though to a much lesser extent on the path of the racquet, some small measure of attention must be left over for the movement of the arm. Short-term memory and knowledge are a good test of what occupied the attention at a point in time. Then since, immediately after playing a tennis stroke, one invariably has some sort of short-term memory and knowledge of one's arm movement, that arm movement must have been proprioceptively perceived at the time. Indeed, it is clear that this proprioception was a necessary condition of the act itself. In short, the theory that proprioception is necessary for our normal physical manipulations of the environment, survives a difficulty posed by the fact that proprioception constitutes no kind of distraction during those activities.

(b) Proprioception in instrumental action: how distraction is avoided

(1) I have been considering a series of active situations—tennis, driving a car, opening a door—in which proprioception is a necessary condition of intentional instrumental action. Yet before I proceed, I must note in passing that there exist other examples of manipulation of the environment in which the role of proprioception is more problematic than in these cases. I have in mind those actions in which the epistemological and attentive recessiveness of the bodily means increases

to such an extent that such bodily phenomena become invisible to their agent—special activities like knacks (whistling) and skills (darts) providing instances of the kind. However, I can at this point do no more than simply mention these problematic acts, because I have still to follow up a further question concerning proprioceptive content in the familiar instrumental situations at present under examination. That is to say, where an instrumental act is intentional both under an instrumental description *and* a determinate bodily description like 'moving my arm forwards', *and* is at the same time such that the attention moves outward onto a focal point lying beyond those bodily means. In a word, in the typical active intervention of mind in physical nature. While we have demonstrated that proprioception is necessary in these cases, we have yet to show how it is that the mind manages to circumvent the problem of 'distraction' in these situations.

(2) I return now to this problem. The difficulty is, that even though the bodily movement necessitates attention, it constitutes no sort of distraction as one engages actively with the environment. Then while it is true that the quantity of attention called upon by proprioception is generally small, it must be emphasized that the resolution of the difficulty is not to be found in quantitative considerations. The following remarks make that clear. They show that attentive *content* rather than *quantity* is the determining factor.

Consider once again the example of hitting the tennis ball. It is important to notice that different *attentive situations* might prevail as one performs an instrumental act of this kind, and that in some of these attentive situations perception does indeed constitute a distraction. Leave proprioception aside for a moment, and consider the relation between playing the stroke and looking at the ball, since that exemplifies the problem just as well. These latter two activities can take different forms, in some of which looking is undoubtedly a distraction. Whether it distracts depends above all on the *content* of that looking. If the content is studying the ball's colour, plainly it will. If it is studying the ball's path, very likely it will not. If it is studying that path to see if it is paraboloid in character, very likely it will once again constitute a distraction. And so it is clear that for perception not to distract, but to enhance and enable performance, the object-content must be of a special and indeed unique kind: it must be the path of the ball *qua* (say) object-of-a-volley. Whatever exactly this content consists in, it must one assumes include direction, speed, relation to the court-space available for that type of shot, and so on. This content cannot be acquired merely additively, but must somehow be realized naturally and synthetically through the offices of the intentional heading under which one acts.

Then once the perceptual activity acquires the required character, it ceases to be in competition for attention with the stroke. The activities of looking and volleying are two, are distinct existents, and each occupies so much of the limited space of one's attention, and yet if the contents of these two activities are of the required kind, they cease to be in competition for the attention. Though attention is divided, it is not the scene of a tug of war—provided the behaviour of the agent is suitably integrated. Such looking as we have described must, one assumes, be functionally subordinated to the playing of the stroke: it appears in a hierarchy, whose presence is manifested in the interdigitated content of the two enterprises. My surmise is that proprioception takes its place even lower down in this hierarchy, and in such a way as likewise to constitute no sort of distraction. Here, too, internal object or content must play a decisive role. At this point the problem of 'distraction' seems to me to be more or less solved.

(3) And yet a residual difficulty remains. It concerns the character or type of the proprioception involved in this case (and others). Thus, a genuine *activity* of looking at the tennis ball takes place as one engages in this instrumental action, but does a parallel second *activity* of proprioceptive attending join it? On the face of it, one would say not. While one is conscious of engaging in an activity of looking as one plays a tennis stroke, one seems not to have embarked upon any parallel project of proprioception. Such an answer poses a problem for the theory that the resolution of the problem of distraction lies in the harmonious content of a sequence of hierarchically related intentions.

An example assists us here. Let us suppose that I am engaged in playing the violin. Then what goes on in my feet and legs is of less interest to me than what goes on in my fingers and arms, is known and remembered less, and presumably therefore must be proprioceptively perceived less. Now nothing but an intention and act-desire with an indexically given present-tense time content set me in active motion, and this deed was co-present with and surely essentially dependent upon an enhanced attentive awareness of certain body parts. Accordingly, the increased proprioception must owe its existence to that same initiating intention and act-desire, and must one assumes be actively determined, which is to say that a project of proprioception must be going on (however recessively). Then the situation does not seem significantly different in the case of the tennis player. Thus, if we bear in mind that his intention is to use an arm of which he is aware to stroke a ball he can see, it is difficult to avoid the conclusion that an active process of proprioception must here too have been generated along with the act of stroking the ball. In short, despite its recessiveness, in such situations we must be engaged actively in determining our own proprioceptive perceivings. In that case, three simultaneous and internally linked activities—looking, proprioceptive perceiving, and stroking—will have been ushered into being by a single decision to act. The internal content of these three activities form a hierarchy which is such that harmony rather than dissension reigns within the attention. Within this hierarchy, proprioception will normally play a role that is at once recessive and harmonious. This squares with our experience. And it constitutes a defence of the main proposition that I have been at pains to defend in this Section 2: that proprioception is a necessary condition of physical acts of intentionally manipulating the environment. It shows the way in which this necessity is satisfied.

634

(c) Objections to the claim that proprioception is needed for instrumentality

Not everyone is of the same mind on this important issue. On the one hand we discover the following comment by M. T. Turvey[3] (in the course of expounding views
in line with the discoveries of the Russian scientist Bernstein). 'What must be
understood is that in the course of performing *any* activity, the *perceptual information available* is of these three kinds. In order to *guide any activity* you need to be able
to pick up on the properties of the environment, you need to have *some appreciation
of where your limbs are with respect to each other*, and you need to know where you are
with respect to the layout of the environment' (my italics). Meanwhile Bill Brewer
remarks[4] (speaking of his own claims concerning simple visually guided motor acts)
that 'it' (the short-term body image i of the moment)[5] 'is not essential for Brewer's
simple reaching and grasping, on the Bernsteinian account he develops', and also
states[6] that 'little to no knowledge of current bodily configuration is required for
this kind of task'.

These look like opposed theoretical positions. Then what perplexes me is that
Turvey explicitly takes himself to be giving expression to the 'Bernstein Perspective'. How can Bill Brewer's account simultaneously be 'Bernsteinian'? In any case,
how are we to understand Turvey's 'some appreciation of where your limbs are with
respect to each other'? I can only assume that he means 'some knowledge of *some*
of the internal spatial properties of one's limbs'. What else? And his claim that 'in
order to guide *any* activity' one needs such knowledge, is in agreement with the
position I have been urging (above). In short, I seem to find myself in agreement
with Tovey and at loggerheads with Bill Brewer on this issue.

I shall briefly repeat the reasons which support the view in question, viz. that proprioception is a necessity if one is to manipulate the environment. Thus, we know
that acts fall under multiple descriptions, under some of which they are intentional,
and that intentional action necessitates beliefs whose content matches those intentional headings. Accordingly, one thing that seems to be at issue with Bill Brewer is
whether simple acts like visually guided reachings are sometimes (often? mostly?)
not intentional under *any* descriptions which make *some* mention of the internal
spatial properties of the limbs. I do not mean under beautifully precise exhaustive
descriptions. I merely mean under descriptions making mention of *some* internal
spatial properties. Then surely they are thus intentional. When I reach for a cup of
tea, do I not intend to move my hand *out* from my body? And in *this direction* out
(very roughly demarcated)? And some *relatively short* way out? Is not this familiar
act intentional under at least *some* of these spatial descriptions? Would not one be

---

[3] In *Human Motor Behaviour*, ed. J. A. Scott Kelso, Lawrence Erlbaum, 1982:286.

[4] In *Spatial Representation*, Blackwell, 1993: 274.

[5] I stipulate the sense of this expression in Sect. 3 of the present chapter. The sense in question is: the
internal content of the proprioceptive perceptual experience of the moment. This is what Bill Brewer is
speaking of at this point.

[6] Op. cit., p. 273.

grossly surprised by *some* hand movements (e.g. by a zigzag)? And would not such surprise indicate a loss of *control* over the act? But control implies a match of intention and deed. The characterization offered by Bill Brewer of everyday acts of reaching imports a cognitive hiatus that is simply not present—a hiatus that is in fact encountered in more extreme examples of the species. Thus, the normal acts of reaching are scarcely on a par with (say) sudden high-speed duckings from what shows as a mere blur in one's visual field! These latter wild unpremeditated lurch-ings are acts in which one's expectations of spatial path are minimal, and the act is intentional under 'avoiding something that I glimpsed nearby'—but under pre-cious few other spatial headings. One more or less 'finds' oneself at a point in space at the end of these convulsive deeds. That, precisely, does not happen with 'simple reaching and grasping'.

Then if we can agree that everyday reaching necessitates some knowledge con-cerning 'where your limbs are with respect to each other', which as Turvey points out is to be acquired through perception, the question arises as to the mode of per-ception through which this is accomplished. It has to be either proprioceptive, visual, or a combination of both. While Bill Brewer seems to think that both postural knowledge *and* short-term image are inessential to these familiar acts, I shall consider whether sight alone might meet one's cognitive needs in such cases. Suppose I am playing tennis, coordinating sight and physical action with a measure of skill, and that my right arm of a sudden becomes completely anaesthetic, indeed suddenly does not seem present at all! Would not this have *some* detrimental effect on my serve? It may be that in some imaginable realms it would fail to do so, but on the tennis courts I have bestrode I have little doubt that most of us would botch the shot! Then if *some* aesthesia is a necessary condition of the normal stroke, why so? It can scarcely be that one needs *intellectual reassurance* that the limb still exists! Then in the first place what reason can there be for refusing the hypothesis that proprioception meets the binding need for *an immediate concrete seeming-presence* (which sight cannot provide)? And can proprioception occur without spatial content, and thus without *short-term image*? Second, what reason can there be for refusing the hypothesis that feeling plays some part in informing us of the *where-abouts* of the active limb? Or are we to believe that reaching for (say) a cup of tea depends upon an 'appreciation of where your limbs are with respect to each other' which is *wholly visual* in origin? It is one thing to suppose that in such cases sight is to a degree an informant concerning body configuration, it is quite another to confer upon it the role of sole informant. Is reaching for a visible cup of tea so unut-terably different from reaching into one's pocket for one's handkerchief? As remarked above, Bill Brewer describes the former familiar cases along lines which better fit exceptional cases like a high-speed ducking that is triggered by sudden visual stimulus.

In the light of these considerations I conclude that simple acts like reaching require a *measure of proprioceptive awareness*, a proprioceptive perception whose content is what we (later) call a 'short-term body image' or 'i'. Indeed, the few apparent exceptions (such as inhaling) depend upon an already established present proprioceptive setting. I suspect that Bernstein's valuable findings are of less philosophical import than Bill Brewer supposes. Personally, I would surmise that the well-worn philosophical concept of 'under a description' (that is, of *intentional aspect*) already captures much of what is philosophically interesting in these findings. While philosophers ought not to be insensible of scientific achievement, it is desirable at the same time that they have some faith in their own methods and discoveries. Out of the frying pan (of factual ignorance) into the fire (of scientism)!

(d) Proprioceptive attending and the whole body

I have so far discussed problems arising over the reality, and the perceptual content of proprioception in two sorts of cases: introspective proprioception, in which limb presence and posture are the focus of immediate active interest, and intentional manipulative instrumental action, where they are not. Before I leave the question of proprioceptive content, I should like to say a little about (proprioceptive) perception of the body *as a whole*, not in the atypical case of introspective proprioception, but such as occurs for most of our waking (and perhaps sleeping) lives. In the light of the observations just made concerning proprioception in instrumental action, I think I should at this point disavow a theory I have endorsed in several places in print.[7]

The theory in question recommended itself to me for the following reasons. Struck by the extraordinary recessiveness of proprioceptive perception, and above all by the fact that whenever we need intentionally to move a limb or site a sensation we can do so immediately and without further ado, it seemed to me that at any particular moment we must be aware of the presence and position of every sensuously differentiable point on the body-outside. If I feel a tickle on my chin, I scratch it; if I see a missile near my head, I duck automatically; and so on. These facts made it seem as if in some nearly subliminal way the entire body-outside is continually perceived in all its detail, even though consciousness seems not to *record* the multifarious detail such perception would involve, and despite the fact that this theory implies the absence in proprioception of the familiar and important phenomenon of *attentive selectivity*. This latter implication certainly troubled me, since perception of its very nature is a phenomenon in which the attention culls what it needs, and discards what it does not, from out of a richer given. But I could see no alternative at the time I endorsed these views.

However, the above theory now strikes me as both unparsimonious and ill-sorted with certain facts. Those facts are that when I attend self-consciously to a limb, or intentionally use one body part to the exclusion of the rest, that excluded remainder inevitably recedes in my awareness. The limb stands out on a 'ground' of the body as a whole, which is perceived also to be sure, but less differentially and vividly

---

[7] B. O'Shaughnessy, *The Will*, vol. I., ch. 7., CUP, 1980.

than the limb in question. Then unless we are to embrace the improbable idea that *two* qualitatively different varieties of perception go on simultaneously all the time, one vastly complex and nearly subliminal, the other selective and accessible to memory centres, there seems no alternative but to abandon the doctrine of comprehensive detailed proprioception. Accordingly, a more economical theory suggests itself, namely that we all the time perceive the body as a whole, recessively and with a limited measure of differentiation of detail, and that particular sensations and/or intentional bodily actions usher into being a perceptual awareness of the body-point or part sensuously or actively singled out, an awareness that takes place on the 'ground' of the body as a whole. Since every differentiable point or part on the body-outside is capable of playing such a role, and since we are continually aware of the body as a whole, it is easy to misconstrue the latter property as identical with the property of being actually, albeit nearly subliminally perceived.

3. The Short-Term Body Image

(a) The distinction between short-term and long-term body image

I want to say something at this point about the distinction between what I have (elsewhere) called the 'short-term' and 'long-term' body image.[8] When most people speak of the 'body image', they have in mind something approximating more closely to what I called the 'long-term body image' than to what I described as the 'short-term body image'. Nevertheless, a case exists for singling out several different items and giving them these various titles. Indeed, I will argue that the expression 'short-term body image' might with justice be applied to three diverse though closely related phenomena. But for the moment, let me briefly try to justify the prime distinction, that between long-term body image and short-term body image.

When I postulated the existence of a long-term body image, I was entertaining a particular complex hypothesis. Namely: that there exists a perceptual sense of 'how at instant t one seems to oneself to be disposed in spatial respects R in space',[9] which is such that what it singles out is to be causally explained by the joint operation of *two* causal factors. The first of these factors is something present and phenomenal that is causally sensitive to, and probably causally explained by, the spatial properties singled out in the perceptual experience: for example, the factor in question might be postural or kinaesthetic sensations, but could instead be neurological phenomena. The second causal factor is something that is singled out by a different and *quite special* sense of 'how at instant t one seems to oneself to be disposed in spatial

---

[8] B. O'Shaughnessy, *The Will*, vol. i., ch. 7., CUP, 1980.

[9] I mean 'a proprioceptive "seeming" whose content is R'. R could be ostensively explained as 'the sort of thing you now immediately spatially perceive with regard to your limbs'.

respects R_a in space'.[10] An example of this kind of causal explanatory claim would be the following: 'At instant t one seems to be aware of a flexed arm *because* in general (and in fact over a period of decades) one takes oneself to be a being endowed with an arm which can adopt postures like flexed, straight, etc.; and *because* of the operation of postural sensations (etc.) at t' (the sense of 'takes oneself to be' being something quite other than that of 'imagines oneself to be' or 'has the cognitive attitude that one is' or 'perceptually experiences oneself as'). The hypothesis is, that if in general one took oneself to be (say) octopus-shaped instead, then despite having a human shape and despite the presence of posture-caused phenomena like sensations of posture, one could not have the experience of seeming to be in the presence of a flexed (very roughly) arm-shaped thing.

Thus, the supposition is that *some something* (call it 'the long-term body image' or 'I'), whose content encompasses arm-shape, functions as a necessary but insufficient condition of these experiences of shape and posture. That is, that one continuously carries within one's mind/brain certain (probably) mental 'luggage' that one's mind/brain brings to bear upon the data of the moment (which is in fact probably sensational and possibly also neurological in character), whose nature is such that the causal conjunction of these several factors results in a proprioceptive perception whose spatial content in part repeats and is in any case tightly constrained by that psycho/cerebral 'luggage' (I). Just what kind of a thing this item I is supposed to be, and whether anything answers to it in reality, remain to be considered. And so does the validity of the above complex hypothesis. But for the moment I want to take a look at what the item I is supposed to explain, namely what I have called the 'short-term body image'.

(b) Three different kinds of short-term body image

It turns out that more than one thing might naturally qualify for this title. Three closely related phenomena can be distinguished, which I shall call (α), (β), and (γ). The first (α) is the *content of the proprioception* of the body at any moment. This is something that mutates from instant to instant, and not just because body posture continually changes but also because attentive focus shifts, whether because of the odd passing bodily sensation or else in accord with the intentional bodily occupations of the moment. Thus, you could have the same bodily spatial state on two occasions t_1 and t_2, but because you were physically active in one way at t_1 and either physically inactive or active in some other way at t_2, different proprioceptive experiences would almost certainly occur at t_1 and t_2. Here we have one reality, the proprioceptively *perceived* of the moment (α), which it is natural to describe as a 'body image'. However, another equally significant reality is the proprioceptively *perceptible* of the moment, which I shall call (β). For any given bodily spatial state,

[10] R_a is more comprehensive than R, and (roughly) coincides with the spatial properties of the outside of a physical object (here, the body of the animal subject).

this latter (β) will, one presumes, be a fixed content. We would arrive at the value of that content by distributing the attention all over the body, while the body remained in one given posture, and synthesizing the multiple findings in a single spatial image. This single spatial image (β) is what is available for perception, or as we say what is perceptible, given a determinate bodily posture.

Now (α) and (β) have certain common features. Thus, whatever in (α) stands out upon the ground of the body as a whole, for example the spatial properties of the bowing arm of a violinist, is certain to find itself in (β), or the perceptible variety of 'body image at that instant'. But another important common property between (α) and (β) consists in the *very kind* of those common contents. Crudely expressed one might say that they are alike in a quite peculiar impoverishment of detail/parts. Whatever the exact description of this special feature may be, it is evident that (α)- and (β)-type body images will be alike in lacking the presence of the full complement of tactilely differentiable parts of the body-outside. This property of (α) and (β) suggests the need for a third sense of 'short-term body image', for it brings to our notice a third reality which is—like (α) and (β)—causally determined by the conjunction of long-term body image and postural sensations, etc. (and ultimately therefore by posture itself). This concept manages to make good the spatial impoverishment of (α) and (β). It is of what one might call the *potentially perceptible* of the moment.

This third reality (γ) is arrived at in the following manner: we take the content of the (β) image of the moment and augment it with all the points and parts that *might in principle* come to consciousness were a highly localized tactile sensation to take up residence at that point. This image fills in the lacunae of (α) and (β), and is in this sense an image of a continuity. Then whereas the (α)-type body-image was the content of a particular perception, the (β)-type was not, and it goes without saying that the (γ)-type likewise is not—irrespective of whether the entire body outside happens to be clad in a hairshirt or whatever. Despite their unrealizability in experience, the (β) and (γ) images are, I think, genuine fixed realities, which correspond to any determinate posture, whether static or mobile.

(c) The constitutive raw material of body images

A problem arises as to the 'metal' in which these images are cast. We know that (α) is the content of a special variety of perception, namely proprioception, and that (β) and (γ) are constructs out of such; but precisely *what sort of thing* goes to constitute (α)? At the very least (α) contains what can be brought by the subject under concepts, and expressed in his language: for example, 'My right hand rested on my right knee, and my right arm was straight.' But this tends to conceal the problem. Thus, when we say 'straight', how exactly are we using this term? Are we merely opposing it to 'crooked', or do we literally mean that the arm is as rulers and Roman roads are? Neither answer strikes me as altogether satisfactory. The first because the same problem must break out over 'crooked', the second because it seems to go beyond what we strictly perceive, and in any case assumes a synthesis of points which it is hard to credit. The content seems somehow 'sub-conceptual', as one might say, not ineffable but forged out of something other than the concepts enshrined in one's language. After all, the proprioceptions of non-rational animals probably do not differ from those of rational animals in the dramatic way the visual perceptions cannot help doing. Does speaking a language *help one to run*? While it would certainly help one to look for next Saturday's theatre tickets, it is surely irrelevant to locomotion! For whatever reason, the content of proprioception seems best expressed in a practical medium rather than in conceptual terms: for example, in the act of raising one's arm to catch a ball. Finally, the content of a (γ)-type image is, I believe, best and concretely given by a physical model of the body surface. And what this means is, not that one might in principle perceive such a thing, but that for any given body posture all the acts of pointing to all the sensuously differentiable perceptible points on one's body surface would in the end delineate such a surface. Since this content includes (β) content, it seems fair to describe it as putting on display the sum total of what might in principle at any instant be perceived.

Whatever the answer to these questions concerning content, the justification for speaking of these three kinds of body image (α), (β), and (γ), which is to say the evidence for believing they stand for realities, is twofold. In the first place it is conceptual: each sense of 'body image' can be precisely expressed as a bona fide concept. Thus, the (α) image is of the *perceived* at any instant, the (β) image is of the *perceptible* at any instant, and the (γ) image is of the *potentially perceptible* at any instant. The second justification is available only for (β) and (γ) images, and consists in the fact that for any given posture one and only one (β) and (γ) value exists—a property which doubtless follows simply from the first justification. While only one of these three phenomena can be accounted an event, let alone an experience, they are phenomenal realities nonetheless. Their cause lies in body posture, together with whatever mind-impinging phenomena body posture regularly causes, whether it be postural sensations or neurological events, taken in conjunction with the presence of something else which I have called 'the long-term body image' (about which I speak in a moment). Posture and long-term image causally determine the (β) and (γ) image at any instant, while posture and long-term image, together with attention distribution, jointly determine the (α) image of the instant. Since what is perceived depends upon what is perceptible, the (β) image of the moment must encompass the (α) image, and since they each depend on what is potentially perceptible, the (γ) image must encompass both.

4. The Long-Term Body Image

(a) Conceptual considerations

None of the three phenomena I have labelled 'short-term body image' seem to be what most people who speak of 'the body image' have in mind. While what they in fact have in their minds is in my view for the most part an unformed or vague or mal-formed concept, I think it likely nonetheless that people are conscious here of something that is a fourth reality, to be set alongside the other three. However, this claim needs to be hedged in somewhat, because of an *ambiguity* in the use of 'body image'. Thus, there exists on the one hand a *mentalistic* concept of 'body image', which is exemplified in such familiar comments as 'Anorexics often have a distorted body image'. But there also exists what is probably a less overtly mentalistic concept, which we find at work in assertions like 'Infants already possess a body image' and 'Amputation has no instantaneous effect on one's body image'. I see no prospect of unifying these two usages, for the simple reason that they are in my opinion concerned with different realities. Then when I speak of a 'long-term body image', it is the second less overtly mentalistic phenomenon that I have in mind. I am convinced that something real exists here, to which it is natural to append the label 'body image' or 'long-term body image'.

In fact, it seems to me that a large part of the philosophical problem of the body image consists in putting together a proper and veridical concept of this latter entity, and in setting out what kind of considerations would constitute an adequate justification for launching that concept into use. It should not be thought that the *mere expression* 'body image' carries us through to that destination; indeed, one might say that it is itself so far little more than a verbal picture, and in any case the existence of ambiguity disposes of the suggestion without further ado. Now when I remark that the concept is for the most part unformed or vague or malformed in people's minds, I mean *either* that they have not engaged in the work of fashioning a concept *or* that they assume that the mere expression is self-explanatory *or* that they have not even noticed the existence of an ambiguity. And yet I think it often enough the case that people are aware of this elemental phenomenon. We find our-selves in the curious situation where not merely does awareness precede delineation of an individuating concept, but in addition an improperly differentiated double awareness precedes both. In any case, I emphasize that my concern in the ensuing discussion is with the particular something that those who have resort to the *less overtly mentalistic usage* have in all probability actually noticed.

(b) The peculiarities in our concept of long-term body image

(1) Why do we believe there exists something it is natural to describe as a 'long-term body image'? And why do we think it is endowed with a spatial content (call it C) matching the body-outside? Well, what preliminary data makes us posit that something? The first thing is, that C is common to all examples of the three varieties of short-term image (to all i's, as we called them) over an extended period—like decades. And yet this common property of experiences cannot on its own constitute reason for believing in a distinct image of the body, in any natural sense of 'image'. Doubtless the regularity demands causal explanation, and in terms of something

with value C, but this still falls far short of what needs to be the case if we are to feel obliged to posit anything of the kind of the long-term body image. After all, the above complex causal property happens to be possessed by the body itself. For we assume all the short-term images are veridical perceptions of body shape, and we know that C is common to all instances of body shape, so the regularity in question must be caused by something with value C, viz. the body.

Clearly, there is more to the concept of long-term body image than the inherence of value C in something which explains the regular presence of C amongst an extended sequence of proprioceptive experiences. What we are looking for *at the very least* is something with value C, set in the mind/brain, intervening causally between the body itself and the regularity amongst the short-term images (the i's), and explaining that regularity. And yet it has to be said that it is not immediately clear why exactly is it that we feel impelled to posit an explanation of such an *internal kind* of those i's? And in any case is that the *only* function whose necessary discharge makes us wish to posit a 'long-term image'? Is our concept of long-term body image merely of 'the whatever in mind/brain explains the regularity amongst the i's'? Is that all there is to the concept?

(2) It takes us an important step nearer to grasping what goes into the concept of long-term body image (I), to understand just how the latter specification still falls significantly short of the necessary requirements for I. It does so in an interesting way. A visual example helps to bring out how. This particular example functions above all as a contrasting case, through the aid of which we manage to bring to light the fundamental *structural role* that is played by the long-term body image in proprioceptive and body experience generally.

Let us suppose a person is confronted with a dense array of coloured points on a page, and that this array harbours the clearly visible outline in red points of a beetle of type X; assume he is confronted by a succession of such point-arrays, in each of which an X-type red beetle appears, only differently postured each time; and suppose this person identifies the red X beetle every time. Then he might do so in two different ways. He might know each profile as 'a particular profile of the X beetle': a piecemeal collection of individual cognitions, not unlike that possessed by 'airplane spotters' in Britain in 1940. But he might instead simply know what X beetles *look like*—just as we all know what (say) hands or cups look like—and come to recognize the beetles in innumerable postures on the page as a result of this knowledge. Then if this is how he managed to identify X beetles, this latter piece of visual knowledge will have intervened in the viewer's mind, sandwiched between the beetle's appearance in his visual field and the event of visual recognition, and done so again and again in the course of many recognitions. It thus explains the common presence of a spatial content (call it C′) in an extended sequence of visual experiences. Bearing this in mind, one might be inclined to say of the viewer that he harbours a 'long-term image of beetle shape' (with content C′) in a sense which at first blush seems to closely parallel that invoked when we speak of a 'long-term body image'. However, in fact the two senses differ quite fundamentally. And that they do, brings out just how easy it is to misunderstand the concept and role of the long-term body image.

(3) Here are some of the characteristics of the visual case. A viewer is presented with a complex array of points within which he discerns a shape, and then another array within which he discerns another shape, and so on. Then it *so happened* that those shapes had a common content—*and* that the viewer was aware of it—*and* that this knowledge helped him single out each shape. Thus, in each perception he imposed one possible interpretation out of many possible others on a complex datum with a spatial character all of its own, and he might have done this through knowing many particular structures or one general structure. Here we have some of the significant features of the visual situation. Then the respects in which that visual situation is a flawed model for proprioception, highlight the peculiarities of the long-term body image.

Note first of all that a limb completely devoid of all feeling is usually propriocep-tively imperceivable, so that proprioceptive bodily sensations must generally help to make proprioception possible. Note also that the visual perception of physical objects is mediated by the perception of the secondary quality colour-brightness. Then it is clear that this man must have singled out beetle postures through seeing an array of red dots *and* knowing beetle shape, in a quite different way from that in which we perceive body-postures through experiencing an array of proprioceptive sensations *and* having a long-term body image. Several features of this visual situa-tion find no analogue in proprioceptive situations. In particular:

A. The parts of the immediate perceptual datum (here, the visual field) can be differentiated and ordered without employing the perceived (beetle) material object as individuating framework. Thus, I might individuate a point in my visual field either as 'red and at mid-point in my visual field', or else as 'red and directly out in front of my head'. (By contrast, we individuate proprio-ceptive sensations by positioning them in relation to the outside of the mate-rial object they make perceptible.)

B. The secondary quality or sensation (here, the colour red) mediating the per-ception of the (beetle) material object is not as such of any *specific* material object, nor as such of any specific *type* or *shape* of material object, nor as such of *material objects* at all—red in the visual field being susceptible of multiple interpretations. (By contrast, proprioceptive sensations are as such of one's unique, determinately shaped, human body.)

C. Many points are perceived that fall a perceptible distance away from the per-ceived (beetle) object: for example, all the other visible points on the page may be blue. (By contrast, we do not feel sensations outside our own body.)

(4) We are trying to explain why it is we hypothesize the existence of something we call 'a long-term body image'. Clearly, if there exists some kind of image with

value C mediating the causal transactions between the body and the proprioceptive perceptual-contents or the i's, that image must have a radically dissimilar function from that of the visual image with beetle-shape value (C') in determining visual perceptions of beetle postures. While the latter was the *imposition* of a spatial structure upon something with a spatial structure of its own that is expressible in multiple structuring systems, the former seems not so much the imposition of a (secondary) structure upon something already (primarily) structured, as the *acquisition* of a structure for what otherwise would lack structure and indeed being. This bodily image seems not so much something perceptually discerned in its object, as something which is at once truly instantiated in its object *and yet* imposed somehow from within.

The peculiarities of the proprioceptive situation that determine this divergence in function between the visual image (of a beetle) and the long-term image (of a body), stem above all from the vitally important property A (above). Here we encounter a unique situation in perception, and a very strange one at that: namely, the *revealed* (material object) constitutes the very system of ordering/individuation/differentiation of the *revealer* (bodily sensations). This property is a direct corollary of the immediacy of proprioceptive perception: the fact that proprioceptive sensations do not attentively mediate the perception of the object they help make perceptible; for if they did, they would have an ordering system that was independent of their object. In short, they would constitute something akin to the visual field.

(c) The origin of the concept of a long-term body image

Then how did we come by this unusual concept of a long-term body image? I think it all begins in the following way. It arises out of the fact that the very existence and general veridicality of proprioception *stands in need of explanation*. There is a puzzle as to how such a phenomenon as proprioception can so much as exist, which will soon become apparent. To begin let us remember that since bodily sensation is a necessary condition of almost all proprioception, bodily sensation must help cause proprioception and must help therefore to explain its veridicality. Now the bulk of the content of proprioception is the *spatial state* of the body. Yet how can bodily sensation help to generate such spatial content? And how can it help to explain the veridicality of that content?

One theory is that bodily sensation occupies much of the body-outside when proprioception occurs, that this entire complex of sensation maps reliably onto the body-outside, and that awareness of these sensations and their spatial properties is *epistemologically prior* to awareness of the body and its space. In short, bodily sensations are said to make possible and explain proprioceptive spatial content, first by bringing to awareness *its own* shape, which then secondly *represents* that of the body. This theory would fill in the lacuna between efficacious bodily sensations and proprioception, and would in addition explain how proprioception is possible. It is a representational theory. However, the theory faces overwhelming difficulties. Thus, sensations require a framework of differentiation; and even in the case of sight the body helps satisfy this need through providing directional differentia, while the body certainly provides the framework for bodily sensations. It follows that the spatial properties of bodily sensations cannot be the epistemological foundation of the spatial content of proprioception. In any case, relative to what would these epistemologically prior sensations acquire a place in space for their owner? If we say relative to the body, we are thinking in a circle, while if we say relative to nothing, how can spatial differences be given to the perceiver? The conclusion must be that a sensation-representationalist theory of proprioception is false, and that bodily sensations come *in the first place* to awareness with a body-space as the required framework of location, differentiation, and individuation.

It is at this point that the aforementioned puzzle concerning proprioception appears. *Whence* the spatial content of proprioception if not via that of postural/bodily sensations? Whence that content, particularly if bodily sensation is the *means* through which we experience such a content? This is the puzzle, and it requires a drastic solution. The only way out of this difficulty is to posit a massive contribution on the subject's own part to the formation of the content of the proprioceptive experience—something which ought in principle to be possible, bearing in mind that in proprioception we continually perceive one and the same object throughout our entire lives. It seems therefore that we ourselves must bring the spatial content to the proprioceptive experience, and do so upon receiving the stimulus of sensation. More exactly, remembering that sensations mutate as posture alters, we must bring all of the space that we encounter in proprioception—minus the differentia of posture. It is, I think, *in this way* that we come by the theory of the long-term body image. Once we recognize the untenability of sensation-representationalism in proprioception, such a theory seems unavoidable.

(d) Filling in the concept of the long-term image

(1) We arrive via this route at the concept of a something (which we are calling I) permanently ensconced in the mind/brain, endowed with a relatively rich spatial content, and playing a significant part in the determination of the spatial content of proprioception. And upon this foundation we build up in stages a richer conception of that something (I). Then as noted already in Section 3, the delineation of I begins with our entertaining a complicated *double hypothesis*, the first part of which takes the following form. We first of all hypothesize that there exists an entity I in the mind/brain which is endowed with the following properties *at least*:

    (i) It is natural to say of it that, in a very special sense that needs spelling out, it is of 'how at time t one seems to oneself to be disposed in spatial respects R_a in space' (where R_a as a general rule tends to coincide with the stable surface properties of one's body).

(ii) The content of R_a transcends *particular postures*: for example, while the content includes arm and leg shapes, it excludes posture-values, such as those of being crooked or straightened.

(iii) The entity I transcends one's *states of consciousness* and *states of aesthesia*, indeed one's *psychological states* generally. That is, a man will retain this image, he will in the special sense seem to himself thus-shaped (etc.) when comatose or stunned, and were it (improbably) to be the case that some drastic brain event switched off all sensation (and proprioception) while waking consciousness continued unabated. More, it would survive an attack of madness in which he seemed to himself to be an octopus.

(iv) The contents of this entity (I) tend to change very slowly, generally paralleling changes in actual body size and shape: the image may be presumed to change its dimensions during the time of our life when we are growing, and to change its shape during adolescence or maybe somewhat during pregnancy and very likely over the decade in which we became hugely fat.

So much for the first hypothesis. The second hypothesis—which is *explanatory* in type—is that the something (I) answering to the above characterization, when it is conjoined with certain phenomena of the moment which probably include the sensational and/or cerebral effects of posture, helps causally to explain the short-term body images of the moment, and in particular the first proprioceptive-perceptual (or α) variety of short-term image. That is, I helps to cause the short-term image i_x at each instant t_x. Then if something happens to answer to this dual specification, if something actually has the above constitutive and causal properties, such a something will be what we are calling 'the long-term body image'. But if nothing does, the concept and usage fizzle out.

(2) Let me now expand the characterization of the hypothesized long-term image. Since, apart from content, its properties are almost entirely causal, and since these causal properties pertain mostly to origins, I will begin with an account of its *origin properties*.

The hypothesis is that I is largely innately determined, but exhibits a malleabil-ity at the hands of protracted coordinated experience. More specifically, it seems on the one hand unlikely that natural developmental alterations, such as growing or the changes of adolescence, are going to find themselves represented in the body image *solely* as a result of coordinated motor-perceptual experience; and even more unlikely that the representations of the presence and shape of one's limbs (e.g. fingers) can be *largely* the product of experience. It is on the other hand simultane-ously hypothesized that experience, and therefore one's own personal experiential history, leave their mark on the image of the present moment. The supposition is, that especially in the case of novel, and most of all unnatural shapes—such as a newly acquired hump, which could not have been genetically anticipated, sustained coordinated experience can enable their incorporation in the image. This malleability at the hands of experience might be thought to have functional, and therefore also selective, value for the individual in facilitating veridical proprioceptions and therefore accurate intentional manipulations of the environment. In sum, I have hypothesized the existence of three kinds of origin-properties: changeless-innate (e.g. fingers), developmental-innate (e.g. growing), and experience-acquired (e.g. hump, corpulence). To these I add what might be described as *conditions of persistence*: for example, the property of transcending postural change, indeed body shape of the moment, together with psychological states generally, including states of consciousness and aesthesia. To learn that I is such as to be unaffected by sudden changes of body shape or states of aesthesia, is to learn something significant about its conditions of origin.

The richness of the origins of I attests to its links with genetics and personal history. By contrast, the *effect-property* of I—there seems to be only one—is indicative surely of *natural function*. The conjectured effect of I is (as I have already noted) that it causes the short-term body image i_x of the moment t_x, when assisted (in all probability) by two kinds of contemporaneous phenomena. The first of these agencies is the standard effect of present posture, notably postural/kinaesthetic sensations and maybe also certain cerebral effects; while the second may well be short-term memory of recent movement, bearing in mind the effect upon proprioception of protracted immobility. That is, the explanatory half of the double hypothesis is that I, together with certain contemporaneous effects of present and immediately past posture, causes the proprioception of the moment. The upshot of these several causal hypotheses is that I proves to be a natural device whereby the changeless innate, the developmentally innate, and a certain past history wherein the contingencies of development find due recognition, are brought to bear upon the data of the present and immediate past, in generat-ing the proprioception of the moment. Perhaps the most noteworthy feature of this causal hypothesis is that the present body shape is simply *by-passed* in this causal transaction, and that present posture is merely associatively operative! Despite being the object of perception, it is not directly operative in the causal transaction! Here we have a dramatic unlikeness to the visual perception of shape, and an eccentric phenomenon to be accommodated by the Causal Theory of Perception!

(e) The type and ontological status of the long-term body image

But what *kind of thing* is the long-term body image? In particular, is it a *psychological* phenomenon? A preliminary note of caution before attempting to come to grips with these two questions. In speaking of the long-term body image, I remarked earlier that it is (in a special sense yet to be spelled out) 'how at a certain time one seems to oneself to be in spatial respects R_a' (R_a being specified in the text). Then it has at this point to be admitted that this sentence is somewhat misleading. Whatever variety of 'seeming' it is we are talking of, it can be none of the familiar psychological 'seemings': it is not a perceptual experience of a certain shape, nor an imagining-of or imagining-that one is possessed of some shape; indeed, it is no kind of experience at all. And neither is it a cognitive attitude with such a content, whether we are thinking of a belief, an expectation, an inclination or tendency to believe, and so on. And in fact we ought to abandon any attempt to fit the long-term body image into any familiar psychological box. It is not just that it is wrong. By importing the element of psychological self-reference, with its overtones of self-consciousness, as these concepts invariably do, such an approach suffers in addition from the fundamental failing of construing the body image in far too *elevated* terms. In reality, we are dealing here with something extremely primitive. There can be no doubt that in the less overtly mentalistic sense of 'body image' that is my concern, the body image is present in animals of all kinds and levels of complexity in precisely the sense it is present in rational self-conscious adult humans. In my opinion, we simply ought not to assume that it is or that it is not psychological in status. Let us for the moment agree that it is cerebral *at the very least*. And let us note in passing that there is, as I observed earlier, another phenomenon worthy of the title 'long-term body image', which unquestionably is psychological in status, and is almost certainly a type of *imagining*. 'Many anorexics have a distorted body image' undoubtedly refers to some such imaginative phenomenon: in short, to something vastly less primitive than the body image that is our concern.

What can we say in a positive vein about the type and status of that less overtly mentalistic body image? It is ringed in with causal properties, some of which are surely of definitional import. These properties ought to provide a lead on the two questions above, in particular upon the issue of ontological status. Thus, I hypothesized the long-term body image as: something at least cerebral, with relatively fixed content C, mostly innately determined—whether developmentally in advance (e.g. breasts) or so to say timelessly (e.g. fingers), but malleable in ways by protracted coordinated experience; and having the unique and vitally important function of being such as to cause i_x when assisted by the postural/kinaesthetic sensations of the moment (and possibly also by short-term memory of just-passed short-term images). It is plain that the latter functional causal power is centrally important to I's being the kind of thing it is, and it seems probable that malleability at the hands of protracted coordinated experience is also of near central significance. Then it is noteworthy that the long-term image is thus defined in terms of causal properties which link it above all to *psychological* items, such as proprioceptive experiences and bodily sensations. This suggests the likelihood of its being a dispositional property that is cast in psychological terms, and presumably therefore of its being psychological in status. It may be that I is a disposition to harbour i_x's at the instigation of the postural/kinaesthetic sensations Σs_x. More exactly, I define I (with content C) as a differential causal element in the genesis of i_x's that manage to realize C-content. It is not just that I and Σs_x cause i_x (with content matching the posture P_x of the moment): I is hypothesized as responsible for the realization of C-ness in the latter

i_x which has a content matching P_x. These considerations lead me to assume that I is psychological in status.

5. The Univocality of 'Long-Term Body Image'

(1) The long-term body image is hypothesized as a necessary causal intermediary between present postural/kinaesthetic bodily sensations (and/or cerebral effects of posture/motion) and present proprioceptive perceptions of body space. Meanwhile it has also been suggested that the long-term body image is a necessary condition, and thus a causal agency, in the generation of veridical perceptions of the location of bodily sensations. Might the long-term images involved in these causal transactions be *different phenomena*? Might these non-identical definite descriptions, these indirect identificatory causal recipes, single out different items? Could there be *several* 'long-term body images'? I shall argue against this view. That is, in support of the theory that 'long-term body image' is univocal in 'The long-term body image is a necessary condition of immediate proprioceptive perception of presence, posture, and motion in limbs', and 'The long-term image is a necessary condition of veridical perceptions of sensation location'; indeed, that it is univocal also in 'The long-term body image is a necessary condition of successful intentional body-directed physical acts, such as scratching oneself.' My claim is, that one and the same I makes these veridical phenomena possible.

(2) I believe we misunderstand the nature of the long-term body image if we suppose that any empirical phenomena could demonstrate the existence of *several* long-term body images. In general the long-term body image is veridical: animals of all kinds successfully manœuvre their way in the environment, and accurately enough (say) flick away irritating insects from their body (without looking), etc. These achievements require that their agent be apprised of the spatial properties of limbs and tickles and suchlike. And in general most animals veridically perceive these existents, whether body parts or bodily sensations, as endowed with the objective spatial properties they in fact have. Such proprioceptive perceptions depend upon the existence and veridicality of an inhering long-term body image. But veridical long-term images represents body parts and surfaces as where in body-relative physical space they actually are. Then how could there be a *variety* of veridical body images? Since we locate bodily sensations precisely in the body, and the body in the space occupied by physical realities generally, it is difficult to make sense of the idea of multiple veridical images. Then how could we suppose that there might be one long-term body image for sensations and another for active limbs?

We must never lose sight of the fact that representationalism is false of proprioception, that bodily sensations are located by the mind absolutely immediately in parts of the body, and that in proprioception there is no analogue of the visual field. In a word, no autonomous bodily sensation-system exists with an ordering principle that is independent of the body-object they bring to awareness. I suspect that confusion on these matters underlies the supposition that one long-term body image might determine proprioceptive perception of body-space, and a second long-term image govern the perception of 'sensation space'. It is easy to feel that in the very first place bodily sensations come to awareness as standing in certain relations to one another, and only secondly find themselves assigned by the mind to particular limbs. Such a state of affairs would seem to open the door to the existence of separate representational schemas for sensations and limbs.

6. Is the Long-Term Body Image an A Priori Postulate?

(1) The justification for positing a long-term body image (I, as I call it) begins with the fact that a common content C exists in all short-term body images (the i's, as I call them) over an extended period. This justification is immeasurably strengthened by the consideration that, while the content of proprioception is spatial and while postural (etc.) sensations cause proprioception, postural sensations cannot be the *original bearer* of spatial content in proprioception. Accordingly, I hypothesized the existence of an I with spatial content C, transcending posture and psychological states of all kinds, which joins with postural/kinaesthetic sensations Σs_x of the moment t_x, and maybe also with cerebral events and short-term memory of the immediate past $i_{x-\epsilon}$, to cause the i_x of the moment. Now this hypothesis is a purely empirical explanatory hypothesis. And so it cannot possibly be construed as a priori necessary. And yet it seems to me that once we assume the presence of certain vastly familiar features of the animal condition, the theory of a long-term body image is forced upon one with something resembling necessity. At the very least, possession of a long-term body image is a deeply embedded element in animal existence as we know it, indeed is a sort of foundation stone of that phenomenon. The demonstration of this claim is the aim of the ensuing discussion.

Since the hypothesis of a long-term image, of an I, is an empirical explanatory hypothesis, alternative hypotheses ought to be possible. I propose at this point to advance such an alternative, and draw out the implications of that hypothesis with a view to establishing the above claim concerning the centrality of I to animal life. The following possibility comes to mind. Let us suppose it were the case that all points on the body-outside cast a versimilitudinous literal image in the brain, thanks to the mediation of certain neurological events, an image which constantly mutated as body-posture changed. Suppose also that the content of this 3D image (which we shall call I_{3D}) automatically determined matching immediate bodily perceptual 'seemings', even though cast in the spatially impoverished respects that are typical of proprioception generally. And let us assume that these are all the immediate body perceptions that exist.

If this was how matters stood, we would I suggest have no grounds for postulating a long-term body image: its explanatory rationale would have been removed. And much else would vanish along with the long-term image. For example, a natural conservatism in relation to one's own bodily being would be supplanted by a permanent readiness for 'revolutionary change'. Thus, were it to be the case that one's body suddenly rebelled against the constraints of nature and adopted an octopus shape, then all of one's immediate bodily perceptual 'seemings' would instantaneously acquire an octopoid spatial character: one would not, so to say, recognize oneself from the inside! And the past would drop out altogether as a causal determinant of present bodily perceptual content. And so too would innate or genetic determining factors. Spatial content would be constantly renewed, instant by instant, in this wholly a-historical account. Everything causally relevant would be at once literally physically superficial and in the 'here and now'.

(2) Certain difficulties begin to appear for this theory. The a-historical character, the possibility of sudden octopoid body 'seemings', are disconcerting to say the least; but not, I think, essentially unintelligible. The first real problem arises when we ask the question: how necessary is it, in the supposed generation of body 'seemings' by the literal image I_{3D}, that it act in conjunction with the bodily sensations of the moment Σs_x?

One's first thought is, that it can hardly be necessary. After all, the posture of the moment P_x is presumed to have the cerebral effect I_{3D}, so the informational basis for a veridical perception of P_x must already be installed within the organism, quite independently of the existence of sensation Σs_x. Why should not an anaesthetic perception of the body exist? Well, I can see no reason why it should not. But this fails to prove that we can dispense with Σs_x in arriving at body 'seemings'. The trouble with such a suggestion is that it considers the phenomenon of perception from too *abstract* a point of view. For it is not just perception of a limb that we are supposing might be possible in the absence of a long-term body image: after all, we can see the limb already! Nor is it merely immediate knowledge of limb presence and posture: there seems to be nothing especially problematic in supposing that the posture of the moment P_x might generate an immediate knowledge of P_x in the absence of sensation. What we are asking is whether the *short-term body image*, the i_x of the moment, might be possible without I and possibly also without Σs_x. And what *is* this i_x? It is not merely the perception of a limb (for we can see the limb already), nor knowledge (since sight breeds knowledge), nor even the immediate perception of a limb with a content matching the normal impoverished spatial content of proprioception. A new sense might arise that managed to match the latter specifications, yet failed to realize the kind of phenomenon whose conditions of existence we are considering. For what we are specifically asking is whether, in the absence of a long-term body image, the perceptual phenomenon that we call 'i_x' might be possible. That is, an event endowed with the complex property of being at once a perceiving *and* immediate *and* with a spatial content matching that of normal proprioception—*and* in addition endowed with the further vitally important property of giving to the bodily will its *immediate bodily object*. (For this is the natural function of proprioception.)

(3) We know that proprioception possesses this vital property. Then might I_{3D} manage to cause *proprioception* of the limb? Might I_{3D} manage to lead to the instantiation of the above vitally important property via this particular route? Perhaps so, perhaps not. But if it is to do so, it cannot but make use of the proprioceptive sensations of the moment Σs_x. This is because proprioception is an immediate mode of feeling one's limbs to be present and disposed in a certain way, and it is as trivially impossible to immediately feel the presence of a limb in the absence of feeling as it is to have visual experience in the absence of visual secondary qualities and/or visual sensations. Accordingly, we must abandon the idea of engendering short-term body images (i_x's) purely at the hands of I_{3D} and in the absence of bodily sensation. This is not to deny that I_{3D} might, without the assistance of bodily sensation, manage to produce an immediate perception of limbs that had the requisite kind of spatial content *and* the vitally important property of giving to the bodily will its immediate bodily object. It simply affirms that such an unprecedented variety of perceiving would not be a form of proprioception, which is as essentially a 'feeling so' as is sight a 'looking so' and hearing a 'sounding to one so'. Whether or not this unusual possibility is in principle realizable somewhere somehow, it is at the very least a great remove from the animal condition as it is realized terrestrially. For this reason, I have chosen to confine my discussion to the proprioceptive mode of realizing the property of giving to the bodily will its immediate bodily object. But if we do thus opt for the proprioceptive mode, we have no choice but to assign a perceptual role to Σs_x.

(4) The question remains: might I_{3D} (rather than I), acting in conjunction with Σs_x, manage to conjure up a truly proprioceptive 'feeling it so', namely i_x? Here another difficulty stands in the way. It is that of managing simultaneously to involve Σs_x essentially in the perceptual transaction, and discover a function which confirms that involvement. Now we earlier noted that Σs_x cannot spatially represent the body to its owner, so that all spatial representational function must, one assumes, be held by I_{3D}. Then what informational function is left for Σs_x? None? But can Σs_x succeed in discharging its necessary function of ensuring that the body 'feel thuswise', and at the same time pass informational function completely over to I_{3D}? It seems to me that it cannot. Wherever there exists a perceptual relation, wherever the attention can truly land upon a distinct existent, *latent knowledge* is instantiated in the situation. How can Σs_x ensure a 'feeling so' and shed all cognitive import? For the attention to pass 'feelingly' via sensation to a limb, surely the 'feel' Σs_x must relate to that limb in a manner which accords with a regularity of some kind, and therefore through a relation bearing cognitive import. These considerations force me to the conclusion that if a properly proprioceptive 'feeling it so', if a true i_x is to be caused by I_{3D}, then Σs_x will have to be of cognitive significance—and thus capable of *interpretation*. More, since representationalism is false of proprioception and the content of proprioception is spatial, Σs_x will have to admit of a *non-projective spatial* interpretation. That is, Σs_x will be thus interpreted by something present in the

subject's mind/brain. This latter item must be such that, acting in conjunction with Σs_x, it automatically interpretationally generates i_x. And this is in effect to say that the something in question must be close in character to the long-term body image (rather than to I_{3D}).

Thus, once we opt for a truly proprioceptive 'feeling' perception of the body, such as would give to the bodily will its immediate body object, and once we recognize the inapplicability of sensation-representationalism in the case of proprioception, we are more or less compelled to posit a long-term body image. I conclude, that the long-term body image is as deeply embedded in animal existence as proprioception. To be sure, it is no kind of a priori necessity. However, once we introduce into the scene such fundamentals of the animal condition as proprioception and the bodily will, it is strictly unavoidable.

(5) Figure 23.1 is a diagrammatic representation of the possible origins of the proprioceptive experience i_x of the present moment t_x. I have opted for the near necessity of the following historical theory.

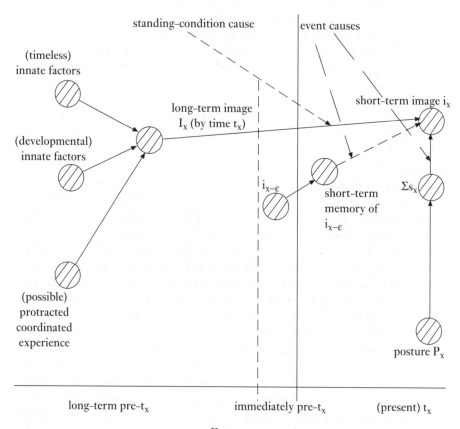

FIG. 23.1

654

But I recognized the possibility—maybe only in different life-systems—of the following a–historical account of the origins of i_x, as shown in Figure 23.2.

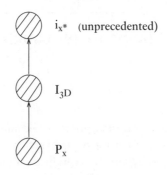

(present) t_x

FIG. 23.2

And I rejected the following a–historical accounts:

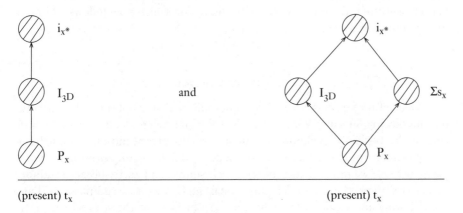

FIG. 23.3

655

24

The Sense of Touch

Through the phenomenon of proprioception we become aware of our bodies, and this is a necessary condition both of the physical actions which are such an important part of animal life generally, and of the individuation of the perceptual sensations which enable the attention to travel beyond its confines onto the world outside in perceptual experiences of a sensuous order. Meanwhile this immediate awareness of the body enables the attention to pass in a non-sensuous manner beyond the surface of the body onto nearby physical objects, for it is through these specific means that there comes to be such a thing as the sense of touch. These two senses, proprioception and touch, might with justice be described as primordial in character. Together they form a closed circle, a unit which stands in no need of epistemological input from the other senses. The discussion which now follows addresses itself to the second element in this 'unit'.

1. Pre-eminence

(1) Which of the senses is No. 1? A silly question, no doubt; but since I have a weakness for picking XI's or XV's or XVIII's as the case may be, let us pursue it a little further. Pretty plainly, by almost any yardstick smell and taste must share fourth and fifth position. And a good case can be made out for relegating hearing to No. 3: partly because we intuit sounds but not their source, and partly because auditory space perception is largely merely directional and is in any case rudimentary. Then the following are reasons why sight, the most brilliant of the senses, is a strong claimant for No. 1 position. Thus, it is far and away the most used of the senses, being far and away the most informative; for an entire sector of space, with its contents already labelled along with their spatial properties, is in sight with fine differentiation instantaneously presented to view. Indeed, epistemologically we conduct much of our lives through the sense of sight, precisely because it serves up a sector of the world directly to our awareness (as no other sense does). What more could one ask of a sense?

And yet by a different set of criteria touch is a strong contender for first place. It is not just that with touch we perceive material objects and their spatial properties, albeit less finely and abundantly than with sight. (These last, presumably, being

656

necessary conditions of any pre-eminence worth the having.) Where touch may prove to be pre-eminent is, in being fundamental to the animal condition as such, something which seems to follow from the fact that tactile-sense is broad enough to overlap with the sheer capacity for physical action on the part of its owner. Whereas sight is a highly contingent addition to animality—being a direct product of the superabundance and rectilinearity of transmission of light-rays in the natural setting—it is far from obvious that touch is the same. Which part of the natural setting gave rise to touch? Was it the sheer solidity of dry land? Our confusion at this question suggests that this sense is at least a special case, and perhaps something more. Could a species of animal lack such elementals as shelter under its umbrella? In my opinion, not without entailing radical adjustments to our concept of animality, at the very least. I will offer reasons for this view in Section 2.

(2) The following property may be proposed as a test of pre-eminence. A sense such that an animal might be equipped with it alone of the five senses, and yet through it become aware of the realities of physical space-time and some of its main extra-psychological physical contents. This test would manage to detect the joint properties of complete autonomy and adequacy, and prima facie it seems unlikely that any sense other than touch could measure up on this count. Then ought we to settle for this property as the criterion of pre-eminence, and award the accolade to touch? However, a difficulty is posed by the theoretical possibility of innate knowledge of what could—at least on this test—confer on a sense a pre-eminence which seems unjustified. Thus, a child might be born knowing much, including an entire language, whereupon the mere hearing of informative speech would suffice to acquaint him with goings on in the world at large. Surely it would be absurd to deduce, even if these circumstances generally prevailed, that hearing was the most fundamental of the senses? After all, its natural capacities lag far behind those of sight and touch. Outlandish possibilities such as the above cannot alter the fact that the spatial data of hearing is rudimentary and validated only through appeal to extra-auditory facts of the kind sight and touch provide. We must not allow the various possibilities opened up by innate knowledge to obscure the fact that some senses naturally depend upon others as those others may not depend on them.

If this is Scylla, then there is Charybdis to match. Namely: there is reason to think that *any* sense requires *some* knowledge if we are to gain *more* knowledge through its use. How could the mere experiencing of what Quine described as 'irritations of the nervous system' (however regular), simply on its own generate knowledge of the state of the environment? Must it not be supplemented by knowledge of the ways of the world if it is to yield knowledge? Do we not need to know that we can trust these sensuous deliverances?

Steering between these two difficulties, I suggest the following as a sufficient condition of a reasonable, though stipulated, 'pre-eminence'. The sense in question (a) enables us to assemble the bare bones of a physical world, without (b) the use of other senses, and (c) without depending upon a fund of innate knowledge that is such that some other sense could with its use satisfy requirement (a). On this count also, touch rates as pre-eminent and sight not, for the immediate objects of sight require interpretation in the light of other data, since nothing about the visual sensory objects which we experience necessitates that they present to view what they do, or indeed anything at all. Again, touch is the one sense that necessarily is concerned with the spatial properties of material objects, for sight might have taken a much simpler form than that known to us, but it is difficult to see how touch could (as will emerge at the end of Section 2). Conjoining the latter two properties with the aforementioned near necessity to the animal condition, it seems justifiable to conclude that, even though touch is continually recessive in relation to sight, in that the attention concentrates the vast bulk of its resources upon the contents of the visual field, touch is in a certain respect the most important and certainly the most primordial of the senses. The reason is, that it is scarcely to be distinguished from the having of a body that can act in physical space.

What must be emphasized about touch is that it involves the use of no mediating field of sensation, no mediating secondary quality. There is in touch no analogue of the visual field of visual sensations which mediates the visual perception of the environment. Such a thing is possible only because in touch a body investigates bodies as one body amongst others, for in touch we directly appeal to the tactile properties of our own bodies in investigating the self-same tactile properties of other bodies. Whereas we do not smell or hear or see through smelling or hearing or seeing ourselves, the space and solidity of our bodies provides the access to the space and solidity of other bodies. This coinciding of means and object ensures that sense-mediation drops out. This is the source of the pre-eminence of touch.

2. Why the Sense of Touch is Necessary to Animality

Why say the sense of touch *must* obtain in an animal, and *must* be potentially veridical? The following considerations suggest that it is so.

We set out with the assumption that animals have bodies, that they necessarily adopt physical and enmattered form. Presumably also they necessarily have awareness of those bodies, which is to say awareness of themselves *qua* physical object— indeed, of themselves *qua* physical object in the special immediate mode we all know. But why should we believe this latter claim? It is a consequence of the necessity to the animal condition of the capacity for supporting psychological phenomena. Whereas scientific considerations might force us to re-classify a natural kind like the whale, causing us to detach it from the class of fish, no empirical data could lead us to classify a living species that had *no* potentiality for psychologicality (whether mislaid, hopelessly lost, etc.) as an animal. The reason being, first that the concept of animality is transcendent of all life-systems in the universe, second that animality is no more a natural kind than is psychologicality or matter. (Taking 'natural kind' in the following familiar sense: that the essence of such a kind is one of nature's secrets that has to be wrested out of her by empirical and indeed scientific means—so that naming typically precedes defining.) If an object in some remote galactic system is alive and capable of experience, it is an animal come what may. No classificatory exigencies can make it not.

Then the necessity of the capacity for psychologicality in animals, leads to the necessity of body-awareness, thanks to the mediation of a further necessity, action. Thus, behaviourism, neo-behaviourism, Wittgensteinian devotees of outer criteria of a largely active kind, together with latter-day functionalists, all recognize that active animal behaviour is no mere contingent associate of the animal mind. All accept that the animal mind must at some point have the capacity to express itself in active behaviour. What sort of active behaviour? Physical or bodily action. Indeed, not just mere bodily movings, but intentional manipulative physical action. That is, informed intentional instrumental deeds which effect change in the environment through intentional movings of the animal's own body.

Then it seems that these intentional bodily movings require *awareness* of the animal's body: more, an *attentively immediate* awareness of the primitive variety that obtains in us all. The following makes this clear. Consider a situation in which a man's right arm does not in this primitive way seem to its owner to be postured in any way, indeed does not in this way even seem *there*. Then irrespective of whether he vividly sees his arm, and knows exactly how it is spatially disposed, such a man is not in a position to immediately move it. Although he is not paralysed, in these circumstances his bodily will is simply unavailable for use upon his right arm. Thus, he can instrumentally move his right arm with his left arm, he may even be able to somehow instrumentally move it via a mental act like visualizing, but he will not be able to immediately move it. This is because the bodily will takes an immediately given bodily object. What else?

This claim is not to be confused with the following rather crass assertion: if we are to immediately move a limb we must know all its postural properties. What knowledge at each instant has a pianist of the posture of his left little finger during the *presto* of Beethoven's op. 27, no. 2 sonata? And yet when an act is both 'basic' *and* intentional under *some* spatial description or other—like 'move my fingers suchwise as to play op. 27, no. 2 (at such and such a stage)'—which the act of playing this fragment of the sonata precisely is—then an immediate proprioceptive knowledge of the spatial property thus singled out is a necessary condition of the act. Thus, this pianist was immediately aware of the movements of his *left-hand fingers*, even though unaware of that of his left little finger. And yet his left little finger was at all times *immediately perceptible* to him, for it was an element of an *immediately perceived* collective. And that is to say, that it was 'immediately given' to his awareness, as were all his other fingers. As a general phenomenon, physical action could not exist in the absence of the property of being immediate and intentional under some spatial description. It follows that physical action could not in general exist in the absence of proprioception.

But might we not be able to satisfy the principle that the animal mind express itself in behaviour without the behaviour needing to be bodily movings? The only alternative is, that the behaviour consists in mental instrumental action which in a-nomic but non-chance manner relatively frequently effects desired bodily phenomena: for example, getting goose pimples by thinking of poetry. Then note that this animal is to be divested both of body-sense and of a bodily will—and not *qua* pathological deprivation, but in hale health and of its very nature as a type! Is such a condition of quasi-Cartesian isolation from the body credible? It may well be conceptually exceptionable, for reasons I will not enter into. But I shall not argue the issue. Let me say that at the very least what we have here is a *colossal* departure from the animal condition as we know it. In a powerful sense of 'necessity', the potential for body-sense and bodily will is necessary to the animal state. I am content to express my claims in terms of such a brand of necessity. As colossal as is the colossalness of the above departure from the norm, so necessary is the necessity in question.

To repeat: the non-accidental inner–outer relation remarked by twentieth-century philosophers of many persuasions, is such that we must in general have immediate awareness of our bodies of a type that makes possible intentional bodily actions which are at the same time physical instrumental acts in which the body is brought into known physical relation with the environment. Then how does this conclusion bear upon the thesis of the supposed necessity of touch in animal life? Might we lack tactile sense even as we meet this constraint? For example, even though the knowledge required for intentional basic bodily actions must in the first place come from immediate body-sense rather than (say) sight, might the knowledge of the environment required for intentional manipulative actions come uniquely from (say) sight? Might we be 'feel beings' with the body, and 'visual beings' with all else?

Well, the deliverances of sight can inform our physical instrumental actions, even to the complete exclusion of the sense of touch. But this is irrelevant to the point at issue: namely, whether we can meet the above constraint and lack a sense of touch. Then note that it already postulates a body-sense acquired knowledge of the body's spatial properties sufficient to make possible informed intentional bodily deeds. We shall now show that this alone guarantees a sense of touch. Thus, the subject may be presumed to know that some limb L_1 (a right arm, say) is moving forwards (say) in relation to the front of his body, say out from some point P_1. Then what if L_1 meets an obstruction at point P_2, and can advance no further? Presumably, this subject will know he has moved L_1 from P_1 on his body to P_2 lying beyond in space, and not to desired further point P_3. If he does not, how can he perform intentional bodily actions? Then why cannot he *repeatedly* discover that in just this tract of physical space, L_1 cannot advance beyond P_2? And discover the same with limb L_2, and repeatedly; and with L_3, and again repeatedly; and so on? Surely with this data behind him he may conclude: 'there is *something solid* at P_2'? Then this is evidence of a tactile-perceptual power. After all, he could in a comparable situation move his arm rapidly around the perimeter of some object, directing attention beyond his body onto that object as he does, emerging in the end with awareness of its shape. In short, this man is endowed with tactile-sense. But how could he lack it? How could one have informed command over the spatial properties of one's body, without knowledge of its limits and thus of external limiting factors? Therefore even though a man might integrate visual data with bodily action without utilizing tactile-sense, it is not really possible to suppose a man might have full command over his limbs and lack tactile-sense. Insofar as intentional physical action necessitates body-sense, it equally necessitates tactile-sense.

It is for reasons of this kind that I believe that the capacity for tactile-sense is as essential to the animal condition as the capacity for body-sense: that is, for immediate body-awareness. In my view, each requires the other. But we have seen that body-sense is a necessary feature of animality. So therefore is tactile-sense. (It follows that touch cannot take a significantly simpler form. For the necessity of touch is the necessity of intentional bodily action, and there seem to be no rudimentary forms of that.)

3. The General Characteristics of the Sense of Touch

(a) The justification for speaking of a 'sense of touch'

Tastes and smells are culled in simple uniform manner. By contrast, in the case of sight variegation exists both in the methods and contents of perception, ranging from the momentary glimpsing of an after-image's colour, to walking around an object in order to inspect its layout in three-dimensional space. A similar variegation occurs with touch. The simplest of all cases is that of momentarily feeling something contact a point on one's body. Probably the next most simple case is feeling something extensive momentarily contact one. Complexity appears when time, motion, and activity appear as additional variables. Thus, one might passively feel an insect wander across one's forehead. Or actively run one's hand around the outside of a box with a view to discovering its shape. Finally, one might feel one's way around a room in total darkness; or, if blind, navigate one's way across an entire city.

All these cases are exercises of the sense of touch. Why? Is it because one uses the sensation of contact as access to the object? But the following example casts doubt on that suggestion. One's right hand may be numb, and yet by discovering that we cannot push it through something it is touching, we might come to know of the presence of an object, indeed manage by movement to be aware of its shape. Would we not have tactilely perceived that object? But, it may be objected, one must all the same have and put to use bodily feeling elsewhere in the body in becoming aware of the immobility of the arm. This may be so, but those bodily feelings, say in elbow and shoulder, do not play an attentive perceptual role in this transaction. That is, they do not represent the solidity of the impediment, for we do not become aware of that solidity in becoming aware of the sensations. The position is rather that these bodily sensations *non-representationally* cause awareness of the immobility of the arm, which in turn helps cause awareness of the obstructive object. In any case, there is no a priori reason why body awareness must have a sensation cause. It is conceivable that one be immediately aware of the presence and posture of a limb merely through neurological causes. Intuition without sensation is a theoretical possibility.

In a word, tactile sensation is inessential to tactile perception. Then is it body-awareness that is the necessary mediator in the case of tactile perception? I believe it is. I think that in touch we become aware of extra-bodily objects through becoming aware of the unique body-object. That is, in touch we gain epistemological access to the world at large through immediate epistemological access to one small part of it: our own body. Indeed, it is in principle possible that this be our only epistemological access to the outer world. Awareness of our own bodies might have been our sole epistemological route to the physical domain. This can be said of no other sense.

Note that the structural situation in tactile perception is significantly different from that in other examples of sense-perception. In particular, because there is no analogue of the sense-mediators of the visual field of visual sensations and elsewhere, the attention does not discover its outer objects through landing upon inner sensuous objects. Therefore we would do well to treat the expression 'sense-perception' with caution when it is used in connection with touch. If tactile perception is a case of sense-perception, it differs on the count of 'sense' from the other four senses, and differs perhaps on the count of 'perception' also (as will emerge). We can if we wish talk of 'the five senses', but we should recognize significant differences between them, and especially between touch and the others.

(b) The varieties of tactile sense

The above discussion has brought to our notice the vital role of body awareness in tactile perception. But it does not show that the bodily sensation is not also of great importance. Indeed, I am happy to affirm as a principle that the simplest case of tacile perception, in which we feel something momentarily contact a point on our body, is the unit out of which are fashioned the more complex structures of tactile perception. Accordingly, I shall at this juncture offer an account of the several modes of tactile perception, cast in terms of that unit case. But first a brief account of the unit case itself.

A. *Momentary point contact.* Here we feel something at a point on the body. What information do we gain? Precious little: merely that something solid contacts us at that point. The internal or qualitative information concerning the 'something' being meagre to vanishing point, the relational spatial information all but everything. 'Something solid here.' Then how is the 'here' specified? The first thing to note is, that it is not specified *purely spatially*. Thus, not by mentioning a point relative to the fixed stars, nor to the revolving earth, and not even by mentioning a point relative to the body: say, by fixing its position on an xyz co-ordinate system running from head to feet. It is not just that we are not like tin soldiers, and flex and move much of the time. More importantly, a qualitative element inevitably enters the picture, viz. the body part involved. This qualitative determinacy is an inescapable part of our experience of a body-point. We experience the point touched as on or of some given limb.

And yet the data is not *purely qualitative* either: say, merely the right index finger (wherever that may be). Spatial information also enters. To begin with, this spatial content shows in the structurally determinate character of body-part awarenesses. Thus, the data will be at least as complex as, on-right-index-finger-attached-to-hand-attached-to-arm-attached-to-etc. For we can import into the specification of the experience of the moment, descriptions of the containing body that are for its owner determinate both with regard to its parts *and* their structural spatial relations. These widening descriptive circles remain true to the experience of the subject, for a pain in the foot is experienced as located in *one end of the body* just as much as it is experienced as in the foot. Why stop at the foot? Or the shin? Or the knee?

Yet such descriptions are still largely qualitative. To realize full spatial determinacy we need to augment them with an additional internal spatial element: namely, with the posture adopted by this thus-structured entity. For example: by-forehead-of-standing-at-attention-saluting-body. And so the information that is conveyed by mere point-contact turns out to be determinate about part, in a determinately spatially structured and membered whole, that is internally spatially disposed in determinate manner. In sum, the information conveyed at that moment concerns a point in a body-relative space that is qualitatively determinate both locally and globally. Roughly speaking, this almost totally body-relative information that *something* is at such a point is the unit out of which the deliverances of the sense of touch are fashioned. Indeed, it could in principle be that upon which depended our entire knowledge of the physical world. For example, had we been animals lacking all other senses but that of touch.

B. *Extensive contact*. The interest of this case is twofold: first on the count of spatial determinacy, second on that of mediation. Suppose an object of approximately saucer size contacts one's body. What spatial information do we gather from this tactile experience? We have a rough idea of the size of the item and next to none of shape, rather as we have indeterminate perception of shape and colour at the edge of the visual field—where 'large', 'bright', 'moving' tend to be conserved, even as determinables like 'circle of 1 ft. diameter', 'yellow', 'moving upwards' are lost. Now this latter state of affairs is not the product of a want of attention, but of a want of differentiation in the visual sensations occurring at the peripheries of the visual field. Then from what does it derive in tactile experience?

Two possible answers suggest themselves to this question: the character of bodily sensations, or the character of body awareness. Consider them in turn. Following the visual analogue one might wish to say: these sensations just do not have it in them, either to line up in a straight line, or to arrange themselves in a way that correlates with or maps onto straightness. Alternatively, one might wish to say: the character of body awareness is such that body parts cannot be experienced as straight, curved, equidistant, in a straight line; in a word, in the way the objects of sight are experienced. So the first answer says that the sensation of contact of the large-ish object is indeterminate in these respects. While the second answer claims that the body as immediately experienced is not endowed with such determinations. One answer puts the blame on the sensations through which the object is experienced, the other puts the blame upon body awareness through putting the blame on the character of its internal objects.

Consider the first answer. It is flawed through depending upon an inadequate theory of sensation location. In failing to distinguish the spatial experience of sensation from the spatial properties of sensations, we implicitly endorse the existence of an autonomous sensation-space. While pains are not *experienced* as lying in straight lines, they can nonetheless do just that. This is because, in the familiar sense in which we locate bodily sensations, they are set down by our minds in actual places in the physical space of the body. While a toothache may perhaps literally be in the brain, in the sense that we know so well it is located just where the tooth is. Then what is to prevent those physical places from composing a straight line? And so the first answer, which models the proprioceptive upon the visual situation, must be rejected: the indeterminacy in question lies in our spatial *experience* of bodily sensation rather than in the *sensations* themselves. As a result of this fact, the earlier question should now be rephrased as follows. Does indeterminacy of spatial content in 'extensive contact' derive from the character of sensation-space awareness, or does it stem instead from that of body-space awareness?

Let us compare these two answers. Now it is true that a pain does not come to consciousness as (say) 'equidistant from two other sensations' or as 'composing a straight line'. On the other hand, it is equally true that (say) three parts of the body that are simultaneously touched and that lie in a straight line, will not be experienced as 'in a straight line', any more than is one's nose experienced as a triangular wedge. In short, the poverty of spatial determinations applies alike to the sensation as experienced, and the body part as experienced that the sensation brings to consciousness. How could it be otherwise? It seems therefore that it is a mistake to say, concerning this somewhat rudimentary example of tactile perception: the information that we gather is indeterminate with regard to the shape of the contacting object *because* our experience of bodily sensations is indeterminate in the same regard. And it seems equally mistaken to attribute it to the identical indeterminacy in the experienced object of body-awareness. Yet surely both factors are implicated. So I suggest that we attribute it alike to either, as different aspects of the one situation.

C. *Active exploratory movement.* This is the prime case of tactile perception. Whereas the first two rudimentary cases could as easily be understood merely as examples of body-awareness, in this phenomenon the attention unambiguously goes beyond the body and we unquestionably perceive the object which actively we explore. But before I consider this case, a brief mention of two passive examples involving movement. First, suppose that something moves across one's neck. Then in this case the same indeterminateness appears in the object as given to perception as was noted in the previous static examples, for whereas we here intuit a movement we hardly intuit a shape. The second rather absurd example brings us nearer that goal. Thus, your left foot is placed upon some object and is moved by a third-person around the peripheries of the object. Here, for the first time in these examples, we encounter a case in which we might discover, very imperfectly no doubt and probably assisted by processes of thought, a shape of the kind of a square or circle (say).

The fully fledged active exploratory case of tactile perception has a form like this. Keeping one's hand on an object, one runs it around the edge and attends to the shape of the object as one does. This phenomenon seems to be constituted out of the simplest perception of all, for as one acts one continues to have an unchanging sensation of contact at the same point on the body. Then while at first one might actively follow the outline of the object part by part, one might thereafter actively initiate the entire movement that one remembers tracing out *qua* follower: for example, act now under 'move the hand to the right in a near straight line in such a way as to retain contact'. Thus, our capacity to tactilely discover spatial properties like being straight is all one with our capacity to intentionally initiate movements possessed of just such properties. Then the transformation of spatial data from the relatively indeterminate 'large' or 'moving'—found in the simpler perceptions—to the relatively determinate 'straight' or 'rectangular' or 'parallelepiped'—which we discover in this developed variety of perception—cannot be due merely to the introduction of time or movement into the situation, for these were present when something wandered across one's body. But neither is it entirely due to the element of activity, for a new type of spatial data already began to separate itself out in the example of the passive movement of the left foot. The novel and crucially important factor is I suggest the movement of one's limbs.

4. Tactile Representationalism

(a) Tactile representationalism in simple cases

(1) Let us suppose that with the right hand we actively feel a straight edge. We say: 'it feels straight'. What is the role of feeling here? And do we intuit or notice-*of* something straight? One thing is clear, and that is that nothing like a visual representative sensuous model can be applied in this active exploratory situation. 'Feels straight' is here most unlike 'looks straight'. For the comparison to be accurate, we should need to be immediately aware of bodily sensation either set somehow in space in a straight line, or else immediately given in such a way as to correlate with straightness in map-like projective manner.

A variety of considerations quash the suggestion. The first is, that the bodily sensation is never at any instant experienced as either straight or a projective analogue of straight. The second consideration begins by noting that the perceptual process under discussion is a procedure through time (by contrast with visual perception, where the contents of visual fields are presented to view simultaneously). Then the bodily sensation of contact upon the palm of the feeling hand is unchanged throughout the tactile enterprise, beginning and ending as a single sensation at a single body-place. In short, this sensation does not at each moment of the enterprise extend in a line *across space* or any mental analogue of space. But in addition neither does it persist in consciousness *across space and time* in linear form as we act, say in the manner of a rocket which visibly traces out a straight line, for this would require of bodily sensations that they be experienceable as 'straight', 'curved', etc. In sum, we do not perceive the straightness of an edge through perceiving the straightness or quasi-straightness of a sensation which represents that straightness, whether instantaneously or across time. The role of bodily sensations in tactile perception must be wholly disanalogous to the representational role of visual sensations in visual perception. There is no possibility that sensation representationalism holds of the active fully fledged form of tactile perception.

(2) And so if an intuition of straightness occurs in this developed example of tactile perception, it cannot be an intuition of sensation. Therefore it is of act, or movement, or edge, or several at once, or it is non-existent. Since the act of limb moving is not the limb movement, I cannot suppose that the act itself is straight, and hence that it could be the object of the spatial intuition. And I see no reason for resisting the conclusion that we intuit or notice-*of* the limb movement.

But do we intuit the object's shape as well? Well, we at least discover through tactile perception that it is straight, and in that restricted sense perceive its shape. But is that a sufficient condition of *intuition* of shape? I do not think it is. Whether or not intuition occurs in this simple case, complexity in an object presents a real problem for any general intuitionist analysis of tactile discovery as such. Let us suppose that I clamber all over an object in the dark and come to the conclusion that it is a hexahedron; then whereas I discovered by feel that it was a hexahedron, it is far from obvious that I intuited hexahedron-ness. Might I not simply have worked the shape out from tactile data? Then if that is how matters stood, I cannot have perceived the shape. In short, discovering X through perceptual means need not be through the *noticing* of X. The noticing or intuition of (say) shape requires that the synthesis of that shape takes place within the perceptual experience itself.

Thus, in the case of many complex entities which we identify through perception, we should be wary in assuming we have perceived (say) their shape or (say) overall structure. And this is true of more than just touch. And yet there can be no principle *proscribing* such perceptions. It is clear we sometimes perceive complex structures. Take the case of a symphony. Do we not intuit such items for what they are? Even though there is no such sound as (say) the Eroica Symphony, I have heard the work often enough, and cannot see how to avoid the conclusion that this (complex) object came in suitable manner to my attention or intuition (across time, assisted by attending-activity). An item can come to *attention*, and be *recognized* in the process for what it is, even though it is a complex structure across time, and despite the fact that active attending was a necessary condition of the attention recognizing and individuating it. This active mental element introduced the required synthesizing agency into the perceptual situation. Indeed, in the case of complex intelligible perceptibles like speeches or symphonies, absence of the active synthesizing factor of attending is liable to result in the objects of perception being experienced as a mere 'sound salad' or 'word salad'! In such cases the mental will is a causally necessary condition of an identificatory 'perceiving as—'.

(3) In the section immediately below I discuss the special problems raised by the tactile perception of complex shapes. Meanwhile, I note that in simple cases like the perception of straightness, there can be little doubt that we intuit the shape both of the limb movement *and* of the felt object. More, since we intuit the latter only because we intuit the former, this tactile perception has to be classed as *representational* in type. Then even though this is an example of sense-perception, and even though we 'feel that the object is straight', the representational element is not sensation. It is the spatial properties of the immediately experienced actively executed body movement.

Tactile representationalism differs in one important respect from the full-blown visual variety. Thus, to visually perceive a red object I need do no more than notice the red sensation it causes, a fact which we acknowledge in saying that '*in* seeing the sensation we see the represented object'. It is different with touch. For it is not enough to notice the straightness of an edge that I notice the straightness of the hand movement that discloses it to me. In addition, the latter perception has to be subordinated to an active perceptual project which is directed beyond the body to the spatial properties of the object. It follows from this that 'the transitivity of the attention' must take a different form in the case of touch from elsewhere. And yet despite this difference, it remains true that awareness of the external spatial property only occurs through the mediation of a body-awareness with matching spatial content. It is the conjunction of match of content and causal link that makes the relation representational. But for the attention to utilize this relation and make the journey across, the further condition is necessary.

(b) The limits of tactile representationalism

(1) According to the representational theory of tactile perception, whereby the mediate perceptions of tactile-sense match the immediate perceptions of body-sense, the deliverances of tactile and body-sense coincide, e.g. straightness of perceived edge matching straightness of hand movement. How wide is the scope of this theory? Such a match holds when we are concerned with simple body-relative limb movement and the corresponding simple spatial property of an object.

But does it hold in complex cases? Do we body-sense perceive the movement of the limb when we tactilely perceive the spatial properties of complex objects?

I do not think so. Suppose that in the dark I run my hand all over a multi-faceted object. Then normally my concern will be with the shape of the *object* and not with the overall shape of the *hand movement*. In that case I will perceive the former but not the latter, for these are different and my mind records only one of these shapes. This signals the breakdown of representationalism in such perceptions. It is true that exceptionally I could be interested in discovering both shapes at once in tactile perception. Then in that case I will engage in a peculiarly self-conscious project of mentally synthesizing my already accomplished movements (rather as I might watch the trail left in the sand by the car I am driving by peering in the driving mirror), and simultaneously I will engage in the usual (and distinct, second) project of mentally synthesizing what tactilely I discover of the object. In such a bizarre case I will perceive both the shape of the object by tactile means *and* the shape of my hand movement by body-sense—and these are two *distinct* perceptual projects. Nonetheless, I will not have accomplished the former through accomplishing the latter. Therefore the relation is non-representationalist.

The summary account of the tactile perception of complex shape is this. Mostly only the outer-directed tactile project is undertaken when we are concerned to perceive complex shape, so that mostly the deliverances of tactile-sense will be vastly more rich than those of body-sense. Exceptionally however one might undertake both perceptual projects at once. In either case the perceptual relation is non-representationalist in character. Representationalist is inexistent in the bizarre case because I do not perceive the shape of the object *through* perceiving that of the limb movement, and it is inexistent usually because I do not usually *perceive* the shape of the limb movement. Nevertheless, it seems to me that these qualifications scarcely blunt the real force of representationalism. Representationalism continues to hold piecemeal in these complex cases. Thus, I become aware of each part of the shape of the complex object that I become aware of, only through becoming aware of the matching spatial properties of the movement of the limb.

(2) One other variety of tactile perception has to be considered, if we are to gain an appreciation of the scope and limits of tactile representationalism generally. Namely, tactile perceptions in which the entire body is put to active use in the perceptual process.

How do the deliverances of tactile and body-sense relate in cases of tactile perception in which we circumnavigate a large object that we are feeling with a view to discovering its shape? Does one perceive by tactile-sense or body-sense that one's body moves in a circle? Surely, tactilely. For body-sense is defined, not just by its objects, but by the characteristics of the perceptual situation, for body-sense immediately reveals the presence and body-relative spatial properties of body and limbs. Therefore we do not perceive by body-sense that our own body has revolved on an axis running from head to feet, and still less do we perceive by body-sense that our body has moved in a circle when we circumnavigate (say) a sphere or cylinder. Therefore whereas we (exceptionally) could by body-sense perceive the movement of an arm when tactilely we investigate some complex multi-faceted object, we could never by body-sense perceive the circular movement of the body that the perceiver effects in perceiving the circularity of a circumnavigated object. Representationalism fails to hold of these cases also, however simple or complex the shape may be.

(3) It follows from the above discussions in (1) and (2) that even though we can know an object is straight by knowing through body-sense that a limb movement is straight, we do not *in general* know that tactilely an object has the shape S it has through knowing through body-sense that the perceiving body-movement also has shape S. The reason being, first that when the object is complex and the method of investigation *hand movement*, we do not as a rule body-sense perceive the overall shape of that hand movement; second that when the method of investigation involves *circumambulation*, then (a) we do not body-sense perceive the movement of our body, and (b) even when we happen tactilely to perceive the movement of our body, this is no more immediate than the perception of the object and so cannot be the representational means of our tactilely perceiving that object, despite the fact that it is (ultimately) through immediate awareness of leg movement that we are aware of the shape of the object, and (c) in complex cases we do not even tactilely perceive the movement of the body. This gives us an idea of the limitations of a representationalism which, as I emphasized earlier, holds nonetheless at all times in piecemeal fashion in the case of this sense.

5. The Cognitive Presuppositions of Tactile-Sense

(a) The dependence of tactile experience and discovery upon cognition

While tactile perception can be physically passive and mentally active, as when one actively attends to a passively moved limb that contacts an object; or even mentally and physically passive, as when one merely notices the movement of that contacting limb; the most successful and complex examples of the type are active in mind and body. Then the active project of feeling an object for shape, breaks up into two distinct but synthesized activities: namely, running the hand around the object, and attending to the object's shape as it is disclosed piecemeal across time to the unifying and attentive mind; for the shape of an object reveals itself to an exploring hand and mind, rather in the way an unfolding utterance discloses its content to an attentive ear and mind.

It is of the first importance that this complex tactile project rests on certain cognitive assumptions: first concerning one's body, second concerning the object. Thus, concerning one's own body we assume that, even though it constantly disposes itself differently, its size and parts do not much change. Of course, things might have been different. Were we able intentionally to change size of body or limbs at will, rather like a balloon fish, or were we so to say chameleons of shape, we would doubtless engage in tactile investigations during static norms—though it is conceivable we acquire the capacity to read shape even as we intentionally enlarge or alter ourselves (somewhat as we make estimations that a car is moving at 120 m.p.h. from the vantage point of a 70 m.p.h. fellow car). The other assumptions concern the object of tactile investigation. Here, too, we mostly assume that the object does not significantly alter in size and shape, and in position relative to the environment. Think of a blind man trying to circumnavigate and estimate the size of an object that imperceptibly slides parallel to him on a sheet of ice. He will *seem to perceive* something larger than he actually perceives, and doubtless make erroneous *judgements*, in each case because his beliefs were erroneous. Then if the above are the presumed fixtures in this situation, the presumed variables are, first the body-relative position of the exploring limb, second the environmental position of the circumambulating perceptual subject. But of course the assumptions vary with the situation. Given one set of assumptions one shape will seem to come to consciousness, given another set another will seem to do so. Whatever they are, those assumptions play the role of necessary cognitive background to the tactile project.

So both the shape one *seems to perceive* and what one *actually perceives and discovers* from the tactile project, depend on what one assumes and knows concerning the shape and stability of one's body, and the stability of the object and its spatial relation to the environment and/or the body engaged in feeling it. Without such knowledge, one will not come by knowledge of things by tactile means. Indeed, this dependence of perceptual inquiry upon a fund of knowledge is found with all the senses. It is a variant upon 'Unto him that hath shall be given', for only he who already knows something can by these means come to know more. Only he who knows something about the character of the environment and his relation to that environment, can by sense-perceptual means make discoveries therein. Even the primitive senses of smell and taste can provide information only if supplemented by the knowledge of what smells thus and tastes thus, and the knowledge that (say) smell informs us of what stuff is on the breeze rather than (say) pervading the interior of a distant star. And plainly the same holds of the more sophisticated senses of sight and hearing, whose sensuous offerings likewise receive interpretation in the light of known or believed facts.

(b) The significance of cognitive assumptions in tactile-sense

(1) Then why is it that this dependence of sense-experience and sense-discovery upon knowledge of one's body and its environment, seems to be so significant and even disturbing in the case of tactile perception? By contrast, we can easily enough accommodate the fact that the other senses likewise require cognitive bolstering. Why the difference? Let me by way of reply list a few of the properties of those other senses which together constitute the reason for our complacency in their case. To begin with, these senses are highly contingent features of the animal condition;

and might have taken different form; and interpose as object for the attention a sensory entity between perceiver and object: an entity which does not carry its own interpretation, indeed which might have had a different or even no interpretation, being interpretable only when there exists a regular relation with outer objective fact. Finally, these four senses have the sense of touch to fall back on as source of the knowledge through which their sensuous offerings can be interpreted.

When we turn to the sense of touch a very different picture emerges. Thus, we have given reason for believing that this sense is a near necessary feature of animality as such. Again, it is difficult to see how touch could take a significantly different form or correlate with significantly different facts. Again, of all the (outer) senses touch is the one sense that necessarily is concerned with spatial properties, which is to say with the fundamental individuating characteristic of physical realities. This is because in tactile perception no intervening third sensuous entity gets between one and the object; while what does intervene, namely the bodily movement of the subject, is the bearer of the selfsame property which is its interpretation: a publicly perceptible spatial condition. Again, while the other perceptual sensations might never have had an interpretation, nothing like this can hold in the case of touch, seeing that touch is as primordial a feature of animality as the capacity for physical action or sense-perception generally. Finally it seems that the interpretations of touch, when operating in the settings for which it is designed, must in general be veridical. How could touch be a necessity, and all its deliverances illusions? And it seems also to follow that animals could exist that as a species were endowed with no more than the sense of touch. Those wedded to doctrines like functionalism cannot contemplate such a possibility in the case of any other sense. This underlines the uniqueness of touch amongst the senses.

If there is anything of special import in the fact that touch requires supplementation by knowledge, it must have its source in these special features of the sense. The problem as I see it derives from the fact that touch might be the one and only sense of a species. For whereas the other four senses have touch to fall back upon as cognitive base, upon what could a solitary sense of touch fall back if we are to interpret its findings?

(2) One interesting but misguided suggestion must be rejected forthwith. Namely, that body-sense provides an immediate cognitive foundation for tactile sense without itself depending on knowledge. That is, that we might immediately and without cognitive assistance *just know* what we body-sense discover. (Note that this is not the same as claiming that in body-sense we have near-infallible knowledge of the kind we have of our own sensations.) Then one can see why one might be inclined to endorse the above misguided theory. The reason is, that the role played by supplementary knowledge in body-sense perception is markedly unlike its role in the familiar examples of sense-perception. It is a recessive and silent role, being repetitious and scarcely so much as receiving a mention. After all, it concerns one and the same object, again and again and again, like the one house inhabited for a

lifetime, the one car one can never think of changing. This makes the relevant knowledge appear functionless. But in fact even though body-sense is immediate and the five senses are mediate transactions through sensation, we have no more superior access to bodily facts through body-sense than we have through visual or tactile means. To suppose otherwise, a sort of variant on the Cartesian soul alone with its thoughts, only here with its body, is plainly unacceptable.

There can be no doubt that body-sense is grossly corrigible as inner sense is not. It is easy to imagine systematic dislocations between the immediate deliverances of body-sense and the objective facts of the body. For example, the body image might undergo seasonal changes even though the body stays unaltered, so that it might perhaps be that in autumn one's right arm systematically seemed larger than it is. In that case, knowledge of this fluctuation would be a necessary supplement through which we could reach through body-seemings to bodily facts. Systematic illusions must be possible here as elsewhere. It is not as if, feeling one's left arm with one's right hand, and making use as one does of normal tactile cognitive assumptions, one is a less reliable observer than oneself immediately reporting the posture of the left arm—wholly independently of knowledge! In fact the two findings must make use of knowledge, in their own distinctive and diverse ways, and simultaneously must arrive at the identical truths—if truths they be.

(c) The necessity of innate knowledge in tactile-sense and body-sense

Accordingly, we reject this improbable solution of the difficulty posed by the need for knowledge in interpreting touch in a purely tactile species. Then where is that knowledge to come from? One obvious possibility is that there exists innate knowledge of some of the more general properties of material objects. I can see nothing the matter with this suggestion. If animals ever know *anything*, presumably a newly born foal knows something as, tipped out of the womb, it walks across the grass. Does an animal ever know anything? If not, why does it have eyes? Either the visual sensations produce behaviour mediated by nothing psychological, or this causal relation is mediated by information and/or expectations. The first account, while condescending to allow psychological phenomena in animals, so cuts down on what it will allow as to dispense altogether with psychological causal explanation. This preposterous idea would mean we could never explain animal behaviour by invoking animal desire. The unacceptability of these claims pushes us towards the second account, which allows mental content for animals, bearing in mind that one cannot have contentless expectations or unheld information, and inevitably retains mental causation. Then how can we avoid the view that some animals sometimes know something? What kind of natural function can cognitive attitudes have, if they are never to be well-formed and well-derived? It seems we must opt for the view that the newly born foal, and probably therefore all animals, are born with some knowledge of some of the more general characteristics of physical reality.

What alternative is there? Consider the following suggestion. Suppose that, instead of postulating a fund of innate knowledge, we assume that consciousness preceded knowledge of the ways of the world. Evidently this cognitive void does not last. Then we must suppose that the transition is accomplished purely through experience. Consider the idea carefully. The supposition must be, that somehow through repeated associations in experience, consciousness graduated to a state in which it was equipped with knowledge. But why? How? It cannot be through the usual learning from experience, since that depends on already given knowledge. Then can mere association on its own accomplish so much? Frankly, I doubt whether a coherent account can be given of the crossing of this weirdest of Rubicons, nor of the evidence that would attest to it. And is this transition any less mysterious than the hypothesis of innate knowledge? Again, if we refuse to credit these beings with innate knowledge, what account are we to offer of body-sense? Are they not to know how their own limbs are disposed? And how in the present context is such ignorance to be evidentially revealed? Actively? The whole account is shot through with difficulties that vanish once we suppose that animals are born with knowledge of the ways of working of particular environments and of their own bodies. The hypothesis is at once intelligible, highly explanatory, and near obligatory.

It seems that the mere existence of animal consciousness necessitates that the capacity for tactile experience be co-present with *some* measure of innate knowledge of the ways of the physical world, such that new knowledge can be generated by tactile experience. This is not true of any other sense, though it is true of the senses as a whole. It must be possible to learn from tactile experience, whether in this or some other environment, and doubtless in the environment for which it was designed, which is to say the environment in which the species evolved. That is, animals are items which are such that they can learn from experiences—of a certain kind—in a certain setting, so that there must be a setting in which this power can be displayed. This holds of sense-perception as a whole, of tactile perception in particular, and of body-sense willy-nilly.

We noted earlier that something in us shies at the suggestion that in the case of touch (and equally with body-sense) perceptual knowledge requires supplementation by knowledge if it is to generate new knowledge. The reason now seems clear. It is because the relation holding between perceptual experience of these primordial kinds, and the physical realities they disclose, is not a mere relation of empirical association. It is closer. Because there is no possibility that we might in general discount either touch or body-sense as failed putative senses, as it might have been that auditory sensation no more correlated with environmental phenomena than do itches or tingles, the relation must be more intimate. Since we can scarcely be animals and lack either body-sense or tactile-sense, and since these senses could scarcely be senses without the potential for use and hence veridicality, the association of perceptual experience with perceptible fact must in their case be a near certainty. Innate knowledge is therefore a necessity with them. It can hardly be said to depend upon mere fortunate empirical fact. At the root of the unease produced in us by the need of knowledge in the case of tactile-sense (and body-sense), lies the feeling that knowledge of such matters cannot but be experientially associative in origin. But such a supposition would threaten too much. The bond must be at once tighter and guaranteed.

6. The Dependence of Tactile-Sense on Body-Sense

(1) My concern at this point is with the relation between tactile-sense and body-sense. It is a remarkable, and little remarked, kinship. As it were, mirror-image senses. One sense leading us outwards beyond ourselves, the other taking us back into ourselves, the latter being part of the means utilized by the former. And while the forms taken by the perceptions are unlike, the content is astonishingly similar. Now the mode of perceiving employed in the case of body-sense—which on the face of it seems almost non-existent, for it is immediate and we are rarely aware of singling out body-parts for proprioceptive attention—is almost invariably recessive and (when active) subordinated to other attentive projects (as in car-driving). By contrast, the central tactile perceptual process is a double and active project, generally taking place in full awareness and often working hand in glove with thought-processes. For while we might intuit straightness in a movement of our limbs, and perhaps also in some object which we experience through such means, and while more complex tactile intuitions can occur if we engage in active attending, we only manage by exploratory touch to discover much if we supplement the procedures by inference linking tactile findings. Whereas a man can visually take in the contents of a room at a glance, if he is to make a comparable discovery through touch he will almost certainly have to assemble a mass of inferentially linked tactile data.

So much for the unlikeness in the methods of sensing in the case of tactile- and body-sense. What of the likeness in what they disclose? The common content is spatial: on the one hand the shape and position of objects, on the other hand the relative position and disposition of limbs. To be sure, there are differences in the spatial concepts in terms of which the perceptual data is structured. Thus, body-sense avails itself of such concepts as 'straight', 'crooked', 'moving', 'near face', 'away from the body', whereas the data of touch is structured in terms of concepts like 'straight', 'spherical', 'rectangular'. Nevertheless, they are both spatial and necessarily overlap, e.g. 'straight'. Meanwhile, a whole set of common properties bind these two senses in the tightest of unions. I am thinking of the following. Being necessary features of animality. Putting to use the same kind of sensation, viz. bodily sensation. Being unable to take significantly different or rudimentary form. Being unable to exist without the other sense. Being capable of co-existing in the absence of all other senses. Failing to interpose mediating sensations between consciousness and its perceptual object. Being necessarily concerned with spatial properties. Being necessarily supplemented with knowledge sufficient to ensure the passage from perceptual experience to further knowledge. Being in general necessarily veridical.

(2) A formidable array. Indeed, so formidable that one wonders whether we may not be dealing with two modes of a single sense. But the differences are sufficiently striking to make this idea unacceptable. To begin with, the relation of the attention to its object is of a different kind in each case. In body-sense it is immediate, in tactile-sense it is mediated by awareness of the body. Again, sensation is the causal mediator in body-sense, whereas awareness of the body is the causal mediator in the case of touch. Then these differences highlight the most obvious and fundamental difference of all: namely, that tactile-sense depends attentively and causally on body-sense, whereas body-sense stands in no such relation to tactile or any other sense. But there are other important differences as well. For example, a striking difference is to be found in both the type and the role played by supportive knowledge. We have seen that knowledge is needed to get us from immediate body experience to knowledge of the body, and that it is recessive and repetitive: roughly, it concerns the stability and matching of body and long-term body image. By contrast, while the knowledge put to use in tactile perception similarly concerns stability in various items, it in the first place varies from locale to locale (e.g. one may discover that what one is feeling at this place is moving), second it is self-consciously put to use in ratiocinative procedures (e.g. as one feels one's way across a city), third it postulates specific spatial relations holding between us the perceiver and the object (e.g. that both are moving at different speeds). And so on.

(3) In general, we may say that these two modes of perception are closely akin, and in their diverse ways mutually supportive of one another. What is the explanation of the closeness of this bond? Is it that in each case the same variety of sensation, namely bodily sensation, plays a vital role? But a man with drastic tunnel vision who could see only a mere spot at a time, could in a fashion tactilely perceive the shape of an object through awareness of the motion of his head as he examined the perimeter of the object his gaze was trained upon. Would he not *feel* rather than *see* that the object has the shape it has? Further, we earlier noted that a man whose hand was anaesthetized might manage to detect obstructions to the progress of his arm, and it is probable that this is a tactile perception. In a word, we cannot attribute the kinship of these two varieties of perception to the type of the sensation they utilize.

I suggest instead that it lies in the essential mutual interdependence of these two senses. For despite the obvious dependence of tactile-sense upon body-sense, which might lead us to suppose that body-sense has some kind of priority in the scheme of things, it will in fact emerge that there is a mutual though different form of dependence of either sense upon the other. Now the dependence of body-sense upon tactile-sense is both more covert and more subtle than the other, and requires to be teased out into the light of day. For the moment my concern is with the more obvious reverse dependence. Thus, we know that tactile perception interposes between consciousness and the perceived object an item wholly unlike the sensory given of the four other senses: namely, the bodily movements of the perceiver. Thereby it interposes an example across time of a shape in space. That is, an item

PERCEPTION AND THE BODY

the same in kind as the perceived. A sort of mimicry occurs, so that perception of one type of item depends on an already achieved immediate other instance of perception of the same kind of item. This at least holds of the simple objects of tactile-sense. Thus, it is because we know our hand has travelled roughly in a circle that we know the object we have just felt likewise traverses a sort of circle in space. For the most part, with one or two exceptions where complexity of structure obtains, the important and revealing cases of tactile perception follow this rule. Indeed, even the perception of warmth is accomplished only through the warming of one's body. In short, uniquely in the case of this sense, perception seems to depend upon an already achieved example of perception of an item the same in kind as itself.

Then given the primacy of the sense of touch among the senses, in that it is the essential sense and the one that of necessity concerns itself with the ultimate differentia of the physical, namely space; and given that tactile-sense functions as the final cognitive 'back up' on which visual-sense and the rest may count; the whole edifice of sense-perception now seems in a certain sense to depend upon the perception of our own bodies. That is, coming to know what goes on in the physical world seems in a sense ultimately to depend upon our knowing what is going on in our own bodies. That is, perception of physical reality depends in a certain sense upon immediate perception of the body.

7. The Dependence of Body-Sense upon Tactile-Sense

Instead of the Cartesian consciousness alone with its thoughts, attempting to build a bridge to the beyond, we might seem to have put in its place the animal alone with its body and its immediately given postures and movements, attempting to build a cognitive bridge, if not to another ontological realm, to the remainder of the physical realm. Clearly, there is something the matter with such an account. But what? Three separate properties of body-sense raise difficulties for this kind of theory. One is, the *fallibility and the dependence upon knowledge* of the findings of body-sense; another is, the *dependence of body-sense on tactile-sense*; a third is, the binding need of *coherence* between the findings of the two senses. Consider these properties in order.

(a) The dependence of body-sense content on body image content

(1) We have already commented on the first property. We noted the fallibility of the deliverances of body-sense, which are unproblematically corrigible as those of sensation-perception are not, and saw too that the findings of body-sense require supplementation by knowledge if new knowledge is to be gained. Where is that knowledge to come from? Hardly uniquely from the findings of body-sense. We need knowledge concerning the stability of the body, the reliability of body-sense, and suchlike, and this can be acquired only by going outside

676

body-sense, and in any case depends at some point upon a fund of innate knowledge about the ways of the body. Here we have a first corrective of the Cartesian
analogue.

(2) The second corrective seems to me of some interest. It turns upon the
differences between the *experienced objects* of body-sense and tactile-sense. We shall
begin this discussion by spelling out the dependence of body-sense on the
body image, for this enables us to bring to light a latent dependence of body-
sense on tactile-sense that is obscured by the differences in their experienced
objects.

The objects of body-sense are such things as 'presence of arm', 'flexedness of
arm', 'hand near chin', 'body presence'. But they do not include the *three-
dimensional shape* of the limb whose presence and posture one perceives. Now body-
sense depends on the possession of a long-term body image. Then how do the contents of that image compare with the contents of body-sense experience? Like the
latter the body image is constituted out of superficial experienceable body-parts,
linked at particular points. But it also includes the property of 3D-shape. Thus, the
long-term body image etches in a surface in three-dimensional space, a surface that
is revealed above all in one's actions, whether they be acts of manoeuvering amongst
other objects, self-concernful acts like clutching one's head, or acts of sensation
locating—though it is manifest also in one's body-related beliefs and expectations.
Then we have just seen that this 3D-surface is no part of the content of body-sense
experience. Rather, it is the *presumed shape* of that whose presence and posture is the
content of that experience: it is a necessary condition of that content. The body
image provides the *subject* onto which are pinned the predicates which are disclosed
in body-sense experience. Now we have seen that those predicates are drawn from a
special grid of concepts that include 'flexed', 'moving', 'fast', but do not include
'equidistant', '30°', 'cylindrical', 'seventeen-sided'. That is, a more limited system
of concepts than the universal spatial concepts put to use in characterizing the long-
term body image. Then to repeat: without the existence of something which in a
special sense is given as of a relatively determinate 3D-shape which we characterize
in the general abstract terminology of spatial language, in other words a particular
part of the *long-term body image*, no content could be conveyed in body-sense. And
the reason is, that it is that something which provides the subject for predication.
Yet while it *makes possible* body-sense experience, it is no part of the content of
body-sense experience. Contrast: *looking* at one's arm. Here one perceives arm,
position, and flexedness, of that whose 2D-profile and 3D-face one simultaneously
perceives, all in the one perceptual package.[1]

[1] The claim that the long-term body image provides the subject for predication of the properties perceived
by body-sense, does not contradict the claim that in body-sense the attention finds immediate bodily objects.
The body image is not a mediating experienced entity, but a necessary schema in terms of which the immediately experienced body is experienced. The point may be summed up in the slogan: we body-sense immediately experience only what is long-term body imaged. It is in this special sense that it provides a subject.

(b) The dependence of body-sense content on tactile-sense content

(1) The deliverances of body-sense are (say): the straightness or the semi-flexedness, the fast-movingness or stillness, of a something that is *in some sense* given but never experienced as endowed with a relatively determinate 3D-shape described in the general abstract terminology of spatial language. Now this lack can be experienced as a failing of kinds. Somehow the absence of the 3D-shape from body-sense experience can make the latter appear essentially vague, even in a way as *blind*, a matter for instinct more than anything else. And body-sense *is* blind in this sense: that it is not made for accord with the sense of sight, since it is in itself *pre-visual* and has nothing to do with sight, being so to say born in the dark. However, it is scarcely blind in any other sense. It has necessary links with sight which cannot be shaken off, for body-sense has a content that significantly overlaps with that of normal seeing. Thus, one can see not just 'equidistant', '30 °', 'cylindrical', which are obscured to body-sense, but also 'flexed', 'moving', 'fast', which are revealed to it. In short, body-sense has no special space of its own. Its space is open to, and perceptible by, the senses at large. It presents to awareness the universal physical space under a select few concepts, whose most obvious characteristic is that they are specifically tailor-made for use in intentional physical action. The absence of certain spatial determinations has this specific functional origin.

(2) What we have just noted in the case of developed seeing, holds also of the essentially space-oriented sense, touch. It likewise is concerned with the same public spatial subject-matter as body-sense. And so there exist two ways in which one might perceive one's body, which seem to stand in particularly close relation to one another. Namely: immediately by body-sense, and mediately by reflexive or self-directed tactile-sense. Then how do these two perceptual modes of relating to one's body, say to one's right arm, themselves interrelate? What kind of a *modus vivendi* have they?

More specifically: how does the immediate giveness in body-sense of a something—which enters the body image as a part endowed with a non-experienceable 3D-shape S—*as* at once 'flexed', 'out from the torso', 'moving left' (say), *relate* to the giveness to simultaneous exploratory (if harassed) touch in which I discover (in myself): 'arm', 'flexed', 'moving left', 'roughly cylindrical'? There is overlap of content, viz. 'flexed', and failure of overlap, viz. 'roughly cylindrical'. However, 'roughly cylindrical' enters the presumed but inexperienced shape S of that which is the *subject* of body-sense. And this is no coincidence. For the dependence of body-sense experience on the long-term body image carries tactile implications. It is of some interest that the body image is characterized by the very system of concepts that tactile-sense employs. This, too, is no accident. The reason is, that the body image manifests its existence and content in tactile encounters in which tactile-sense is employed. For example: holding one's chin, walking through a doorway, scratching one's foot. Therefore the body image must be the image of what would reveal itself in tactile encounters with oneself and others as having just such a content. This shows in the above example in which we related by body-sense and tactile-sense to the one arm. We saw there that 'roughly cylindrical' occurred non-accidentally in both presupposed body image subject of body-sense-experience *and* experienced object of tactile-experience. For generally the inexperienced presupposed image subject of body-sense will coincide with the findings of tactile perception of the body-part represented therein. Clearly they need not, for illusions are possible. But they should and doubtless mostly do. This spells out the essential dependence of body-sense upon tactile-sense that is our present concern.

(3) At this point it seems that the 'fog' pervading one's conception or imagery of body-sense clears somewhat. I mean, the indefiniteness that tends to characterize one's idea of body-sense when one starts to think about it, which is traceable to the fact that the body is not experienced as *fully determinate* spatially. The rationale underlying the experience of vagueness being, that we readily (and falsely) conclude that the body must be experienced as spatially *indeterminate*, and the reason for this is that we have sight as covert model. Determinacy enters by another door. Thus, the 'fog' clears when we bring into intelligible relation, as I have attempted to do, the findings of tactile-sense and the content of the body image that is implicitly put to use in body-sense. In both cases we encounter space, warped it may be just a little in that rectangles can emerge as rhombuses, but with all its determinations intact. Then for tactile-sense to be veridical we require that body-sense be veridical; while if body-sense is to be veridical we require that that which is the subject-matter of the content, be presumed to be endowed with properties open to tactile investigation which would be the perceived content of a veridically exploring tactile project. That is, we require the long-term body image to be veridical and therefore such that veridical tactile perception of the body would arrive at an identical content. This is the door through which appears the determinacy that illusorily seemed absent because it was no part of the experience of body-sense. It all boils down to the fact that our experience of our own body is an experience of a physical reality with an objective spatial envelope. That is, of something transcending all immediate proprioceptive experience.

(c) The necessary coherence of body-sense and tactile-sense

What is left of the suggestion that body-sense is epistemologically prior to tactile-sense, let us say in the way in which the perception of visual sensations (truly) is epistemologically prior to the visual perception of material objects? I rejected this suggestion for three reasons.

First, because of the fallibility of body-sense experience, which requires supplementation by knowledge if it is to yield more knowledge: namely, knowledge of the body's stability, and the reliability of this particular body-sense. The second consideration arose out of a specific difficulty: that even though the deliverances of body-sense are couched in a special grid of concepts ('flexed', etc.) that merely overlapped with those pressed into use by tactile-sense, they are yet appended to a seemingly shadowy something not perceived as endowed with comparable spatial traits. Thereby one might come to suppose that, somewhat as the immediate objects of visual experience have an immediate personal verification which is largely independent of the perceptions of a third person and indeed of anything else, so here we have perceptual data which is set in a space all of its own, an analogue of so-called visual space. Then the corrective to this line of thought is, that the data of body-sense gain reality and content only through the presumption of a subject for that content which is endowed with fully determinate spatial properties of a kind accessible to tactile-sense. Thus, the potential findings of tactile-sense enter the deliverances of body-sense, not as *content* but as *subject* of that content. That is, the supposed priority of body-sense is a myth, since even the immediate and possibly erroneous deliverances of body-sense rest on a foundation in which tactile findings are conditionally presupposed. In a word, the analogy with immediate acquaintance with private objects, to wit visual sensations, set in some (supposed) private analogue of physical space, to wit (so-called) visual space, breaks down. Physical space that is open to tactile exploration enters in at the very beginning. After all, there is no autonomous bodily sensation sensory schema, analogue of the visual field, for the reason that it is of the essence of a bodily sensation to be putatively referred to a known or unknown part of the body. Projectively, we locate bodily sensations in the body and nowhere else. They either projectively 'land' or merely putatively 'land'. There is no third alternative. Hence a pain in a phantom limb is projectively nowhere: it is, one might say, a 'projective failure'. It fails to realize its projective 'hopes', and is doomed to inhabit a sort of limbo of space.

The third and final consideration that disposes of the suggestion that body-sense is epistemologically prior to tactile-sense is, that the findings of tactile-sense and body-sense must intelligibly cohere. If one's right hand proprioceptively seems to one to be moving in a straight line, and if this is to generate *knowledge* concerning one's right hand and thereby also of the material object the hand is contacting in some tactile exploration, that right hand must in general to one's exploring left hand tactilely seem to be doing what immediately and so to say internally it seems to be doing. Once again, the immediate proprioceptive given is not comparable to that of visual perception, for its putative object (viz. a limb) is (unlike visual sensations) the kind of item open to the exploration of the mode of sensing (viz. tactile) it is supposed to originate. These two vital differences between on the one hand body-sense and touch, and all the other senses on the other hand, constitute the reason why, even though tactile-sense depends on body-sense in a way body-sense does not on tactile-sense, yet in another and equally essential manner body-sense depends just as fundamentally on tactile-sense. In a creature in which these were the only senses, the dependence of each upon the other would be absolute and total. Of course, without prior knowledge the whole epistemological show would not get off the ground. But, as we have observed already, that is true of the senses as a whole and is not peculiar to touch and body-sense.

Conclusion

In this concluding section I shall go over some of the main topics which form the body of this work, and in terms which give some idea of their overall significance. In particular, I want once more to articulate just why it is that consciousness is so closely tied to the phenomenon of perception. In my opinion it is because consciousness is as such directed to the World, and perception is our ultimate mode of access to the World. This connects these phenomena in two quite different ways. On the one hand if the mind and consciousness are to so much as exist, to have substance of any kind, one needs before all else to be capable of being aware of outer reality, so that perception emerges as part of the very foundation of consciousness. On the other hand perception is a vitally important part of the functional rationale of consciousness, for it is an essential power of the state, one of its prime uses, a necessary condition of one's leading a life of any kind. Thus perception is of a double and elemental import for consciousness.

1. The Primacy of Epistemology and Perception

The main topic of this work is consciousness. Now the most fundamental characteristic of consciousness is the closeness of its links with the World. Indeed, since representation is essential to consciousness, consciousness could be said to be born of the World or Reality, and even in its image. Moreover, the conscious uniquely are 'in touch' with the World. Consciousness might be compared to a window, through which for the one and only time we actually catch sight of Reality. While the comparison is misleading, since consciousness is not the perception of anything let alone of the World, consciousness nonetheless realizes a distinctive relation to the World which it is proper to describe as one of awareness. In particular, an experiential readiness and capacity to follow the path of truth in relation to an intuitionally encountered Reality, indeed to follow the path of truth generally.

Then if the most fundamental characteristic of consciousness is the closeness of its links with the World, the most fundamental of its relations to the World is the perceptual relation of sheer awareness of sectors of the world. I think it is clear from the considerations set out above that the perceptual cognitive properties of consciousness must lie at its very heart. It was this which led me to devote so much space in this work to the task of linking consciousness intelligibly with perception, and then going on to describe the manner in which in perception consciousness interacts with the world. As we have just seen the perceptions of the conscious have a dual role to play in the life of the mind, each of fundamental import. Thus perception is a major part of the *immediate natural purpose* of consciousness, for it enables its owner actively to engage with, indeed simply to lead a life in an environment. At the same time perception has a long-term *formative* function, for it has the function of being the avenue via which internalization of the world can occur, and therefore of enabling mind and consciousness to so much as exist. Accordingly, perception must be accounted as both a functional cognitive device like a natural instrument of investigation, not unlike a probe or telescope, and at the same time as akin to something of an altogether different order, something of the nature of a life-line or umbilical cord. This dual role, one of an immediate practical character and the other long-term and formative in its aims, reveals how it is that perception is of such significance so far as consciousness is concerned.

But there is one other rather more general reason for supposing perceptual cognitive function to be of central, indeed of pre-eminent significance for consciousness. It seems to me intuitively evident that the epistemological properties of consciousness are more closely linked to its nature than are any other properties, including its vastly important executive powers. A natural image for the emergence of consciousness is of a light going on in the mind, and the main significance of light for human kind is epistemological, that which makes visible and knowable. As I have remarked at several places in the text, the non-accidental ambiguities in 'awareness', ranging from (sheer) awareness (ie. consciousness), to (directed, experiential) awareness (ie. the 'stream of consciousness'), to (sheer, extensional) awareness (i.e. perception), emphasize the closeness of the tie between consciousness and perceptual empirical knowledge. It seems clear that epistemology, more precisely epistemology based upon contemporaneous perception, lies closer to the heart of consciousness than its expression in informed intentional action upon the environment—or any other manifestation of the state.

For these reasons most of my inquiry into consciousness has concentrated on its epistemological properties, and because that epistemology is empirical epistemology mostly on the perceptual function of consciousness. The two phenomena are linked at the deepest possible level. Perception is a condition of the mind's very existence, renewing its content from instant to instant, helping to enrich that which of its nature is ultimately totally dependent-on and oriented-to the world, and simultaneously concretely sets before the mind the world in which it is to live and engage with in informed active constructive manner.

2. Consciousness and Epistemology

(1) Thus, the natural purpose of consciousness pre-eminently includes perception of a contemporaneous sector of physical reality. Meanwhile the function of

perception is to lead the mind cognitively onto that sector of reality. Accordingly, the end of the line in this transaction is the world as encountered in the perceptions and cognitions of the conscious. Then in the foregoing discussion, in concentrating my energies largely upon the epistemological properties of consciousness, I was led naturally to investigate the following four fundamental elements in this basic empirical epistemological interaction.

α. Consciousness.
β. Perception.
γ. The interpretational processes of consciousness in empirical epistemology.
δ. The world as encountered in the perceptions of the conscious.

In this Conclusion I shall briefly review the claims made concerning these four elements of the situation. I will do so roughly in the order set out above, but for the moment concentrate my comments both upon (α) consciousness and the rational processes (γ) it involves, since such a procedure helps to elucidate the nature of (α) consciousness.

(2) After an initial inquiry in Part I into the *experience*, which is the phenomenal core of consciousness and an occurrence with time and flux at its very heart in so far as the events and processes of experience are the mutations of—nothing, I turned to the topic of consciousness. When I approached this phenomenon at close quarters, it seemed to lend itself to analysis into parts. However those parts proved to be quite other than the atomistic parts of a psychological molecule. This is above all true of the rationalistic apparatus of consciousness, since each constituent element of that rationalistic structure necessitates the presence of all of its brethren elements. Thus the various properties jointly responsible for the rational self-conscious character of human consciousness must in the course of evolution have appeared absolutely con-temporaneously with one another, doubtless in gradualistic fashion, but of necessity always in the form of an ensemble or *totality*. Then the character of the parts into which the state consciousness resolved, confirms the above surmise that the episte-mological powers of consciousness are essential properties. They include accessibil-ity of the perceptual attention, together with availability of the mental apparatus requisite for the epistemological interpretation of the data of perception and so for acquiring knowledge of the realities thus encountered. This epistemological prop-erty is to be found right across the board of animal kind: if consciousness is to be real-ized in a mind, the mode of belief-formation operative at that moment has to be well-formed, whether in the rational mode of self-conscious beings or the merely regularistic/innate mode of non-rational animals.

The epistemological capacity is built out of two powers. The power of concrete intake of the environment in the form of perception, together with the mental machinery through which conscious subjects come via perception to learn about the environment. Part I of this work addressed itself to the latter power, while Parts II–IV were primarily concerned with the former, the power of perception. Thus,

Part 11 was an attempt to transparently link perception and consciousness by means of a universal theory of perception which took such a form as makes clear how naturally and in predestined manner perception emerges from consciousness. Meanwhile, the remaining Parts 111–1v examined the three senses expressly directed to spatial data and thus to object-constitution and ultimately to world-constitution: sight, proprioception, and touch. The bulk of my energies went into an analysis of the sense of sight, since of these three it alone was concerned to assemble the object in a way that was largely detached from the body. More exactly, it was for that reason together with the comprehensiveness and general impressiveness of the sense. So much for the moment for the first of the four main elements involved in the fundamental epistemological transaction, that of consciousness (α). I pass now to a consideration of the rationalistic constitution (γ) of the self-conscious variety of consciousness.

(3) In Chapters 5–6 I examined the mental processes which accompany perceptual experience in the self-consciously conscious. That is, the rational 'processing' to which the minds of conscious beings subject the data of perceptual experience. But to begin (in Chapter 3) it seemed desirable to delineate the distinctive character of the perceptions upon which those processes are brought to bear. After all, the perceptual experiences of the conscious must be significantly dissimilar from the circumscribed perceptions of somnambulists and subjects in hypnotic trance. I described them as 'realistic' 'perceptions as—', in an extra-perceptual sense of the latter expression. This is because while the conscious perceive objects as embedded in reality, they do not do so in the sense one sees (say) a table as set in a room full of furniture. Rather, those objects are 'perceived as—' in such conceptual terms as evidence their being correctly sited in the cognitive representation of Reality with which conscious beings are normally 'in touch'. The perceptions of the conscious are relations of awareness-of a sector of the world, cast in the broadest possible or realistic terms, in which the data give to awareness is positioned in one's cognitive representation of reality. That is, one's K-Syst. is brought to bear by the understanding upon the perceptual experience, so that the objects that we see as (say) we scan a scene are almost invariably labelled in experience for what they are, set in a cognitive picture of the world which has the properties of truth, consistency, and a perspectivalism in which those items are located in their proper spatio-temporal site. Thus, the data of perception finds itself embedded in a veridical cognitive map of reality, and not just the circumscribed regions accessible to (say) somnambulists. Even the delusive B-Syst. of the insane rates as a cognitive map of reality, and in consequence their perceptual experiences when awake exhibit the trait of 'realism'.

This property of conscious perceptual experience was examined in Part 1. However, much of Part 1 was concerned with the *mental conditions* making possible the cognitive epistemological interpretation of perceptions of this type (which I discuss (below) in 3). Those conditions at once underlie and are part of that sub-set of the properties constitutive of consciousness which I described as 'The

Apparatus of Rationality'. And by that I meant the closely bonded totality of traits that are necessary conditions of an occurrent rationality: rationality itself (which is to say the rational determination of those mental phenomena susceptible of rational determination, such as belief and desire), self-knowledge, thinking, self-determination, and so forth. In consciousness this totality is called upon to rationally interpret the data of perceptual experience, namely the 'realistic' perceptions characteristic of the state, and lead in the end to the augmenting of one's cognitive representation of the world, given from the perspective of here, now, myself, at such a point in space-time and history. That is, to perspectival knowledge of a local sector of the world, cast in universal terms.

3. The Mental Conditions of Epistemology in the Self-Conscious Conscious

(1) I want at this point to set down the above-mentioned mental conditions which underlie rational epistemology. Thus it seemed to me in examining consciousness that there are certain properties of the state which are at once *part* of the rationalistic apparatus of consciousness and yet *supportive* of certain other elements of that complex of properties. It is these particular traits that I want now to consider. Now we know that consciousness involves rationality of state, and it emerged in Part 1 that rationality necessitates certain examples of mental activity and pre-eminently the activity of *thinking*. Equally, we saw that a measure of *self-knowledge* was a necessary condition of rationality and consciousness, and the discussion of gross inebriation and psychotic mental states helped uncover the mental mechanics whereby atrophy or deformation of consciousness resulted from breakdown in this capacity. Here we have two conditions of rationality and a proper example of wakeful self-conscious consciousness. When they are present they have the function of enabling the rational powers of the mind to be harnessed, and consciousness to pass from perceptual experience to knowledge of a sector of the world. In this way the vitally important epistemological function of consciousness can under such conditions be fulfilled.

Given the 'realistic' perceptions typically experienced by the conscious, together with the satisfaction of the above conditions of rationality, the normal epistemological relation between consciousness and the world can be realized. Then to see the part which those conditions play in the establishing of that relation, it is illuminating to compare the two *relata* involved: the inner domain of self-conscious consciousness, and that of outer reality which is the object of cognition. These domains, which differ significantly, share nonetheless certain properties which help make possible the epistemological interaction between the two.

Physical reality has these characteristics:

1. The rule of causality is universal.
2. The ultimate rationale, whose existence is a necessity, is universal in its scope and character and timelessly true.

3. Both physical reality itself, and the content of the ultimate rationale, namely the fundamental laws and basic existents, are contingencies.
4. Rational causation is inexistent.
5. Absolute causal isolation of particular systems is a realistic possibility.
6. Predictability of a high order is possible in such systems.
7. Superficial regularities abound.

Meanwhile the stream of consciousness of self-consciously conscious subjects exhibits the following properties:

1. The rule of causality is universal.
2. No system of universal governing laws exists.
3. Both mental reality itself, and at least some mental explanatory factors, are contingencies.
4. Rational causation is the norm for some phenomena.
5. Absolute causal isolation of particular systems is impossible.
6. Predictability is limited, and hemmed in with conditions.
7. Regularities in experience tend (in whatever manner) to generate beliefs.

(2) The properties in common to these two domains are significant. Thus, merely on account of being phenomenal continuities, the following similarities already exist. Both domains are in the same time-system, are subject to causality, and contingent a posteriori existentially and explanatorily. Then the stream of experience of self-conscious consciousness introduces two further properties essential to epistemological function. The first is the internal intelligibility of the rational progression of the cognitively significant experiences of the self-conscious conscious, which parallels the openly accessible intelligibility of the cognitively significant experiences of the unself-conscious and of the outer phenomena that are their objects. The second epistemologically significant property of rational conscious experience is the continuous and immediate acquaintance with all three temporal dimensions, encountered in this state.

The presence of the active thinking process guarantees the inherence of both, and permits the intelligibility of one flow of experience to be brought to bear in detecting the intelligibilty of the other. Despite the ontological difference between the experiential and physical domains, and the marked dissimilarity of the governing explanatory rationales, the required conditions are realized whereby one type of rationale can be brought to bear in detecting the other, and thus for certain events in the experiential domain to be deemed identifications of items in the physical. Identification of objects necessitates understanding of their causal properties, and the internal intelligibility of rational progressions of experience imports the possibility of understanding the outer progression of events. Likewise the immediate acquaintance with an originating past and an actively determined future imported by the mental will, introduces the temporal framework necessary for the identification across time of outer items (notably, material objects) which preserve identity across time.

If on the other hand the stream of consciousness had the properties of the dreaming flow of experience, the epistemological office of consciousness could not be discharged. Even if items could be perceived, and as what in fact they are, they could not be reliably identified, since identificatory knowledge of existents depends on the above property of the understanding, and the dreaming progression of experience is not internally intelligible to a dreaming subject, whether at the time of dreaming or even retrospectively on waking. If the understanding is to be accessible and harnessed to the epistemological task of interpreting the flow of outer phenomena, the experiential flow within must be comparably intelligible, indeed in the case of self-consciousness must be rationally accessible to the understanding of the subject. But this cannot be realized if as in the case of dreaming the rationale governing the progression of the stream of experience is hidden from the view of the subject. Again, dream experience is such that the past drops out of sight and the future is never visible, and this likewise is inconsistent with the identification of items which preserve identity across time.

(3) It was in part for reasons of this kind that I argued for the view, first that a measure of *self-knowledge* is a necessary condition of consciousness in the self-conscious, and secondly for the necessity of mental activeness in the cognitively significant experiential processes of consciousness, and pre-eminently for the presence of the *active thinking process*, the ultimate custodian of present operative rationality. The reason mental activeness is essential for consciousness is twofold. It lay first in the close links between action and reason, something that is manifest in the fact that the class of mental phenomena capable of being rationally determined and the class of phenomena implicated in the causal determination of intentional action (belief, desire, intention, decision, choice, will, the act itself) are one and the same. Then it is through this property and ultimately through the required mental activeness taking the form of the active thinking process that the internal intelligibility of reason is introduced into the progression of cognitively significant experiences (perceptual, thinking, planning, etc) of consciousness. And it lay secondly in the fact that intentional action makes its own future and continues its recent still-intended past, in each case avowedly so. Then through these means the subject is empowered to detect the profile across time of outer phenomenal objects, which is likewise essential to their identification and individuation.

4. Consciousness and Perception

In the state consciousness thus constituted from experience, rationality, activity, thinking, self-knowledge, awareness of the temporal dimensions, together with accessibility of the perceptual attention, we typically encounter the 'realistic' perceptions unique to this condition. Now when one is conscious perception plays the steady role of informant concerning the outer world, and stage-setter for a life in which informed intentional action looms large and consciousness realizes in that phenomenon what is perhaps its ultimate function. Consciousness marshals the mind's resources as no other state, avails itself of the information conveyed through 'realistic' perception and inference, and thanks in part to its rational character tends to call forth intentional projects directed towards such 'realistically' revealed scenes (for rationality discloses desirable ends). For much of the time perception plays this role of handmaiden in the service of intentional behaviour that probably realizes the primary function of consciousness. But perception is in any case an essential function of consciousness.

Then how does perception arise in the midst of consciousness? It occurs in the stream of consciousness, a systemic phenomenon analytically entailed by consciousness and barely to be distinguished from it. This 'stream of consciousnesses' is a 'stream of experiences', and the first (and essential) property of perception is that it is an experience, since perception is nothing but extensional experience-of a phenomenal reality. Accordingly, perception takes its place in that system. However, it is a unique example of the phenomena constituting the system, for it is (so to say) the chosen event in which the system opens onto the rest of the world, given to awareness in its ultimate (i.e. physical) ontological form. Perception is uniquely the phenomenon in which consciousness becomes concretely aware of the outer world, and as it ultimately is. This confers a special epistemological status upon perception. Perception must be the original epistemological relation between consciousness and the world, and the basis of all more developed or thought-mediated intentional consciousnesses. If awareness goes beyond itself uniquely in this phenomenon, it must be so.

Thus perception is *nothing but* the occurrent extensional *awareness-of* distinct phenomenal realities. The theory of perception formulated in Part 11 demonstrated that there are no modes of perceptual awareness, there are merely modes of presentation through which objects comes to awareness, as it were multiple suits of sensuous clothing available for the one and same item, but no variegation in our relation to the variously clad objects. For example there is no such thing as visual noticing, there is merely the noticing of visibles. Then it is scarcely surprising that the bare awareness-of physical reality should be part of the foundation upon which knowledge of extra-mental phenomena ultimately depends. While innate knowledge is a necessary condition of empirical knowledge, since the senses alone cannot convey knowledge, in the absence of the possibility of awareness taking consciousness out of itself onto outer reality little could be known of that domain. Nor should it surprise us that awareness of outer reality is part of the foundation of mind and consciousness, when one remembers that these phenomena are essentially directed to the world and above all to outer reality. Thus in the state consciousness the limited system 'stream of experiences' typically encompasses one unique phenomenon in which the genus 'Experience' is put to use in determining a species merely through the formal device of giving to it an extensional object. Here we have the means of demonstrating, not that consciousness necessitates accessibility of the perceptual attention, but that it carries within itself the conceptual raw material for the constitution of the concept of perception. It shows just how naturally perception arises in the midst of the state consciousness. In this way perception can be seen as a predestined phenomenon through which consciousness keeps an appointment with the world.

5. Visual Perception

(1) The primal epistemological meeting of the mind with the world is the perceptual encounter. The point of departure in this phenomenon is consciousness, the point of arrival the fully constituted physical object in its universal 'realistic' setting, the connecting relation that of mere awareness. Certain simple truths set these few facts in an interesting light. One is, that consciousness is awareness of the world in a non-perceptual sense of 'Aware'. Another, that perception is no more than awareness of a sector of the world. And another, that consciousness is a state which empowers one to learn of the world through perceptions in which the object is experienced as embedded in its universal world-setting.

The following conclusion can be drawn. Namely, that when 'realistic' or uncircumscribed sheer awareness-of the fully constituted physical object and setting occurs, and generates knowledge with matching content, the mental phenomenon that non-perceptually yet experientially *is* awareness of the world—viz. the state that we call 'consciousness'—is realizing a potential central to its nature. Consciousness involves an occurrent experiential empowerment for harbouring phenomena precisely of this kind. And so awareness of the world of one kind must carry within itself the potential for awareness of a sector of the world mentally embedded in its widest or world-setting. This helps to explicate the sense of 'Consciousness is awareness of the world'. Consciousness is awareness of the world in that it is specifically apt for the generation of events of awareness of sectors of the world mentally embedded in their world-setting and causing knowledge with matching content. While this may not exhaust the content of consciousness, it records what is probably its most fundamental property. It seems appropriate to describe as 'awareness of the world' a state mentally apt for realizing awarenesses of sectors of the world that locate those sectors cognitively in their universal or world setting.

(2) Thus the point of arrival of the 'primal epistemological meeting of mind and world' is the fully constituted physical object in its universal 'realistic' setting. Now if we are to illustrate how this is realized through perception, we are obliged to consider those senses whose perceptual content is pre-eminently spatial, since space is part of the framework of physical reality and the constitution of the object the goal of the epistemological interaction. This narrows the possibilities down to proprioception, touch, and sight, because they alone unite spatial content with the capacity

to perceptually assemble physical objects in three spatial dimensions out of perceptual experience. Then proprioception is automatically discountable, since it is necessarily concerned uniquely with the space of the perceiver's own body. And even though touch manages to go beyond the body of the perceiver to in principle any object, it has yet to cut the rope linking the object to the body.

It is true that sight is a directional sense, and from a point in the body, and to this extent is no different. Nevertheless, whereas the space given to touch is at once objective and relative to the body, the space accessible to sight achieves a measure of autonomy beyond that of touch. Thus one sees the spatial relations between objects set at a distance from the body, indeed sees also in some sense the very space around those things in a way not open to touch. In any case sight has a multitude of assets which make it the most effective example to demonstrate how in the perceptions typical of consciousness we encounter the fully constituted physical object in its universal 'realistic' setting. I am thinking of the properties of differentiation, organization, and projective reliability, which are of such an order that the items we see come to us in the very first place already labelled like exhibits in a museum. In fact, so great are the assets of this sense that Nature has so arranged things that we cannot *not* look at the visual field even if we want to. It is a benign compulsion, like that of thinking. For reasons such as these we tend epistemologically to lead our lives through our eyes. And it is for those same reasons that I devoted the whole of Part III to a study of visual perception. It enabled me to substantiate in the particular general claims concerning the perceptual experiences typical of consciousness.

(3) Those claims were concerned in part with the formation of the internal objects of perceptual experience. However, as a general rule these achievements of the understanding have to be matched by those of the attention, and in the case of sight those achievements are considerable. When we came to investigate this sense we found that the attention had a lengthy journey to undertake from its first and psychological object to its final outer physical object, and the understanding correspondingly extensive labours of an interpretational order. It seems that in the instantaneous visual experience of the moment the work of interpretation is assigned to the understanding and that of organization to the attention, and that the organization/spatial structure is in the very first place imposed by the attention upon an ordered array of sensory data, a phenomenon which I saw fit to describe as 'The Given'. While structures objectively exist in that 'given', no structures have priority over others, none are absolute as the others not, and the structures are limitless in number. That discerned in the visual experience is merely one out of an array of possibles, selected by the attention for reasons internal to itself and the mind, caused from without but not received in the manner in which a *tabula rasa* acquires an impressed imprint. The mere fact that mental causation is an ineradicable element of the situation is demonstration of this truth.

Interpretation is imposed upon the first object singled out by the attention, which is experienced as structured, and of necessity since the internal object of sight cannot be spatially indeterminate. My suggestion was that this first object is a structured sense-datum, a thing of sensations and spatial structure and nothing more, something of the ilk of a round sensation of red, located from the very beginning (merely) directionally in body-relative physical space. I advanced a theory to the effect that an instantaneous causal sequence is set in motion between the several internal objects of the experience, culminating in the final complex content of the perception. Then if the cognitive function of sight is to be discharged, it is necessary in general though not in particular that the sequence of causally linked internal objects match the later elements of the sequence of outer objects encountered by the attention in its 'journey outwards' from mind to physical objects at a distance in space. However, for it to be possible for an internal object legitimately to be set in three spatial dimensions in the instant, it must be possible for the mind to assemble the object in three spatial dimensions 'in the round'—across space—and across time. And this introduced a whole new order of tasks, on the one hand for the attention, on the other for the understanding.

6. The Object

(1) The summary picture that emerged is this. Starting from the state that non-perceptually is awareness of the World, constituted out of phenomena like experience and an occurrent rationality together with accessibility of the attention, perception occurs. In a general sense this is a momentous occurrence, for it is part of the foundation of consciousness and simultaneously a major function of that state. While sheer mentality necessitates *knowledge* of reality, and consciousness realises an *occurrent awareness* of reality, perception is bare concrete extensional *awareness-of* a sector of reality. Then since perception is awareness of what lies beyond the mind, it must in general be the source of objects for mental states, and in the particular indexically provide objects for many experiences in the self-conscious and all but all in the unself-conscious. In short, despite the existence of a limited endowment of innate knowledge, this concrete contact with reality is causally prior to either intentional or thought-mediated contact. It is not as if all three modes of access to outer reality were on a footing, three different windows opening onto the one scene. The bare and concrete awareness-of outer reality is a causal condition of the others.

To illustrate how consciousness augments one's cognitive representation of the world through perception, I turned to the visual sense and exclusively to fully developed examples. This is necessary because visual perception adopts forms which fall short in the above regard, such as the perceptions of somnambulists or animals. These beings do not perceive objects as embedded in a universal setting, nor do those perceptions engender knowledge with such content. By contrast, the typical visual perceptions of conscious humans do precisely that. They unite distinctive informational assets peculiar to sight with access to spatial properties sufficient to enable the perceptual constituting of physical objects set in three-dimensional space and time and in universal terms. In short, an object embedded in the World. In the discussion in Part III I described the lengthy 'journey of the attention' of sight: starting from a Given presented for awareness, it organizes its first sensory object and proceeds on its 'journey' through light, surface, side, and mediators of various kinds, arriving in the end at a physical object lying at a remove in space, all of which is made possible through the existence of psycho-physical regularities of several kinds. And I supplemented this with an account of the corresponding labours of the understanding, whose final goal is the most ambitious internal object of the experience. When this leads naturally to knowledge with matching content, the rounding out of what one might call the 'empirical epistemological module of the mind' is complete.

(2) Certain internal conditions are necessary for this to happen. In particular, and quite apart from the a priori forms of intuition of Kant, because the senses are not literally 'ports of knowledge' perception can engender knowledge only with the aid of already acquired knowledge which rests ultimately upon an innate cognitive base. This is one condition, of a cognitive order. However others exist pertaining to perception itself which one might fail to discern through misunderstanding the nature of this phenomenon. There is a danger of conceiving of perception as a merely passively received imprint imposed from without—something in the nature of a blow to the mind. And it is indeed a passive occurrence, since seeing and hearing etc. happen to us. However, to construe it as akin to the reception of a blow would be to suppose the cognitive apparatus of the mind to lie dormant, whereupon neither the understanding nor attention would make any contribution to the constitution of the perceptual experience. In fact both agencies are called upon, the attention to structure the first and thereby also all subsequent objects, the understanding to interpret the objects and arrive at the most ambitious internal object. Thus the inactiveness of the perceptual experience has a tendency to obscure the causal contributions of the mind, and most especially the understanding, to the formation of perceptual experience. These mental contributions constitutively develop the typical (say) visual perceptual event to a level of complexity and meaningfulness far removed from rudimentary visual perceptions, such as those of a sleeper who merely sees the light.

(3) But the momentary visual experience, so illuminating in many ways in that its highly developed character allows one pellucidly to trace out the attentive and interpretational achievements of the mind, culminating in a complex ordered experience, can nonetheless mislead. And it is precisely on account of that very richness. For it makes the experience appear self-sufficient in a way it is not: it conceals an essential dependence. This is why seeing 'in the round', and likewise touch 'in the round', are so instructive. It is not just that they underscore the situatedness of perception: they bring to light a further dimension to this phenomenon, concealed by the highly interpretational visual accomplishments of the instant. Namely, the

existence of something one could call 'the perceptual constituting of the material object out of situated momentary experiences', a conditional process upon which perceptions of the moment are in a certain respect dependent. An all-important property of both varieties of perception 'in the round' is that they do not involve experiencing an 'appearance-thing'. First because while in the visual experience we experience a succession of sensation-things *and* the look across space and time of the material object, the latter is not an individual stretched across space and time, second because in touch we do not come across anything that is the tactile appearance of the object. Then the absence of appearance-things opens a door, behind which lie a multitude of interrelated phenomena: the processes we called 'constituting of the object out of experiences'. It shows quite clearly that, once the content of perceptual experience acquires the complexity and structure introduced by three spatial dimensions and the presence of (say) materiality, we have need of an altogether different kind of explanation of the existence of perceptual content than can be provided by a mental thing like (say) a sensation. It is a content that can crystallize only with the aid of the understanding.

The positing of appearance-things in such perceptual situations is tantamount to denying to the understanding any role in the visual individuation of objects. The beauty of seeing 'in the round' is, that this doctrine is patently unacceptable in the case of a phenomenon of this kind, since without intellectual grasp nothing could synthesize the momentary experiences which would otherwise flash past senselessly. What emerged in the discussion of appearances in Chapter 21 was, that even to experience something so seemingly subjective as an appearance, one had to posit a sequence of positions across space and time for the perceiver and a rationale linking those multiple values with the experiential sequence. To endorse appearance-things is to suppose one could dispense with the rationale, arriving at the destination without the journey! The perceptual findings across space and time corroborate the content of the highly interpretational visual experience of the moment, and are by implication conditions of the veridicality of the latter. Thus the visual individuation of the material object in the instant involves more than the material object: by implication the mind radiates out perceptually across space and time, and a spatio-temporal logic binds the many experiences into one whole. And all of this is necessary if we are to justify the visual experience of the moment! Rather as understanding the sense of a word necessitates grasp of an entire language, so visually to posit in the instant a material object as object is to posit a containing spatio-temporal setting and an open-ended array of triples consisting of visual experience, position, and time. Visual identification in the instant visually implicates a spatio-temporal container radiating out into space and time with no clear limits.

And not just beyond the spatial envelope of the object. A kind of mirror effect exists within: not so much radiating out as reverberating within its confines. Pascal speaks somewhere of the infinitude concealed within things, as opposed to that encompassing all existents: the 'small infinity' as against the 'large infinity'. Implicit

693

in the 'seeing as—' of humans who in the instant recognize material objects, lies an unending corroborative evidential confirmation which takes observation within the confines of the material object, utilizing the concepts of side, surface, outside, interior, and above all of part, involving once more an unending sequence of intelligibly knit visual experiences which constitute a sort of perceptual dismembering of the object. This is of course not undertaken each time one visually identifies in the instant, but it is implicit notwithstanding, and, like the painter and his painting, complete only when one decides so, and in principle always resumable.

In sum, the momentary fully interpretational visual experience, in which the attention travels beyond the surface of the perceiver's body and lights upon a material object at a distance in three-dimensional physical space—a 'journey' that is for the most part veridically paced by the understanding, which in the instant develops the internal object of the experience to an extent precisely matching the later attentive achievements—this experience rests upon a complex foundation. If it is to count as a recognition of its object, a series of conditionals having application far and wide without, and near and narrow within, are by implication endorsed. On the one hand the wide physical world in which the object is set, on the other hand the limitless density of its inhabitants: each have claims upon the experience which must be recognized. Thus, the end of the line in the momentary visual experiences of the waking self-conscious cannot be divorced in the experience from the containing world. In this sense such experiences may be said to be continuations of the task of world-constituting which consciousness continually undertakes.

7. Perception and Things

The theoretical position regarding perception which I have endorsed in this work is at loggerheads with certain theoretical accounts of this phenomenon and its place in the mind. For example, with the theory that perception is an incidental so far as consciousness is concerned, the supposition that accessibility of the perceptual attention is no part of the essence of consciousness. This was rejected on several grounds, turning mostly on the fact that consciousness necessitates a content which has ultimately to be acquired through awareness of outer reality: no other final court of appeal seems conceivable than that of experience which takes the mind outside of itself in the concrete mode of awareness-of. Likewise my theoretical stance on these questions is inconsistent with any doctrine which, from the point of view of epistemology, fails to accord primacy to perception, conceiving of it as merely one out of a possible range of modes of original access to outer reality, a contingent one out of a ruck, to be set on an equal footing with thought-contact and imagination-contact and who knows what else. If, for the sake of convenience, the first of these rejected doctrines could be dubbed 'Angel-ist' or even 'Solipsist', the latter might be described as 'Spinozist' in view of its non-preferential multi-aspectist character.

694

The third theory of perception which I have been at pains just now to disprove might be described as 'monadic bare particularist', even as 'thing-ist'! Paradoxically, one of the main pitfalls in providing a satisfactory theory of perception lies in taking the thingishness of their thing-objects a little too seriously. These ultimately opaque outer realities conceal behind their exterior a logic of sorts, by which I mean the principle of organization of largely spatial differentia that is recognized by the understanding when, in following an intelligible line through a sequence of momentary experiences, it arrives in suitably justified manner at a point where a fully constituted material object seems in the concrete to have just then been perceptually experienced. 'Thing-ist' theory turns its back on all this, has resort to appearance-things as an escape from the mental meaning intelligibly linking the multiple situated experiences, and by implication endorses as a model for perception those rudimentary examples of the phenomenon in which the intellect is dormant, such as that of a sleeper who momentary sees merely the light.

The proper counter to this doctrine takes the following form, as it seems to me. It is not as if I am claiming that in perception things are not just things, but are in addition propositions incarnate. Rather, there is a tendency to think that in perception we get the material object *first* and *then* structure it, as if the intellect were an intruder from outside in the perceptual experience. Thus, a tendency towards a 'bare particularist' account, in which in the first place the intellect is wholly dormant. This theory may be viewed as a misreading of the fact that the objects of the perceptual attention are non-propositional, are nothing more and nothing less than—things (broadly understood). Conversely, the theory that in perception the attention takes propositional objects, might be seen as a misconstrual of the falsity of 'bare particularism'. In fact the process across space and time which results in the attention having singled out a material object 'in the round', which of necessity can be realized only if the understanding intelligibly threads the pieces together, culminates in a 'conclusion' which is neither a proposition nor a 'bare particular'—so to say, the Scylla and Charybdis of the situation—but a concrete determinately constituted particular which can give rise to knowledge with matching content and thereby enable perception and consciousness to fulfil their cognitive functions. After all, the material object is an intelligible item, and so too are its varieties.

What this implies is, that as consciousness expresses its nature in the perceptions typical of the state, the mind is led out onto entities in which the world is mentally visible as the framework through which those entities are constituted by the attention and understanding for what they are. Thus, what they are in experience is not of the order of undecipherable particles of Being of such a nature as to be cut adrift from Reality: 'bare particulars' as I have called them. The fact that to be conscious is to be 'in touch' with Reality is a property which is harnessed in the perceptions of the conscious. In short, at one end of the perceptual attentive line of the conscious is a state specifically engaged with the World, at the other end concrete sectors of the World in which the setting of the World is mentally visible in the form of individuating container. This is what I had in mind in claiming that in the perceptions of the conscious, consciousness keeps an appointment with Reality, and in its true or ultimate (physical) ontological form. In linking consciousness with perception in this way, I am providing a metaphysics of consciousness fit for believers in the physical metaphysics of today.

Index

hallucination (*cont.*):
  and prevailing mental state 511, 547
  as 'unreal' presence in visual field 509–12
health, *see* disease
hearing:
  as essentially inactive 389
  as probabilistic part of listening 400
  puzzle over origin-of in listening 393–406
heat:
  distinguished from (secondary) 'feel'
    quality 463–4, 516
Hegel, G. F. 162
Heidegger, M. 19, 99, 169
Heifetz, J. 445
Heracliteanism 60–1, 65
holes:
  nature of and perception of 333
holograms:
  and the visibility of light 440–1
Hume, David 342, 365, 386, 544
hypostatization:
  of internal objects of seeing 466

Id Freudian 170–3
  posited as developmentally prior to
    representation 171
'idle active drift':
  (in stream of consciousness) 216–19
illusions:
  'objective' 350
  'subjective' 350–1
imagination:
  actor and 364, 366, 369–70
  attention and 355–7
  classification of varieties 340–1
  constituting the concept 362–70
  'corelessness' of direct-object imaginings
    367–70
  definition 358–9, 361, 366
  discovery-experience distinguished from
    377–8
  'filler' phenomenal prototype, concept of
    363–4
  hallucinatory form, definition 350–1
  identifying-heading of perceptual-
    imaginings 364
  imagination, theories of priority of
    357–61, 366–7
  imagining, theories of priority of 357–61,
    366–7
  intentional object of 363–4
  negation and the imagination 372–5,
    377–8

non-cognitive value of 345, 352–3
perception distinguished from 352–3,
    355–7, 371, 375–8
perceptual 340, 349–57, 392–3
propositional 340–6
as quasi- 'the real thing' 349, 359–64
'resemblance' and 'confusion' 364–6
super-definability 369–70
thought distinguished from 375–8
imaginative perception 346–9
  conditions of 347–8
  determinants of 348–9
  as sub-variety of perception 347
indefinability of some mental types 39, 64
insanity:
  and contamination of belief-system
    144–5
  and consciousness-disturbance 146–8
  insane action 139
  insane belief 140–1, 144–6
  and consciousness 135–41
  and knowing what one is doing 136–41
  and loss of insight 149–51
  and loss of the World 150–1
  occurrent delusion 137–9
instinctive behaviour 52–5
intentionality:
  breakdown (of indifference-to-inexistence)
    with sensation-experience 15–21,
    509–12
  of change of mental state 178–9
  and consciousness 6
  perception and 15–21
interiority:
  of conscious state 158–9, 237–9, 256–8
  diminutions of 253–6
  and thinking 239
internal intelligibility of flow of conscious
    experience 216–31

Julesz, J. 195

Kant, I. 24
Khayyam, Omar 339
knowing what one is doing 126, 131,
    135–41
  literal necessity of 136–7
  mental-state sense 126, 137–41
  and self-determination 139–41

Lewis, D. 479
libido:
  Freudian theory of 282

outsides of material objects 605–7
  pre-eminence of as individuating aspect 606

Parmenides 63–4
parts of material objects 604
past:
  dream and 91–2
  experience and 55–60
Peacocke, C. 471
perception:
  of 'collectives' 483–7, 490–2
  of complex objects 323–4, 338
  concrete core of 327–8, 334–6
  consciousness and 1, 6–33
  constituting the concept 302–11, 314–15
  discovery-experience, difference from
  as falling in specific mode under genus
    'experience—' 311
  'Given' and 30
  'Given' as cause and object of visual
    experience 539–40
  idiosyncraticity theory, falsity of 17–19, 292–301
  imagining, difference from 375–8
  intentionality and 15–21, 293–5, 302–4, 313
  internal development within 28, 563–4, 568–9
  mediation and 27–30, 549–52
  mirror and 20
  modelessness of 18, 311–12
  nature of 14–19, 273, 302–17, 688–9
  negative objects, inexistence of 329–34
  objects of 24–7, 411
  propositional objects, inexistence of 24–7, 318–38
  psycho-physical and psycho-causal
    determinants of 542–44
  synthesis in 206–7
  thought-experience, difference from 375–7
  work of understanding in 556–69, 623–5, 691
phantasy:
  directed active 220
Picasso, P. 326, 578
Poe, E. A. 131
process:
  event and 44–6, 173–4
  experience and 44–9, 175–7
  as form of 'experiential consciousness' 49, 229

  nature of 44
  non-experiential examples of 46–7, 178–9
  in physical nature 173–4
proprioception:
  bond with touch 674–80
  compared with touch 629–30
  as framework for individuation of sensation 558, 594, 624, 626–7
  need for in instrumental action 632, 635–7
  problem of distraction in instrumental action 628–34
  a true perceiving 628–30
  of whole body 637–8

ratiocinative progression 220–2
  and fishing 221
  internal intelligibility of 220–2
rationality:
  as ingredient of consciousness 157–8
  thinking as custodial agency of 257–8, 261–3
Reality:
  consciousness and 1, 5, 12–13, 31–3, 78–9, 115–16
  inner and outer 149–51
reason:
  as sole access to Reality 157–8
reasoning:
  absence of in animals 196
recollecting:
  mechanism in 382–3
'red':
  as name of the look of the sensation of red 530–1
relations:
  insight into between (some) psychological *relata* 185–6
representationalism:
  inexistence of light and sound
    representation of light and sound 445–7
  inexistence of sensation representation of body 645–6, 650–1
  by light of material objects 448–50, 454
  by sense-data of light and material objects, *see* sense-data
  tactile, scope and limits of 665–9
Russell, B. 212

Sartre, J.-P. 169, 182, 286, 330
Schopenhauer, A. 99, 162, 170–3, 193
Searle, J. 16, 189–90, 325, 332, 338
secondary qualities 461–4, 515–37